UITGAVEN VAN HET
NEDERLANDS HISTORISCH-ARCHAEOLOGISCH INSTITUUT TE ISTANBUL

Publications de l'Institut historique-archéologique néerlandais de Stamboul
sous la direction de
Machteld J. MELLINK, C. NIJLAND, J.J. ROODENBERG,
J. de ROOS ET K.R. VEENHOF

LXIX

BABYLONIA 689-627 B.C.

A Political History

BABYLONIA 689-627 B.C.
A Political History

by

GRANT FRAME

NEDERLANDS HISTORISCH-ARCHAEOLOGISCH INSTITUUT
TE ISTANBUL
1992

CIP-GEGEVENS KONINKLIJKE BIBLIOTHEEK, DEN HAAG

Frame, Grant

Babylonia 689-627 B.C.: a political history / by Grant Frame. — Istanbul: Nederlands Historisch-Archaeologisch Instituut; Leiden: Nederlands Instituut voor het Nabije Oosten [distr.]. — (Uitgaven van het Nederlands Historisch-Archaeologisch Instituut te Istanbul, ISSN 0926-9568: 69)
ISBN 90-6258-069-6
NUGI 641/941
Trefw.: Babylonië: politieke geschiedenis; 689-627.

Printed in Belgium

To my parents
Norman and Edith Frame

CONTENTS

ILLUSTRATIONS

Permission to publish the photograph on the cover and figures 2-7 was kindly granted by the Trustees of the British Museum. Maps 1-2 and figure 1 were made by L.M. James; figure 1 was prepared from the photographs of the stela in F. von Luschan, *Ausgrabungen in Sendschirli* 1: *Einleitung und Inschriften* (Berlin, 1893), pls. 1 and 3. Figure 8 (© Réunion des musées nationaux) was supplied by the Louvre Museum.

TABLES

ABBREVIATIONS

AAA	*Annals of Archaeology and Anthropology.*
ABL	Harper, R.F. *Assyrian and Babylonian Letters Belonging to the K(ouyunjik) Collection(s) of the British Museum.* 14 volumes. Chicago, 1892-1914.
Acta Antiqua	*Acta Antiqua Academiae Scientiarum Hungaricae.*
Adams, *Heartland of Cities*	Adams, R.McC. *Heartland of Cities: Surveys of Ancient Settlement and Land Use on the Central Floodplain of the Euphrates.* Chicago, 1981.
Adams, *Land Behind Baghdad*	Adams, R.McC. *Land Behind Baghdad: A History of Settlement on the Diyala Plains.* Chicago, 1965.
Adams and Nissen, *Uruk Countryside*	Adams, R.McC., and Nissen, H.J. *The Uruk Countryside: The Natural Setting of Urban Societies.* Chicago, 1972.
ADD	Johns, C.H.W. *Assyrian Deeds and Documents Recording the Transfer of Property, Including the So-Called Private Contracts, Legal Decisions and Proclamations, Preserved in the Kouyunjik Collections of the British Museum, Chiefly of the 7th Century B.C.* 4 volumes. Cambridge, 1898-1923.
ADOG	*Abhandlungen der Deutschen Orient-Gesellschaft.*
AEM	*Archives épistolaires de Mari.*
AfO	*Archiv für Orientforschung.*
AfO Bei.	*Archiv für Orientforschung, Beiheft.*
AfK	*Archiv für Keilschriftforschung.*
Ahmed, *Asb.*	Ahmed, S.S. *Southern Mesopotamia in the Time of Ashurbanipal.* The Hauge and Paris, 1968.
AHw	von Soden, W. *Akkadisches Handwörterbuch.* 3 volumes. Wiesbaden, 1959-81.
AJSL	*American Journal of Semitic Languages and Literatures.*
AKA	Budge, E.A.W., and King, L.W. *Annals of the Kings of Assyria: The Cuneiform Texts with Translations, Transliterations, etc., from the Original Documents in the British Museum.* Volume 1. London, 1902.
ANET	Pritchard, J. B., ed. *Ancient Near Eastern Texts Relating to the Old Testament.* 3rd edition with supplement. Princeton, 1969.
AnOr	*Analecta Orientalia.*

AnSt	*Anatolian Studies.*
AOF	*Altorientalische Forschungen.*
AOTU	*Altorientalische Texte und Untersuchungen.*
ARINH	Fales, F.M., ed. *Assyrian Royal Inscriptions: New Horizons in Literary, Ideological, and Historical Analysis.* Rome, 1981.
ArOr	*Archiv Orientální.*
ARRIM	*Annual Review of the Royal Inscriptions of Mesopotamia Project.*
ASJ	*Acta Sumerologica.*
Aynard, *Asb.*	Aynard, J.-M. *Le Prisme du Louvre AO 19.939.* Bibliothèque de l'École des Hautes Études 309. Paris, 1957.
B	siglum (prefix) for objects in the Babylon collection of the Archaeological Museums, Istanbul; siglum (infix) for excavation numbers from the Iraqi excavations at Babylon.
Bagh. Mitt.	*Baghdader Mitteilungen.*
Barnett, *North Palace*	Barnett, R.D. *Sculptures from the North Palace of Ashurbanipal at Nineveh (668-627 B.C.).* London, 1976.
Bauer, *Asb.*	Bauer, T. *Das Inschriftenwerk Assurbanipals.* 2 volumes. Assyriologische Bibliothek, Neue Folge 1-2. Leipzig, 1933.
BBSt	King, L.W. *Babylonian Boundary-Stones and Memorial Tablets in the British Museum.* 2 volumes. London, 1912.
BDB	Brown, F., Driver, S.R., and Briggs, C.A. *A Hebrew and English Lexicon of the Old Testament.* Based upon the lexicon of W. Gesenius as translated by E. Robinson. Revised edition. Oxford, 1968.
BE	*The Babylonian Expedition of the University of Pennsylvania*, Series A: *Cuneiform Texts.*
BHT	Smith, S. *Babylonian Historical Texts Relating to the Capture and Downfall of Babylon.* London, 1924.
BIN	*Babylonian Inscriptions in the Collection of J.B. Nies.*
BiOr	*Bibliotheca Orientalis.*
B-K	Brinkman, J.A., and Kennedy, D.A. "Documentary Evidence for the Economic Base of Early Neo-Babylonian Society: A Survey of Dated Babylonian Economic Texts, 721-626 B.C." *Journal of Cuneiform Studies* 35 (1983): 1-90. With supplement in *Journal of Cuneiform Studies* 38 (1986): 99-106.

BM	siglum (prefix) for objects in the collection of the British Museum, Department of Western Asiatic Antiquities.
Borger, *Esarh.*	Borger, R. *Die Inschriften Asarhaddons, Königs von Assyrien.* Archiv für Orientforschung Beiheft 9. Graz, 1956.
Borger, *HKL*	Borger, R. *Handbuch der Keilschriftliteratur.* 3 volumes. Berlin, 1967-1975.
Borger, *Zeichenliste*	Borger, R. *Assyrisch-babylonische Zeichenliste.* With the assistance of F. Ellermeier. Alter Orient und Altes Testament 33. Kevelaer and Neukirchen-Vluyn, 1978.
Börker-Klähn, *ABVF*	Börker-Klähn, J. *Altvorderasiatische Bildstelen und vergleichbare Felsreliefs.* Baghdader Forschungen 4. Mainz am Rhein, 1982.
Brinkman, *MSKH* 1	Brinkman, J.A. *Materials and Studies for Kassite History.* Volume 1: *A Catalogue of Cuneiform Sources Pertaining to Specific Monarchs of the Kassite Dynasty.* Chicago, 1976.
Brinkman, *PKB*	Brinkman, J.A. *A Political History of Post-Kassite Babylonia, 1158-722 B.C.* Analecta Orientalia 43. Rome, 1968.
BRM	*Babylonian Records in the Library of J. Pierpont Morgan.*
BSA	*Bulletin on Sumerian Agriculture.*
BSMS	*Bulletin. The (Canadian) Society for Mesopotamian Studies.*
CAD	*The Assyrian Dictionary of the Oriental Institute of The University of Chicago.* Chicago and Glückstadt, 1956-.
CAH	*Cambridge Ancient History.* 3rd edition. Cambridge, 1970-.
Cameron, *HEI*	Cameron, G.G. *History of Early Iran.* Chicago, 1936.
Carter and Stolper, *Elam*	Carter, E., and Stolper, M.W. *Elam: Surveys of Political History and Archaeology.* Berkeley, Los Angeles, and London, 1984.
Cocquerillat, *Palmeraies*	Cocquerillat, D. *Palmeraies et cultures de l'Eanna d'Uruk (559-520).* Ausgrabungen der Deutschen Forschungsgemeinschaft in Uruk-Warka 8. Berlin, 1968.
Cogan, *Imperialism*	Cogan, M. *Imperialism and Religion: Assyria, Judah and Israel in the Eighth and Seventh Centuries B.C.E.* Missoula, Montana, 1974.
Combe, *Sin*	Combe, É. *Histoire du culte de Sin en Babylonie et en Assyrie.* Paris, 1908)
CT	*Cuneiform Texts from Babylonian Tablets in the British Museum.*

Cuneiform Archives	Veenhof, K.R., ed. *Cuneiform Archives and Libraries: Papers Read at the 30e Rencontre Assyriologique Internationale, Leiden, 4-8 July 1983*. Leiden, 1986.
Curtis, *Bronzeworking Centres*	Curtis, J., ed. *Bronzeworking Centres of Western Asia c. 1000-539 B.C.* London, 1988.
Dalley, *Edinburgh*	Dalley, S. *A Catalogue of the Akkadian Cuneiform Tablets in the Collections of the Royal Scottish Museum, Edinburgh, with Copies of the Texts*. Edinburgh, 1979.
Dalley and Postgate, *TFS*	Dalley, S., and Postgate, J.N. *The Tablets from Fort Shalmaneser*. Cuneiform Texts from Nimrud 3. London, 1984.
Dandamaev, *Slavery*	Dandamaev, M.A. *Slavery in Babylonia from Nabopolassar to Alexander the Great (626-331 B.C.)*. Revised edition. Translated by V.A. Powell; edited by M.A. Powell and D.B. Weisberg. DeKalb, 1984.
Death in Mesopotamia	Alster, B., ed. *Death in Mesopotamia. Papers Read at the XXVIe Rencontre Assyriologique Internationale*. Mesopotamia 8. Copenhagen, 1980.
Deimel Festschrift	*Miscellanea orientalia dedicata Antonio Deimel annos LXX complenti*. Analecta Orientalia 12. Rome, 1935.
Deller Festschrift	Mauer, G., and Magen, U., eds. *Ad bene et fideliter seminandum: Festgabe für Karlheinz Deller zum 21. Februar 1987*. Alter Orient und Altes Testament 220. Kevelaer and Neukirchen-Vluyn, 1988.
De Meyer, *Tell ed-Dēr* 3	De Meyer, L. *Tell ed-Dēr*. Volume 3: *Soundings at Abū Ḥabbah (Sippar)*. Louvain, 1980.
Diakonoff Festschrift	Dandamayev, M.A., et al., eds. *Societies and Languages of the Ancient Near East: Studies in Honour of I.M. Diakonoff*. Warminster, 1982.
Dietrich, *Aramäer*	Dietrich, M. *Die Aramäer Sudbabyloniens in der Sargonidenzeit (700-648)*. Alter Orient und Altes Testament 7. Kevelaer and Neukirchen-Vluyn, 1970.
van Dijk, *Rēš-Heiligtum*	van Dijk, J. *Texte aus dem Rēš-Heiligtum in Uruk-Warka*. With the assistance of W.R. Mayer. Baghdader Mitteilungen Beiheft 2. Berlin, 1980.
Divination	Nougayrol, J., ed. *La divination en Mésopotamie ancienne et dans les régions voisines*. Paris, 1966.
Donbaz and Grayson, *Clay Cones*	Donbaz, V., and Grayson, A.K. *Royal Inscriptions on Clay Cones from Ashur now in Istanbul*. Royal Inscriptions of Mesopotamia, Supplements 1. Toronto, Buffalo, and London, 1984.

Dougherty, *Sealand*	Dougherty, R.P. *The Sealand of Ancient Arabia.* Yale Oriental Series, Researches 19. New Haven, 1932.
Durand, *DCEPHE* 1	Durand, J.-M. *Documents cunéiformes de la IV*^{e} *Section de l'École pratique des Hautes Études.* Volume 1: *Catalogue et copies cunéiformes,* Hautes Études Orientales 18. Geneva and Paris, 1982.
Durand, *TBER*	Durand, J.-M. *Textes babyloniens d'époque récente.* Recherche sur les grandes civilisations, Cahier 6. Paris, 1981.
Eisenstadt, *Origins*	Eisenstadt, S.N., ed. *The Origins and Diversity of Axial Age Civilizations.* Albany, 1986.
Environmental History	Brice, W.C., ed. *The Environmental History of the Near and Middle East Since the Last Ice Age.* London, New York, and San Francisco, 1978.
Eph'al, *Ancient Arabs*	Eph'al, I. *The Ancient Arabs: Nomads on the Borders of the Fertile Crescent, 9th-5th Centuries B.C.* Jerusalem and Leiden, 1982.
Fall of Assyria	Zawadzki, S. *The Fall of Assyria and Median-Babylonian Relations in Light of the Nabopolassar Chronicle.* Poznan, 1988.
FB	*Forschungen und Berichte.*
Finet Festschrift	Lebeau, M., and Talon, P., eds. *Reflets des deux fleuves. Volume de mélanges offerts à André Finet.* Akkadica Supplementum 6. Leuven, 1989.
FLP	siglum (prefix) for objects in the John Frederick Lewis collection of the Free Library of Philadelphia.
FO	*Folia Orientalia.*
GAG	von Soden, W. *Grundriss der akkadischen Grammatik, samt Ergänzungsheft zum Grundriss der akkadischen Grammatik.* Analecta Orientalia 33+47. Roma: 1969.
GCCI	*Goucher College Cuneiform Inscriptions.*
Gibson, *Eleventh Season*	Gibson, McG., et al. *Excavations at Nippur, Eleventh Season.* Oriental Institute Communications 22. Chicago and London, 1975.
Gibson, *Kish*	Gibson, McG. *The City and Area of Kish.* Coconut Grove, Florida, 1972.
Gibson, *TSSI* 2	Gibson, J.C.L. *Aramaic Inscriptions, including Inscriptions in the Dialect of Zenjirli.* Textbook of Syrian Semitic Inscriptions 2. Oxford, 1975.
Gibson, *Twelfth Season*	Gibson, McG., et al. *Excavations at Nippur, Twelfth Season.* Oriental Institute Communications 23. Chicago, 1978.
Gonçalves, *L'expédition de Sennachérib*	Gonçalves, F.J. *L'expédition de Sennachérib en Palestine dans la littérature hébraïque ancienne.* Louvain-la-Neuve, 1986.

Grayson, *ARI*	Grayson, A.K. *Assyrian Royal Inscriptions.* 2 volumes. Wiesbaden, 1972 and 1976.
Grayson, *Chronicles*	Grayson, A.K. *Assyrian and Babylonian Chronicles.* Texts from Cuneiform Sources 5. Locust Valley, New York, 1975.
Haller, *Gräber*	Haller, A. *Die Gräber und Grüfte von Assur.* Wissenschaftliche Veröffentlichungen der Deutschen Orient-Gesellschaft 65. Berlin, 1954.
HHI	Tadmor, H., and Weinfeld, M., eds. *History, Historiography and Interpretation: Studies in Biblical and Cuneiform Literatures.* Jerusalem and Leiden, 1983.
Hinz, *Elam*	Hinz, W. *The Lost World of Elam: Re-creation of a Vanished Civilization.* Translated by J. Barnes. London, 1972.
Iconic Book	Tucker, G.M., and Knight, D.A., eds. *Humanizing America's Iconic Book: Society of Biblical Literature Centennial Addresses 1980.* Chico, California, 1982.
IM	siglum (prefix) for objects in the collections of the Iraq Museum, Baghdad.
JA	*Journal asiatique.*
JAC	*Journal of Ancient Civilizations.*
Jacobsen, *Salinity*	Jacobsen, T. *Salinity and Irrigation Agriculture in Antiquity. Diyala Basin Archaeological Projects: Report on Essential Results, 1957-58.* Bibliotheca Mesopotamica 14. Malibu, 1982.
Jacoby, *FGrH* III C/1	Jacoby, F. *Die Fragmente der griechischen Historiker.* Volume III/C/1: *Aegypten-Geten Nr. 608a-708.* Leiden, 1958.
JANES	*Journal of the Ancient Near Eastern Society of Columbia University.*
JAOS	*Journal of the American Oriental Society.*
Jastrow, *Dictionary*	Jastrow, M. *A Dictionary of the Targumim, the Talmud Babli and Yerushalmi, and the Midrashic Literature.* Volume 1. London, 1903.
JCS	*Journal of Cuneiform Studies.*
JEOL	*Jaarbericht van het Vooraziatisch-Egyptisch Genootschap "Ex Oriente Lux".*
JESHO	*Journal of the Economic and Social History of the Orient.*
JNES	*Journal of Near Eastern Studies.*
Joannès, *TEBR*	Joannès, F. *Textes économiques de la Babylonie récente (Étude des texts de TBER - Cahier n° 6).* Recherche sur les civilisations, Cahier 5. Paris, 1982.
JRAS	*Journal of the Royal Asiatic Society of Great Britain and Ireland.*
JSS	*Journal of Semitic Studies.*

JTVI	*Journal of the Transactions of the Victoria Institute.*
K	siglum (prefix) for objects in the Kuyunjik collection of the British Museum.
KAH 1	Messerschmidt, L. *Keilschrifttexte aus Assur historischen Inhalts.* Part 1. Wissenschaftliche Veröffentlichungen der Deutschen Orient-Gesellschaft 16. Leipzig, 1911.
KAH 2	Schroeder, O. *Keilschrifttexte aus Assur historischen Inhalts.* Part 2. Wissenschaftliche Veröffentlichungen der Deutschen Orient-Gesellschaft 37. Leipzig, 1922.
KAI	Donner, H., and Röllig, W. *Kanaanäische und aramäische Inschriften.* 3 volumes. Revised edition. Wiesbaden, 1969-1973.
KAV	Schroeder, O. *Keilschrifttexte aus Assur verschiedenen Inhalts.* Wissenschaftliche Veröffentlichungen der Deutschen Orient-Gesellschaft 35. Leipzig, 1920.
Kessler, *Nordmesopotamien*	Kessler, K. *Untersuchungen zur historischen Topographie Nordmesopotamiens nach keilschriftlichen Quellen des 1. Jahrtausends v. Chr.* Tübinger Atlas des Vorderen Orients Beiheft B/26. Wiesbaden, 1980.
Al Khalifa and Rice, *Bahrain*	Al Khalifa, H.A., and Rice, M., eds. *Bahrain through the Ages: The Archaeology.* London, New York, Sydney, and Henley 1986.
King, *LIH*	King, L.W. *The Letters and Inscriptions of Ḫammurabi, King of Babylon, about B.C. 2200, to Which are Added a Series of Letters of Other Kings of the First Dynasty of Babylon.* 3 volumes. London, 1898-1900.
Kinnier Wilson, *Wine Lists*	Kinnier Wilson, J.V. *The Nimrud Wine Lists: A Study of Men and Administration at the Assyrian Capital in the Eighth Century, B.C.* Cuneiform Texts from Nimrud 1. London, 1972.
Kitchen, *Third Intermediate Period*	Kitchen, K.A. *The Third Intermediate Period in Egypt (1100-650 B.C.).* 2nd edition with supplement. Warminster, 1986.
Klauber, *Beamtentum*	Klauber, E. *Assyrisches Beamtentum nach Briefen aus der Sargonidenzeit,* Leipziger semitistische Studien 5/III. Leipzig, 1910.
Knudtzon, *Gebete*	Knudtzon, J.A. *Assyrische Gebete an den Sonnengott für Staat und königliches Haus aus der Zeit Asarhaddons und Asurbanipals.* 2 volumes. Leipzig, 1893.

Koldewey, *Pflastersteine*	Koldewey, R. *Die Pflastersteine von Aiburschabu in Babylon.* Wissenschaftliche Veröffentlichungen der Deutschen Orient-Gesellschaft 2. Leipzig, 1901.
Koldewey, *Tempel*	Koldewey, R. *Die Tempel von Babylon und Borsippa.* Wissenschaftliche Veröffentlichungen der Deutschen Orient-Gesellschaft 15. Leipzig, 1911.
Koldewey, *WEB⁴*	Koldewey, R. *Das wieder erstehende Babylon. Die bisherigen Ergebnisse der deutschen Ausgrabungen.* 4th edition. Leipzig, 1925.
König, *EKI*	König, F.W. *Die elamischen Königsinschriften.* Archiv für Orientforschung, Beiheft 16. Graz, 1965.
Kümmel, *Familie*	Kümmel, H.M. *Familie, Beruf und Amt im spätbabylonischen Uruk: prosopographische Untersuchungen zu Berufsgruppen des 6. Jahrhunderts v. Chr. in Uruk.* Abhandlungen der Deutschen Orient-Gesellschaft 20. Berlin, 1979.
Kwasman, *NALD*	Kwasman, T. *Neo-Assyrian Legal Documents in the Kouyunjik Collection of the British Museum.* Studia Phol: Series Maior 14. Rome, 1988.
L	siglum (prefix) for objects in the Lagash collection of the Archaeological Museums, Istanbul.
Laessøe, *Bît rimki*	Laessøe, J. *Studies on the Assyrian Ritual and Series* bît rimki. Copenhagen, 1955.
Lambert, *BWL*	Lambert, W.G. *Babylonian Wisdom Literature.* Reprint edition with corrections. Oxford, 1967.
Landsberger, *Brief*	Landsberger, B. *Brief des Bischofs von Esagila an König Esarhaddon.* Mededelingen der Koninklijke Nederlandse Akademie van Wetenschappen, Afd. Letterkunde, N.R. 28/6. Amsterdam, 1965.
Langdon, *Kish*	Langdon, S. *Excavations at Kish.* Volume 1. Paris, 1924.
Langdon, *NBK*	Langdon, S. *Die neubabylonischen Königsinschriften.* Vorderasiatische Bibliothek 4. Leipzig, 1912.
LAS	Parpola, S. *Letters from Assyrian Scholars to the Kings Esarhaddon and Assurbanipal.* 2 volumes. Alter Orient und Altes Testament 5/1-2. Kevelaer and Neukirchen-Vluyn, 1970 and 1983.
LBAT	Sachs, A.J. *Late Babylonian Astronomical and Related Texts Copied by T.G. Pinches and J.N. Strassmaier.* With the cooperation of J. Schaumberger. Providence, 1955.

Lehmann, *Ššmk*	Lehmann, C.F. *Šamaššumukîn, König von Babylonien 668-648 v. Chr., inschriftliches Material über den Beginn seiner Regierung.* 2 volumes. Assyriologische Bibliothek 8. Leipzig, 1892.
Lie, *Sar.*	Lie, A.G. *The Inscriptions of Sargon II King of Assyria.* Volume 1: *The Annals.* Paris, 1929.
lišān mitḫurti	Röllig, W., ed. lišān mitḫurti: *Festschrift Wolfram Freiherr von Soden zum 19.VI.1968 gewidmet von Schülern und Mitarbeitern.* With the assistance of M. Dietrich. Alter Orient und Altes Testament 1. Kevelaer and Neukirchen-Vluyn, 1969.
Livingstone, *Explanatory Works*	Livingstone, A. *Mystical and Mythological Explanatory Works of Assyrian and Babylonian Scholars.* Oxford, 1986.
Livingstone, *SAA* 3	Livingstone, A. *Court Poetry and Literary Miscellanea.* State Archives of Assyria 3. Helsinki, 1989.
LKU	Falkenstein, A. *Literarische Keilschrifttexte aus Uruk.* Berlin, 1931.
LSS	*Leipziger Semitistische Studien.*
Luckenbill, *Senn.*	Luckenbill, D.D. *The Annals of Sennacherib.* Oriental Institute Publications 2. Chicago, 1924.
MAH	siglum (prefix) for tablets in the collection of the Musée d'Art et d'Histoire, Geneva.
Malbran-Labat, *Armée*	Malbran-Labat, F. *L'armée et l'organisation militaire de l'Assyrie d'après les lettres des Sargonides trouvées à Ninive.* Geneva and Paris, 1982.
McCown and Haines, *Nippur* 1	McCown, D.E., and Haines, R.C. *Nippur.* Part 1: *Temple of Enlil, Scribal Quarter and Soundings.* With the assistance of D.P. Hansen. Oriental Institute Publications 78. Chicago, 1967.
McCown, Haines, and Biggs, *Nippur* 2	McCown, D.E., Haines, R.C., and Biggs, R.D. *Nippur.* Part 2: *The North Temple and Sounding E.* With the assistance of E.F. Carter. Oriental Institute Publications 97. Chicago, 1978.
McEwan, *Priest and Temple*	McEwan, G.J.P. *Priest and Temple in Hellenistic Babylonia.* Freiburger altorientalische Studien 4. Wiesbaden, 1981.
MDAIK	*Mitteilungen des Deutschen Archäologischen Instituts Abteilung Kairo.*
Mesopotamien und seine Nachbarn	Nissen, H.-J., and Renger, J., eds. *Mesopotamien und seine Nachbarn: Politische und kulturelle Wechselbeziehungen im Alten Vorderasien vom 4. bis 1. Jahrtausend v. Chr.* 2 volumes. Berliner Beiträge zum Vorderen Orient 1. Berlin, 1982.

MMA	siglum (prefix) for objects in the Metropolitan Museum of Art, New York.
Moorey, *Kish*	Moorey, P.R.S. *Kish Excavations 1923-1933, with a Microfiche Catalogue of the Objects in Oxford Excavated by the Oxford-Field Museum, Chicago Expedition to Kish in Iraq, 1923-1933.* Oxford, 1978.
Moran Festschrift	Abusch, T., Huehnergard, J., and Steinkeller, P., eds. *Lingering Over Words: Studies in Ancient Near Eastern Literature in Honor of William L. Moran.* Harvard Semitic Studies 37. Atlanta, 1990.
N	siglum (prefix) for tablets from Nippur in the University Museum; siglum (infix) for tablets found by the recent American expedition to Nippur (1948-present).
NABU	*Nouvelles Assyriologiques Brèves et Utilitaires.*
NAPR	*Northern Akkad Project Reports.*
Nbk	Strassmaier, J.N. *Inschriften von Nabuchodonosor, König von Babylon (604-561 v. Chr.).* Leipzig, 1889.
Nbn	Strassmaier, J.N. *Inschriften von Nabonidus, König von Babylon (555-538 v. Chr.).* Leipzig, 1889.
ND	siglum (prefix) for the excavation numbers from the British expedition to Nimrud.
NRVU	San Nicolò, M., and Ungnad, A. *Neubabylonische Rechts- und Verwaltungsurkunden übersetzt und erläutert.* Volume 1: *Rechts- und Wirtschaftsurkunden der Berliner Museen aus vorhellenistischer Zeit.* Leipzig, 1935.
Oded, *Deportations*	Oded, B. *Mass Deportations and Deportees in the Neo-Assyrian Empire.* Wiesbaden, 1979.
OECT	*Oxford Editions of Cuneiform Texts.*
OIAR	*The Oriental Institute Annual Report.*
OIC	*Oriental Institute Communications.*
OIP	*Oriental Institute Publications.*
Olmstead, *Assyria*	Olmstead, A.T. *History of Assyria.* Chicago and London, 1951.
OLZ	*Orientalistische Literaturzeitung.*
Oppenheim, *Ancient Mesopotamia*	Oppenheim, A.L. *Ancient Mesopotamia: Portrait of a Dead Civilization.* Revised edition completed by Erica Reiner, with an appendix on chronology by J.A. Brinkman. Chicago and London, 1977.
Oppenheim, *Letters*	Oppenheim, A.L. *Letters from Mesopotamia: Official, Business, and Private Letters on Clay Tablets from Two Millennia.* Chicago and London, 1967.
Or. NS	*Orientalia*, Nova Series.

OrAnt	*Oriens Antiquus.*
Oriental Studies	*Oriental Studies: A Selection of the Papers Read before the Oriental Club of Philadelphia 1888-1894.* Boston, 1894.
Palais	Garelli, P., ed. *Le palais et la royauté (archéologie et civilisation).* Paris, 1974.
Papyrus and Tablet	Grayson, A.K., and Redford, D.B. *Papyrus and Tablet.* Englewood Cliffs, New Jersey, 1973.
Parpola, *Toponyms*	Parpola, S. *Neo-Assyrian Toponyms.* Programming and computer printing by K. Koskenniemi. Alter Orient und Altes Testament 6. Kevelaer and Neukirchen-Vluyn, 1970.
PBS	*Publications of the Babylonian Section* (University Museum, University of Pennsylvania).
Petschow, *Pfandrecht*	Petschow, H. *Neubabylonisches Pfandrecht.* Abhandlungen der Sächsischen Akademie der Wissenschaften zu Leipzig, Philologisch-historische Klasse 48/1. Berlin, 1956.
Piepkorn, *Asb.*	Piepkorn, A.C. *Historical Prism Inscriptions of Ashurbanipal,* Volume 1: *Editions E, B_{1-5}, D, and K.* Assyriological Studies 5. Chicago, 1933.
Pinches, *Berens Coll.*	Pinches, T.G. *The Babylonian Tablets of the Berens Collection.* Asiatic Society Monographs 16. London, 1915.
Pinckert, *LSS* 3/4	Pinckert, J. *Hymnen und Gebete an Nebo.* Leipziger Semitistische Studien 3/4. Leipzig, 1920.
Postgate, *FNALD*	Postgate, J.N. *Fifty Neo-Assyrian Legal Documents.* Warminster, 1976.
Postgate, *Royal Grants*	Postgate, J.N. *Neo-Assyrian Royal Grants and Decrees.* Studia Pohl: Series Maior 1. Rome, 1969.
Postgate, *Taxation*	Postgate, J.N. *Taxation and Conscription in the Assyrian Empire.* Studia Pohl: Series Maior 3. Rome 1974.
Potts, *Dilmun*	Potts, D.T., ed. *Dilmun: New Studies in the Archaeology and Early History of Bahrain.* Berliner Beiträge zum Vorderen Orient 2. Berlin 1983.
Power and Propaganda	Larsen, M.T., ed. *Power and Propaganda: A Symposium on Ancient Empires.* Mesopotamia 7. Copenhagen, 1979.
Prelude	Brinkman, J.A. *Prelude to Empire: Babylonian Society and Politics, 747-626 B.C.* Occasional Publications of the Babylonian Fund 7. Philadelphia, 1984.
PRS	siglum (prefix) for objects in the collection of the Philosophical Research Society.

PRT	Klauber, E.G. *Politisch-religiöse Texte aus der Sargonidenzeit.* Leipzig, 1913.
PSBA	*Proceedings of the Society of Biblical Archaeology.*
PTS	siglum (prefix) for objects in the collection of the Princeton Theological Seminary.
R	Rawlinson, H.C., ed. *The Cuneiform Inscriptions of Western Asia.* 5 volumes. London, 1861-84.
RA	*Revue d'assyriologie et d'archéologie orientale.*
RB	*Revue biblique.*
Reiner Festschrift	Rochberg-Halton, F., ed. *Languages, Literature, and History: Philological and Historical Studies Presented to Erica Reiner.* American Oriental Series 67. New Haven, 1987.
Reuther, *Merkes*	Reuther, O. *Die Innenstadt von Babylon (Merkes).* Wissenschaftliche Veröffentlichungen der Deutschen Orient-Gesellschaft 47. Leipzig, 1926.
RGTC	*Répertoire géographique des textes cunéiformes.*
RIMA	*Royal Inscriptions of Mesopotamia. Assyrian Periods.*
RLA	*Reallexikon der Assyriologie und Vorderasiatischen Archäologie.* Leipzig and Berlin, 1928-.
Rm	siglum (prefix) for objects found by H. Rassam in the collection of the British Museum, Department of Western Asiatic Antiquities.
ROMCT	*Royal Ontario Museum Cuneiform Texts.*
Rost, *Tigl. III*	Rost, P. *Die Keilschrifttexte Tiglat-Pilesers III. nach den Papierabklatschen und Originalen des Britischen Museums.* 2 volumes. Leipzig, 1893.
RP	*Records of the Past.*
RT	*Recueil de travaux relatifs à la philologie et à l'archéologie égyptiennes et assyriennes.*
SAA	*State Archives of Assyria.*
SAAB	*State Archives of Assyria Bulletin*
Sachs, *Astronomical Diaries* 1	Sachs, A.J. *Astronomical Diaries and Related Texts from Babylonia.* Volume 1: *Diaries from 652 B.C. to 262 B.C.* Completed and edited by H. Hunger. Vienna, 1988.
Saggs, *Assyria*	Saggs, H.W.F. *The Might That Was Assyria.* London, 1984.
SANE	*Sources from the Ancient Near East.*
San Nicolò, *BR 8/7*	San Nicolò, M. *Babylonische Rechtsurkunden des ausgehenden 8. und des 7. Jahrhunderts v. Chr.* Abhandlungen der Bayerischen Akademie der Wissenschaften, Philosophisch-historische Klasse, Neue Folge 34. Munich, 1951.

San Nicolò, *Prosopographie*	San Nicolò, M. *Beiträge zu einer Prosopographie neubabylonischer Beamten der Zivil- und Tempelverwaltung*. Sitzungsberichte der Bayerischen Akademie der Wissenschaften, Philosophisch-historische Abteilung, 1941, 2/2. Munich, 1941.
Scheil, *Sippar*	Scheil, V. *Une saison de fouilles à Sippar*. Cairo, 1902.
Schnabel, *Berossos*	Schnabel, P. *Berossos und die babylonisch-hellenistische Literatur*. Leipzig and Berlin, 1923.
Schollmeyer, *Šamaš*	Schollmeyer, A. *Sumerisch-babylonische Hymnen und Gebete an Šamaš*. Paderborn, 1912.
Seux, *Épithètes*	Seux, M.-J. *Épithètes royales akkadiennes et sumériennes*. Paris, 1967.
Sjöberg Festschrift	Behrens, H., Loding, D., and Roth, M.T., eds. *dumu-e_2-dub-ba-a: Studies in Honor of Åke W. Sjöberg*. Occasional Publications of the Samuel Noah Kramer Fund 11. Philadelphia, 1989.
Smith, *Assyrian Discoveries*	Smith, G. *Assyrian Discoveries; an Account of Explorations and Discoveries on the Site of Nineveh, during 1873 and 1874*. 3rd edition. London, 1875.
Smith, *First Campaign*	Smith, S. *The First Campaign of Sennacherib, King of Assyria, B.C. 705-681*. London, 1921.
Smith, *MAT*	Smith, S.A. *Miscellaneous Assyrian Texts of the British Museum, with Textual Notes*. Leipzig, 1887.
Smith, *Senn.*	Smith, G. *History of Sennacherib Translated from the Cuneiform Inscriptions*. Edited by A.H. Sayce. London and Edinburgh, 1878.
Speleers, *Receuil*	Speleers, L. *Recueil des Inscriptions de l'Asie Antérieure des Musées Royaux du Cinquantenaire à Bruxelles*. Brussels, 1925.
Stamm, *Namengebung*	Stamm, J.J. *Die akkadische Namengebung*. Mitteilungen der Vorderasiatisch-Ägyptischen Gesellschaft 44. Leipzig, 1939.
Starr, *SAA* 4	Starr, I. *Queries to the Sungod: Divination and Politics in Sargonid Assyria*. State Archives of Assyria 4. Helsinki, 1990.
Steve Festschrift	De Meyer, L., Gasche, H., et Vallat, F., eds. *Fragmenta Historiae Elamicae: Mélanges offerts à M.J. Steve*. Paris, 1986.
Stier Festschrift	*Antike und Universalgeschichte. Festschrift Hans Erich Stier*. Münster, 1972.
StOr	*Studia Orientalia* (Societas Orientalis Fennica).

Strassmaier, *8e Congrès*	Strassmaier, J.N. "Einige kleinere babylonische Keilschrifttexte aus dem Britischen Museum." In *Actes du Huitième Congrès International des Orientalistes, tenu en 1889 à Stockholm et à Christiania*, 2/IB, pp. 279-83 and Beilage. Leiden, 1893.
Streck, *Asb.*	Streck, M. *Assurbanipal und die letzten assyrischen Könige bis zum Untergange Niniveh's.* 3 volumes. Vorderasiatische Bibliothek 7. Leipzig, 1916.
Studies Landsberger	Güterbock, H.G., and Jacobsen, T., eds. *Studies in Honor of Benno Landsberger on His Seventy-fifth Birthday, April 21, 1965.* Assyriological Studies 16. Chicago, 1965.
Studies Oppenheim	Biggs, R.D., and Brinkman, J.A., eds. *Studies Presented to A. Leo Oppenheim.* Chicago, 1964.
Symbolae van Oven	David, M., et al., eds. *Symbolae ad jus et historiam antiquitatis pertinentes Julio Christiano van Oven dedicatae.* Leiden, 1946.
Tadmor Festschrift	Cogan, M., and Eph'al, I., eds. *Ah, Assyria ... Studies in Assyrian History and Ancient Near Eastern Historiography Presented to Hayim Tadmor.* Scripta Hierosolymitana 33. Jerusalem, 1991.
Tallqvist, *APN*	Tallqvist, K.L. *Assyrian Personal Names.* Acta Societatis Scientiarum Fennicae 43/1. Helsinki, 1914.
Tallqvist, *NBN*	Tallqvist, K.L. *Neubabylonisches Namenbuch zu den Geschäftsurkunden aus der Zeit des Šamaššumukîn bis Xerxes.* Acta Societatis Scientiarum Fennicae 32/2. Helsinki, 1902.
TAVO	*Tübinger Atlas des Vorderen Orients.*
TCL	*Textes cunéiformes du Louvre* (Musée du Louvre, Département des Antiquités Orientales).
TCS	*Texts from Cuneiform Sources.*
TDP	Labat, R. *Traité akkadien de diagnostics et pronostics médicaux.* 2 volumes. Paris, 1951.
Thompson, *PEA*	Thompson, R.C. *The Prisms of Esarhaddon and Ashurbanipal found at Nineveh, 1927-8.* London, 1931.
Thompson, *Rep.*	Thompson, R.C. *The Reports of the Magicians and Astrologers of Nineveh and Babylon in the British Museum.* 2 volumes. London, 1900.
Thureau-Dangin, *Rit. Acc.*	Thureau-Dangin, F. *Rituels accadiens.* Paris, 1921.
TUAT	*Texte aus der Umwelt des Alten Testaments.*
TuM	*Texte und Materialien der Frau Professor Hilprecht Collection of Babylonian Antiquities im Eigentum der Universität Jena .*

25th Congress	*Proceedings of the 25th Congress of Orientalists.* Volume 1. Moscow, 1962.
U	siglum (prefix) for excavation numbers from the British-American expedition to Ur.
UCP	*University of California Publications in Semitic Philology.*
UE	*Ur Excavations.*
UET	*Ur Excavations, Texts.*
Unger, *Babylon*	Unger, E. *Babylon, die heilige Stadt nach der Beschreibung der Babylonier.* 2nd edition with introduction by R. Borger. Berlin, 1970.
UVB	*Vorläufiger Bericht über die ... Ausgrabungen in Uruk-Warka.*
VA	siglum for objects in the Vorderasiatische Museum, Berlin.
VAS	*Vorderasiatische Schriftdenkmäler der Königlichen Museen zu Berlin.*
Veenhof, *Aspects*	Veenhof, K.R. *Aspects of Old Assyrian Trade and its Terminology.* Studia et Documenta ad Iura Orientis Antiqui Pertinentia 10. Leiden, 1972.
Vleeming and Wesselius, *Studies* 1	Vleeming, S.P., and Wesselius, J.W. *Studies in Papyrus Amherst 63. Essays on the Aramaic Texts in Aramaic/Demotic Papyrus Amherst 63.* Volume 1. Amsterdam, 1985.
Voix de l'opposition	Finet, A., ed. *La voix de l'opposition en Mésopotamie.* Brussels, n.d..
W	siglum (prefix) for excavation numbers for tablets found by the German expedition to Warka.
Wachsmuth, *Einleitung*	Wachsmuth, C. *Einleitung in das Studium der alten Geschichte.* Leipzig, 1895.
Waetzoldt, *Textilindustrie*	Waetzoldt, H. *Untersuchungen zur neusumerischen Textilindustrie.* Rome, 1972.
Walker, *CBI*	Walker, C.B.F. *Cuneiform Brick Inscriptions in the British Museum; the Ashmolean Museum, Oxford; the City of Birmingham Museums and Art Gallery; the City of Bristol Museum and Art Gallery.* London, 1981.
Watanabe, *Vereidigung*	Watanabe, K. *Die* adê-*Vereidigung anlässlich der Thronfolgeregelung Asarhaddons.* Baghdader Mitteilungen Beiheft 3. Berlin, 1987.
Watelin and Langdon, *Kish*	Watelin, L.C., and Langdon, S. *Excavations at Kish.* Volumes 3 and 4. Paris, 1930 and 1934.
Waterman, *RCAE*	Waterman, L. *Royal Correspondence of the Assyrian Empire.* 4 volumes. Ann Arbor, 1930-36.
WBJ	*Wissenschaftskolleg zu Berlin. Jahrbuch.*
Wetzel, *Stadtmauern*	Wetzel, F. *Die Stadtmauern von Babylon.* Wissenschaftliche Veröffentlichungen der Deutschen Orient-Gesellschaft 48. Leipzig, 1930.

Wetzel and Weissbach, *Hauptheiligtum*	Wetzel, F., and Weissbach, F. *Das Hauptheiligtum des Marduk in Babylon, Esagila und Etemenanki.* Wissenschaftliche Veröffentlichungen der Deutschen Orient-Gesellschaft 59. Leipzig, 1938.
Winckler, *AOF*	Winckler, H. *Altorientalische Forschungen.* 3 volumes. Leipzig, 1893-1905.
Winckler, *Sar.*	Winckler, H. *Die Keilschrifttexte Sargons nach den Papierabklatschen und Originalen.* 2 volumes. Leipzig, 1889.
Wiseman, *Chronicles*	Wiseman, D.J. *Chronicles of Chaldaean Kings (626-556 B.C.) in the British Museum.* London, 1956.
Wiseman, *Treaties*	Wiseman, D.J. "The Vassal-Treaties of Esarhaddon." *Iraq* 20 (1958): 1-99 and pls. I-XII and 1-53.
WO	*Die Welt des Orients.*
WVDOG	*Wissenschaftliche Veröffentlichungen der Deutschen Orient-Gesellschaft.*
WZKM	*Wiener Zeitschrift für die Kunde des Morgenlandes.*
YBC	siglum (prefix) for tablets in the Yale Babylonian Collection.
YOS	*Yale Oriental Studies, Babylonian Texts.*
ZA	*Zeitschrift für Assyriologie und vorderasiatische Archäologie*; previously *Zeitschrift für Assyriologie und verwandte Gebiete.*
Zadok, *West Semites*	Zadok, R. *On West Semites in Babylonia during the Chaldean and Achaemenian Periods: An Onomastic Study.* Jerusalem, 1977.
zikir šumim	van Driel, G., et al, eds. zikir šumim: *Assyriological Studies Presented to F.R. Kraus on the Occasion of his Seventieth Birthday.* Leiden, 1982.
ZK	*Zeitschrift für Keilschriftforschung und verwandte Gebiete.*

PREFACE

This book had its beginnings as a doctoral dissertation defended at the University of Chicago in August 1980. The long lapse between its submission to the University and its current appearance in this revised form is due to several reasons, in addition to the pressure of other commitments. Initially, I wished to leave the topic for a period of time in order that I might return to it with fresh—and it is to be hoped improved—insights. Numerous important publications dealing with the period of concern appeared over the following few years and time was then required to digest and account for them in this study. In addition, the dissertation used numerous unpublished documents and at that time it was not possible to cite them in a published form.

In 1977, J.A. Brinkman suggested that the topic of this study form the subject of my doctoral dissertation; he closely supervised its progress in that form and has continued to offer his advice and encouragement as I revised it for publication. No words can express the gratitude I feel for his aid, counsel, and patience in the completion of this manuscript. The many enlightening discussions I had with S. Parpola on the topic of this study added greatly to my understanding of this period of Mesopotamian history, even on matters where we disagree. My sincere thanks must also be expressed to E. Reiner for her sage counsel in the preparation of the manuscript in its dissertation form and for her deep concern in my proper progress as an Assyriologist. Without the help of these three individuals, who served on my doctoral committee, this study would never have been completed.

J.A. Brinkman and the late D.A. Kennedy gave me access to their transliterations of a large number of unpublished Babylonian economic documents from this period and my appreciation must be offered to them for their great generosity. The free exchange of information between myself and J.A. Brinkman over the years has been invaluable in preparing this volume and it is not possible to designate all the statements influenced by him. In many cases, it is no longer possible to determine who is ultimately responsible for any particular idea or suggestion.

I wish to express my gratitude to the authorities and staff of several museums for permission to examine documents in their collections and for their cooperation and assistance. In particular, my gratitude must be extended to P.R.S. Moorey, Ashmolean Museum; C.B.F. Walker and the late E.

Sollberger, British Museum; B. André, Louvre; E. Leichty, University Museum, Philadelphia; and L. Jakob-Rost and E. Klengel-Brandt, Vorderasiatische Museum.

Thanks are also due to J.A. Armstrong, R.D. Biggs, P.E. Dion, J.-M. Durand, McG. Gibson, O.R. Gurney, J. Johnson, G.J.P. McEwan, D. Pardee, J.E. Reade, D.B. Redford, A. Sachs, W.H. van Soldt, J.W. Wevers, and L.S. Wilding for their aid in the course of the preparation of this study.

I would like to offer my appreciation to the Social Sciences and Humanities Research Council of Canada (formerly part of the Canada Council) for their financial aid to my studies during the years 1975-79 and for their award of a research grant which allowed me to collate tablets in museums in the United Kingdom, France, and Germany in the spring of 1978.

For stimulating my interest in ancient Mesopotamia and for guiding my initial footsteps in Assyriology, I am grateful to A.K. Grayson and R.F.G. Sweet of the University of Toronto. As Director of the Royal Inscriptions of Mesopotamia Project, A.K. Grayson has continued to be interested in my work and has allowed me the time and facilities with which to revise this work for publication. My special thanks must be expressed to him.

In addition, my appreciation must be extended to A. Gallagher-Ellis for her assistance in editing my somewhat murky prose, to L.M. James for preparing the maps and the drawing of the Zinjirli stela, and to the editors of the series *Uitgaven van het Nederlands Historisch-Archaeologisch Instituut te Istanbul*, especially C. Nijland and K.R. Veenhof, for accepting this study for publication. This book was prepared on an Apple Macintosh Plus computer and printed on a PS Jet+ laser printer with a font developed by W.H. van Soldt to print Akkadian transliterations; tables 3-6 were typeset by the publisher. The General Index was for the most part computer-generated.

My greatest debt of gratitude is to my parents, Norman and Edith Frame. I will never be able to repay them for the constant support and encouragement they have given me over the years.

CONVENTIONS

PROPER NOUNS

The spelling of Akkadian personal names will not attempt to reproduce the pronunciation current (or thought to be current) in Babylonia during the years 689-627 B.C. since to do so would often introduce spellings which are not readily recognizable or might be confusing to the reader. Names which have a generally accepted English form (e.g., Ashurbanipal, Esarhaddon, Merodach-Baladan, Nabopolassar, and Sennacherib) will retain that customary form. In general the spelling of personal names will follow the patterns indicated by the examples in J.J. Stamm, *Die akkadische Namengebung*, Mitteilungen der Vorderasiatisch-Ägyptischen Gesellschaft 44 (Leipzig, 1939), pp. 325-53. Thus, a number of names which are transcribed into English in a certain way (e.g., Šamaš[1] and Enlil[2]) will keep that form here; and nouns in personal names will be written with the grammatically correct case endings (e.g., the accusative "-a" in Šamaš-šuma-ukīn and Šuma-iddin) even though the vowel may have been elided before the initial vowel of the following word[3] or some other vowel may have been pronounced. In addition, "y" rather than "j" will be used to indicate the front glide; thus in certain hypocoristic-style personal names "y" will be employed (e.g., Ṣillaya not Ṣillaja)[4] since "j" does not usually stand for this sound in English.

The spelling of place names which do not have customarily accepted forms (e.g., Babylon, Euphrates, and Assyria) will in general follow those given in S. Parpola, *Neo-Assyrian Toponyms*, Alter Orient und Altes Testament 6 (Kevelaer and Neukirchen-Vluyn, 1970) or R. Zadok, *Geographical Names According to New- and Late-Babylonian Texts*, Répertoire géographique des texts cunéiformes 8 (Wiesbaden, 1985). In order to distinguish the name of the god from the name of the city, Aššur will be used for the god and Assur for the city. The writing of the Chaldean tribal names will follow Brinkman

1 I.e., "m" will be kept even though in intervocalic position it may have been pronounced "w" (cf. von Soden, *GAG*, §§31a and 21b-h).

2 I.e., assimilation of "n" to the following consonant is not indicated. (EN.LÍL was almost certainly pronounced "Illil" at this time.)

3 In Babylonia during the following century this was occasionally indicated in the writing (e.g., ^{m}*šu-um*-GI.NA for Šum-ukīn, *Nbn.* 243:2).

4 In agreement with the review of I.J. Gelb, "Notes on von Soden's Grammar of Akkadian," *BiOr* 12 (1955): 106, the penultimate syllable of such hypocoristics is transcribed with a short vowel.

in *Or.* NS 46 (1977): 306.[5] As in the personal names, "y" will be used in place of "j."

DATES

Unless otherwise stated, all dates given in this study (excluding those in bibliographical citations) are B.C. Each Babylonian year has been given a single Julian year equivalent; this is even though the ancient year actually encompassed parts of two Julian years, with the Babylonian year beginning around the time of the vernal equinox. For example, events which occurred late in what is cited here as 652 actually took place early in Julian year 651. Days are cited in Arabic numerals and months in capital Roman numerals by the order in which they occurred in the Babylonian year. Thus, 19-V-651 stands for the nineteenth day of the month of Abu in the year 651 B.C. As an aid to the reader, when a Babylonian month name is given in this study, it will be followed by its month number—e.g., Ayyaru (II).

I	Nisannu	March/April
II	Ayyaru	April/May
III	Simanu	May/June
IV	Du'ūzu	June/July
V	Abu	July/August
VI	Ulūlu	August/September
VI_2	Intercalary Ulūlu	
VII	Tašrītu	September/October
VIII	Araḫsamna	October/November
IX	Kislīmu	November/December
X	Ṭebētu	December/January
XI	Šabaṭu	January/February
XII	Addaru	February/March
XII_2	Intercalary Addaru	

MISCELLANEOUS ABBREVIATIONS

DN	divine name
GN	geographical name
PN	personal name
RN	royal name

[5] For simplification, the spellings Bīt-Dakkūri and Bīt-Yakīn will be used rather than Bīt-Dak(k)ūri and Bīt-Jakīn(i).

NA	Neo-Assyrian
NB	Neo-Babylonian
obv.	obverse
rev.	reverse
Asb.	Ashurbanipal
B.u.	Bēl-ušallim
Esar.	Esarhaddon
Kan.	Kandalānu
N.u.	Nabû-ušabši
Senn.	Sennacherib
Ššu	Šamaš-šuma-ukīn

CHAPTER 1

INTRODUCTION

On the first day of the month Kislīmu in the year 689 B.C., a victorious Assyrian army entered Babylon, the revered capital of Babylonia. Having spent more than five years in putting down a rebellion in that land, the Assyrian king, Sennacherib, was not inclined to be merciful to the city and ordered it to be destroyed. Just over sixty years later, however, an individual by the name of Nabopolassar was to ascend the throne of Babylonia and begin the process leading up to the destruction of the Assyrian empire. What happened in Babylonia during these years is the focus of this study.

It can be argued that with Sennacherib's victory in 689 Babylonia reached the nadir of its political existence. The land lay devastated by Assyrian military actions conducted over the previous years. Babylon itself was abandoned and destroyed, and the separate kingship of Babylonia was abolished. The final insult was the destruction or removal of the statue of the god Marduk, which left Babylonians bereft of their chief deity. At the same time, Assyria was approaching its zenith—with Babylonia as its greatest prize. During the succeeding years, however, unrest in Babylonia, in particular the Šamaš-šuma-ukīn Revolt, taxed Assyrian power to the limit and played an important role in bringing about the collapse of its empire. As the sixty-year period drew to a close, forces in Babylonia were undoubtedly regaining strength and building up the momentum that was to bring about the formation of the Neo-Babylonian empire and the shift of hegemony over western Asia from Assyria to Babylonia.

In attempting to learn about the history and culture of ancient Mesopotamia, we are fortunate that hundreds of thousands of contemporary inscriptions have been preserved. The sheer bulk of source material has, however, tended to discourage scholars from presenting detailed studies of the various periods of Mesopotamian history.[1] Considerable documentary evidence is available for the study of Babylonia during the seventh and sixth centuries, when that land developed into the major power in the Near East, and the period in question, 689 to 627, is particularly in need of study in view

---

1 Among the more important exceptions to this are D.O. Edzard's study of the Isin-Larsa period, *Die "Zweite Zwischenzeit" Babyloniens* (Wiesbaden, 1957), and J.A. Brinkman's of the post-Kassite period, *A Political History of Post-Kassite Babylonia, 1158-722 B.C.*, Analecta Orientalia 43 (Rome, 1968).

of the number of new sources which have become known over the last few years.[2] Copies of a large number of letters, official correspondence of the Assyrian kings Esarhaddon and Ashurbanipal, have recently been published but most of these have yet to be edited and studied.[3] Other documents have appeared only in catalogue form and wait to be presented in full.[4] Also, revised editions are required for many texts published years ago, when our knowledge of the Akkadian language was not as great as it is today. Many kinds of texts (i.e., royal inscriptions, letters, economic documents, chronicles, and omen requests) provide information on this period, and each genre has its own particular uses and problems of interpretation. Chapter 2 surveys and briefly evaluates the source material.

Fortunately, the basic chronology of the period is known so that there is a firm backdrop for the reconstruction of events. Accordingly, the chapter on chronology (chapter 3) is quite short, concentrating on a few unresolved matters.

The population of Babylonia comprised a number of different groups. The most important were the "Akkadians" (mainly identifiable as the residents of urban centres and the bearers of classical Babylonian culture) and the various Chaldean and Aramean tribes. These are described in chapter 4; their respective social relationships and cultural backgrounds are outlined since these factors influenced their actions and reactions in the important events of the time.

The main body of this study is a detailed chronological reconstruction of the major political events from 689 to 627 (chapters 5-9). Each chapter covers one short period of time, either the reign of one king or a part of a king's reign distinguished by a different political situation. These shorter spans are as follows: the reign of the Assyrian king Sennacherib after his destruction of Babylon (689-681); the reign of Esarhaddon (681-669); the first three quarters of the reign of Šamaš-šuma-ukīn (669-653), during which

---

[2] Studies involving this period include S.S. Ahmed, *Southern Mesopotamia in the Time of Ashurbanipal* (The Hauge and Paris, 1968) (cf. the review by G. van Driel in *BiOr* 26 [1969]: 367-68); M. Dietrich, *Die Aramäer Südbabyloniens in der Sargonidenzeit (700-648)*, Alter Orient und Altes Testament 7 (Kevelaer and Neukirchen-Vluyn, 1970) (cf. the review by Brinkman in *Or.* NS 46 [1977]: 304-25); and J.A. Brinkman, *Prelude to Empire: Babylonian Society and Politics, 747-626 B.C.*, Occasional Publications of the Babylonian Fund 7 (Philadelphia, 1984).

[3] Parpola, *CT* 53 and Dietrich, *CT* 54. The letters of Assyrian scholars to the Assyrian kings Esarhaddon and Ashurbanipal have been edited and studied by Parpola in *LAS* and Dietrich (*Aramäer*) used many of the Babylonian letters in his study of the Arameans in southern Babylonia during the Sargonid period. M. Dietrich, S. Parpola, G.B. Lanfranchi, and P. Machinist are currently preparing new editions of all the letters of the Sargonid period as part of the Neo-Assyrian Text Corpus Project.

[4] Brinkman and Kennedy's index of economic texts for the years 721-626 (*B-K*) includes numerous unpublished documents. I am grateful to them for allowing me to make use of their preliminary transliterations of these texts.

time he ruled over Babylonia under the overlordship of his brother, Ashurbanipal, the king of Assyria; the Šamaš-šuma-ukīn Revolt (652-648); and the reign of Kandalānu (647-627). During the first period (chapter 5), there was no "king of Babylon"; Sennacherib reigned directly over Babylonia as king of Assyria. The land lay devastated and quiescent. Few records have survived from Babylonia for these years and consequently little is known of the events of the time. In 681 Esarhaddon succeeded his father as ruler of Assyria and assumed anew the title "king of Babylon." During his reign (chapter 6), he sought to win favour with his Babylonian subjects by various actions, including the rebuilding of Babylon. Nevertheless, several attempts were made by individuals and groups to throw off the Assyrian yoke. After the death of Esarhaddon in 669, the separate kingship of Babylonia was restored. One of Esarhaddon's sons, Šamaš-šuma-ukīn, became ruler of Babylonia, though under the overlordship of his brother Ashurbanipal, the new Assyrian king (chapter 7). Again there was some unrest, often caused or exacerbated by the king of the neighbouring state of Elam. Between 652 and 648, Babylonia was wracked by a revolt led by Šamaš-šuma-ukīn against Assyria (chapter 8). Although the rebellion lasted for more than four years, it was eventually put down, in large part because the rebels had not been able to win the support of all their compatriots. Indeed, various cities and individuals actively supported the Assyrian cause. After defeating the rebels, Ashurbanipal installed as vassal Kandalānu, of whom little more than his name is known. The twenty-one years of Kandalānu's reign (647-627) form a minor dark age in Babylonian history, an age that was to end with the deaths of both Kandalānu and Ashurbanipal in 627 (chapter 9). A new era began at that time, as Nabopolassar founded a new dynasty, fought to evict Assyrian troops from Babylonian soil, and went on to defeat the Assyrians in their homeland and to create the foundations of the Neo-Babylonian empire.

The two following chapters deal with the internal structure and the external relations of the Babylonian state. Chapter 10 examines the superstructure and infrastructure of the state and includes an outline of the administrative system used to govern Babylonia. Chapter 11 explores the relations between Babylonia and its neighbours Assyria and Elam, with emphasis on the reasons for their actions and policies.

A brief summary statement is presented in chapter 12. There are then a number of appendices (A-F) on special problems which may be overly detailed for the general reader but of interest to specialists.

We are fortunate in having available a large body of contemporary source material for this important period in Babylonia's political history. In piecing together the nature and order of events from these records, we can see the relationships at work between the various groups in the land, and we may arrive at a better understanding of the relationship that existed between

Babylonia and its age-old neighbour, rival, and enemy, Assyria. This relationship was a determining factor in many of the actions of both countries over the centuries. The present study will make use of documents unavailable to previous studies and attempt to distinguish between what is reasonably certain and what is conjecture.[5] As present gaps in our knowledge of the period in question are filled with information gained through further discoveries in ancient sites and modern museums, and as research on particular problems is carried out,[6] some matters presented in this study will undoubtedly require revision. Nevertheless, the time is now ripe for a reconsideration of the political history of Babylonia during the years 689-627.

---

5 Regrettably, the damaged state and ambiguous nature of many of the sources will make the use of such terms as "may," "perhaps," "possibly," "appears," and "seems" more frequent that one would desire.

6 The information that can be gathered from a close and systematic examination of even fragmentary letters can be quite extensive and important, as demonstrated by Parpola's work with the Assyrian scholarly letters (*LAS*).

CHAPTER 2

SOURCES

In order to present this history of Babylonia during the sixty-three years of interest, it has been necessary to examine a wide range of source material, much of which is unpublished or published only in either a preliminary or an outdated manner. This chapter presents a brief survey of the various types of sources available. A full study of the material, describing each individual source (e.g., inscription or archaeological artifact) and evaluating its usage, would require several monographs. The source material for this study can be divided into two main areas: written material (ancient texts) and non-written material (archaeological evidence, including reliefs).

I. Written Sources

The textual evidence for the years 689-627 is extensive and includes many different kinds of texts such as kinglists, chronicles, royal inscriptions, letters, economic texts, and omen queries. Almost all of the texts are from Assyria or Babylonia.[1] Thus no attempt is made here to list and discuss each individual document because of the large numbers of texts involved (e.g., approximately four hundred and seventy-five economic texts and several hundred letters). Since a relatively short period of time is of concern here, the dating of some texts (particularly letters) to this period may be a matter of dispute; the dates of such texts will be discussed in the body of the study as each of these texts is cited. Unless otherwise indicated, all texts are written in the Akkadian language; a few documents were composed in Sumerian (primarily inscribed bricks), Aramaic (a letter, a "historical tale," and a section of Ezra), Hebrew (a few passages in the Old Testament), and Greek (Berossos and the Ptolemaic Canon). Akkadian texts can be divided into two groups—Babylonian and Assyrian, the criterion for the distinction being the dialect in which the texts were written (and not the provenance of the texts); the exceptions are the royal inscriptions of Sennacherib, Esarhaddon, and

---

[1] For an evaluation of some of these sources, and similar types of sources, the reader is referred to Brinkman, *PKB*, pp. 24-36. See also Ahmed, *Asb.*, Appendices A and B (though with regard to Appendix B, note the reservations expressed by van Driel in *BiOr* 26 [1969]: 367-68); Grayson, *Or.* NS 49 (1980): 140-94; Eph'al, *Ancient Arabs*, pp. 40-59; and Brinkman, *Prelude*, pp. 113-22.

Ashurbanipal, which are listed here uniformly as Assyrian, even those which were written in Babylonian dialect and script and found in Babylonia.

Chronological Sources

The basic framework for this period is established by kinglists and chronicles. Almost all were composed after 627, but they seem to have relied upon earlier material for their statements.

Kinglists

Six kinglists preserve information about this period. The first three are simple lists of Babylonian kings (sometimes with the lengths of their reigns) presented in chronological order; the other three are synchronistic kinglists, recording both Assyrian and Babylonian kings.[2] Unfortunately, Babylonian Kinglist A (BM 33332), which contains a complete record for this period, does not preserve the lengths of the reigns of Esarhaddon, Šamaš-šuma-ukīn, and Kandalānu (abbreviated to Aššur-aḫa, Šamaš-šuma, and Kandal respectively); also, both the length of reign allotted to Sennacherib after the defeat of Mušēzib-Marduk and the name of the successor to Kandalānu are uncertain.[3] The Uruk Kinglist (IM 65066) begins sometime before Kandalānu (who is given a reign of twenty-one years) and continues into the Seleucid period. The entry before Kandalānu is unclear, although various proposals have been made by scholars; immediately following him are the reigns of Sîn-šumu-līšir and Sîn-šarra-iškun (for a combined total of one year), and Nabopolassar (twenty-one years).[4] The Ptolemaic Canon, written in Greek and attributed to Claudius Ptolemaeus, who lived in the second century A.D., lists the kings of Babylonia, together with their lengths of reign, and begins with the reign of Nabonassar (747-734). According to the Canon, following the four-year reign of Mušēzib-Marduk (Μεσ ησιμορδάκου, genitive case) were an eight-year kingless period (ἀβασίλευτα), the thirteen-year reign of Esarhaddon (᾿Ασαραδίνου, gen.), the twenty-year reign of Šamaš-šuma-ukīn (Σαοσδουχίνου, gen.), and the twenty-two year reign of Kandalānu (Κιν ηλαδάνου, gen.); Kandalānu's successor was Nabopolassar (Ναβοπολασσάρου, gen.) who reigned twenty-one years.[5] The Synchronistic

---

[2] For editions of the kinglists, see Grayson in *RLA* 6, sub "Königslisten und Chroniken. B. Akkadisch." In addition to the bibliography listed *ibid.* and Grayson, *Chronicles*, pp. 267-71, note also for the Uruk Kinglist van Dijk, *Rēš-Heiligtum*, no. 88. For the definition of simple and synchronistic kingslists, see Brinkman, *PKB*, pp. 15-16; see *ibid.*, pp. 26-30 for an evaluation of the reliability and usefulness of these documents.

[3] Grayson in *RLA* 6, pp. 90-96 §3.3.

[4] Grayson in *RLA* 6, pp. 97-98 §3.5; Borger, *AfO* 25 (1974-77): 165-66.

[5] Grayson in *RLA* 6, p. 101 §3.8. The following variants in the writing of the royal names are attested: Μεσησιμοράκου and Μεσησημορδάκου (Mušēzib-Marduk);

Kinglist A 117 originally extended from Ērišum I and Sumulael of Assyria and Babylonia respectively through to Ashurbanipal and Kandalānu; the later portion of the text is totally preserved. After referring to Sennacherib and Mušēzib-Marduk as kings of Assyria and Akkad respectively, this text gives (a) Sennacherib, king of Assyria and Babylon; (b) Esarhaddon, king of Assyria and Babylon; (c) Ashurbanipal, king of Assyria, and Šamaš-šuma-ukīn, king of Babylon; and (d) Ashurbanipal, king of Assyria, and Kandalānu, king of Babylon. The lengths of their reigns are not stated; however, "scholars" (*ummânu*) are named for Sennacherib (Bēl-upaḫḫir and Kalbu), Esarhaddon (Nabû-zēru-līšir and Ištar-šuma-ēreš), and Ashurbanipal (Ištar-šuma-ēreš).[6] Also available for use are synchronistic fragments VAT 11931 and Assur 13956dh (*KAV* 9 and 182 respectively). For this period, the former retains only portions of a few names in the column of kings of Babylonia; following Šū[zubu?] (=Mušēzib-Marduk) are Sennach[erib], Esar[haddon] and Ashur[banipal]. The latter, as far as it is preserved, lists the Assyrian kings and scholars, and basically follows A 117, although it adds Aššur-etil-ilāni as the successor of Ashurbanipal and has a few differences in the names of the scholars.[7]

No major disagreements are found among the statements of these kinglists, though some differences do exist. The Ptolemaic Canon considered the period of Sennacherib's reign over Babylonia after the destruction of Babylon in 689 (as well as his earlier reign) to have been kingless, in contradiction to the assignment of the period to Sennacherib in Babylonian Kinglist A and the Assyrian synchronistic kinglists; thus it reflected either resentment toward Sennacherib because of his destruction of Babylon or the fact that Sennacherib never claimed the title "king of Babylon." In addition, there was some confusion concerning the king to whom the year 668 should be assigned and concerning the succession to Kandalānu; these problems will discussed in elsewhere in this study.

Chronicles

Four chronicles preserve information for this time.[8] All are Babylonian documents, although one, the Esarhaddon Chronicle, may show a pro-Assyrian (or pro-Esarhaddon) bias. The Babylonian Chronicle, part of what has been termed the Neo-Babylonian chronicle series, is preserved in three exemplars. Only one of these exemplars is reasonably complete and it was

---

'Ισαρινδῖνος (Esarhaddon); Σαοσκουλιχίνου (Šamaš-šuma-ukīn); and Ναβοπολασάρου and Ναβοπολάσαρος (Nabopolassar); see Wachsmuth, *Einleitung*, p. 305.

6 Grayson in *RLA* 6, pp. 116-21 §3.12.

7 Grayson in *RLA* 6, pp. 121-22 §3.13 and 124-25 §3.17.

8 For information on Assyrian and Babylonian chronicles, see in particular Grayson, *Chronicles* and *RLA* 6, sub "Königslisten und Chroniken. B. Akkadisch."

copied (from an original) probably in 500. The chronicle extends from the mid-eighth century to the accession year of Šamaš-šuma-ukīn (668).[9] After this point, there is a major gap in the series, for which nothing has survived until just before the accession of Nabopolassar to the throne of Babylonia in 626. Fortunately, some information for this time is preserved in three individual chronicles. The Esarhaddon Chronicle contains entries from the beginning of the reign of Esarhaddon (the first clear entry is for his first regnal year, 680, although there were earlier entries) through to the first year of Šamaš-šuma-ukīn (the last identifiable year). This chronicle and the Babylonian Chronicle frequently have similar entries and likely had at least one source in common.[10] After an entry for the sixth year of Aššur-nādin-šumi (694), the Šamaš-šuma-ukīn Chronicle records events from that king's fourth and fourteenth through eighteenth years (664 and 654-650). In addition, entries for two earlier kings of Babylonia (Širikti-Šuqamuna and Nabû-šuma-iškun) are found at the end of the tablet.[11] Finally, the Akītu Chronicle records interruptions in the New Year's festival during the years 689-626 and occasionally gives the reasons for these interruptions by referring to military actions;[12] thus the period of concern for this chronicle and that of our study are virtually identical.

Each of the chronicles appears to be quite reliable for this period; where overlaps occur, no major conflicts are found. Occasionally minor differences occur when the exact day of the month is mentioned (such as the date of the return of the statue of the god Marduk to Babylon).[13] On two occasions, the Esarhaddon Chronicle does not include events, related in the Babylonian Chronicle, which may have reflected poorly upon the Assyrian king (an Elamite attack on Sippar in 675 and an Assyrian defeat in Egypt in 674). Whether this reflects a pro-Assyrian bias on the part of the composers of the Esarhaddon Chronicle or not remains uncertain.[14] These texts are a record of events considered important by the ancients and constitute extremely valuable source material; criteria for their use have been established by others.[15]

---

[9] Grayson, *Chronicles*, no. 1. This chronicle has been recently examined by Brinkman in an article in *Moran Festschrift*, pp. 73-104. He feels that there are at least two substantially differing versions of the text and that the nature of the series to which the chronicle belonged is unclear; the matter has little relevance to the present study.

[10] Grayson, *Chronicles*, no. 14. Note also Brinkman, *Moran Festschrift*, pp. 88-95.

[11] Grayson, *Chronicles*, no. 15.

[12] Grayson, *Chronicles*, no. 16.

[13] Eph'al points out two errors of dating in the chronicles in *Ancient Arabs*, pp. 53-54, one from the period of concern here and one from the time of Nabonidus.

[14] Brinkman points out that it could equally be suggested that the compilers of the Babylonian Chronicle had an anti-Assyrian bias or that they had additional outside material, i.e., material not available to the compilers of the Esarhaddon Chronicle (*Moran Festschrift*, pp. 92-94).

[15] E.g., Brinkman, *PKB*, pp. 30-33.

Contemporary Sources

Royal Inscriptions[16]

The only strictly Babylonian royal inscriptions during this period are those of Šamaš-šuma-ukīn—no inscriptions by Kandalānu are known, and Esarhaddon was primarily an Assyrian king. The royal inscriptions of Šamaš-šuma-ukīn, like most Babylonian royal inscriptions, contain little political or historical information but concentrate instead on religious and building matters.[17] The most important inscription left by Šamaš-šuma-ukīn is a Sumerian-Akkadian bilingual inscription in pseudo-archaic script; it deals with the rebuilding of the wall of Sippar (Lehmann, *Ššmk*, no. 1).[18] Two inscriptions dealing with his work on the Ezida temple (*ibid.*, no. 2 and Pinckert, *LSS* 3/4, no. 6) are known, as is one brick inscription, in the Sumerian language, which deals with the Ebabbar temple in Sippar (Walker, *CBI*, no. 77). A poorly preserved copy of a votive inscription that records a dedication to the god Nabû by Šamaš-šuma-ukīn is also attested (Lambert, *AfO* 18 [1957-58]: 385-87 no. 2 and pl. 25, the second text on the tablet). Two kudurrus (both of stone and in the shape of stelae) are attested: VA 3614 (Steinmetzer in *Deimel Festschrift*, pp. 302-306; *B-K* K.163) and BM 87220 (*BBSt* 10; *B-K* K.169). The former records the grant of a temple prebend in Sippar by Šamaš-šuma-ukīn and the latter his confirmation of the ownership of a large tract of land. In addition, BM 77611++ records that Šamaš-šuma-ukīn renewed the gift of a prebend originally granted by Aššur-nādin-šumi (see *B-K* Fn.4 and Kn.5).

Royal inscriptions of Sennacherib, Esarhaddon, and Ashurbanipal, both those from Assyria and those from Babylonia, frequently mention the southern kingdom. These include annalistic documents as well as votive and building inscriptions. The principal editions of the royal inscriptions of Sennacherib and Esarhaddon are those of Luckenbill (*The Annals of Sennacherib* [Chicago, 1924]) and Borger (*Die Inschriften Asarhaddons, Königs von Assyrien* [Graz, 1956]) respectively.[19] Much work has been

---

16 For a form-critical study of royal inscriptions from Assyria and Babylonia, as well as other types of historical texts, see Grayson, *Or.* NS 49 (1980): 140-94. Note also the series of studies on Assyrian royal inscriptions published in *ARINH* and *HHI*.

17 See Brinkman, *PKB*, pp. 24-25 for a general evaluation of the information contained in Babylonian royal inscriptions of the late second and early first millennia.

18 The text has been recently re-edited and studied by Jacobsen in *Tadmor Festschrift*, pp. 279-91.

19 For texts of Esarhaddon dealing with Babylonia, note in particular the following additional works: Heidel, *Sumer* 12 (1956): 9-37 and pls. 1-12; Borger, *BiOr* 21 (1964): 143-48; Millard, *AfO* 24 (1973): 117-19 and pls. 13-14; Tsukimoto, *ARRIM* 8 (1990): 63-69; and the study by Brinkman in *JAOS* 103 (1983): 35-42.

done on the inscriptions of Ashurbanipal since just over seventy years ago Streck published his edition of all the texts known to him in his monumental work *Assurbanipal und die letzten assyrischen Könige bis zum Untergange Niniveh's* (Leipzig, 1916). In particular, editions and studies by Aynard, Bauer, Piepkorn, Thompson, and Weidner, and more recently by such scholars as Cogan, Gerardi, Grayson, Knudsen, Millard, Spalinger, and Tadmor have added much to our knowledge of Ashurbanipal's royal inscriptions.[20] In Babylonia, votive and building texts of Esarhaddon have been found at, or deal with, Babylon, Borsippa, Nippur, and Uruk; those of Ashurbanipal mention Babylon, Borsippa, Cutha, Dēr, Nippur, Sippar, Uruk, and possibly Akkad.[21] The annals of Esarhaddon and Ashurbanipal are of particular importance because they report those kings' political and military actions in Babylonia; their inscriptions from Babylonia are for the most part regular Babylonian royal inscriptions and contain little historical data.[22] Sennacherib's annals contain nothing about Babylonia after his destruction of Babylon in 689. The royal inscriptions of Esarhaddon and Ashurbanipal present a number of problems; in particular, the dates, and sometimes the order, of various campaigns and events described in these texts are often uncertain.[23] Criteria for the use of royal inscriptions have been established by Olmstead among others.[24]

---

[20] For details about the publications of the royal inscriptions of these three kings, see the references in Borger, *HKL* 3, pp. 23-24 and 26-27 (with additions in the index of Assyriology in recent issues of *Archiv für Orientforschung*). For the numbering and publication of the various editions of the annals of Ashurbanipal and for references to recent studies, see Grayson, *ZA* 70 (1980): 227-45; note also Tadmor in *25th Congress*, pp. 240-41; Cogan and Tadmor, *Or.* NS 50 (1981): 229-40; and Eph'al, *Ancient Arabs*, especially pp. 46-52. Editions C, D, E, H, and K of Ashurbanipal's annals and Ashurbanipal's tablet inscription from the Ištar temple at Nineveh are poorly preserved and require new editions; they will not generally be cited in this study unless they provide information not contained in better preserved editions. Except for the building section at the end, edition D appears to be basically a duplicate of edition B. New editions of the royal inscriptions of these three kings are being prepared by the Royal Inscriptions of Mesopotamia Project, under the direction of A.K. Grayson.

[21] Some of Ashurbanipal's brick inscriptions were in the Sumerian language (*PBS* 15 74; Walker, *CBI*, nos. 79-80; and Gerardi, *ARRIM* 4 [1986]: 37).

[22] Exceptions being some inscriptions of Esarhaddon from Babylonia dealing with the rebuilding of Babylon and edition H of Ashurbanipal's annals, some exemplars of which were found at Babylon.

[23] In a recent article (*ZA* 70 [1980]: 227-45), Grayson attempts to deal with the internal chronology of the reign of Ashurbanipal.

[24] E.g., A.T.E. Olmstead, *Assyrian Historiography: A Source Study* (Columbia, 1916). Note the recent comments by Cogan in *Tadmor Festschrift*, pp. 121-28.

Officials' Inscriptions

Inscriptions belonging to Sîn-balāssu-iqbi and Sîn-šarra-uṣur, governors of Ur from the time of Šamaš-šuma-ukīn, have been preserved. All but one of the votive and building inscriptions (including bricks) of Sîn-balāssu-iqbi are in Sumerian (*UET* 1 168-171 and 173-183); *UET* 8 102 is in Akkadian.[25] One of his texts (*UET* 1 172) is a copy of a Sumerian inscription by Amar-Suen, a ruler of the Third Dynasty of Ur, at the end of the third millennium. Three of these inscriptions (*UET* 1 168 and 170, and 8 102) mention Ashurbanipal; none refer to Šamaš-šuma-ukīn, the king of Babylonia at that time. A dedicatory inscription (*TCL* 12 13 and duplicate Durand, *DCEPHE* 1, HE 144)[26] records a gift of land by Sîn-šarra-uṣur to the goddesses Ištar of Uruk and Nanaya "for the life of Šamaš-šuma-ukīn." While these texts show the activity of these governors of Ur and possibly reflect their loyalties, they contain little historical data. The numerous inscriptions of Sîn-balāssu-iqbi referring to building projects may well reflect a period of increased prosperity at Ur during the first half of Ashurbanipal's reign.

Adê-Agreements

A sizeable number of documents recording treaties or loyalty oaths (Akkadian *adê*) imposed upon vassal rulers and individuals living within the Assyrian empire (including members of the Assyrian royal family) have been preserved from the seventh century and these have recently been collected and re-edited by Parpola and Watanabe (*SAA* 2).[27] The number of such documents may be the result of an increasing concern to ensure the proper succession as a result of the problem arising at the end of Sennacherib's reign. Of those texts of interest here, most are in Assyrian script and dialect; those which are Babylonian are described as such below. The earliest document, VAT 11449, is an oath of loyalty imposed by Sennacherib; the exact date and circumstances of its composition are unclear, but it may date to the time of the appointment of Esarhaddon to be crown prince.[28] The longest and most important is the *adê*-agreement imposed by Esarhaddon upon a

---

[25] Eight clay disks with this inscription are known; they record work done by Sîn-balāssu-iqbi on a well at Ur; see Brinkman, *Or.* NS 38 (1969): 339-42 and 348, addendum.

[26] *B-K* Kn.11. Note the study by Durand in *RA* 75 (1981): 181-85.

[27] Other recent editions and studies of some of these texts include Grayson, *JCS* 39 (1987): 127-60; Parpola, *ibid.*, pp. 161-89; and Watanabe, *Vereidigung*. For discussions of the term *adê*, its meaning, and the structure of this type of text, see these three works and Parpola and Watanabe, *SAA* 2, pp. XV-XXV and XXXV-XLII (which also provide references to previous studies).

[28] Parpola and Watanabe, *SAA* 2, no. 3.

number of his eastern vassals in 672;[29] it reveals Esarhaddon's plans for the succession to the thrones of Assyria and Babylonia upon his death. Two further Assyrian loyalty oaths imposed on behalf of Esarhaddon are preserved on the tablet fragments 83-1-18,420(+)83-1-18,493(+)91-5-9,131 and 91-5-9,22.[30] Zakūtu, the mother of Esarhaddon, required Šamaš-šuma-ukīn, his brothers, and other Assyrians to take an oath of allegiance to Ashurbanipal, likely soon after the death of her son late in 669; this oath is recorded in *ABL* 1239.[31] *ABL* 1105, written in both Babylonian dialect and script, records an oath of allegiance to Ashurbanipal by some Babylonians; the poor state of preservation of the text makes its exact interpretation uncertain but it can be argued that it dates to the start of the Šamaš-šuma-ukīn Revolt in 652.[32] Also from the reign of Ashurbanipal is Bu 91-5-9,178, an *adê*-agreement between Ashurbanipal and the Arab tribe of Qedar which likely dates to the period just before the start of the revolt of Šamaš-šuma-ukīn.[33] Finally, one might also mention BM 50666+50857+53678+53728(+)51098, a fragmentary tablet written in Babylonian script and dialect; while it may not be an *adê*-agreement itself, it does appear to describe the agreement imposed by Esarhaddon in 672.[34] These documents recording treaties or loyalty oaths are of great historical importance and present some idea of the political authority and plans of the parties imposing them.

Legal and Adminstrative Documents

A recent catalogue of the dated economic texts from the eighth and seventh centuries published by J.A. Brinkman and D.A. Kennedy[35] includes approximately 475 texts from the years 689-627. Most of these record either sales (of houses, fields, gardens, temple prebends) or loans, although other matters are also recorded (such as court cases, rental agreements, and

[29] Parpola and Watanabe, *SAA* 2, no. 6. Note in particular the recent, thorough edition in Watanabe, *Vereidigung*.

[30] Parpola and Watanabe, *SAA* 2, nos. 4 and 7 respectively. Watanabe and Parpola (*ibid.*, p. XXVIII) suggest that the former may have been imposed shortly before Esarhaddon ascended the throne since he is not called king in what is preserved ot the text and Parpola (*JCS* 39 [1987]: 175) suggests that the latter may date to 670, following an unsuccessful coup d'état. Note also the fragment K 4439 whose date and particulars are uncertain but which Parpola and Watanabe tentatively suggest may be Esarhaddon's *adê*-agreement with Hazael of Qedar or his son Yauta' (*SAA* 2, no. 13 and p. XXXIV).

[31] Parpola and Watanabe, *SAA* 2, no. 8.

[32] Parpola and Watanabe, *SAA* 2, no. 9.

[33] Parpola and Watanabe, *SAA* 2, no. 10.

[34] Parpola and Watanabe, *SAA* 2, no. 14.

[35] *JCS* 35 (1983): 1-90, with a supplement in 38 (1986): 99-106 (abbreviated in this study as *B-K*). When an economic text is cited in this study, the Brinkman-Kennedy catalogue number will be given in addition to the major publication reference (or museum number in the case of unpublished texts).

administrative accounts). Only three documents, less that one per cent of the total number of economic texts from this period, are dated by the regnal years of Sennacherib; the approximate percentages for the reigns of Esarhaddon, Ashurbanipal, Šamaš-šuma-ukīn, and Kandalānu are six per cent, nine per cent, thirty-nine per cent, and forty-five per cent respectively. (These documents are presented in tabular form in Appendix A.) Two texts are dated by the tenure of a governor of Ur (possibly from the reign of Sennacherib after the destruction of Babylon), three by non-canonical Babylonian eponym officials, and four posthumously to an earlier king, Aššur-nādin-šumi; for a discussion of these texts, see Appendix C. A number of other economic documents can be dated to this period by internal evidence (e.g., prosopography).

The date formulae of these texts attest to the acceptance of a specific king's reign at a certain place at a particular point in time. Thus they reflect the extent of the given king's realm and are helpful in determining his exact length of reign. The body of these documents give some idea of the social and economic life of Babylonia at the time, and occasionally refer to historical events (e.g., a famine or a siege). In addition, they frequently contain statements about who held certain offices within the Babylonian provincial system. (Appendix B contains a list of Babylonian officials during this time period.) The presence of two texts dated by the tenure of a governor of Ur, Ningal-iddin, could indicate that in this instance substantial authority was either delegated to or assumed by a provincial official (see Appendix C). Assyrian influence in Babylonia is indicated by the temporary carry-over and adaptation of the practice of dating by eponyms at Babylon. Because economic texts were private documents, not intended for public display and propaganda, they may generally be regarded as unbiased. The abundance of texts from the years 669-627 may be a sign of increased activity and prosperity in Babylonia during the time Ashurbanipal was king of Assyria while the relative scarcity of texts from 689-681 may reflect an impoverished or uncertain state of affairs in Babylonia as a result of Sennacherib's defeat of Mušēzib-Marduk and the destruction of Babylon. Accident of discovery may, however, play a part here, making these suggestions tentative.

A few Assyrian administrative texts also provide useful information. These include a document dealing with the return of Babylonian cultic objects that had been taken to Elam (*ADD* 930) and two texts that refer to tablets taken from Babylonia to Assyria shortly after the Šamaš-šuma-ukīn Revolt, namely *ADD* 943(+)944 and 1053.[36]

---

[36] For editions of the latter two texts, see Parpola *JNES* 42 (1983): 1-29 nos. 1 and 3.

Letters

Several hundred Assyrian and Babylonian letters and reports provide information on the history of Babylonia during the period in question.[37] Only one of these, *UET* 4 167, a letter to an individual by the name of Ningal-iddin, was found in Babylonia (at Ur) and it is not absolutely certain that it refers to the Ningal-iddin who was governor of Ur around 680. Since no letters from this period have been found at Babylon, we are deprived of the correspondence between the Babylonian kings Šamaš-šuma-ukīn and Kandalānu and their subjects; this undoubtedly results in a distorted view of conditions.[38] Almost all the letters were found in the royal archives at Kuyunjik, the citadel of Nineveh. These have been published in copy primarily by Harper (*ABL*), Thompson (*Rep.*), Parpola (*CT* 53), and Dietrich (*CT* 54). Reliable editions of the Harper letters have long been wanting.[39] New editions of the letters of Assyrian and Babylonian scholars (e.g., exorcists and haruspices) to Esarhaddon and Ashurbanipal have recently been published by Parpola (*LAS*);[40] his systematic study of these has provided much new information and many new ideas for our understanding of this period. He, Lanfranchi, and Machinist are currently preparing new editions of the remainder of the Sargonid letters from Assyria[41] and Dietrich is working on new editions of the letters from Babylonia found at Nineveh. In addition to these letters written in cuneiform on clay tablets, a fragmentary Aramaic letter written on a potsherd was found at the city of Assur in the early part of this century. This letter, the Assur Ostracon, was sent by an Assyrian official to his brother (or colleague) during the time of the Šamaš-šuma-ukīn Revolt, refers to the events of that time, and mentions individuals known from other letters.[42]

The majority of the letters preserved from the years 689-627 are dated to the final part of the reign of Esarhaddon, the beginning of the reign of Ashurbanipal, and the years around the Šamaš-šuma-ukīn Revolt.[43] They

---

[37] A valuable survey by Parpola of the Neo-Assyrian letters appears in *ARINH*, pp. 117-42. See also his article in *Cuneiform Archives*, pp. 223-36 and Malbran-Labat's comments in *Armée*, pp. 1-4.

[38] Some letters excavated in Babylonia (particularly from Nippur and Uruk) may date to this period; however, this remains to be proven.

[39] The editions of the Harper letters by L. Waterman (*RCAE*) and R.H. Pfeiffer (*State Letters of Assyria*, American Oriental Series 6 [New Haven, 1935]), while useful in their time, contain numerous errors and are badly outdated.

[40] When a letter has been edited by Parpola, both the *ABL* number and the *LAS* number will be given in this study.

[41] One volume of letters from the reign of Sargon II has already appeared (*SAA* 1, by Parpola).

[42] Donner and Röllig, *KAI*, no. 233 and Gibson, *TSSI* 2, no. 20.

[43] With regard to the Assyrian letters, see Parpola, *ARINH*, p. 136.

deal with a wide range of topics, including political, military, economic, scholarly, cultic, and legal matters. Since letters were not normally intended for public perusal, they are generally considered more candid, less guarded, and therefore more reliable than official statements; however, since all but a few of the letters under consideration were intended to be seen by the king of Assyria, they may present a distorted view of conditions. Officials in Babylonia reporting to the Assyrian king might well have had their own reasons for giving a false view of affairs in their area and thus might conceal or report inaccurately upon certain matters.

The use of these letters poses many problems for the modern historian. Many of them are poorly preserved and they often lack the introductory section which gives the names of author and recipient. Only rarely are these documents dated or is the name of the king specifically stated. The author of a letter expected the recipient to be familiar with the background against which the letter was written and thus often alluded to places and events that are obscure to us, as well as to individuals whose identities are unknown to us. Different individuals of the same name are known to have written to the king and/or be mentioned in the letters, making it sometimes difficult to be sure who is meant. Although we may assume that only important officials and individuals would have corresponded directly with the king, we can rarely be certain exactly what official position was held by any such individual. Frequently it is not even possible to tell where a letter originated, although the gods mentioned in the introductory section were often important locally and therefore provide a clue.[44] Finally, these letters sometimes use idiomatic expressions which are difficult to understand. The letters provide tantalizing allusions to people, places, and events; however, their use for historical purposes is often hazardous, particularly when we must rely on our often uncertain understanding of the text and its historical background for restoring broken or damaged passages. Thus, although these letters are extremely valuable sources of evidence, they must be used judiciously. In order to avoid lengthy argumentation and running the risk of "creating" a history for this period based upon conjectured interpretations of letters whose meaning and background cannot be proven with some reasonable degree of probability, I have not attempted to account for every letter or letter fragment which may conceivably date to this period. It is inevitable, however, that other scholars will have different views as to the interpretation of some of the letters used in this study. It is to be hoped that the forthcoming editions and studies of the individual letters and letter fragments by the Neo-Assyrian Text Corpus Project, and future joins of fragments, will allow us to eliminate some of the uncertainties in the use of these texts. Astronomical references in the

---

44 For example, letters from Uruk tended to mention the goddesses Ištar and Nanaya, two deities whose cults were well known at Uruk.

scholarly letters published in *LAS* allowed Parpola to propose precise dates for many of those letters; however, such references are lacking in most of the remaining letters and we are unlikely to be able to do more than suggest approximate dates for the vast majority of them.

Omens and Oracular Material

Approximately twenty-five oracle queries (questions placed before Šamaš, the god of omens and oracles) and extispicy reports (reports of diviners on the results of their inspection of the entrials of sheep) deal with matters involving Babylonia in the time of Esarhaddon and Ashurbanipal. They form only a small part of the corpus of omen queries and reports from the reigns of these two Sargonid kings. The matters of concern in these texts include proposed campaigns to Babylonia, the return of the statue of the god Marduk, and the appointment and loyalty of officials. The original publications of most of these are by Klauber (*PRT*) and Knudtzon (*Gebete*). I. Starr has recently re-edited all these texts for the Neo-Assyrian Text Corpus Project (*SAA* 4) and they will be cited according to their number in his work. These texts, many of which were dated in antiquity, are valuable for the insight they give into what the Assyrian kings contemplated doing, thought possible, or were eager to learn about.

A Babylonian tablet dated in the tenth year of Šamaš-šuma-ukīn and containing a number of astrological omens has been preserved (*UET* 6/2 413); also dating to the reign of Šamaš-šuma-ukīn is a tablet containing diagnostic omens (*TDP* no. 12, text C). These two texts are of use for their date formulae and for the light they shed on scholarly activity at this time. Two texts, found in Assyria but written in Babylonian script, record historical omens about Ashurbanipal and Šamaš-šuma-ukīn (*CT* 35 pls. 37-38 and Starr, *AfO* 32 [1985]: 60-67). They were undoubtedly composed after the events they describe and show pro-Assyrian sympathies. They refer to a number of incidents in Babylonia and Elam; for example, one omen portending the annihilation of the army was declared to be an omen of Šamaš-šuma-ukīn who had been defeated in battle by the army of Ashurbanipal (*CT* 35 pl. 38 rev. 14-17).

Miscellaneous Inscriptions

There are a number of informative texts that do not fit neatly into any of the above categories. These include a copy of a dedicatory inscription of the Babylonian king Marduk-šāpik-zēri (1081-1069) made during the reign of Kandalānu (King, *LIH* 1 70), a copy of an incantation of the *maqlû* type written for Šamaš-šuma-ukīn (*PBS* 10/2 18),[45] a hymn to the goddess Ištar written or copied at Nippur during the seventh year of Šamaš-šuma-ukīn and mentioning Enlil-bāni, the governor of Nippur (BM 78903; *B-K* Kn.9), and a number of Babylonian religious texts (prayers and rituals to ward off evil) that refer to Šamaš-šuma-ukīn.[46] These attest to scholarly activity in Babylonia during this period and the latter reflect concern for Šamaš-šuma-ukīn's well-being.

The earliest astronomical diary known, BM 32312,[47] records information for the year 652; it also contains historical references which may be compared with entries for that year in the Akītu Chronicle. Besides confirming the chronology of this period (year 16 of Šamaš-šuma-ukīn in the Akītu Chronicle is to be equated with the absolute year 652 B.C.), this text confirms the reliability of at least some of the historical statements in the Akītu Chronicle. It is unlikely that this contemporary scholarly text, not designed for general use, would have given incorrect historical data. Another tablet in the British Museum records observations of the movement of the planet Saturn during the year 647 to 634, thus during the reign of Kandalānu.[48]

Two Assyrian texts published by A. Livingstone as *SAA* 3, nos. 29-30 appear to be denunciations of a Babylonian by the name of Bēl-ēṭir son of Ibâ, who was active in the time of Ashurbanipal.[49] These two documents, although poorly preserved and very difficult, give some insight into Assyrian feeling towards a Babylonian rebel.

One text which likely dates to this period is the so-called "Marduk Ordeal," most recently edited and studied by T. Frymer-Kensky in *JAOS* 103 (1983): 131-41 and by A. Livingstone in *Explanatory Works*, pp. 205-53 and as *SAA* 3, nos. 34-35. Although the two scholars are not in agreement over the exact date of the composition or its interpretation, it seems clear that this Assyrian text's description of the captivity of the god Marduk is to be connected with the fate of the god and his statue following Sennacherib's capture and destruction of Babylon in 689.

K 4730(+)Sm 1816, a document which is commonly referred to as the "Sin of Sargon," purports to be a pseudo-autobiography of Sennacherib in which he recorded how he had attempted to discover the reason his predecessor Sargon II had died in battle and his body had not been recovered for burial in Assyria. It is likely, however, that the text dates from the time of

---

45 See also Lambert, *AfO* 18 (1957-58): 288-99, text B (CBS 1203).

46 For a list of the texts, see pp. 116-17 n. 77.

47 A. Sachs kindly provided me with information on this piece before its publication as *Astronomical Diaries* 1, no. -651.

48 See Walker, *BSMS* 5 (1983): 20-21.

49 See also Parpola, *JNES* 42 (1983): 11 n. 39. Parpola kindly allowed me to make use of his own transliterations of the two documents before Livingstone's publication appeared.

Esarhaddon and was intended to justify that king's restoration (or creation) of a statue of the god Marduk, and by implication his favourable policy towards Babylonia.[50]

Non-contemporary Sources

A number of later texts contain statements that refer to the period in question. Since they were written after the events they describe, their evidence must be used with great caution.

Several inscriptions composed during the time of the Neo-Babylonian monarchs refer to events in our period. A text probably coming from the time of Nabopolassar and describing that king's war with Assyria refers to Sennacherib's looting of Babylon (Gerardi, *AfO* 33 [1986]: 30-38). A royal inscription of Nabonidus (Langdon, *NBK*, Nabonid no. 8) describes the destruction of Babylon in 689 and Marduk's twenty-one-year sojourn in Assyria. Unfortunately the description is rather more literary than historical in nature. Another of his texts (*CT* 34 pls. 26-37) refers to the destruction of the city of Sippar-Anunītu and its temple Eulmaš by Sennacherib, though when this took place during Sennacherib's reign is not stated. An inscription of Nabonidus' mother, Adad-guppi' (Gadd, *AnSt* 8 [1958]: 35-92 and pls. 1-16), contains statements about the lengths of reigns of kings who had ruled during her lifetime. She states that Ashurbanipal ruled forty-two years, the only known definite statement as to the exact length of his reign.

Several late texts include references to astronomical observations made (or astronomical events calculated to have occurred) during this period. In particular, BM 33809 is a list of specific years in the reigns of various kings of Babylonia; the years recorded are usually at nineteen-year intervals and extend from 732 to the time of the Seleucids. This list includes the sixth year of Esarhaddon (675), the thirteenth year of Šamaš-šuma-ukīn (655), and the twelfth year [of Kandalānu] (636). Some of the entries may have been calculated back from a later time since the dates do not always match nineteen-year intervals; for example, one expects the seventh year of Esarhaddon (674), not his sixth year.[51] In addition, five fragmentary texts (Pinches,

[50] The text will be referred to by its recent edition in Livingstone, *SAA* 3, no. 33. The primary edition (upon which Livingstone's is based) and study of the text is that by H. Tadmor, B. Landsberger and S. Parpola in *SAAB* 3 (1989): 3-51. With regard to the text, note also Tadmor in *Eretz Israel* 5 (1958): 150-63 and 93*; Tadmor in Eisenstadt, *Origins*, pp. 212-14; and Garelli in *Voix de l'opposition*, pp. 193-96.

[51] Information on the text courtesy J.A. Brinkman and C.B.F. Walker. For the meaning and importance of the nineteen-year cycle, see Hunger in *RLA* 5, p. 298.

LBAT 1414-1418) record lunar eclipses, arranged in eighteen-year cycles, for this period.[52]

Berossos, whose work written in Greek around 300 B.C. is known only via the statements of later writers, refers briefly to the events of this period, generally citing the names of kings and the lengths of their reigns.[53] Some of what is attributed to him is clearly incorrect (e.g., Esarhaddon is given a reign of eight years and Šamaš-šuma-ukīn one of twenty-one years). His statement that Šamaš-šuma-ukīn was succeeded by his brother (variant Sardanapallos) has led many scholars to identify Kandalānu with Ashurbanipal. In view of the complexity of the tradition that preserves the statements of Berossos and of the existence of clearly incorrect statements, information attributed to Berossos must be weighed very carefully.[54]

The Old Testament may be of use at at least one point. Ezra 4:9-10 (the preamble to a letter in Aramaic) refers to one Asnappar (variant Osnappar) who had exiled people from Babylonia and Elam to Syria-Palestine. The most likely person to have done so was Ashurbanipal; there is, however, no contemporary evidence for this event. In addition, 2 Chronicles 33:11-13 describes Manasseh being taken captive to Babylon and may possibly be connected with some punishment for involvement with the Šamaš-šuma-ukīn Revolt; however, this remains to be proven.[55]

Of particular interest is an Aramaic document in demotic script from Egypt now in the Pierpont Morgan Library (Amherst papyrus 63). It was found in a jar near Thebes together with eighteen other papyri, three of which bore dates ranging between 139 and 112 B.C. The document is actually a collection of several different texts, one of which is a lengthy tale about the rebellion of Šamaš-šuma-ukīn against Ashurbanipal or the diplomatic manoeuvres at the start of that revolt.[56] The text is difficult to undertand; parts are poorly preserved and the interpretation of various sections of the story is uncertain.

---

52 *LBAT* 1416 (BM 35115) records the various eighteen-year cycles in which lunar eclipses occurred between 703 and 378 and includes lunar eclipse possibilities in the accession and 18th years of Šamaš-šuma-ukīn (668 and 650) and the 16th year of Kandalānu (632). See Walker, *BSMS* 5 (1983): 23.

53 For the fragments attributed to Berossos of interest here, see Jacoby, *FGrH* III C/1, pp. 385-87 and 404 and Schnabel, *Berossos*, pp. 268-71. For a recent translation of Berossos, see Burstein, *SANE* 1/5 (1978).

54 See Brinkman, *PKB*, pp. 34-35 and Burstein, *SANE* 1/5 (1978): 6 and 10-11.

55 Other sections of the Old Testament may refer to events of interest during this period, but this remains uncertain.

56 On the document see Bowman, *JNES* 3 (1944): 219-31; Nims, *OIAR* 1980-1981, pp. 47-48; Nims and Steiner, *JAOS* 103 (1983): 261-74, *JNES* 43 (1984): 89-114, and *RB* 92 (1985): 60-81; and Vleeming and Wesselius, *BiOr* 39 (1982): 501-509, *JEOL* 28 (1983-84): 110-40 (with further bibliography listed on p. 140), and *Studies* 1. Nims and Steiner (*JAOS* 103 [1983]: 261) and Lipiński (*BiOr* 44 [1987]: 413) date the document to the late second century B.C.; Vleeming and Wesselius argue for a date in the fourth century B.C. (*JEOL* 28 [1983-84]: 111).

Two translations of the tale have appeared—one by C.F. Nims and R.C. Steiner and one by S.P. Vleeming and J.W. Wesselius—but they disagree on a number of points important to the interpretation of the text (e.g., whether or not the text refers to Šamaš-šuma-ukīn ceasing to send tribute to Ashurbanipal at the start of the revolt and whether or not it describes Šamaš-šuma-ukīn leaving Babylon to submit to his brother and dying en route).[57] Although the document itself is of late date, various correct historical details (e.g., the mention of the brothers' sister Šērū'a-ēṭerat) indicates that the composer of the story had earlier sources (written or oral) at his disposal.[58] The text is a literary work clearly intended to cast Ashurbanipal as the hero and to vilify Šamaš-šuma-ukīn.[59] Because of its literary nature and late date, we must be circumspect in using the tale to reconstruct the events of the period.

II. Non-written Sources

The period of concern to this study is quite short, only sixty-three years, and was not isolated from the preceding and following periods by any major cultural changes. Criteria for dating archaeological levels and objects have not yet been defined closely enough for our purposes and thus it is rarely possible to use archaeological evidence in this study. Usually levels are dated by inscribed objects found in them. Since archaeological periods are not necessarily identical to historical periods, defining such criteria may prove impossible. Only the destruction of Babylon, the starting point for this study, may prove identifiable by stratigraphy alone.

Surface Surveys

Surface surveys encompassing this time period have been carried out over a large part of Babylonia—the lower Diyala basin, Akkad, and the regions around Tell ed-Dēr, Kish, Nippur, Lagash, Uruk, and Ur.[60] However, the

---

[57] Steiner and Nims, *RB* 92 (1985): 60-81; their commentary to the text is to appear in a future article. Vleeming and Wesselius, *Studies* 1, pp. 31-37.

[58] Vleeming and Wesselius argue that "the story underlying this text, if not the actual composition, must be dated quite close to the events it describes, certainly not later than the sixth century BC" (*Studies* 1, p. 32). Some historical details in the text are clearly incorrect (e.g., Ashurbanipal is described as being older than Šamaš-šuma-ukīn).

[59] See in particular the statement that the year of Ashurbanipal's birth was good while that of Šamaš-šuma-ukīn was bad (Steiner and Nims, *RB* 92 [1985]: 70 and Vleeming and Wesselius, *Studies* 1, p. 33).

[60] Brinkman estimates that less than one third of the settled area of the alluvium between the Tigris and Euphrates rivers in southern Mesopotamia has been subject to detailed survey (*Prelude*, p. 3). Not all areas, however, appear to have been surveyed with equal thoroughness and not all of these surveys have been published as yet. See Adams, *Land*

ceramic typology for the period in question is not sufficiently established for exact usage here, and to complicate matters, the various surveyors have not always used the same boundaries for the time periods cited within their studies. For example, the period 689-627 is included within the time from the fall of the Kassite dynasty (*c.* 1158) till approximately the start of the Neo-Babylonian period (626) in the Diyala and Akkad surveys;[61] within the period 800 till 120 in the Uruk area survey; and within the period *c.* 1000 till 539 in the Kish area survey. It is therefore difficult to extract even general trends for the period 689-627 from the data available.[62] Still, the surveys might suggest a decrease in settled area, and thus population, in Babylonia. As tabulated by Brinkman, when you compare the area occupied during the period 1150-626 with that during the period 1600-1150, the greatest decline is found around the lower Diyala (loss of about three-quarters of the population) with less drastic declines the further south one goes (down to the loss of only about one quarter of the population in the area around Ur); the information would also suggest that a greater percentage of the population lived in towns and villages than in cities.[63] In an important re-evaluation of the material, however, Brinkman has recently questioned this.[64] He has pointed out various problems involved in using the data and has noted that both the main centres of urban population after the mid-ninth century (in the northwest, around Babylon, Borsippa, Cutha, and Dilbat) and the major tribal areas (to the west of Nippur and Uruk, along the old course of the Euphrates and in the marsh area east of Ur and Uruk) lay outside the areas that have been subject to intensive survey.[65] Thus the conclusions that one might draw from the surveys are not necessarily valid for the land or the period as a whole and indeed may well be contradicted by the textual evidence. The average number of economic texts per year rises dramatically around 720, and particularly after 668; this would suggest an increase in economic activity in the land and could well reflect an increasing population.

Behind Baghdad; Adams and Nissen, *Uruk Countryside*; Gibson, *Kish*, with an appendix by Adams; de Meyer, *Tell ed-Dēr* 3, pp. 1-13 and plan 1; Adams, *Heartland of Cities*, with an appendix by H.T. Wright. Note also Roux, *Sumer* 16 (1960): 20-31, map following p. 30, and pls. 1-8; Jacobsen, *Salinity*; and the articles on research in the Hamrin area in *Sumer* 40 (1984).

61 The chronological boundaries for the Akkad survey are not explicitly stated by Adams (in Gibson, *Kish*); the information for this period was provided to me in a personal communication from Adams.

62 Note also the reservations by P.J. Parr on the reliability of our interpretations of the evidence gained from current surface surveys in *Man, Settlement and Urbanism*, edited by P. Ucko *et al* (London, 1972), pp. 805-10.

63 See Adams, *Heartland of Cities*, pp. 152-54 and Brinkman, *Prelude*, pp. 4-6.

64 See Brinkman in *JNES* 43 (1984): 169-80 and note also *Prelude*, pp. 3-10 and *Sumer* 41 (1985): 110-12.

65 Brinkman notes, however, that it might prove difficult to detect the tribal peoples in any survey in view of their generally nomadic life-style.

Excavations

The fact that economic texts were composed at various sites, including Babylon, Borsippa, Cutha, Dilbat, Kish, Marad, Nippur, Sippar, Ur, and Uruk, leaves no doubt that these cities were occupied during the years 689-627. Since dated texts can be useful in dating the levels in which they are found, it is unfortunate that only about ten per cent of these were found in archaeological excavations—at Babylon, Kish, Nippur, Ur, and Uruk.[66] Archaeological evidence confirms that these five cities were occupied at this time.[67]

At Babylon, extensive archaeological excavations were carried out by the Deutsche Orient-Gesellschaft under the leadership of R. Koldewey between 1899 and 1917 A.D. and more recently, work has been done by the Iraqi State Organization for Antiquities and Heritage. Information for the period of concern here comes primarily from the Merkes quarter, where there is some evidence of destruction or abandonment and a later rebuilding (see chapter 5). This may be associated with the destruction of Babylon by Sennacherib in 689 and the subsequent rebuilding beginning under Esarhaddon, though at present there are insufficient clear data to consider this proven. No clear archaeological evidence has been found to confirm Sennacherib's assertion that he destroyed Babylon's city walls, Esarhaddon's claim to have rebuilt them, or Ashurbanipal's to have repaired them. Although bricks, foundation tablets, and other texts record the building and restoration of various temples at Babylon (in particular Esagila) by Esarhaddon, Ashurbanipal, and Šamaš-šuma-ukīn, many of these were not found in situ and clear archaeological evidence of work at this time on the sites mentioned is unknown. Nebuchadnezzar's restoration of the city and his major building projects have undoubtedly destroyed much of the earlier work at the site.[68]

Between 1923 and 1933 A.D. an expedition from Oxford and the Field Museum (Chicago) led by S. Langdon and L.Ch. Watelin conducted excavations at the dual city Kish-Ḫursagkalama. Work at Ḫursagkalama revealed a thriving religious centre in the seventh century; levels are dated by

---

66 Note also, F. Safar, *Sumer* 5 (1949): 154-72. Some texts were found by Rassam at Borsippa and by Scheil at Sippar, but details on their findspots are not generally known.

67 For detailed bibliography on the archaeological work at these sites up until 1971, see R.S. Ellis, *A Bibliography of Mesopotamian Archaeological Sites* (Wiesbaden, 1972) and A.R. al-Haik, *Key Lists of Archaeological Excavations in Iraq*, 2 volumes (Coconut Grove, Florida, 1968-71).

68 The most important publications on archaeological work at Babylon include: Koldewey, *Ischtar-Tor*; Koldewey, *Pflastersteine*; Koldewey, *Tempel*; Koldewey, *WEB*[4]; Koldewey and Wetzel, *Königsburgen*; Reuther, *Merkes*; Unger, *Babylon*; Wetzel, *Stadtmauern*; Wetzel and Weissbach, *Hauptheiligtum*.

the presence of texts dated to kings during that time. Regrettably, clear, reliable data on this site are unavailable.[69]

Archaeological excavations have been carried out at Nippur by the University of Pennsylvania from 1888 to 1900 A.D. and by teams led by the Oriental Institute of the University of Chicago in recent decades.[70] The temple of the god Enlil at Nippur may have experienced changes in circulation and functioning as a result of work done by Ashurbanipal since alterations in that structure may be associated with a floor containing inscribed bricks of that king (level II).[71] The excavators also speculate that Ashurbanipal was responsible for a wall around the site.[72] The Inanna temple continued to be used throughout this period and Esarhaddon seems to have rebuilt it on a different line to that of its predecessor.[73] From late Kassite times down to the very end of the Assyrian period, the site of the earlier North Temple was probably unoccupied; after that time, the area appears to have been a residential quarter.[74] In addition, house levels in TA (levels III_2 and III_1) and WC-2 may be dated to this time by the presence of dated texts in them.[75] Some glazed pottery that is related to Assyrian palace wares was found in WC; although a general date during the period of Assyrian domination over Nippur seems likely for this pottery, no more exact date can be determined as

---

69 The major publications of Kish are: Gibson, *Kish*; Langdon, *Kish* 1; Moorey, *Kish Excavations*; and Watelin and Langdon, *Kish* 3 and 4. The texts mentioned by Moorey, *Kish Excavations*, pp. 48 and 179 as coming from this period presumably include *OECT* 10 4 and 7 (*B-K* K.53 and K.134; the latter was actually composed at Babylon), which were found at Tell Inghara (C-6,4) and Mound W (see *OECT* 10, p. 1).

70 Note the following publications in particular: Crawford, *Archaeology* 12 (1959): 74-83; C.S. Fisher, *Excavations at Nippur* (Philadelphia, 1905-1906); Gibson, *Eleventh Season*; Gibson, *OIAR* 1981-82, pp. 40-48, 1984-85, pp. 20-30, and 1987-88, pp. 18-29; Gibson, *Twelfth Season*; Gibson, Zettler, and Armstrong, *Sumer* 39 (1983): 170-90; Hansen and Dales, *Archaeology* 15 (1962): 75-84; H.V. Hilprecht, *Explorations in Bible Lands during the 19th Century* (Philadelphia, 1903), pp. 289-568; McCown and Haines, *Nippur* 1; McCown, Haines, and Biggs, *Nippur* 2; J.P. Peters, *Nippur or Explorations and Adventures on the Euphrates* (New York and London, 1897); and *Iraq* 45 (1983): 217. A doctoral dissertation by J.A. Armstrong on the archaeology of Nippur at this time ("The Archaeology of Nippur from the Decline of the Kassite Kingdom until the Rise of the Neo-Babylonian Empire") was submitted to the University of Chicago in 1989; however, it was not available for use by the author.

71 McCown and Haines, *Nippur* 1, pp. 18 and 27.

72 Gibson, Zettler and Armstrong, *Sumer* 39 (1983): 177 and 189.

73 See Hansen and Dales, *Archaeology* 15 (1962): 75-76 and R.L. Zettler, "The Ur III Inanna Temple at Nippur" (unpublished doctoral dissertation, University of Chicago, 1984), pp. 80-84.

74 McCown, Haines, and Biggs, *Nippur* 2, p. 69.

75 McCown and Haines, *Nippur* 1, pp. 69-71 and 76; Gibson, *OIAR* 1981-1982, pp. 40-48; *Iraq* 45 (1983): 217; and Gibson, Zettler and Armstrong, *Sumer* 39 (1983): 172, 184-89. Area WB appears to have been unoccupied at this general time and used for trash pits and burials; see Gibson, *Twelfth Season*, pp. 55 and 74-75.

yet.[76] Inscriptions refer to building activities having been carried out at Nippur by both Esarhaddon and Ashurbanipal.

Between the years 1922 and 1934 A.D., Sir Leonard Woolley directed extensive excavations at the site of Ur for the British Museum and the University Museum (Philadelphia). From Woolley's work, it was discovered that one of the governors of Ur during the reign of Ashurbanipal, Sîn-balāssu-iqbi, had carried out an ambitious building programme at the site, a programme which suggests that the city had experienced a period of prosperity under him. Among other places, work by Sîn-balāssu-iqbi has been identified on the Ningal temple, Edublalmaḫ, the Gipāru, and along the northwest temenos wall. A useful summary of the archaeological and textual evidence has been presented by Brinkman in *Or.* NS 34 (1965): 241-58 (particularly pp. 248-55) and 38 (1969): 310-48 (particularly pp. 336-42).[77]

Systematic archaeological excavations began at Uruk in 1912 A.D. by J. Jordan and have continued under various directors up until the present time.[78] A continuous series of house levels stretching from the time of Sargon II through the Achaemenid period, dated by tablets found in those levels, has been discovered in the area southwest of the Eanna enclosure wall at Uruk.[79] Esarhaddon and Ashurbanipal both claim to have done work in temples at Uruk,[80] and a brick with an inscription of Esarhaddon found in the Anu ziggurat attests to work done by him on that structure. His work on that ziggurat is the first known in historical times.[81]

Work at Borsippa, Cutha, and Sippar is also recorded by various kings during this time;[82] but as far as I am aware, there is no clear archaeological evidence to support those claims.[83]

---

76 Information courtesy Gibson; and see Brinkman, *Prelude*, p. 120 and n. 588.

77 The major publications on the archaeological work at Ur are found in the series *Ur Excavations* (*UE*); in particular, *UE* 8 and 9 deal with the period of concern here. Note also L. Woolley, *Ur 'of the Chaldees,'* revised and updated edition by P.R.S. Moorey (Ithaca, 1982).

78 Major publications include: J. Jordan, *Uruk-Warka nach den Ausgrabungen durch die Deutsche Orient-Gesellschaft* (WVDOG 51) (Leipzig, 1928); the series *Vorläufiger Bericht über die ... Ausgrabungen in Uruk-Warka* (*UVB*) and *Ausgrabungen in Uruk-Warka: Endberichte*; and North, *Or.* NS 26 (1957): 185-256.

79 Lenzen, *UVB* 18, pp. 12-15 and *UVB* 19, pp. 15-16.

80 E.g., Borger, *Esarh.*, pp. 73-78 §§47-51; and *YOS* 1 42.

81 Schmidt, *UVB* 26-27, pp. 13 and 30.

82 E.g., Borger, *Esarh.*, p. 32 §20; Streck, *Asb.*, pp. 176-89 and 228-33; Lehmann, *Ššmk*, no. 1; Walker, *CBI*, no. 77.

83 For Rassam's work at Borsippa and Cutha between 1879 and 1882, see Reade, *Iraq* 48 (1986): 105-16 and pls. 13-19 (with further references). Excavations are currently being carried out at Borsippa by the Austrian Archaeological Expedition to Iraq and at Sippar by the University of Baghdad. Note also the archaeological evidence of work on the temple of Nergal by Ashurbanipal at Tell Haddad (see in particular Hannoun, *BSMS* 2 [1982]: 5-6 and Rashid, *Sumer* 37 [1981]: 72-80 [Arabic section]) and the fact that a brick with an

Thus, except at Babylon, Nippur, and Ur, archaeological data add little usable information for this period. There may well be evidence at Babylon that the city was destroyed by Sennacherib and subsequently abandoned and rebuilt. Evidence of an Assyrian presence at Nippur is suggested by the ceramic wares found there which are similar to Assyrian palace wares, and these could date to the time after the revolt of 652-648 when that city was kept under Assyrian control. At Ur, a period of prosperity during the first half of the reign of Ashurbanipal is indicated by the ambitious building programme of Sîn-balāssu-iqbi. So little concrete information is available that no broad trends can be discerned. Where relevant, the archaeological evidence for individual buildings and building projects will be presented in the body of this study.

Art

Few studies have been made of the art of Babylonia during the first half of the first millennium and few items can be dated reliably to the period of concern here.[84] Reliefs of divine symbols can be found on two kudurrus from the reign of Šamaš-šuma-ukīn (BM 87220 and VA 3614). VA 3614 also shows a "presentation" scene: the king and an individual standing before him (presumably the person receiving the prebend described in the text on the kudurru). These have been studied by U. Seidl as part of her work on Babylonian kudurru reliefs.[85] A few stelae describing the building activities of Ashurbanipal and Šamaš-šuma-ukīn also bear reliefs showing one or the other of the two carrying a work-basket on his head, presumably depicting him aiding in the reconstruction of the temple described on the stela. One of these comes from Babylon (photograph on cover) and two from Borsippa (figs. 2-3).[86] On the front of a stela from Zinjirli describing Esarhaddon's

inscription of Ashurbanipal was found at the ziggurat of Dūr-Kurigalzu (al-Jumaily, *Sumer* 27 [1971]: 89 and pl. 14 fig. 30 [Arabic section]; see below, pp. 112-13).

84 For cylinder seals, note especially Porada's study in *Or.* NS 16 (1947): 145-65 and pls. 3-8. With regard to bronze objects, see E.A. Braun-Holzinger in Curtis, *Bronzeworking Centres*, pp. 119-34. Note also Brinkman, *Prelude*, pp. 120-21 and his references to a number of minor works (small terracotta plaques and molds, mainly from Nippur) which may date to around our period.

85 Seidl, *Bagh. Mitt.* 4 (1968): 1-220 as nos. 109-10, note especially pp. 62-63 and 209 (the article is reprinted with an addendum as *Die babylonischen Kudurru-Reliefs: Symbole mesopotamischer Gottheiten*, Orbis Biblicus et Orientalis 87 [Freiburg and Göttingen, 1989]). For drawings of the reliefs, see *BBSt* pl. 6 (BM 87220) and *Bagh. Mitt.* 4 (1968): 62 fig. 24 (VAT 3614).

86 BM 90864, 90865, and 90866 (see Börker-Klähn, *ABVF*, nos. 224-26, with further bibliography); note also BM 22533 (see Reade and Walker, *AfO* 28 [1981-82]: 119 no. 4). BM 90864 was found in the area of the temple of Marduk at Babylon and BM 90865 and 90866 in a room of the temple of Nabû at Borsippa; see *ibid.* and Reade, *Iraq* 48 (1986): 109.

conquest of Egypt in 671 (VA 2708), the king is shown in relief with two captives, likely Tirḫaka of Egypt (or his son Ušanaḫuru) and Ba'lu of Tyre (or Abdi-milkut of Sidon). Two individuals are depicted on the sides of the stela (one on each side) and these are probably Ashurbanipal and Šamaš-šuma-ukīn since one figure wears Assyrian attire and the other Babylonian attire and since the stela was made after the appointment of the two to be crown princes (fig. 1).[87] Šamaš-šuma-ukīn and Ashurbanipal are probably also to be identified with the damaged figures carved on the sides of two stelae of Esarhaddon from Til Barsip which are now in the Aleppo Museum.[88] A fragment of a bronze relief published by Parrot and Nougayrol in the journal *Syria* about thirty years ago is sometimes thought to come from the temple of the god Marduk at Babylon and to depict Esarhaddon and his mother Naqi'a (Akkadian: Zakūtu). The inscription on the piece is poorly preserved; the original purpose and location of the relief and its ascription to Esarhaddon are all open to question. The fragment may actually be part of the same relief as a piece which appears to duplicate an inscription of Sennacherib dealing with a temple in the city of Assur.[89]

No wall reliefs found in Babylonia or known to have been made by or for Babylonians are attested for the period, and none of the reliefs of Sennacherib or Esarhaddon from Assyria can be convincingly shown to represent scenes of Babylonia during this period. A number of wall reliefs from the North Palace of Ashurbanipal at Nineveh depict actions of Assyria against Šamaš-šuma-ukīn, Elam, and the Gambūlu and show fighting in the marshes, the capture of Chaldeans, and the taking of booty, among other incidents.[90] However, as Brinkman points out, much work remains to be done on the use of Assyrian wall reliefs for historical purposes.[91] Details of individual scenes can sometimes be identified by epigraphs inscribed on the reliefs themselves; when epigraphs are not present, identifications can sometimes be difficult. Nevertheless, these reliefs are valuable in that they give a view of the flora and topography of the land as well as some idea of the lifestyles of various population groups, their clothing (and armour), and, occasionally, their battle tactics.

---

87 See Börker-Klähn, *ABVF*, no. 219 (with further bibliography).

88 See Börker-Klähn, *ABVF*, nos. 217-218 (with further bibliography).

89 See Parrot and Nougayrol, *Syria* 33 (1956): 147-60 and pl. 6; Börker-Klähn, *ABVF*, nos. 220-21 (with further bibliography, to which add E.A. Braun-Holzinger, *Figürliche Bronzen aus Mesopotamien* [Munich, 1984], p. 105 and pls. 68-69 nos. 356-57, and Curtis, *Bronzeworking Centres*, pp. 88-89 and fig. 87).

90 Barnett, *North Palace*, especially pls. 16-26, 28-30, 34-35, 60-61, and 63-69. For a few of these, see figs. 4-8.

91 *Prelude*, p. 121. In connection with the topic of our work, note in particular Reade's study of Ashurbanipal's sculptures in *Bagh. Mitt.* 10 (1979): 96-110 and his comments in *ARINH*, pp. 165-66.

CHAPTER 3

CHRONOLOGY

The essential framework of both the absolute and relative chronologies of Babylonian history from the destruction of Babylon by Sennacherib until the death of Kandalānu has been so well established by the evidence of kinglists, eponym lists, chronicles, and date formulae of economic texts that there is little need to reconsider the matter here. In absolute dates, this period is identified with the years 689 to 627 B.C.[1]

One point of disagreement among scholars concerns the date when Ashurbanipal died or relinguished control of Assyria. He is last attested in a date formula from his thirty-eighth year (20-III-631),[2] and some writers have suggested that his reign ended at about that time, with either his death or his abdication.[3] These proposals are in conflict with the only known source mentioning the length of Ashurbanipal's reign, the Harran inscription of the mother of Nabonidus, which states that he ruled for forty-two years, thus until 627. There is, however, some inconsistency in the dates given in that text; it claims that she was born in the twentieth year of Ashurbanipal and died in the ninth year of Nabonidus, having passed through the forty-second year of Ashurbanipal, the third year of Aššur-etil-ilāni, the twenty-first year of Nabopolassar, the forty-third year of Nebuchadnezzar, the second year of Amēl-Marduk, and the fourth year of Neriglissar, a total of 104 years.[4] By modern reckoning the twentieth year of Ashurbanipal was 649 and the ninth year of Nabonidus was 547; thus a total of 102 years would be expected. It is premature to assume that the error lay in the statement about the length of Ashurbanipal's reign and not somewhere else, for example, in a possible overlap in the reigns of Aššur-etil-ilāni and Nabopolassar.[5] Berossos is said to have stated that after the reign of Šamaš-šuma-ukīn, the latter's brother (var. Sardanapallos) ruled for twenty-one years.[6] If this refers to

---

[1] The standard statement on Mesopotamian chronology is that of Brinkman in Oppenheim, *Ancient Mesopotamia*, pp. 335-48. Note that BM 32312 confirms that year 16 of Šamaš-šuma-ukīn is to be identified with the year 652 (see pp. 289-90). In *LAS* 2, pp. 382-83, Parpola has presented an attempt to determine the exact Julian equivalents of Assyrian dates for the years 681-648.

[2] N 4016 (*B-K* J.38).

[3] E.g., Reade, *JCS* 23 (1970-71): 1-9; and von Soden, *ZA* 58 (1967): 241-55.

[4] Gadd, *AnSt* 8 (1958): 46-50 i 29-33 and ii 26-28 and see the discussion 69-72.

[5] See for example J. Oates, *Iraq* 27 (1965): 142.

[6] Jacoby, *FGrH* III C/1, pp. 386-87 §§33-34.

Ashurbanipal, it would support the belief that he reigned until 627. However, Kandalānu may have been meant since the text was primarily concerned with the rulers of Babylonia. The complex problem of Kandalānu's successors and their dates, and the question of the Assyrian succession upon the death of Ashurbanipal, are closely connected with the subsequent years leading up to the fall of Assyria. Because that period is beyond the scope of this study, these matters will be discussed only briefly (chapter 9).[7]

For the dating of Assyrian inscriptions, we are fortunate that the Assyrian eponym canon is preserved down to 649, the eponymy of Aḫi-ilaya. In addition, it is clear that the eponym for 648 was Bēlšunu.[8] The exact sequence of the remaining post-canonical eponyms, however, remains uncertain, although an attempt to order them has been made by M. Falkner.[9] Of particular importance are the dates of the three eponyms Nabû-nādin-aḫḫē (or Nabû-nādin-aḫi), Nabû-šar-aḫḫēšu, and Šamaš-danninanni; during their eponymies various editions of Ashurbanipal's annals were composed. The dates of these eponymies, of the various inscriptions coming from the post-canonical period, and thus of the events described in these inscriptions have been much discussed, although no consensus has been reached. Scholarly opinion tends to date (1) the eponymate of Nabû-nādin-aḫḫē, during which edition C of Ashurbanipal's annals was composed, to 647 or 646,[10] (2) the eponymate of Nabû-šar-aḫḫēšu, during which editions F and T were composed, to 646 or 645,[11] and (3) the eponymate of Šamaš-danninanni, when edition A was composed, to 643 or 642.[12] The basic problem about the dating of the eponymy of Nabû-šar-aḫḫēšu is the statement in *ADD* 927 that there were six years between the eponymy of Sagabbu (651) and that of Nabû-šar-aḫḫēšu. If the six years are inclusive, then Nabû-šar-aḫḫēšu was

---

7 The most recent treatments of these matters are those of Zawadzki, *Fall of Assyria* and J. Oates, *CAH* 3/2 (in press); J. Oates kindly made a draft of her manuscript available to me.

8 See Ungnad in *RLA* 2, pp. 428-29.

9 *AfO* 17 (1954-56): 100-20. Note the additions, comments, and corrections in the following: Deller, *Bagh. Mitt.* 15 (1984): 246; Dalley and Postgate, *TFS*, especially pp. 5, 10, and 14-15; and Pedersén, *AfO* 35 (1988): 172-73.

10 647: e.g., Tadmor, *25th Congress*, p. 240 (date later retracted, see below) and Reade and Walker, *AfO* 28 (1981-82): 121-22. 646: e.g., Grayson, *ZA* 70 (1980): 245 and Cogan and Tadmor, *Or.* NS 50 (1981): 239 and n. 24. See *ibid.*, p. 235 n. 15 for the date of edition C.

11 646: e.g., Falkner, *AfO* 17 (1954-56): 113-14 no. 28 and 118; Reade and Walker, *AfO* 28 (1981-82): 121-22; Parpola in *ARINH*, p. 121 n. 4; and Finkel, *SAAB* 3 (1989): 65. 645: e.g., Aynard, *Asb.*, pp. 12-15 and Cogan and Tadmor, *Or.* NS 50 (1981): 229 and 239 n. 24.

12 643: e.g., Cogan and Tadmor, *Or.* NS 50 (1981): 230. 643 or 642: e.g., Tadmor, *25th Congress*, p. 240 and Grayson, *ZA* 70 (1980): 245.

eponym in 646; if not, he was eponym in 645.[13] If his eponymy is to be dated to 645, then two eponymies would separate it from that of Bēlšunu (648). While one of these would be that of Nabû-nādin-aḫḫē, no candidate for the remaining eponymy has as yet been proposed. It is possible that the eponymy of Šamaš-danninanni could date even earlier than 643, that is, to the year following the eponymy of Nabû-šar-aḫḫēšu.[14] Editions A and F, which were composed in these two eponymies, both commemorate the rebuilding of the House-of-Succession (*bīt ridûti*) at Nineveh and thus are likely to date quite closely in time.[15] Although the exact dates of the three eponymies are uncertain, their relative order is clear: Nabû-nādin-aḫḫē, Nabû-šar-aḫḫēšu, Šamaš-danninanni.

A chronological chart for the period 689-627 (Table 1) is included to aid in correlating the regnal years of the kings of Assyria and Babylonia and their absolute year equivalents. For convenience, Elamite kings are included in this chart in the order they appear in Assyrian and Babylonian sources, although in some cases their dates are uncertain.[16]

---

13 On this matter, see in particular Falkner, *AfO* 17 (154-56): 113-14.

14 Parpola (*ARINH*, p. 121 n. 4) suggests that the eponymy of Šamaš-danninanni is "unlikely to be much later than 645."

15 Falkner (*AfO* 17 [1954-56]: 116 no. 37 and 118) originally suggested 636 for the eponymate of Šamaš-danninanni and the composition of edition A. She assumed that this edition had been composed after "die grosse Triumphfeier" of Ashurbanipal in Nineveh and that that occurred around 637 or 636, relying upon Streck (*Asb.*, p. CDLXVII) for the date of that event. Streck's reasoning for the dating of the celebration is, however, not sound.

16 There could be more than one Elamite king at a time (e.g., Ḫumban-nikaš II on the throne of Elam and Tammarītu on the throne in Ḫîdalu). Possibly the older plan of succession to the Elamite throne still held some force. For this older order of succession, see Stolper in Carter and Stolper, *Elam*, pp. 24-25. In the table, the Babylonian forms of the names of Elamite kings are given in parentheses where it might prove useful. The dates given for Elamite rulers include their accession years. In this study, I will follow the practice of the *CAH* in referring to the rulers of Elam, except for Teumman, by the Elamite form of their names; the Elamite form for Urtak is unknown.

TABLE 1

Chronological Table for the Years 689-627

	ASSYRIA	BABYLONIA	ELAM
	Sennacherib	Mušēzib-Marduk	
689	year 16	year 4	(Ḫumban-nimena died 7-XII)
	(Babylon captured by Assyrians 1-IX)		Ḫumban-ḫaltaš I 689-681
688	year 17	Sennacherib (2nd reign)	
		year 1*	
687	year 18	year 2*	
686	year 19	year 3*	
685	year 20	year 4*	
684	year 21	year 5*	
683	year 22	year 6*	
682	year 23	year 7*	
681	year 24	year 8*	(Ḫumban-ḫaltaš I died 23-VII)
	(Sennacherib died 20-X)		Ḫumban-ḫaltaš II 681-675
	Esarhaddon accession year		
680	year 1		
679	year 2		
678	year 3		
677	year 4		
676	year 5		
675	year 6		(Ḫumban-ḫaltaš II died 5/7-VI)
			Urtak 675-664?
674	year 7		
673	year 8		
672	year 9		
671	year 10		
670	year 11		
669	year 12		
	(Esarhaddon died 10-VIII)		
	Ashurbanipal accession year		
668	year 1	Šamaš-šuma-ukīn accession year	
667	year 2	year 1	
666	year 3	year 2	
665	year 4	year 3	
664	year 5	year 4	Tepti-Ḫumban-Inšušinak (Teumman) 664?-653?
663	year 6	year 5	
662	year 7	year 6	
661	year 8	year 7	
660	year 9	year 8	
659	year 10	year 9	
658	year 11	year 10	
657	year 12	year 11	
656	year 13	year 12	
655	year 14	year 13	

	ASSYRIA	BABYLONIA	ELAM
	Ashurbanipal	Šamaš-šuma-ukīn	
654	year 15	year 14	
653	year 16	year 15	Ḫumban-nikaš II (Ummanigaš) 653?-652?
652	year 17	year 16	
	(Rebellion began *c*. II; hostilities commenced 19-X)		
651	year 18	year 17	Tammarītu (II) 652?-649?
650	year 19	year 18	
	(Babylon besieged 11-IV)		
649	year 20	year 19	Indabibi 649?-648?
648	year 21	year 20	Ḫumban-ḫaltaš III (Ummanaldaš) 648?-*c*. 645
	(Babylon fell to the Assyrians sometime after 30-V)		
647	year 22	Kandalānu year 1	Ḫumban-ḫabua (Umbaḫabua) 647? Tammarītu (II) 647?
646	year 23	year 2	Pa'e 646?
645	year 24	year 3	
644	year 25	year 4	
643	year 26	year 5	
642	year 27	year 6	
641	year 28	year 7	
640	year 29	year 8	
639	year 30	year 9	
638	year 31	year 10	
637	year 32	year 11	
636	year 33	year 12	
635	year 34	year 13	
634	year 35	year 14	
633	year 36	year 15	
632	year 37	year 16	
631	year 38	year 17	
630	year 39	year 18	
629	year 40	year 19	
628	year 41	year 20	
627	year 42	year 21	
	Aššur-etil-ilāni accession year?	(Kandalānu died between 8-III and 1?-VIII)	

NOTE: * "kingless" according to the Ptolemaic Canon and the Babylonian Chronicle (Grayson, *Chronicles*, no. 1 iii 28).

CHAPTER 4

THE BABYLONIAN PEOPLE

In the middle of the seventh century, Babylonia was not a unified, homogeneous state. Over the centuries various different groups and peoples had migrated into the Babylonian plain and settled there. Some had become assimilated and adopted Babylonian ways, while others had preferred to keep their own customs. The outlook of residents of one of the old cities such as Babylon or Uruk would have been different from that of rural farmers who cultivated crops along the banks of rivers and canals,[1] or of those who pastured animals on the inland steppe or who exploited the resources of the southern marshes.[2] The documents of the period indicate a basic division in the population between tribal and non-tribal inhabitants of the land. The latter were what we may term "Akkadians," an amalgam of several older groups who had merged their distinctive identities by this time.[3] They are mainly distinguishable as the residents of urban centres, the bearers of traditional Babylonian culture. Among the numerous tribal groups,[4] the documents make a clear distinction between the Chaldean and the Aramean tribes; Assyrian texts often refer to these two groups in parallel.[5] The tribal groups could lead settled or nomadic existences (or a mixture of the two) and although a tribesman might involve himself in affairs of state, he remained in close affinity with his tribe. The Akkadian on the other hand tended to identify himself by his family descent or occasionally by his city or town. In addition to the Akkadians, Chaldeans, and Arameans, a fourth group often appears in texts of the period, namely the people of the Sealand, an area of marshes at the head of the Persian Gulf. Since the major group living in the

---

[1] Of course, urban residents often cultivated crops in or near their cities.

[2] For the geography of the region, the reader is referred in particular to Adams, *Heartland of Cities*, pp. 1-26 and *Land Behind Baghdad*, pp. 3-12; and W.B. Fisher, *The Middle East: A Physical, Social and Regional Geography*, seventh edition (London, 1978), pp. 363-97.

[3] The use of the term "Akkadians" for this group may be confusing to some because we often think of Akkadians as opposed to Sumerians and because at this time Akkad sometimes stood for Babylonia as a whole. Nevertheless, the term was used for this group in some ancient sources (see below) and seems the best choice available.

[4] Zadok (*WO* 16 [1985]: 74) refers to one hundred West Semitic tribal groups appearing in texts of the first millennium (five Chaldean tribes, forty-four Aramean tribes, six Arab tribes, and approximately forty-five tribes of uncertain affiliation).

[5] E.g., Luckenbill, *Senn.*, p. 25 i 39 (LÚ *aramu* LÚ *kaldu*).

Sealand was likely the Chaldean tribe of Bīt-Yakīn, the people of the Sealand will discussed with the Chaldeans in this chapter.

The diverse nature of the Babylonian state is echoed in the fact that no single term existed in common usage for "Babylonia" as a whole. Rulers generally assumed the title "king of Babylon" or occasionally "viceroy of Babylon," that is, ruler of the most important city and the traditional seat of government for Babylonia. Otherwise they had to revert to the old titles of "king of Sumer and Akkad" or "king of Karduniaš." The terms "Akkad" and "Akkadians" often appear in texts from our period, particularly in Assyrian inscriptions. Akkad sometimes refers to the the city by that name, sometimes to the land as a whole (as in scholarly reports and some chronicle passages), and sometimes only to the northern part of the land, that is the region originally called Akkad, as opposed to the southern part (ancient Sumer) which was now inhabited mainly by tribal groups. When the Assyrian sources wanted to distinguish the old settled population of the land from the tribal groups, the term people of Akkad or Akkadians was used for the former. For example, in edition A of Ashurbanipal's annals we find UN.MEŠ KUR URI.KI KUR *kal-du* KUR *a-ra-mu* KUR *tam-tim*, "the people of Akkad, Chaldea, Aramu, (and) the Sealand," and in an extispicy report from the time of the rebellion of 652-648 *lu-ú* <LÚ.>URI.KI *lu-ú* LÚ *kal-da-a-a lu-ú* LÚ *aḫ-lam-i*, "either Akkad(ians), or Chaldeans, or Aḫlamû (Arameans)."[6] The term "Akkadians" was employed because this section of the population was imbued with classical Babylonian culture and because it used, or was most familiar with, the Akkadian language, the language of Babylonian civilization for over one thousand years.[7] Thus, in this study Akkadians will be used only to refer to this segment of the population.

In order that the reader may understand better the various forces at play in Babylonia from 689 to 627, a brief description of each group follows. While a fair amount is known about the residents of various cities, less is known about individual tribes. Thus, it is often necessary to refer to earlier or later material.[8]

I. Akkadians

The term Akkadians is used in this study to describe the descendants of various older groups (e.g., the Akkadians of the third millennium, Sumerians, Amorites, and Kassites) which were now so intermixed as to be

---

6 Streck, *Asb.*, pp. 30-31 iii 97-98 and Starr, *SAA* 4, no. 280 rev. 11-12.

7 For the growing importance of the Aramaic language, see p. 48.

8 Many of the statements about the general character of the various groups are based upon the works of Brinkman (*PKB*, pp. 246-88; *Power and Propaganda*, pp. 223-50; and *Prelude*, pp. 11-15 and 27-28).

no longer distinguishable.[9] Akkadians were the foundation of the Babylonian state and the bearers of what is considered to have been classical Babylonian culture. They were a sedentary population, mainly identifiable as the inhabitants of the urban centres and especially of the old cult centres of the northwestern part of the land (Babylon, Borsippa, Cutha, Dilbat, and Sippar) and of the southwest (Ur and Uruk), where they probably formed the majority of the population. In the north, many Akkadians were likely settled in the countryside, farming the fertile land along the rivers and canals, but our documentation tends to emphasize the urban segment of the population. In the extreme south, where the swampy condition of the land and the higher salinity of the soil made settled life based upon agriculture more difficult, the Akkadians may be distinguished more in the ancient cult centres, with most of the hinterland given over to the various tribal groups. Thus, the term Akkadians should be considered to have more socio-cultural implications than specifically ethnic ones.

The basic social unit for the Akkadian was the family. In documents, members tended to identify themselves as "PN_1 son of PN_2," with PN_2 representing the individual's father (e.g., Nabû-bēlšunu *mār/māršu ša* Dābibi), although occasionally also by the city from which they came (e.g., Itti-Marduk-balāṭu *Urukayu*).[10] A tendency to identify oneself with a larger group or clan, however, can be noted. It became increasingly common to identify an individual as "PN_1 son of PN_2, descendant of PN_3" (e.g., Mušēzib-Marduk *māršu ša* Kiribtu *mār* Sîn-nāṣir). PN_3 can sometimes be proven to be not the grandfather of PN_1, but rather some more distant ancestor who was looked upon as the founder of the family. Often this ancestral name was derived from an occupation, resulting in such family names as "Carpenter," "Smith," "Doctor," "Weaver," "Fuller," and "Priest-of-Ištar-of-Babylon." Sometimes the paternal name was omitted and only the individual's name and family name were given. It is often difficult to be certain if a paternal or family name is meant by PN_2 in a name PN_1 *mār* PN_2. The practice of giving one's family (or ancestral) name may reflect a greater interest in genealogy or a need to distinguish homonymous individuals in an increased population, although it may well indicate a desire to attach oneself in unsettled times to a larger unit, possibly in imitation of the tribal structure. Some of these larger families came to play major roles in the political and economic life of the land. For instance, the Arkât-ilī-damqā, Iliya, and Nūr-Papsukkal families appear to have monopolized the chief offices in the civil and religious administration of Borsippa during these sixty-odd years.[11]

---

9 Kassite names are still occasionally attested—Kurigalzu (e.g., *BRM* 1 32:1; *B-K* I.26) and Kadašman-Enlil (IM 57925:9, time of Aššur-etil-ilāni; *B-K* Mn.1).

10 The latter method is generally used to refer to third parties, often in letters.

11 See Appendix B sub 3 and Frame, *JCS* 36 (1984): 67-80.

The Akkadians and their cities formed the core of the Babylonian state. The control of much (if not most) of the wealth of the land was in their hands; the important civil and religious offices were regularly held by Akkadians; and in their assemblies they met to decide legal matters. Their cities were certainly the intellectual and cultural centres of the country. There were located the scribal schools and there astronomical observations were made.[12] Their political support, or at least acquiescence, was earnestly desired by the Assyrians in order to facilitate Assyria's control of Babylonia. Assyrian rulers carried out ambitious building programmes in their cities (particularly Babylon, Borsippa, Nippur, and Sippar) and often granted special privileges to them and their citizens.[13] While most information on these privileges comes from the time of the Neo-Assyrian kings, the concept of the citizens of certain Babylonian cities having special rights seems to have originated before that time. The inhabitants of these cities did not regard their privileges simply as royal gifts but rather insisted that they were their rights.[14] Esarhaddon claims to have re-established for the citizens of Babylon the rights covered by the terms *andurāru*, *šubarrû*, *kidinnūtu*, and *zakûtu*; he also reinstated the *šubarrû* of Borsippa, Nippur, and Sippar.[15] Similarly Ashurbanipal states that he confirmed the *kidinnūtu* of Babylon.[16] In the past, Shalmaneser III had referred to the people of Babylon and Borsippa as *ṣābē kidinni šubarê ša ilāni rabûti*, "men of *kidinnu* (status), freed (of taxes?) by the great gods," and given them food, drink, and fine garments.[17] Besides referring to the people of Babylon, Borsippa, Sippar, and Nippur as the people of *kidinnu*, Sargon II claims to have established the *šubarrû* of Babylon, Nippur, and Sippar and granted *andurāru* to a number of other cities including Ur, Uruk, Larsa, and Eridu;[18] however, there is no reference these latter cities having special privileges during the period under study here. In contrast to these kings, Sennacherib never claims to have granted such privileges to Babylonian cities. Exactly what these privileges entailed is uncertain; they apparently

---

12 Astronomical observations from about this time are reported to have been made at the cities of Akkad, Babylon, Borsippa, Cutha, Dilbat, Nippur, Uruk, and perhaps Sippar (see, for example, *ABL* 337:6-8 [*LAS*, no. 278] and 895:7-10; Thompson, *Rep.* 101A and 274:8-9; Parpola, *LAS* 2, p. 268 and n. 481).

13 On the privileged position of certain cities and their citizens, see in particular Leemans in *Symbolae van Oven*, pp. 36-61 and Reviv, *JESHO* 31 (1988): 286-98. The privileges appear to have had to be confirmed by each new king and could change according to the will of the new monarch.

14 See in particular the Babylonian Fürstenspiegel (Lambert, *BWL*, pp. 110-15 and Reiner and Civil in *Diakonoff Festschrift*, pp. 320-26).

15 Borger, *Esarh.*, pp. 25-26 §11 episode 37 and p. 81 §53:41.

16 E.g., Streck, *Asb.*, pp. 226-27:10.

17 Michel, *WO* 4 (1967-68): 32 vi 4-5.

18 E.g., Lyon, *Sar.*, pp. 30-31:4 and Winckler, *Sar.*, pp. 60-61:362-63, 80-81:3-4, and 96-97:5-7.

included various provisions at different times. It is likely that *kidinnūtu* could include freedom from certain taxes (e.g., customs dues) and the expropriation of land by civil authorities, exemption from military draft and corvée duty, and the right of appeal to the king in court cases. A certain territoriality may have been involved in the privileges since the people of Babylon appear to claim that not even a dog that entered Babylon could be slain.[19] While encouraging co-operation of the citizens, these privileges probably lessened Assyria's control over and income from these cities, and it is perhaps no accident that only Babylon is known to have had any special privileges during the reign of Ashurbanipal.[20]

As already noted, there is really no unambiguous or indigenous term to describe this group and there is no reason to assume that they viewed themselves as a homogeneous group. Various different classes of Akkadians existed, not all having the same rights in the community.[21] Intercity rivalries may have been frequent and, since the exact conditions and interests of the various cities were different, it is not surprising that they often did not act in common.

II. Chaldeans

Chaldeans are first attested in Babylonia in the time of Ashurnasirpal II of Assyria, in 878.[22] Although five tribes are known—Bīt-Amukāni, Bīt-Dakkūri, Bīt-Yakīn, Bīt-Ša'alli, and Bīt-Šilāni—only the first three are attested during the years 689-627.[23] There is some evidence to indicate that the Chaldeans were West Semites, possibly related to the Arameans, but not sufficient to make any definite statement on the matter.[24] They were located predominantly in southern and western Babylonia and are mentioned as both

---

[19] *ABL* 878; in view of references to "the kings, our lords," the text is to be dated to the reign of Ashurbanipal before the rebellion of 652-648. Reviv argues that the letter indicates that the privileged position only extended to the permanent residents of Babylon and that the people of that city were trying to obtain that position for all its residents, in particular foreign wives (*JESHO* 31 [1988]: 291).

[20] K 6232, a Neo-Assyrian tablet fragment which is probably to be assigned to Ashurbanipal and which mentions Šamaš-šuma-ukīn, may refer to Sippar as a "city of *kidinnu*-status" (URU *ki-din-ni*), but the context is broken. The text is to be published by G. Frame and A.K. Grayson.

[21] See Dandamaev, *Acta Antiqua* 22 (1974): 433-44 for a study of social stratification during the Neo-Babylonian period and note also Oelsner, *AOF* 4 (1976): 131-49.

[22] On the Chaldeans, see in particular Brinkman, *PKB*, pp. 260-67 and *Prelude*, pp. 14-15; Edzard in *RLA* 5, pp. 291-97; and Zadok, *WO* 16 (1985): 49-63.

[23] Little is known about the Bīt-Ša'alli and Bīt-Šilāni at any time. With regard to these two tribes, see Zadok, *WO* 16 (1985): 51-52 and 57-58. For the spelling of the tribal names, see Brinkman, *Or.* NS 46 (1977): 306.

[24] See Brinkman, *PKB*, pp. 265-67 and Edzard in *RLA* 5, pp. 291-92.

a people (LÚ *kaldu/kaldayu*) and a land (KUR *kaldu*).[25] There was also a province named after them (*pīḫat* URU *kaldu*), possibly in the area of Babylon.[26] From earliest times the Chaldeans were at least partially settled; Chaldeans and Arameans are said to have lived in Cutha, Ḫursagkalama, Kish, Nippur, Sippar, and Uruk in the time of Sennacherib[27] and they are known to have had walled cities of their own. In the first part of his reign, Sennacherib claims to have conquered 88 walled cities and 820 villages which belonged to the Chaldeans.[28] Reliefs of Assyrian kings suggest that Chaldeans engaged in agriculture (including date-palm cultivation) and animal husbandry (horses and cattle). Inscriptions from the time of Shalmaneser III refer to silver, gold, tin, bronze, elephant tusks, elephant hides, ebony, and sissoo-wood being brought by two Chaldean leaders as tribute to Assyrian kings.[29] This would suggest that the Chaldeans (or at least their sheikhs) prospered at times, possibly benefiting from trade routes that ran through their territories.[30]

Individual Chaldeans appear to have become "Babylonianized," taking Babylonian names,[31] becoming involved in Babylonian political life, and turning to agriculture for their livelihood, but as a whole the Chaldeans maintained their tribal structure and distinct identity. Tribes were referred to as the "House of PN" (e.g., Bīt-Yakīn), with PN in this usage standing for the eponymous ancestor of the clan or tribe. Usually individual Chaldeans were described as "PN_1 son of PN_2," with PN_2 indicating the eponymous ancestor of the individual's tribe (e.g., Ea-zēra-qīša *mār* Amukānu). Descendants of Merodach-Baladan II of the ruling family of the Bīt-Yakīn, who had become deeply involved with the political events of the period and more "Babylonianized," were often referred to by the more conventional Babylonian order (e.g., "Nabû-zēr-kitti-līšir *mār* Merodach-Baladan," not "Nabû-zēr-kitti-līšir *mār* Yakīn") in letters and Assyrian royal inscriptions. Each tribe was united under one leader; the leaders of the various tribes were called collectively *ra'šānu* (NB) or *ra'sānu/re'sānu* (NA).[32] An individual

---

25 See Parpola, *Toponyms*, pp. 188-90 and Zadok, *RGTC* 8, pp. 191-92.

26 *OECT* 10 400:2 (time of Sîn-šumu-līšir; *B-K* N.3). The location is suggested by the fact that the text is dated at Babylon.

27 Luckenbill, *Senn.*, p. 25 i 39-41. On the Urbi who are also said to have been living in these cities, see below, p. 50 n. 112.

28 Luckenbill, *Senn.*, p. 54:50; *ibid.*, p. 56:11, a later source, contains the variant 89 walled cities.

29 E.g., Hulin, *Iraq* 25 (1963): 56:49.

30 Particularly the routes from the Persian Gulf passing through the Sealand and along the Euphrates river.

31 The majority of Chaldeans whose names are known bore Babylonian names; see Zadok, *WO* 16 (1985): 53-54.

32 Brinkman, *PKB*, p. 265, n. 1075; Edzard in *RLA* 5, p. 294; and *AHw*, p. 959 sub voce *ra'su*.

tribal ruler was often designated simply as the son of the eponymous ancestor of his tribe (e.g., *mār Amukāni*). The fact that Assyrian sources sometimes referred to particularly important Chaldean tribal leaders as kings (e.g., Šamaš-ibni of Bīt-Dakkūri) attests to their power and influence. No concrete details are known about the internal organization of the individual tribes.

The Chaldeans, divided up into their tribes and ruled by their own traditional leaders, formed semi-autonomous units within the state and appear to have been supervised less closely than the city populations. They occasionally proved to be a disruptive element within the country both before and during this period.[33] It proved continually difficult for the Assyrian overlords of Babylonia to maintain close control over the Chaldeans and it was the leaders of the Chaldean tribes who frequently led rebellions against Assyrian authority during the eighth and seventh centuries. Although many dwelt in towns and villages, and were thereby vulnerable to Assyrian raids, the Chaldeans were still more practiced in making use of the natural environment to escape Assyrian advances and to harry them. Although Chaldean tribes on occasion gave allegiance to the rulers of Babylonia, they remained essentially independent of them. Each of the three major tribes, however, had provided at least one king of Babylonia before this period began—(Nabû)-mukīn-zēri of Bīt-Amukāni, Nabû-šuma-iškun and Mušēzib-Marduk of Bīt-Dakkūri, and Erība-Marduk and Merodach-Baladan II of Bīt-Yakīn. The tribal affiliation of the earliest Chaldean ruler of Babylonia, Marduk-apla-uṣur (*c.* 775), is unknown.[34] Occasionally Assyrian rulers killed or deposed Chaldean chieftains, presumably allowing individuals more friendly to Assyria to replace them as leaders of their tribes. This is not to imply, however, that the Chaldeans always opposed Assyria; indeed some are known to have served in the Assyrian army and to have opposed fellow Babylonians in rebellion against Assyria.[35]

There is some indication, although no absolute proof, that Bīt-Amukāni[36] was the largest Chaldean tribe in the time of Sennacherib. In a list of places belonging to Bīt-Amukāni, Bīt-Dakkūri, Bīt-Ša'alli, and Bīt-Yakīn, which Sennacherib claims to have conquered, the Bīt-Amukāni were accorded more walled cities and villages (39 and 350 respectively) than any of the other tribes.[37] We cannot be sure that all these places were inhabited by the Bīt-

---

33 The idea of Chaldeans as lawless tribesmen even enters the Bible in Job 1:17; this passage was kindly brought to my attention by P.E. Dion. Generally, the Bible uses the term Chaldeans to refer to the people of Babylonia as a whole.

34 See Brinkman, *PKB*, p. 215.

35 See for example *ABL* 1292:5'-7' (Parpola, *SAA* 1, no. 18) and Dalley and Postgate, *TFS*, pp. 35 and 38-39 (time of Sargon II).

36 On this tribe, see in particular Unger in *RLA* 2, pp. 35-36. For attestations of the tribe, see Parpola, *Toponyms*, 77-78 and Zadok, *RGTC* 8, pp. 80-81.

37 Luckenbill, *Senn.*, pp. 52-54:36-50.

Amukāni, as opposed to simply being located in the area where they dwelt. They may merely have been spread over a greater area than any other tribe. The exact area occupied by this tribe is not clear; most of the places mentioned in Sennacherib's list as belonging to this tribe are otherwise unknown or cannot be located with any degree of certainity. Larak (likely located east or northeast of Nippur)[38] is listed as belonging to the Bīt-Amukāni and the tribe is known to have been active in the area of Uruk during the Šamaš-šuma-ukīn Revolt. Thus Bīt-Amukāni may have stretched between these two cities.[39] According to Assyrian inscriptions, Sapiya (likely Babylonian Šapiya) had been the capital of Nabû-mukīn-zēri of Bīt-Amukāni (731-729),[40] but the Bīt-Amukāni are not known to have had any particular centre during the years 689-627. An individual by the name of Kudurru appears to have held some authority over this tribe during part of this time and to have had to deal with incursions by Puqūdu tribesmen.[41]

In the reign of Sennacherib, Bīt-Dakkūri is said to have had 33 walled towns and 250 villages, many more settlements than Bīt-Ša'alli and Bīt-Yakīn and somewhat less than Bīt-Amukāni.[42] With the decline in the importance of the Bīt-Yakīn as a result of the actions of Assyrian kings against that tribe, the Bīt-Dakkūri appear to have assumed a more important position in Babylonia. This tribe provided a king of Babylonia in the middle of the eighth century (Nabû-šuma-iškun, *c.* 760-748) and one just before the period in question (Mušēzib-Marduk, 692-689), and one of its rulers, Šamaš-ibni, was termed a king in Esarhaddon's inscriptions.[43] The Bīt-Dakkūri appear to have been concentrated around the Euphrates south of Babylon and Borsippa.[44] Marad (likely modern Wannat as-Sa'dūn, located about 55 km southeast of Babylon) and Dūr-Ladīni (possibly Tell Khaled, located several

---

38 See Zadok, *RGTC* 8, p. 210. Edzard suggests that the city lay not far from Isin; see *RLA* 6, p. 494.

39 *TCL* 12 90, from the time of Nabonidus, refers to land in Bīt-Amukāni which appears to have lain near Uruk. See also Smith, *Senn.*, p. 24 and Zadok, *WO* 16 (1985): 58-62.

40 Rost, *Tigl. III*, pp. 60-61:23; Zadok, *RGTC* 8, p. 287.

41 *ABL* 258, 275, and 279. The reference to Nabû-šarra-uṣur the *rab kiṣri* in *ABL* 275 rev. 5 suggests a date around the time of the Šamaš-šuma-ukīn Revolt since this individual also appears in *ABL* 462 (rev. 27'), a letter dating to shortly after the revolt.

42 Luckenbill, *Senn.*, pp. 52-53:36-39. Although Sennacherib claims to have conquered thirty-three walled towns, only twenty-six are listed by name. For the other three tribes mentioned (Bīt-Amukāni, Bīt-Ša'alli, and Bīt-Yakīn), the totals agree with the number of towns cited. Since the combined total for all four tribes requires the Bīt-Dakkūri to have had thirty-three walled towns, it seems likely that a line containing the names of seven towns belonging to the Bīt-Dakkūri had been omitted in this copy of the text. On this error, see also Eph'al, *Ancient Arabs*, p. 40 n. 106. See Unger in *RLA* 2, pp. 38-40 and Zadok, *WO* 16 (1985): 54-57 for discussions of this tribe and Parpola, *Toponyms*, pp. 80-81 and Zadok, *RGTC* 8, pp. 85-86 for textual attestations.

43 E.g., Borger, Esarh., p. 52 §27 episode 12.

44 See Smith, *Senn.*, pp. 19-22.

km southeast of Hilla)[45] were said by Sennacherib's scribes have been among the cities of Bīt-Dakkūri captured by the Assyrian king and Šamaš-ibni is known to have seized land belonging to citizens of Babylon and Borsippa.[46]

The Bīt-Yakīn[47] were the most important Chaldean tribe until about the end of the eighth century, when actions by Assyrian monarchs (particularly deportations by Sargon II and Sennacherib)[48] greatly weakened the tribe. Indeed during the period 689-627, the Bīt-Yakīn are mentioned by name in only two texts.[49] Sennacherib, in his list of conquests, mentions only eight walled towns (including Larsa, Eridu, Kissik, Kullab, and Dūr-Yakīn) and one hundred villages for the Bīt-Yakīn[50] and yet it is clear that not all the cities were inhabited by or even on good terms with the Chaldeans. In *ABL* 210 the people of Kissik stated that the Chaldeans hated them and this was reiterated in *ABL* 736, where they claimed that all the people of the region hated them because they reported loyally to Ashurbanipal. Until its destruction in 707, the town of Dūr-Yakīn had served as the tribe's major centre.[51] The Bīt-Yakīn were closely connected with the Sealand, the area of swamp-marsh around the lower courses of the Tigris and Euphrates rivers at the head of the Persian Gulf.[52] Tiglath-pileser III refered to the "sea of Bīt-Yakīn," apparently as one of the extremities of his realm.[53] Sargon stated that

---

45 For the location of Marad, see Zadok, *RGTC* 8, p. 220 and Edzard in *RLA* 7, p. 351. For the location of Dūr-Ladīni, see Zadok, *WO* 16 (1985): 54-55.

46 E.g., Borger, *Esarh.*, p. 52 §27, episode 12.

47 With regard to this tribe in general, see Unger in *RLA* 2, pp. 43-44 and Zadok, *WO* 16 (1985): 52 and 62-63. For textual attestations, see Parpola, *Toponyms*, pp. 84-85 and Zadok, *RGTC* 8, p. 93.

48 E.g., Winckler, *Sar.*, pp. 118-19:116 and Luckenbill, *Senn.*, p. 35 iii 59-70. Note also Bīt-Yakīn's mass flight to Elam to escape Sennacherib's military actions (*ibid.*, p. 38 iv 32-36).

49 *ABL* 1131:3 (partially restored), 7, and 11; *CT* 54 22 rev. 27. *ABL* 576, which may deal with the same general incident as *ABL* 1131, refers to the Sealand (rev. 9 and 11), not to the Bīt-Yakīn.

50 Luckenbill, *Senn.*, p. 53:48-49.

51 Although Dūr-Yakīn was captured by Sargon II in 709, it does not appear to have been destroyed until two year later; see van der Spek, *JEOL* 25 (1977-78): 56-66.

52 The location of the head of the Persian Gulf in antiquity is uncertain. Some of the most important articles on the position of the head of the Persian Gulf in antiquity are Lees and Falcon, *Geographical Journal* 118 (1952): 24-39; Larsen, *JAOS* 95 (1975): 43-57; Larsen and Evans, and Vita-Finzi in *Environmental History*, pp. 227-44 and 255-61 respectively; MacFadyen and Vita-Finzi, *Geological Magazine* 115 (1978): 287-300; Hansman, *Geographical Journal* 144 (1978): 49-61; and Waetzoldt in *Strandverschiebungen in ihrer Bedeutung für Geowissenschaften und Archäeologie*, Ruperto Carola Sonderheft (Heidelberg, 1981), pp. 159-83 and figs. 1-3. The most detailed discussion of the Sealand is that of Dougherty (*Sealand*); however, many of his conclusions cannot be accepted, including his views that the terms "Karduniaš" and "Sealand" could be used interchangeably (*ibid.*, p. 141) and that a large part of the Sealand was in Arabia (*ibid.*, especially pp. 122-23 and 157). See also Ahmed, *Asb.*, pp. 17-20 on the marsh area.

53 Rost, *Tigl. III*, pp. 54-55:3-4.

Bīt-Yakīn was situated "on the shore of the sea as far as the border of Dilmun,"[54] although it seems unlikely that this tribe actually occupied the area along the northern coast of the Arabian Peninsula to Bahrain.[55] The exact extent of the marshes is unclear; it varied as climactic changes caused the marshes to expand or recede.[56]

The identification of Bīt-Yakīn with the Sealand, or at least part of it, seems clear from the following considerations:

1. The Sealand appears to have been at least partially co-extensive with what has been described as Bīt-Yakīn territory.

2. In his inscriptions, Sargon II consistently separates Bīt-Yakīn from the other Chaldean tribes when mentioning them by name; he terms these other tribes "all of Chaldea."[57]

3. One Yakīn (or [*mār*] Yakīn), presumably the ruler of Bīt-Yakīn, was called king of the Sealand by Shalmaneser III.[58]

4. Erība-Marduk, leader of the Bīt-Yakīn and ruler of Babylonia at some point in the first half of the eighth century, was later said to have been of a Sealand dynasty.[59]

5. Merodach-Baladan II of Bīt-Yakīn was called king of the Sea(land) in an Assyrian inscription describing Tiglath-pileser III's campaign in 729.[60]

---

54 E.g., Winckler, *Sar.*, pp. 84-85:25-26.

55 Or should Dilmun be taken to include Failaka here? Sargon may suggest that some of the Bīt-Yakīn lived along the border with Elam (Winckler, *Sar.*, p. 60:364-366) although this is not clear because the names of five cities are mentioned between the references to the Bīt-Yakīn and the Elamite border, and because none of these cities is known to have belonged to the Bīt-Yakīn.

56 Dietrich, *Aramäer*, pp. 4-5, suggests that the Sealand was divided into two parts: the Northern Sealand with its capital at Nagītu and the Southern Sealand with its capital at Ur; however, there is no real evidence for this. Dietrich refers to *ABL* 540 rev. 7—LÚ.GAR.KUR *tam-tim ṣa-pu-nu*—and understands this to refer to an entity called the Northern Sealand, taking *ṣa-pu-nu* to be a northwest Semitic loan word meaning "north" (Dietrich, *Aramäer*, p. 161 n. 1, and see *AHw*, p. 1083); but this word is a hapax legomenon in Akkadian. Zadok reads *za-bu-nu* and takes it to be an Aramaic name; see *WO* 16 (1985): 62 n. 207. As far as I am aware, there is no other evidence to support the division to the Sealand into two parts or the statement that Nagītu and Ur were capitals of the two.

57 See Winckler, *Sar.*, pp. 100-101:21-22 and 152-53:82-86; note also *ibid.*, pp. 84-85:25-26, 138-39 no. 1:18-19 and no. 2:14-15, 144-45:17-19, and 160-61:24-26. Sennacherib's inscriptions clearly include the Bīt-Yakīn among the Chaldean tribes (Luckenbill, *Senn.*, pp. 49:11 and 52-54:36-50). The reason for the division in Sargon's inscriptions is unclear. Possibly it was intended to emphasize the importance of the Bīt-Yakīn at that time (partially due to the fact that Merodach-Baladan II was ruler of Babylonia during a large part of the reign of Sargon) or to indicate its distinct geographical location.

58 Michel, *WO* 4 (1967-68): 34 vi 7; Michel reads [*mār*] ^{m}*ia-ki-ni*, "[des (Fürsten von) Bīt-]Jakin." See also Brinkman in *Studies Oppenheim*, p. 8.

59 For Erība-Marduk, see Brinkman, *PKB*, pp. 221-24.

60 2 *R* 67:26. For Merodach-Baladan II, see Brinkman in *Studies Oppenheim*, pp. 6-53 and especially pp. 11-12.

6. The leaders of the Sealand whose affiliation is clear during this period were all members of the Bīt-Yakīn tribe (Nabû-zēr-kitti-līšir, Na'id-Marduk, and Nabû-bēl-šumāti).[61]

7. The Bīt-Yakīn are rarely mentioned by name during the years 689-627 and it is unlikely that they vanished totally.[62]

Probably the Bīt-Yakīn formed a large part of the population of the Sealand and encouraged anti-Assyrian actions there although it seems likely that other groups, including tribeless individuals (e.g., refugees and outlaws hiding from the authorities), also dwelt there. The lay of the land was ideally suited for hiding from pursuers and for guerilla warfare. Many of the Sealanders may have lived as the marsh Arabs did until recently, dependent upon animal husbandry, hunting, gathering, and fishing for their livelihood. The rulers of the Sealand, however, could control great wealth, as attested by the goods sent by Merodach-Baladan II to Tiglath-pileser III: a large quantity of gold ore, objects made of gold, precious stones, wooden beams, plants, coloured garments, aromatic plants, and cattle.[63] The Assyrian king recognized Meodach-Baladan's importance as ruler of the Sealand, and of all the Chaldean leaders called only him "king."

The Bīt-Yakīn had frequently opposed Assyria before this period began and were deeply involved in Babylonian affairs. Merodach-Baladan II had wrested Babylonia from Assyrian control in 722 when the new Assyrian king Sargon II was preoccupied at home and had maintained himself on the throne of Babylon for twelve years despite opposition from Assyria. Although he had been forced to abandon Babylon in 710, he did not give up and managed to regain the throne for nine months in 703 before again fleeing from Assyrian forces. Although the tribe did not act as a unit by the name Bīt-Yakīn during the period in question (or at least there is no record of their having done so), they provided a number of notable rebel leaders—Nabû-zēr-kitti-līšir, Nabû-ušallim, and Nabû-bēl-šumāti—all members of the tribe's ruling family (two sons and one grandson of Merodach-Baladan II) and were undoubtedly active under the terms Sealand and Sealanders. Though Na'id-Marduk, another son of Merodach-Baladan, ruled the Sealand as a loyal official of Assyria, he had been involved earlier in Nabû-zēr-kitti-līšir's

---

61 All three were descendants of Merodach-Baladan II. Nabû-bēl-šumāti is called a Sealander in Starr, *SAA* 4, no. 280 rev. 1, where the final element of his name is erroneously written *šīmāti* (NAM.MEŠ).

62 See p. 40 n. 49 for the two texts referring to the tribe at this time. It is unclear why they appear so seldom in the texts of the period, though the deportations by Assyrian kings (including Sennacherib) had undoubtedly reduced their numbers and importance. Possibly some of those who remained found it expedient to merge themselves with the other inhabitants of the area in which they lived. Or it may simply have become more fashionable to use the term "Sealand" rather than "Bīt-Yakīn."

63 See 2 *R* 67:26-28.

rebellion[64] and had submitted to Assyria only when he saw that Elam could not be trusted to give him asylum. Nabû-bēl-šumāti may have been a loyal official before he joined the Šamaš-šuma-ukīn Revolt,[65] but once he had done so, he proved to be Šamaš-šuma-ukīn's most important Babylonian ally. The Sealand bordered on Elam, and at times parts of it may have fallen under Elamite control as the marshes expanded and receded and as tribes migrated. At one point a king of Elam claimed that the Sealand was legitimately part of his realm.[66] Inevitably the Bīt-Yakīn leaders of the Sealand had close contacts with Elam, sometimes taking refuge there from the Assyrians, and sometimes receiving Elamite military aid against Assyrian forces.

The Chaldean tribes consistently provided the impetus, leadership, and manpower for anti-Assyrian actions, both during this period and earlier, in spite of numerous punitive actions directed against them by Assyrian kings. Apparently the Chaldean chieftains managed to mobilize the military and economic resources of their tribes more easily than did the leaders of the urban populations and to make use of their natural environment to effectively oppose the Assyrians. There is no evidence of fighting among the Chaldean tribes at this time but neither are they known to have acted in concert with one another or to have united under a common Chaldean leader. This lack of unity among the Chaldean tribes was a principal cause of the failure in anti-Assyrian actions. During the Šamaš-šuma-ukīn Revolt some cooperated with the Aramean Puqūdu, though at other times they are known to have been at enmity with that tribe.[67] There is no evidence of anti-Chaldean sentiment on the part of Akkadians, although the two could occasionally be in conflict; the Chaldeans were generally both important and accepted members of the Babylonian community.

III. Arameans

At different times Aramean tribes were found throughout most of the Near East.[68] The term "Aramean" first occurs in a clear context in the beginning of

---

64 Since Na'id-Marduk fled from Elam when Nabû-zēr-kitti-līšir was killed, it is likely that he had gone there with his brother in order to escape from Assyrian troops which were advancing to relieve Ur.

65 Nabû-bēl-šumāti reported to the king in *ABL* 839 (possibly feigning loyalty, see pp. 128-29).

66 Or at least that he wished to consider it as such (*ABL* 1114:14'-rev. 2 and rev. 7-11).

67 See in particular *ABL* 275.

68 With regard to the Arameans, see in particular Brinkman, *PKB*, pp. 267-85 and *Prelude*, pp. 12-14 (and the bibliography *ibid*., n. 44); Dietrich, *Aramäer*; Forrer in *RLA* 1, pp. 131-39; Moritz in *Oriental Studies Published in Commemoration of the Fortieth Anniversary (1883-1923) of Paul Haupt as Director of the Oriental Seminary of the Johns Hopkins University, Baltimore, Md.*, edited by C. Adler and A. Ember (Baltimore and

the twelfth century, where Tiglath-pileser I uses it to describe the land of the Aḫlamû located west of the Euphrates from Palmyra to Anat and Rapiqu.[69] In the early texts they are generally pictured as hostile, or as disruptive elements in the land,[70] and this is also true for the years 689-627. During this period, the Arameans in Babylonia appear to have been concentrated in rural areas, primarily in the eastern part of the country, along the Tigris River, although their presence is also known around Uruk and Nippur. Nippur, in particular, appears to have had a long history of conflict with the Arameans inhabiting the surrounding area. The Akkadian word *aramu* is used to refer to both the people themselves (LÚ *aramu*) and the area of the country in which they lived (KUR *aramu*).[71] The Arameans were divided into a great many more tribes than the Chaldeans—at least forty as opposed to five—each being led by one or more sheikhs (singular: *nasīku*), the larger tribes perhaps having more than one and the smaller tribes having only one.[72] With so many tribal leaders they appear to have been far less capable of united or co-operative action than the Chaldeans.

The Gambūlu and the Puqūdu may have been among the largest of the Aramean tribes in Babylonia and it is only for these two tribes that there is any significant information for the years 689-627.[73] In fact, very few of the tribes are well attested at this or any other time.[74] The Puqūdu inhabited the marshy region in eastern Babylonia along the Elamite border. During the reign of Sargon II they appear along the Uqnû river (generally identified with either the modern Karkheh or Kārūn rivers),[75] but in this period they are known to have been active in the area of Uruk. The Puqūdu were at least

---

Leipzig, 1926), pp. 184-211; and Zadok, *West Semites* (especially pp. 1-21), *WO* 16 (1985): 63-70, and *Tadmor Festschrift*, pp. 104-17.

69 Weidner, *AfO* 18 (1957-58): 350 lines 34-36. See Brinkman, *PKB*, p. 267 n. 1717.

70 See for example Gadd, *Iraq* 16 (1954): 192-93 and pl. 50 vii 45-72.

71 See Parpola, *Toponyms*, pp. 35-37 (sub *Arumu*) and Zadok, *RGTC* 8, p. 27. The latter designation was likely secondary in derivation, that is to say that the land of Aramu simply referred to the area in which the Aramu dwelt and not to an organized state. A city of Aramu appears once (likely located in Assyria), in *ADD* 1168:8; since the gentilic form (URU *ar-ma-a-a*) is actually found in that text, URU may simply have been used instead of LÚ in this instance.

72 Brinkman, *PKB*, pp. 270 and 274-75 and *Power and Propaganda*, p. 241 n. 14; Zadok, *WO* 16 (1985): 68-69. The great majority of Aramean tribes were likely smaller in size than the Chaldean ones.

73 For textual attestations for the Puqūdu and Gambūlu, see Parpola, *Toponyms*, pp. 128-29 and 280-81 and Zadok, *RGTC* 8, pp. 137 and 249-50 (sub Piqūdu).

74 See Brinkman, *PKB*, pp. 270-72. Among the other Aramean tribes finding mention in the texts of this period are the Ḫudadu (as the name of a lowland, *tāmirtu*, *BIN* 1 159:20 [*B-K* L.29]), the Lītamu (as the name of a lowland, *TCL* 12 11:1 [*B-K* K.86]), the Radê (as the name of a town in Elam, *ABL* 281 rev. 16) and the Ru'a (as the name of a town, *ABL* 268:10). See also Zadok, *WO* 16 (1985): 68-69.

75 For the modern identification of the Uqnû river, see Brinkman, *PKB*, p. 269; Parpola, *Toponyms*, p. 406; Nashef, *RGTC* 5, pp. 322-23; and Carter and Stolper, *Elam*, p. 188.

partly settled since there is reference to a Puqūdu town.[76] With regard to their size, we may note that they had more than one sheikh at a time[77] and frequently appear in texts. Most of our information about the tribe comes from the time of the Šamaš-šuma-ukīn Revolt, when some actively supported the rebellion. There may have been some fighting between the Puqūdu and the Gurasimmu tribe in the time of Esarhaddon[78] and strife with the Chaldean Bīt-Amukāni tribe is also attested.[79] Located in the Babylonian-Elamite border region, the Gambūlu were naturally in contact with Elam and at times appear to have been allied with, or under the control of, that country. Sargon II mentions eight Gambulian sheikhs who dwelt along the Uqnû river and attributes to the tribe six districts and forty-four fortified towns.[80] During part of the period in question Ša-pī-Bēl appears to have been their stronghold, the seat of the Gambulian leader Bēl-iqīša who submitted to Esarhaddon and was rewarded by him. The town was destroyed by Ashurbanipal in 653 because Bēl-iqīša and his sons had turned from Assyria and encouraged Elam to invade Babylonia.[81]

Some Arameans dwelt in towns and cities of their own and others in the older cities of the land (Cutha, Ḫursagkalama, Kish, Nippur, Sippar, and Uruk).[82] For the most part, however, they seem to have been less sedentary, or less tied to permanent settlements, than the Chaldean tribes, and therefore probably more dependent upon animal husbandry (horses, oxen, sheep, and goats) for their livelihood.[83] Some Aramean tribes known in Babylonia provided soldiers for Assyria, though exactly when is not clear. Members of the Itu' tribe, for instance, served as permanent units of infantry within the Assyrian army and kept garrison duty for the Assyrian king at Borsippa.[84]

Like the Chaldeans, the Arameans, with their own traditions and lifestyles, appear to have formed semi-independent units within the Babylonian state. Rulers of Babylonia often found it difficult to maintain control over them;

---

[76] *ABL* 268:9.

[77] *ABL* 622+1279 rev. 4.

[78] *ABL* 947 rev. 3'-8'. The reference to Sîn-šarra-uṣur (likely the son of Ningal-iddin) in rev. 9'-10' suggests that the letter was written during the reign of Ashurbanipal (see below) and thus that the action described in rev. 3'-8' occurred during the reign of Esarhaddon.

[79] *ABL* 275.

[80] Lie, *Sar.*, pp. 45 n. 9 (partially restored) and 48-49:1. See also Brinkman, *Prelude*, p. 13 n. 47 and Zadok, *WO* 16 (1985): 38-42.

[81] E.g., Borger, *Esarh.*, p. 53 §27 episode 13 and Piepkorn, *Asb.*, pp. 70-73 vi 17-49. Ša-pī-Bēl may be identical with the towns Šapiya and Sapiya; see p. 265 n. 3. Zadok prefers to read the name Šapi-Bēl (*WO* 16 [1985]: 38).

[82] E.g., Lie, *Sar.*, pp. 48-49:1; *ABL* 268:9-10; and Luckenbill, *Senn.*, p. 25 i 39-41.

[83] See Brinkman, *PKB*, p. 275.

[84] See Postgate in *RLA* 5, pp. 221-22; *ABL* 349; and Reade, *Iraq* 34 [1972]: 104-105. These Arameans may well have been from Assyria itself, not Babylonia, since this tribe was located the west bank of the Tigris around modern Samarra. See also *ABL* 685 and 883 and note Garelli in *Mesopotamien und seine Nachbarn*, pp. 441-43.

tribal groups, in effect, appear to have lain outside the normal provincial structure. Arameans tend to have been less Babylonianized than Chaldeans even though their presence in Babylonia preceded the Chaldeans'. To a certain extent, Arameans were less likely to take Babylonian names than their Chaldean counterparts. An individual Aramean was usually identified with the gentilic form of his tribe rather than his father's name (e.g., ^{m}*na-ṭè-ru* LÚ *ru-ú-a-a*).[85] *BIN* 2 132 records the names of large number of Puqudians who had been dedicated to the goddesses Ištar of Uruk and Nanaya by Sargon II and Sennacherib and about whom some dispute arose in the time of Esarhaddon and Ashurbanipal. Most of these individuals bore good Akkadian names as did their fathers, who are also cited. However, these Puqudians had been in the service of the goddesses for a good many years, and thus perhaps in closer contact with city ways than other Arameans.[86] Arameans rarely became involved in Babylonia's political life and are never known to have provided a king of Babylonia.[87] Few individual Arameans, or at least few individuals with clearly Aramaic names, are attested during this time although there were clearly many Arameans present in the land. It is likely that some individuals whom we assume to have been Akkadians were in fact Arameans (or Chaldeans), that is individuals who had taken Akkadian names and who have simply not been identified as members of a particular Aramean (or Chaldean) tribe in the text(s) mentioning them. Some tribesmen, particularly those living in the ancient cities of the land (the area from which most of our information derives), may have consciously attempted to assimilate with the group which dominated those cities and which practiced the "higher" culture of the land (i.e., the Akkadians) in the hope of gaining a share of that group's power, influence, and prestige. During the years 689-627, the Arameans are not known to have provided any major leader or to have led any country-wide anti-Assyrian action, though they did support actions against Assyria.[88] In the past Aramean tribes had been a disruptive element within the Babylonian state; there is some evidence that this was the case during this period also.[89] However, no anti-Aramean sentiment on the part of other Babylonians is attested at this time. The Puqūdu do not appear to have been always viewed with suspicion by the urban populations, since at

[85] NBC 6142:13 (*B-K* J.5); see Brinkman, *Prelude*, p. 13 n. 46 and Zadok, *RGTC* 8, p. 427.
[86] With regard to *BIN* 2 132, see Zadok, *West Semites*, pp. 181-82.
[87] It has sometimes been thought that Adad-apla-iddina, a ruler of Babylonia in the eleventh century, was an Aramean, but see Walker in *zikir šumim*, pp. 414-15.
[88] Bēl-iqīša of the Gambūlu was one of those who instigated Urtak's invasion of Babylonia and Nabû-ušēzib of the Puqūdu was an active supporter of the Šamaš-šuma-ukīn Revolt.
[89] *ABL* 275 and see Parpola, *LAS* 2, p. 281, commentary to no. 284 rev. 4 (*CT* 53 75).

one point the flocks of the temple of Uruk grazed freely with those of the tribe.[90]

Arameans (particularly the Gambūlu) were often in contact with Elam; indeed they may be found living in both countries. As the border fluctuated or tribes migrated, they could come within the sphere of Elamite authority and Elam would have frequently encouraged disruptive elements among the tribes in order to cause problems for the Assyrians, or at times the Babylonian government. While the Gambūlu, in alliance with Elam, appear to have been anti-Assyrian before the Šamaš-šuma-ukīn Revolt, it was only during that revolt that the Puqūdu are known to have supported any rebellion against Assyria during the years 689-627. At that time, they are known to have been divided in their support for Šamaš-šuma-ukīn; some, at least, aided Ashurbanipal.[91] The Assyrian king stated that Šamaš-šuma-ukīn had roused the Arameans to revolt, which would suggest that other Aramean tribes also aided the rebels.

A tribal group by the name of the Gurasimmu[92] is present in the area of Ur during the time of Ashurbanipal and one letter appears to refer to their having subdued the Sealand and the Puqūdu for Esarhaddon.[93] They are never explicitly called Arameans, but it seems likely that they were. They appear in texts only from the reign of Ashurbanipal, thus after the time the lists of Aramean tribes were compiled. Like the Arameans, they are referred to by the tribal gentilic (LÚ *gurasimmaya*).[94] The Gurasimmu were under the jurisdiction of the governor of Ur, at least during the tenure of Sîn-balāssu-iqbi and probably during that of Sîn-tabni-uṣur, before they joined the rebels in the Šamaš-šuma-ukīn Revolt. The exact area they inhabited is unclear; Bēl-ibni claims to have subjugated them from the town of Kapru as far as the watercourse of É.MEŠ-GAL (reading uncertain), a distance of twelve *bēru* (over 120 kilometers); unfortunately, neither place can be located, although Kapru was considered to be part of Bīt-Yakīn in the time of Sargon II.[95]

---

90 *ABL* 268:8-10. The flocks were grazing in URU *ru-'-ú-a*, a settlement probably inhabited by members of the Ru'a tribe (Zadok, *RGTC* 8, pp. 262-63).

91 *ABL* 1195 rev. 1-5.

92 On this tribe, see Dietrich in *RLA* 3, pp. 702-703. For references to the tribe, see Parpola, *Toponyms*, p. 136 and Zadok, *RGTC* 8, pp. 142-43. For the writing of the name, see these works and Brinkman, *Or.* NS 38 (1969): 341 n. 2. The name could be preceded by the determinatives denoting a people, a land, and a city.

93 See p. 45 n. 78.

94 See Brinkman, *Or.* NS 46 (1977): 308.

95 *ABL* 790+*CT* 54 425:7-9. On Kapru, see Dietrich, *Aramäer*, p. 101 n. 1 and Zadok, *RGTC* 8, p. 194. For the length of the *bēru*, see *CAD* 2 (B), pp. 208-11, Thureau-Dangin, *JA* 13 (1909): 98-99, and Streck, *Asb.*, p. 74 n. 1. If *ABL* 942:7-8 refers to towns belonging to the Gurasimmu which the Puqūdu (Piqūdu) and Sealand had plundered, instead of towns which the Gurasimmu, Puqūdu, and Sealand had plundered, then either some Gurasimmu were settled in towns or some towns were located in the area in which the Gurasimmu inhabited.

In summary, there is only scant information for the Aramean tribes during the years 689-627 and what there is deals mostly with only two of the more than forty tribes. Although the Gambulian Bēl-iqīša (and his sons) and the Puqudian Nabû-ušēzib were prominent in anti-Assyrian movements, neither played a national role and there is no evidence of any united Aramean action during this time. The Arameans had their profoundest effect on Babylonia in the realm of language.[96] It was during these years that the Aramaic tongue was replacing Akkadian as the language of the people; it has even be argued that Aramaic was wide-spread as the common language in Babylonia by the late seventh century.[97] One may note that in the previous century Sargon II had refused to allow an official in Babylonia to send his reports in Aramaic. He was ordered instead to write in Akkadian, perhaps because fewer (i.e., only authorized) people would have been able to read that language.[98] The importance of the Aramaic language in Babylonia can also be detected by such matters as Aramaic dockets on Babylonian economic documents, an Aramaic letter dated to the time of the Šamaš-šuma-ukīn Revolt, Aramaic influence on topographic names, and the presence of Aramaic words in Babylonian documents.[99]

IV. Other Population Groups

According to a Babylonian letter to Ashurbanipal, there were many foreign peoples (individuals speaking different languages) in Nippur under the protection of the king of Assyria (EME.MEŠ *ma-ʾ-da-a-ti ina* EN.LÍL.KI *ina* GIŠ.MI LUGAL).[100] This likely refers to groups in addition to those mentioned above.[101] Perhaps some were Elamite refugees who had fled from

---

96 For the Babylonian-Aramaic relationship in general, see Greenfield in *Mesopotamien und seine Nachbarn*, pp. 471-82.

97 Greenfield in *Mesopotamien und seine Nachbarn*, p. 471.

98 *CT* 54 10:15-22; see Dietrich, *WO* 4 (1967-68): 90 and Parpola, *ARINH*, pp. 123-24 n. 9. Note also the scribe writing Aramaic (*sepīru*) mentioned in Strassmaier, *8e Congrès* no. 3:7 (*B-K* I.7; Babylonian text composed at Assur).

99 Dockets: YBC 7166 and 80-B-4 (*B-K* J.20 and K.99). Aramaic letter: *KAI* no. 233 (found at Assur but written in Babylonia). Toponyms: see Zadok, *WO* 12 (1981): 39-69 and *RGTC* 8, pp. XIV-XXV (Aramaic toponyms gradually replaced Akkadian ones in first millennium Babylonia). Aramaic words in Babylonian and Assyrian texts: see von Soden, *Or.* NS 35 (1966): 1-20, 37 (1968): 261-71, and 46 (1977): 183-97, and Greenfield in *Mesopotamien und seine Nachbarn*, pp. 472-73. Note also possible Aramaic influence in the "dialogue documents" (*ibid.*, pp. 473-74). See also Brinkman, *Prelude*, p. 14 n. 53.

100 *ABL* 238 rev. 6'; see *CAD* 9 (L), p. 214. The heterogeneous nature of the population at Nippur may help explain why this city frequently gave trouble to the Assyrians and was placed under direct Assyrian control during the second half of the reign of Ashurbanipal.

101 Zadok has written a number of works on foreign population groups in Babylonia during the Chaldean and Achaemenian periods, sometimes mentioning earlier material. In

the political upheavals in Elam;[102] others may have been traders, conducting business in Nippur. The presence of several Egyptians (usually described as descendants of Egyptians) in Babylonia is attested in contemporary documents. During the reign of Esarhaddon, Šarru-lū-dāri, "the Egyptian" (LÚ *miṣiraya*) appears to have been one of several individuals who prodded the governor of Nippur into actions which Bēl-ušēzib criticized in a letter to the king.[103] He is the only Egyptian recorded as playing any role in events during these years, though many others appear as participants in or witnesses to legal and administrative transactions. Some of these had undoubtedly been deported to Babylonia by Esarhaddon and Ashurbanipal, who at times controlled Egypt; still others may have come for private or commercial reasons.[104]

There would have been a certain number of Assyrians present in Babylonia as government officials, on military duty, and as merchant traders. There is no clear evidence of an "Assyrian community" there, although a fair number may have been settled at (or on garrison duty in) Nippur during and after the time of Kandalānu when that city was directly controlled by the Assyrians and served as their base of operations in the south. The presence of ceramic wares similar to Assyrian palace wares at the site would tend to support this view.[105] At one time it was thought that there were persons of Assyrian descent among the temple personnel at Borsippa; however, this was based upon the misinterpretation of A ^{m}AŠ-ŠUR as "descendant of the Assyrian" rather than as "descendant of Ēda-ēṭir."[106] Two individuals of Assyrian descent do, however, appear in economic documents from Babylon during

---

particular, see Zakok, *Tel Aviv* 6 (1979): 164-81 and *West Semites*; and Eph'al, *Or.* NS 47 (1978): 74-90. As just mentioned, Aramaic may well have been adopted as the language of a large, and ever-increasing, number of the urban population. Basically nothing is known of the Chaldean language. It is not impossible that the Chaldeans spoke Aramaic, or a dialect of that language, at this time. One should note that the Aramaic language was later called Chaldee. See Brinkman, *PKB*, pp. 265-67 (especially p. 267 n. 1716) and Edzard in *RLA* 5, pp. 291-92.

102 Elamite refugees are known to have sought asylum in Assyria at this time (e.g., Ḫumban-nikaš II and Tammarītu, the sons of Urtak).

103 *CT* 54 22 rev. 11-13 (see chapter 6). Because the surface of the tablet is badly damaged at this point, readings are only tentative.

104 On Egyptians in Babylonia, see Eph'al, *Or.* NS 47 (1978): 74-90 and Zadok, *Göttinger Miszellen* 26 (1977): 63-68. In addition to the Egyptians listed by him for this period, note also the following references: BM 77907:26 (Bēl-iddin, descendant of Miṣiraya); BM 78167:9-10, 11, 18 and 20 (⌜^{m}⌝[...], descendant of Miṣiraya; Bēl-ēṭir, descendant of Miṣi[raya]; Ninurta-ušabši, descendant of Miṣiraya; and Lā-qīpi, descendant of Miṣiraya); Gurney in *Diakonoff Festschrift*, p. 121 no. 1:3 and 6 (Bēl-uballiṭ, descendant of Miṣiraya); BM 46799+46928+47309:17 (descendant of Miṣiraya); and BM 36347 rev. 14' (Nabû-zēra-ušabši, descendant of Miṣiraya; scribe) (*B-K* K.1, K.6, K.16, K.59, and L.177 respectively).

105 See pp. 23-24.

106 See pp. 247-48 on this matter.

this time, one in 662 (Anu-nāṣir) and the other at the end of Kandalānu's reign (Marduk?-ēreš).[107] Aššur-bēla-uṣur who was *qīpu* of Eanna at some point between 665-648[108] may have been an Assyrian or a member of a family that wished to demonstrate its loyalty to Assyria by using the name of the god Aššur in a member's name.

"Arabs" are sometimes found in Babylonia at this time; however, it is uncertain if many were actually living there.[109] Arab troops came to the aid of Šamaš-šuma-ukīn against Ashurbanipal, as they had when Merodach-Baladan II was fighting Sennacherib.[110] Likely dating to this period are two letters which report that two families from Tema had fled from Eridu and that a merchant from Tema had visited the king of Babylonia.[111] Several towns with Arab names are mentioned in Sennacherib's inscriptions as lying in western Babylonia, in the areas of the Bīt-Amukāni and Bīt-Dakkūri tribes.[112] In addition, a number of objects that may have Arab or Phoenician origin and several inscriptions that may be connected to proto-Arabic script have been discovered in Babylonia, although these have been found in first-millennium contexts, their exact dates are uncertain.[113]

Babylonia was inhabited by several different population groups with varying cultures, life-styles, and backgrounds. Most of the documents of the period come from the cities and thus the hands of Akkadians. Therefore, our

---

107 BM 78086:11, ^{md}*a-nù*-PAB DUMU ^{m}*aš-⸢šur⸣-a-a*, or possibly ^{m}DINGIR!-*a-a* (collation courtesy C.B.F. Walker; *B-K* K.17); and MMA 86.11.181:10-11, ^{md}AMAR?.UTU?-APIN-*eš* A LÚ *aš-šur-⸢a?⸣-a* (*B-K* L.164). See also Zadok, *Assur* 4/3 (1984) and *West Semites*, p. 13 for Assyrians in Chaldean and Achaemenian Babylonia.

108 He is attested as *qīpu* in a document which mentions that Nabû-ušabši was governor of Uruk. The maximum possible period during which Nabû-ušabši could have been governor is 665-648. See Appendix B sub 15a and c.

109 Following Eph'al (*JAOS* 94 [1974]: 108 n. 1 and *Ancient Arabs*, pp. 5-11), the term "Arab" is used here to refer to the desert nomads found east of Babylonia in the Syro-Arabian desert and northern Arabia. See also Zadok, *West Semites*, pp. 192-93.

110 Luckenbill, *Senn.*, p. 51:25-29. An Arab raid on Sippar, likely dating to the reign of Sargon II, is reported in *ABL* 88 (see Eph'al, *Ancient Arabs*, pp. 115-16 and Parpola in *ARINH*, p. 133).

111 *UET* 4 167 (the reading of the verb "fled" is uncertain) and *ABL* 1404. On the date, see Eph'al, *Ancient Arabs*, p. 190.

112 Eph'al, *JAOS* 94 (1974): 108-15 and *Ancient Arabs*, pp. 112-16. See also Zadok, *ZDMG* 131 (1981): 42-84. The Urbi, who are mentioned as being resident in some Babylonian cities (Luckenbill, *Senn.*, p. 54:52) and whom some scholars have taken to be Arabs, are now thought to be a type of warrior (see Eph'al, *JAOS* 94 (1974): 110-11 n. 16). In Adams, *Heartland of Cities*, p. 333, Wright reports on finding a number of settlements (some of which were quite small in size) on the south side of the southernmost channel of the Euphrates in the area of Ur; these were not protected from the neighbouring desert. Perhaps these border villages were inhabited by Arabs, though there is no real evidence for this.

113 See Eph'al, *JAOS* 94 (1974): 109-10 and Brinkman, *Prelude*, p. 28. With regard to the people called the Sutians, see M. Heltzer, *The Suteans* (Naples, 1981), pp. 94-98.

view of conditions is undoubtedly skewed. However, it does seem clear that the cities and their citizens dominated the intellectual, religious, and economic life of Babylonia. Each of the major groups—Akkadians, Chaldeans, and Arameans—rarely acted as a cohesive unit, let alone in concert with the others. The differences between and within the tribal groups on the one hand and the urban populations on the other served only to hinder a common outlook or policy. Their failure to band together politically and militarily kept the Babylonians vulnerable to domination by Assyria. Although cities had on occasion supported Chaldean rulers—for example, Merodach-Baladan II and Nabû-mukīn-zēri—against Assyria in the past, not once during the years 689-627 were the various groups able to present a united front against Assyria. In general, it was the Chaldean tribes, and in particular the Bīt-Yakīn rulers of the Sealand, who tended to oppose the Assyrians at this time.

It is not possible to estimate the size of the population of Babylonia during this time or to determine the relative size of the tribal groups as opposed to that of the urban population. Archaeological surface surveys carried out for some parts of the country have been interpreted as indicating that there was a major drop in occupation (and thus presumably population) in the late second and early first millennia and that it was only during the time of the Neo-Babylonian empire that the trend was reversed and the population began to increase. However, as was mentioned in chapter 2, the areas surveyed may not be representative of Babylonia as a whole and the period of greatest decline in population may well have ended by the middle of the eighth century. Record-keeping continued to increase during the period in question,[114] indicating more legal, economic, and administrative activity and thus perhaps a growing population. Finally, in connection with the size of the population, it is useful to note that during the approximately fifty years preceding our period, the Assyrian kings Tiglath-pileser III, Sargon II, and Sennacherib claim to have deported almost half a million people from Babylonia, over half of them Chaldean tribesmen.[115] Although we may question the accuracy of these figures, the numbers were surely large and must indicate that a considerable number of people had been living in the tribal areas of the land. These deportations (and the military campaigns connected with them) caused the disappearance of the Bīt-Šilāni and Bīt-Ša'alli tribes and the eclipse of the Bīt-Yakīn.

---

[114] At least we have an increasing number of texts preserved.

[115] A study of the practice of deportation as carried out by the Neo-Assyrian monarchs has been presented by B. Oded (*Deportations*). See also Brinkman, *Prelude*, p. 20, especially n. 81, and *Power and Propaganda*, p. 227 and nn. 27-31.

CHAPTER 5

SENNACHERIB AND THE "KINGLESS YEARS" (689-681)

After a long and bloody struggle, Babylon fell to Sennacherib on the first day of Kislīmu (IX) in 689, having been in revolt against Assyria since 694 when Elamite troops led by their king Ḫallušu-Inšušinak had invaded Babylonia, carried off Aššur-nādin-šumi, Sennacherib's son and appointee as king of Babylonia, and replaced him with Nergal-ušēzib of the Babylonian Gaḫal family. When Nergal-ušēzib was defeated and captured by the Assyrians in 693, Mušēzib-Marduk, a Chaldean of the Bīt-Dakkūri tribe, became ruler over Babylonia and continued the rebellion.[1] Starving under siege by Sennacherib, Babylon was already in dire straits by the twenty-eighth day of Abu (V) in 690 and unimaginable deprivation must have followed before the city finally fell or surrendered fifteen months later.[2] Sennacherib had had to carry out several costly campaigns in Babylonia during the course of his reign and as a result his feelings towards that land had hardened. In retaliation for the Babylonians' rebellious actions, and in particular for their handing his son over to Elam, Sennacherib took his revenge on Babylon. Assyrian inscriptions describe his actions. The squares of the city were filled with the corpses of its defenders. The city was looted, its gods smashed, and its people dispersed. Mušēzib-Marduk, his family, and possibly the statue of Marduk, the tutelary god of Babylon, were carried off to Assyria. The fate of Mušēzib-Marduk and his family after being taken to Assyria is not known but the statue of Marduk was to remain absent from Babylon for twenty years, making the performance of the rituals of the New Year's festival impossible.[3] In addition, the statues of the god Adad and the goddess Šala, which the Babylonian king Marduk-nādin-aḫḫē had stolen

---

[1] Events in Babylonia from 694 to 689 are narrated in Grayson, *Chronicles*, no. 1 ii 39-iii 24. See also Brinkman, *Or.* NS 34 (1965): 244-46 and Levine, *JCS* 34 (1982): 28-58. Aššur-nādin-šumi had apparently been handed over to the Elamites by some of his own subjects (see Parpola, *Iraq* 34 [1972]: 21-34 and pl. 19:26-30).

[2] See Brinkman, *JCS* 25 (1973): 93-94. As Brinkman points out, the possibility that Babylon may have been relieved for a time between 28-V-690 and 1-IX-689 cannot be excluded.

[3] Luckenbill, *Senn.*, pp. 83:43-48 and 137:36-37; Grayson, *Chronicles*, nos. 1 iii 22-23, 14:31-33, and 16:1-4. On the removal or possible destruction of the statue of Marduk, see pp. 56-59.

from the Assyrian city of Ekallāte 418 years earlier, were returned to Ekallāte.[4] Sennacherib burned Babylon completely and demolished its houses, temples, and city wall, dumping the debris into the Araḫtu canal. When debris washed away by the rivers eventually reached Dilmun, the people of that country were so overcome with fear of the god Aššur (and Assyrian might) that they sent gifts to Sennacherib and provided tools and workmen to aid in the demolition of Babylon. Canals were dug through the midst of the city to flood it and turn it into a swamp "in order that it would not be possible to recognize the site of that city and (its) temples in the future."[5]

The destruction of Babylon marked a turning point in the history of Babylonia and undoubtedly had a great affect on how Babylonians regarded their northern neighbours. Previously, the old important Babylonian cities had been treated generously by Assyrian monarchs. Now, Babylonia's special position in Assyrian eyes (or at least the eyes of the Assyrian king) was ended with the destruction of its capital. The centre for Mesopotamian culture and scholarship for a millennium and a focal point for opposition to Assyria, Babylon was no more. Its destruction was intended to break the back of Babylonian resistance to Assyrian overlordship and to serve as an example to other would-be rebels. Sennacherib appears to have been successful in accomplishing these ends; Babylonia gave him no more trouble during the remainder of his reign.

Only three of Sennacherib's inscriptions describe the destruction of Babylon: the Akītu-House stela, the Bavian inscription, and K 1634, a fragment of a hexagonal prism which merely duplicates (as far as it is preserved) the account of the Bavian inscription.[6] Sennacherib's other inscriptions may have avoided the subject because it was a sensitive topic. The stela mentions that some dust from Babylon was stored in the Akītu-House at the city of Assur to serve as a reminder of the power of Assyria.[7] The statements in the Bavian text about the destruction provide a contrast to those describing the king's building activities to provide for the prosperity of Nineveh.[8] In the Bavian text the destruction of Babylon's gods and the looting of the temples are attributed to the king's men, not to the king himself, thus exempting Sennacherib from any charge of impiety. Still he must have

---

[4] Luckenbill, *Senn.*, p. 83:48-50. The reference to 418 years presents some chronological problems since this would date the removal of these statues from Ekallāte to 1107 while according to the most widely used chronological scheme (Brinkman in Oppenheim, *Ancient Mesopotamia*, p. 338) Marduk-nādin-aḫḫē is thought to have reigned from 1099 to 1082. The statues had perhaps become dilapidated during their sojourn in Babylonia since *ABL* 662 (*LAS*, no. 191) appears to record the repair of statues of the two deities.

[5] Luckenbill, *Senn.*, pp. 83-84:50-54 and 137-38:36-44.

[6] Luckenbill, *Senn.*, pp. 78-85 and 135-39; Reade, *JCS* 27 (1975): 194.

[7] Luckenbill, *Senn.*, p. 138:44-47.

[8] See Galter, *StOr* 55 (1984): 161-73.

been hated by the Babylonians for destroying their capital and abducting (or possibly destroying) their god Marduk. This is surely why Sennacherib was not always included in the canon of Babylonian kings; his two reigns (704-703 and 688-681) were labelled "kingless" in the Ptolemaic Canon and a Babylonian chronicle.[9] However, although Babylonian Kinglist A and the Assyrian kinglists considered him to have been king of Babylonia,[10] Sennacherib himself never took the title "king of Babylon"; nor was that title ever accorded him by his son, Esarhaddon, or his grandsons, Ashurbanipal and Šamaš-šuma-ukīn.[11]

Confirmation of the destruction and depopulation of Babylon can be found in Esarhaddon's texts describing his rebuilding and resettlement of the city. According to his inscriptions, in the reign of an earlier king the Araḫtu canal overflowed its banks, swept destructively across the site of the city, and turned it into a ruin. The gods of Babylon left the city, flying up to the heavens, and the citizens fled or were given into slavery. To restore Babylon, Esarhaddon had first to clear away the trees and reeds which had grown up on the site and to redirect the river waters back into their old channel. Not wishing to appear to criticize his father's actions, Esarhaddon did not mention Sennacherib in these accounts; instead, the blame for Babylon's fall was placed upon its own citizens who were being punished by the god Marduk for their evil deeds.[12]

ABL 418, a letter from the reign of Esarhaddon, refers to that king having returned prisoners and booty taken from Babylon and having repopulated that city, confirming the fact that Babylon had been looted and depopulated at some point in the fairly recent past. A damaged Babylonian text likely dating to the reign of Nabopolassar calls Sennacherib the "[plund]erer of Akkad" and mentions the killing of the elders of Babylon and the taking of booty from Babylon to Assyria.[13] An inscription from the time of Nabonidus also recalls

---

9 Grayson, *Chronicles*, no. 1 iii 28; the evaluation of Sennacherib's first reign is unclear. Two Babylonian chronicles mention Sennacherib as ruler for 688-681, but do not specifically state that he was ruler of Babylonia (as opposed to Assyria): Grayson, *Chronicles*, nos. 14:31 and 16:1.

10 Babylonian Kinglist A iv 12 and 19, Synchronistic Kinglist A 117 iv 1 (restored) and 10, and the synchronistic kinglist fragments *KAV* 9:4' and 182 iv 1' (the latter two mostly restored); see Grayson in *RLA* 6, pp. 93, 120, 122, and 125.

11 In contrast, Esarhaddon frequently gave his grandfather, Sargon II, the titles "viceroy of Babylon" and "king of Sumer and Akkad" (e.g., Borger, *Esarh.*, p. 8 §5:2). Ashurbanipal and Šamaš-šuma-ukīn gave similar titles to Esarhaddon and Sargon but not to Sennacherib (e.g. Lehmann, *Ššmk*, no. 2:9-11 and Rashid, *Sumer* 37 [1981]: 80 nos. 1:4-7 and 2:4-7 [Arabic section]).

12 Borger, *Esarh.*, pp 12-15 and 19 §11 episodes 2-9 and 18.

13 Gerardi, *AfO* 33 (1986): 30-38, note lines 2-9 and rev. 7-8. Gerardi interprets the text as a "declaration of war" in which Nabopolassar justified his attack on Assyria as retaliation for Sennacherib's action against Babylon.

the destruction of Babylon and the removal of the god Marduk to Assyria. Although Sennacherib is not mentioned by name in what is preserved of the document, it is undoubtedly he who is said to have plotted evil against the land, to have turned Babylon's sanctuaries into ruins, to have desecrated their cult, and to have taken Marduk to Assyria. Even though the text says that he had acted in conformity with the will of the god Marduk, he was still punished for these actions by being killed by his son.[14] Thus, about a century and a half later, Babylon's destruction was still remembered and the Assyrian king blamed. Sennacherib is said to have acted in conformity with the will of the god(s), but only because it was not possible to conceive of Babylon having been destroyed without divine consent. Nabonidus also attributed the destruction of the city of Sippar-Anunītu and its temple Eulmaš to Sennacherib, again because a god (Sîn) had become angry with them. There is no other evidence to support this destruction or to indicate when during his reign it might have occurred.[15] The same may be said for Sennacherib's action against the Bīt-Amukāni; booty taken from that tribe was given to Esarhaddon at some point after he had been named crown prince.[16]

Archaeological evidence from the Merkes quarter of Babylon may support the belief that Babylon was devastated and probably abandoned for a time. Reuther,[17] the excavator, states that at one point in what he terms the Middle Babylonian-Assyrian stratum, there was a level of rather poor house remains above a level of flimsily built, but relatively substantial houses. Frequently there were no recognizable structural remains in this upper level, and the debris consisted of layers of sand and clay with sherds, fragments of bricks, hearths, and ash layers. Above this were widely scattered and poorly built houses. Finally, above this in turn, in what he terms the Neo-Babylonian stratum, were the remains of a more prosperous settlement. Reuther suggests that the layers of sand and clay represent the abandonment of the area following the city's capture by Sennacherib. He states that since traces of burning were found in only two places, most of the houses were simply abandoned, possibly having first been stripped of their wood. He notes that there is no evidence that the area was destroyed by flooding, even though

---

[14] Langdon, *NBK*, Nabonid no. 8 i 1'-41'.

[15] *CT* 34 pl. 34 iii 26-29. Archaeological evidence from Tell ed-Dēr has yet to throw any light on this matter. For the likely identification of Tell ed-Dēr with Sippar-Anunītu, see Charpin, *RA* 82 (1988): 13-32, particularly pp. 14 and 16-17.

[16] *ABL* 1452. Since fighting with the Bīt-Amukāni is known to have occurred earlier in the reign of Sennacherib (e.g., Luckenbill, *Senn.*, pp. 53-54:42-47 and 50-51), it is possible that this text refers to booty acquired as a result of a military action dating before 689. Note the Tukultī-Ninurta-Šagarakti-Šuriaš seal which Sennacherib took from Babylon after conquering that city (see *RIMA* 1, A.O.78.28). In *Prelude*, p. 69, Brinkman speculates that Sennacherib may also have taken some action against the city of Dēr.

[17] Reuther, *Merkes*, especially pp. 21-25 and 60-64.

Sennacherib claims to have obliterated the site by flooding it. Thus, no evidence of systematic destruction has been found in this residential area. Possibly Sennacherib focused his attention on the religious and administrative areas and on the fortifications, leaving the less important residential quarters to be looted, abandoned, and eventually destroyed by the erosive actions of wind and rain. Reuther also argues that the layer of widely scattered houses represents tentative rebuilding on the site before the restoration by Esarhaddon and that the upper prosperous stratum represents that restoration.[18] Support for this interpretation is said to come from the fact that various tablets dated to the reigns of Šamaš-šuma-ukīn and Kandalānu were found in levels associated with the foundations of the more prosperous houses.[19] The scheme presented by Reuther is plausible, but hardly proven; one could wish for a clearer and more detailed presentation of the evidence and for better chronological linkage. The major building projects carried out by the Neo-Babylonian monarchs have undoubtedly made it difficult to find traces of Sennacherib's destruction.

None of the chronicles mention the destruction of Babylon by Sennacherib, or its later rebuilding by Esarhaddon, instead they concern themselves with the presence or absence of the god Marduk. Two state that Marduk stayed in the city of Assur for the last eight years of the reign of Sennacherib, as well as for all of the reign of Esarhaddon, being returned to Babylon only in 668.[20] However, Sennacherib's inscriptions state that the gods of Babylon were destroyed along with the city and Esarhaddon's say that they had flown up to the heavens. None refer to a separate fate for Marduk. The first clear mention of the idea that Marduk resided in Assyria during his absence from Babylon is during the time of Ashurbanipal when it is said that in the reign of a previous king Marduk had sat in Assyria before the father who had begotten him (i.e., the god Aššur).[21] Certainly a statue of Marduk went from the city of Assur to Babylon during the reign of Ashurbanipal and it is known that Esarhaddon had intended to send a statue of Marduk to Babylon, actually saying he had done so in one text. But that text and one other of Esarhaddon's inscriptions say that the god Bēl (Marduk)

---

18 The level of more prosperous houses is referred to as the Neo-Babylonian level, but that is defined as commencing with the restoration of Babylon after the city's destruction by Sennacherib (Reuther, *Merkes*, p. 6), thus we appear to have a circular argument.

19 Reuther (*Merkes*, p. 22) says that a large number of tablets dated to the reign of Kandalānu were found in two clay vessels about one metre deeper than the bottom of the foundation of a house of the Neo-Babylonian level. Since these tablets were found below the houses of that level, one may wonder if that level does indeed represent Esarhaddon's restoration. Some of the texts have been published by L. Jakob-Rost in *FB* 10 (1968): 39-62.

20 Grayson, *Chronicles*, no. 14:31-32 and 35-36, and no. 16:1-7.

21 E.g., Streck, *Asb.*, pp. 232-33:7-9.

had been born in Assyria: "the god Bēl, the goddess Bēltiya ... were duly born in Ešarra, the temple of their progenitor, and (their) form(s) took (their) beautiful shape" and "the god Bēl and the goddess Bēltiya ... according to their command were made inside the city of Assur and duly born in Eḫursaggalkurkurra." (Eḫursaggalkurkurra was the name of the principal cella within Ešarra, the temple of the god Aššur.) Both texts also mention the materials used in fashioning these and several other gods.[22] This would suggest that the original statue of Marduk no longer existed and had in fact been destroyed at the time of Sennacherib's capture of Babylon. In order to show his concern for Babylonia and try to reduce resentment in that land, Esarhaddon would then have created a new statue of the god Marduk. But the idea that the statue of Marduk sent to Babylon in 668 was not the original one is not found in the texts from the time of Ashurbanipal or later,[23] and it is not impossible that Esarhaddon was describing the restoration of the original statue and doing so in a "mystical" way in order to associate Marduk with and under the national god of Assyria for political-ideological reasons.

Whether the statue of Marduk was destroyed or not must remain uncertain. Either its destruction or its presence in "captivity" in Assyria would have helped Sennacherib in his increasing promotion of Assyria's god, Aššur, as the most important of all gods. During the reign of Sargon II, Aššur had begun to be identified with the god Anšar, who belonged to the oldest generation of the gods and was one of Marduk's ancestors in the Babylonian Epic of Creation. Sennacherib continued this identification and had statues of "Aššur (written ^{d}AN.ŠÁR) and the (other) great gods" constructed.[24] He described Anšar as "king of all the gods, creator of himself, father of the gods ... king of heaven and earth, lord of all the gods ... who fashioned heaven and netherworld."[25] The main temple of the god Aššur at Assur was renovated; and in place of the Akītu-House (the temple for the celebration of the New Year's festival) in Babylon, Sennacherib restored and embellished one near the city of Assur, one in which the god Aššur would play the role of hero, not Marduk as in the Babylonian Epic of Creation. Indeed, Sennacherib had the decoration on the gate of this temple show Anšar/Aššur marching against Tiamat.[26] It is no accident that one of the two main inscriptions describing this building, the Akītu-House stela, also describes

---

22 Borger, *Esarh.*, pp. 83-84 §53 rev. 35-38 and pp. 88-89 §57 rev. 11-24.

23 Though this fact may have been forgotten or supressed by the scribes for political-religious motives.

24 E.g., *KAH* 1 49 (composed before the death of Aššur-nādin-šumi).

25 Luckenbill, *Senn.*, p. 149 no. 5:1-4.

26 Luckenbill, *Senn.*, pp. 135-43. Sennacherib claimed to be reviving an ancient, lapsed ritual when he rebuilt the temple, but he may in fact have been instituting a new one. In two texts of the Epic of Creation from Assur the god Aššur (written AN.ŠÁR) replaces Marduk as the hero of the tale (*KAR* 117 and 173).

the destruction of Babylon and that dust from the rubble of Babylon was stored in that temple "in order that the people should proclaim the praise of his (the god Aššur's) might."[27] In an important text from Nineveh, Sennacherib gave Aššur (writen AN.ŠÁR) epithets which were normally associated with Marduk and, most importantly, stated that Aššur held the Tablet of Destinies, "a symbol of supreme rule that in *Enūma Eliš* is strongly identified with Marduk and his supremacy over the universe," thus causing Aššur to usurp Marduk's role even further.[28] Inevitably, in lists of gods mentioned in royal inscriptions from the reign of Sennacherib, Marduk appears less frequently and less prominently than in texts from the reign of Sargon II. As further evidence of the "usurption" of Marduk's place by Aššur, we may note that the ceremonial bed belonging to Marduk was removed from Babylon at the time of its destruction, set up in the temple of Aššur, and rededicated to that god.[29]

The Neo-Assyrian composition which is generally referred to as the "Marduk Ordeal" appears to be connected with the captivity of Marduk in Assyria, or at least with his absence from the city of Babylon. With regard to the text itself, A. Livingstone states: "Marduk's Ordeal is not one single composition with a fixed arrangement of lines or subject matter to which all manuscripts conform ... In the present state of knowledge of the work five versions are to be distinguished ... The arrangement of the subject matter varies from version to version."[30] Because of the number of different versions, their varying arrangements of the material, and their damaged or fragmentary nature, it is often difficult to be certain of the meaning of the text. Livingstone and T. Frymer-Kensky have recently and independently re-edited and studied the composition and come to conflicting opinions about a number of matters,[31] but it seems clear that the composition refers to Marduk (Bēl) as a criminal being held in captivity and one who is prosecuted on behalf of the god Aššur. The text mentions looting and desecration, possibly ordered by the gods, and may connect this with the destruction of Esagila, Marduk's

---

27 Luckenbill, *Senn.*, p. 138:44-47.

28 George, *Iraq* 48 (1986): 133-46; Michalowski, *Moran Festschrift*, p. 392. As Lambert notes (*Iraq* 45 [1983]: 86), Sennacherib's attempt to put an end to the cult of Marduk and to set up Aššur in his place, ironically "often meant making Aššur more like Marduk than he had been previously."

29 The bed was returned to Babylon in 654. See K 2411 (Streck, *Asb.*, pp. 292-303), K 8664 (*OECT* 6 pp. 70-72 and pls. 2-3), and Millard, *Iraq* 26 (1964): 19-23. On the question of the destruction/removal of the statue of Marduk, the promotion of the god Anšar/Aššur, and the place of Marduk in lists of gods in royal inscriptions from the reigns of Sargon and Sennacherib, see in particular Tadmor, *JCS* 12 (1958): 82; Landsberger, *Brief*, pp. 20-27; Borger, *BiOr* 29 (1972): 36; Machinist, *WBJ* 1984-85, pp. 353-6; Tadmor in Eisenstadt, *Origins*, pp. 213-14; and Tadmor, *SAAB* 3 (1989): 23-31.

30 Livingstone, *Explanatory Works*, p. 205.

31 Frymer-Kensky, *JAOS* 103 (1983): 131-41; Livingstone, *Explanatory Works*, pp. 205-53 and *SAA* 3, nos. 34-35.

temple in Babylon. Livingstone feels that the text shows the god Aššur as the supreme authority and Marduk in a humiliating position, a position brought about by the god Aššur. In his opinion, the text may have been composed "under the influence of Sennacherib's involvement with religious reforms, especially Assyrianisation of the religion and the captivity of Marduk" (i.e., the promotion of the idea that the god Aššur was superior to the god Marduk).[32] Frymer-Kensky argues that the captivity of Marduk portrayed in the text was not permanent, that Marduk did not undergo an ordeal in the story, nor was he condemned, and that there may have been a final section in which the gods fought to free Marduk. She feels the composition must have been composed "to justify and celebrate, not the subjugation of Marduk, but his ultimate vindication." Thus she dates the text not to the reign of Sennacherib but rather to 669 when the statue of Marduk was returned to Babylon.[33] Due to the current state of the text(s), it is not possible to be certain about the exact interpretation of the story, though it almost certainly attempts to explain Marduk's captivity in Assyria. It is to be hoped that further exemplars will be found and that these will enable us to understand the text better.

Very little information is available about Babylonia from the time following the destruction of Babylon until the end of Sennacherib's reign. The only events considered worthy of mention in the chronicles for this period were the following: the death of the Elamite king Ḫumban-nimena on the seventh day of Addaru (XII) of 689 and the subsequent accession of Ḫumban-ḫaltaš I; the cancellation of the important New Year's festival for the last eight years of Sennacherib's reign (and the twelve years of Esarhaddon's reign) due to Marduk's absence; the return of the gods of Uruk to Uruk on the third day of Du'ūzu (IV) in 681; and the death of Ḫumban-ḫaltaš I of Elam on the twenty-third day of Tašrītu (VII) of the same year and the subsequent ascension of Ḫumban-ḫaltaš II to the throne of Elam.[34] An entry for the year 693 in the Babylonian Chronicle states that the gods of Uruk had been removed from that city during that year. It has sometimes been thought that that entry stated that it was Elamites who carried them off and that the later entry stated that it was from Elam that they returned in 681.[35] Since there is no record of an Assyrian campaign against Elam in 681, this would presumably indicate that Ḫumban-ḫaltaš I had allowed the gods of Uruk to return to Babylonia in order to establish or confirm peaceful relations with Assyria. However, it is far from certain that it was the Elamites who had carried off the gods in 693. The passage in the chronicle describing their removal is somewhat complex

---

32 Livingstone, *Explanatory Works*, pp. 230-35.
33 *JAOS* 103 (1983): 138-41.
34 Grayson, *Chronicles*, nos. 1 iii 25-33, 14:31-33, and 16:1-4.
35 E.g., Grayson, *Chronicles*, no. 1 iii 2-3 and 29.

and the name of the country from which they returned in the later entry is badly damaged. It seems more likely that it was Assyrians who removed the gods from Uruk in 693 since the chronicle had just clearly stated that it was they who had entered Uruk and plundered its gods and people[36] and since it is also possible to read the name of the country from which they returned as Assyria.[37] Possibly Sennacherib returned the statues of these gods to Uruk in an attempt to alleviate some of the anti-Assyrian feeling there. He may have had some particular regard for Uruk and its deities since a document from the time of Ashurbanipal states that Sennacherib (and Sargon II) had given some Puqudians to the goddesses Ištar of Uruk and Nanaya.[38]

Sennacherib's royal inscriptions are silent on Babylonia after 689,[39] and none of his reliefs has been shown to depict Babylonian events during this time. A fragmentary Babylonian astronomical text may indicate that there was a revolt in 686 but this is far from certain; in any case, no further details are known about the incident.[40] No letters can be dated with certainty to the period 689-681, although a few later letters may refer to events of that time. According to one letter from the governor of Nippur to the king Esarhaddon (*ABL* 327), the governor of Babylon was denying Nippur access to the water of the Banītu canal even though Sennacherib had granted Nippur access to that water. Possibly Sennacherib had allowed Nippur to use the water because the now-destroyed Babylon no longer needed it. With the restoration of Babylon by Esarhaddon, however, dispute arose over the control of the water of the canal.

During all or part of this time, Nabû-zēr-kitti-līšir, son of Merodach-Baladan II, and Ningal-iddin may have held the offices of governor of the Sealand and governor of Ur respectively, since they occupied those positions at the very beginning of Esarhaddon's reign. The actual dates of their appointments to these offices are, however, unknown.[41]

---

36 Grayson, *Chronicles*, no. 1 ii 48-iii 1.

37 Collation by Brinkman (see Brinkman, *Moran Festschrift*, p. 103). For a translation of the full passage in the Babylonian Chronicle which would indicate that it was the Assyrians who carried off the gods of Uruk, see Oppenheim, *ANET*, p. 302. See also Levine, *JCS* 34 (1982):44-45 n. 52 on this matter.

38 *BIN* 2 132:1-4 (read ^{md}30-ŠEŠ.<<PAP>>.ME-SU in line 3). It is not known when Sennacherib gave the Puqudians to the goddesses (i.e., before or after the death of his son Aššur-nādin-šumi).

39 Few Assyrian royal inscriptions, however, were written during the years 688-681.

40 *LBAT* 1417 i' 1, [MU.3.KÁ]M? *bar-tú* (collation by C.B.F. Walker). Or should we take this to indicate the third year after the rebellion of 694-689?

41 Grayson, *Chronicles*, no. 1 iii 39-42; Borger, *Esarh.*, pp. 46-47 §27 episode 4. On Ningal-iddin's appointment, see below. It is possible that Nabû-zēr-kitti-līšir received his appointment at some point after the battle of Ḫalulê, which likely took place in 691 and during which his brother Nabû-šuma-iškun was captured by the Assyrians (Luckenbill, *Senn.*, p. 46 vi 16-19; see Dietrich, *Aramäer*, pp. 12-13). Nabû-šuma-iškun was one of only two persons (excluding the kings of Elam and Babylonia) mentioned by name as

Only a few economic documents are securely dated to this period and none of these refers to Sennacherib as king of Babylonia. Two from Nippur and one from Ḫursagkalama were dated according to the years of Sennacherib as king of Assyria. Two texts from Borsippa were dated to the twelfth and thirteenth years "after Aššur-nādin-šumi"; thus Sennacherib's reign in Babylonia was ignored and the years were reckoned according to the last ruler who would have been considered legitimate in both Assyrian and Babylonian eyes. In addition, two texts from Ur may also date to this "kingless" period in Babylonia; their unique date formulae use the year of office of the city's governor, Ningal-iddin, as reference point: "year eight of Ningal-iddin, governor of Ur" and "year twelve of Ningal-iddin."[42] The only secure date we have for Ningal-iddin's governorship is 680, the first year of Esarhaddon.[43] If these two texts come from the time of Sennacherib's "non-kingship" over Babylonia, this would mean that Ningal-iddin had become governor either before the rebellion of 694-689 or immediately after it had begun. Either Ur had not joined that rebellion, or Ningal-iddin had been pardoned by Sennacherib and allowed to retain his position, or Ningal-iddin had been appointed governor by Assyria around the time Assyrian forces campaigned in southern Babylonia in 693 and captured the nearby city of Uruk in the seventh month of that year.[44] The texts could conceivably come from the reign of Esarhaddon, with Ningal-iddin having been appointed governor after the destruction of Babylon in 689.[45] It seems more likely, however, that documents dated by the office of a city governor would have come from a "kingless" period in Babylonia than during the time there was a recognized king of Babylonia, although this can not be considered certain since no texts dated by the regnal years of Esarhaddon have been found at Ur. In view of these different dating systems, it is clear that Assyria had not issued a decree ordaining how years were to be reckoned. On the one hand,

---

having taken part in the battle of Ḫalulê on the rebel side. Thus it is clear that he was an important and prominent leader, possibly the head of the Bīt-Yakīn tribe and governor of the Sealand since these two offices sometimes overlapped; however, there is no direct evidence which records the position Nabû-šuma-iškun held or the date Nabû-zēr-kitti-līšir became governor of the Sealand.

42 See Appendix C and note also *UET* 4 9 (*B-K* Sn.3; although the date is not preserved, Ningal-iddin, the governor of Ur, appears as witness). Note also A 33248, a document from Sumundanaš(?) dated to the fifteenth year of Ḫallušu, and BM 49318, which comes from the reign of either Sennacherib, Sîn-šumu-līšir, or Sîn-šarra-iškun (*B-K* Q.2 and On.6 respectively). On Ningal-iddin, see below and Brinkman, *Or.* NS 34 (1965): 246-48.

43 See p. 269 n. 2 and p. 278.

44 Grayson, *Chronicles*, no. 1 ii 48-iii 1. Our knowledge of what happened in Babylonia during the rebellion (and particularly the years 692-689) is limited and it is possible that Ur and Uruk were held by Assyria during these years.

45 San Nicolò suggests that the two texts might come from the reign of Esarhaddon, with the twelfth year of Ningal-iddin being 669, which was also the twelfth year of Esarhaddon (*Or.* NS 19 [1950]: 218-19).

the relative lack of documentation for this time may be an accident of archaeological discovery; but, on the other hand, it may reflect a period of uncertainty and weakness in Babylonia caused by Assyrian military actions. The few economic texts preserved suggest that life carried on in a relatively normal way. Land and slaves were sold and transactions involving loans were made.

At some point, having ascertained divine approval by means of omens, Sennacherib appointed his son Esarhaddon to be his heir and on an auspicious day, Esarhaddon entered the House-of-Succession (*bīt ridûti*). Sennacherib made his other sons and the people of Assyria swear to accept his choice of successor.[46] A copy of the oath taken by Assyrians may be preserved on VAT 11449, but due to damage to the tablet this cannot be considered certain.[47] Esarhaddon was not the eldest son of Sennacherib[48] and it is thus unclear why he was chosen heir. Perhaps his influential mother Zakūtu (Aramaic Naqiʾa) had played some role in the choice.[49] H. Winckler suggested that Esarhaddon was made governor of Babylonia during his father's lifetime and that Zakūtu ruled Babylonia during the reign of her son.[50] These ideas were accepted by some later scholars, in particular by F. Schmidtke, who proposed that Esarhaddon had been appointed ruler of Babylonia after the fall of Babylon in 689, and by H. Lewy, who suggested that Zakūtu had held the regency of Babylonia between roughly 683 and 670 (i.e., that she held it already during the reign of Sennacherib).[51] As R. Borger has pointed out, these suggestions were based upon misreadings and misunderstandings of the ancient sources and there is no concrete evidence to support either of these suggestions,[52] though it does seem clear that Zakūtu

---

46 Borger, *Esarh.*, pp 40-41 §27 episode 2 i 8-22. Tadmor (*Iconic Book*, p. 147) points out that according to the available evidence this was "the first time in the history of Assyria that the court and citizenry were obliged to take a loyalty oath to the heir apparent." Tadmor suggests that the reason Sennacherib formally appointed an heir to the throne and imposed a loyalty oath was because he was well aware of the danger of a usurper seizing the throne after his death. Sennacherib's father, Sargon II, appears to have been a usurper, seizing the throne from the direct line of Tiglath-pileser III.

47 Parpola and Watanabe, *SAA* 2, no. 3. Esarhaddon's name is not preserved on the tablet but Parpola (*JCS* 39 [1987]: 163-64) argues that the text best fits this interpretation and suggests that the ceremony may have taken place in the first month of 683 or 682.

48 Borger, *Esarh.*, p. 40 §27 episode 2 i 8; see Parpola in *Death in Mesopotamia*, pp. 175 and 178 nn. 31-32.

49 On this matter, see Borger, *ARRIM* 6 (1988): 6-7 (with further bibliography). His view that both Esarhaddon and his mother had pro-Babylonian sympathies remains to be proven. On Zakūtu, see *ibid.* and below, pp. 92-93.

50 Winckler, *AOF* 2, pp. 56-57 and 189.

51 Schmidtke, *AOTU* 1/2, pp. 86-90 and H. Lewy, *JNES* 11 (1952): 272-77 respectively.

52 *BiOr* 29 (1972): 33-34. On these matters, see also Ahmed, *Asb.*, pp. 56-57 n. 45.

had some interests in, or property located at, Laḫīru, near the Assyro-Babylonian border.[53]

According to Esarhaddon's later inscriptions, his brothers opposed his appointment as heir and did all they could to remove him from favour. They managed to alienate Sennacherib from Esarhaddon, but Esarhaddon claims that his father never changed his mind about keeping him as his heir. Still, Esarhaddon does appear to have had to leave the court. He states that the gods sent him to dwell in a secluded place, where they protected him and kept him ready to assume the throne.[54] He was thus far from home when his father was killed by his treacherous brothers. M.T. Larsen has pointed out that one Assyrian document was dated on 5-II of the "eponymy after Nabû-šarra-uṣur," i.e., 681. He suggests that trouble after the appointment of Esarhaddon as heir may have prevented the appointment of the new eponym at the right time.[55]

Thus, the period from the destruction of Babylon in 689 until the death of Sennacherib in 681 is poorly known. The destruction likely cowed the rest of Babylonia into submission and this demonstration of Assyrian might may have made the new king of Elam, Ḫumban-ḫaltaš I, unwilling to incur Assyrian enmity by attempting any military incursions into Babylonia or by stirring up rebel movements in that land. It was, however, probably during this decade that the Bīt-Dakkūri tribe was gaining power in northwestern Babylonia by encroaching upon the lands of Babylon and Borsippa and that Nabû-zēr-kitti-līšir of the Sealand was building up his position in the south. Esarhaddon had to deal with trouble in these two areas early in his reign. Possibly Assyrian control had been somewhat lax, encouraging the Bīt-Dakkūri to appropriate land. While Sennacherib may have encouraged others to make use of the land now lying vacant around Babylon, there is no evidence that Borsippa had been singled out for punishment by Sennacherib.

---

53 For the location of Laḫīru, see p. 220 n. 37.

54 Borger, *Esarh.*, pp. 41-42 §27 episode 2 i 23-40.

55 *RA* 68 (1974): 22 (referring to *ADD* 213).

CHAPTER 6

ESARHADDON, KING OF ASSYRIA AND BABYLONIA (681-669)

Sennacherib died in Assyria on the twentieth day of the month of Ṭebētu (X) in 681, murdered by one or more of his sons. The murderer(s) undoubtedly hoped to usurp power at that time, while Esarhaddon, the officially designated heir, was temporarily in disfavour and exile. Dispute over the succession to the throne of Assyria continued for about six weeks, until the second day of Addaru (XII), by which time Esarhaddon had gained the upper hand over his brother(s), although his formal accession to the throne did not take place until the eighth/eighteenth/twenty-eighth day of that month. Arda-Mulišši, the brother who may have actually killed Sennacherib, escaped Esarhaddon's hands; according to 2 Kings 19:37 and Isaiah 37:38, the patricides managed to flee to "the land of Ararat" (Urartu).[1] Fear that one or more of his brothers might return and try to seize the throne may have been one of the reasons Esarhaddon imposed oaths of loyalty on some of his subjects[2] and was deeply concerned to settle the succession for after his own death. Esarhaddon reigned over Assyria and Babylonia for twelve years, dying on the tenth day of Araḫsamna (VIII) in 669 while on a campaign against Egypt. No major rebellions broke out in Babylonia during the king's reign, but despite his numerous efforts to win the support of the Babylonian people several local or minor disturbances did occur.

Information on Babylonia becomes more plentiful with the accession of Esarhaddon. He occasionally took the title "king of Babylon"[3] and was

---

1 Grayson, *Chronicles*, no. 1 iii 34-38 (accession of Esarhaddon on day 18 or 28); Borger, *Esarh.*, pp. 40-45 §27 episode 2 (accession of Esarhaddon on day 8); Streck, *Asb.*, pp. 38-39 iv 70-71; Langdon, *NBK*, Nabonid no. 8 i 35-41; 2 Chron. 32:21; Schnabel, *Berossos*, p. 269 lines 24-25 and p. 270 line 6; Josephus, *Antiquities*, x i 5. See also the discussions cited by Oppenheim in *ANET*, p. 288 n. 1 and in addition Schmidtke, *AOTU* 1/2, pp. 82-86; Landsberger and Bauer, *ZA* 37 (1927): 65-73; Parpola, *Death in Mesopotamia*, pp. 171-82; Tadmor, *HHI*, pp. 38-41; von Soden, *NABU* 1990, pp. 16-17 no. 22; Ishida, *Tadmor Festschrift*, pp. 166-73; and Grayson, *CAH* 3/2 [in press]. With regard to the mistaken assumption that Sennacherib was killed in Babylon, see Landsberger and Bauer, *ZA* 37 (1927): 215-21.

2 Parpola and Watanabe, *SAA* 2, nos. 4 and 7. Parpola and Watanabe suggest that no. 4 was composed shortly before Esarhaddon's accession in 681 and that no. 7 was composed after an abortive coup d'état early in 670 (*ibid.*, pp. XXVIII and XXXI).

3 Generally on brick inscriptions from Babylon, Nippur, and Uruk (for references, see Seux, *Épithètes*, p. 302).

acknowledged as such by the compilers of Assyrian and Babylonian kinglists.[4] More frequently, he used the titles "viceroy of Babylon" and "king of Sumer and Akkad" in his royal inscriptions.[5] He is never accorded such titles in chronicles or said to have ascended the throne of Babylonia; instead, chronicles state that he "sat upon the throne in Assyria," "ruled Assyria," and was "king of Assyria."[6] In the date formulae of Babylonian economic texts from his reign, Esarhaddon was clearly given the title "king of Babylon" only once, in a text from Babylon, although a second case may exist.[7] Instead, Esarhaddon was called "king" (eleven times), "king of Assyria" (seven times), "king of the world" (six times), or "king of (all) lands" (three times). The twenty-nine Babylonian legal and administrative texts dated by Esarhaddon's regnal years show that his rule was accepted in cities such as Babylon, Borsippa, Dilbat, Nippur, Sippar, Šapiya, and Uruk.[8] Political events in Babylonia are mentioned in Esarhaddon's royal inscriptions and in letters, and two chronicles provide a firm time frame for the reign. Regrettably, the king's royal inscriptions do not always present the events of the period in chronological order, with the result that the correct sequence of events is not always clear.

The disorder in Assyria following the death of Sennacherib provided an ideal setting for rebellion in Babylonia. Nabû-zēr-kitti-līšir, governor of the Sealand and son of Merodach-Baladan II (the infamous rebel leader and sometime king of Babylonia), seized this opportunity to break his oath of loyalty and attack Ningal-iddin, the governor of Ur, in 680. The city was besieged by Nabû-zēr-kitti-līšir and his forces, but did not fall to the rebels. This effort to extend the area under his control may have been the first step in a planned attempt to re-establish the Babylonian kingdom ruled by his father, who had also made use of some irregularity in the succession in Assyria to declare Babylonia's independence.[9] Exactly what elements of the population provided Nabû-zēr-kitti-līšir's base of support is uncertain, but it is likely that

---

4 Ptolemaic Canon; Babylonian Kinglist A iv 20'; Synchronistic Kinglist A 117 iv 12; and Synchronistic Kinglist fragment *KAV* 182 iv 4' (RN restored).

5 E.g., Borger, *Esarh.*, p. 8 §5:1.

6 Grayson, *Chronicles*, no. 1 iii 38 and iv 30 and 32, and no. 14:28 and 30. In the view of the composers of at least the second chronicle (the Esarhaddon chronicle), there could be no true king of Babylonia while the statue of Marduk was absent and the New Year's festival could not be performed. Although Esarhaddon was not called "king of Babylon," years were numbered according to the years of his reign and not described as years in which there was no king in Babylon, as had been done for the years of Sennacherib following the destruction of Babylon.

7 Jakob-Rost, *FB* 12 (1970): 52-53 no. 3 (*B-K* I.9) and possibly *OECT* 10 393 (*B-K* Fn.3).

8 See Appendix A, Table 3. A document from Babylonia was already dated by the accession year of Esarhaddon (Owen and Watanabe, *OrAnt* 22 [1983]: 37-48; *B-K* I.1).

9 For a discussion of the career and family of Merodach-Baladan II, see Brinkman in *Studies Oppenheim*, pp. 6-53.

his native tribe the Bīt-Yakīn, which had supported rebellions in the past, were the mainstay of his force.[10]

Once Esarhaddon had settled affairs in Assyria, he turned his attention to the south. A message was sent to Ningal-iddin which told him to take courage because Esarhaddon had ascended the throne and which presumably implied that the new Assyrian king would send aid. It appears, however, that the message did not reach the governor of Ur but fell instead into the hands of Nabû-zēr-kitti-līšir.[11] Esarhaddon sent troops to deal with Nabû-zēr-kitti-līšir and when the rebel heard of their advance, he fled to Elam, a country which had served as a refuge for his tribe in the past. Ḫumban-ḫaltaš II, the new king of Elam, had Nabû-zēr-kitti-līšir put to death, possibly because he did not feel the time was ripe for opposing Assyria. Esarhaddon then appointed Na'id-Marduk, another son of Merodach-Baladan II, as ruler of the Sealand. Na'id-Marduk had fled to Elam with his brother, but after seeing the treatment given Nabû-zēr-kitti-līšir he had submitted to Esarhaddon. The king's inscriptions written in 673 record that Na'id-Marduk came to Nineveh every year, bringing substantial tribute to offer to Esarhaddon.[12] Things did not always go well for Na'id-Marduk. Although damaged, *ABL* 958 appears to indicate that at one time the king was angry with him; Na'id-Marduk's subjects wrote to the king stating that he was indeed totally loyal to the king. In leaving the Sealand in the charge of Na'id-Marduk, Esarhaddon continued the usual Assyrian policy of leaving vassal areas under the control of members of the native ruling families, simply replacing rebellious individuals by ones who it was hoped would be more submissive.

Opposition to Esarhaddon's rule may also have broken out (or been suspected) at Nippur. A damaged chronicle entry for 680 refers to the governor of Nippur (*šandabakku*); when it is compared with entries for 678 and 675, which mention governors of Nippur being removed from office or killed, it seems likely that here too the governor was being punished.[13] In addition, an unsigned denunciation from Babylonia sent to Esarhaddon alleged that there was a conspiracy against the Assyrian king led(?) by one Nabû-aḫḫē-iddin son of Kuppuptu. It was reported that this man had sent

---

[10] For possible support at Uruk, see the following note.

[11] *ABL* 589. Uruk was involved in the matter in some way since the position of *ša muḫḫi āli* ("one in charge of the city") of Uruk is mentioned immediately after the statement that the message had been given to (Nabû)-zēr-kitti-līšir (rev. 4). It is possible that this position (or the promise of this position) was given by the rebel to the messenger as a reward for handing over the letter (see *CAD* 17/1 [Š], p. 2), but the passage is damaged and there is no proof of this.

[12] Grayson, *Chronicles*, no. 1 iii 39-42; Borger, *Esarh.*, p. 33 §21:21 and pp. 46-48 §27 episode 4; Heidel, *Sumer* 12 (1956): 16-17 ii 26-33; *CT* 54 22 rev. 38-39; possibly *ABL* 1107 and 1248:4-9 (see Dietrich, *Aramäer*, pp. 202-203 no. 159 for possible restorations).

[13] Grayson, *Chronicles*, no. 1 iii 43; cf. *ibid.*, no. 1 iv 1-2 and 14-15, and no. 14:10-11 and 19.

valuable gifts to the king of Elam and had apparently written to persuade him that Esarhaddon's forces were not as large as Sennacherib's had been; the rebel was undoubtedly trying to win Elam's military support against Assyria. Since the letter states that Sennacherib had just died—literally "Sennacherib <has gone to> (his) fate"—it seems likely that the incident should be dated shortly after his death. Where the centre of the conspiracy originated is not mentioned and nothing further is known of Nabû-aḫḫē-iddin.[14]

Soon after Esarhaddon became king, possibly already in 680, he began the rebuilding and resettlement of Babylon.[15] The restoration of Babylon is mentioned in an inscription of Esarhaddon's dated in the second month of his MU.SAG.NAM.LUGAL.LA.[16] Since Esarhaddon did not take the throne until the twelfth month of 681, this phrase cannot be identified with his actual accession year and must refer to the early part of his reign in general (in contrast to the practice in Babylonia where the same phrase regularly refers to a king's accession year). Some recensions, including one which has the date MU.SAG.NAM.[LUGAL.LA], refer to Babylonian gods having been returned from Elam, an event which took place in the twelfth month of 674 according to two chronicles and thus these recensions must date after that time.[17] If one accepts Esarhaddon's statement that Babylon lay abandoned for eleven years, then the resettlement should not have begun before 679 (with both 689 and 679 counted as part of the eleven years).[18]

Esarhaddon claims to have mobilized all Babylonia in rebuilding Babylon and even states that he aided personally in the manual labour of the project,

---

14 Weidner, *AfO* 17 (1954-56): 5-9. One of the individuals mentioned in the document as having contributed gifts to be sent to the king of Elam is probably mentioned in a document from Babylon dated to the eponymy of Ubāru (Bibēa son of Dugullakê; see *ibid.*, p. 7). Babylon is mentioned in the text, albeit in broken context (*ibid.*, p. 6, line 30). Since that city was supposedly abandoned at this time, it would be difficult to locate the conspiracy there, although Babylon may not have been as totally destroyed as Sennacherib had claimed.

15 The most complete description of the rebuilding of Babylon is found in Borger, *Esarh.*, pp. 16-26 §11 episodes 12-37; see also Borger, *BiOr* 21 (1964): 145-47 and Millard, *AfO* 24 (1973): 116-19. The Babylon inscriptions of Esarhaddon have been studied most recently by Cogan in *HHI*, pp. 76-87 and by Brinkman in *JAOS* 103 (1983): 35-42.

16 Borger, *Esarh.*, p. 29 §11 recension G and cf. A^1, C^2, and E^3; for the date of E^3, see Nougayrol, *AfO* 18 (1957-58): 314, 318, and pl. 22 vi 32'-35'.

17 Borger, *Esarh.*, p. 25 §11 episode 36 recension C; Grayson, *Chronicles*, nos. 1 iv 17-18 and 14:21-22.

18 Borger, *Esarh.*, p. 15 §11 episode 10. Borger (*BiOr* 29 [1972]: 34-35) assumes that MU.SAG.NAM.LUGAL.LA refers to the year 680 and explains the eleven years as commencing with 691, the year of the particular event which had caused Marduk to abandon his people. With regard to the use of the phrase MU.SAG.NAM.LUGAL.LA, see in particular: Borger, *BiOr* 29 (1972): 34-35; Tadmor in *ARINH*, p. 22; Frame, *RA* 76 (1982): 157-59 n. 5; Brinkman, *JAOS* 103 (1983): 36 n. 7; Owen and Watanabe, *OrAnt* 22 (1983): 37-38 n. 3. Cogan (*HHI*, pp. 85-87) argues that some of the texts dated with this formula may come from the king's accession year and others from as late as 674.

demonstrating his true concern for the welfare of Babylon and symbolizing the new Assyrian policy with regards to Babylonia. The Euphrates was channeled back into its old bed, rituals were performed, and Babylon was built anew. Specifically, Esarhaddon claims to have rebuilt Esagila, its ziggurat, the processional street, and the two city walls (Imgur-Enlil and Nēmed-Enlil).[19] Statues of the great gods were restored and returned to their shrines. Esagila was provided with new furnishings of gold and silver, and cult personnel (priests, exorcists, musicians, etc.) were re-appointed to serve there. Once again rites could be performed and offerings made in the temple.[20] The king states that he re-opened the city's streets and allowed Babylon to be again in contact with all lands, possibly implying that its people could re-establish Babylon's important position in commerce.[21] Esarhaddon was extremely proud of his restoration of Babylon and frequently mentioned it in his inscriptions, even in those from Assyria.[22] The rebuilding was a lengthy process and continued into the reign of his successor, Ashurbanipal,[23] although, as was mentioned earlier, it is possible that Babylon had not been destroyed as utterly as Sennacherib had claimed. Esarhaddon states that he resettled Babylon with its former inhabitants. He redeemed those who had fallen into slavery when the city was destroyed, gave them clothing, and returned their property to them. He considered them again to be citizens of Babylon, confirmed their privileged status, and encouraged them to dwell in the city, build new homes, plant new orchards, and dig new canals.[24] Babylon was repopulated at least partially by the end of 679 since a document was dated at that site in the middle of the tenth month of that year.[25] Towards the end of the last month of 678 an assembly of Babylonians met to decide a law case, an indication that the civic structure of the city was again in place.[26]

---

[19] Borger, *Esarh.*, pp. 19-21 and 24-25 §11 episodes 18-23, and 34-35. The processional street is mentioned on one of his brick inscriptions (*ibid.*, p. 30 §13).

[20] Borger, *Esarh.*, pp. 23-24 §11 episodes 32-33.

[21] Borger, *Esarh.*, pp. 25-26 §11 episode 37a.

[22] E.g., Borger, *Esarh.*, p. 9 §7:5, p. 33 §21:5, and p. 66 §29 Nin. G:3.

[23] See *ABL* 119. Parpola suggests that although the rebuilding began earlier in Esarhaddon's reign, little was accomplished until after the conquest of Egypt in 671 (*Death in Mesopotamia*, pp. 179-80 n. 41).

[24] Borger, *Esarh.*, pp. 25-26 §11 episode 37, and possibly *ABL* 702 rev. 1-4 (cf. Landsberger, *Brief*, pp. 32-33). Since it is not certain that Babylon was totally destroyed by Sennacherib, it is possible that the city was not completely depopulated by him. Reuther detected traces of what he believed to be temporary or insubstantial dwellings in the Merkes quarter after that area's general abandonment or destruction and before its major rebuilding (see above). It must be pointed out, however, that there is no clear textual evidence for settlement on the site of Babylon between 688 and the end of 679, in particular, no economic texts have been found which were composed at Babylon during these years.

[25] FLP 1833 (*B-K* I.3a), dated on 14-X-year 2 of Esarhaddon.

[26] Strassmaier, *8e Congrès*, no. 4 (*B-K* I.6), dated at Babylon on 23-XII_2-year 3 of Esarhaddon.

That Babylon did not immediately recover its former pre-eminent position (at least in the economic sphere) may be suggested by the fact that only six of the thirty economic texts from Babylonia coming from the reign of Esarhaddon were composed at Babylon.[27] During the following reigns of Šamaš-šuma-ukīn and Kandalānu, Babylon produced a higher proportion of texts.[28] Although inscriptions on bricks attest to work on the processional street, Esagila, and the ziggurat,[29] there is no direct archaeological evidence that can be clearly assigned to Esarhaddon's rebuilding, much of which was undoubtedly obscured by the later rebuilding of Nebuchadnezzar II.[30] The restoration of Babylon is not mentioned in any of the chronicles; to their compilers it was the return of the statue of Marduk that was important.

The restoration of Babylon was an attempt to reconcile the Babylonians to Assyrian rule. The single greatest obstacle in winning their favour would have been the sight of Babylon in ruins. Babylonia was Assyria's most prized possession, and Assyria's special efforts to keep it quiet and submissive are not surprising. Sennacherib's decision to destroy Babylon may have been taken in the heat of the moment, the result of anger at the lengthy resistance of Babylon to Assyrian forces and the loss of his son and heir, Aššur-nādin-šumi, due to Babylonian treachery. Esarhaddon was simply returning to Assyria's normal policy towards Babylonia up until Sennacherib's destruction of Babylon after the rebellion of 694-689. Pragmatically, he may have felt that it would be easier to keep Babylonia quiet with the carrot instead of the stick. He would not have wanted to risk losing the wealthy southern kingdom; its loss would have been a dangerous sign of weakness to other vassals. As rebuilder of Babylonia's venerable capital, Esarhaddon could pose as its benefactor and thereby hope to lessen Babylonian discontent.

Possibly not all Assyrians had supported Sennacherib's decision to destroy Babylon since at least part of Assyria's ruling element tended to revere Babylonian culture. Esarhaddon himself had great respect for Babylonian scholarship and frequently requested astrological reports from

---

27 This total includes one text composed at Babylon and dated to the eponymy of Ubāru, governor of Babylon; this eponymy dates almost certainly to the reign of Esarhaddon (see below and Appendix C).

28 Babylon provided approximately forty per cent of those texts whose place of composition and date are known both for the reign of Šamaš-šuma-ukīn (including texts dated by Ashurbanipal down to 648) and for the reign of Kandalānu (including texts dated by Ashurbanipal between 647 and 627).

29 Borger, *Esarh.* p. 30 §§13-18.

30 The archaeological evidence for this rebuilding in the Merkes quarter was presented in chapter 5. Although Esarhaddon claims to have rebuilt the city walls (Borger, *Esarh.*, p. 21 §11 episode 23 and p. 25 episode 35), no evidence of that rebuilding is identified by the excavator of the walls (see Wetzel, *Stadtmauern*, p. 66). With regard to work on the ziggurat, see Bergamini, *Mesopotamia* 12 (1977): 148-50.

Babylonians;[31] he assumed Babylonian titles and frequently mentions Babylonian gods in his inscriptions, including those from Assyria. It has sometimes been suggested that there were two parties at the Assyrian court, one pro-Babylonian and the other nationalist/anti-Babylonian (i.e., against granting favours or special status to Babylonia), and that Esarhaddon was a "member" of the former group.[32] Further, it has been suggested that the conflict in the Assyrian court over the treatment of Babylonia was long-standing and that one of the factors involved in Sennacherib's murder was his violent treatment of Babylon. The situation has been compared with that at the time of Tukultī-Ninurta I (1243-1207) who also conquered Babylonia, removed the statue of Marduk to Assyria, and was deposed and killed by one of his sons.[33] However, Tukultī-Ninurta did not destroy Babylon totally and there is again no evidence that he was killed for his actions with regard to Babylonia. While Esarhaddon did reverse his father's policy on Babylonia as soon as he became king, there is no indication that Sennacherib's policy was at all involved with his murder. If Esarhaddon belonged to a pro-Babylonian party which opposed Sennacherib's policy with regard to Babylonia, why had Sennacherib chosen him as his heir? As already mentioned, in viewing Babylonia with favour, Esarhaddon was reverting to the normal practice of Neo-Assyrian kings. It was Sennacherib who had changed Assyrian policy, and he had done so only toward the end of his reign and then out of a desire to exact revenge on Babylon for its particular sins. Undoubtedly there would have been differing and conflicting views upon the best way to control Babylonia (various methods were tried over the years); however, no evidence has yet been produced to indicate that these views had led to the formation of political factions or lay behind any of the important political events of the period (e.g., the choice of Esarhaddon as Sennacherib's heir or the murder of Sennacherib). I am not aware of any direct evidence to indicate strong opposition in Assyria to Esarhaddon's policy of reconciliation with Babylonia or to suggest that Esarhaddon restored Babylon in order to appease a pro-Babylonian party in Assyria which had been shocked by Sennacherib's "impiety" in destroying Babylon.[34] Although Esarhaddon does appear to have

---

[31] See Thompson, *Rep.* and Parpola, *LAS*.

[32] See Landsberger, *Brief*, pp. 14-16; Machinist, *WBJ* 1984-85, p. 358; Pečírková, *ArOr* 53 (1985): 164 and n. 37; and Borger, *ARRIM* 6 (1988): 6.

[33] Machinist, *JAOS* 104 (1984): 570 and *WBJ* 1984-85, pp. 358-62. Machinist's use of *ABL* 1216 in this matter is not convincing. The author of the letter had wanted Babylon rebuilt and had prodded the crown prince Esarhaddon to that end, but there is no evidence as to where the prince(s) who murdered Sennacherib stood on this matter.

[34] Unless the "Sin of Sargon" text is taken to have been composed in the reign of Sennacherib to spur him to honour the god Marduk by stating that Sargon II had suffered an ignominious fate because that king had not done so (see below). See Garelli in *Voix de l'opposition*, pp. 196-98 for a valuable critique of the question of a pro-Babylonian party in Assyria. It has sometimes been suggested that Esarhaddon's wife and mother were

appreciated and respected Babylonian scholarship and culture, his actions to win Babylonian support may have arisen simply out of a desire to do whatever seemed likely to be most effective in keeping Babylonia quiet so that he could concentrate his energies, and perhaps more importantly his army, elsewhere.

Out of respect for his father and, surely, out of a desire to avoid antagonizing his Assyrian supporters, Esarhaddon's inscriptions emphasize the will of the gods when discussing the destruction and rebuilding of Babylon. Babylon was not destroyed by Sennacherib but rather by the gods. Because of the evil of its citizens and their impiety in having given the property of Esagila to Elam in exchange for military aid against Assyria, the gods had given the people into slavery and had caused the Araḫtu canal to overflow its banks, turning Babylon into a swampy ruin. The gods had abandoned the city of their own free will.[35] Again, in describing his own restoration of Babylon, Esarhaddon was only acting in conformity with the will of the gods. Marduk's anger against the city had abated and the god had altered the city's fate so that it could be rebuilt beginning only eleven years after its destruction, instead of after seventy years as had previously been ordained. The god did this by a piece of ingenious trickery; he turned the number seventy upside down, thereby changing it to eleven in the cuneiform script. Various signs in the heavens and on earth were given by the gods to indicate that the time had come to rebuild Babylon.[36] With this divine framework, Babylonians could not blame Sennacherib for the destruction of Babylon and Assyrians could not find fault with Esarhaddon for altering what Sennacherib had done.[37]

A document we refer to as the "Sin of Sargon" text was most probably composed during the reign of Esarhaddon to defend his reversal of Sennacherib's policy with regard to Babylon. This Assyrian document describes how Sennacherib sought to determine by means of divination the reason Sargon II had died violently on the battle-field, far from home. He

---

Babylonians and that they influenced his policy with regard to Babylonia. There is no clear evidence for this; the one piece of evidence suggesting that one of Esarhaddon's sons, Šamaš-šuma-ukīn, was born in Babylonia can be interpreted in more than one way (see p. 96). Landsberger has suggested that Esarhaddon's feelings with regard to Babylonia were essentially the same as Sennacherib's (*Brief*, pp. 14-16), but see Borger, *BiOr* 29 (1972): 35-36.

35 Borger, *Esarh.*, pp. 12-15 §11 episodes 2-9. It would have been unthinkable that such a city as Babylon could have been destroyed without the approval of the gods and the abandonment of a city by its gods prior to its destruction was a common motif (see for example the lamentation over the destruction of Ur).

36 Borger, *Esarh.*, pp. 15-19 §11 episodes 10-17 and see Cogan in *HHI*, pp. 76-87.

37 With regard to the divine framework within which the destruction and rebuilding of Babylon were described in Esarhaddon's inscriptions ("divine alienation—devastation: divine reconciliation—reconstruction"), see Brinkman, *JAOS* 103 (1983): 35-42.

appears to have learned that Sargon had exalted the gods of Assyria over those of Babylonia and had thereby committed a sin against the gods. In order to avoid the same fate, Sennacherib made a statue of the god Anšar (Aššur), but was prevented by Assyrian scribes from making a statue of a second deity. Although the name of the other diety is not preserved at this point in the text, there is an earlier reference to a statue of Marduk (in broken context) and the modern editors of the document have reasonably suggested that the statue which had not been made was that of the god Marduk. The document next records Sennacherib urging the reader to "Take [heed] to what I have explained to you, [and] reconcile [the gods of Akkad] with your gods!" It seems likely that the real purpose of the text is to state that Sennacherib, like Sargon II, had died violently because he too had failed to honour the gods of Babylonia, and in particular the god Marduk. In other words, in order to avoid a similar fate, and in conformity with the will of the gods, Esarhaddon was correct in restoring the cult of Marduk. The text would have been composed in order to convince any Assyrians who had supported Sennacherib's actions in 689 and who now opposed bestowing favours on Babylonia that Esarhaddon was only following the wishes of both the gods and his father in honouring Marduk (and the other gods of Babylonia) and, through implication, in rebuilding Marduk's city of Babylon.[38]

The (unknown) author of *ABL* 1216 reminded the king that when he was still prince, he (the author of the letter) had reported an "omen of the kingship of Esarhaddon," that Esarhaddon would rebuild Babylon and restore Esagila.[39] Parpola suggests that if this had become publicly known, he would have found it difficult not to carry out the rebuilding; however, it is unlikely

---

[38] For an edition and study of the text, see Tadmor, Landsberger, and Parpola, *SAAB* 3 (1989): 3-51; an edition of the text based upon their edition is found as Livingstone, *SAA* 3, no. 33. See also Tadmor, *Eretz Israel* 5 (1958): 93* and 150-63; Tadmor in Eisenstadt, *Origins*, pp. 212-14; and Garelli in *Voix de l'opposition*, pp. 193-96. If the editors' restoration in rev. 23' is correct (*...-ma ba-l[a?-ṭi ú-qat-tu-ú* ...], "and (thus) [*shortened my li*]*fe*"), the text would imply that Sennacherib's was indeed dead at the time it was composed. The emphasis in the text upon omens can be compared with a similar emphasis in royal inscriptions of Esarhaddon (see above). Parpola (*SAAB* 3 [1989]: 47) suggests that the text dates to 671 or 670 because an inscription of Esarhaddon composed after the conquest of Egypt describes the extispicy performed before the decision to fashion a new statue for the god Marduk and because both that text and the "Sin of Sargon" indicate that the extispicy was performed in the same unusual manner. If he is correct, the composition of the "Sin of Sargon"—and its justification of the creation of a statue of the god Marduk in Assyria by an Assyrian king—may have been connected with the appointment of Šamaš-šuma-ukīn as heir to the throne of Babylon in 672 (see below) since it was intended that Šamaš-šuma-ukīn would take that statue back to Babylon.

[39] *ABL* 1216:13'-15' and cf. rev. 14-15.

that the author of this letter would have originally made such a statement if Esarhaddon had been opposed to the restoration of Babylon.[40]

Upon initiating the rebuilding of Babylon, or soon thereafter, one Ubāru was appointed governor (*šākin ṭēmi*) of Babylon. Although he is not included in the canon of Assyrian eponyms, one document from Babylon refers to him as eponym, obviously attesting to his important position within the provincial administration. The fact that the text has a large number of important officials as witnesses (including a military officer, the chief administrative officials of temples in Babylon, Borsippa, Kish, and Sippar, and a provincial governor) may suggest that these persons had gathered in Babylon for some special reason, possibly for some ceremony in connection with Babylon's rebuilding.[41] This (Babylonian and non-canonical) eponymate may have been assigned to him in order to "celebrate" the rebuilding of Babylon and thus date to around the time the restoration began; it could, however, date as late as the early part of the reign of Šamaš-šuma-ukīn since no other individual is known to have held the position of governor of Babylon until 654.[42] In *ABL* 418, one of his letters to the Assyrian king, Ubāru wrote:

> When I entered Babylon, the Babylonians received me in a friendly fashion. They bless the king daily, saying that he is the one who returned the prisoners and booty (taken) from Babylon. From Sippar as far as Bāb-Marrati ("Gate-of-the-Sea") the sheikhs of Chaldea bless the king, saying that he is the one who (re)settled Babylon. All the lands put their trust in the king, my lord.

While the governor surely exaggerated matters to win favour with the king, it seems likely that most Babylonians would have welcomed Esarhaddon's actions. Little is known about the extent of Ubāru's authority, but he did control a potential water supply for Nippur.[43]

Esarhaddon's attempt to win Babylonian support was not limited to the resettlement of Babylon. He also revived the ancient city of Akkad.[44] That

---

40 *Death in Mesopotamia*, pp. 179-80 n. 41. He dates this letter to II-680 based upon astronomical statements in the document; see also Labat, *RA* 53 (1959): 113-18.

41 Pinches, *AfO* 13 (1939-41): 51-55 and pls. 3-4 (*B-K* S.7); see Appendix C. The individual who heads the witness list, the military officier (*rab kiṣri*) Mannu-kî-Arba'il (name partially restored), appears to have been an Assyrian. As the leader of an army unit, he may have been sent to command troops who guarded the newly rebuilt city or who were engaged in supervising its continued restoration.

42 See Appendix B sub 2b.

43 *ABL* 327 rev. 5-14. For other references to Ubāru, see Appendix C.

44 The exact location of the city of Akkad remains a matter of debate. In a recent study, C. Wall-Romana has argued that it lay in the lower Diyala region close to the ancient Tigris and that Tell Muhammad is the best candidate for the site (*JNES* 49 [1990]: 205-45). Landsberger has suggested that at this time Akkad was another name for Babylon (*Brief*,

Esarhaddon was the one responsible for the city's new importance is indicated by the statement of Mār-Ištar, an agent serving in Babylonia, that "when the king, my lord [caused] the city of Akkad to be (again) inhabited ..."[45] After the fall of the Sargonic empire in the late third millennium, there are few references to this city, and none for approximately five hundred years before the time of Esarhaddon. In Addaru (XII) of 674 statues of "the goddess Ištar of Akkad and the gods of Akkad" returned from Elam and re-entered Akkad on the tenth day of that month. Presumably they had been sent back to Babylonia by the new Elamite king Urtak in order to demonstrate his friendship to Esarhaddon.[46] We also hear of offerings being sent to the goddess "Lady-of-Akkad" by the governor of Laḫīru,[47] rituals being performed in the city of Akkad,[48] and astronomical observations being made there.[49] Nabonidus later credited Esarhaddon (and Ashurbanipal) with being the first to have restored the Eulmaš (the temple of Ištar of Akkad) since the Kassite king Kurigalzu.[50] It remains unclear exactly when in his reign Esarhaddon decided to restore the city of Akkad. It may have been the return of its gods at the end of 674 that prompted the king to turn his attention to that city, but it is also possible that the Elamite king had chosen to send those particular gods back to Babylonia because he knew that Esarhaddon had already begun work on Akkad, or had at least expressed his intention of doing so.[51] While the city may not have disappeared entirely during the time it

---

pp. 38-39), but this is most unlikely; see Parpola, *LAS* 2, p. 263-64 and Wall-Romana, *JNES* 49 [1990]: 215.

45 *ABL* 746:7-8 (*LAS*, no. 275), *kî šarru bēlī* (URU) *akkad* [*ušē*]*šibūni*.

46 Grayson, *Chronicles*, no. 1 iv 17-18 and no. 14:21-22. The writing A.GA.DÈ.KI suggests that the city of Akkad, not the land of Akkad, was meant.

47 *ABL* 746:4-12 (*LAS*, no. 275). Note also the references to property (socle, stars, and censors) of the Lady-of-Akkad in *ADD* 930, a document which may date to the reign of Esarhaddon (see below, p. 99).

48 E.g., *ABL* 437 and 629 (*LAS*, nos. 280 and 279 respectively).

49 *ABL* 337:5-9 (*LAS*, no. 278). This city may not have been a site where observations were made regularly (see Parpola, *LAS* 2, p. 268).

50 *CT* 34 pl. 30 ii 28-45. Although the two Assyrian kings searched, they were not able to find the foundation inscription (*temennu*) of Eulmaš from the time of the Sargonic kings Sargon and Narām-Sîn. I am currently preparing an article on the history of the Eulmaš temple at Akkad.

51 Urtak could instead have returned the statue of the goddess Nanaya of Uruk which was not recovered from Elam until the time of Ashurbanipal. Parpola (*LAS* 2, pp. 262-63) feels that the order to repopulate Akkad can have been issued only after the return of the goddess of that city; however, the absence of the ancient statue did not mean that the city could not be inhabited or restored. A substitute statue may have been set up in the temple by an earlier ruler of Babylonia or Esarhaddon may have intended to make one. It is also possible that the original statue had been removed from Akkad only the previous year (see below), possibly while work was in progress at the site. While the texts mentioning the city of Akkad seem to come from the later years of the Esarhaddon's reign, they cannot be considered proof that the city was not restored until then since most similar texts preserved for the reign of Esarhaddon come from that time. The restoration of the city would have

is unattested, it is clear that it found new importance in the reign of Esarhaddon.[52] Possibly he restored Akkad as a further concession to the Babylonians; in addition to rebuilding Babylon, the country's capital, he had rebuilt Akkad, its ancient capital.

Esarhaddon claims to have restored the privileged position held by certain old cult centres of Babylonia. The *kidinnūtu, šubarrû, zakûtu,* and *andurāru* of Babylon were granted or confirmed, as was the *šubarrû* of Borsippa, Nippur, and Sippar.[53] As mentioned earlier (chapter 4), exactly what these privileges entailed is not clear, though they likely included financial and judicial benefits to the citizens of those cities and were certainly prized by them. Although damaged, *ABL* 702 may describe a dispute over whether or not certain taxes should be paid; Ubāru and the citizens of Babylon appear to argue against paying the taxes, stating that when the king resettled their city he had given it privileges with regard to taxation.[54] The author of a letter to Esarhaddon mentions the privileges of Sippar, Babylon, and Nippur and argues that Nippur was as privileged as Babylon.[55] Temples and other buildings were built or restored throughout the country: Borsippa (Ezida and temple of the goddess Gula),[56] Dēr (a temple),[57] Nippur (temple of the goddess Inanna, Ekur, processional street, and a well),[58] and Uruk (Eanna, including the ziggurat and the sanctuaries Enirgalanna and Eḫilianna).[59] In addition, work may have been contemplated on the temple of the god Nergal

---

taken several years and thus references in these texts to work-in-progress are not clear evidence that the restoration of the city had begun only then.

52 For a study of the existence of Akkad after the end of Sargonic period, see McEwan, *AfO Bei.* 19, pp. 8-15. *CT* 53 106 rev. 10'-11' (*LAS*, no. 283) refers to the father of the king having appointed a canal inspector of the city of Akkad. As noted by Parpola (*LAS* 2, p. 276), if this letter dates to the time of Esarhaddon rather than to that of Ashurbanipal, it would refer to an action by Sennacherib.

53 Borger, *Esarh.* pp. 25-26 §11 episode 37 and p. 81 §53:41.

54 See Landsberger, *Brief*, pp. 32-33.

55 *CT* 54 212; see Reiner in *Diakonoff Festschrift*, pp. 320-26.

56 Borger, *Esarh.*, p. 32 §20, p. 76 §48:8, and p. 95 §64 rev. 10-14 (with significant restorations). Note also *ABL* 1214:12'-17' (*LAS*, no. 291), assuming that the Ezida mentioned was located in Borsippa and not in Babylon. An inscription from the time of Adad-apla-iddina found on a gold belt presented to Nabû was recopied during the reign of Esarhaddon; Gadd, *StOr* 1 (1925): 28-33.

57 *ABL* 476 rev. 11-29 (*LAS*, no. 277).

58 Goetze, *JCS* 17 (1963): 119-31 and Borger, *Esarh.*, pp. 70-71 §§39-42. The Inanna temple had an elaborate entrance with a rabbeted doorway and flanking towers and appears to have been built on a different line than the earlier temples on the site. For archaeological evidence on the Inanna temple, see Crawford, *Archaeology* 12 (1959): 79; Hansen and Dales, *Archaeology* 15 (1962): 75-84; and R.L. Zettler, "The Ur III Inanna Temple at Nippur" (unpublished doctoral dissertation, University of Chicago, 1984), pp. 80-84.

59 Borger, *Esarh.* pp. 73-78 §§47-51. See also *UVB* 8, pp. 54-55, and 26-27, pp. 13 and 30. With regard to Uruk, note also the king's confirmation of previous Assyrian kings' dedication of Puqudians to goddesses of Uruk (*BIN* 2 132:5-7) and his reassembling of the scattered herds of the goddess Ištar of Uruk (*LKU* 46).

in Cutha.[60] Gods that had been taken to Assyria by Sennacherib were returned to Dēr (Anu-rabû [exact reading uncertain], Šarrat-Dēr, Niraḫ, Bēlet-Balāṭi, Kurunītum, Sakkud of Būbê, and Mār-bīti), Larsa (Šamaš), Sippar-Aruru (Ḫumḫumia, Šuqamuna, and Šimaliya), and Uruk (Uṣur-amāssa). Two of Babylon's gods may have been sent back as well (Abšušu and Abtagigi).[61] The gods of Dēr and Sippar-Aruru (Dūr-Šarrukku) probably returned to their respective cities in 680 while Uṣur-amāssa of Uruk apparently did not return home until 671.[62] The return of captured gods was a practice commonly used by Assyria to win the support of erstwhile enemies.[63] Divine statues were repaired or made anew, given rich adornment, and remounted.[64] The income and offerings due to the gods were restored and confirmed.[65] The cost of all Esarhaddon's work in Babylonia must have been enormous and may have been financed in part from booty taken in his conquest of Egypt. Booty from a campaign to Šubria (to the west of Lake Van) entered Uruk late in 673, perhaps as a gift to one or more of Uruk's temples.[66]

Esarhaddon thus took many steps to reconcile Babylonians to Assyrian rule: restoration and resettlement of Babylon; revival of the city of Akkad; renovation or construction of temples throughout Babylonia; restoration and embellishment of statues of Babylonian gods and their return to Babylonia; renewal of offerings to various Babylonian gods; granting of privileges to

---

60 *ABL* 1214:17'-rev. 3 (*LAS*, no. 291); context broken and interpretation uncertain.

61 Borger, *Esarh.*, p. 46 §27 episode 3 and p. 84 §53 rev. 40-44. Unger (*Babylon*, pp. 137 and 185) suggests that Enamtaggadua ("E-namtaggatuḫa"), to which the god ᵈAN.MAR.TU (reading uncertain) was taken, was in Babylon.

62 Grayson, *Chronicles*, no. 1 iii 44-46 and no. 14:3-4. *ABL* 467:13-19 (*LAS*, no. 277); for the date of the letter, see *LAS* 2, pp. 265-66. For the identification of Dūr-Šarrukku with Sippar-Aruru, see p. 220 n. 36. Esarhaddon claims to have taken the hands of the goddesses Ištar of Uruk and Nanaya and to have led them back to their temples in Uruk (Borger, *Esarh.*, p. 76 §48:14 and p. 77 §49:14) but it is not clear that they had previously been taken to Assyria.

63 See Cogan, *Imperialism*, pp. 35-41. Divine statues were also returned to Arab tribes in order to keep the western border quiet. For Esarhaddon's involvement with the Arabs, see Eph'al, *Ancient Arabs*, pp. 125-42.

64 See for example Borger, *Esarh.* pp. 83-84 §53 rev. 35-41; *ABL* 404, 1202:5-7, 340:5-17, 476:12-26, and *CT* 53 75:5-9 (*LAS*, nos. 58, 281, 276, 277, and 284 respectively).

65 Borger, *Esarh.*, p. 74 §47:23; *ABL* 746 and 1202 (*LAS*, nos. 275 and 281); and cf. *LKU* 46.

66 Grayson, *Chronicles*, no. 1 iv 19-21. There is some confusion in the chronicles about the exact date of this incident (see *ibid.*, p. 84). While this chronicle says that the booty entered Uruk in the ninth month of 673, it also states that Šubria was captured in the tenth month. The Esarhaddon chronicle (*ibid.*, no. 14:24-25) says that Šubria was captured in the twelfth month of 673; no reference is made to booty going to Uruk in this source. See Brinkman, *Moran Festschrift*, pp. 94-95 for a possible explanation for these inconsistencies, an explanation which would eliminate the sending of booty from Šubria to Uruk. For the location of Šubria, see Grayson, *Chronicles*, p. 263 and Kessler, *Nordmesopotamien*, pp. 106-107 and 121 (as Šupria).

Babylon, Borsippa, Nippur, and Sippar; consultation of (and respect for) Babylonian scholars; use of Babylonian royal titles; and depiction of himself in his inscriptions as a true king of Babylonia concerned for the welfare of that land.[67] In view of all these actions to win the support and goodwill of Babylonians, it is perplexing that he did not return the statue of Marduk, Babylon's patron deity; that was not to occur until the time of his successor. Esarhaddon states that he repaired it or, perhaps more accurately, made a new statue of Marduk. The basic purpose behind the "Sin of Sargon" text may have been to justify the making of a new statue of that god. The restoration or "rebirth" of Marduk's statue is described as being under the sponsorship of the Assyrian god Aššur (who is sometimes called Marduk's father), obviously for both political and religious reasons.[68] Esarhaddon contemplated returning the statue of Marduk and in some of his inscriptions he actually claims to have returned it to Babylon.[69] These latter texts may reflect aborted attempts to return the statue. An unsuccessful attempt appears to be described in *ABL* 32 (*LAS*, no. 29) which says that Bēl and other gods were at Labbanat and that an inauspicious event had occurred there, presumably causing the statue to be returned to Assyria.[70] Likely the statues had gone to

---

[67] In her unpublished doctoral dissertation "Symbols of Power: Figurative Aspects of Esarhaddon's Babylonian Policy (681-669 B.C.)" (University of Pennsylvania, 1987), B.N. Porter argues that the images of king and nation used in Esarhaddon's royal inscriptions were intended to affect public opinion in Assyria and Babylonia and that different emphases can be found in the texts intended for the two different countries.

[68] For the creation/restoration of the statue of Marduk, see pp. 56-57. Note also Starr, *SAA* 4, no. 200 which mentions Esarhaddon and the god Marduk and which Starr suggests may refer to the making of the statue of that god. Too little is preserved of the text to make any conclusions about the matter.

[69] Borger, *Esarh.*, p. 74 §47:18-19, pp. 88-89 §57 rev. 8-24, and cf. pp. 45-46 §27 episode 3 ii 22-26. See also Lambert in *Deller Festschrift*, pp. 157-74. Borger, *Esarh.* pp. 88-89 §57 rev. 8-24 contains the most complete description of Marduk's "return" and must have been written sometime after the tenth year of Esarhaddon (671) since the text refers to the conquest of Egypt. In *CT* 54 22:19-20, dated to 676 (see p. 84 n. 104), the author predicted that Esarhaddon would take the hand of Bēl in Babylon for many years, obviously anticipating the return of the statue of Marduk to Babylon during the king's reign. Two undated omen queries ask if the statue of Marduk should be loaded on a boat at Assur and sent back to Babylon (Starr, *SAA* 4, nos. 264-65). They are currently attributed to the early part of the reign of Ashurbanipal in comparison with a query composed on 23-I-668 which asks if Šamaš-šuma-ukīn should take the statue back (*ibid.*, no. 262 and cf. no. 263), but it is not impossible that they come from the reign of Esarhaddon.

[70] Landsberger, *Brief*, p. 68. Parpola (*LAS* 2, pp. 32-35) discusses this letter in detail and suggests that the incident took place in II-669. *ABL* 1214 (*LAS*, no. 291) refers to the possibility or expectation that the king would come to Borsippa (at some point in or after the fourth month); Parpola dates the letter to the same year and suggests that the purpose of the visit was to be present at the ceremonial return of Marduk's statue to Babylon (*LAS* 2, p. 294). *CT* 53 121 (*LAS*, no. 297) may suggest that the king of Elam had intended to go to Babylon at one point, possibly in the latter part of the reign of Esarhaddon (if the letter can be ascribed to Mār-Ištar); the context, however, is broken and any conclusions are

Labbanat on their way to Babylon.[71] The evidence for the planned or attempted return of the divine statues all appears to come from the end of Esarhaddon's reign (*c.* 673-669). The restoration of Esagila may not have been sufficiently completed to warrant the return until then[72] and the installation of Šamaš-šuma-ukīn as crown prince of Babylon in 672 (see below) may have prompted the return of the statue. After the aborted attempt(s) described above, the final delay in returning the statue may have been caused by Esarhaddon's decision to conduct a third campaign against Egypt.[73]

Esarhaddon's actions in promoting the prosperity of Babylonia may be at least in part responsible for the increased level of economic activity attested in Babylonia during this reign. Twenty-nine Babylonian economic texts dated by his regnal years have been found and, as already mentioned, a document dated by the eponymy of a governor of Babylon likely comes to his reign as well.[74] While this is much fewer than for the following two reigns, it is an improvement over almost all similar periods of time during the past five hundred years.[75] Approximately two-thirds come from the north (from such cities as Babylon, Borsippa, and particularly Dilbat) and one-fifth from the extreme south (Uruk and Šapiya). The documents record normal business transactions (the sale of houses, orchards, and fields, the making and repayment of loans, the redemption of individuals, and the division of property), as well as court cases involving disputes over the payment for a prebend in the temple of Šamaš at Sippar, a land sale, and a debt.[76]

A high official, the *rab bīti* ("steward"), carried out some activity in Babylonia during the year 679; since two chronicles considered it worthy of mention, it must have been of some importance in the land. In comparison with similar entries for 677 and 652, it seems likely that the official was

---

uncertain. Parpola suggests that the Elamite king may have intended to be in Babylon in order to honour the return of the statue of Marduk (*LAS* 2, p. 304).

71 Labbanat appears to have been located near the border between Assyria and Babylonia on the route between Assur and Babylon, possibly near modern Baghdad (see Landsberger, *Brief*, p. 68 n. 136 and Parpola, *LAS* 2, p. 33).

72 Work continued on Esagila into the reign of Ashurbanipal (see *ABL* 119).

73 See Borger, *BiOr* 29 (1972): 36.

74 See *B-K* I. Note, however, that two of the economic texts were composed at Assur (80-B-12 and Strassmaier, *8e Congrès*, no. 3; *B-K* I.4 and I.7).

75 The twelve-year reign of Merodach-Baladan (721-710) provides a larger number of texts (thirty-seven), but almost two-thirds of these are pierced ovoids, all but one of which were found in Assyria. The fourteen-year reign of Nabonassar (747-734) is also attested by a reasonable number of economic texts (twenty-two, most of which probably come from the same archive) and the various rulers of Babylonia during the time of Sennacherib on the throne of Assyria (704-681) provide approximately twenty texts. For text references, see *B-K*.

76 Strassmaier, *8e Congrès*, no. 4, *OECT* 10 396, and *TCL* 12 4 (*B-K* I.6, I.15, and I.25).

choosing or examining something, perhaps levying troops; the reason for his action is unknown.[77] If the steward was levying troops, his action may have been prompted by the activities of individuals in Babylonia who were giving trouble to the authorities there and who were presumably not loyal to Assyria.

Not all Babylonians welcomed Esarhaddon's accession to the throne or continued Assyrian rule and the Assyrians had to put down some unrest in Babylonia in the following year. Chronicles state that in 678 DN-aḫḫē-šullim (the governor of Nippur) and Šamaš-ibni (leader of Bīt-Dakkūri) were transported to Assyria and executed.[78] Nothing further is certain about the governor of Nippur; however, Esarhaddon's inscriptions give some details about Šamaš-ibni's crime. This important ruler of Bīt-Dakkūri, who was called a "king" in some Assyrian texts, had forcibly taken possession of fields belonging to the inhabitants of Babylon and Borsippa, probably while Babylon lay abandoned. With the restoration of that city, dispute arose over the ownership of the land. Esarhaddon claims to have plundered Bīt-Dakkūri, returned the fields to their original owners, and replaced Šamaš-ibni with Nabû-ušallim, son of Balāssu, who retained his authority over Bīt-Dakkūri into the reign of Šamaš-šuma-ukīn.[79] A kudurru from the time of Šamaš-šuma-ukīn refers to land which had been illegally appropriated by two Chaldean officials (LÚ *šá-kan u* LÚ *šá-pi-ru šá* KUR *kal-du*) at a time in the past when there had been disorder and insurrections in the land of Akkad. The land had been restored to its rightful owner by Esarhaddon and Nabû-ušallim had been involved with the matter in some way, at least he had given testimony about the proper ownership of the land at the time the kudurru was made.[80] This may describe the seizure of land in northern Babylonia by Šamaš-ibni; the disorder in the land which the text mentions may refer to the

---

77 Grayson, *Chronicles*, no. 1 iii 48 and no. 14:6 (both damaged); cf. no. 1 iv 4, no. 14:12, and no. 16:10. On the meaning of *biḫirtu beḫēru*, see chapter 10, section III.

78 Grayson, *Chronicles*, no. 1 iv 1-2 and no. 14:10-11. The theophoric element at the beginning of the first name is not preserved in the first chronicle and indistinct in the second; for the divine names attested in personal names of this type, see Tallqvist, *NBN*, p. 333. In *Or*. NS 34 (1965): 247 n. 6, Brinkman queries whether Šamaš-ibni was indeed executed since Esarhaddon's inscriptions do not mention his fate and since the verb used in the chronicles (*dâku*) does not have to mean "kill." This Šamaš-ibni is probably the individual by that name whose corpse was later returned to Babylonia by Aššur-etil-ilāni (*YOS* 1 43 and 9 81-82).

79 Borger, *Esarh*., p. 33 §21:22-23 and p. 52 §27 episode 12; Heidel, *Sumer* 12 (1956): 16-19 ii 34-45. *ABL* 336 reports that various individuals who had fled from Šamaš-ibni were then before Nabû-ušallim (presumably after the latter had been made leader of the Bīt-Dakkūri) and that the latter would not give them up without a direct command from the king. The author of that letter also thought that it would interest the king that two of Nabû-ušallim's officials had a large sum of money and were were planning on buying horses. Perhaps he feared that the horses might be used in some rebellion against Assyria. On Šamaš-ibni, see Meissner, *OLZ* 21 (1918): 220-23.

80 *BBSt* 10 rev. 1-13 (*B-K* K.169).

troubles at the death of Sennacherib and when Nabû-zēr-kitti-līšir attacked Ur. Esarhaddon's action against Bīt-Dakkūri may have been prompted by a request from Bēl-ušēzib that the king send troops and seize persons who had destroyed Babylon and looted its property; these persons were described as "nobles (LÚ.NUN.MEŠ) of the land of Akkad whom the king, your father, had appointed."[81] In *ABL* 223 (*LAS*, no. 30) it is reported that it had been revealed that a rebel, Ṣillaya,[82] had asked about Šamaš-ibni, Ningal-iddin, and Na'id-Marduk and had spoken about an uprising in the land (*ina muḫḫi šabalkute ša māti*), urging that the fortified positions be seized. Possibly Ṣillaya had been attempting to discover where these three important Babylonian leaders stood with regard to rebellion, and whether they would support anti-Assyrian actions. If Šamaš-ibni had agreed to support the rebellion, this may have been the reason he was deposed from his position over the Bīt-Dakkūri.[83]

ABL 403, a letter from an Assyrian king to the "non-Babylonians" (*la* LÚ.TIN.TIR.KI.MEŠ), may have some bearing here. These non-Babylonians may have been persons who had acquired land in or near Babylon while the city lay destroyed and who now claimed the status of citizens of the restored city. In this purposefully curt and insulting letter, the king states that he had not even opened the letter they had written to him because: "You are pretending to be Babylonians against the command of the god (of the city of Babylon) and you charge my servants with the unspeakable things that you and your master used to commit." Only if the letter had been from true Babylonians, individuals who were loyal to him and loved him, would he have opened it. The "master" of these "non-Babylonians" may well have been Šamaš-ibni and their "crimes" the seizure of land at Babylon.[84] The restoration of the land around Borsippa to its legitimate owners may have also prompted the order by the king expressed in *ABL* 1202 (*LAS*, no. 281) that an account of the livestock belonging to the

---

81 Thompson, *Rep.* 272 rev. 13-18. On the basis of astronomical statements contained in the report, Parpola dates it to 679 (*LAS* 2, pp. 18 and 37). Note the reference to the land of Akkad and the kings of Amurrû when mentioning those who were to be affected by omens portended by an eclipse (Thompson, *Rep.* 272 rev. 9-10). Note also *ABL* 1006:18-rev. 2 (Thompson, *Rep.* 268) where the king is advised to remove from office(?) one of the noblemen of Chaldea, Aram or(?) [...]; Parpola discusses this incident and states that the text describes the total lunar eclipse occurring in III-678 (*LAS* 2, p. 37).

82 The Assyrian form of the name, Ṣallaya, is used in the letter.

83 The letter may date to 679 (see Parpola, *LAS* 2, p. 516, contra p. 35). There is no concrete evidence that Na'id-Marduk ever supported anti-Assyrian actions after his appointment over the Sealand or that he was deposed from office (cf. Dietrich, *Aramäer*, p. 34). With regard to the possibility that Ningal-iddin may have been removed from his post as governor of Ur by Esarhaddon, see below.

84 A translation of *ABL* 403 is found in Oppenheim, *Letters*, no. 116. While the letter would fit well with this incident, there is nothing in it which explicitly dates it to this time.

god Nabû be taken as it had in former times and that the offerings to the god be made properly.[85]

The demonstration of Assyrian might against the Chaldean tribe and a presumably successful campaign against the land of the Barnakians north of Elam at about the same time[86] may have been what caused the Gambulian leader, Bēl-iqīša son of Bunanu, to submit to Assyria and take tribute to Nineveh at some point before the end of Ayyaru (II) 676. Desiring the support of this large and important Aramean tribe located on the border with Elam, Esarhaddon treated Bēl-iqīša favourably, fortified his stronghold in the marshes, Ša-pī-Bēl, and looked upon the presence of Bēl-iqīša's archers there as a garrison against Elam.[87] *ABL* 541 shows that Bēl-iqīša was regarded as a loyal vassal;[88] he could travel through northern Babylonia, give his daughters in marriage to Babylonians, and, apparently illegally, be given land located between Cutha and Kish in the province of Babylon.[89]

Two chronicles report that in 677, the *rab bīti* carried out an action (*biḫirtu ibteḫir*) in Babylonia, though exactly what was done remains uncertain.[90] For the following year, the chronicles report that the Assyrian army captured the city of Bazza (Assyrian Bāzu) in the seventh month.[91] I. Eph'al argues that since the campaign against Bazza is mentioned on a prism dated to 22-II-676, it should have taken place before 676; he also suggests that with the evidence presently available Bazza was most likely located "in the northeastern part of the Arabian peninsula, west of the Persian Gulf."[92] If this location is correct, the Assyrian army probably marched through Babylonia to reach its goal.

---

85 See Parpola, *LAS* 2, p. 273.

86 Borger, *Esarh.*, p. 34 §21:28, p. 51 §27 episode 10, and p. 100 §66:20; Heidel, *Sumer* 12 (1956): 16-17 ii 16-19. The campaign against the Barnakians is mentioned in the Nineveh inscription before his defeat of the Bīt-Dakkūri; however, the order of events in Esarhaddon's inscriptions is not always chronological. It must have taken place before 673, when the text was composed and likely before Urtak ascended the throne of Elam in 675 (when peaceful relations between Assyria and Elam were established). For the location of the Barnakians, see Unger in *RLA* 2, p. 38 and Young, *Iran* 5 (1967): 13 and n. 21.

87 Borger, *Esarh.*, pp. 52-53 §27 episode 13; Heidel, *Sumer* 12 (1956): 22-25 iii 37-52 (prism dated to 22-II-676). In leaving Bēl-iqīša in charge of Ša-pī-Bēl Esarhaddon was simply accepting the current situation. It might have required a military campaign to remove him.

88 In view of the references to Elam and to Bēl-iqīša having control over a region, it seems likely that the Bēl-iqīša mentioned in *ABL* 541 was the Gambulian leader.

89 *ABL* 336. The exact dates of *ABL* 336 and 541 are uncertain; dates in the time of Šamaš-šuma-ukīn cannot be excluded.

90 Grayson, *Chronicles*, nos. 1 iv 4 and 14:12. See below, chapter 10.

91 Grayson, *Chronicles*, nos. 1 iv 5-6 and 14:13. See also Borger, *Esarh.*, p. 33 §21:24-27, pp. 56-57 §27 episode 17, and p. 86 §57:4-5; and Heidel, *Sumer* 12 (1956): 20-23 iii 9-36.

92 *Ancient Arabs*, pp. 53-54 and 130-37 and see Zadok, *RGTC* 8, p. 73. No reason for the campaign is stated in the sources, but Eph'al speculates that it may have been economic in nature (i.e., a desire for booty); see Eph'al, *Ancient Arabs*, p. 137.

Possibly the action of the *rab bīti* was connected in some way with this campaign.[93]

Although the Elamite king Ḫumban-ḫaltaš II had earlier resisted involvement with anti-Assyrian elements in Babylonia,[94] in 675 he felt the time was right to open hostilities with Assyria. Possibly worried about Assyria's intentions in view of its campaign against the Barnakians on Elam's northern border, and choosing a moment when some at least of the Assyrian army was occupied in far-off Anatolia,[95] or taking advantage of the unsettled conditions in Babylonia caused by the actions of Ṣillaya (see below), he marched into northern Babylonia and entered Sippar early in 675. Because of the presence of Elamite troops in Sippar, or its neighbourhood, the statue of the city's tutelary god, Šamaš, was kept in its temple and not taken out to take part in religious ceremonies.[96] There is no direct evidence that any other city was attacked by the Elamites at this time, though the city of Akkad may have been (seen below). Sippar was back in Assyrian hands by the end of 675 since a document was dated there under Esarhaddon on the second day of the twelfth month of that year.[97] Likely the Elamite troops had already abandoned Sippar and returned to Elam by the month of Ulūlu (VI), when the chronicles state that Ḫumban-ḫaltaš died unexpectedly "in his palace" and was succeeded by his brother Urtak.[98] It is uncertain what caused the Elamites to abandon Sippar; possibly Assyrian troops had advanced to give battle, or perhaps the

---

93 Possibly he had been raising auxilary troops or gathering supplies for the Assyrian army.

94 He had refused asylum to Nabû-zēr-kitti-līšir.

95 Grayson, *Chronicles*, no. 1 iv 10 and no. 14:15 mention an Assyrian campaign to Melīdu in 675; the former chronicle refers to it between entries about the Elamite entry into Sippar and the death of Ḫumban-ḫaltaš II (see below). For the location of Melīdu, see Streck, *Asb.*, pp. CCCL-CCCLI.

96 Grayson, *Chronicles*, no. 1 iv 9-10; exactly why the statue did not leave the temple is not stated. The Esarhaddon chronicle (*ibid.*, no. 14) does not mention the capture of Sippar. This chronicle may have omitted the incident because it reflected poorly on Esarhaddon that Elamites had been able to capture an important city under his control, but the pro-Esarhaddon nature of this chronicle has been recently brought into question by Brinkman (*Moran Festschrift*, pp. 92-94). Brinkman has also pointed out that the composer of the Babylonian Chronicle may have added the entry about Sippar in error, inserting it for the sixth year of Esarhaddon instead of for the sixth year of his somewhat similarly named brother Aššur-nādin-šumi who reigned in Babylon two decades earlier and for whom there is a similar entry (*Prelude*, pp. 78-79 and n. 380). Brinkman argues that an Elamite invasion of Babylonia would be out of place at this time since relations between Assyria and Elam were otherwise peaceful between 690 and 665 and since there is no record of an Assyrian response to this hostile action. It should be pointed out, however, that Elam is known to have supported an attempt to oust the ruler of the Sealand during the reign of Esarhaddon and to replace him by an individual with ties to Elam (see below).

97 *VAS* 5 2 (*B-K* I.16).

98 Grayson, *Chronicles*, nos. 1 iv 10-13 and 14:16-18. The former source says that Ḫumban-ḫaltaš II died on 7-VI while the latter states that he died on 5-VI. On the spelling of the name Urtak, see Brinkman, *Prelude*, p. 79 n. 381 and the references cited there.

attack on Sippar was intended merely as a raid with no intent to maintain control of the city.

The new king of Elam restored friendly relations with Assyria by sending messengers of "friendship and peace" to Nineveh where they swore an oath by the great gods. According to Assyrian inscriptions, Urtak did so out of fear of Assyrian might and in order to protect his land from possible Assyrian attack. As proof of his friendship, Urtak sent statues of the gods of Akkad to Babylonia in the month of Addaru (XII) in 674.[99] When these statues had been taken to Elam is unknown; they may have been carried off as booty after a raid in the distant past or they had been taken the previous year in the course of the invasion of Babylonia by Ḫumban-ḫaltaš II. Esarhaddon and Urtak corresponded on friendly terms and may even have exchanged their own children as hostages.[100] Peaceful relations presumably lasted for the remainder of Esarhaddon's reign; when Urtak did invade Babylonia early in the reign of Ashurbanipal, the Assyrian king described the move as unexpected.[101] Babylonia was basically quiet during the second half of Esarhaddon's reign, possibly in part because would-be rebels could no longer look to Elam for support.

While there is no direct indication that Ḫumban-ḫaltaš II had acted in conjunction with anti-Assyrian elements in Babylonia when attacking Sippar, such may have been the case. The chronicles record that at some point in the same year (675) Šuma-iddin, the governor of Nippur, and Kudurru, the Dakkurian, were taken to Assyria, presumably for punishment.[102] Possibly they had supported or been implicated in the Elamite invasion or their activities may have served as a diversion for the Elamite move. The fact that the head of the Bīt-Dakkūri tribe and a governor of Nippur had been executed in 678 (see above) points to a continuing involvement between that tribe and city. Kudurru is probably to be identified with Kudurru son of Šamaš-ibni, the author of *ABL* 756, who wrote to the king asking him not to let him die

---

99 Borger, *Esarh.*, pp. 58-59 §27 episode 19; the name of the Elamite king is not stated, but copies of text date to 673, i.e., after the accession of Urtak. Grayson, *Chronicles*, no. 1 iv 17-18 and no. 14:21-22. Cf. Borger, *Esarh.*, p. 25 §11 episode 36. Note the extispicy request Starr, *SAA* 4, no. 74 which dates to the reign of Esarhaddon and which appears to ask if Urtak's words were true. The agreement between Esarhaddon and Urtak may be the one mentioned in *CT* 54 580 (see Dietrich, *Aramäer*, pp. 58-59 n. 9).

100 *ABL* 918; see Parpola, *Iraq* 34 (1972): 34 n. 66.

101 Piepkorn, *Asb.*, pp. 56-59 iv 18-34. But note the extispicy request concerning the trustworthiness of Urtak's words (Starr, *SAA* 4, no. 74) and the fact that in *ABL* 476 rev. 11-26 (*LAS*, no. 277, dated by Parpola to 671) distrust may be expressed with regard to Elam's involvement at Dēr.

102 Grayson, *Chronicles*, no. 1 iv 14-15 and no. 14:19. The reading of the first name as Šuma-iddin is shown by the writing [m]MU-SUM.NA in *CT* 54 22 rev. 1.

from hunger like a dog.[103] Since Kudurru is called "the Dakkurian" (*mār Dakkūri*) in the chronicles, a term often employed for the leader of the tribe, it may be that he had replaced Nabû-ušallim as head of that tribe or had led an attempt to oust him. Šuma-iddin was only the latest in a series of governors of Nippur who had fallen out of favour with Assyria within five years. In 678 the governor was removed from office and something had happened to another governor in 680. Although the passage is damaged at a crucial spot, *CT* 54 22 appears to state that there had been three different governors within the space of a single year, the latest being Šuma-iddin. In this letter, Bēl-ušēzib accused Šuma-iddin of having removed the old dias of Nippur, of having performed an apotropaic ritual concerning the matter, and of being in association with several rebels (or persons suspected of being opposed to Assyria), in particular Ṣillaya and Sāsiya (see below).[104] Perhaps it was this letter that resulted in Šuma-iddin's arrest.

According to *ABL* 327, at one point actions of anti-Assyrian elements had placed Nippur in a precarious position. The governor claimed that because of his city's loyalty to Assyria all the lands hated it, its citizens could not leave the city safely, and the city gates had to remain locked. Ṣillaya had even denied the city access to water from the Banītu canal. The governor asked the Assyrian king to have Ubāru, the governor of Babylon, provide Nippur with access to the water. He implies that no one would support Assyria if they saw the way the people of Nippur were left without access to water (i.e., without aid from Assyria in time of need). The exact date of this letter is open to question, although the references to Ubāru and Ṣillaya (see below) point to a date in the early or middle years of Esarhaddon's reign.

A person (or persons) by the name of Ṣillaya (Assyrian: Ṣallaya) appears in a number of letters that may be dated to the reign of Esarhaddon with either certainty or reasonable confidence. It is not clear whether all references deal with only one man; however, most do seem to present a uniform picture, so it is quite possible that they describe one individual.[105] This Ṣillaya may have

---

103 Possibly this letter dates to the time after Kudurru had been taken to Assyria, where he may have been kept in captivity. *ABL* 447 (see Parpola, *LAS* 2 pp. 458-59) refers to a son of the *šandabakku* (governor of Nippur) who was in fetters in the House-of-Succession in Nineveh. Since several governors of Nippur got into trouble with Assyria during the reigns of Esarhaddon and Ashurbanipal, it is unclear whose son he was.

104 On *CT* 54 22 rev. 9-11, see p. 229. In rev. 1 read ⸢LÚ *šá*⸣-*an-da-bak-ka* not ⸢ŠEŠ *šá*⸣-*an-da-bak-ka*; see Brinkman, *Or.* NS 48 (1977): 318 sub 24. The letter may be dated to the end of 676, the year after Sidon was captured (see lines 13-15 and Dietrich, *WO* 4 [1967-68]: 234-35).

105 The fact that the letters refer to Ṣillaya by this name only (i.e., without his father's name, or his city or tribal affiliation, or his occupation) may indicate that their authors felt that there would be no confusion over the identity of the Ṣillaya mentioned. However, since Ṣillaya is a reasonably common name in the economic texts of the period and since

held an official position at some time since he reported to the Assyrian king about events that probably took place at some point between 680 and 675. At that time, he was, or pretended to be, loyal; he told the king that "evil things are done behind the king's back" and that he wanted to come and speak to the king.[106] The choice of gods invoked by Ṣillaya in *ABL* 1131 suggests that he was associated with Nippur;[107] references to him in connection with Nippur and its governors in *ABL* 327 and 540, and *CT* 54 22 (see above) point to the same conclusion.

Complaints about Ṣillaya were expressed in several letters. In *ABL* 702, an individual by the name of Zākir appears to have charged that Ṣillaya opposed the resettlement of Babylon;[108] and in *ABL* 416, Zākir claimed that Ṣillaya had stolen his property and wished to kill him (Zākir). The author of *CT* 54 527 states that Ṣillaya had said that he (Ṣillaya) wished to kill a Gambulian by the name of Iḫīru and to write to the Chaldean leaders to tell them (falsely) that he (Ṣillaya) wished to kill Ningal-iddin and Šamaš-ibni.[109] The reference to Šamaš-ibni dates this last text prior to 678 when Šamaš-ibni was executed. Nabû-zēru-līšir states in *ABL* 223 (*LAS*, no. 30) that it was reported that Ṣillaya had spoken about rebellion and ordered the seizing of fortified places. Since this letter may date to 679,[110] it would show Ṣillaya already in revolt early in the reign of Esarhaddon. Ṣillaya had also inquired about three officials—Ningal-iddin, Šamaš-ibni, and Na'id-Marduk (the governor of Ur, the leader of the Bīt-Dakkūri, and the governor of the Sealand respectively). Presumably he had wanted to discover what they were doing or how they stood with regard to anti-Assyrian actions.[111] *CT* 54 22 may also connect Ṣillaya with anti-Assyrian activities in 676, this time in collaboration with Sāsiya, another individual whose name is broken, and possibly the governor of Nippur, Šuma-iddin, or the latter's son;[112] however,

---

we are not fully conversant with the background against which these letters were written, any identifications we make must be considered tentative.

106 *ABL* 1131. Ṣillaya reported on actions of Nabû-ušallim (son of Merodach-Baladan II) against the Sealand (here Bīt-Yakīn); it is shown below that these actions probably took place between 680 (at the earliest) and 675.

107 Ṣillaya invoked [Enlil], Ninurta, and Nusku in the introduction of *ABL* 1131 (lines 1-2; according to a collation by I. Finkel there is room to restore Enlil at the end of line 1); these three gods were elsewhere invoked by governors of Nippur (e.g., *ABL* 327:3-4 and 328:3-4).

108 *ABL* 702 rev. 7; exact interpretation not certain.

109 *CT* 54 527 rev. 1-5 (see Dietrich, *Aramäer*, pp. 150-51 and 156-57 nos. 35 and 50). The letter is damaged and some points are open to dispute. See p. 100 n. 178 on the interpretation of this letter.

110 See Parpola, *LAS* 2, p. 516 (contra p. 35). In view of the mention of Šamaš-ibni in the letter (rev. 4), a date before 678 seems likely.

111 With regard to the interpretation of this letter, see also p. 100 n. 178.

112 For the date of the letter, see p. 84 n. 104. Rev. 3-8 appear to suggest that the son of the governor of Nippur had held back four minas of silver and given them to Sāsiya,

since this section of the letter is poorly preserved any conclusions must remain uncertain. As was mentioned earlier, *ABL* 327 shows Ṣillaya preventing Nippur from taking water from the Banītu canal and he is likely one of those mentioned in that letter who are said to hate the people of Nippur because of their loyalty to Assyria. The governor of Nippur had claimed: "We are not safe anywhere; wherever we might go we would be killed ... We have now locked our gates tight and do not go out ..."[113] Thus at times Ṣillaya appears to have acted with the governor of Nippur and at times against him. In view of the rapid changeover of governors at this time, this is not surprising since not all of the governors would have had the same political views. Although the exact interpretation of *ABL* 540 is uncertain, it has been taken to indicate that rebellious former governors of Nippur had mobilized troops and gone to the aid of Ṣillaya in the land of Akkad and the Sealand. The author of the letter (likely the king) orders the addressee to take troops and support Nabû-ēṭir, governor of the Sealand, presumably in opposing Ṣillaya and the latter's followers.[114] Finally, *ABL* 1255 may show Ṣillaya

---

[...]-x-ŠEŠ, and Ṣillaya, though the damage at the ends of rev. 3 and 4 allows the possibility that the son of Šuma-iddin was not the subject of the verbs *ušeklâššu* and *inamdin* in rev. 5 and 6 respectively. The author of this letter may then state that the king should not believe favourable comments about Šuma-iddin because an insurrection was then in progress; again damage to the text makes any reading most uncertain (*ina ūmu agâ? sīḫi? ipšu*, rev. 7-8; see Dietrich, *Aramäer*, pp. 158-59 no. 55). No connection between the giving of the money and the revolt is expressly stated but such a connection is implied. Dietrich has identified the Sāsiya mentioned in the letter with an individual by that name (actually the Assyrian form of the name, Sāsî) who was involved with a conspiracy at Harran (*Aramäer*, pp. 50-56). After re-examining the evidence, Brinkman denies any connection between a Sāsiya who was a Babylonian official and any conspiracy at Harran, and indeed questions the idea of a widespread revolt led by a Sāsiya/Sāsî and centred at Harran (*Or.* NS 46 [1977]: 312-15). Parpola (*LAS* 2, pp. 238-40) reasserts the idea of a rebellion whose base was at Harran or in an adjacent region and which was led by, or on behalf of, an individual called Sāsiya late in the reign of Esarhaddon. However, he avoids any clear statement conecting a revolt in the north with the activities of Ṣillaya in the south (though see *ibid.*, p. 35 and p. 239 n. 420). It seems likely that more than one person by the name of Sāsiya/Sāsî appears in the texts of the period. It is uncertain if the Sāsiya of *CT* 54 22 is to be connected with the individual by that name in *ABL* 445 who was called "mayor" (with regard to his full title, see p. 99 n. 174) and who received one mina of gold from Sîn-balāssu-iqbi of Ur, and/or with the individual in *CT* 54 37 (*ABL* 1345+) who was also called "mayor" ([m]*sa-si-i*[*a*] LÚ *ḫa-za-an-nu*, lines 15-16) and who was said to be loyal to the king.

113 *ABL* 327:13-20 (for a translation of the letter, see Oppenheim, *Letters*, no. 121).

114 See Dietrich, *Aramäer*, pp. 48-49. It may also be possible to interpret the letter as criticizing the addressee for not acting like the governor of Nippur and thus not aiding Ṣillaya. In this case, the letter would have to refer to another Ṣillaya or be dated while Ṣillaya was still in favour in Assyrian eyes (but see below).

Although the beginning is not preserved, *ABL* 540 can probably be assigned to the king since the author refers to an action by his grandfather (rev. 1-2) and can order the addressee to raise troops (rev. 4-9). The reference to the author's grandfather points to the author being Esarhaddon (grandson of Sargon) or Ashurbanipal or Šamaš-šuma-ukīn (grandsons of

attempting to win the support of two important individuals at Dilbat,[115] but this could date to the period before he began his rebellious activities.

Thus it seems that during the early and middle years of Esarhaddon's reign a person by the name of Ṣillaya carried out some anti-Assyrian actions in Babylonia, particularly in the area around Nippur. No clear details are known except that he helped bring Nippur to sad straits and that one or more governors of Nippur aided him. There is no evidence how widespread his support was, or indeed if his rebellious activities had any real success. No references to him can be dated clearly before 680 or after about 675 and his fate is unknown.[116] In summary, although the official Ṣillaya who reported loyally to the king in *ABL* 1131[117] may be a different person than the rebel Ṣillaya, it seems reasonable to assume that all the texts mentioning a troublemaker by the name of Ṣillaya during the early and middle years of the reign of Esarhaddon refer to the same person.

According to the Esarhaddon chronicle, on the eighth day of Addaru (XII) in 674 the army of Assyria went(?) to Šamēlē,[118] presumably the fortified town of this name located in the area of Bīt-Amukāni.[119] Undoubtedly the

---

Sennacherib). The incident described does not fit well into what is known to have happened in Babylonia during the latter two kings' reigns; thus the letter should likely be assigned to the reign of Esarhaddon. Although *ABL* 540 is in Babylonian script, there are some indications that it was written by an Assyrian (e.g., the spelling Ṣallaya in line 14' instead of Babylonian Ṣillaya). The reference to Nabû-ēṭir as governor of the Sealand (rev. 6-7; with regard to the phrase *tam-tim ṣa-pu-nu*, see p. 41 n. 56) suggests that he had replaced Na'id-Marduk sometime before the conclusion of Ṣillaya's rebellious activities. Borger, *Esarh.*, p. 47 §27 episode 4 edition A ii 63-64 imply that Na'id-Marduk was still in office in 673 when the text was composed; however, its scribe(s) simply may not have chosen to mention the fact that Na'id-Marduk had been replaced as governor of the Sealand. On the other hand, there is no proof exactly when Ṣillaya's actions came to an end.

115 Possibly Bēl-īpuš, one of the two persons, is to be identified with the man by that name before whom a trial took place in Dilbat in 674 (*TCL* 12 4:3-5; *B-K* I.25). It is also possible that Bēl-i[ddin?], the second individual mentioned in *ABL* 1255, is to be identified with the Bēl-iddin whose sons are said to have been related to a governor of Dilbat appointed by Šamaš-šuma-ukīn in *ABL* 326.

116 K 1351:2 (Livingstone, *SAA* 3, no. 29) may indicate that Ṣillaya was not caught and punished by the Assyrians but had fled for his life (*ul-tu a-*⌜*di?-ni?*⌝ ᵐ*ṣal-la-a la im-me-du* KUR-*šú*, "before Ṣallaya disappeared forever"), if the Ṣallaya referred to in this text (a denunciation of an individual by the name of Bēl-ēṭir [cf. *CT* 54 22 rev. 12?]) is to be identified with the rebel Ṣillaya active in the reign of Esarhaddon.

117 Possibly see also *ABL* 540 and 1255.

118 Grayson, *Chronicles*, no. 14:20. The reading of the verb is unclear; however, some verb of motion seems reasonable. Dietrich, *Aramäer*, p. 56 suggests [*ittal*]*kū*. The reading of the year in which this incident took place is not completely certain; it may be either Esarhaddon's seventh year (674) or his eighth year (673). See Brinkman, *Moran Festschrift*, p. 95 n. 128.

119 Luckenbill, *Senn.*, p. 53:43. *CT* 54 507, written during the revolt of 652-648, also connects Šamēlē with Bīt-Amukāni by stating that there were members of that tribe there (line 13). In view of the fact that this letter was written by an official of Uruk (see the introductory blessing), and that these persons had apparently come to him (lines 13-17), it

campaign was intended to put down some rebellion. Perhaps it was to deal with Ṣillaya's actions,[120] although there is no other evidence to connect him with Šamēlē. The Babylonian Chronicle replaces this entry with the statement that the army of Assyria was defeated in Egypt. The compiler of the Esarhaddon chronicle may have omitted the defeat in Egypt because it reflected unfavourably on the Assyrian king.[121]

Sometime between 680 and 675 Elam supported an attempt by Nabû-ušallim son of Merodach-Baladan II to gain control of the Sealand from, or possibly in succession to, his brother Na'id-Marduk. Nabû-ušallim had fled to Elam some time during the reign of Sennacherib.[122] The date post quem is indicated by the fact that Na'id-Marduk did not become ruler of the Sealand until 680, when he replaced Nabû-zēr-kitti-līšir. The date ante quem is suggested by the accession of Urtak to the throne of Elam after the death of Ḫumban-ḫaltaš II in VI-675 when friendly relations were established between Assyria and Elam (see above). If the Ṣillaya who was the author of *ABL* 1131 is to be identified with the sometime rebel active in Babylonia during the early and middle years of the reign of Esarhaddon, then the attack by Nabû-ušallim and Elamite troops on Bīt-Yakīn, reported in that letter, should antedate Ṣillaya's period of open rebellion. The actions of Nabû-ušallim and his ally the king of Elam are described in *ABL* 576 and 1114.[123] Asserting

---

seems likely that they had gone to Uruk; this may suggest that Šamēlē was located in the area of Uruk. The name of the town is perhaps to be read (Ālu)-ša-amīlē/amēlē.

120 See Dietrich, *Aramäer*, p. 56. Dietrich (*ibid.*) and Parpola (*LAS* 2, pp. 36-37) postulate that Ṣillaya was the head of Bīt-Amukāni.

121 See Grayson, *Chronicles*, p. 30. G. Fecht has attempted to reconcile the two accounts by suggesting that Šamēlē was an Assyrian form for the name of an Egyptian city (*MDAIK* 16 [1958]: 116-19), but Spalinger points out several linguistic problems in accepting Fecht's proposed identification (*Or.* NS 43 [1974]: 300-301). In view of the well known town Šamēlē in Babylonia, it is best to assume that town was meant by the Esarhaddon chronicle.

122 Piepkorn, *Asb.*, pp. 74-75 vi 70-72.

123 The names of the authors of these texts are not preserved; however, the contexts indicate that they were written by the people of the Sealand or their elders. *ABL* 328, a letter from the governor of Nippur to the king of Assyria, states that the brothers of the king of Elam had tried to persuade the latter to attempt to remove the Chaldeans from Assyrian control (lines 9-13; read LÚ *kal-di* in lines 10 and 12 [collated]). Although he initially refused to break his alliance (*adê*-agreement) with the king of Assyria (lines 14-15), the king of Elam appears to have changed his mind later (lines 19-22). Since Nabû-ušallim son of Merodach-Baladan acted against the Sealand, an area inhabited by Chaldeans, with the support of Elam, it is possible that the incident described in *ABL* 328 was connected with the actions of Nabû-ušallim. The *adê*-agreement between Elam and Assyria mentioned in the letter, however, could suggest the treaty between Urtak and Esarhaddon (see above) and one would assume Nabû-ušallim's actions had taken place before that agreement was made. Possibly the king of Elam did not change his mind in *ABL* 328 or Ḫumban-ḫaltaš II had also had a treaty with Assyria and the action described in the letter is to be connected with his invasion of Babylonia in 675. The relation of the incident described by Na'id-Marduk to the Assyrian king's mother in *ABL* 917 to this incident is uncertain. *ABL* 917:6-15 shows

that Na'id-Marduk was dead, Nabû-ušallim and Elam sent messengers to the Sealand demanding it accept Nabû-ušallim as its lord. The leaders of the Sealand refused to receive Nabû-ušallim unless instructed to do so by the king of Assyria. Since they claimed that Na'id-Marduk, their lord, was still alive, it is reasonable either that the enemies' claim that Na'id-Marduk was dead was a *ruse de guerre*[124] to get the Sealand to support Nabû-ušallim or that Na'id-Marduk had only just died and his death was not yet known widely. In the latter case, one would have expected his own subjects to have known of his death before word reached the king of Elam and he was able to react. The Elamites settled Nabû-ušallim with the Targibātu and gave him several tribes on the border of Na'id-Marduk's domain so that he could use their territories as bases from which to launch operations against the Sealand. Nabû-ušallim continued to demand that the elders of the Sealand submit to him and that they provide him with support, threatening to destroy their land and houses if they did not. When the rebels captured one of the Sealanders garrisoning an outpost in the Naḫal region, the king of Elam sent him back to the Sealand with a message claiming that the Sealand did not belong to Assyria but rather to Elam, and thus implying that they should obey him and accept Nabû-ušallim. The people of the Sealand reported all this to Esarhaddon and asked him to give instructions that the Chaldean tribes help them if the king of Elam should attack. Elam supported Nabû-ušallim's endeavours in order to remove the Sealand from Assyrian control and bring it within the Elamite sphere of influence. Further actions by Nabû-ušallim are unknown; possibly the accession of Urtak to the throne of Elam in 675 and the subsequent peace between Assyria and Elam (lasting into the reign of Ashurbanipal)[125] removed his Elamite backing. The date of Na'id-Marduk's death or departure from office is uncertain; Nabû-ēṭir may have assumed power over the Sealand by about 675.[126]

It is unclear how often Esarhaddon was in Babylonia during the course of his reign. He claims to have been there on at least three occasions—when he aided personally in the rebuilding of Babylon, when he defeated Šamaš-ibni in 678, and when he grasped the hands of the goddesses Ištar of Uruk and

---

that Na'id-Marduk was attacked from Elam at one point, or at least that Elamite troops had seized a border crossing and that Na'id-Marduk wanted to make sure that troops from Assyria would be sent to aid him if they advanced (see Dietrich, *Aramäer*, pp. 144-45 no. 24 for the passage in question).

124 See Dietrich, *Aramäer*, p. 2.

125 See above, p. 83.

126 See above, pp. 86-87. Note, however, that copies of Esarhaddon's inscription stating that Na'id-Marduk "came to Nineveh every year without fail with his weighty gifts (for me) and kissed my feet" were made in 673 (Borger, *Esarh.*, p. 47 §27 episode 4 ii 63-64 and p. 64 Datierungen). For the suggestion that Na'id-Marduk was deposed from office for disloyalty, see p. 100 n. 178.

Nanaya, led them back to their temples in Uruk, and offered sacrifices there.[127] Assyrian kings, however, often claimed to have done things (especially lead campaigns) which they in fact did not, and Esarhaddon's claim to have aided in the restoration of Babylon may have been simply intended to show his great interest in that project. A document dated at Sippar on the second day of the twelfth month of 675 mentions two *qurbūtu*-officials—likely servants of the Assyrian king—and the "chief bird catcher of the king."[128] Is it possible that these individuals were in Sippar in the entourage of the king, who had come to visit the city after its recapture from Elamite control earlier that year? As long as Babylonia remained reasonably quiet his presence (at the head of an army) was not required; he could concentrate instead on more troublesome areas (Phoenicia and the northern border) and undertake his grand project, the invasion of Egypt. While Esarhaddon may have spent very little time in Babylonia, he was well informed of how matters stood there. Officials in Babylonia naturally reported to him as their king, often in great detail about minor matters. He exercised final authority over Babylonia and gave orders about even trivial concerns. He sent "special agents" to the south bearing royal orders and empowered to ensure that they were carried out. These agents were to report on conditions, including the actions of Babylonian officials, from the Assyrian point of view, since local officials might well give him biased views of conditions in the areas they administered. One such trusted agent was Mār-Ištar who reported on conditions in Babylonia during the last few years of Esarhaddon's reign. He seems to have been responsible for supervising the restoration of temple buildings and cultic statues and the re-organization of cultic services. His letters contain information on administrative affairs as well as astronomical and magical matters. His numerous reports mention Akkad, Babylon, Borsippa, Cutha, Dēr, Dilbat, Dūr-Šarrukku, Ḫursagkalama, Laḫīru, Nippur, Sippar, and Uruk—too large an area to have been under the political authority of a single local official. The exact nature of his authority is not clear. Although he appears to have been able to issue direct orders to the chief local officials (including governors) on his own, without specific direction from the king, when dealing with these officials he

---

127 Borger, *Esarh.*, p. 20 §11 episode 21, p. 52 §27 episode 12, p. 76 §48:14-15, p. 77 §49:14-15, and p. 77 §50:16-17. It is not improbable that two (or all) of these occurred in the course of the same visit to Babylonia. General statements by Esarhaddon to have built such-and-such a temple or to have returned the statue of such-and-such a god to its temple are not considered to be evidence of a real claim by him to have been present at the accomplishment of the act.

128 *VAS* 5 2 (*B-K* I.16). The name of one of the *qurbūtu*-officials contains the divine name Aššur, suggesting that he was an Assyrian. One of the *qurbūtu*-officials was in charge of the harbours (*ša muḫḫi karrānu*) and the other in charge of outlying districts (*ša muḫḫi birranāti*).

generally asked the king to issue orders that matters be examined or corrected. The fact that he reported directly to the king on a wide range of topics shows that his position was of some importance and that his reports were valued.[129]

As one method of checking unrest in Babylonia, Esarhaddon appears to have held certain Babylonians hostage in Assyria,[130] presumably as guaranty for their relatives' loyalty to Assyria. Some may have been boys to be educated in a proper pro-Assyrian attitude, with the intention that they would one day assume positions of authority in Babylonia.

Esarhaddon frequently consulted Assyrian and Babylonian scholars and diviners and listened to reports from ecstatic prophets. In contrast to the situation with regards to the reigns of Sargon and Sennacherib, large numbers of omen queries and religious and astrological reports have been preserved from this king's reign. This could simply be an accident of discovery, but the large number of such texts and the evident concern expressed in certain of Esarhaddon's letters to receive reports from these people would suggest otherwise. This is supported by the fact that the king's royal inscriptions frequently refer to celestial signs and other omens.[131] The omen queries sought information about political and military matters concerning both his empire and its neighbours (e.g., the success of campaigns and the possibility of insurrection), the appointment of officials, and the health of the king and his family.[132] Esarhaddon was clearly interested in determining the will of the gods and his own fate. In Mesopotamian culture, however, it was commonly believed that one could determine the will of the gods and alter or avoid one's fate by performing certain actions. Thus, Esarhaddon should not necessarily be considered abnormally superstitious.[133] Acting upon the advice of scholars, on perhaps eight separate occasions Esarhaddon relinquished his throne to a substitute (*šar pūḫi*) for a period of time in order that evil portended for the king by certain lunar eclipses might affect the substitute

---

129 See Parpola, *LAS*, nos. 275-297, with special reference to nos. 275 (*ABL* 746), 276 (*ABL* 340), 277 (*ABL* 476), 280 (*ABL* 437), 281 (*ABL* 1202), 284 (*CT* 53 75), 291 (*ABL* 1214), and 293 (*ABL* 339). A view of Mār-Ištar's actions may also be gained from a letter from the head of the Esagila temple in Babylon to the king (Landsberger, *Brief*, pp. 5-13). Landsberger, *Brief*, pp. 38-57 discusses the career of Mār-Ištar and see also Pecírková, *ArOr* 53 (1985): 165-67. Parpola (*LAS* 2, p. XVI) describes Mār-Ištar as being connected with the "inner circle" of persons advising the king; thus his "career" in Babylonia may have been an atypical one. For the date of Mār-Ištar's activities, see *ibid.* 2, p. 418.

130 See Parpola, *Iraq* 34 (1972): 33-34 and pl. 19 lines 37-39.

131 See Cogan in *HHI*, pp. 78-80.

132 See Parpola, *LAS*; Thompson, *Rep.*; 4 *R* pl. 68; and Starr, *SAA* 4. With regard to Neo-Assyrian prophecies, see Weippert's articles in *ARINH*, pp. 71-115 and in K.R. Veenhof, *Schrijvend Verleden: Documenten uit het Oude Nabije Oosten Vertaald en Toegelicht* (Leiden, 1983), pp. 284-89 (with further bibliography).

133 Esarhaddon was aware that it was unwise to rely upon the interpretation or report of any one scholar/diviner and sometimes had matters checked by another person. See Lanfranchi, *SAAB* 3 (1989): 109-11.

instead.[134] Although another individual formally sat on the throne, Esarhaddon retained control and authority over affairs of state and acted under the cognomen "the Farmer" (LÚ.ENGAR). As king of both Assyria and Babylonia, he was in danger if the omens portended the death of the ruler of either land. On four occasions (in 679, 674, and twice in 671) a substitute king appears to have been enthroned in the city of Akkad, Babylonia's ancient capital.[135] At the end of his term as "ruler," the substitute was put to death. On the fourth occasion the ritual was performed in Akkad, some fear was exhibited by citizens and officials at the death of the substitute, perhaps because in this case it was the son of a high official who was killed, Damqî, the son of the temple administrator (*šatammu*) of Akkad, and not a criminal or simpleton as may have been the case previously. The official reporting to Esarhaddon on this incident claims that they were able to quiet the people.[136]

Esarhaddon's concern with the will of the gods and his fate may have been connected, at least in part, with his apparent ill health in his later years.[137] A study of references to the king's health has led S. Parpola to suggest that Esarhaddon was suffering from *lupus erythematosus disseminatus*, a lethal and (at present) incurable disease. Sufferers experience muscular pain, articular stiffness, fever, eye affection, and buzzing in the ears. Physical appearance becomes greatly altered (as a result of cutaneous eruptions, papules, blisters, etc.) and depression is a serious side effect. If Esarhaddon had this disease, it would not be surprising that he tried to determine (and perhaps alter) his fate by consulting diviners and acting upon their advice.[138]

The queen mother Zakūtu (Aramaic: Naqi'a) played an important role during the reigns of Esarhaddon and Ashurbanipal and possibly earlier.[139] She may in fact have been involved in Sennacherib's choice of Esarhaddon to be his heir; Esarhaddon is known to have had older brothers, but they may not have been sons of Zakūtu. She may also have been influential in the choice of Ashurbanipal and Šamaš-šuma-ukīn as Esarhaddon's heirs. While it has been suggested in the past that Zakūtu was of Babylonian origin and

---

[134] A detailed study of the substitute kingship ritual is found in Parpola, *LAS* 2, pp. XXII-XXXII. The following information is taken from that work.

[135] For the dates the substitute king should have been enthroned in Akkad, see Parpola, *LAS* 2, pp. XXIII, XXV, and 428-29.

[136] *ABL* 437 (*LAS*, no. 280).

[137] An omen query with regard to the reason the king was ill was composed in 672 (Starr, *SAA* 4, no. 183). The other omen queries dealing with the king's health either do not indicate the year in which the query was made or do not have the date preserved.

[138] Parpola, *LAS* 2, pp. 230-36. Parpola relied upon Dr. J. Rantasalo for medical assistance in his study of the problem. In her review of Parpola's work, M. Roth states that Dr. B. Rosner has suggested that several alternative diagnoses are possible, particularly Reiter syndrome, a cause of arthritis (*ZA* 75 [1985]: 309 n. 3).

[139] On Zakūtu, see in general Lewy, *JNES* 11 (1952): 264-86; Seux in *RLA* 6, p. 162; Borger, *ARRIM* 6 (1988): 6-7; and Grayson in *CAH* 3/2 (in press).

that she influenced Esarhaddon to treat Babylonia favourably,[140] there really is no evidence of this. On occasion Babylonian officials sent reports to her about political events,[141] although there is no proof that she ever held an official position in or over Babylonia.[142] Quite likely she had some influence over her son, and officials may have found her a useful channel of communication to the king. Possibly Esarhaddon's ill health led him to rely upon his mother for aid in carrying out his royal duties. It is well attested in the ancient and mediaeval world that a resourceful and energetic queen or queen mother could become a power behind the throne. Following the death of Esarhaddon she had influence enough to exact an oath of loyalty to Ashurbanipal from his brothers, relatives, and officials. Dedicatory and building inscriptions of hers are also known and she may be depicted on a bronze relief in a position of prominence, standing beside the Assyrian king.[143]

Of major importance to Babylonia's political future was Esarhaddon's appointment in the second month of 672 of two of his sons, Ashurbanipal and Šamaš-šuma-ukīn, as heirs to the thrones of Assyria and Babylonia respectively.[144] The ceremonies involved with their installation as crown princes lasted several days. Two of Esarhaddon's royal inscriptions state that loyalty oaths were made to the crown prince Ashurbanipal on the eighteenth day of the month. Ashurbanipal later stated that his father had gathered all the people of Assyria on an auspicious day, the twelfth (variant: eighteenth) day of the month, and had them enter into a sworn agreement (*adê nīš ilāni*) to recognize Ashurbanipal's (future) right to the throne.[145] Although Šamaš-

140 E.g., H. Lewy, *JNES* 11 (1952): 272-73 n. 42.

141 *ABL* 917; the letter is from Na'id-Marduk of the Sealand to the mother of the king and deals with troubles with Elam. Cultic matters were also of concern to her; see *ABL* 368.

142 See chapter 5.

143 Parpola, *SAA* 2, no. 8 (*ABL* 1239); *ADD* 645 (dedication to the goddesses Ninlil and Lady-of-Nineveh); Borger, *Esarh.*, pp. 115-16 §86 (construction of a palace at Nineveh for Esarhaddon); and see p. 26.

144 With regard to the succesion, see in particular Seux in *RLA* 6, pp. 156-57; Wiseman, *Treaties*, pp. 3-9; and Watanabe, *Vereidigung*, pp. 2-5. Starr, *SAA* 4, no. 149 asks whether Esarhaddon should have his son Sîn-nādin-apli enter the House-of-Succession (i.e., be the king's heir). The text does not bear a date and Sîn-nādin-apli is otherwise unknown. Either Esarhaddon had previously thought of appointing another son to be heir or Sîn-nādin-apli was renamed Ashurbanipal when he was chosen to succeed Esarhaddon (i.e., just as Esarhaddon had been renamed when he became crown prince). On this matter, see Parpola, *LAS* 2, p. 106.

145 Borger, *Esarh.*, p. 72 §43:40 and Hulin, *Iraq* 24 (1962): 116 ND 11308:63-64. Streck, *Asb.*, pp. 2-4 i 11-30 and Aynard, *Asb.*, pp. 28-31 i 10-24 (largely restored). See also Cogan, *JCS* 29 [1977]: 98-99). Oathtaking ceremonies possibly connected to this event may be described in *ABL* 33, 384, and 386 (*LAS*, nos. 2, 3, and 1 respectively; see *ibid.* 2, pp. 3-6). A similar ceremony had occurred when Esarhaddon had been formally designated heir by Sennacherib; see Borger, *Esarh.*, pp. 40-41 §27 episode 2.

šuma-ukīn is not mentioned by Ashurbanipal, it is likely that he was announced as heir to the throne of Babylon at the same time. Copies of the oaths of loyalty imposed on a number of vassal rulers, dated on sixteenth and eighteenth of the month, refer to Ashurbanipal as crown prince of Assyria and Šamaš-šuma-ukīn as crown prince of Babylon.[146] After their appointment, special concern was shown for their safety and good health.[147] The king was told that if it suited him "statues of the sons of the king" would be set up in the temple of the moon-god at Harran and this may well refer to statues of the two crown princes.[148] The two of them appear to have been depicted with Esarhaddon on his stelae from Zinjirli (fig. 1) and Til Barsip.[149] It is unclear how old the two sons were at their appointment, but Ashurbanipal was old enough to have a wife while he was crown prince.[150] Šamaš-šuma-ukīn was older than Ashurbanipal, but it is not clear that he was in fact Esarhaddon's eldest son.[151] This attempt to settle the succession to the throne(s) was intended to try to avert such strife as had occurred at the death of Sennacherib. The recent death of his beloved wife[152] coupled with his poor health may have made Esarhaddon think of his own mortality, or it may have

---

[146] Parpola and Watanabe, *SAA* 2, no. 6. Note the apparent reference to this *adê*-agreement in an inscription of Esarhaddon (Parpola and Watanabe, *SAA* 2, no. 14).

[147] For example, Marduk-šākin-šumi asked the king if prayers and rituals should be performed to protect the two crown princes from evil (*ABL* 23 rev. 9-13 [*LAS*, no. 185]) and Aššur-ušallim mentioned them in the introductory blessing of a letter he wrote to the king (*ABL* 434).

[148] *ABL* 36 (*LAS*, no. 7). Parpola (*LAS* 2, p. 10) argues that there were only two statues and that these are likely to have been statues of the two crown princes.

[149] For the stelae from Zinjirli and Til Barsip, see pp. 25-26 and Börker-Klähn, *ABVF*, nos. 217-219. On the stela from Zinjirli and on at least one of the two stelae from Til Barsip the figure which is usually identified with Ashurbanipal was placed on the side of the stela closest to the figure Esarhaddon; this required Ashurbanipal to be depicted on the left side of the stela from Zinjirli and on the right side of the one from Til Barsip. The figure usually identified with Šamaš-šuma-ukīn was thus placed on the side furthest from Esarhaddon. While this might indicate that Ashurbanipal's position was more important than that of his brother, it could instead simply reflect the fact that the area from which the stelae came would eventually be controlled by Ashurbanipal not Šamaš-šuma-ukīn. The identities of the figures on the sides of the third stela are not clear.

[150] See *ABL* 308 (for a translation, see Oppenheim, *Letters*, no. 97).

[151] See p. 96. The vassal treaties refer to older and younger sons of Ashurbanipal (Parpola and Watanabe, *SAA* 2, no. 6:69). Parpola, *LAS* 2, p. 231 n. 390, suggests that Šamaš-šuma-ukīn must have been born in 693 at the latest, under the assumption that Assyrian princes could not have entered the House-of-Succession until they were at least twenty years old; however, this remains unproven. Ashurbanipal is known to have had a wife while he was crown prince (*ABL* 308), but it is not known when he married her or how old he was at the time.

[152] His wife died on 5/6-XII-673 according to Grayson, *Chronicles*, no. 1 iv 22 and no. 14:23. Brinkman raises the possibility that she actually died a year later, in 672 (*Moran Festchrift*, pp. 94-95). This lady may be Ešarra-ḫamât (see Lambert, *RA* 63 [1969]: 65-66 and Parpola, *LAS* 2, pp. 190-91) and the funeral rites after her burial may be described in *ABL* 26, 378, and 379 (*LAS*, nos. 197, 195, and 198 respectively).

been the planned invasion of Egypt that spurred him to put the affairs of his kingdom in order.[153] By the formal installation of Ashurbanipal and Šamaš-šuma-ukīn as crown princes and the taking of oaths of allegiance by all and sundry, Esarhaddon did the best he could to ensure the desired succession, although he would undoubtedly have remembered that he himself had had to fight for the throne even though he had been the designated heir whom his brothers and the people of Assyria in general had promised to support.

The division of the realm between two sons was unprecedented, an attempt to win Babylonian support (and submission) during the remainder of Esarhaddon's reign and thereafter by promising the Babylonians their own king, and possibly to avoid strife in Assyria itself if the two brothers had strong followings within that land. Exactly what Esarhaddon intended the relationship between the two kings to be is not clear. Šamaš-šuma-ukīn is mentioned only twice in the oaths taken by Esarhaddon's Iranian vassals (once in the body of the text and once in the colophon), while Ashurbanipal appears numerous times. This could suggest that Šamaš-šuma-ukīn's position was considered less important than that of his brother, but more likely it reflects the fact that these oaths were to be taken by vassals who would have had to deal with Ashurbanipal and not his brother. No stipulations show that Šamaš-šuma-ukīn was expected to be subordinate to his brother, but the titles accorded Šamaš-šuma-ukīn may reflect a lesser status. Šamaš-šuma-ukīn is called "prince of the House-of-Succession of Babylon" on both occasions he appears, while the title accorded Ashurbanipal, who is also mentioned in both passages, was prefixed by the adjective "great" ("great prince of the House-of-Succession" and "great prince of the House-of-Succession of Assyria").[154] After the death of Esarhaddon, Ashurbanipal seems to have held final authority over Babylonia while Šamaš-šuma-ukīn was king of that land. This may well have been Esarhaddon's intent since no conflict or complaint about this arrangement is known to have arisen for sixteen years.[155]

---

153 The Assyrians marched against Egypt in the beginning of the following year (Grayson, *Chronicles*, no. 1 iv 23-28 and no. 14:25-26); cf. Starr, *SAA* 4, no. 84 (see Parpola, *LAS* 2, p. 64 n. 120). Leichty (*Tadmor Festschrift*, pp. 56-57) argues that in 673 Esarhaddon had campaigned against Šubria in order to deal with his brothers (the murderers of Sennacherib) before he appointed his successors, i.e., to eliminate possible pretenders to the throne.

154 See Parpola and Watanabe, *SAA* 2, no. 6:84-87 and 666-669. Note, however, that one exemplar omits the title "great" for Ashurbanipal and another describes Šamaš-šuma-ukīn by that term (see *ibid.*, no. 6:667 and 669; the latter variant is omitted from the list of variants on p. 58 but is found on the microfiche at the back of the volume).

155 It is suggested in the following chapter that Ashurbanipal held a type of "protectorship" over Babylonia, controlling its foreign affairs and defence and that Babylonia was in effect a vassal state of Assyria.

The king's plans for the succession caused some astonishment. Adad-šuma-uṣur, the king's exorcist, praised the decision but commented that "the king, my lord, has done upon earth what has not been done in heaven"; while he had appointed one son to succeed him in Assyria, his eldest son (*apilka rabû*) was to be king of Babylonia.[156] It is thus clear that Šamaš-šuma-ukīn was older than Ashurbanipal though they may not have had the same mother.[157] Possibly Ashurbanipal was the son of Esarhaddon's principal (or favourite) wife while Šamaš-šuma-ukīn was the eldest son of a secondary wife. It was not the succession of a younger son which was unprecedented; Esarhaddon himself had not been Sennacherib's eldest son. It was the division of the realm between two brothers that caused for comment. It has sometimes been stated that the mother of Šamaš-šuma-ukīn was a Babylonian; however, this is based upon an ambiguous statement in a bilingual inscription from the time of Šamaš-šuma-ukīn which says that the goddess Erua had designated him to rule the people ki sig_7-alam ama-ugu-mu / *a-šar nab-ni-it um-mi a-lit-ti-ia*. The passage can be interpreted to mean that he had been designated to rule the place where his mother had been born or that he had been chosen to rule while he was still in his mother's womb. The idea that an individual could chosen by the gods before his birth is well attested in Mesopotamian tradition.[158] While it would seem logical that Esarhaddon might have decided to entrust the future rulership of Babylonia to Šamaš-šuma-ukīn because the latter's mother came from that land, there is in fact no other evidence that she did so.

While heir-designate to the throne of Babylon, Šamaš-šuma-ukīn assumed some authority over his future realm. As required by loyalty oaths presumably imposed as a result of his appointment, he now received reports

---

156 *CT* 53 31:5-11 (*LAS*, no. 129 and Deller in *lišān mitḫurti*, pp. 56-57).

157 See also Parpola, *LAS* 2, pp. 116-17. Šamaš-šuma-ukīn was mentioned first, immediately preceding Ashurbanipal (actually the tomb for Ashurbanipal), in a document listing amounts of food for various children of Esarhaddon (Weidner, *AfO* 13 [1939-41]: 214 and pl. 14). A late Aramaic text (Amherst papyrus 63) describes Ashurbanipal as having been born before Šamaš-šuma-ukīn (see Steiner and Nims, *RB* 92 [1985]: 70 and Vleeming and Wesselius, *Studies* 1, p. 33); however, it may have done so under the (mistaken) assumption that as king of Assyria and overlord of Babylonia Ashurbanipal would naturally have been the elder of the two, or because it felt that the hero of the tale, Ashurbanipal, should be the elder. Watanabe (*Vereidigung*, p. 3) believes that the two were both sons of Esarhaddon's main wife, Ešarra-ḫamât.

158 Lehmann, *Ššmk*, no. 1 i 6 and ii 6. Compare in particular the description of Ashurbanipal having been created by the gods to become ruler of Assyria while he was still in his mother's womb (Streck, *Asb.*, pp. 2-3 i 3-5). On this matter, see Borger, *Esarh.*, p. 88 commentary to lines 13-14, and *BiOr* 29 (1972): 34; Landsberger, *WO* 3 (1964-66): 77 n. 116; *CAD* 1/1 (A), p. 340; Seux, *Épithètes*, p. 292 and n. 154; and most recently Jacobsen, *Tadmor Festschrift*, pp. 279-81.

from Babylonia which he then passed on to Esarhaddon.[159] We might expect that Šamaš-šuma-ukīn would visit or take up residence in Babylonia at this time, but, while there are indications that he might have done so (the presence of some of his servants/officials in Laḫīru and Labbanat), there is as yet no clear proof. References to his servants or officials being in Babylonia (or across the border in Laḫīru),[160] officials in Babylonia writing to him, concern by Babylonians for his welfare, and rites and ceremonies being performed for him in Babylonia are only circumstantial evidence; these would be expected whether or not he was actually present.[161] Certainly he was in Assyria at one point when he fell ill[162] and again later when he took the statue of Marduk back to Babylon in 668. Ashurbanipal also seems to have assumed some authority over his future realm. He later claimed that he issued orders to the great men (of the land) in the presence of his father and that no governor was appointed without his approval.[163] While this could simply refer to a period of training under the supervision of his father, it is also possible that illness on the part of Esarhaddon, or possibly his preoccupation with other matters (e.g., the campaign to Egypt), made it necessary or desirable for Ashurbanipal to take over some of the king's duties.[164]

Toward the end of Esarhaddon's reign, when information is more abundant, it appears that Assyrian control over Babylonia was somewhat lax. At some point between Šamaš-šuma-ukīn's appointment as heir and the death of Esarhaddon the persons who had delivered up Sennacherib's son Aššur-nādin-šumi to Elam in 694 were alive and free in Babylonia, presumably

159 See the letter edited by Parpola in *Iraq* 34 (1972): 21-34 and pl. 19. *ABL* 534-536 were sent by Šamaš-šuma-ukīn to his father, but the exact dates of these are unknown. *ABL* 535 and 536 are fragmentary and *ABL* 534 is quite brief; thus none provides much useful information. Note also the letter to "the son of the king" reporting on the actions of Ningal-iddin's son Sîn-balāssu-iqbi (*ABL* 445). Although the letter is Assyrian and the name of the author not given, the reference to Sîn-balāssu-iqbi and the introductory blessing mentioning Nabû and Marduk suggest that the letter was sent by a Babylonian. Waterman (*RCAE* 1, p. 311) assumes the addressee was the crown prince Ashurbanipal; while this seems reasonable, it is not impossible that the letter was sent to Šamaš-šuma-ukīn.

160 See *ADD* 625 (Kwasman, *NALD*, no. 46; contract composed on 1-II-670 involving land in the area of Laḫīru leased by Atar-ilī, the *ša rēši* of the crown prince of Babylon) and possibly *ABL* 32 (*LAS*, no. 29; see *ibid.* 2, pp. 32-33).

161 The presence of Šamaš-šuma-ukīn in Babylonia during this period has been argued most strongly by H. Lewy (*JNES* 11 [1952]: 275-76) and more recently by Parpola (*LAS* 2, p. 271); in particular it is thought that Šamaš-šuma-ukīn resided in Laḫīru for at least some of this time. The exact interpretation of the circumstances described in *ABL* 1383 (*LAS*, no. 70), which is used by Parpola to indicate a journey by Šamaš-šuma-ukīn from Babylonia to Assyria, is uncertain.

162 *ABL* 439 (*LAS*, no. 140).

163 Streck, *Asb.*, pp. 258-59 i 27-28. It may be during this period that Ashurbanipal wrote several letters to his father: *ABL* 1001, 1026(+)*CT* 53 226, and 1257; *CT* 53 147.

164 See Parpola, *LAS* 2 pp. 235-36; note Parpola's references to the "(joint) rule of the king and the (crown) prince."

stirring up trouble.[165] Some fugitives from Assyria (quite possibly individuals who had been implicated in a conspiracy against Esarhaddon) were actually given refuge by the *qīpu*-official, who later sent them on to Borsippa.[166] Elsewhere it was proposed by a son of Ningal-iddin (likely Sîn-balāssu-iqbi) that he block a canal in order to withhold water from those who relied upon it;[167] presumably those to be deprived of water were being punished for some action or were being coerced into submission. The letters of Mār-Ištar, Esarhaddon's special envoy, reveal instances of poor management and corruption in some Babylonian cities. There was civil unrest at Babylon when the governors of Babylon, Borsippa, and Cutha imposed heavy taxes upon their citizens; the governor of Babylon had some of the protestors imprisoned upon the (supposedly) trumped up charge that they had thrown clumps of earth at his messengers.[168] At Borsippa, the shepherds of animals belonging to Nabû had bribed their governor and the administrative head of the temple with the result that there was no accounting of the animals and offerings were not being made in the way the king had commanded.[169] The governor of Dūr-Šarrukku had taken silver and animals belonging to the gods Šimaliya (Šimalū'a) and Ḫumḫum without proper authorization.[170] The governor of Cutha may also have been accused of having illegally taken property of the citizens of Cutha.[171] Finally, in one fell swoop, the *qīpu*-officials of the temples of Cutha, Dilbat, Ḫursagkalama, and Sippar were dismissed and new ones appointed; the reason for this action is unknown, but likely they were being dismissed for mismanagement or corruption.[172]

The dates and manner in which Ningal-iddin assumed and relinguished the governorship of Ur are uncertain. We know from a comparison of chronicles

---

165 Parpola, *Iraq* 34 (1972): 22-23 and pl. 19:26-30; Parpola dates the text to 670 (*ibid.*, pp. 27-28).

166 Landsberger, *Brief*, p. 11 lines 33-37. Landsberger states that the *qīpu*-official served in Babylon (ibid., p. 6); this is reasonable since the author of the letter, Šuma-iddin, was likely the *šatammu* of Esagila (see Appendix B sub 2c) and since the letter refers to work on Esagila and the (other) temples of Babylon.

167 *CT* 53 75 rev. 14-18 (*LAS*, no. 284).

168 *ABL* 340:23-rev. 23 (*LAS*, no. 276).

169 *ABL* 1202 (*LAS*, no. 281).

170 *ABL* 339 (*LAS*, no. 293); this city may have been annexed to Assyria at this time (see pp. 222-24).

171 *CT* 53 75 rev. 19-21 (*LAS*, no. 284); for the restoration of rev. 21, see Parpola, *LAS* 2, p. 282.

172 *ABL* 1214 rev. 4-9 (*LAS*, no. 291). Parpola (*ibid.* 2, p. 296) suggests that the dismissal may have been occasioned by evil portents which had just occurred. There are several other possible instances of problems in Babylonia about this time. *ABL* 349 refers to civil unrest in Borsippa; Röllig dates this letter to *c.* 675, but without giving any reason for this dating (*RLA* 5, p. 232). If restored correctly, *ABL* 23 rev. 21-25 (*LAS*, no. 185) refers to rebellious plots conceived by Babylonians; Parpola dates this letter to the year 671 (*ibid.* 2, pp. 176-77).

and royal inscriptions that he was governor in 680 and from economic texts that he held office for at least twelve years. As mentioned in the previous chapter, Ningal-iddin may have been become governor around the time of the rebellion of 693-689 and the two texts dated by his eighth and twelfth years may well come from sometime during the last eight years of Sennacherib's reign, though they could conceivably date to the reign of Esarhaddon since no texts dated by the regnal years of that king have been found at Ur. There is no evidence suggesting that Ningal-iddin was alive in the reign of Ashurbanipal, and Sîn-balāssu-iqbi, one of his sons, is attested as governor in 658.[173] Since Sîn-balāssu-iqbi could send the large sum of one mina of gold to Sāsiya, an official, during the reign of Esarhaddon,[174] and since an individual simply referred to as the "son of Ningal-iddin" could act independently, and presumably with some official position or recognition, during the reign of that king,[175] it seems possible that Ningal-iddin had left office and been replaced by Sîn-balāssu-iqbi during the time of Esarhaddon. Ningal-iddin held an important position in the provincial administration of Babylonia. Texts were dated by the years of his tenure in office; his position passed in turn to three of his sons, Sîn-balāssu-iqbi, Sîn-šarra-uṣur, and Sîn-tabni-uṣur;[176] and *ABL* 223 (*LAS*, no. 30) mentions (ranks?) him with two of the most important individuals in Babylonia: Šamaš-ibni, the "king" of Bīt-Dakkūri, and Na'id-Marduk, the governor of the Sealand. *ADD* 930, an account of valuables belonging to Babylonian deities (including the Lady-of-Akkad), some of which had apparently been in Elam, may date to the twelfth month of 674, when the gods of Akkad taken to Elam were returned to Babylonia (see above). This text suggests that Ningal-iddin had been in Elam before that time and that while there had taken a silver object weighing fifteen minas.[177] Possibly he had gone to Elam in order to help escort the divine statues back to Elam and had taken this object into his custody in order to safeguard it on the journey back. It has sometimes been suggested that

173 See Appendix B sub 14a. For Sîn-balāssu-iqbi, see in particular Brinkman, *Or.* NS 34 (1965): 248-53. *ABL* 920, a letter from a son of Ningal-iddin to Ashurbanipal, states that certain persons had served Ningal-iddin during the time of the present king's (Ashurbanipal's) fathers (lines 7-12). This could imply that Ningal-iddin had not lived (or remained in office) into the reign of Ashurbanipal, though it could simply indicate that these persons had left Ningal-iddin's service before Ashurbanipal became king of Assyria.

174 *ABL* 445. The title that Sāsiya (PN written in its Assyrian form, Sāsî) bore in rev. 1 is not clear. I am informed by Parpola that his collation of the passage shows that Harper's LÚ *ḫa-za-nu* [*ša*] DUMU MAN ("mayor [of] the son of the king") may be LÚ *ḫa-za-nu* [*ša*] ⌜URU x⌝, where x could be either NINA or KASKAL.

175 *CT* 53 75 rev. 14-18 (*LAS*, no. 284); Parpola dates this letter to 670 (*ibid.* 2, p. 278).

176 See Appendix B sub 14a and Appendix C.

177 *ADD* 930 i ("ii") 7-10; see Postgate, *Taxation*, pp. 311-14 and Parpola, *ZA* 65 (1975): 295-96. Ningal-iddin took the silver object "in exchange(?)" ([*ina p*]*u-ḫi it-ti-ši*); the use of the term "in exchange" is unclear (see Postgate, *FNALD*, p. 37 §3.2.4).

Ningal-iddin and his colleague Na'id-Marduk of the Sealand were removed from office for disloyalty, by 675 at the latest and possibly already in 678, but there is no real evidence to support the idea that they were deposed.[178] Exemplars of Esarhaddon's inscription which refers to Ningal-iddin as his loyal subject (*ardu dāgil pāniya*) and which states that Na'id-Marduk brought tribute to Nineveh year by year without fail were composed in 673. If the two officials had proved disloyal and been removed from office or killed, these passages might have been altered.[179] Furthermore, reference to their punishment might well have been made in the chronicles since these mention the punishment of some other important Babylonian officials during the reign of Esarhaddon.[180] As far as we can tell, under Ningal-iddin and his sons Sîn-

[178] For the view that Ningal-iddin of Ur and Na'id-Marduk of the Sealand were removed from office, see Dietrich, *Aramäer*, pp. 33-36 and Parpola, *LAS* 2, p. 37. This view is based primarily upon interpretations of events described in *ABL* 917, *CT* 54 527, and *ABL* 223 (*LAS*, no. 30). In *ABL* 917, Na'id-Marduk criticized a "son of Ningal-iddin" for having written to the king of Elam at a time when there was some conflict between the Sealand and Elam. It is proposed from this that the son had been acting on his father's command or had been imitating his father in being in league with Assyria's enemy. *CT* 54 527 is taken to indicate that Ningal-iddin and Šamaš-ibni had been in league with Ṣillaya against Assyria because the letter appears to state that Ṣillaya had been lying when he had told Chaldean leaders that he wanted to kill Ningal-iddin and Šamaš-ibni. *ABL* 223 is said to show Ṣillaya trying to stir up rebellion by referring to three prominent Babylonians—Ningal-iddin, Šamaš-ibni, and Na'id-Marduk—who had suffered a humiliating fate. The case against Ningal-iddin and Na'id-Marduk has not been proven. In brief, *ABL* 917 does not refer to Ningal-iddin at all and could merely imply that one of his sons had not been as careful with regard to his contacts with Elam as Na'id-Marduk had. *CT* 54 527 is badly damaged and the context in which Ṣillaya made his statement is lacking. Ṣillaya may have been lying to the Chaldeans only to give them a false idea of his plans; it is not necessary to assume that Šamaš-ibni and Ningal-iddin were actually in league with him or were themselves allied in all matters. Finally, it is possible that *ABL* 223 simply shows Ṣillaya trying to determine how Ningal-iddin, Na'id-Marduk and Šamaš-ibni stood with regard to anti-Assyrian actions. (Parpola's original interpretation of *ABL* 223 was based upon his dating of the letter to 674; he later determined that 679 was more likely [see *LAS* 2, p. 516].) One could use *ADD* 930 (see above) to suggest that Ningal-iddin had taken refuge in Elam for some reason and acquired the silver object "illegally" before it could be sent back to Babylonia, but due to the damaged condition of the text, the exact circumstances behind the event are open to more than one interpretation. For another interpretation of the letter, see above. In sum, there is no reason to assume that Ningal-iddin and Na'id-Marduk were removed from office for collusion with Šamaš-ibni or Ṣillaya, or for any disloyalty to Assyria.

[179] Borger, *Esarh.*, pp. 46-47 §27 episode 4; for the dates of A^1, A^2, and A^{16}, see *ibid.*, p. 64. However, it cannot be considered absolutely certain from this that the two were still in office in 673. If they had died or been replaced for reasons unconnected with disloyalty, the scribes may simply not have bothered to state that the two were no longer in office. The fact that one of Ningal-iddin's sons freely referred to his father by name in a letter to Ashurbanipal (*ABL* 920:11-12 and cf. *ABL* 1248:4-6 as restored by Dietrich, *Aramäer*, pp. 136-37 no. 6) may suggest that he felt there was no reason to avoid mentioning his father to the king (i.e., his father had not fallen out of favour with Assyria).

[180] Grayson, *Chronicles*, no. 1 iv 1-2 and 14-15, and no. 14:10-11 and 19.

balāssu-iqbi and Sîn-tabni-uṣur Ur was a bastion of pro-Assyrian sentiment in southern Babylonia, an area whose tribal groups frequently provided support for rebel movements.[181]

The execution of a large number of important individuals (LÚ.GAL.MEŠ) in Assyria is recorded for 670 by two chronicles and possibly referred to in two letters.[182] This does not appear to have been complemented by any similar measure in the south, or by any unrest there, although some persons fleeing from Esarhaddon's wrath on that occasion may have sought refuge in Babylonia.[183] In spite of all Esarhaddon's efforts to win Babylonia's acceptance of Assyrian rule, the country was still a likely place of asylum for those fleeing Assyrian anger.

In summary, during his reign Esarhaddon made great efforts to win the support of Babylonia and to promote peace between Assyria and Babylonia. Nevertheless, Babylonia remained restless under Assyrian control. Although no major countrywide revolt occurred, the texts show that there was frequent unrest, highlighted by several local rebellions and that Esarhaddon found it necessary to send Assyrian troops south on a number of occasions in order to restore order.[184] Resistance to Assyrian rule appears to have been led most often by Chaldean tribal leaders and to have frequently involved governors of Nippur. The Aramean tribes appear to have remained quiet; in fact an Aramean leader was even entrusted with the task of guarding the border against Elam.[185] On occasion the rebels were supported by Elam; however, this country's policy vis-à-vis Assyria was not consistent. On the one hand Elam aided Nabû-ušallim and invaded Sippar, and on the other hand it killed Nabû-zēr-kitti-līšir and apparently made a treaty with Esarhaddon in the time of Urtak. Still, Esarhaddon was able to pass the thrones of Assyria and Babylonia to his sons peacefully and to leave Babylonia in such condition that no rebellion broke out there for another sixteen years.

---

181 The sentiments of Ningal-iddin's third son, Sîn-šarra-uṣur, are less clear, and it is possible that he came to support Šamaš-šuma-ukīn against Ashurbanipal.

182 Grayson, *Chronicles*, no. 1 iv 29 and no. 14:27; *ABL* 1217 and 584+1370 (*LAS*, no. 247). The executions apparently took place in the month of Nisannu (see Larsen, *RA* 68 [1974]: 22 and Parpola, *LAS* 2, p. 238). With regard to *ABL* 1217, see Parpola, *LAS* 2, p. 464 no. 59. Parpola identifies those being punished as the individuals who had conspired with, or on behalf of, Sāsî (*LAS* 2, pp. 238-40). With regard to Sāsî (Babylonian Sāsiya), see pp. 85-86 n. 112.

183 Landsberger, *Brief*, p. 11:33-35. The references to Mār-Ištar (lines 10 and 46) point to the end of Esarhaddon's reign when he was active in Babylonia. *CT* 53 75:24-25 (*LAS*, no. 284) may also refer to this incident.

184 Against Nabû-zēr-kitti-līšir (leader of the Sealand and head of the Chaldean tribe of Bīt-Yakīn) in 680, Šamaš-ibni (the head of the Chaldean tribe of Bīt-Dakkūri) in 678, and the town of Šamēlē (located in the area of the Bīt-Amukāni) in 674.

185 Although Esarhaddon may simply have been recognizing the fact that the individual (Bēl-iqīša of the Gambūlu tribe) controlled that region.

CHAPTER 7

ASHURBANIPAL, KING OF ASSYRIA, AND ŠAMAŠ-ŠUMA-UKĪN, KING OF BABYLONIA (669-653)

After ruling for twelve years, Esarhaddon died on the tenth day of Araḫsamna (VIII) in 669 while on a campaign to Egypt.[1] Of the three Assyrian kings during the period 689-627, he was the only one who was not obliged to become involved in an all-out conflict with Babylonia at some point during his reign.[2] His plans for the royal succession were carried out smoothly, and in the ninth month of that year his son Ashurbanipal became king of Assyria.[3] Assyria reached the height of its power during the reign of Ashurbanipal, with his victories in Egypt and Elam. Babylonia remained quiet during the first part of his reign and, from the evidence of increasing economic activity and ambitious building programmes, appears to have prospered.

Soon after Ashurbanipal ascended the throne, his grandmother Zakūtu, who had proven herself influential during the reign of Esarhaddon, imposed an oath of allegiance on behalf of her grandson upon Šamaš-šuma-ukīn, his other brothers, relatives, officials, and the citizens of Assyria. They were not to discuss, propose, or perform any act against Ashurbanipal, king of Assyria, but were to report any talk of rebellion to him and Zakūtu, and to arrest any individual who tried to instigate a rebellion or spoke seditiously. Šamaš-šuma-ukīn is given no royal title in the text, though he is called Ashurbanipal's favourite brother (*aḫi talīmešu*). It thus seems likely that the incident must be dated to the brief period between Ashurbanipal's accession to the throne of Assyria and that of Šamaš-šuma-ukīn to the throne of Babylonia. The facts that it was Zakūtu, and not Ashurbanipal, who imposed the oath and that people were to report to her as well as Ashurbanipal show that she maintained her influential position into the reign of her grandson.[4]

---

1 Grayson, *Chronicles*, no. 1 iv 30-32 and no. 14:28-30 (day restored).

2 Sennacherib's conflict with Babylonia had actually taken place before the period of interest here.

3 Grayson, *Chronicles*, no. 14:34.

4 *ABL* 1239 (Parpola and Watanabe, *SAA* 2, no. 8). Loyalty oaths to the Assyrian king were also taken in various cities of Babylonia (see *ABL* 202 [translated as Oppenheim, *Letters*, no. 91]), but the exact date this was done is not clear (possibly after the revolt of 652-648).

Šamaš-šuma-ukīn[5] assumed the kingship of Babylonia the following year when he took to Babylon a statue of the god Marduk.[6] In theory he was returning the statue taken by his grandfather at the sack of Babylon, but in practice he may have been bringing a new one, since the original statue may well have been destroyed in 689. Late in the month of Nisannu in 668 (23-I),

---

[5] The name Šamaš-šuma-ukīn means "The-God-Šamaš-Has-Established-A-Name (i.e., a son)." On the writing of the royal name, see Lehmann, *Ššmk*, pp. 6-16 and *ZK* 2 (1885): 360-64; and Streck, *Asb.*, pp. CCXLIV-CCXLVI. In Akkadian chronological texts (kinglists and chronicles) the name is written $^{\mathrm{(m)d}}$GIŠ.NU$_{11}$-MU-GI.NA (Synchronistic Kinglist iv 14; Grayson, *Chronicles*, no. 1 iv 33-34, no. 14:35 and 40 [partially restored], no. 15:2 and 7 [partially restored], and no. 16:5 and 9) and ^{m}20-MU (Babylonian Kinglist A iv 21). Similar to the latter writing is 20-MU-GIN in the late Babylonian astronomical text *LBAT* 1417 ii' 1 and iii' 1, and perhaps in BM 33809:5 (reading unclear [information courtesy C.B.F. Walker]; on this text, see p. 18). In other cuneiform texts (letters, economic texts, royal inscriptions, etc.), $^{\mathrm{(m)d}}$GIŠ.NU$_{11}$-MU-GI.NA is again the predominate form, used approximately 90 per cent of the time. The following variations to this have been noted:

$^{\mathrm{(m)d}}$GIŠ.NU$_{11}$-	a) omission of divine determinative (*TCL* 12 8:37; Starr, *SAA* 4, nos. 282 rev. 7 and 283 rev. 5; *CT* 35 pl. 38 rev. 10, 14, 17 and 21; Wiseman, *Treaties*, pl. 49 no. 44B:4' [only the first text is not Assyrian])
	b) ^{md}GIŠ.NU$_{11}$.GAL (Starr, *SAA* 4, no. 290:22; Bauer, *Asb.*, pl. 3 v 9)
	c) NU for NU$_{11}$ (*ABL* 117:5, 534:2, 536:2, 740 rev. 19; *BRM* 1 34:31! [copy: GIŠ.ŠÚ]; it is not absolutely certain that *ABL* 534 and 536 refer to the son of Esarhaddon)
	d) NA for NU$_{11}$ (*ABL* 1106:14'; probably an error)
	e) followed by the gloss UTU (Starr, *SAA* 4, no. 285 rev. 2'; the gloss is not indicated by Starr, but is copied and noted by Klauber [*PRT*, p. 119 and pl. 64 no. 113]; collation by C.B.F. Walker confirms its presence)
-MU-	a) omitted (Hunger, *Bagh. Mitt.* 5 [1970]: 293 no. 18:18; *TCL* 12 8:37; 81-7-27,204:16; 3 *R* pl. 35 no. 6:5'; Lehmann, *Ššmk*, no. 8:11 and 19)
-GI.NA	a) omission of NA in several texts (e.g., Wiseman, *Treaties*, pl. 2 ii 86 and Lehmann, *Ššmk*, no. 13 iv 14)
	b) GIN for GI.NA in about ten texts (e.g., *CT* 54 17:5, 9 and rev. 15; *VAS* 4 5:19; and *BRM* 1 37:12)
	c) -⌈GIN⌉-*i* [*n*?] (*CT* 53 130:9; see Parpola, *LAS*, no.150)

On no occasion is the first part of the name written ^{d}UTU, the normal writing for Šamaš, although as noted above, the gloss UTU does follow ^{md}GIŠ.NU$_{11}$ in one text. (Note also the comments below, p. 154 n. 101.)

With regard to non-Akkadian texts, the name appears in the Ptolemaic Canon as Σαοσδουχίνου (var. Σαοσδουλιχίνου; see Wachsmuth, *Einleitung*, p. 305), in Berossos as Sammuges, Hamugios and Samoges (see Schnabel, *Berossos*, pp. 269-70), and in an Aramaic text in demotic script as srm(w)gy (Semitic interpretation; see Steiner and Nims, *RB* 92 [1985]: 70-80 xvii 10-11, 15, 16-17, passim).

[6] Grayson, *Chronicles*, nos. 1 iv 34-36 and 14:35-36. The former chronicle implies that both Ashurbanipal and Šamaš-šuma-ukīn ascended their thrones in 669 though it does indicate that the following year was Šamaš-šuma-ukīn's accession year (iv 33-34).

diviners in Assyria were instructed to perform an extispicy to determine whether Šamaš, the god of omens and oracles, and Marduk approved of Šamaš-šuma-ukīn's taking Marduk's statue from Assur to Babylon in the course of that year. Undoubtedly it was Ashurbanipal who ordered that the gods be consulted on this matter. At the same time, he may have been seeking to know whether the gods favoured Esarhaddon's plans for Šamaš-šuma-ukīn since his brother was not called "king of Babylon" or "crown prince of Babylon" in the oracle query.[7] The answer must have been positive since in the following month Šamaš-šuma-ukīn escorted Marduk and other Babylonian gods back to Babylon amidst great pomp and rejoicing. All along the way, from the quay of the city of Assur to the quay of Babylon, offerings were made and bonfires lighted; festivities went on night and day. Various local deities awaited the coming of Marduk at the river bank, and the gods Nergal, Nabû, and Šamaš even left their cities of Cutha, Borsippa, and Sippar to go to Babylon to celebrate the great god's return.[8]

The return of the god Marduk with the new king would have been an auspicious beginning to the reign of Šamaš-šuma-ukīn. Although both the god and the king were "gifts," impositions that the Babylonians would have little choice but to accept, the sight of Marduk, coming hand in hand with Šamaš-šuma-ukīn, ready to offer again his protection and patronage to the land, would have helped the new king win the support of Babylonians. While the statue of Marduk may well have been a new one, fashioned by Esarhaddon's artisans and considered by Assyrians to be the progeny of the Assyrian god Aššur,[9] there is no evidence that Babylonians did other than

---

[7] Starr, *SAA* 4, no. 262. Cf. *ibid.*, nos. 263 (query asking if Šamaš-šuma-ukīn should take Marduk back to Babylon; date not preserved) and 264-265 (queries asking if Marduk should be put on a boat and sent back to Babylon in the coming year; dates not preserved) which may also come from this time. Note also the undated query *ibid.*, no. 266 which asks if a particular individual should be appointed to a position in the shrine of the god Marduk. It is uncertain if the position was in a temple in Babylonia or in one in Assyria. If the former, the appointment may have been connected with preparations for the return of the statue of Marduk to Babylon. The name of the individual to make the appointment is not preserved. Despite Starr's restoration indicating that it was Ashurbanipal, is it possible that it was Šamaš-šuma-ukīn?

[8] The best description of the return of Marduk to Babylon is found in Ashurbanipal's "Schooldays" text (Streck, *Asb.*, pp. 262-69 ii 26-iii 30); this description is very reminiscent of that of Esarhaddon when he claimed to have returned the statue of Marduk (Borger, *Esarh.*, pp. 88-89 §57 rev. 17-24). The exact date of Marduk's re-entry into Babylon is uncertain. The Babylonian Chronicle and the Esarhaddon Chronicle state that it was on 24/25-II-668 (Grayson, *Chronicles*, nos. 1 iv 36 and 14:36). The reading of the exact day upon which it took place is uncertain in both texts; see the collations by Brinkman in *Moran Festschrift*, p. 90. The Akītu Chronicle states that it was on 24-II-668 (Grayson, *Chronicles*, no. 16:7). Frymer-Kensky (*JAOS* 103 [1983]: 140-41) argues that the return of the Babylonian gods to Babylon was what prompted the composition of the so-called "Marduk Ordeal" text. On this text, see pp. 58-59.

[9] See above, pp. 56-57.

welcome it and accept Marduk's return as totally legitimate. For twenty years Marduk had been absent from Babylon and the New Year's festival had not been able to take place.[10] Now the important ceremonies could again be performed.[11]

In his votive and building inscriptions from Babylonia dated before the outbreak of rebellion in 652, Ashurbanipal proudly claimed that it was he who had allowed Marduk to return to Babylon and had appointed Šamaš-šuma-ukīn to the kingship of Babylonia (never mentioning Esarhaddon's wishes).[12] The fact that Ashurbanipal allowed his brother to take up the kingship of Babylonia shows that he was willing, or felt obliged, to carry out his father's wishes and to risk the possibility that his brother might one day oppose him. Not to have done so might have caused civil war in Assyria since Esarhaddon's wishes had been announced publicly and since Ashurbanipal had acquiesced in those wishes by his presence at the formal appointment of himself and his brother as heirs to the thrones of Assyria and Babylonia. If he called into question his brother's right to the throne of Babylonia, his own right to rule Assyria might have been threatened since he was not the eldest of Esarhaddon's sons.[13] In addition, the necessity of dealing with unrest in the western part of his empire may have made him hesitant of stirring up trouble at home. The need to determine an auspicious date for the return of the statue of Marduk, to carry out of the appropriate ceremonies, and simply for the new king of Babylonia to get from Assyria to Babylon may account for the time lag between the accession of Ashurbanipal and that of Šamaš-šuma-ukīn.

During the brief period between Ashurbanipal's accession and that of his brother, transactions were dated at Uruk by the accession year of Ashurbanipal, "king of (all) lands," on the eleventh and nineteenth days of the

---

10 Grayson, *Chronicles*, no. 14:31-33 and no. 16:1-4. The chronicles imply that a New Year's festival was held in 668, after Marduk returned. Langdon, *NBK*, Nabonid no. 8 i 23-25 states that Marduk was in Assur for twenty-one years; this may be explained by counting 689 as the first year of his exile or by noting that the statue returned to Babylon in the twenty-first year of its exile. Parpola uses *ABL* 956 rev. 6-7 (*LAS*, no. 190) to suggest that while the main statue was in exile a "spurious statue was used in the ceremonies to keep the cult of the god alive" (*LAS* 2, p. 188; Parpola dates the letter to 670). If he is correct, we must assume that the compilers of the chronicles had not considered the festivals during that time to have been valid. Note also the case of the statue of the goddess Nanaya of Uruk (see Cogan, *Imperialism*, p. 34).

11 Though note that some of the cultic furniture did not return till later in the king's reign, in 654 and 653 (Grayson, *Chronicles*, no. 15: 4-5 and see below).

12 E.g., Streck, *Asb.*, pp. 226-27:11-12 and 230-31:8-9 and 11-12. Šamaš-šuma-ukīn did not mention his brother when referring to the return of Marduk to Babylon (Lehmann, *Śšmk*, no. 1 i 14-22 and ii 14-22, and no. 2:5-8; Pinckert, *LSS* 3/4, no. 6:15-17).

13 It seems clear that Šamaš-šuma-ukīn was older than Ashurbanipal (see p. 96), and thus perhaps a more likely heir to the throne of Assyria than his brother if Esarhaddon had not declared otherwise.

month of Addaru (XII) in 669.[14] Since Šamaš-šuma-ukīn had not yet formally ascended the throne, Babylonians were undoubtedly waiting to see if Ashurbanipal would permit his brother to be installed as king and felt that it was best to date by the Assyrian king's regnal years in the meantime. The Ptolemaic Canon assigned 668, Šamaš-šuma-ukīn's accession year, to Esarhaddon (even though he had died the previous year) by giving him a reign of thirteen years and his successor Šamaš-šuma-ukīn the correct reign of twenty years.[15] Berossos, however, appears to have assigned 668 to Šamaš-šuma-ukīn by listing for him a reign of twenty-one years.[16] Although Babylonian Kinglist A and the Synchronistic Kinglist record Šamaš-šuma-ukīn as Esarhaddon's successor as ruler of Babylonia, they do not give the length of the reign of either king.[17] A fragment of what appears to be a synchronistic kinglist may give the name Ashurbanipal after that of Esarhaddon in the list of rulers of Babylonia. If so, the list may have been referring to this brief period; however, the text is very badly damaged and no conclusions should be drawn from it.[18]

The extent of Šamaš-šuma-ukīn's realm is indicated by the places at which texts were dated by the years of his reign. Such texts come from nineteen locations, including the important centres of Babylon, Borsippa, Cutha, Dilbat, Ḫursagkalama, Kish, Nippur, Sippar, Ur, and Uruk (see Appendix

---

14 YBC 4016 and BM 118975, with duplicates BM 118969 and MAH 15976 (*B-K* J.1-J.4 respectively).

15 This explanation for the statement in the Ptolemaic Canon that Esarhaddon had a reign of thirteen years is in contrast to that proposed in Grayson, *Chronicles*, p. 240 where the thirteenth year was assigned to the end of Sennacherib's reign under the mistaken assumption that the Ptolemaic Canon only gave seven years for that period.

16 Schnabel, *Berossos*, pp. 269 line 29 and 270 line 7. Note, however, that the immediately preceding statements on the lengths of the reigns of Sennacherib and Esarhaddon are incorrect; they are assigned eighteen and eight years respectively, not the twenty-four and twelve known historically.

17 See Grayson in *RLA* 6, pp. 93 and 120; the lengths of their reigns are not preserved in the former source and not given in the latter. The exact interpretation of the Uruk Kinglist at this point is unclear; see Borger, *AfO* 25 (1974-77): 165-66 and Grayson in *RLA* 6, pp. 97-98.

One Babylonian economic text, BM 26630 (*B-K* K.2), records an intercalary sixth month at Borsippa in the first year of Šamaš-šuma-ukīn (667) and two others, YBC 9120 and duplicate YBC 11391(*B-K* K.10-11), record an intercalary sixth month at Babylon in his second year (666). (The list of intercalary months in Parpola, *LAS* 2, pp. 381-82 erroneously dates the second instance to 667 and does not mention the former document.) Thus, two years in a row would have had an intercalary sixth month. If the texts from Babylon had erroneously considered 668 to have been Šamaš-šuma-ukīn's first regnal year (assuming he ascended the throne at the same time as Ashurbanipal), then both transactions could date to 667. Up till this period, however, months were not always intercalated in regular patterns; thus two successive years could conceivably have had intercalary months.

18 *KAV* 9 iv 5'-6'; see Grayson in *lišān mitḫurti*, pp. 112-13 and in *RLA* 6, pp. 121-22. Only the element Aššur is preserved for the names of both Ashurbanipal and Esarhaddon; the name following Ashurbanipal (if that name is restored correctly) is not preserved.

A). In economic texts, Šamaš-šuma-ukīn was given the title "king of Babylon," or occasionally just "king."[19] In his royal inscriptions, he was called "king of Babylon,"[20] "viceroy of Babylon," "king of Sumer and Akkad,"[21] and "king of Amnanu."[22] In assuming the title "king of Amnanu," Šamaš-šuma-ukīn revived a title used previously only for Sîn-kāšid, Baḫlu-kulim, and perhaps Sîn-gāmil, all kings from the Old Babylonian period.[23] Perhaps he was attempting to identify himself with the country's past and to pose as a true Babylonian ruler. Among the epithets used to refer to Šamaš-šuma-ukīn in his royal inscriptions are "mighty king," "capable," "judicious," "noble vice-regent," "(faithful) shepherd," "wise viceroy," "valiant prince," "provider of Ezida," and "one who reveres the lord of lords."[24] The only new epithets appearing during his reign are "favourite of the gods Enlil, Šamaš, and Marduk" and "one who settled [*the gods who*] are in Esagila."[25] The latter title probably reflects the fact that he returned the statue of the god Marduk to Esagila in 668. A number of others first appear in the time of Esarhaddon or Merodach-Baladan II.[26]

Exactly how much authority Šamaš-šuma-ukīn had within his realm is uncertain although it is likely that he had authority over at least local matters. He could settle a dispute over the ownership of land in Bīt-Ḫaʾraḫu,[27] assign a prebend in Ebabbar, the temple of the god Šamaš at Sippar,[28] renew and increase prebends in the offices of baker, butcher, and brewer which had been previously granted by Aššur-nādin-šumi,[29] regulate water traffic,[30] and

---

19 The latter is written LUGAL.E and only occurs in a few texts (e.g., BM 47535 and BM 82645; *B-K* K.74 and K.115). Or should we take this to be a misunderstood abbreviation for LUGAL E.KI, "king of Babylon"?

20 Lehmann, *Ššmk*, no. 1 i 2 and ii 2, no. 2:3 (partially restored), and no. 3:11.

21 Walker, *CBI*, no. 77:5-6; Lehmann, *Ššmk*, no. 1 i 5 and ii 5, no. 2:3, and no. 3:11; Lambert, *AfO* 18 (1957-58): 387 and pl. 25:14 and 29-30.

22 Lehmann, *Ššmk*, no. 1 i 2 and ii 2.

23 See Seux, *Épithètes*, p. 421 and Dossin, *Syria* 32 (1955): 7 iii 6-7 (title "king of Tutul and Amnanu" given to Baḫlu-kulim by Yaḫdun-Lim). On the use of this title by Šamaš-šuma-ukīn, see Streck, *Asb.*, CCLIX n. 1.

24 See Lehmann, *Ššmk*, no. 1 i 1 and 3-4 and ii 1 and 3-5; no. 2: 2 and 4; and no. 3:12-14.

25 See Seux, *Épithètes*, pp. 163 and 365.

26 See Seux, *Épithètes*, pp. 170-71, 212, 276, 323-24, and 373.

27 *BBSt* 10 (*B-K* K.169).

28 Steinmetzer, *Deimel Festschrift*, pp. 302-306 (*B-K* K.163). This is the only document dated at Sippar by the regnal years of Šamaš-šuma-ukīn. It is worthy of note that although Šamaš-šuma-ukīn is described in the text as the son of Esarhaddon, the brother of Ashurbanipal, and the descendant of Sargon (lines 5-8), the name of his grandfather is not given. Undoubtedly this is because Sennacherib had destroyed Babylon and abolished the kingship of Babylonia.

29 BM 77611+77612+ (*B-K* Fn.4 and Kn.5); the name of the temple in which the prebends were given is not preserved.

30 *ABL* 1385.

carry out building projects in Babylon (enclosure wall of Esagila), Borsippa (wall of the temple Ezida and Eminamabulmeš, a shrine within that temple), and Sippar (city wall and temple of the god Šamaš).[31] Šamaš-šuma-ukīn claims that he had been chosen by the gods "to gather the scattered people of Akkad" and "to carry out the forgotten rites and rituals" and that he had re-established the regular offerings in Esagila for the gods of the land of Sumer and Akkad.[32] Both claims undoubtedly refer at least in part to the king's involvement with the restoration of cultic practices in Esagila occasioned by the restoration of Babylon and the return of the statue of Marduk. At the death of Esarhaddon, however, the people of Ḫalman (perhaps modern Ḫolwan, east of the Tigris) were able to stop sending offerings of sheep to the god Marduk.[33] Possibly they had stopped sending them because Ḫalman was considered part of Assyria, not Babylonia, and they hoped to use this fact to get out of performing a duty imposed when the two lands had a single ruler (Esarhaddon).[34]

There is no concrete evidence that relations between Ashurbanipal and Šamaš-šuma-ukīn were anything but good until rebellion broke out in 652. A pair of stelae describing the restoration of the Ezida temple at Borsippa was found in one room of that temple (figs. 2-3). Each stela depicts one of the two kings and, while ascribing the restoration of the temple to that monarch, mentions the other in a favourable manner.[35] The kings made friendly references to each other in their inscriptions[36] and Šamaš-šuma-ukīn wrote to his brother on occasion.[37] Ashurbanipal came to the aid of Babylonia when it was invaded by Elam (see below); he showed favour to the god Marduk; and

---

31 Babylon: *ABL* 119 rev. 8-15. Borsippa: Lehmann, *Ššmk*, no. 2 (Lehmann states that the stela was found at Babylon [*ibid.*, 1 p. 22], which could suggest that the text refers to the shrine by the name Ezida within the Esagila complex, but the text actually comes from Borsippa [see Reade, *Iraq* 48 (1986): 109]); Pinckert, *LSS* 3/4, no. 6; and note the dedication of part of a boat(?) to the god Nabû of Borsippa in Lambert, *AfO* 18 (1957-58): 385-87 and pl. 25. Sippar: Lehmann, *Ššmk*, no. 1 and Walker, *CBI*, no. 77. Šamaš-šuma-ukīn is depicted on the stela from Borsippa (Lehmann, *Ššmk*, no. 2) carrying a basket on his head, thus aiding personally in the rebuilding.

32 Lehmann, *Ššmk*, no. 1:9-13 and no. 2:8; Pinkert, *LSS* 3/4, no. 6:17.

33 *ABL* 464:11'-17'; for the location for Ḫalman, see Brinkman, *PKB*, p. 195 n. 1195.

34 This assumes that the practice of sending offerings to Marduk had begun in the time of Esarhaddon and that areas east of the Tigris had been annexed by Assyria (see chapter 10).

35 Streck, *Asb.*, pp. 240-45 and Lehmann, *Ššmk*, no. 2. For their provenance, see Reade, *Iraq* 48 (1986): 109 and pl. 13.

36 Šamaš-šuma-ukīn is described as the "favourite/beloved (brother)" (*aḫu*) *talīmu* of Ashurbanipal in the inscriptions of both brothers (e.g., Streck, *Asb.*, pp. 230-33:21-22 and Lehmann, *Ššmk*, no. 3:20), as well as in those of Esarhaddon and Zakūtu (Parpola and Watanabe, *SAA* 2, no. 6:86 and no. 8:3), and Šamaš-šuma-ukīn refers to Ashurbanipal as his "favourite brother" ŠEŠ TAM.MA.BI on his brick inscription from Sippar (Walker, *CBI*, no. 77:9-11). The exact meaning of *talīmu*, however, remains unclear; see Watanabe, *Vereidigung*, p. 4.

37 *ABL* 426 and 1385; probably also *ABL* 809 and *CT* 53 140.

he even claims to have given his brother many more cities, fields, orchards, and people than his father had ordered.[38] However, as will be seen, if Šamaš-šuma-ukīn had expected to rule his realm independently of his brother, he would have had grounds for complaint.

It is not clear what the exact relationship between the two kings was expected to be, though the mere fact that Šamaš-šuma-ukīn had been obliged by Zakūtu to swear allegiance to his brother as king of Assyria suggests that Ashurbanipal was intended to be his overlord and would indicate that he was not expected to be any more than a vassal ruler, albeit ruler of a specially privileged part of the Assyrian empire. Ashurbanipal claimed in some of his building inscriptions from Babylonia that he had "appointed Šamaš-šuma-ukīn, my favourite brother, to the kingship of Babylon,"[39] indicating that he was his brother's overlord. A late Aramaic story describing the war between the two brothers indicates the same when it states that Ashurbanipal had sent Šamaš-šuma-ukīn to be governor of the land of Babylon, telling him to eat its bread and drink its wine.[40] The titles accorded Ashurbanipal in inscriptions of Šamaš-šuma-ukīn show that the latter acknowledged the supremacy of the former. Šamaš-šuma-ukīn refers to his brother as "great king," "king of the world," and "king of the four quarters (of the world)," titles which he never used for himself.[41] It would be useful to know if Babylonia sent tribute to Assyria at this time, but there is no clear evidence on the matter.[42]

The sources available for this period give a one-sided view of conditions. Because we have not found the Babylonian archives, we have as yet no letters from Babylonian officials to Šamaš-šuma-ukīn. Almost all the Assyrian royal inscriptions that contain historical information about Babylonia date after the beginning of the Šamaš-šuma-ukīn Revolt and therefore do not show him in a favourable light, while the few texts left by Šamaš-šuma-ukīn contain scant historical information. However, the surviving evidence shows that Ashurbanipal was deeply embroiled in Babylonian affairs. Ashurbanipal kept a close eye on events in Babylonia and felt free to act there with little or

---

38 Streck, *Asb.*, p. 28 iii 70-77 and see Parpola and Watanabe, *SAA* 2, no. 6:89-90 and 275-78. Parpola considers the fact that Ashurbanipal could have a substitute king quickly enthroned at Akkad (i.e., in his brother's realm) in 666 as an indication that the two brothers were on good terms, though he does note that the action was to protect Šamaš-šuma-ukīn, not the Assyrian king (see *LAS* 2, p. 305).

39 E.g., Streck, *Asb.*, pp. 230-31:11-12 and 242-43:31-32.

40 Amherst papyrus 63. See Steiner and Nims, *RB* 92 (1985): 71 and 73; and Vleeming and Wesselius, *Studies* 1, pp. 34-35.

41 Lehmann, *Ššmk*, no. 2:12; Pinckert, *LSS* 3/4, no. 6:20; *BBSt* 10:11'; and Steinmetzer, *Deimel Festschrift*, p. 303:6-7.

42 Steiner and Nims believe that part of the Aramaic text indicates that Ashurbanipal had told Šamaš-šuma-ukīn to devote himself to sending tribute to Assyria, but the translation by Vleeming and Wesselius does not agree with such an interpretation. On the question of the payment of tribute by Babylonia to Assyria, see p. 131 n. 1 and pp. 238-39.

no reference to his brother, the king of Babylonia. Many persons in Babylonia, including high officials, reported directly to Ashurbanipal about both domestic matters (e.g., building programmes, murders, and the movements of population groups)[43] and foreign affairs (such as contacts with Elam).[44] Even Šamaš-šuma-ukīn's orders with regard to building projects were carefully reported to Ashurbanipal.[45] It is not clear whether Šamaš-šuma-ukīn had the authority to appoint officials in his own realm. According to *ABL* 238, it was the Assyrian king who had sent an individual to be governor of Marad, suggesting that it was Ashurbanipal who had appointed him to be governor of that Babylonian city. *ABL* 326 refers to a governor of Dilbat who had been appointed by Šamaš-šuma-ukīn, but this letter dates to the time of the rebellion of 652-648 and thus it is unclear if the appointment had been made before or during the revolt. Some important officials continued in office from the time of Esarhaddon into the reign of Šamaš-šuma-ukīn,[46] indicating that the latter did not install new officials throughout his realm immediately upon ascending the throne. Deputations from Babylonian cities went to see Ashurbanipal in person and officials sometimes sent individuals to him to be interrogated, without reference to Šamaš-šuma-ukīn.[47] Some officials at least looked to Ashurbanipal for authority to carry out actions, and obeyed his orders.[48] Even the citizens of Babylon, Šamaš-šuma-ukīn's capital, wrote to Ashurbanipal.[49]

Both the people and the administration of Babylonia appear to have felt that the Assyrian king had some authority over them and they kept him well informed about conditions in the southern kingdom. This attitude is shown clearly in the fact that Sîn-balāssu-iqbi, governor of Ur, stated in some of his building inscriptions that his works were "for the preservation the life of Ashurbanipal," who was called "king of kings" or "king of Assyria, mighty king, king of the world";[50] Sîn-balāssu-iqbi never mentioned Šamaš-šuma-ukīn, his legitimate overlord.

---

43 E.g., *ABL* 119, 753, and 839. The exact date of *ABL* 753 is not certain, but the context does not suggest that the Šamaš-šuma-ukīn Revolt was in progress at the time the letter was written.

44 E.g., *ABL* 268.

45 *ABL* 119 rev. 8-15 and see also *ABL* 1247.

46 Two such officials were Nabû-nādin-šumi, the *šatammu* of Ezida in Borsippa, and Aḫḫēšaya, the governor of Uruk. See Appendix B.

47 E.g., *ABL* 268 rev. 6-8 and 753:6-7.

48 E.g., *ABL* 269. The fact that Nabû-ušabši felt able to assemble all Akkad indicates that this text was written before the Šamaš-šuma-ukīn Revolt had divided the land.

49 *ABL* 878. The text is addressed to "the king" although the body of the text refers to "the kings, our lords" (e.g., lines 6 and rev. 3'). In *ABL* 926 Ashurbanipal wrote to the people of Babylon, calling them the people under his protection (or the people granted *kidinnu*-status by him, *ṣābē kidinniy*[*a*]); the letter may, however, come from the time after the rebellion of 652-648.

50 *UET* 1 170:2-4; *UET* 8 102:4-5.

Šamaš-šuma-ukīn himself reported to Ashurbanipal on occasion:

> Concerning the boats of that emissary about which I wrote to my brother, saying: "I have sent word and they will let them go." Because I had written to my brother once or twice but he had not answered my letter(s), I became afraid. With regard to that prince Ḫumban-nikaš, the king knows that he is very *aggressive*. He will do ... of this grain and set ... The king knows that as many as we are, we can offer neither ... nor anything else. (Therefore) I wrote, saying: "Let the boats go! They may pass!" Now I have seen the letter of Bēl-iqīša and I will write, saying: "The boats should not pass! Hold (them) back!" I have sent the letter of Bēl-iqīša to the king. May the king do as he chooses![51]

Šamaš-šuma-ukīn seems to defer to his brother, keeping Ashurbanipal informed of his actions and becoming worried when he had not heard from him. In this instance, however, it may have been a matter of national security which was involved since reference is made to an aggressive(?) (*raṣmu*) Elamite prince and to the head of the Gambūlu tribe (assuming the Bēl-iqīša mentioned is to be identifed with the Gambulian by that name). It is possible that Šamaš-šuma-ukīn was attempting to deceive his brother in this letter and that he was actually in league with the Elamite prince. Knowing that Ashurbanipal would not want the ships to pass, Šamaš-šuma-ukīn may have purposefully sent the order allowing their departure before he could hear from his brother on the matter. When the important tribal leader Bēl-iqīša objected, and when it was probably already too late, he sent a new order to try to cover himself in case Ashurbanipal became angry.[52]

Ashurbanipal authorized a number of building projects in Babylonia while he was king of Assyria; however, when an inscription recording a particular project does not mention his brother Šamaš-šuma-ukīn—in either a hostile or favourable light—it is often impossible to determine in which part of the Assyrian king's reign the project was carried out (i.e., before 652, when Šamaš-šuma-ukīn rebelled against Assyrian overlordship, or after that date). During the time before 652, work was carried out in the name of the Assyrian king at Borsippa on the temple of the god Nabû (Ezida) and on the city wall (Ṭābi-supūršu), at Sippar on the temple of the god Šamaš (Ebabbar), and at Uruk on the temple of the goddess Ištar (Eanna).[53] During this same period,

---

51 *ABL* 1385.

52 This interpretation of the letter was kindly suggested to me by S. Parpola.

53 Borsippa: Streck, *Asb.*, pp. 240-45 (for the provenance of the inscription, see Reade, *Iraq* 48 [1986]: 109); and Weidner, *AfO* 13 (1939-41): 217-18 and pl. 16 (BM 83000, a fragmentary duplicate of the inscription, confirms Weidner's restoration of the building portion of the text). Sippar: Streck, *Asb.*, pp. 228-33; and cf. K 6232, a fragment which is probably to be assigned to Ashurbanipal and which mentions Sippar and Šamaš-šuma-ukīn (to be published by G. Frame and A.K. Grayson). Uruk: Lutz, *UCP* 9/8 (1931): 385-90 and pls. 7-8. *ABL* 464:3'-5' also refers to work on temples at Sippar and Cutha.

various building projects were carried out in the name of Ashurbanipal in Babylon, his brother's capital city. The Assyrian king claims to have completed work begun by Esarhaddon on Esagila, the temple-complex of the god Marduk (including Etuša, the chapel of the god Marduk, and Ekarzaginna, the shrine of the god Ea) and to have done work on the temples of the goddesses Ninmaḫ and Ištar (Emaḫ and Eturkalamma) and on the outer wall and gates of the city.[54] The stela from Babylon recording Ashurbanipal's work on Ekarzaginna depicts him taking part in the restoration of that temple in person (see photograph on cover), although it is unlikely that he actually did so. Various short brick inscriptions indicate that Ashurbanipal had carried out work on Esagila and its ziggurat (Etemenanki), but when these bricks were made during the king's reign is not known.[55] In his votive and building inscriptions from Babylonia dated before the outbreak of rebellion in 652, Ashurbanipal proudly claimed to have (re)-established the privileged position (*kidinnūtu*) of Babylon and the regular offerings of Esagila.[56] In addition, having repaired Marduk's ceremonial bed, which Sennacherib had taken to Assyria and placed in the temple of the god Aššur, Ashurbanipal returned it to Babylon in 654. A richly decorated chariot was also made and presented to the god in 653.[57]

At some point during Ashurbanipal's reign, building projects were carried out in that king's name at a few other sites within Babylonia. According to an inscription of Nabonidus, Ashurbanipal restored Eulmaš, the temple of the goddess Ištar of the city of Akkad at Akkad,[58] and this may be confirmed by an inscription on a cylinder fragment which is likely attributable to Ashurbanipal and which mentions both "the temple of Ištar" and "Ištar of Akkad."[59] However, since Ištar of Akkad also had a temple at Babylon, this inscription could refer to that temple and not to the one at Akkad itself. An inscribed brick from the ziggurat at Dūr-Kurigalzu attests to work by

---

54 Streck, *Asb.*, pp. 226-29, 230-31:12-15, 232-41, and 244-49. With regard to the shrine of Ea, note also the cylinder fragment from Babylon mentioning that god (ibid., pp. XC-XCI); the fragment is currently no. 7893 in the Museum of the Ancient Orient in Istanbul.

55 Streck, *Asb.*, pp. 350-51 nos. a.α and β; Wetzel and Weissbach, *Hauptheiligtum*, pp. 39-40 nos. A.II.2.a-e.

56 E.g., Streck, *Asb.*, pp. 226-27:9-10 and 230-31:10-11.

57 Grayson, *Chronicles*, no. 15:4-5; Millard, *Iraq* 26 (1964): 19-23; Thompson, *PEA*, p. 30 and pl. 14 i 39-51; Weidner, *AfO* 13 (1939-41): 205 and pl. 11 lines 27-31; and Matsushima, *ASJ* 10 (1988): 99-109 and 120-23.

58 *CT* 34 pls. 30-31:28-45.

59 81-2-4,174 (to be published by the author). The name of the king is not preserved on the fragment, but the closest parallels to the text are found in Ashurbanipal's cylinder dealing with the restoration of the outer wall and gates of Babylon (Streck, *Asb.*, pp. 234-39), which dates to the time before the Šamaš-šuma-ukīn Revolt.

Ashurbanipal at that site.[60] The Assyrian king enlarged the courtyard of Ešaḫulla, the temple of the god Nergal at Tell Haddad in the Hamrin,[61] but Tell Haddad was almost certainly under direct Assyrian control at this time (as were several other places on the eastern side of the Tigris)[62] and no longer considered to be part of Babylonia. Work on the temple of the god Enlil was carried out at Nippur in the name of Ashurbanipal at some point during that king's reign. Since Šamaš-šuma-ukīn is not mentioned in any of the inscriptions recording this work, since Nippur was kept under direct Assyrian control after the rebellion of 652-648, and since one of these inscriptions accords Ashurbanipal the title "king of Sumer and Akkad," at least some of this work probably dates a time when Šamaš-šuma-ukīn was not king of Babylonia, or at least not acknowledged as such by scribes at Nippur. Thus, Ashurbanipal's building projects at this city will be described in chapter 9.

Although Ashurbanipal claims to have given his brother soldiers, horses, and chariots,[63] there is no clear evidence that Šamaš-šuma-ukīn had any substantial military forces under his control until the rebellion began. It appears that Ashurbanipal held most of the military authority over Babylonia. When Urtak invaded Babylonia and encamped against Babylon, Šamaš-šuma-ukīn had to wait for Ashurbanipal to send troops to deal with the invading army; the Elamites did not depart until Assyrian troops advanced.[64] The Assyrian king felt free to command the governor of Uruk to assemble troops and to send them against the Gambūlu. That governor could even consider the possibility that the Assyrian king might order him to assemble all (the troops of) the land of Akkad in the campaign against the Gambūlu; no mention is made of Šamaš-šuma-ukīn.[65] This is the only clear reference to Babylonian troops during the period and here it is Ashurbanipal who ordered their levy. Assyrian inscriptions describing the campaign against Elam and the Gambūlu in 653 (see below) never mention Babylonian forces as forming

---

[60] Al-Jumaily, *Sumer* 27 (1971): 89 and pl. 14 fig. 30 (Arabic section). The photo is somewhat unclear, but the inscription appears to read ᵐAN.ŠÁR?-DÙ-A MAN ŠÚ MAN KU[R *aššur* (...)] MAN *kib-r*[*at*] 4-⌜*tim*?⌝ [(...)] (lines 2-3). Al-Jumaily states that although the brick was found built into the southwestern façade of the ziggurat, this was not its original emplacement. It is not possible to tell from the photo if the brick mentions the name of the structure for which it was originally made, but it may well have been for a structure associated with the god Enlil. The first line of the inscription may begin ⌜*a*?-*na*? ᵈEN?.LÍL?⌝ (reading very uncertain); most Kassite royal inscriptions from Dūr-Kurigalzu were dedicated to this god and deal with structures associated with him (including the Eugal temple, with which the ziggurat seems to have been connected).

[61] Rashid, *Sumer* 37 (1981): 72-80 (Arabic section); Hannoun, *BSMS* 2 (1982): 5-6. For further information on this site, see *Iraq* 45 (1983): 210-11 and 47 (1985): 220-21 and the bibliography cited there.

[62] See pp. 222-24.

[63] Streck, *Asb.*, pp. 28-29 iii 74-75.

[64] See p. 120.

[65] *ABL* 269.

part of their army.[66] Perhaps Babylonian troops were not mentioned because the editions of Ashurbanipal's annals describing these wars were composed after the rebellion of 652-648 began and they may not have wished to mention anything remotely favourable to Šamaš-šuma-ukīn.

Thus, the evidence clearly demonstrates that between 669 and 653 Babylonia was not an independent state but rather an integral part of the Assyrian empire. There is nothing concrete to indicate that Šamaš-šuma-ukīn was more than a vassal ruler, though he and his realm were granted preferential treatment by the Assyrian king. Ashurbanipal was Šamaš-šuma-ukīn's overlord and held a type of protectorship over Babylonia, controlling its foreign relations and defence and even involving himself deeply in its internal affairs. Quite possibly Esarhaddon had intended this to be the case and had wanted Šamaš-šuma-ukīn to become king of Babylonia simply to find an effective means to govern that country and keep it within Assyria's sphere of control. Realizing that Ashurbanipal held the military power and final authority, Babylonian officials naturally looked to him for leadership and direction, possibly neglecting their obligations to their own king, Šamaš-šuma-ukīn. In view of the close ties between the two lands, they may have found it easier to gain access to, and the attention of, the Assyrian king than would the subjects of other vassal rulers. It is certain that Šamaš-šuma-ukīn's authority over Babylonia itself was seriously limited by Ashurbanipal, and it is obscure exactly what real power and authority Šamaš-šuma-ukīn held over Babylonian officials.[67]

Economic activity appears to have increased greatly during the second half of the reign of Šamaš-šuma-ukīn. On average, only four legal or administrative documents are attested per year for the period 668-659; but for the remainder of his reign, the average is about eleven texts per year, the highest average for a similar length of time since the Kassite period.[68] This may indicate improved economic conditions in the country. Most of the documents whose place of composition is known come from three neighbouring cities in northwestern Babylonia—Babylon, Borsippa, and

---

66 It is not certain that the incident involving the governor of Uruk described in *ABL* 269 was directly connected with this campaign.

67 The fact that a governor of Babylon was important enough to be assigned an eponymy (non-canonical) likely *c*. 656-653 (see Appendix C) may reflect some limitation upon the Babylonian king's authority at the heart of his realm since the practice of dating by eponyms was an Assyrian custom.

68 Documents dated by the regnal years of both Ashurbanipal and Šamaš-šuma-ukīn are used to compile these statistics; texts whose dates within the reign of Šamaš-šuma-ukīn are unknown or uncertain have not been included (34 documents). If one further divides the period 658-648 into the time before the revolt (658-653) and the time of the revolt (652-648), the averages are twelve and ten respectively. During the thirteenth century an average of more than fifteen economic texts per year is attested for the reigns of several Kassite kings (see Brinkman, *MSKH* 1, pp. 36-37).

Dilbat. Although several documents come from Sippar during the following reign of Kandalānu, only one text, a kudurru, attests to activity there during the reign of Šamaš-šuma-ukīn. Uruk, in the southern part of the land, also provided a considerable number of documents (about eleven per cent of the total number of texts for the period 669-648).

The private sale of temple prebends became common practice in Neo-Babylonian and later times, but it is during the reign of Šamaš-šuma-ukīn that the records of those transactions first appear in significant numbers.[69] The earliest private sales transaction from the first millennium involving a prebend comes from just before our period of concern; that document, dating to the accession year of Aššur-nādin-šumi (700) and coming from Uruk, records that the office of baker for the goddess Nanaya (or the right to the income from that office) for ten days in the month of Ṭebētu (X) was sold for fifty-two shekels of silver.[70] A document dating to the third year of Esarhaddon (678) also refers to the sale of a prebend (*isqu*) at some point in the probably quite recent past; on this occasion the prebend was before the god Šamaš in Sippar.[71] During the reign of Šamaš-šuma-ukīn sales of prebends and the handing over of prebends as security for loans are attested before the revolt of 652-648 at Borsippa (office of scribe in the house of dates in Ezida), Marad (office of butcher for the cella of Lugalmarada and the other gods of Marad), and Uruk (office of baker for the goddess Kanisurra and an office involving the goddess Nanaya),[72] and during the revolt at Babylon (offices of brewer[?] and "temple-enterer"), Uruk (office of baker for the goddess Bēltiya), and Ur (office of scribe before the "Lady-of-Ur" and office of brewer in the shrine of the god Ninazu).[73]

The economic texts of the period also record normal legal and administrative matters. Two individuals appear prominently in a number of texts, indicating their active involvement in the economic life of the time and undoubtedlty the fact that we have found their archives. Bēl-ušallim son of Lē'ēa made a large number of silver loans during a career lasting at least thirty-three years, from the eighth year of Šamaš-šuma-ukīn until the

---

69 Sales of prebends are attested in the Old Babylonian period and other documents often mention royal grants of prebends.

70 Hunger, *Bagh. Mitt.* 5 (1970): 202-203 and 275 no. 3 (*B-K* F.1); on the date, see Brinkman, *Or.* NS 41 (1972): 245. Note also the text mentioned p. 107 and n. 29.

71 Strassmaier, *8e Congrès*, no. 4 (*B-K* I.6).

72 Borsippa: VAT 13392 (*B-K* K.151; exact date uncertain, 22-II-653 or 652). Marad: Driver, *JRAS Cent. Suppl.* (1924): 41-48 and pls. 4-5(*B-K* K.10). Uruk: Hunger, *Bagh. Mitt.* 5 (1970): 203-205, 232-34, 276, and 293-94 nos. 4 and 18-20 (*B-K* K.24, K.97-98, K.165 [year not preserved but Nabû-iqīša, *šatammu* of Eanna, a witness to the transaction, is only attested in office during the pre-rebellion reign of Šamaš-šuma-ukīn]).

73 Babylon: Ellis, *JCS* 36 (1984): 37 no. 3 (*B-K* K.127). Uruk: Hunger, *Bagh. Mitt.* 5 (1970): 205-206 and 277 no. 5 (*B-K* J.6). Ur: BM 113929 (*B-K* J.11; the document was composed at Ninā) and *UET* 4 23 (*B-K* J.39; date uncertain).

twentieth year of Kandalānu (660-628), and attested by appoximately twenty texts. While his centre of activity was Babylon, on one occasion shortly after the end of the Šamaš-šuma-ukīn Revolt, he went to Borsippa and issued a loan to an individual for a business venture. The average loan issued by Bēl-ušallim was for two thirds of a mina of silver, though one loan was for the sum of 1 1/2 mina. The rate of interest charged by him varied between 13.3 and 20 per cent per annum, with the average being about 15 per cent.[74] The normal yearly interest rate charged for loans during the years 689-627 was about 20 per cent, with almost all rates falling between 12.5 and 30 per cent; no marked variation can be noted for specific periods or reigns within this time.[75] The career of Mušēzib-Marduk son of Kiribtu and descendant of Sîn-nāṣir stretched over at least twenty-six years, from the third year of Esarhaddon until at least the fifteenth year of Šamaš-šuma-ukīn (678-653). Although his activities began in the time of Esarhaddon, about three quarters of the texts mentioning him come from the reign of Šamaš-šuma-ukīn. Of the at least eighteen transactions in which he acted, eleven come from Uruk, five from Babylon, and one each from Ur and Šapiya. His activities were centered in the south, but he may have moved to Babylon in 655 since the texts mentioning him which are dated to the years 655-653 only come from that city. All of his transactions involve land in some way and most of the texts record Mušēzib-Marduk's purchase of date palm orchards, fields, or houses specifically stated to be located at Uruk.[76]

Just as there is evidence of great activity in the economic sphere and of widespread building projects, there is also evidence of considerable literary (or scribal) activity in the land. Various religious and scientific texts were composed or copied in Babylonia during the years before strife broke out between the two brothers. These included prayers, incantations, rituals,[77] and

---

[74] The texts involving Bēl-ušallim were published by Jakob-Rost in *FB* 10 (1968): 39-62; see also Jakob-Rost, *FB* 12 (1970): 58 no. 11. The texts published in the first article were found in a clay jar in the Merkes quarter of Babylon (h 26) and the text published in the second article may also have been found there.

[75] These statistics come from a study of approximately fifty-five loan documents which state the rate of interest. A rate of 20 per cent per annum was the standard rate of interest on silver loans in the Neo-Babylonian period (see Petschow, *Pfandrecht*, pp. 15-16 n. 31 and pp. 20-21 n. 43a).

[76] With regard to the career of Mušēzib-Marduk, see Frame, *RA* 76 (1982): 157-66. In addition to the texts cited there, two documents from Uruk dated to the reign of Kandalānu (years two and fifteen) mention a Mušēzib-Marduk (Ellis, *JCS* 36 [1984]: 38-39 no. 4 and 52 no. 17 [*B-K* L.4 and L.94]). It remains uncertain if the same individual is meant, although in each case it is not impossible to restore the passage to indicate that he was the son of Kiribtu (in one case as [A-(*šú šá*) ^{m}*ki?-ri*]*b?-*⌈*ti*⌉ and in the other as A-*šú šá* ^{m}⌈*ki?-rib?-ti*⌉); we may note that in one of the texts he appears to be purchasing land at Uruk. I am currently preparing a detailed study of the texts mentioning this individual.

[77] *PBS* 1/1 12-18 (Šamaš-šuma-ukīn is mentioned in only nos. 12 and 18;); *PBS* 1/2 108, 110, 119-21, 123, 124, 126, 129, and 133 (Šamaš-šuma-ukīn is mentioned in only

diagnostic[78] and lexical texts.[79] Astronomical observations continued to be recorded[80] and the earliest attested astronomical diary comes from the year 652. Besides recording astronomical observances, the diary described weather conditions, the river level, and, on two occasions, military events.[81] In order to avert evil thought to portend for Šamaš-šuma-ukīn because of a lunar eclipse, a substitute king appears to have been installed in the city of Akkad in the fourth month of 666, though actually there may have been no need to install one on that occasion.[82] Substitute kings had been installed in Akkad on several occasions during the reign of Esarhaddon (see above).

Few details about Babylonian political life during the years 669-653 are known.[83] On the twentieth day of Ṭebētu (X) in 668, soon after Šamaš-šuma-ukīn took the throne, Bēl-ēṭir, "the judge of Babylon," was taken prisoner and executed.[84] Whether it was Ashurbanipal or Šamaš-šuma-ukīn who ordered the arrest and execution is unknown, but in view of Ashurbanipal's involvement with Babylonian affairs, he cannot be ruled out. Why Bēl-ēṭir was punished is uncertain. Possibly he is to be identified with the astrologer

---

nos. 108, 110, 119, 120, and 124); *PBS* 10/2 18; Langdon, *RA* 16 (1919): 67-68; Scheil, *Sippar*, nos. 1, 2, 6-8, 18 (=Combe, *Sin*, no. 6), 36 (=Schollmeyer, *Šamaš*, no. 13a), and 59 (Šamaš-šuma-ukīn not mentioned in nos. 7 and 8 [and possibly nos. 1 and 59?]). While the assignment of some of these texts to this time remains unproven (e.g., *PBS* 1/1 15-16), most appear to be tablets of the *bīt rimki* series prepared for Šamaš-šuma-ukīn to ward off evil portended by a lunar eclipse (or by two separate lunar eclipses, one in the month of Kislīmu and one in the month of Ṭebētu). None of these documents bears an actual date and in only two of them is Šamaš-šuma-ukīn specifically called king (*PBS* 1/2 108:1' and Scheil, *Sippar*, no. 6:4'). See Prince, *AJSL* 31 (1914-15): 256-70; Ungnad, *Or.* NS 12 (1943): 293-310; and Laessøe, *Bît rimki*, pp. 93-98; Parpola, *LAS* 2, pp. 164-65 and 351 n. 649; and Brinkman, *Prelude*, p. 89 and n. 439. A large number of these texts come from Sippar and it has been suggested that Šamaš-šuma-ukīn often resided there, preferring it to Babylon where Assyrian supporters and spies were more numerous (Scheil, *Sippar*, p. 71). This remains pure speculation; similar prayers which have not yet been discovered may have been composed at Babylon. Using some of these texts as evidence, Kinnier Wilson suggests that Šamaš-šuma-ukīn "would certainly appear to have become mentally ill in some way" (*Studies Landsberger*, p. 297). Certainly Šamaš-šuma-ukīn was concerned about and wished to protect himself from harm portended by omens. However, in view of the common belief in the possibility of avoiding or counteracting current or portended evil and of winning the favour of the gods by means of certain (ritual) acts, it seems unwise to consider him mentally ill, or even overly superstitious, solely on the basis of these texts.

78 *TDP*, no. 12 text C.

79 VAT 13100 (Erimḫuš).

80 See *LBAT* 1414-1417 (lunar eclipses) and the statements in various letters and reports from this period (e.g., *ABL* 46 [*LAS*, no. 298]).

81 BM 32312 (Sachs, *Astronomical Diaries*, no. -651).

82 *ABL* 46 (*LAS*, no. 298); see *LAS* 2, pp. 304-305.

83 The date and sequence of some events are not certain since Ashurbanipal's royal inscriptions do not always record events in the same order. The most recent attempt to clarify these matters is that of Grayson in *ZA* 70 (1980): 227-45. The present study will differ from his presentation at a few points.

84 Grayson, *Chronicles*, no. 1 iv 38 and no. 14:39.

of that name who had been accused some time between Ayyaru (II) of 672 and the end of Esarhaddon's reign of not doing his duty and of consorting with rebel elements.[85] Or possibly he is to be identified with Bēl-ēṭir son of Ibâ who was castigated strongly in two Assyrian texts; among the terms used to describe him are "servant of a dead god, house whose star has disappeared from the heavens," and "slave girl."[86] These two texts present many difficulties, but they do link him with Šamaš-ibni, whom Esarhaddon had defeated, and Šamaš-ibni's daughter Balīḫītu.[87]

At some point in 668, Assyrian troops were sent to deal with the people of the town of Kirbītu (or Qirbītu) who had been giving trouble to Dēr and plundering the people of Yamutbal, an area east of the Tigris. Kirbītu was captured and looted. Some of its people were resettled in Egypt while individuals from another land were settled in Kirbītu.[88] All or part of the troubled area had been annexed to Assyria.[89]

Most of the information available about political events in Babylonia at this time involves Elam and the Gambūlu tribe. The status of the Gambūlu vis-à-vis Babylonia is not clear. Bēl-iqīša, the Gambulian leader, had submitted to Esarhaddon and had been regarded by the king as a "march warden" against Elam, but it is not absolutely certain that the area of the Gambūlu was considered part of Babylonia proper, even though Bēl-iqīša travelled freely in Babylonia and was given land there.[90] On the contrary, during this period the Gambūlu almost always appear as allies (vassals?) of Elam.[91]

---

85 Parpola, *Iraq* 34 (1972): pl. 19 and p. 29.

86 Livingstone, *SAA* 3, nos. 29-30; S. Parpola kindly provided me with his own transliteration of these texts before Livingstone's book appeared.

87 The family of Ibâ is mentioned in a few additional texts. *ABL* 454, a letter to Ashurbanipal, refers to Ibâ and Balīḫītu (lines 8-16); a second letter to Ashurbanipal, *CT* 54 55, refers to [...] son of Ibâ in broken context (rev. 9'). *CT* 54 490 (dated to the reign of Ashurbanipal) refers to Bēl-ēṭir son of Ibâ in broken context (rev. 15). Parpola (*JNES* 42 [1983]: 11 n. 39) compares similar wording between *ABL* 289:7-8 and K 1351:14 and rev. 4, and 82-5-22,88:2 (Livingstone, *SAA* 3, nos. 29 and 30 respectively), and suggests that since *ABL* 289 dates from the time of the Šamaš-šuma-ukīn Revolt (5-II-650), the other two texts may do so as well. If this dating proves correct, the Bēl-ēṭir mentioned in these texts could not be the individual mentioned in the chronicles.

88 Grayson, *Chronicles*, no. 1 iv 37 and no. 14:38; Piepkorn, *Asb.*, pp. 14-15 iv 1-10 and 48-49 iii 5-15; Bauer, *Asb.*, p. 15 and pl. 8 iv 15-25; Streck, *Asb.*, pp. 166-67 rev. 6-12. For the location of Kirbītu, possibly near Pušt-i Kūh, see Streck, *Asb.*, p. CCCXLIX. Zadok (*WO* 16 [1985]: 48) suggests that the term Yamutbal (Jamūt-bala) was probably an archaic desgination for the region around Dēr.

89 It is suggested below (pp. 222-24) that all or most of the area east of the Tigris had been annexed by Assyria.

90 *ABL* 336. Whether this letter should be dated to the reign of Esarhaddon or Ashurbanipal is uncertain.

91 E.g., Piepkorn, *Asb.*, pp. 58-59 iv 28-32, 72-73 vi 39-41, and 76-77 vii 9-21 (in the last case via the mayor of Ḫilmu, a district of Gambūlu). The normal position of the Gambūlu with regard to Babylonia and Assyria is unclear. They aided Merodach-Baladan II

The friendly relations between Assyria and Elam during the reign of Esarhaddon continued into the first years of Ashurbanipal's reign. The Assyrian king even claims to have aided Elam by sending food supplies during a famine there and by giving shelter in Assyria to starving Elamites.[92] It was likely in 664, or shortly before that date,[93] that Urtak, king of Elam, was persuaded to invade Babylonia by Bēl-iqīša (ruler of the Gambūlu), Nabû-šuma-ēreš (governor of Nippur), and Marduk-šuma-ibni (an Elamite official). In a surprise attack, the Elamite army marched into Babylonia, covered it "like a swarm of locusts," and encamped against Babylon.[94] In the

---

during the reign of Sargon and had been annexed to Assyria by that king (Lie, *Sar.*, pp. 42-45:273-75 and 48-49:1). During the reign of Sennacherib, they had gone to the aid of Merodach-Baladan II and Mušēzib-Marduk, summoned by the ruler of Elam in the latter case (Luckenbill, *Senn.*, pp. 49:10-15 and 42-43 v 37-57). Esarhaddon claimed that Bēl-iqīša of Gambūlu had submitted to him (see above).

92 Piepkorn, *Asb.*, pp. 56-59 iv 20-26 and Nassouhi, *AfK* 2 (1924-25): 101-103 iii 10-22.

93 The date is suggested by the reference to an Elamite prince fleeing to Assyria on 12-VII-664 in the Šamaš-šuma-ukīn Chronicle (Grayson, *Chronicles*, no. 15:2-3). This may refer to the flight of Ḫumban-nikaš, son of Urtak, from Teumman when the latter seized the throne of Elam upon the death of Urtak, which edition B of Ashurbanipal's annals implies took place soon after the incident described below. As is mentioned below, the one text dated by the regnal years of Ashurbanipal at Nippur in V-664 (NBC 6142, *B-K* J.5) might also support a date in 664 (or earlier) for Urtak's invasion of Babylonia. H.W.F. Saggs, (*Assyria*, p. 112) suggests that the invasion took place in 665, i.e., the year before the Elamite prince fled to Assyria. Although the tablet is damaged, Rm 281 (Bauer, *Asb.*, pp. 56-57 and pls. 53-54) appears to state that Urtak attacked while Ashurbanipal was in Egypt and mentions this incident immediately before describing Ashurbanipal's second campaign to Egypt, which resulted in the installation of Psammetichus I to the throne of his father, Necho I. The accession of Psammetichus I is reliably dated to 664 by Egyptian sources, including astronomical data (see Kitchen, *Third Intermediate Period*, pp. 393-94 and the articles mentioned *ibid.*, p. 148 n. 271). If the order of events in Rm 281 is correct, the invasion of Urtak should have taken place in 664 at the latest. If Ashurbanipal was in Egypt during his first campaign to that country, then the invasion of Urtak may have taken place in 667, a view adopted by Grayson in his recent study of the internal chronology of the reign of Ashurbanipal (*ZA* 70 [1980]: 230). (For the date Ashurbanipal's first campaign to Egypt, see Kitchen, *Third Intermediate Period*, p. 392.) However, placement in Ashurbanipal's royal inscriptions does not always have chronological significance. In addition, edition B of Ashurbanipal's annals states that Ashurbanipal was in Assyria when Urtak invaded Babylonia (Piepkorn, *Asb.*, pp. 58-59 iv 35-38). Which of the two sources was correct is uncertain since Assyrian royal inscriptions occasionally stated that a king took part in a campaign in which he probably did not participate personally. Rm 281 refers to Ashurbanipal's first campaign against Ḫumban-ḫaltaš III (left edge), indicating that it was composed after that event. Since edition B was composed before that campaign, its evidence should be given greater credence.

94 Piepkorn, *Asb.*, pp. 58-59 iv 27-48 and Bauer, *Asb.*, p. 16 and pl. 9 v 43-50 (heavily restored). Ahmed (*Asb.*, pp. 78-79) suggests a number of reasons why Bēl-iqīša changed loyalties; however, the exact interpretations and dates of several of the letters used by him are open debate. Ahmed states that Bēl-iqīša had been made a *šatammu*-official by the Assyrian king, but there is no reason to assume the official by that name mentioned in *ABL* 914:4 and rev. 19 is to be identified with the Gambulian leader.

course of this campaign, the Elamites may have raided the city of Uruk, since Nabû-ušabši later claimed that Bēl-iqīša and Elam had destroyed his father's house.[95] It is also possible that Nippur, led by its governor, aided the Elamites. Only one text dated by Ashurbanipal's reign is known from Babylonia during Šamaš-šuma-ukīn's kingship and before the beginning of his revolt in 652; it was composed at Nippur on the twenty-ninth day of Abu (V) in 664. A possible explanation for this unique dating could be that Assyrian troops remained in Nippur after the Elamites were routed because the city or its governor had supported Urtak and that the text was composed during this period of Assyrian "occupation."[96]

Edition B records that Ashurbanipal delayed sending troops to aid Babylonia against the Elamites because of soothing messages from Urtak's ambassadors in Assyria. Upon hearing of the invasion, he first sent a messenger to observe the actions of the Elamite king. Only when the messenger returned and reported that Babylonia had been overrun did Ashurbanipal muster his troops.[97] It is possible that Ashurbanipal was not in Assyria at the time of the invasion and that it was this that caused the delay, and indeed had encouraged the Elamites to invade Babylonia.[98] Assyrian troops moved south and the Elamites retreated home, harried by the Assyrian forces. In the same year, Urtak died "before his time" (*ina ūme lā šīmtišu*) and was replaced by Teumman, presumably the Tepti-Ḫumban-Inšušinak who was a son of Šilḫak-Inšušinak II and therefore a member of the royal family although apparently not the legitimate heir.[99] As a result of Teumman's usurption of the throne, the sons of Urtak and Ḫumban-ḫaltaš II fled to Assyria, accompanied by sixty of their relatives, numerous archers, and freemen.[100] The Šamaš-šuma-ukīn Chronicle states that on the twelfth day of Tašrītu (VII) in 664 an Elamite prince fled to Assyria;[101] this may refer to Urtak's eldest son, Ḫumban-nikaš, who was later placed on the throne of

---

95 *ABL* 269:10-15. This passage could refer to the physical destruction of Nabû-ušabši's paternal home, the economic ruin of his family, or the murder of his relatives. *ABL* 998:1'-8' (see Dietrich, *Aramäer*, p. 166 no. 71 for possibly restorations) may refer to Urtak and his son Ḫumban-nikaš having been at Uruk; however, the text is not totally preserved at this point. In *ABL* 998:5' read ... [m]*um-ma-ni-g*[*a-áš* DUM]U LUGAL ... (collation I. Finkel).

96 NBC 6142 (*B-K* J.5). Nothing about the text, however, suggests any Assyrian influence or presence in the city. Any "occupation" of Nippur would not have been permanent since texts were dated by Šamaš-šuma-ukīn at Nippur in 660, 656, 655, and at the start of the Šamaš-šuma-ukīn Revolt (see Appendix A, Table 5).

97 Piepkorn, *Asb*., pp. 58-59 iv 35-50.

98 See n. 119 n. 93. This delay in sending aid to Babylonia would not have been looked upon with favour by those subject to the invasion.

99 See König, *EKI*, p. 7 and Carter and Stolper, *Elam*, p. 50.

100 Piepkorn, *Asb*., pp. 58-61 iv 51-58 and 72-86; Streck, *Asb*., pp. 210-13:15-rev. 1; and Weidner, *AfO* 8 (1932-33): 190 K 2651:2-5.

101 Grayson, *Chronicles*, no. 15:2-3.

Elam by Ashurbanipal. According to Ashurbanipal's annals, Bēl-iqīša, Nabû-šuma-ēreš, and Marduk-šuma-ibni were punished by the gods for their evil actions. Bēl-iqīša, who had cast off the yoke of Assyrian overlordship, died as the result of "the bite of a *rat*"; Nabû-šuma-ēreš, who had broken his oath of loyalty to Ashurbanipal, died of dropsy; and the god Marduk laid a "heavy penalty" upon Marduk-šuma-ibni, who had induced Urtak to commit evil. They are all said to havel died in a single year.[102]

The successor of Nabû-šuma-ēreš as governor of Nippur was likely Enlil-bāni, who is known to have been governor in 661 and to have been in correspondence with the Assyrian king.[103] At some point Ashurbanipal wrote to him (and the people of Nippur) and Nabû-ušabši (and the people of Uruk) to thank them for their help in a military venture on the other side of the Tigris.[104] This may refer to the campaign against the Gambūlu in 653 (see below). Enlil-bāni was also instructed to take every possible precaution in order to capture an unnamed individual. Every road was to be watched and everyone attempting to pass was to be interrogated. The king commanded: "Just as one places a screen at the opening of an outlet canal in order to filter out twigs, trash, and pebbles, so you will screen (everyone) at all of his (possible escape) routes." The king warned that the fugitive might disguise himself and he promised the fugitive's weight in gold to whoever captured or killed him.[105] Who the fugitive was is unknown. Could he have been Nabû-šuma-ēreš or someone involved with him in encouraging Elam to invade Babylonia? During the time Enlil-bāni governed Nippur, at least one Assyrian official (Aššur-bēla-taqqin, the *šaknu*) was stationed there, officially to forward orders and messengers of the king but presumably also to keep an eye on the city whose governors had proved troublesome in the past.[106]

Although Bēl-iqīša, the Gambulian, had aided the Elamite invasion of Babylonia, it is not clear that immediate retaliation was undertaken against the Gambūlu.[107] In 658 and possibly 657, Ashurbanipal contemplated sending troops against them;[108] but there is no evidence if he did so. When Ashurbanipal finally attacked the Gambūlu, a son of the rebel Bēl-iqīša was ruler of the tribe and in alliance with Elam. Ashurbanipal claims that Teumman, who is described as the "image of a *gallû*-demon," continually

---

102 Piepkorn, *Asb.*, pp. 60-61 iv 59-68.

103 See Appendix B sub 11a.

104 *ABL* 292 (for the restoration of the introduction, see p. 276 n. 50) and 297; see Frame in *Cuneiform Archives*, pp. 269-70.

105 *ABL* 292.

106 *ABL* 238 rev. 8'-11'. He and Enlil-bāni were likely among the authors of *ABL* 617+699 (see p. 276 n. 50).

107 For a possible campaign in 663, see pp. 122-23 n. 112.

108 Starr, *SAA* 4, nos. 271 and 272, and cf. no. 270. *ABL* 269 also refers to a contemplated campaign against this tribe.

demanded the extradition of the sons of Urtak and Ḫumban-ḫaltaš II to whom Ashurbanipal had given asylum. Ashurbanipal refused and detained Teumman's two messengers, Umbadarâ and Nabû-damiq. Despite unfavourable portents, Teumman finally mustered his troops in the fifth month of the year to do battle with the Assyrians, although it is not clear that these troops actually moved outside of Elam.[109] After obtaining the gods' approval, the king of Assyria assembled his own army in the following month and moved to the border city of Dēr. Hearing of the Assyrian advance, Teumman became afraid and retreated to Susa. The Assyrian forces continued their advance and invaded Elam. In brief, after a bloody battle at the Ūlāya river (generally identified with either the Karkheh river or the Kārūn river),[110] the Elamites were defeated and Teumman was killed. Ashurbanipal installed Ḫumban-nikaš II, a son of Urtak who had sought the Assyrian king's protection, on the throne in the city of Madaktu and another son of Urtak, Tammarītu, on the throne of the Elamite city of Ḫîdalu. In order to ingratiate himself with Ashurbanipal, Ḫumban-nikaš II handed over to him Šumaya, a son of Nabû-ušallim and grandson of Merodach-Baladan II.[111] A lunar eclipse which edition B mentions as having taken place immediately before Teumman levied his troops is usually identified with one that took place in July of 653.[112]

---

109 According to one of Ashurbanipal's inscriptions, Teumman intended to conquer Assyria, and in particular the city of Nineveh (Livingstone, *SAA* 3, no. 31:7'-13').

110 With regard to the identification of the Ūlāya river, see Parpola, *Toponyms*, p. 406 and Nashef, *RGTC* 5, p. 322.

111 Aynard, *Asb.*, pp. 38-41 ii 53-71; Piepkorn, *Asb.*, pp. 60-75 iv 74, 87-vi 16, 57-61 and 70-75; Streck, *Asb.*, pp. 26-27 iii 27-49; Weidner, *AfO* 8 (1932-33): 176-91. See also Carter and Stolper, *Elam*, p. 50 on Ashurbanipal's statement that he had also made Ḫumban-nikaš ruler of Susa. For the possible identification of Madaktu with Tépé Patak, see Miroschedji, *Steve Festschrift*, pp. 209-25. Ḫîdalu was apparently located in the mountains east of Susa on the road to Fars (see ibid., pp. 217 and 223; Zadok, *RGTC* 8, p. 146 sub Ḫajdalu; and Stolper in Carter and Stolper, *Elam*, p. 47).

112 See Piepkorn, *Asb.*, pp. 62-63 v 4-8. J. Mayr (*ibid.*, pp. 105-109) identified the eclipse with one that took place on July 13 of 653 and he has been followed by most scholars. F.R. Stephenson (apud Reade and Walker, *AfO* 28 [1981-82]: 122) believes that the description of the eclipse in edition B could equally well refer to an eclipse which took place in August of 663. Reade (*ibid.*, pp. 120-21) points out that if the campaign against Teumman is dated to 653 there is a long gap between the flight of the Elamite princes and Teumman's demand for them (the supposed cause of the fighting) and a short gap between Assyria's great victory over Elam and the outbreak of new trouble (the Šamaš-šuma-ukīn Revolt). If the lunar eclipse is dated to 663, the campaign against the Gambūlu, which is described as being a continuation of the campaign against Teumman, can be seen as a more prompt response to punish the Gambūlu for their support of Urtak's invasion than if Ashurbanipal waited until 653. However, if we accept Mayr and Parpola's reconstructions of the absolute chronology of the period, the eclipse of 663 would have occurred in the fifth month of the Babylonian year and the eclipse of 653 in the fourth month (Mayr in Piepkorn, *Asb.*, pp. 108-109 and Parpola, *LAS* 2, pp. 383 and 403). Since edition B clearly states that the eclipse took place in the fourth month, it seems best to assume that

Oaths of loyalty to Ashurbanipal and friendship with Assyria were likely imposed upon Ḫumban-nikaš and Tammarītu at this time if this had not already been done before Ashurbanipal granted them asylum in Assyria or agreed to help them oust Teumman.[113] In invading Elam to depose Teumman, Ashurbanipal pictured himself not as an aggressor, an enemy of Elam, but rather as the ally of the true rulers of that land. He later claimed in a letter to Elamite elders—who would have known the truth of the matter—that the Assyrian troops whom he had sent with Ḫumban-nikaš to depose Teumman had not raised their hands against any Elamite temples or cities and had not taken any booty.[114] Although editions A and F of Ashurbanipal's annals do not mention any plunder taken from Elam after this campaign, editions B and C state that a large amount of military equipment was carried off. Perhaps the belongings on enemy corpses and the equipment abandoned by a routed army were not considered true plunder, but rather the natural prerogative of the victorious troops.[115]

After the defeat of Teumman, Assyria appears to have claimed suzerainty over Elam. In addition to stating that the one whom he now made king over Elam was a creation of his own hands ([*ši*]*kin qātēya*), Ashurbanipal declared that he had unified that land, settled Assyrians there, and imposed taxes and tribute upon them.[116] In otherwords, Elam was now part of the Assyrian empire and its king a vassal of Assyria.[117] Ḫumban-nikaš may have felt

---

Ashurbanipal's campaign against Teumman took place in 653 rather than 663. Several royal inscriptions of Teumman (assuming he is Tepti-Ḫumban-Inšušinak) mention various building projects and military campaigns carried out by him (see König, *EKI*, pp. 169-72) and these would suggest that he had reigned for a reasonable period of time. Stolper, however, suggests that Teumman may have been the local ruler of Susa during the reign of Urtak (Carter and Stolper, *Elam*, p. 50); thus these building and military actions may have been carried out then.

113 For the existence of oaths taken by Ḫumban-nikaš and Tammarītu, see Piepkorn, *Asb*., pp. 76-77 vii 3-6 and *ABL* 1022 rev. 19-23 (heavily restored; see Parpola and Watanabe, *SAA* 2, p. XXI).

114 BM 132980 (to be published by A.R. Millard). See Parpola and Watanabe, *SAA* 2, p. XX; the letter uses the term "lay hands on (something indicted)" (*aḫu* + *wabālu*), not "set foot in." With regard to this letter, see also W.G. Lambert and A.R. Millard, *Catalogue of the Cuneiform Tablets in the Kouyunjik Collection of the British Museum, Second Supplement* (London, 1968), p. 85 and Millard in *Abstracts of the XXXVIe Rencontre Assyriologique Internationale, 10-14 July 1989* (Gent, [1989]), p. [17].

115 Piepkorn, *Asb*., pp. 70-71 vi 10-16 and Bauer, *Asb*., p. 16 and pl. 10 vii 3-9 (heavily restored).

116 Livingstone, *SAA* 3, no. 31 rev 12-17. With regards to Ashurbanipal making an individual loyal to him ruler of Elam, note also the advice given to him by the Babylonian Nabû-bēl-šumāti in *ABL* 839 rev. 11-18 (see Mattila, *SAAB* 1 [1987]: 27-30).

117 Note also the title "king of Elam" which was given to Ashurbanipal in one omen query (Starr, *SAA* 4, no. 274:2). The text deals with the appointment of an individual to a particular office, possibly to one in or over Elam. No date is preserved on the text and it could conceivably come from the period after the campaigns against Ḫumban-ḫaltaš III. A

compelled to pay lip-service to this view while Assyrian troops remained near, but he was undoubtedly waiting for a opportunity to throw off the Assyrian yoke. In the following year he was to ally himself with rebels in Babylonia and send them aid against Assyrian forces A legal document composed at Ḫîdalu (Ḫādalu) has been found which is dated to the accession year of Tammarītu as "king of Elam" and which refers to an assembly of Babylonians. Possibly the main individual involved in the text (Bēl-īpuš son of Balāṭu) and these Babylonians had gone to Ḫîdalu with Tammarītu.[118]

Having defeated Teumman, the Assyrians marched to the area of the Gambūlu in order to punish them for their present alliance with Teumman[119] as well as for their earlier support for Urtak's invasion of Babylonia. Ashurbanipal claims to have covered the Gambūlu area "like a fog" and to have besieged its capital, Ša-pī-Bēl. Dunanu (Bēl-iqīša's son and the current leader of the Gambūlu) surrendered out of fear; Ashurbanipal took him captive, along with his brothers, wife, children, officials, and artisans. The region was thoroughly looted and the Assyrians totally destroyed Ša-pī-Bēl, making it as if it had never existed. Ashurbanipal claims to have taken away silver, gold, valuables, countless cattle, sheep, and horses, and every single inhabitant of the land. The head of Teumman was hung round the neck of Dunanu and the head of the previous ruler of the city of Ḫîdalu, Šutruk-naḫḫunte (Ištarnandi of the Assyrian inscriptions), was hung around the neck of Samgunu, another of Bēl-iqīša's sons. When the army returned to Nineveh and the two Elamite messengers held there saw Teumman's head, they lost their reason; Umbadarâ tore out his beard and Nabû-damiq committed suicide. In order to demonstrate the might of Assyria, Ashurbanipal put the head of Teumman on display at the gate of Nineveh. Two sons of Nabû-šuma-ēreš, the former governor of Nippur, were among those captured and they were forced to take the bones of their dead father to Nineveh and to crush them there in public. One section of an Assyrian palace relief of the campaign against Teumman and the Gambūlu shows individuals being forced to grind up some objects (fig. 4) and thus probably depicts this incident. Mannu-kî-aḫḫē (Dunanu's deputy) and Nabû-uṣalli, the head of a Gambulian city who Ashurbanipal claims had spoken insolently about the gods, had their tongues torn out and were flayed in the city of Arbela. Dunanu was slaughtered like a sheep in Nineveh. His brothers and Šumaya, the grandson of Merodach-Baladan whom Ḫumban-nikaš had sent to

---

study of Elam as a province of Assyria is being prepared by M. Stolper, who presented a paper on the topic at the American Oriental Society, Atlanta, March 1990.

118 Leichty, *AnSt* 33 (1983): 153-55 and pl. 34 (*B-K* R.1). Leichty suggests that Bēl-īpuš may have been an Assyrian official (*ibid.*, p. 155).

119 This is indicated by the fact that an official of Teumman's who had been sent to aid the Gambūlu was found in Ša-pī-Bēl by the Assyrian forces (Piepkorn, *Asb.*, pp. 72-73 vi 39-41).

Ashurbanipal, were also killed and their flesh was sent throughout the lands to be seen as an example of what happened to those who opposed Assyria.[120]

Sîn-balāssu-iqbi son of Ningal-iddin was likely governor of Ur during most of the reign of Šamaš-šuma-ukīn before the outbreak of hostilities in 652. As was mentioned above, he may have been installed during the reign of Esarhaddon.[121] References in economic texts indicate that he certainly held that position in 658 and 657.[122] He did not take the usual title for governor, *šākin ṭēmi*, or the title *šaknu* which his father had, but preferred to use *šakkanakku* in economic texts and building inscriptions, possibly reflecting some claim to greater authority or power.[123] He claims to have been governor of Eridu and the Gurasimmu tribe as well as of Ur. This is likely since Eridu was close to Ur and may have lain under the jurisdiction of his father.[124] Sîn-balāssu-iqbi's authority over the Gurasimmu was at least such as to allow him to arrest 500 indivudals who had taken refuge among them and to return those arrested to their own lord.[125] Under his administration, Ur experienced a period of prosperity and the most important building programme at the city since the time of the Kassite king Kurigalzu was undertaken. He is known to have done work on Ur's ziggurat, the Ningal temple, the well within the Ningal temple, the Gipāru, the Edublalmaḫ, and along the temenos wall, among other places.[126] While searching for the foundation plan of the temple of Ekišnugal he discovered an inscribed brick from the time of Amar-Suen (*c.* 2046-2038) which referred to the statue of the goddess Ningal. Sîn-balāssu-

---

120 Aynard, *Asb.*, pp. 40-43 ii 72-iii 5; Bauer, *Asb.*, p. 16 and pls. 10-11 vii 10-120 (heavily restored); Piepkorn, *Asb.*, pp. 70-77 vi 17-vii 2; Streck, *Asb.*, pp. 26-29 iii 50-69; Thompson, *AAA* 20 (1933): 85, 94, and pls. 93-94:105-107; Weidner, *AfO* 8 (1932-33): 176-91, particularly epigraphs 3 (stating that the head of Ištarnandi was hung around the neck of a Elamite herald, not Samgunu), 12, 18-22, 24, 26, 28-29, 34, and 36-38 and pp. 186-91. Editions A and F describe the campaign against the Gambūlu as a continuation of the one against Teumman, while editions B and C describe it as a separate campaign. For a discussion of the reliefs depicting the campaigns against Teumman and Dunanu, see Reade, *Bagh. Mitt.* 10 (1979): 96-101.

121 See p. 99.

122 See Appendix B sub 14a.

123 BM 113927:32 and *UET* 4 32:17 (*B-K* K.40 and 45); *UET* 1 168:5, 169:6, and passim.

124 *UET* 1 168:4-6 and 170:5-7; *UET* 8 102:6-9. In *UET* 4 167 the actions of two families from Tema with respect to Eridu were reported to Ningal-iddin; this may suggest that he was overlord of Eridu as well as Ur.

125 *ABL* 839:16-22; see also p. 128 n. 146. Later the Gurasimmu were said to have revolted from Sîn-tabni-uṣur, then governor of Ur (*ABL* 754:4-8), which indicates that they had been under his jurisdiction.

126 *UET* 1 168-171, 173-183, and 8 102. See Brinkman, *Or.* NS 34 (1965): 248-53 and 38 (1969): 336-42 for a summary of the archaeological and textual evidence for Sîn-balāssu-iqbi's building programme.

iqbi had a copy of the inscription put on display.[127] He dedicated some of his works to Ashurbanipal, never mentioning Šamaš-šuma-ukīn, his legitimate overlord,[128] though on at least one occasion he went to see Šamaš-šuma-ukīn in person.[129] It has been suggested that he was disliked by Šamaš-šuma-ukīn for his Assyrian sympathies and that the Babylonian king tried to have him arrested on one occasion. This, however, remains uncertain.[130]

Exactly when Sîn-balāssu-iqbi left office is unknown. It seems that Sîn-šarra-uṣur, another son of Ningal-iddin, was governor of Ur at some point, quite likely just before the revolt began.[131] No texts from Ur have been found which mention him as governor of that city, but in an inscription likely from Uruk, Sîn-šarra-uṣur dedicated some land to two goddesses of Uruk, Ištar and Nanaya, for the life of Šamaš-šuma-ukīn and in doing so called himself governor (*šakkanakku*) of Ur.[132] The exact circumstances that surrounded Sîn-šarra-uṣur's assumption of the governorship and his eventual loss of that office are unclear. J.-M. Durand interprets various texts (in particular *ABL* 290, 947, and 1274) to indicate that Sîn-šarra-uṣur and Sîn-tabni-uṣur, a third son of Ningal-iddin, had disputed the governorship for a period of time, *c.* 655-653, that the former had the support of the Gurasimmu tribe and Šamaš-šuma-ukīn and that the latter had the support of the urban population and the Assyrian king. Durand further argues that during the period of strife Ur suffered badly from famine.[133] It seems clear that at some point in time Sîn-šarra-uṣur and Sîn-tabni-uṣur were at odds with one another (though not necessarily militarily), that some Gurasimmu supported Sîn-šarra-uṣur, that Sîn-šarra-uṣur did not always find favour in the eyes of Ashurbanipal, and that Sîn-tabni-uṣur came out on top;[134] however, the poorly preserved state of the evidence in question and the normal problems with understanding letters means that the exact interpretation of events must remain uncertain.[135]

---

127 *UET* 1 172. See Brinkman, *Or.* NS 34 (1965): 250 and n. 2 for the idea it may have been put in a temple museum formed by Sîn-balāssu-iqbi.

128 See above p. 110.

129 *ABL* 426:7-8; for the understanding of the passage, see Durand, *RA* 75 (1981): 183.

130 See especially *ABL* 426 and Durand, *RA* 75 (1981): 183.

131 See Durand, *RA* 75 (1981): 181-85.

132 *TCL* 12 13 and duplicate Durand, *DCEPHE* 1, HE 144; for the reading of the first line, see Durand, *RA* 75 (1981): 181.

133 *RA* 75 (1981): 181-85. *ABL* 290 and 1274 are assigned to the time of the rebellion in our study (see below).

134 See, for example *ABL* 290 and 523 (the Assyrian king would not listen to Sîn-šarra-uṣur's slanderous remarks about Sîn-tabni-uṣur), 947 (some Gurasimmu requested to see Sîn-šarra-uṣur so that they might live), and 1002 (Sîn-šarra-uṣur only submitted to the author of the letter because he saw that the latter's enemies never succeeded; see p. 163). The exact dates of these letters are uncertain and some may well date to the time after the commencement of the Šamaš-šuma-ukīn Revolt.

135 *ABL* 839 which may date to the middle of 653 depicts Sîn-balāssu-iqbi as then having some authority in the south, thus likely still as governor. This would suggest that

Another important official in southern Babylonia was Nabû-ušabši, the governor of Uruk. He must have assumed that position sometime between 666 and 661; the previous governor, Aḫḫēšaya, is last attested in office in the former year and Nabû-ušabši appears with the title "governor of Uruk" in a document dated in the tenth month of the latter. He maintained control of Uruk well into the Šamaš-šuma-ukīn Revolt.[136] He frequently wrote to Ashurbanipal about both domestic and foreign matters and he and the elders of Uruk appear to have gone to pay their respects to Ashurbanipal on at least one occasion.[137] At some point, possibly between 666 and 659, an Elamite sent a gift of horses to Ištar of Uruk. Shepherds brought the horses to Nabû-ušabši who did not give them to the temple; instead, he sent the shepherds, as well as an inscribed horse-trapping recording the gift, to Ashurbanipal.[138] Nabû-ušabši was probably afraid of the political implications of the gift. Perhaps he felt that he might be accused of having unauthorized contacts with Elam or that the king might think that Elam was trying to win Uruk's favour. On another occasion, Nabû-ušabši warned the king against one Pir'u and his father, Bēl-ēṭir. He recorded their comings and goings to Elam and stated that they had "done all that is detrimental to Assyria in Uruk."[139] Since the king of Assyria ordered Nabû-ušabši to raise troops and send them against the Gambūlu,[140] Nabû-ušabši must have been well trusted. This trust proved justified; Nabû-ušabši was to play a prominent pro-Assyrian role during the rebellion of 652-648.[141]

At some point before the outbreak of rebellion in 652, Nabû-bēl-šumāti, a grandson of Merodach-Baladan II, appears to have been put in charge of the Sealand, although the evidence is ambiguous. There is no clear statement calling him governor of the Sealand, though one chronicle entry for the year

---

any conflict between Sîn-šarra-uṣur and Sîn-tabni-uṣur over the governorship must be dated after that point. On *ABL* 839, see pp. 128-29.

136 See Appendix B sub 15a. For a study of some aspects of his career, see Frame in *Cuneiform Archives*, pp. 260-72.

137 *ABL* 753:6-7.

138 *ABL* 268. The same incident may be described in *ABL* 831 rev. 12'-14' (partially restored); the date is suggested by the maximum possible overlap of the tenures of office of the authors of these letters—Nabû-ušabši, governor of Uruk, and Itti-Marduk-balāṭu, who is probably to be identified with Balāṭu, the *šatammu* of Uruk (see Appendix B). *ABL* 268:17-19 suggests that it was a *teppir* of the Elamite king who sent the gift ([*ša/ištu* ᵐ*ta-a*]*m-ma-ri-ti* [...]-*il te-ep-pi-ir* LUGAL KUR NIM.MA.KI), but *ABL* 831 rev. 12' states that it was the king [of Elam]. On this matter, see Cogan, *Imperialism*, p. 56.

139 *ABL* 266 and 998. The names of neither the author nor the individuals in question are preserved in *ABL* 998; however, the circumstances described in the two letters appear to be the same.

140 *ABL* 269 and see also *ABL* 297, discussed above.

141 One of the very few individuals with an Assyrian name who held office in Babylonia during the years 689-627 was *qīpu* of Eanna during the governorship of Nabû-ušabši, namely Aššur-bēla-uṣur (see Appendix B sub 15c).

651 is sometimes restored to read "[Nabû-bē]l-šumāti, governor [of the Sealand]."[142] Since he was a member of a family that had provided governors (and kings) for the Sealand in the past,[143] and since he wrote to Ashurbanipal about conditions in southern Babylonia and events in Elam,[144] he may well have been chief of the Bīt-Yakīn tribe and governor of the Sealand. He was to be Šamaš-šuma-ukīn's chief ally during the rebellion, but in *ABL* 839 he reported to Ashurbanipal, telling him that he had heard that several towns had revolted against the king of Elam after the latter had suffered a stroke. The stroke mentioned in the letter may be that suffered by Teumman in Du'ūzu (IV) of 653 and thus date the letter to shortly after that incident.[145] A partially preserved postscript appears to advise Ashurbanipal to appoint a loyal prince ("a prince from among his [the king's] servants") to govern Elam and this may further date the letter to during or shortly after Ashurbanipal's invasion of Elam which began in the sixth month of that year. Nabû-bēl-šumāti may well desire the king to appoint Ḫumban-nikaš, a son of the previous Elamite king Urtak, since that prince had taken refuge in Nineveh from Teumman and since he was the one whom Ashurbanipal did make ruler of Elam after the defeat of the Elamite forces and the death of Teumman. Another part of the letter seems to criticize Sîn-balāssu-iqbi for handing over five hundred fugitives to an individual whom Nabû-bēl-šumāti may describe as an enemy of the king.[146] Since this letter may depict Nabû-bēl-šumāti as a supporter of Ḫumban-nikaš (an individual who was to support Šamaš-šuma-ukīn in the revolt which broke out in the following year) and as a detractor of Sîn-balāssu-iqbi (one of Ashurbanipal's strongest supporters in Babylonia), it

---

142 Grayson, *Chronicles*, no. 15:13 and see Millard, *Iraq* 26 (1964): 26.

143 With regard to the genealogy of Nabû-bēl-šumāti, see Brinkman in *Studies Oppenheim*, pp. 28-31.

144 *ABL* 839. On *ABL* 832-838, letters sent by other individuals with the name of Nabû-bēl-šumāti, see Frame, *JCS* 36 (1984): 70 n.16.

145 Piepkorn, *Asb.*, pp. 62-63 v 5-12. Dietrich connects the stroke mentioned in the letter with the sudden death of Ḫumban-ḫaltaš II in 675, thus suggesting that Nabû-bēl-šumāti was already governor at that time (*Aramäer*, p. 37). The letter, however, indicates that the king did not die immediately while the chronicle implies that Ḫumban-ḫaltaš did (see Brinkman, *Or.* NS 46 [1977]: 308 n. 27).

146 On *ABL* 839, see Mattila, *SAAB* 1 (1987): 27-30. Mattila tentatively takes Natan, the individual to whom Sîn-balāssu-iqbi gave the refugees, to be king of the Sealanders (LUGAL *šá* LÚ *tam-da-a-a*) and assumes this denotes a contrast to the Sealand under the authority of Nabû-bēl-šumāti (*ibid.*, p. 29 n. 3). It would not be surprising if there was more than one individual who had a following in the Sealand since that area was large and made up of a diverse and scattered population. Natan and Nabû-bēl-šumāti may have been two of such leaders, with the latter the official responsible for the region in Assyrian eyes. However, the passage does not have to refer to Natan as king of the Sealanders. Zadok suggests that the Tamdu could be an Arab group (*WO* 16 [1985]: 72-73) and that a reading LÚ *ud-da-a-a* is equally possible (*RGTC* 8, p. 303). It is also possible that Natan should be identified with the Puqudian by this name who acted during the rebellion of 652-648 (see below).

may be that Nabû-bēl-šumāti was already working against Assyria in this letter, though in the guise of a loyal supporter of Assyria; however, this remains pure speculation. The author of *ABL* 998, possibly Nabû-ušabši, warned Ashurbanipal that Nabû-bēl-šumāti might not be loyal to Assyria and suggested that the latter be made to take an oath as to where his true loyalities lay.[147] Ashurbanipal later claimed that Nabû-bēl-šumāti had treacherously imprisoned some Assyrians who had gone to aid him, but this comes from inscriptions written after the rebellion had begun and it is unclear if they had been sent before or after news of the revolt had reached Ashurbanipal.[148] The statement in *ABL* 839 that "the Sealand has not been settled since (the time of) Na'id-Marduk"[149] and the reference to the large number of fugitives in connection with this fact would suggest that conditions in the Sealand were not the best at this time.

It is difficult to find any clear indications that Šamaš-šuma-ukīn was preparing matters during this time in order to facilitate the declaration of his independence from Assyria, though his rebuilding of the city wall of Sippar could conceivably reflect a desire to strengthen that city in preparation for a planned rebellion. *ABL* 426 could also reflect the Babylonian king's desire to have a pro-Assyrian official (Sîn-balāssu-iqbi) removed from office and replaced by someone more favourable to Šamaš-šuma-ukīn, but the proper understanding of the passage in question is open to debate.[150] It may be possible to see some last-minute actions by Ashurbanipal to win favour in Babylonia and to discourage rebellion. Could the ceremonial bed and chariot of the god Marduk which were sent to Babylon in 654 and 653 (i.e., shortly before the outbreak of the rebellion early in 652) have been sent in order to show Babylonians that Ashurbanipal still regarded them with favour? Could the long-delayed campaign conducted against Elam and the Gambūlu in 653 have also been made to remind Babylonians first-hand what happened to Assyria's enemies? We may note that after that campaign the flesh of butchered rebels (Gambulians and descendants of Merodach-Baladan) was sent to every country (*ana tāmarti mātitān*) to serve as a vivid example of the consequences of opposition to Assyria.[151]

---

147 *ABL* 998 rev. 7'-9'. Although the name of the author is not preserved, the following indications suggest that the letter was sent by Nabû-ušabši: the author is associated with the governor Aplaya (14'), who helped Uruk during the rebellion; Uruk is mentioned in line 5'; the obverse may describe the same situation as depicted by Nabû-ušabši in *ABL* 266:7-21; and rev. 9'-10' may suggest that the author had some authority over Kudurru (on whom, see below).

148 Piepkorn, *Asb.*, pp. 80-81 vii 81-86 and Bauer, *Asb.*, p. 17 ix 59-62.

149 *ABL* 839:14-15. The passage could also be translated: "concerning the Sealand which ever since Na'id-Marduk ceased to be present"; see *CAD* 2 (B), p. 273.

150 See Durand, *RA* 75 (1981): 183-84. Note also the possibility that Šamaš-šuma-ukīn was in league with an Elamite prince (*ABL* 1385; see above).

151 Piepkorn, *Asb.*, pp. 74-75 vi 90-92.

In summary, although the sources available for this period present a one-sided view of affairs, it is clear that Ashurbanipal exercised a great deal of authority and control over his brother's realm and was indeed his brother's overlord. Babylonian officials recognized this and many reported to him, even about the actions of their king, Šamaš-šuma-ukīn. Thus, Ashurbanipal was kept well-informed about matters in Babylonia. He took it upon himself—quite likely considering it his right and his duty—to carry out building projects throughout Babylonia, to take up arms against Babylonia's enemies, and to give orders to officials nominally under Šamaš-šuma-ukīn. Many questions remain about the exact nature and extent of Šamaš-šuma-ukīn's authority over Babylonia. There is no unequivocal indication that Šamaš-šuma-ukīn was discontented with conditions before he rebelled in 652,[152] but it is temptingly easy to assume that he found Ashurbanipal's involvement in Babylonia as by stages irritating, meddlesome, and finally intolerable.

---

152 The author of *ABL* 960 stated that he had earlier reported to the king that "Šamaš-šuma-ukīn is becoming/will become hostile," 14'-15'), but this could refer to matters at the start of 652.

CHAPTER 8

THE ŠAMAŠ-ŠUMA-UKĪN REVOLT (652-648)

It was nearly forty years since Sennacherib had captured and destroyed Babylon. By 652 Babylonia had recovered sufficient strength to encourage certain elements within the land to once again challenge the might of Assyria. Šamaš-šuma-ukīn led his country into rebellion against Ashurbanipal, a war lasting over four years from which Assyria would emerge victorious but likely exhausted. Although Ashurbanipal went on to have other victories and there is no real evidence of the collapse of the empire until after his death, the Šamaš-šuma-ukīn Revolt may well mark the beginning of the decline of Assyria's fortunes.

It is not known what in particular led Šamaš-šuma-ukīn to choose his timing early in 652, although the Assyrian king's interference in internal Babylonian matters, the limitations upon Šamaš-šuma-ukīn's authority, and Babylonia's dependence upon Assyria in military matters were most likely long-term causes. The payment of tribute to Assyria may be involved; however, this remains unclear since it is uncertain if Babylonia actually did pay tribute to Assyria at this time.[1] Šamaš-šuma-ukīn may have harboured a grudge against his brother ever since 672, feeling that as the elder brother he should be the one with higher authority. Between the second and tenth months of 652 an official (*rab bīti*) carried out some action in Babylonia. If he was acting for the Assyrian king and levying troops, as some scholars suppose (see below), this might have prompted Šamaš-šuma-ukīn to rebel.

---

[1] See pp. 238-39. *ABL* 301 rev. 3-5 has sometimes been interpreted to show that Ashurbanipal had required the Babylonians to pay (new) tribute and to suggest that Šamaš-šuma-ukīn used their discontent at this to win them over to rebellion (e.g., Ahmed, *Asb.*, p. 91). Moran, however, has recently shown that the text uses the word *piltu/pištu*, "insult, reproach, scorn," not the word *biltu*, "tax, tribute, etc." (*Tadmor Festschrift*, pp. 320-31). Steiner and Nims understand the Aramaic story on Amherst papyrus 63 to say that Ashurbanipal had obliged his brother to send tribute ("*Devo<te> yourself* to the payment of tribute to [A]⌜ssy⌝ria") but that Šamaš-šuma-ukīn had stopped doing so at the commencement of his rebellion (*RB* 92 [1985]: 63 and 71). Vleeming and Wesselius (*Studies* 1, p. 34) offer a different interpretation of the text and translate this passage as "be inactive on my goodness: the share which is [yours]!" In view of the difficulties in interpreting the text and of the fact that it is a late literary source, it must be used with caution and cannot be taken to prove that Babylonia did pay tribute to Assyria at this time or that Šamaš-šuma-ukīn stopped doing so in 652.

Undoubtedly Šamaš-šuma-ukīn was encouraged by anti-Assyrian elements within Babylonia that were willing to forget his Assyrian origin if he could unite the country and re-establish Babylonia's independence. It is surprising, however, that Babylonia risked a rebellion so soon after the demonstration of Assyrian might against Elam and Gambūlu in 653.

The sources for this period are uniformly one-sided in their perspective. No accounts are preserved from the rebel side, and thus we receive an essentially Assyrian view of events. From this perspective, Šamaš-šuma-ukīn's action in declaring Babylonia's independence from Assyria was that of a perfidious villain. The gods, of course, were on the side of Assyria and saw to it that Ashurbanipal defeated the Babylonian rebels and their allies, including various Elamite kings who, like Šamaš-šuma-ukīn, were depicted as treacherous knaves who had forgotten the favours shown to them by the king of Assyria. A number of letters report on events at this time and give insight into the actual social and political climate. Regrettably, many of these are damaged, making their exact interpretation uncertain and, since they are only rarely dated, it is usually difficult to determine even the relative order of the events described in them. Editions B and D of Ashurbanipal's annals were composed during the revolt, but they provide information only with regard to some Elamite involvement in the revolt, as does edition F, composed in 646 or 645. Probably the authors of the editions written while the rebellion was still in progress felt that it was too sensitive a subject for detailed description as Assyria had not yet proven victorious and punished the rebels. Edition K was the first edition of Ashurbanipal's annals composed after the fall of Babylon; unfortunately it is poorly preserved.[2] Only it and the later editions A and C (the latter also poorly preserved) deal with the revolt in any detail.[3]

Because of the nature of the sources, it is not possible to present a chronologically precise description of events during the revolt. Frequently even the relative order of events is uncertain, although the Šamaš-šuma-ukīn and Akītu Chronicles do provide some footholds. (Table 2 presents a brief outline of the major datable events.) After a discussion of the general extent of the revolt, the period will be dealt with under the following headings:[4]

---

[2] For the information on the fall of Babylon in this edition, see Cogan and Tadmor, *Or.* NS 50 (1981): 229-40.

[3] Editions T and H (as far as the latter is preserved) do not mention the revolt although both were composed after the rebellion (in 646/645 and 639 respectively). The Ištar Tablet mentions the revolt, but provides little detail (Thompson, *AAA* 20 [1933]: 86, 95, and pl. 94:110-113).

[4] The nature of the evidence makes some overlap among the various sections unavoidable.

I. Northern and Central Babylonia[5]
II. Uruk
III. Ur and Its Neighbours
IV. The Arameans
V. The Chaldeans
VI. The Sealand
VII. Elam

According to edition A of Ashurbanipal's annals, Šamaš-šuma-ukīn incited a rebellion among the people of Akkad, Chaldea, Aramu, and the Sealand, from the town of Aqaba as far as Bāb-Salīmēti;[6] he won the support of the kings of Elam, Gutium, Amurrû, and Meluḫḫa, and even the Arabs allied with him.[7] While there is no other evidence that the kings of Gutium, Amurrû, and Meluḫḫa (Nubia) supported Šamaš-šuma-ukīn,[8] more detailed descriptions of the revolt indicate that Ashurbanipal was correct in assigning Akkadians, Chaldeans, Arameans, Sealanders, Elamites, and Arabs to the rebel cause. However, it is also clear that not all of these groups gave their undivided support to Šamaš-šuma-ukīn.

---

5 Comprising roughly Nippur and the area north of that city.

6 Streck, *Asb.*, pp. 30-31 iii 96-100. Despite Dougherty (*Sealand*, pp. 99-105), it is not certain that the phrase "from the town of Aqaba as far as Bāb-Salīmēti" refers only to the Sealand and not to all four preceding groups. If the town Aqaba is to be identified with the town on the Gulf of Aqaba, then this term may have been meant to include all the elements (including the Arabs) who supported the rebellion. For a possible location for Aqaba in northern Babylonia, see the literature cited in Ahmed, *Asb.*, p. 92 n. 118 and note also Zadok, *WO* 16 (1985): 62. The location of Bāb-Salīmēti is uncertain, although Luckenbill, *Senn.*, p. 74:69-70 suggests that it may have been located on the Euphrates. The Ištar Tablet refers to Šamaš-šuma-ukīn having estranged Akkad, Chaldea, and Aramu from Ashurbanipal (Thompson, *AAA* 20 [1933]: 86, 95, and pl. 94:111).

7 Streck, *Asb.*, pp. 30-31 iii 100-106 and 64-65 vii 82-106.

8 The term Gutium is presumably being used to refer to the mountainous area east of the Tigris. Some groups living there may have provided support for the rebellion, or at least used the opportunity to throw off any subservience to Assyria. Edition B of Ashurbanipal's annals refers to some fighting/trouble in Amurrû caused by Arabs (Piepkorn, *Asb.*, pp. 84-85 viii 39-50), but no direct connection is made between this incident and the revolt; see p. 135 n. 16. For the identification of Nubia with Meluḫḫa, see Borger, *Esarh.*, p. 112 §76:15. There is no evidence to suggest that Nubia or Egypt was in contact with, or allied to, Šamaš-šuma-ukīn. Egypt had apparently been lost to Assyria by the mid-650s (see Cogan and Tadmor, *Or.* NS 46 [1977]: 84 and Kitchen, *Third Intermediate Period*, p. 406). According to Herodotus, *History* 2.157, Psammetichus I besieged Ashdod for 29 years before taking that city; however, here is no other evidence for this action. If the Egyptian king did indeed attack Ashdod (part of the Assyrian empire), he is likely to have done so towards the end of his lengthy reign (664-610), when the Assyrian empire was in decline. Edition A of Ashurbanipal's annals records that the Assyrian king conducted military actions against Akko and Ušû (near Tyre) after putting down his brother's rebellion (see below). If Ashdod had been besieged by Psammetichus at that time, Ashurbanipal would undoubtedly have gone to its aid and his action would have been mentioned in the annals.

Not all Akkadians, who were concentrated in the urban centres of the country, appear to have been loyal to Šamaš-šuma-ukīn. Edition A of Ashurbanipal's annals states that only Babylon, Borsippa, and Sippar closed their gates to the Assyrians at the start of the rebellion,[9] although date formulae of economic texts indicate that Nippur and probably Dilbat also supported the rebellion. However, Cutha, Ur, Uruk, and several towns in the extreme south remained loyal to Assyria at the start of the revolt.[10] Thus support for the rebellion among this group seems to have been concentrated in the cities of northern Babylonia.

There is little clear evidence about the actions of the Chaldean tribes during the time of the revolt. Although some of the Bīt-Amukāni aided the rebels, at one point Ashurbanipal felt able to appoint a leader for the troops/people (LÚ.ÉRIN.MEŠ) of that tribe.[11] At least some members of the Bīt-Dakkūri appear to have aided Šamaš-šuma-ukīn.[12] Bīt-Yakīn is unattested during this period except by the term "Sealand" and the individual Nabû-bēl-šumāti, who was a member of the ruling family of the tribe. Following a well established tradition, the Sealand, led by Nabû-bēl-šumāti, was a mainstay of the rebel cause. However, some towns in the area of the Sealand that were considered by Sennacherib to belong to Bīt-Yakīn remained loyal to Ashurbanipal at the start of the revolt and there is other evidence that not all the inhabitants of the Sealand were united behind Nabû-bēl-šumāti (see below). Among the Arameans, only two tribes are known to have played any significant role—the Puqūdu, who were also not unanimous in their support for the rebellion,[13] and the Gambūlu, located on the Elamite border, who were generally involved in association with Elam. At least part of the Gurasimmu tribe remained loyal to Assyria until forced to desert because of rebel actions against them.[14]

An extispicy report for Ashurbanipal dated on the fourth day of Nisannu (I) in 651 shows that Ashurbanipal had Akkadians, Chaldeans, and Aḫlamû (Arameans), either among his troops or supporting the Assyrian cause. In the

---

9 Streck, *Asb.*, pp. 30-31 iii 107-108.

10 Texts at Ur and Uruk were dated by Ashurbanipal's regnal years during the revolt (see Appendix A). Since Cutha was later captured by the rebels (see below), it must have supported the Assyrians prior to that time. *ABL* 1241+*CT* 54 112:14'-19' shows that such towns as Eridu, Kissik, Kullab, and Šāt-iddin supported Assyria during the early part of the rebellion.

11 Starr, *SAA* 4, no. 290 rev. 6-12.

12 Weidner, *AfO* 8 (1932-33): 194-95 no. 60 (passage damaged); see below.

13 Starr, *SAA* 4, no. 289 rev. 1-5 (*ABL* 1195) shows that there were some Puqudians on the Assyrian side. The fact that the author of this extispicy report considered it possible that Tammarītu might attack Nippur shows that it must be dated after that city came under Assyrian control (after the beginning of IX-651, see below).

14 *ABL* 1241+*CT* 54 112:8'-13' (see Dietrich, *Aramäer*, pp. 200-201 no. 155 for restorations).

text, Ashurbanipal sought to find out if Nabû-bēl-šumāti—who is said to have broken his oath of allegiance to the Assyrian king—would come and fight with the Assyrian army, or with the Assyrians, Akkadians, Chaldeans, or Arameans (Aḫlamû) who supported Assyria.[15] The most important supporters of Ashurbanipal in Babylonia were Nabû-ušabši (governor of Uruk), Sîn-tabni-uṣur (governor of Ur), and Bēl-ibni (an official appointed over the Sealand). All three had to deal with the actions of Nabû-bēl-šumāti, who appears to have led the rebellion in the south.

Šamaš-šuma-ukīn wisely sought to win outside support for his rebellion (occasionally paying for it) in order to gain military aid and to prevent the Assyrian forces from concentrating on Babylonia alone. Under its various kings, Elam aided Šamaš-šuma-ukīn, as did rulers of at least two nomadic groups to the west (Abiyate', ruler of the Qedarites, and Uaite', ruler of Sumu'ilu). Although there is evidence of contact between the Babylonian king and Natnu, king of the Nabayateans, during the revolt, there is no evidence that Natnu or his tribesmen provided Šamaš-šuma-ukīn with aid.[16] It is also possible that Ḫundaru, the ruler of Dilmun, was involved in some way with the revolt. Goods belonging to Nabû-bēl-šumāti were found there and Bēl-ibni, who rewon the Sealand from Nabû-bēl-šumāti, asked if Ashurbanipal wanted to pardon Ḫundaru for his offence.[17]

According to 2 Chronicles 33:11-13, Manasseh, king of Judah (*c.* 697-642), was put in fetters and carried off captive to Babylon by the commanders of the Assyrian army, although he was later returned to his kingdom. Because Manasseh was obviously being punished by the Assyrians for some reason and because Babylon is mentioned, this has led to the belief that he

---

15 Starr, *SAA* 4, no. 280; the supporters of Assyria are described as the ones "who have grasped the feet of Ashurbanipal" (rev. 12-13).

16 The question of Mesopotamian relations with the nomadic groups to the west during this period has been recently examined by Weippert (*WO* 7 [1973-74]: 39-85) and Eph'al (*Ancient Arabs*, pp. 46-52 and 142-69). This study will follow the the latter's reconstruction of events since it seems to make the best historical sense of the admittedly confusing and at times inconsistent statements in the ancient sources. Thus, it is assumed here that the Qedarite raids on southern Syria and Transjordan led by Yauta' and Ammuladi(n) date to 652 or earlier and were not conducted in co-ordination with Šamaš-šuma-ukīn's actions in Babylonia (see *ibid.*, pp. 142-55).

17 *ABL* 791; note the reference to Nabû-bēl-šumāti in Thompson, *AAA* 20 (1933): 103-104 and pl. 100, a letter from Ashurbanipal to Ḫundaru. For mentions of Dilmun at this time, see Kessler in Potts, *Dilmun*, pp. 149-51. D. Oates (in Khalifa and Rice, *Bahrain*, p. 431) suggests that *ABL* 458 indicates that Dilmun had two rival rulers, Ḫundaru and Idru, with the former supporting Šamaš-šuma-ukīn and the latter Ashurbanipal. He arrives at this by assuming that the word *muribbānu* which is used to describe Idru's relationship to Ḫundaru means "rival," but the *CAD* 10/2 (M), p. 219 takes the word to refer to some type of profession.

may have been involved, or suspected of being involved, in the rebellion.[18] Perhaps after the revolt had been put down, Manasseh was taken to the recently conquered Babylon to be shown what happened to rebels. However, Manasseh's crime is never stated explicitly and no mention of a rebellion in Babylonia is found in the Biblical passage.

Two cuneiform documents found at Gezer are dated to the seventeenth day of Simanu (III) of "the eponymy after Aššur-dūra-uṣur, governor of Bar-Ḫalzi" (651), and the fourth day of Šabaṭu (XI) of "the eponymy of Aḫi-ilaya, governor of Carchemish" (649), respectively.[19] Assyrian eponyms would not have been used to date these texts if Gezer was in revolt against Assyria at those times. M.T. Larsen suggests that while the use of the posthumous (*arki*) eponym date in 651 may simply indicate that news of the name of the eponym for that year (Sagabbu) had not yet reached Gezer, unrest in the lands between Assyria and Gezer may instead have delayed or prevented the news of the name of the new eponym reaching that city, or the Assyrian bureaucracy may have been too pre-occupied with the war in Babylonia to worry about circulating the name of the eponym for that year.[20] Shortly after 648, Ashurbanipal had to surpress rebellions in Ušû (near Tyre) and Akko.[21] These cities may have made use of the fact that Assyria was busily involved in Babylonia to throw off the Assyrian yoke, although they may not have had acted in league with Šamaš-šuma-ukīn.[22]

Thus, although Šamaš-šuma-ukīn did manage to raise a widespread and impressive coalition against Assyria, Babylonia itself was not united solidly behind him; in particular, the important cities of Uruk, Ur, and initially Cutha held out against him. His support within his own country was concentrated in the cities of northern Babylonia and in the tribal areas of the south. Unfortunately, the exact postion of many elements within the country remains unclear or unknown.

There is no contemporary evidence that Šamaš-šuma-ukīn tried to claim the throne of Assyria at the time of his rebellion, though he was an elder son

---

18 See for example Eph'al, *Ancient Arabs*, pp. 158-59. Cogan (*Imperialism*, pp. 67-70) prefers to connect this incident with Esarhaddon's campaign to Egypt in 671. For other suggested dates for this incident, see J.M. Miller and J.H. Hayes, *A History of Ancient Israel and Judah* (Philadelphia, 1986), pp. 374-76. Josephus, *Antiquities*, x iii presents a variant account of the passage in 2 Chronicles.

19 Gezer, located just outside the kingdom of Judah, had been incorporated into the Assyrian empire in the previous century. See Becking in *JEOL* 27 (1981-82): 76-89 for the most recent edition and discussion of these texts and for the older bibliography.

20 Larsen, *RA* 68 (1974): 22-23.

21 Ashurbanipal's campaign is described as part of his action against the Arabs who had aided Šamaš-šuma-ukīn (Streck, *Asb.*, pp. 80-83 ix 115-128) and would date to *c.* 645.

22 This would seem more likely than that they had revolted just after Ashurbanipal had demonstrated Assyria's might by reconquering Babylonia and severely punishing Elam for its support of Šamaš-šuma-ukīn (see below).

of Esarhaddon than Ashurbanipal. The only place we may find this is in the late Aramaic literary-historical tale found in Egypt, Amherst papyrus 63. There, in initiating his revolt, Šamaš-šuma-ukīn tells Ashurbanipal that he (Šamaš-šuma-ukīn) is king of Babylon while his brother is merely governor of Nineveh, thereby implying that his brother is his subordinate.[23] Even if Šamaš-šuma-ukīn had felt that he had no hope of toppling his brother, he might well have put forward a claim to the throne of Assyria in order to try to cause civil strife in that land and lessen its ability to concentrate its forces against Babylonia. Perhaps Šamaš-šuma-ukīn had made himself so much a king of Babylonia that he could no longer pose as a true contender for the throne of Assyria, or perhaps he felt that his Babylonian subjects would have been less willing to follow him in an attempt to gain the throne of Assyria than in a war of liberation from Assyria. While he may well have tried to win over to his side old friends in Assyria, there is no clear evidence that he had any Assyrian support during the rebellion, though unrest in Assyria in 651 may have been connected with it (see below).

Ashurbanipal could not ignore his brother's actions and allow Babylonia to leave Assyria's sphere of influence. If ever Šamaš-šuma-ukīn were to become master in his own kingdom, he might later attempt to conquer Assyria. In any case, an independent and potentially hostile Babylonia could not be tolerated on Assyria's southern border. Thus, even if it meant temporarily weakening his control over other areas, Ashurbanipal felt that it was necessary to deal decisively with Babylonia. For about four years Assyria was kept busy with the rebellion and time after that was required to settle accounts with those non-Babylonian groups who had aided the rebellion or who had taken advantage of Assyria's pre-occupation with Babylonia for their own ends.

I. Northern and Central Babylonia

Šamaš-šuma-ukīn rebelled against Assyrian domination early in 652 and by the twenty-third day of Ayyaru (II) news of the revolt had reached Assyria. Exactly what Šamaš-šuma-ukīn did to begin the rebellion is unknown, though as already mentioned, Amherst papyrus 63 states that he

---

23 Steiner and Nims, *RB* 92 (1985): 71 and Vleeming and Wesselius, *Studies* 1 p. 34. According to the translation by Steiner and Nims, Šamaš-šuma-ukīn stated that Nineveh was tributary to him (Šamaš-šuma-ukīn) and asked why he (Šamaš-šuma-ukīn) should pay homage to Ashurbanipal ("I am the king of [!] Babylon, and you are the governor of Ni<ne>veh, *my* tribut*ary city*. Why should I pay homage to you?"). According to the translation of this passage by Vleeming and Wesselius, Šamaš-šuma-ukīn told his brother to hand something over for him to assign ("I am the king from Babylon and you are a governor in Niniveh [*sic*]. Give over the share, so that I can assign it!"). In either case, Šamaš-šuma-ukīn is clearly portraying himself as Ashurbanipal's superior.

had sent a message to Ashurbanipal in which he claimed that he was the king of Babylon while his brother was (only) governor of Nineveh, thus implying that the latter was subject to his authority. According to edition A of Ashurbanipal's annals, Šamaš-šuma-ukīn had treated his brother villainously and broken his oath of loyalty to his brother. He had deceived Babylonians who were loyal to Assyria and sent them to his brother in Nineveh in order to bear him greetings, while at the same time he had plotted murder. This could imply that Šamaš-šuma-ukīn had attempted to gain time to build up his support by sending a delegation to Assyria to try to put at rest initial suspicions about his activities. After winning the support of Akkadians, Chaldeans, Arameans, Sealanders, and various outside forces, in particular Ḫumban-nikaš of Elam, Šamaš-šuma-ukīn locked the gates of Sippar, Babylon, and Borsippa against the Assyrians, mounted his soldiers upon the walls of these cities, and prevented Ashurbanipal from sending offerings to their gods. According to edition A, the moon-god Sîn sent word to assure Ashurbanipal that the rebels would be defeated. It was reported that a seer had dreamed that he had seen a message inscribed upon the pedestal of the statue of that god. The god had written: "I will grant a horrible death to (all) those who plot against Ashurbanipal, the king of Assyria, (or) act in a hostile way. I will put an end to their lives with the quick iron dagger, conflagration, famine, (and) pestilence."[24]

On the twenty-third day of Ayyaru (II), Ashurbanipal sent the letter *ABL* 301 to the people of Babylon in an attempt to persuade them not to commit themselves to his brother's cause.[25] He undoubtedly wished to crush the revolt at its heart before it achieved full momentum. Denouncing Šamaš-šuma-ukīn as one who has been "rejected by the god Marduk," Ashurbanipal beseeched them not to listen to Šamaš-šuma-ukīn's lies but rather to remember his own kindness to them. The Assyrian king denied Šamaš-šuma-ukīn's charge that he (Ashurbanipal) planned to do something evil, presumably against the people of Babylon. Šamaš-šuma-ukīn, he said, had lied to them to try to persuade them to support the rebellion. He stated that he held them in high regard and asked them not to ruin their reputation by joining the rebellion.

> I have heard the lying words which that unbrotherly brother (of mine) said to you; (I have heard) everything he said. (They are) lie(s)! Do not trust him! I swear by Aššur and Marduk, my gods, that I have

---

[24] Streck, *Asb.*, 28-33 ii 78-127.

[25] For a full translation and philological study of this letter, see Moran, *Tadmor Festschrift*, pp. 320-31. It remains uncertain if the letter indicates that Ashurbanipal felt that the people of Babylon had already given evidence of siding with his brother—but that he would forgive them if they now abandoned the rebellion—or that he simply did not know what their initial feelings were and wished them to declare themselves one way or the other.

> neither planned in my heart nor spoken with my mouth any of the bad things that he spoke concerning me! That one has thought of nothing but trickery. (He says to himself:) "I will ruin the reputation of the Babylonians who love him (Ashurbanipal) along with my own!" I have not listened to this. Up until now, my mind has been on your brotherhood with the Assyrians and on your privileged position which I established. Accordingly, do not listen to his lies! Do not ruin your reputation which is good in my eyes and in the eyes of every land! Do not do wrong in the eyes of (your) god! I know that there is another matter about which you are concerned. (You say to yourselves:) "Now, the (very) fact that we have continually opposed against him/it (Ashurbanipal/Assyria) will become our reproach." This is no reproach. It is nothing when (your) reputation is (so) excellent ... Now then, I have written to you. If you have not sullied yourselves with him in this affair, let me see an answer to my letter immediately!

The reaction of Babylon's inhabitants to this appeal is unknown; there is no evidence that the letter ever reached Babylon or was made public there.

The Akītu Chronicle states that from the second through the tenth month of 652 the steward (*rab bīti*) carried out some action (*biḫirti ibteḫir*) in Akkad. He was evidently choosing something(s) or some person(s), possibly levying troops.[26] It is uncertain for whom this official was acting. Possibly Šamaš-šuma-ukīn was having troops collected so that he could defend himself against expected Assyrian retaliation. Or possibly he was acting in support of the Assyrian king, as he had for Esarhaddon in 677 and probably 679 (see above). On the one hand, it seems unlikely that an Assyrian would have been able to carry out such an action in Babylonia for eight months without some armed conflict having occurred (and hostilities did not commence until the tenth month), but, on the other hand, one would not expect Ashurbanipal to have allowed Šamaš-šuma-ukīn to gather troops unimpeded for such a long period of time.[27] If the official was acting for Ashurbanipal, it may have been this action that caused the revolt to break out when it did. The action commenced in the second month and Ashurbanipal's letter dated on the twenty-third day of Ayyaru (II) implies that the revolt had just begun. This was the first time that the *rab bīti* had carried out this action in Babylonia since Šamaš-šuma-ukīn had assumed the throne, though it had been done in the time of Esarhaddon. Possibly Šamaš-šuma-ukīn saw it as the final encroachment upon his authority. Or, if the action was carried out for Šamaš-šuma-ukīn, it may have been what made Ashurbanipal realize that his brother had declared his independence of Assyria and what caused him to write to the

---

26 Grayson, *Chronicles*, no. 16:9-10 and see chapter 10 section III for a discussion of the Akkadian phrase in question.

27 If indeed the official was gathering troops.

citizens of Babylon. It was in the final month that the *rab bīti* acted that open hostilities finally commenced. Thus, his action may well have been what indicated to Ashurbanipal that his brother was seeking to declare his independence from Assyria (assuming the official was acting for the Babylonian king) or been the final Assyrian action which caused Šamaš-šuma-ukīn to declare his independence (assuming the official was acting for the Assyrian king), and its completion may have been what finally allowed, or made practical, the commencement of actual warfare.

During the months the *rab bīti* was acting, the two sides were probably jockeying for position, trying to shore up their own support and to increase the number of their followers among the various elements within Babylonia. Most likely Ashurbanipal was attempting to end the revolt by diplomacy before resorting to force of arms. He may have felt it better for the future control of Babylonia if he could get its people to see reason and submit; he would thus avoid increasing their resentment by using force of arms, which would undoubtedly leave the land devastated, depleted of lifes and property. He may have sent appeals to other groups and prominent individuals in Babylonia—promises to forgive transgressions and reward loyalty, and reminders of Assyria's power and the consequences of rebellion in the past. Earlier Assyrian kings had used similar appeals to try to persuade the people of rebel cities to disobey their leaders and submit. Tiglath-pileser III had sent such a message to the people of Babylon urging them to abandon Nabû-mukīn-zēri and Sennacherib had appealed to the people of Jerusalem not to support Hezekiah against Assyria.[28] The late Aramaic story on Amherst papyrus 63 records that Ashurbanipal sent his sister Šērū'a-ēṭerat to Babylon to appeal to Šamaš-šuma-ukīn to abandon his rebellious activities and submit to his brother. When her plea was ignored by Šamaš-šuma-ukīn, Ashurbanipal sent another emissary, this time a high military officer. Again Šamaš-šuma-ukīn is said to have refused to submit.[29] Since the text is a late literary work, with the motif of the good, patient, and forebearing brother (Ashurbanipal) versus the evil, treacherous brother (Šamaš-šuma-ukīn), its evidence cannot be accepted without question; however, it would not be surprising if such appeals had been made. At the same time he was using diplomacy in Babylonia, Ashurbanipal may have been examining the situation in Assyria and elsewhere. He would have needed to know if trouble was likely to break out in Assyria in support of his brother and how the remainder

---

[28] For the letter from the time of Tiglath-pileser III, see Saggs, *Iraq* 17 (1955): 23-26 and pl. 4 no. 1; see also von Soden in *Stier Festschrift*, pp. 46-48; Grayson in *Papyrus and Tablet*, pp. 106-107; and Gonçalves, *L'expédition de Sennachérib*, pp. 407-409. For the appeal in the time of Sennacherib, see 2 Kings 18:17-37 and Isaiah 36:1-22.

[29] Steiner and Nims, *RB* 92 (1985): 73-78 and Vleeming and Wesselius, *Studies* 1, pp. 34-37. For references to Šērū'a-ēṭerat, see Parpola, *LAS* 2, p. 118.

of the empire was likely to act if he became occupied in Babylonia for several years.

Although *ABL* 1105 is badly damaged, it appears to represent an oath of allegiance imposed (or to be imposed) on behalf of Ashurbanipal upon certain Babylonians, possibly Babylonians who had been implicated in the rebellion in some way.[30] A Babylonian origin or destination for the text is suggested by the facts that it is in Babylonian script and dialect and that although Aššur heads the list of gods mentioned in the concluding formulae, Marduk follows him. The individuals swore to support the Assyrian king, to report any word or deed against him, to arrest his foes, and to raise troops and stand against the king's enemies. Sections of the text mention Šamaš-šuma-ukīn, apparently in parallel with individuals or groups hostile or potentially hostile to Ashurbanipal. Except for perhaps one instance, Šamaš-šuma-ukīn is given no title in the text, in contrast to Ashurbanipal, who is constantly described as "king of Assyria." Thus, the document may have been composed soon after the outbreak of the rebellion to be imposed on those who had decided (by choice or under duress) to support the Assyrian cause.[31]

In the middle of the month of Duʾūzu (17-IV-652), Ashurbanipal considered attacking Babylon with the hope that he would capture Šamaš-šuma-ukīn and crush the revolt quickly before it spread. The omens for this scheme were unfavourable[32] and there is no evidence that such a campaign took place. After recording the action of the *rab bīti* in the second through tenth months of the year, the Akītu Chronicle states that it was on the nineteenth day of the tenth month that hostilities commenced between Assyria and Akkad (Babylonia), although exactly what happened on that date is not mentioned.[33] Initial skirmishes must have gone badly for the rebels since it is recorded that Šamaš-šuma-ukīn retired into Babylon in the face of the enemy on the eighth day of Šabaṭu (XI), less than three weeks later.[34]

---

30 See Parpola and Watanabe, *SAA* 2, no. 9. For the possibility that the people had been implicated in the rebellion, see lines 26-28 (heavily restored). Dietrich (*Aramäer*, pp. 82-85) argues that the oath was imposed upon the people or elders of Uruk, Grayson (*JCS* 39 [1987]: 139-40) upon the citizens of Babylon, and Parpola and Watanabe (*SAA* 2, p. XXXII) upon the people of the Sealand. Damage to the text makes any particular attribution difficult.

31 Grayson's edition of *ABL* 301 rev. 12 would suggest that this oath is mentioned in the letter: *adû altaprakkunūši* as "I am now sending you the treaty" (*JCS* 39 [1987]: 139). We should instead take *adû* with the *enna* of the previous line and translate "Now then, I have written to you"; for the phrase *enna adû*, see *CAD* 4 (E), p. 169. There is no clear evidence that *adê* "loyalty oath/treaty" ever appears in the form *adû* (see Watanabe, *Vereidigung*, pp. 9-23).

32 Starr, *SAA* 4, no. 279.

33 Grayson, *Chronicles*, no. 16:11.

34 Grayson, *Chronicles*, no. 15:6. The Akītu Chronicle (*ibid.*, no. 16:12) does not give a separate date for Šamaš-šuma-ukīn's retreat to Babylon, but mentions it after the statement about the start of hostilities on 19-X.

As mentioned, edition A of Ashurbanipal's annals states that Babylon, Borsippa, and Sippar locked out the Assyrians. Šamaš-šuma-ukīn mounted his fighters on the walls of these cities and prevented Ashurbanipal's offerings from being made to Marduk, Nabû, Šamaš, and Erra, the gods of those three cities and Cutha.[35] Borsippa, situated close to Babylon, naturally followed that city's lead. Economic texts were dated at Borsippa by the regnal years of Šamaš-šuma-ukīn through to the twenty-eighth day of Abu (V) in 648 and attest to the fact that the city remained on the rebel side until the end of the revolt.[36] Little detailed information is available about Borsippa during the revolt although an epigraph for one of Ashurbanipal's reliefs refers to the defeat of citizens of Borsippa who had joined Šamaš-šuma-ukīn in rebellion.[37] Sippar, the northernmost important city of Babylonia, might be expected to have borne the brunt of Assyrian action. Again, little is known about this city during the course of the revolt. At one point, it was the target of a contemplated Assyrian campaign; Ashurbanipal requested that an extispicy be performed to determine if his brother would flee Babylon with his troops and officials if Assyrian forces entered Sippar. The extispicy was indecisive.[38] In the end, the city fell or surrendered to the Assyrians. The dating of documents from Nippur by the regnal years of Šamaš-šuma-ukīn at the start of the rebellion—on the twenty-fifth (or later) day of Abu (V) of 651 and on the third (or later) day of Kislīmu (IX) of the same year[39]—is evidence that this city also sided with the rebel king. It was, however, to fall to the Assyrians late in 651.

It is likely that Dilbat also stood on the rebel side.[40] A transaction was dated there by Šamaš-šuma-ukīn's regnal years on the twenty-fifth day of Simanu (III) in 652, more than a month after news of the rebellion had reached Assyria, although admittedly before hostilities had actually broken out. The document describes a lawsuit carried out before an assembly of

---

35 Streck, *Asb.*, pp. 30-33 iii 107-114. Erra is to be identified with Nergal, the patron deity of Cutha. With regard to Sippar's closing its gate, note *ABL* 804 rev. 4-5: "Sippar is a door which is [closed] in our face" (*CAD* 3 [D], p. 55).

36 At least, the last document known to have been dated by the regnal years of Šamaš-šuma-ukīn from Babylon was composed only two days after the last document dated by that king's years at Borsippa. See Appendix A. *OECT* 10 399 (*B-K* J.24), dated at Dilbat on 29-I-646, describes the sale of a date palm orchard in the vicinity of Dilbat which one individual received from another *ina e-de!-el* KÁ *ki-i* 1 MA.NA 1 GÍN KÙ.BABBAR *ina bar-sip*.KI (line 5). It remains uncertain if this refers to a transaction which had taken place during the revolt while Borsippa had been besieged or, perhaps less likely, while Dilbat had been besieged (i.e., "during the closure of the gate [of Dilbat]").

37 Weidner, *AfO* 8 (1932-33): 194-95 no. 54 (partially restored).

38 Starr, *SAA* 4, no. 290:21-24 (date not preserved).

39 IM 57924 and IM 57923 (*B-K* K.114 and K.116).

40 Dilbat is usually identified with Tell Dulaihim/Dēlam (about 15 km southeast of Borsippa), or less frequently with Muḫaṭṭaṭ (about 5.5 km southeast of Tell Dulaihim); see Unger, *ArOr* 3 (1931): 21-22 and Groneberg, *RGTC* 3, p. 51.

people from Babylon and Dilbat, showing that the two cities were in contact at that time.[41] No other documents have been found which were dated at this city until after the revolt had been crushed, but three documents from Borsippa (located about 15-20 kilometres away) may provide some information about Dilbat's loyalties. The first was composed in the month of Kislīmu (IX) of Šamaš-šuma-ukīn's eighteenth year (650) and describes a loan to Uraš-bēlanni son of Lāgamāl-ušēzib.[42] The second comes from the fifteenth day of Duʾūzu (IV) of Šamaš-šuma-ukīn's twentieth year (648) and records the sale of land located at Dilbat. The names of several individuals acting in the second transaction or witnessing it include the divine name Uraš and two other individuals are described as belonging to the family of the "Priest-of-Dilbat."[43] The third, composed on the twenty-eighth day of Abu (V) of that year (648), describes a loan involving an individual by the name of Uraš-ušallim.[44] Since Uraš was the patron deity of Dilbat and Lāgamāl his son, it seems likely that at least some of the individuals whose names mention them came from Dilbat, as may have those whose family name mentions Dilbat. Thus, either Dilbat and Borsippa were still in contact or these individuals had gone to Borsippa on some earlier occasion (possibly to give aid to the rebels).[45]

Two letters provide some further insight on Dilbat's position during the rebellion. *ABL* 326, written sometime after the start of the revolt, seems to indicate that Šulaya, a governor of that city, supported the rebellion. The letter states that he had been been given his position by Šamaš-šuma-ukīn and that several of his relatives had given trouble to Assyria. His maternal uncles had been arrested by Aplaya, the author of the letter, while they were on the road to Babylon, presumably to join the rebels there. Although they claimed to be fugitives, Aplaya told the king that they had done much evil and reminded him that they were the sons of the troublemaker Bēl-iddin and the uncles of Šulaya.[46] Marduk, the author of *ABL* 804 suggests that rebels

---

41 BM 29029 (*B-K* K.107).

42 BM 54216 (*B-K* 121). The interpretation of the second part of the individual's name (-EN-*an-ni*) is not certain.

43 *BRM* 1 38 (*B-K* K.141).

44 BM 134973 (*B-K* K.142); the reading of the individual's name is not completely certain.

45 The possibility that these individuals or their families had moved to Borsippa at some point in the past, unconnected with the rebellion, cannot be excluded.

46 *ABL* 326:4-10. For a date during the rebellion, see *ibid.*, rev. 1'-13'. The possibility that Šulaya was appointed governor before the rebellion and/or that he did not have the same political sympathies as his relatives cannot be excluded from consideration. The fact that Aplaya invokes two deities of Dilbat—Uraš and Bēlet-Ekalli—in the letter would suggest that he was from that city. This would indicate that even if the city as a whole supported the rebellion, at least one citizen did not. He may have left the city because of his pro-Assyrian views; he refers to having been in the Assyrian camp when the rebel forces went against it.

planned to use Dilbat as a base from which to raid Assyrian convoys to the south or to control caravans passing in the neighbourhood. He wrote to Ashurbanipal: "I have heard the following from the mouths of the nobles: 'We will set up a camp at Dilbat.' If they set up a camp at Dilbat people will cross over and no caravan will be able to pass by without their *ḫiyālu* troops coming out and plundering it."[47]

Nothing concrete is known about Kish during the time of the revolt, even though this important city was located only about fifteen kilometres east of Babylon, thus close to the rebel centre.[48] One individual who may have come from this city, Zababa-erība, did support the rebels,[49] but it is uncertain if his views were those of the city as a whole. The fact that edition A of Ashurbanipal's annals does not mention Kish and Dilbat as among those cities who closed their gates to the Assyrians could be taken as indicating that these cities did not support the rebellion actively, but the composer of this edition may simply have not included all the cities who joined the rebellion.

Cutha is the only city in northern Babylonia known to have been held by the Assyrians or their supporters at the outbreak of the rebellion, although it later fell to the Babylonians. Assyrian sources omit it from the list of cities that initially closed their gates to the Assyrians, but include it among those cities which Ashurbanipal had to besiege. They also mention Erra, a god of that city, among the deities to whom Ashurbanipal was prevented from sending offerings by his brother's actions.[50] Since Šamaš-šuma-ukīn fought Assyrians when he took Cutha (see below), there was likely an Assyrian garrison in or near the city at least during the first part of the revolt.[51]

An astronomical diary records that on the twelfth day of Addaru (XII) in 652 "the troops of Akkad did battle with the troops of Assyria; the troops ...

---

47 *ABL* 804 rev. 8-16. The letter must date to at least the second year of the revolt in view of rev. 17-19: "Let them set up a camp opposite ([*m*]*eḫir*) the Babylonian camp, just as they did last year!" It is possible, however, to assume that the nobles were supporters of Assyria and thus that they were advising the Assyrian king that a camp should be established at Dilbat so that the enemies' caravans could be captured. For the possibility that Dilbat was besieged during the revolt, see above p. 142 n. 36.

48 *OECT* 10 7 (*B-K* K.134), which was composed on 12-XII-649 (year 19 of Šamaš-šuma-ukīn) and which records the sale of land located at Kish, was found at mound W of that city (see *OECT* 10, p. 1); however, the text was composed at Babylon and may have been taken to Kish after the revolt ended. The owner of the property had presumably been trapped inside Babylon by Ashurbanipal's siege. There is no proof, however, that he had the same sympathies as the other citizens of Kish or indeed that he was himself from that city.

49 See p. 148.

50 Streck, *Asb.*, pp. 30-33 iii 112-114 and 128-132.

51 *ABL* 944, a letter from Ashurbanipal to two persons dated on 5-VII-652, refers to the people of Cutha and the town Sūr-mirrāte (=Sūr-marrāti=Samarra?) (lines 4-9). Unfortunately the context is broken.

[...]."[52] Regrettably, the outcome and location of the battle are not preserved. The Akītu Chronicle states that on the twenty-seventh day of that month, the Assyrian and Babylonian armies met in battle at Ḫirītu; the Babylonians retreated and many were killed. A similar entry is found in an astronomical diary, which also states that Ḫirītu was situated in the province of Sippar. Editions B and C of Ashurbanipal's annals record that early in the revolt Assyrian troops stationed in the town of Mangisi defeated an army sent by Ḫumban-nikaš II, king of Elam, to aid Šamaš-šuma-ukīn; the battle appears to have taken place in northeastern Babylonia, perhaps in the region of the Diyala River. The battles described in the chronicle and astronomical diary, on the one hand, and editions B and C, on the other, may actually be one battle, but this is by no means certain since the former say that the Assyrians defeated a Babylonian army while in the latter it was an Elamite army that was defeated.[53] In any case, the Babylonian rebels and their Elamite allies appear to have been defeated on at least one or two occasions early in the revolt. However, these early losses did not discourage the rebels; the Akītu Chronicle records that "there was war; fighting continued."[54] Because of the unsettled conditions in the land caused by military activities, the important New Year's festival did not take place in Babylon in 651, nor was it held during the remainder of the rebellion.[55]

Both Ashurbanipal and Šamaš-šuma-ukīn would have been doing all they could to discover the other's plans and the movements of the other's forces. Ashurbanipal frequently turned to the gods for advice on what to do and on what the enemy was planning. Extispicies were performed to determine the truth of reports which had reached him and the potential for success of various planned military movements. In 651, an extispicy was performed to find out if the Elamite army would assemble, march, and fight with Assyrian forces at some point between the eighth day of Abu (V) and the eighth day of Ulūlu (VI). The omens were unfavourable.[56] It is impossible to determine if Ashurbanipal was requesting this information because he had received a

---

52 Sachs, *Astronomical Diaries* 1, no. -651 iv 10'. This entry follows an astronomical observation for the twelfth day of the month and precedes an entry for the thirteenth day. As is the case with another passage (see Appendix D), the historical entry should be assigned the date of the preceding astronomical observation (i.e., day 12 not day 13).

53 On the two battles, their locations, and possible identification, see Appendix D.

54 Grayson, *Chronicles*, no. 16:16.

55 Or at least it did not take place in its full and normal form since the Akītu Chronicle states that during these years Nabû did not go out from Borsippa for the procession of Bēl and that Bēl did not come out (for the procession). Grayson, *Chronicles*, no. 16:18-23.

56 Starr, *SAA* 4, no. 281. Starr tentatively reads the month in which the extispicy was performed as Addaru (XII), but the sign is damaged and it would seem unlikely that a report on the matter would have been requested seven months after (or five months before) the period of concern. Klauber, the original publisher of the report, read Abu (V)—^{arah}*a*[*b*]*u*(!) (*PRT*, p. 140 no. 128 rev. 13)—which seems more likely.

report that the Elamites were planning to do precisely that or if he was simply trying to cover all conceivable possibilities.

The next military engagement considered worthy of mention by the chroniclers occurred in the middle of the following year. On the ninth day of intercalary Ulūlu (VI_2) in 651 Šamaš-šuma-ukīn mobilized his forces, marched to Cutha, and took the city by force, defeating the Assyrians and possibly their Cuthian supporters who were holding the city.[57] Cutha held strategic importance for both sides. The rebels would have considered it dangerous to leave a city close to Babylon in Assyrian hands since the Assyrians would have been able to use it as a base from which to make raids throughout the core of Šamaš-šuma-ukīn's territory. If it were held by the rebels, it would be more difficult for Assyrian forces to go to the aid of their supporters in the southern towns since all the major cities in northern Babylonia would appear have been in rebel hands.[58] When some Nabayatean sheikhs later came to see him, Šamaš-šuma-ukīn gave them 105 individuals as a gift for Natnu, their ruler. These 105 individuals were made up of one hundred Ḫitayans and five Assyrians who had been captured in Cutha.[59] In sending these prisoners to Natnu, Šamaš-šuma-ukīn was undoubtedly trying to win the military support of this important tribal leader. After his capture of Cutha, he also took something or someone from the city to Babylon. Because of damage to the text, it is unclear if the king of Babylon carried off the statue of the god Nergal, or some other object belonging to Nergal, or a person whose name ended with the element Nergal.[60] This person or object was probably taken to ensure Cutha's future loyalty to the rebel cause. Towards the end of the second month of that year (26-II-651), an extispicy was performed because Ashurbanipal was ill.[61] Possibly Šamaš-šuma-ukīn had been encouraged to go on the offensive and attack Cutha with the knowledge that his brother was still sick and unable to lead his forces.

Despite this victory, matters may not have been going well for the rebels. A rumour reached Assyria that Šamaš-šuma-ukīn had fled to Elam and an extispicy was performed on the fifteenth of Tašrītu (VII) to determine the truth of the story. The omens proved unfavourable.[62] A month later, on the

---

[57] Grayson, *Chronicles*, no. 15:7-10. If Grayson's restoration of C[uthians] in line 9 is correct, and Cuthians opposed Šamaš-šuma-ukīn's attempt to take the city, then Cutha would have been the only city in northern Babylonia known to have actively supported the Assyrian cause.

[58] The position of Kish is actually not known and that of Dilbat not absolutely certain (see above).

[59] *ABL* 1117:6-12; the letter is presumably to be dated before 11-IV-650 when Babylon was besieged. The Ḫitayans may have been captured at Cutha or on some other occasion.

[60] Grayson, *Chronicles*, no. 15:10.

[61] Starr, *SAA* 4, no. 317.

[62] Starr, *SAA* 4, no. 282; a recent translation of this extispicy report by K. Hecker is found in *TUAT* 2/1, pp. 73-74.

sixteenth day of Araḫsamna (VIII), another extispicy was performed to see if Šamaš-šuma-ukīn would fall into the hands of Assyrian troops if they went against him. The omens were favourable this time, but proved incorrect if the Assyrian troops did indeed meet him in battle.[63] Assyrian forces or their allies may have been moving about northern Babylonia at that time, making movement by the supporters of the rebellion difficult. An economic text dated at Borsippa on the fifth of Araḫsamna (VIII) seems to indicate that a matter could only be settled when a particular individual was able to get to either Babylon or Borsippa.[64] Another extispicy report, dated sometime in 651, also shows that Ashurbanipal contemplated undertaking a major campaign in that year. Ashurbanipal wished to determine if his troops should cross the marshes, set up camp in Bāb-Sāme, and then fight with the rebel forces. Unfortunately, the location of Bāb-Sāme is not known and it is not clear if the campaign ever took place.[65]

Several other extispicy reports are preserved which deal with the rebellion; however, either the dates of these are not preserved or the texts themselves are so damaged as to preclude definite conclusions about their contents. One, composed on eleventh day of Šabaṭu (XI) in 651, may inquire if Šamaš-šuma-ukīn or his army would flee Babylon, but the damaged condition of the text precludes any certainty about the matter.[66] A second, composed on day 13 of an unknown month in 651, asked if an individual ([...-d]annin or [...-d]a''in) would join with the enemy; the omens were unfavourable.[67] Presumably the enemy whom the individual might have joined was Šamaš-šuma-ukīn or his allies, but there is no proof of this. A badly damaged report appears to refer to archers whom Ashurbanipal had sent to Babylon against Šamaš-šuma-ukīn, but the date and details of the matter are not preserved.[68] Finally, another poorly preserved report, possibly composed in the second month (year not preserved), may ask if the Assyrian forces would be

---

63 Starr, *SAA* 4, no. 283.

64 BM 82645 (*B-K* K.115). The passage reads "When Bēl-iqīša son of Munnabitti has come either to Babylon or to Borsippa and has not established the case with ..." (lines 1-7). While the text does not have to indicate that he was finding it difficult to reach either city because of enemy actions (as opposed to him simply needing to hear of the matter and go to one of them), it may well do so.

65 Starr, *SAA* 4, no. 287. This campaign may have had some connection with events known to have taken place that year (e.g., at Cutha or Nippur). See Streck, *Asb*., pp. CXCIV-CXCV on the location of Bāb-Sāme.

66 Starr, *SAA* 4, no. 285.

67 Starr, *SAA* 4, no. 293.

68 Starr, *SAA* 4, no. 284.

victorious over the forces of Šamaš-šuma-ukīn; again the details of the matter are not preserved.[69]

At some point, probably before the siege of Babylon began in 650, Šamaš-šuma-ukīn and his forces gave battle, or sought to give battle, to the Assyrian forces at Kār-Nergal. This may have been connected with the conquest of Cutha because Kār-Nergal appears to have been located in the general area of Cutha.[70] It was reported to Ashurbanipal that Zababa-erība, who had gone with Šamaš-šuma-ukīn to Kār-Nergal against the Assyrian forces, had killed Rīmanni-ilu (a military official and presumably supporter Ashurbanipal), put the slain man's head-dress upon his own head, and boasted about the matter. Since the head-dress now appears to have been in Assyrian hands and since the Assyrian king was warned that "these men are not friends; they are enemies," it may be that Zababa-erība and several other rebels had been captured and were claiming that they were not in fact enemies of Assyria. The man who reported all this was thus informing Ashurbanipal that their claims should not be believed.[71]

It seems clear that Šamaš-šuma-ukīn did not remain behind Babylon's walls, leaving the conduct of the war to his generals. As mentioned, he had gone with his troops to Kār-Nergal to give battle to the enemy. The Šamaš-šuma-ukīn Chronicle states that he had mustered his troops and gone and captured Cutha, and the Akītu Chronicle reports that in 651 he had had to withdraw into Babylon before the enemy.[72] Despite this, it is uncertain how actively Šamaš-šuma-ukīn actually took part in military actions either as strategist or fighter. It is possible that at one point he was wounded by an arrow in the course of battle, but the text recording this is damaged and the exact context is uncertain.[73]

A poorly preserved entry in the Šamaš-šuma-ukīn Chronicle dated to the second half of 651 may refer to Assyrian officers or nobles. It has been

---

69 Starr, *SAA* 4, no. 288. Several extispicy reports date to the years of the revolt but are so badly damage as to make it impossible to determine if they dealt with matters involving the war or not (see Starr, *SAA* 4, nos. 318-319, 323-324, 326-327, 329-330, and 333-334).

70 For the location of Kār-Nergal, see Saggs, *Iraq* 18 (1956): 50-51 no. 35:20-23; and Black, *NAPR* 1 (1987): 18. Saggs suggests that Kār-Nergal was located on a canal linking Cutha and Sippar, while Black prefers a location on the Tigris at approximately the latitude of Cutha.

71 *ABL* 326; see p. 216 n. 12. Zababa-erība may have been a citizen of Kish since the god Zababa was the patron diety of that city.

72 *ABL* 326 rev. 1'-2' and Grayson, *Chronicles*, nos. 15:7-10 and 16:12.

73 Knudsen, *Iraq* 29 (1967): 53 and pl. 20 i' 5-7, [...] ^{md}GIŠ.NU$_{11}$-MU-GI.NA [... *ša ina* M]È-*ia ina ú-ṣi maḫ-ṣu* [... *la iq*]-*tu-ú nap-šat-su*, "[...] Šamaš-šuma-ukīn [... who] was wounded by an arrow [in bat]tle with me [... (but) did not] die." Since there is a gap in the text immediately before the name of Šamaš-šuma-ukīn, it is possible that some official or servant of his was actually meant; note also that Knudsen's spacing suggests that something may be missing between the name of Šamaš-šuma-ukīn and the actual reference to wounding in battle.

suggested that the passage stated that these had rebelled; however, this remains speculation since the key section word "rebelled" is totally restored.[74] If the passage does refer to a rebellion in Assyria or among Assyrian officers, this event could be connected to a damaged entry for the same year in the Akītu Chronicle which may indicate that there was turmoil in both Assyria and Babylonia ("There were [insur]rections in Assyria and Akkad").[75] In connection with this, one should also note the indecisive extispicy report from Nineveh composed on the fourth day of Šabaṭu (XI) in 651 "concerning the land" (*ina muḫḫi māti*). Could the extispicy have been performed to determine the current state of feeling in Assyria? To determine if the Assyrian people supported Ashurbanipal in the war with his brother or if they supported individuals or forces opposed to Ashurbanipal in Assyria itself?[76] If Ashurbanipal was having trouble at home, this would explain why sufficient troops were not sent to Babylonia at the start of the revolt, allowing the situation there to deteriorate. His opponents in Assyria may have even been supporters of his brother.

The capture of Cutha by the rebel forces is the only major victory known for them during the course of the revolt but the reason for this may be the fact that our sources come almost entirely from the Assyrian side, and thus were unwilling to record rebel victories. The rebel gain at Cutha was soon balanced by their loss of Nippur in central Babylonia. Although the fall of Nippur is not recorded in letters or historical texts, the dating of economic texts indicates that the city changed hands sometime between the beginning of Kislīmu and the middle of Šabaṭu. Early in the month of Kislīmu (IX) of 651, a text was dated at Nippur by the regnal years of Šamaš-šuma-ukīn, while on the eighteenth day of Šabaṭu (XI) of that year, one was dated under Ashurbanipal.[77] The Assyrians undoubtedly stationed troops in Nippur; and it was now liable to attack by Tammarītu, the successor of Ḫumban-nikaš as king of Elam, and likewise a supporter of Šamaš-šuma-ukīn. An extispicy was performed to determine if the troops of Tammarītu would mobilize and

---

74 Grayson, *Chronicles*, no. 15:11, [x (x) U]D 27.KÁM LÚ.GAL.ME *šá* KUR *a*[*š-šur*(?) x x x (x)]. Note that the country to which these individuals belonged is mostly restored. The following lines are also poorly preserved and it is possible that line 11 should be taken with them (thus Millard in *Iraq* 26 [1964]: 26-27). The event described in the passage presumably dates to the second half of the year since an earlier entry is dated to an intercalary sixth month (line 7).

75 Grayson, *Chronicles*, no. 16:17. With regard to the restoration [*saḫ-m*]*a-ša*?-*a-tú*, see *ibid*., p. 132, commentary to line 17.

76 Starr, *SAA* 4, no. 318.

77 IM 57923 (likely dated on the third day of the month) and IM 57901 (duplicate IM 57902) respectively (*B-K* K.116 and J.8-9). The next text dated at Nippur is IM 57906 (and duplicate IM 57912, *B-K* J.16-17), dated on 25-XII-648 under Ashurbanipal.

attack Assyria or Nippur during the course of the next month.[78] At some point during the second half of the revolt, the Assyrian king was advised to station five hundred horses and a high military official (*rab munga*) at Nippur. At the same time it was suggested that only one hundred horses be stationed at Uruk, which may reflect the relative strategic importance (or needs) of the two cities at that time.[79]

The Assyrians were gaining ground in northern Babylonia by the first half of 650. On the eleventh day of Du'ūzu (IV) of that year, Babylon was besieged and was to remain so for more than two years.[80] The goal of the Assyrians was to force the city into surrendering by cutting off its access to supplies of food and military aid and the Assyrian blockade did make life difficult for the inhabitants of Babylon. At least six economic documents dated between the thirteenth day of Araḫsamna (VIII) in 650 and the twenty-ninth day of Ayyaru (II) in 648 mention that the city was under siege or state that conditions were bad because of the resultant scarcity and high price of food.[81] Probably the Assyrians did not set up a continuous encirclement about the city but rather established a number of camps in the area in order to keep a close eye on it. Borsippa, Cutha, and Sippar were also besieged by Assyrian forces,[82] although exactly when and for how long is unclear. Since

---

78 Starr, *SAA* 4, no. 289:5-10; the date on which the report was written is not given. A second extispicy report refers to Nippur (*ibid.*, no. 291); however, the text is badly damaged and it is impossible to determine when it was composed in the reign of Ashurbanipal or in what context Nippur was mentioned.

79 *ABL* 622+1279:20'-rev. 3. This text refers to messengers of Indabibi, who is attested as king of Elam only towards the end of the revolt. *ABL* 617+699 may also come from Nippur during the revolt since the author of the letter, Enlil-bāni, appears to discuss military matters. However, Enlil-bāni is only clearly attested as governor of Nippur before the revolt and we know that he and Nippur were involved in military matters at that time (see above).

80 Grayson, *Chronicles*, no. 15:19.

81 Documents dated at Babylon which refer to the siege and/or famine in the city were composed on 13-VIII-650 (Budge, *PSBA* 10 [1887-88]: 146 and pls. 4-6; *B-K* K.119), 24-IV-649 (Oppenheim, *Iraq* 17 [1955]: 77 n. 26; *B-K* K.128), 5-X-649 (YBC 11404; *B-K* K.132), 9-X-649 (Pinches, *RP* NS 4, pp. 96-99 no. 1; *B-K* K.133), 22-I-648 (YBC 11317; *B-K* K.139), 29-II-648 (Strassmaier, *8e Congrès*, no. 6; *B-K* K.140; the place at which the text was composed is not preserved, but the land sold in the transaction was located at Babylon), and possibly 15-XII-649 (BM 40038; *B-K* K.135). In addition, a document, dated at Babylon (GN only partially preserved) on 20-III of presumably either 649 or 648, describes a woman selling herself in order to acquire food to live (Weidner, *AfO* 16 [1952-53]: 37-38 no. 2 and pl. 3; *B-K* K.153). *OECT* 10 400 (*B-K* N.3), composed at Babylon in the reign of Sîn-šumu-līšir, refers to the siege in the twentieth year of Šamaš-šuma-ukīn, i.e., 648 (MU.20.KÁM ^{d}GIŠ.NU$_{11}$-MU-GI.NA *ina e-del* KÁ, line 13).

82 Streck, *Asb.*, pp. 32-33 iii 130-132, and *OECT* 10 399 (*B-K* J.24; see p. 142 n. 36). Some scholars have suggested that the siege described in *ABL* 1186 may refer to this incident (e.g., Waterman, *RCAE* 3, p. 315 and Ahmed, *Asb.*, p. 104); while this is possible, the letter could refer just as well to some other incident, and not necessarily during the reign of Ashurbanipal.

Borsippa lay close to Babylon, it may have been besieged and have fallen at about the same time as Babylon.[83] Lengthy sieges were not usual because they required the attacking force to tie up a large number of troops for a considerable period of time in hostile territory.[84] In this case, however, it was clear that the rebellion could not be crushed until Babylon had fallen.

Rebels attempted to break through or slip past the besieging forces on a number of occasions. The sons of Bēl-iddin (who is described as an enemy, a troublemaker) were arrested while they were on their way to Babylon. Their captor sent them on to Ashurbanipal, but warned the king not to believe their claims to be fugitives (i.e., individuals fleeing from Babylon).[85] They may have been rebels or rebel sympathizers going to join Šamaš-šuma-ukīn. Help came to the king of Babylonia from the nomadic tribes to the west of Mesopotamia. Arab (Qedarite) troops under the command of two brothers, Abiyate' and Ayamu, sons of Te'ri, together with forces sent by Uaite', another tribal ruler, went to aid Babylon and in doing so Abiyate' at least was breaking an oath of loyalty to Ashurbanipal.[86] This was not the first time that western tribes had come to the aid of Babylonians fighting against Assyria; in 703, a brother of the queen of the Arabs had led troops to aid Merodach-Baladan II against Sennacherib.[87] Although Abiyate' and some of his troops managed to enter the city, the Assyrians claim to have killed a number of them in the process. The deteriorating conditions caused by the siege, however, forced these tribal forces to abandon Babylon and as they fled more were killed by the Assyrians.[88]

Several letters from one Nabû-šumu-līšir to Ashurbanipal describe armed conflict which likely occurred either during or around the time of the rebellion; two letters, *ABL* 259 and 1117, certainly refer to incidents during

83 As was mentioned above, Borsippa was still in rebel hands on 28-V-648.

84 See Eph'al in *HHI*, pp. 94-95.

85 *ABL* 326:4-6.

86 For a loyalty oath imposed by Ashurbanipal upon the Arab tribe of Qedar, and possibly Abiyate' (though the name is restored), see Parpola and Watanabe, *SAA* 2, no. 10. Abiyate' is known to have taken an oath of loyalty to Ashurbanipal at some point in his reign (Piepkorn, *Asb.*, pp. 84-85 viii 32-35) and Parpola and Watanabe (*SAA* 2, p. XXXIII) suggest that the treaty was concluded just before the beginning of the rebellion in 652.

87 Luckenbill, *Senn.*, p. 51:28.

88 Streck, *Asb.*, pp. 68-69 viii 30-41. Although it is clear that the tribal forces abandoned the city while it was under siege (i.e., after IV-650), it is not certain when they entered. Eph'al (*Ancient Arabs*, pp. 154-55) prefers a date before IV-650 since it would have been easier for the troops to have entered before the Assyrian forces were encamped about the city. However, the fact that the sources state that Assyrian troops had inflicted a defeat on them before they entered the city would suggest otherwise. Troops of Uaite' are not specifically mentioned in the text as having gone to the relief of Babylon, but Uaite' is said to have listened to seditious talk from Babylonia, given troops to Abiyate' and Ayamu, and sent them to the aid of Šamaš-šuma-ukīn. Uaite' is also said to have incited the Arabs to revolt and to plunder Ashurbanipal's subjects. See Streck, *Asb.*, pp. 64-65 vii 82-106.

the revolt. *ABL* 259 records how Nabû-šumu-līšir had sent men of the town of Bīrtu to the marshes of Babylon where they had been attacked by supporters of Šamaš-šuma-ukīn. They had killed four of the attackers and captured nine more, whom the author sent to the king. The letter also states that Bīrtu had been demolished and deprived of its gods. The letter does not indicate who was responsible for these actions, or when they had occurred, but it would be reasonable to assume that it had been supporters of the rebellion who had destroyed and looted the town. As mentioned above, *ABL* 1117 describes Šamaš-šuma-ukīn's gift of one hundred and five prisoners to Natnu, ruler of the Nabayateans. Besides *ABL* 1117, three other letters of Nabû-šumu-līšir mention the Arabs in a hostile connection. *ABL* 262 reports on losses suffered by Assyrians and their supporters from Bīrtu as the result of a raid by some Arabs and apparently on the author's response to this. Nabû-šumu-līšir ends the letter by stating that he was sending seven individuals to the king for interrogation. In *ABL* 350 Nabû-šumu-līšir wrote to the king about his victory over some Qedarites who had violated the oaths they had sworn to Ashurbanipal. Finally, *ABL* 260 tells of an attack by Aya-kabaru of the Maš'a tribe on a caravan setting out from the territory of the Nabayateans.[89]

Despite the state of siege, life went on in the cities of northern Babylonia. On the same day that the Assyrians encamped outside Babylon's walls (11-IV-650), a contract was drawn up at nearby Borsippa recording the sale of a date-palm orchard in the lowland (*ugāru*) of Uruk.[90] During the course of the siege individuals in Babylon sold land located within the city and outside it,[91] and property near Dilbat was sold by an individual at Borsippa.[92] Undoubtedly many persons were selling land in an attempt to dispossess themselves of property which was not presently accessible due to the war or was in danger of being looted or damaged by enemy actions. Others were selling off land, prebends, slaves, and even themselves to buy food which

---

89 A translation of *ABL* 260 is found in Oppenheim, *Letters*, no. 118. The letters of more than one Nabû-šumu-līšir were found at Nineveh. For the assignment of the letters to this individual acting around the time of the Šamaš-šuma-ukīn Revolt and for a discussion of these incidents, see Eph'al, *Ancient Arabs*, pp. 54-59, 153-54, and 219. Ashurbanipal was particularly interested in hearing from Nabû-šumu-līšir about the actions of the Arabs (*ABL* 260:8-12). The location of Nabû-šumu-līšir's activities is unknown although two of his letters mention the town of Bīrtu or its people (*ABL* 259 and 262). Zadok keeps the reference to the town of Bīrāti in *ABL* 1128:10, a letter likely to be assigned to Nabû-šumu-līšir, separate (*RGTC* 8, pp. 75-76), but one may wonder if it was not the same place.

90 BM 118977 (*B-K* K.117). Since *ugāru* (A.GÀR) is usually found associated with water and rivers, Stol prefers to translate the term "irrigated fields" (*zikir šumim*, p. 352).

91 Budge, *PSBA* 10 (1887-88): 146 and pls. 4-6 (land located in the province of Qutayanu), BM 78107 (land located in the town of Zuḫrinu), and *OECT* 10 7 (land located at Kish-Ḫursagkalama); *B-K* K.119, 126, and 134 respectively.

92 *BRM* 1 38 (*B-K* K.141).

had risen dramatically in price because of the siege.[93] The few loan documents available indicate no corresponding rise in interest rates and one even states that the loan did not have to be repaid until the land was again at peace.[94] However, according to editions A, C, and K of Ashurbanipal's annals, conditions in the besieged cities had reached a terrible state as a result of starvation and disease by the time these cities finally fell or surrendered to the Assyrians. Each person came to care only about his/her own survival: "A man deserted his wife; a father abandoned [his] beloved son." Ashurbanipal's inscriptions claim that to assuage their hunger the besieged chewed leather and even resorted to cannibalism, eating the flesh of their sons and drinking the blood of their daughters. They state that people wandered about in misery and despair and that disease and death were everywhere in the land of Akkad.[95] Documents from Babylon dated during the siege refer to the distress; the earliest, composed on the thirteenth day of Araḫsamna (VIII), only about four months after the siege began, states: "At that time famine and hardship were established in the land and a mother would not open the door (of her house) to (her own) daughter."[96] One document from Babylon records that "the rate (of equivalency) was three silas of barley for one shekel of silver purchased in secret" and this is to be compared to an approximate rate of one hundred and eighty silas per shekel in the Neo-Babylonian period.[97] Because of the scarcity of food and the resultant high cost of those supplies still available, "people died from lack of food."[98] What the conditions were like in the other cities held by the rebels is unknown; either we do not have any economic texts from them (Cutha and Sippar), or the ones we do have do not refer to abnormal conditions (Borsippa).

The situation in Babylon eventually became hopeless. The siege and the rebellion ended with the death by fire of Šamaš-šuma-ukīn. Ashurbanipal claims that the gods cast his brother into a fire and this could imply either

---

93 E.g., Oppenheim, *Iraq* 17 (1955): 77 n. 26 and Weidner, *AfO* 16 (1952-53): 37-38 and pl. 3 no. 2 (*B-K* K.128 and 153).

94 Literally until "the land has been opened (*ittaptû*)," i.e., until it was possible to move around the country freely. Pinches, *RP* NS 4, pp. 96-99 no. 1 (*B-K* K.133).

95 Streck, *Asb.*, pp. 36-40 iv 41-45 and 79-85 (edition A); Livingstone, *SAA* 3, no. 44 rev. 8-10. For edition C, see in particular ND 5406 ii 1'-22' (Knudsen, *Iraq* 29 [1967]: 55-57 and pl. 19) and Bauer, *Asb.*, p. 17 and pls. 11-12 ix 4-23; for edition K, see in particular BM 134436 a 2'-15' (Cogan and Tadmor, *Or.* NS 50 [1981]: 231-33).

96 Budge, *PSBA* 10 (1887-88): 146 and pl. 6:63-64 (*B-K* K.119).

97 Strassmaier, *8e Congrès*, no. 6:44-45 (*B-K* K.140). For normal prices in the Neo-Babylonian period, see Dubberstein, *AJSL* 56 (1939): 26-27 and Powell, *AOF* 17 (1990): 94. When Nippur was besieged in the time of Sîn-šarra-iškun, one shekel of silver could buy six silas of barley (Oppenheim, *Iraq* 17 [1955]: 89 2 NT 300-301 [*B-K* O.33 and O.47]).

98 Pinches, *JTVI* 26 (1893): 163:20-21 (*B-K* K.133).

suicide or murder.[99] He may have taken his own life or been killed by some of his own people who, with all hope of success dashed, would rather surrender to Ashurbanipal than attempt to hold out any longer.[100] While political necessity may have made his own men kill him in order to get the city to open its gates to the Assyrians, one might have expected them to have instead delivered him up to Ashurbanipal in the hope of receiving a reward. It has sometimes been suggested that Šamaš-šuma-ukīn was thrown into the fire by an official of his by the name of Nabû-qātē-ṣabat, but it is not clear that this individual was in Babylon when the city fell.[101] According to a document purporting to be from the god Aššur to Ashurbanipal, the god had decreed for Šamaš-šuma-ukīn the same fate as that of Išdu-kīn, who is described as an earlier king of Babylon. No individual by the name of Išdu-kīn is otherwise attested as ruler of Babylon and thus exactly what his fate had been is unknown, although the context would surely suggest that it had been an unfortunate one.[102] Whether or not the Aramaic tale on Amherst papyrus 63 describes the death of Šamaš-šuma-ukīn remains uncertain, although it does appear to state that Ashurbanipal had wanted to take his

---

99 Streck, *Asb.*, pp. 36-37 iv 46-52 and Cogan and Tadmor, *Or.* NS 50 (1981): 231 a 17'-21' (partially restored). See also the Ištar Tablet which Thompson restored to indicate that the people of Akkad had killed Šamaš-šuma-ukīn (*AAA* 20 [1933]: 86, 95, and pl. 94:112-113). Barnett (*North Palace*, pp. 46-47) states that one of Ashurbanipal's reliefs shows Šamaš-šuma-ukīn surrendering to the Assyrian king, but as Brinkman (*Prelude*, p. 100 n. 503) points out, the relief only shows the presentation to Ashurbanipal of Šamaš-šuma-ukīn's crown and sceptre. For the relief itself, see figs. 5-6.

100 If Ashurbanipal's first campaign against Ḫumban-ḫaltaš III of Elam is to be dated before the fall of Babylon (see Appendix E), it may have been the Assyrian victory over Babylonia's ally that caused Šamaš-šuma-ukīn and/or his followers to realize that little hope of success remained for the rebellion and that prompted the suicide or murder of the king.

101 See von Soden, *ZA* 62 (1972): 84-85. The idea is based mainly upon *ABL* 972 rev. 8-9 which informs us that Nabû-qātē-ṣabat had placed his lord [into] a fire: *Nabû-qātē-ṣabat ša bēlšu* [*ana*] *išāti ikruruni*. This Nabû-qātē-ṣabat is then identified with the *simmagir*-official of Šamaš-šuma-ukīn by that name whom edition A of Ashurbanipal's annals reports went with Nabû-bēl-šumāti to rouse Elam against Assyria and who ended up in Assyrian hands. Edition A goes on to say that Ashurbanipal hung the severed head of Nabû-bēl-šumāti upon the back of Nabû-qātē-ṣabat (Streck, *Asb.*, p. 62 vii 47-50). If it is the same Nabû-qātē-ṣabat in both cases, we must then assume that he had returned to Babylon from Elam (presumably prior to the commencement of the siege), where he fell into Assyrian hands when the city capitulated, and thus that he had not been delivered up by Ḫumban-ḫaltaš to Ashurbanipal at the same time as the body of Nabû-bēl-šumāti (*c.* 646), as we might assume from edition A. Otherwise, how and why would he have escaped from Babylon after killing Šamaš-šuma-ukīn and have gone to Elam, where he was to be eventually rendered up by Ḫumban-ḫaltaš? Von Soden's use of *ABL* 617+699 in connection with this episode is unwarranted since it is unlikely that Šamaš-šuma-ukīn is mentioned in the text. He reads *Šamaš*-[*šuma-ukīn*] in rev. 5, but Šamaš is written ^{d}UTU and the first element of Šamaš-šuma-ukīn's name is never written with this logogram (see above, p. 103 n. 5). In addition, one would not expect the ruler of Babylon to have been mentioned after one of his own official's (*ana muḫḫi Nabû-qātē-ṣabat u Šamaš*-[...]).

102 Livingstone, *SAA* 3, no. 44 rev. 7.

brother alive.[103] According to Ctesias, when Ashurbanipal (Sardanapallos) was besieged in Nineveh, the Assyrian king had himself burned alive on top of a pyre in his palace. Perhaps it was a faulty memory of the death of Šamaš-šuma-ukīn that was behind this account, but since nothing is known of the circumstances surrounding the death of Ashurbanipal, it is not inconceivable that Ashurbanipal had (also) committed suicide or died by fire.[104]

Babylon and the neighbouring city of Borsippa fell or surrendered at some point after the end of the fifth month of 648. The last texts dated under Šamaš-šuma-ukīn at Borsippa and Babylon come from the twenty-eighth and thirtieth days of Abu (V) respectively.[105] While the Akītu Chronicle states that the New Year's festival was not celebrated from 651 to 648, it does not say that it did not take place in 647; thus, the city was undoubtedly in Assyrian hands by the end of 648.[106] Surprisingly the fall of Babylon is not mentioned in any chronicle. When the Assyrians gained control of such other cities as

---

103 Steiner and Nims (*RB* 92 [1985]: 64-65 and 76-81) understand the text to say that following the advice of his sister Šamaš-šuma-ukīn built a chamber and went into it together with his children and advisers with the intention of setting it on fire. However, he changed his mind and set out to go and submit to Ashurbanipal, dying en route as the result of an accident. Vleeming and Wesselius (*Studies* 1, pp. 32-33 and 37) understand the text in a totally different way and do not appear to believe that the readable portions of the text describe the actual death of Šamaš-šuma-ukīn.

104 See König, *EKI*, pp. 130 and 159-60. In addition to arguing that the description of the death of Ashurbanipal in Greek tradition is an embellished version of the death of Šamaš-šuma-ukīn, MacGinnis (*Sumer* 45 [1987-88]: 40-43) argues that elements of the story in Ctesias about the fall of Nineveh (length of the siege and composition of the forces allied against Assyria) come from traditions in Babylonia about the siege of Babylon during the rebellion of 652-648. After mentioning the defeat of Šamaš-šuma-ukīn, Rm 4,455 (*CT* 35 pls. 37-38) refers to the seizing of someone (the Babylonian king?) or something in the midst of battle and possibly the taking of that person or thing to Ashurbanipal. In view of the contrary evidence of the annals and the uncertainty about the proper understanding of the passage due to damage to it, it is not clear whether this text preserved another account about the end of Šamaš-šuma-ukīn or not. The lines in question read: ... *amūt Šamaš-šuma-ukīn* [*aḫu lā kīnu*(?) (...) *š*]*a*(?) *itti ummāni Aššur-bāni-apli nāram ilāni rabûti tāḫāza īpušuma dabdêšu* [*iškunū*(?) (...) *q*]*ereb tamḫāru iṣbatūnimma ina pān Aššur-bāni-apli šar kiššati* [... *amū*]*t Šamaš-šuma-ukīn lā ṭābti*, "omen of Šamaš-šuma-ukīn, [*the disloyal brother* (...) *wh*]*o* did battle with the army of Ashurbanipal, the beloved of the great gods, but [*was*] defeat[ed (...)], captured in the midst of battle, and [...] before Ashurbanipal, king of the world, [(...). Ome]n of Šamaš-šuma-ukīn: not favourable" (rev. 14-17; for the first part of this passage, see Starr, *AfO* 32 [1985]: 61).

105 BM 134973 and BM 40577 (*B-K* K.142-143).

106 The city may have fallen by 1-XI-648 (see p. 156 n. 107). Its fall was first reported in edition K of Ashurbanipal's annals, dated to *c*. 647, and was also described in editions C and A. The capture of the city and the end of the rebellion may have been the reason for the composition of edition K (see Cogan and Tadmor, *Or*. NS 50 [1981]: 239). It has sometimes been thought that *ABL* 1339 describes the final assault on Babylon (e.g., Waterman, *RCAE* 3, pp. 346-47); the use of the introductory phrase *ana dinān* [*šarri bēli*]*ya lullik* would, however, suggest an earlier date.

Sippar and Cutha is unknown; it is unlikely to have been long after the Assyrians entered Babylon and may well have preceded that point by some period of time.

Ashurbanipal claimed that when he entered the rebel cities he dealt with all of Šamaš-šuma-ukīn's principal supporters, allowing none to escape. He states that he punished all the guilty, mutilating their faces, skinning them alive, and cutting away their flesh. Some he dealt with on the spot; others he took back to Assyria. The latter were sacrificed as funerary offerings to Sennacherib—a nice touch since Sennacherib had destroyed Babylon for rebellion in 689—and their remains were fed to birds, animals, and fish. Following standard Assyrian practice, a number of the rebels may have been deported to other lands. Ezra 4:9-10 reports that Osnappar (likely to be identified with Ashurbanipal) had deported to Syria-Palestine people from various places, including Uruk, Babylon, and Susa. Those from Uruk and Babylon may have been supporters of the rebellion. Looting and confiscation of rebel property was carried out by the victors. Ashurbanipal claims to have taken away his brother's garments, royal paraphernalia, and all the equipment of the palace, including the chariots.[107] A relief from the North Palace at Nineveh actually shows the Assyrian king standing in his chariot while his brother's crown, sceptre, chariot and women are brought before him. The same relief shows men and women being led away, presumably into exile or for punishment (figs. 5-6).[108] As a result of starvation and disease during the siege and vengeful actions by the Assyrians when the cities finally fell, the streets became full of corpses which were devoured by scavenging animals. When Ashurbanipal's vengeance was sated, he states that he cleared the dead bodies from the streets of Babylon, Cutha, and Sippar, purified their shrines, appeased their gods, re-established the regular offerings to the gods which had diminished during the course of the revolt, and resettled Babylon with the surviving residents of these three cities. Having brought Babylonia to heel,

---

[107] Streck, *Asb.*, pp. 36-39 iv 53-76; Bauer, *Asb.*, p. 17 and pl. 12 ix 44-53; Thompson, *Iraq* 7 (1940): 107 and figs. 19-20 no. 34 a 22-37; Wiseman, *Iraq* 13 (1951): 25-26 and pl. 12 viii 1'-15'; Cogan and Tadmor, *Or.* NS 50 (1981): 231-33 a 22'-37'; Weidner, *AfO* 8 (1932-33): 196-97 no. 61; and see Livingstone, *SAA* 3, no. 44:10, 22-25 and rev. 1-2. Ashurbanipal's men may well been responsible for the effacing of Šamaš-šuma-ukīn's stela at Borsippa after that city fell (see Reade, *Iraq* 48 [1986]: 109). Parpola (*JNES* 42 [1983]: 7 and 11) shows that large numbers of literary texts were taken to Assyria from Babylonia, particularly from Nippur and Bīt-Ibâ, late in 648 (1-XI and 29-XII) and suggests that some were taken as spoils of war. It is possible that it was the fall of Babylon which prompted or facilitated the removal of goods to Assyria. This would then suggest that Babylon had fallen before 1-XI-648; however, looting could easily have began outside of Babylon before that city fell. Since one Bēl-ēṭir son of Ibâ is known to have been an enemy of Assyria at some point during the reign of Ashurbanipal (see above, p. 118), it seems possible that Bīt-Ibâ had supported the revolt and that it was now being punished by being looted. Why Bīt-Ibâ had a large number of literary texts is unknown.

[108] See also p. 154 n. 99.

the Assyrian king now extended the velvet glove, in contrast to Sennacherib's earlier behaviour. Finally, when all Babylonia was reconquered, Ashurbanipal appointed new officials who he hoped would be loyal. New taxes, tribute, and offerings for the gods of Assyria were imposed upon the Babylonians.[109]

II. Uruk

As a result of the preservation of the correspondence between officials in southern Babylonia and the Assyrian court, there is more information available about that area during the revolt than about northern and central Babylonia, though regrettably many of the statements in the letters are damaged or ambiguous. Although Uruk had supported the rebellion of 693-689, it was the most important pro-Assyrian bastion in Babylonia during the revolt of 652-648 and it is unlikely that Uruk was ever held by the rebels. During the revolt, texts from Uruk were dated by the regnal years of Ashurbanipal, not Šamaš-šuma-ukīn—two in 651, and one each in 650 and 649.[110] Economic texts refer to Nabû-ušabši as governor of Uruk in 651 and 649,[111] as well as before the revolt began, and it is likely that his pro-Assyrian attitude was at least partially instrumental in keeping Uruk on the Assyrian side.[112] He actively opposed the rebels and was aided by various individuals, including Kudurru, Marduk-šarra-uṣur, three Assyrian governors, and possibly Bēl-ibni of the Sealand.[113] It may well have been Nabû-ušabši who

---

109 Streck, *Asb.*, pp. 38-41 iv 77-109. It is unclear why Borsippa is not mentioned since it too had closed its gates to the Assyrians and is known to have held out until at least 28-V-648. Had the scribe omitted it inadvertently or had it eventually surrendered to the Assyrians and escaped the worst punishment?

110 Hunger, *Bagh. Mitt.* 5 (1970): 277 no. 5; Langdon, *JRAS* 1928, p. 322; Revillout, *PSBA* 9 (1886-87): 234-35; and Smith, *MAT*, pl. 28 (*B-K* J.6-7, 10, and 12). One economic text (Hunger, *Bagh. Mitt.* 5 [1970]: 294 no. 19; *B-K* K.97) is dated at Uruk by the regnal years of Šamaš-šuma-ukīn on ⌜17-VII⌝-652 (after the rebellion was known in Assyria but before hostilities had commenced); however, this text is a duplicate of one dated on 14-VII-653 (Hunger, *Bagh. Mitt.* 5 [1970]: 294 no. 20; *B-K* K.98). Thus, it may be best to follow the editor of those texts and assume a scribal error in the date of the former document.

111 See Appendix B sub 15a. In 651 he is attested as governor on 15-II and in 649 on 20-I (Hunger, *Bagh. Mitt.* 5 [1970]: 277 no. 5 and Smith, *MAT*, pl. 28; *B-K* J.6 and J.12).

112 If Watanabe and Parpola's understanding of the text is correct, *ABL* 539 records Ashurbanipal's commendation of Nabû-ušabši for supporting Assyria instead of the enemy and for imposing oaths of loyalty upon his countrymen (*SAA* 2, pp. XXXII-XXXIII).

113 The official position held by Kudurru at this time is unknown; he is likely to have been a subordinate of Nabû-ušabši. Piepkorn, *Asb.*, pp. 78-79 vii 67 refers to Marduk-šarra-uṣur as the *šūt rēši* of Ashurbanipal. Could he also be identified with the *qurbūtu*-attendant mentioned in the time of Esarhaddon (*ABL* 956 rev. 12-13 [*LAS*, no. 190]; note also Parpola, *LAS* 2, p. 188)? The three Assyrian governors undoubtedly brought levies from their nearby provinces.

warned Ashurbanipal about Nabû-bēl-šumāti's anti-Assyrian sympathies and suggested that the latter be made to take an oath about his true allegiance.[114]

The author of *ABL* 1387, whose name is not preserved, records that several individuals from Uruk had urged him to kill the palace overseer and had offered him two minas in silver. They had claimed that they stood with him and said that they should lock the city gate and support Assyria. Because of damage to the text, the author's response to their proposal is uncertain. The palace overseer may have been an envoy sent by Šamaš-šuma-ukīn to try to win the support of Uruk at the start of the rebellion and this letter could record encouragement given to Nabû-ušabši to stand with Ashurbanipal. Nabû-damiq, Na'id-Marduk, and Gimillu—the three Urukians mentioned by name as having promoted the death of the palace overseer—are likely to be identified with three individuals with the same names who appear in *ABL* 815. In that letter, these three men, an individual by the name of Širiktu, and "the people of Uruk," wrote to fellow Urukians in Assyria. The letter is damaged but the writers urged that troops be led to Uruk in that month of Nisannu to rescue the city and its gods. Possibly they were requesting aid against the rebels led by Šamaš-šuma-ukīn. However, it is perhaps more probable that these two letters describe events at Uruk following the death of Ashurbanipal, when control of Uruk appears to have changed hands several times between followers of Nabopolassar and those of Assyria. Support for the later date is found in the fact that Nabû-damiq, Na'id-Marduk, and Gimillu are perhaps to be identified with officials by those names who served at Uruk either at the end of the reign of Kandalānu or shortly thereafter, when texts were dated while the city gate of Uruk was closed due to unsettled conditions in the land.[115]

ABL 1106 contains important evidence on the course of events in Uruk during the rebellion; however, the damaged condition of the text makes many points uncertain. Apparently the author of this letter had been taken from Uruk to Babylon by two of Šamaš-šuma-ukīn's men.[116] Before leaving Uruk, he had ordered Nabû-zēra-iddin, an official at Uruk (*ša muḫḫi āli*) to bring Aplaya (the governor of Arrapḫa) and Marduk-šarra-uṣur into the city with reinforcements so that Uruk would not fall to the rebels.[117] After he was taken away to Babylon, his brother Sîn-ibni was killed while he himself was rescued or spared through the intercession of his maternal uncles in

---

114 See p. 129.

115 See Kümmel, *Familie*, pp. 139 and 141.

116 *ABL* 1106:17'-19'. Probably these two persons are to be identified with the [*rab*] *mugi* of the king of Babylon and [PN], the Urukian, mentioned in 5'-6'. I would like to thank S. Parpola for various suggestions with regard to the understanding of this letter.

117 *ABL* 1106:9'-17'. Although Nabû-zēra-iddin's title is only partially preserved, the restoration [LÚ *šá* UG]U URU *šá* UNUG.KI (line 11') seems reasonable (restoration proposed by Dietrich in *Aramäer*, pp. 178-79 no. 107).

Babylon.[118] The fact that the author of *ABL* 1106 wrote that letter to Ashurbanipal suggests that he had managed to leave Babylon, possibly by feigning loyalty to Šamaš-šuma-ukīn. The letter goes on to warn Assyrian officials that Babylonian forces were moving against them.[119] The name of the author of *ABL* 1106 is not preserved. Since he had the power to issue orders to an official of Uruk, he was probably a high official of that city, or a representative of Ashurbanipal. It may well have been Nabû-ušabši, himself.[120] It was not likely Kudurru since an Urukian by that name is mentioned in the letter.[121] The incident reported in *ABL* 1106 may have happened early in the revolt because such a rebel action (the taking of an official from Uruk to Babylon) would surely have been easier to accomplish then; in any case, it is likely to have occurred before Babylon was besieged in the fourth month of 650.[122]

Uruk was so important that, among others, the governors of Arrapḫa and Laḫīru were sent there in order to support the Assyrian cause in southern Babylonia.[123] Even Bēl-ibni (Ashurbanipal's appointee to rewin the Sealand from the rebels) may have campaigned with the Urukians on one occasion.[124] The Assyrians assembled troops at Uruk, causing concern for those of the Puqūdu who supported the rebels. Saḫdu, the brother of the Puqudian rebel leader Nabû-ušēzib, sent troops to capture someone from the vicinity of Uruk[125] who could tell them why the Assyrians were massing troops there and

---

118 *ABL* 1106:17'-21'.

119 *ABL* 1106 rev. 8'-10'. If the author of *ABL* 1106 sent an individual to the king of Babylon to warn him that it was not safe to go out (rev. 5'-7'), then he may have purposely been giving the Babylonian king bad advice, since he also proceeded to send warnings to Assyrian officials that rebel troops were going against them (rev. 8'-10'). However, various different interpretations of rev. 5'-7' are possible and it is not necessary to assume that the author of the letter was in communication with Šamaš-šuma-ukīn.

120 Although *ABL* 859:7-9 is damaged, this passage seems to state that either Nabû-ušabši had seized someone and led him away or someone had seized Nabû-ušabši and led him away. (For a possible restoration of these lines, see Dietrich, *Aramäer*, pp. 176-77 no. 102.) If the latter, this might support the identification of Nabû-ušabši as the author of *ABL* 1106.

121 *ABL* 1106 rev. 8'-9'. Since Kudurru is a relatively common name, this reference cannot be considered absolute proof against a Kudurru being the author of this letter.

122 *ABL* 1106 rev. 13'-16' states that the king had given the Sealand to Nabû-kudurrī-uṣur, the colleague (or brother) of the author, and that Bēl-ibni was angry at this (or that Nabû-kudurrī-uṣur was not pleased with Bēl-ibni). Since Bēl-ibni is described as the son or heir of Nabû-kudurrī-uṣur (rev. 14'), either sounds strange. The reference to a servant of Sîn-balāssu-iqbi in rev. 6' may suggest a date before Sîn-tabni-uṣur was appointed governor of Ur (see below). There is no need, however, to assume Sîn-balāssu-iqbi was alive or in office simply because a servant of his is mentioned.

123 See below.

124 *ABL* 752 rev. 12-13. This letter from Nabû-ušabši to Ashurbanipal says: "Bēl-ibni, the Sealande[r], wandered about (*is-se-gi!*) with us for [x] months."

125 Literally "from the *tamirti* of Uruk." For the meaning of *tamirtu* ("irrigation district," or similar), see Joannès, *TEBR*, p. 118 and Stol, *BSA* 4 (1988): 177-81.

what they planned to do. The Puqudians were initially successful and captured ten men; however, forces went out against the Puqudians and defeated them. Saḫdu's intentions were discovered by questioning a captured troop leader.[126]

It was desirable for the rebels to gain control of Uruk because of its own importance as a city and in order both to deprive the Assyrians of their major base in the south and to isolate Ur, located in the extreme southwestern corner of Babylonia, even further from Assyrian aid. Šamaš-šuma-ukīn appears to have appointed one Nabû-nāṣir to be governor of Uruk, presumably intending that he replace Nabû-ušabši and rally the Urukians to the rebel cause. There is no evidence that he ever actually held office in Uruk and he was arrested by supporters of Ashurbanipal.[127] In addition, according to a report from a pro-Assyrian official in Uruk (likely Nabû-ušabši) a sort of "government-in-exile" had been created for those Urukians in Elam, presumably supporters of the rebellion. The king of Elam had promised one individual the office of governor and had put the others under his authority.[128]

As was mentioned, Ashurbanipal sent Assyrian troops to aid Uruk against the rebellious tribes of the south. The governors of Arrapḫa (Aplaya), Zamū (Nūrea), and Laḫīru led their provincial levies there. In addition, the king records sending troops led by Aššur-gimilla-tirra, and 200 horses (presumably with their riders) under the command of the captains Bēl-ēṭir and Arbaya.[129] Bolstered by Assyrian military levies, Uruk was presumably more secure than the region around Ur and Nabû-ušabši became concerned about the situation at the neighbouring city. He urged the king not to abandon that city and the Gurasimmu and thereby cause them to desert to the rebels.[130] Sîn-tabni-uṣur of Ur appealed to Uruk for aid against the enemy who were making Ur's situation precarious.

> Messages from Sîn-tabni-uṣur have come to [Apl]aya, the governor, and myself, saying: "A messenger of Šamaš-šuma-ukīn has come to make the land hostile and (to speak) to me. The land of the Gurasimmu

---

126 *ABL* 1028:1'-16'.

127 *CT* 54 496:3'-6' (see Dietrich, *Aramäer*, pp. 178-179 no. 106 for possible restorations). Due to the fact that the verb at the beginning of line 5' is not fully preserved, exactly what Šamaš-šuma-ukīn did for Nabû-nāṣir is uncertain. One might, however, read [*irḫ*]*uṣušu*) or [*ipqid*]*aššu*.

128 *CT* 54 507 rev. 3'-7'; see Stolper, *JNES* 43 (1984): 310 n. 38. Could this be connected with the incident described in *CT* 54 496?

129 *ABL* 273, 543, 1108, and 1244; the number of horses are only mentioned in *ABL* 273. For the relationship of these letters one to another, see Frame in *Cuneiform Archives*, p. 268. Aššur-gimilla-tirra held the position of *mašennu*, which *CAD* 10/1 (M), p. 363 describes as "a high official, 'steward.'" For the names of the governors, see *ABL* 754(+)*CT* 54 250:11-12.

130 *ABL* 1108 13'-18' and 1244:1'-3' (read *gúr-a-sim-mu* and *gúr-sim-mu* after Ur in lines 16' and 2' respectively; suggested by S. Parpola).

has revolted from me. If you do not come here quickly I will die and the land will turn to Šamaš-šuma-ukīn."

Kudurru took five or six hundred archers from Uruk and together with the governors of Arrapḫa and Zamū, and their provincial levies, went to the aid of Ur.[131] The expedition was likely successful since there is no clear evidence that Ur ever fell to the rebels. These officials were empowered to act on their own initiative, without express orders from the Assyrian king, undoubtedly because of the desperate circumstances involved and the uncertainty of communications at that time. Although Kudurru's exact position in Uruk is not known, he was obviously a high official, possibly second in command to Nabû-ušabši. He corresponded directly with Ashurbanipal,[132] assembled archers for Nabû-ušabši,[133] and led troops to the aid of Ur. Probably he is the same Kudurru who governed Uruk after the revolt (see chapter 9).

At one point, possibly early in 650 or shortly before then, some rebels from Bīt-Amukāni based in the town Šamēlē, appear to have surrendered to an official at Uruk (possibly Nabû-ušabši). *CT* 54 507 tells us that some men from that tribe had come before the author and that two further individuals, Bēl-ušallim and Nabû-gāmil of Šamēlē, had sent messengers claiming that they were now servants of Ashurbanipal. As a means of testing their loyalty, they appear to have been ordered to seize and hand over certain officials in Šamēlē, presumably those who still supported the rebellion.[134] Perhaps the Assyrian forces were beginning to gain the upper hand over the rebels around Uruk by that time. There is also some indication that the Urukians captured Natan (another Puqudian leader) and Mukīn-zēri,[135] one of the persons who had acted for Šamaš-šuma-ukīn in *ABL* 1106.[136] After abandoning the

---

131 *ABL* 754(+)*CT* 54 250. Collations by I. Finkel and C.B.F. Walker support the reading of the traces of the name of the author as Kudurru ([ᵐNÍG.D]U), against Olmstead, apud Waterman (*RCAE* 3, p. 229), who preferred Nabû-ušabši.

132 *ABL* 754(+)*CT* 54 250.

133 *ABL* 998 rev. 9'-10'. For the authorship of this letter, see above, p. 129 n. 147.

134 *CT* 54 507:13-21 (see Dietrich, *Aramäer*, pp. 184-85 no. 118 for possible restorations). *ABL* 517, a letter from Ashurbanipal to Nabû-ušabši dated to 19-II-650, refers to a Bēl-ušallim who had sent a report to Ashurbanipal about the leaders of the Bīt-Amukāni. Bēl-ušallim is not an uncommon name, but because both texts date to the Šamaš-šuma-ukīn Revolt, because one is addressed to an official of Uruk and the other written by an official of that city, and because both deal with the Bīt-Amukāni, the same Bēl-ušallim is likely involved in the two letters. A date of composition for *CT* 54 507 before that of *ABL* 517 is proposed here upon the assumption that the individuals are surrendering in the former text and not simply reaffirming their allegiance.

135 *ABL* 1437. Since the names of the authors of this text are not preserved and since "the Urukian" is referred to in the third person (lines 11'-rev. 1), it is quite possible that it was some other group that seized these persons. The exact reading of the name ᵐGIN-NUMUN is not certain; other possibilites in addition to Mukīn-zēri exist.

136 *ABL* 1106:17'-19'. Natan is never actually called a Puqudian, but he is mentioned in association with the sheikhs of the Puqūdu in *ABL* 622+1279 rev. 4 and with the Puqūdu in *ABL* 282:17-18.

rebellion, Bēl-ušallim aided the Assyrians and reported on the actions of the leaders of the Bīt-Amukāni, sending his reports via Nabû-ušabši. In the second month of 650, Ashurbanipal ordered Nabû-ušabši to tell Bēl-ušallim that the Assyrian king was pleased with what he had done; Bēl-ušallim was summoned to report to Ashurbanipal in person.[137]

At some point after the revolt was crushed, some individuals from Uruk may have been deported to Syria-Palestine, possibly because they had supported or sympathized with the rebels.[138]

III. Ur and its Neighbours

Carrying on the sympathies demonstrated by two of its previous governors, Ningal-iddin and Sîn-balāssu-iqbi, Ur was another bastion of pro-Assyrian sentiment in southern Babylonia. Ur and its neighbouring towns of Eridu, Kissik,[139] Kullab,[140] and Šāt-iddin,[141] as well as the Gurasimmu tribe, seem to have borne the brunt of the rebel actions in the south, which were led by Nabû-bēl-šumāti of the Sealand. Ur fell into dire straits until help came from Uruk and Bēl-ibni rewon the Sealand. Eridu and the Gurasimmu were under the jurisdiction of the governor of Ur in the time of Sîn-balāssu-iqbi and probably remained so at the start of the rebellion.[142] Sîn-šarra-uṣur may

[137] *ABL* 517 may be translated as follows:
Command of the king to Nabû-ušabši:
I am well. May you (therefore) be glad! Concerning the report of Bēl-ušallim about which you [N.u.] wrote (to me [Asb.]), write to him [B.u.] the following:
"Concerning the son of Ea-zēra-qīša and the elders of Bīt-Amukāni about whom you [B.u.] wrote, what you have done is good. What you have done is good for the house of your lord."
Also (say to him [B.u.]):
"Concerning the report about Ḫumbušti which you [B.u.] sent, I [N.u.] have written to the palace about it, saying:
'As to the men who came before the king, the king should not decide their case until Bēl-ušallim comes before the king, my lord, and can give advice to the king which is good for the king, my lord.'
Now, go and see the friendly face of the king, your lord! Give him advice which is pleasing to the king, your lord! Let him [Asb.] hear you [B.u]!"
Ayyaru, day 19, eponymy of Bēl-ḫarrān-šadû'a [19-II-650].

[138] See p. 156.

[139] Possibly Tell al-Laḥm, located about 30 km southeast of Ur, in the area of the Bīt-Yakīn; see Röllig in *RLA* 5, pp. 620-22.

[140] A town in the area of Bīt-Yakīn mentioned in royal inscriptions beside Larsa, Kissik, and Eridu. See Edzard in *RLA* 6, p. 305 and Zadok, *RGTC* 8, p. 202.

[141] A town in the territory of Bīt-Yakīn. See Zadok, *RGTC* 8, p. 290; collation supports a reading Šāt-iddin(a). *ABL* 942:2 and 11 have LÚ URU *šá-at*-SUM.NA-*a-a* and URU *šá-⌜at⌝*-SUM.NA respectively.

[142] *UET* 8 102:6-9. The Gurasimmu are said to have revolted from Sîn-tabni-uṣur part way through the revolt (see above). Since a transaction was carried out at Ninā (modern Surghul, about 60 km northeast of Ur) in 650 in the presence of Sîn-tabni-uṣur, who is

well have been the governor of Ur at the time the revolt began and his departure from office, and replacement by his brother Sîn-tabni-uṣur, may have been the result of Assyrian suspicions about his loyalty.[143] Indeed, Sîn-šarra-uṣur may actually have supported the rebellion initially and changed his allegiance only after he heard of Assyrian victories in the north. The author of *ABL* 1002, likely Ashurbanipal, said: "With regard to Sîn-šarra-uṣur about whom you spoke [to me], saying: 'He is not one who loves Assyria,' do I not know that it was because he saw that my gods did not grant any success to my enemy that he crossed over, came here, and seized my feet?"[144]

Sîn-tabni-uṣur was appointed governor of Ur at some point after the revolt began and before the third month of 650; he may have remained in office for the remainder of the rebellion.[145] Before appointing him, Ashurbanipal had consulted diviners to find out if Sîn-tabni-uṣur would be loyal or if he would support Šamaš-šuma-ukīn. Their report was favourable[146] and presumably Sîn-tabni-uṣur was then put in charge of Ur. Sîn-tabni-uṣur is first explicitly called governor in a text dated on the twenty-third day of Simanu (III) of 650 at Ninā.[147] On one occasion during the rebellion, Ashurbanipal had a extispicy performed to determine if Sîn-tabni-uṣur would become hostile to Assyria and join with Šamaš-šuma-ukīn during a particular period of time—from the twenty-second day of the current month until the twenty-second day of Abu (V).[148] The date the extispicy was performed is not preserved and Sîn-tabni-uṣur is not given the title governor; thus, it is not known if the text dates prior to his appointment to the governorship of Ur or not.

The Puqūdu and the Sealanders actively made life difficult for the pro-Assyrian towns in the south through killing and plundering. They sought to cut off the towns' access to food and reinforcements.[149] Pleas to Ashurbanipal for aid initially received no response,[150] presumably because the

called governor of Ur (BM 113929, *B-K* J.11), is it possible that Ninā was also under his jurisdiction?

143 See p. 126. An extispicy report dated to 16-XI-651 refers to Sîn-šarra-uṣur, possibly asking if some individual(s) associated with him will hear of something and escape (Starr, *SAA* 4, no. 286). The text is too badly broken to determine the context or even to be certain that the Sîn-šarra-uṣur mentioned was the son of Ningal-iddin.

144 *ABL* 1002 rev. 3-9. The passage is difficult and this translation slides over a number of problems. The date of the text is uncertain.

145 With regard to the career of Sîn-tabni-uṣur, see Brinkman, *Or.* NS 34 (1965): 253-55.

146 Starr, *SAA* 4, no. 300. The text is dated on 11-V of an unknown year, but it must clearly come from the time of the revolt.

147 BM 113929 (*B-K* J.11).

148 Starr, *SAA* 4, no. 301.

149 *ABL* 942:7-11 and 1241+*CT* 54 112 rev. 4-5. In comparison with the towns mentioned in *ABL* 1241+*CT* 54 112:14'-19', one should perhaps read U[RU! *k*]*i-i*[*s-s*]*ik*.KI in *ABL* 942:10 instead of the x LÍL.KI of Harper's copy (suggestion courtesy S. Parpola).

150 *ABL* 1241+*CT* 54 112:6'-8'. See Dietrich, *Aramäer*, pp. 200-201 no. 155, but read *nadû* at the start of line 6 and note that the *išappar* in line 8 is not perfectly clear.

Assyrian forces were occupied in northern Babylonia or because they could not get through to the south. In attacks against the town of Bīt-Il-aḫtir and against the troops of Sîn-tabni-uṣur, the Puqūdu appear to have managed to take two or three thousand prisoners[151] and Nabû-bēl-šumāti may even have destroyed part of Ur in his raids.[152]

In an attempt to relieve pressure on Ur and to detach the Puqūdu and the Sealand from the rebel cause, Ashurbanipal appears to have considered appointing Sîn-šarra-uṣur over them. Reports had been sent to him saying that if that individual was appointed over them they would switch their allegiance and support Assyria. Ashurbanipal was undoubtedly dubious both of the truth of the reports and of the loyalty of Sîn-šarra-uṣur himself and he sought to determine the accuracy of these reports by means of extispicy. Regrettably, the document recording the extispicy request does not have its date preserved or record whether or not the omens were favourable. Thus it is impossible to determine if it dates before or after Sîn-šarra-uṣur's removal from office as governor of Ur.[153] There is no evidence to suggest that he was ever put in charge of the Puqūdu or the Sealand.

For more than two years these towns held out against rebel actions and gave refuge to those who were loyal to Ashurbanipal,[154] but finally some began to drop away out of desperation when no help arrived. Eventually Kullab, Eridu, and the Gurasimmu deserted to the rebels. Those in the south who remained loyal to Assyria wrote:

> With regard to us, who (live) in the middle of [Akkad], the enemy from the Sealand and the Puqūdu lie against us. We write to the king, our lord, but the king, our lord, does not send any troops to aid us. The Gurasimmu are situated on our [bord]er. [When] the enemy went

---

151 *ABL* 1028 rev. 4-8; see Dietrich, *Aramäer*, p. 114 n. 2. The passage is damaged and it is not impossible that it states that the Puqūdu were taken captive by the troops of Sîn-tabni-uṣur. On the reading of the name of the town, see Zadok, *RGTC* 8, p. 92. Its exact location is not known.

152 *ABL* 1248:9-rev. 2 (damaged). See Dietrich, *Aramäer*, pp. 202-203 no. 159 for possible restorations. The letter is from Sîn-tabni-uṣur to Ashurbanipal.

153 Starr, *SAA* 4, no. 302. It is not absolutely certain that Ashurbanipal was being asked to put Sîn-šarra-uṣur in charge of the Puqūdu and Sealand. It is possible that individuals from Ur were requesting that Sîn-šarra-uṣur be put over that city and were telling Ashurbanipal that if that happened the Puqūdu and Sealand would support Assyria (i.e., the latter supported and would be guided by Sîn-šarra-uṣur). While unlikely, it is not impossible that the text was composed before the rebellion actually broke out. Šamaš-šuma-ukīn is not mentioned in the document (i.e., in neither a hostile nor a positive manner). Although Starr's translation implies that they would be changing their allegiance ("... will switch their allegiance to ...", the text actually uses the verb "establish/set" (*liš-šuk-na*).

154 *ABL* 210:11-16, "After the enemy encamped against us, the king, our lord, instructed us, saying: 'Shelter and send to me all who come to you!' When the Nuḫānu came to us, [we] sheltered them ..."

against them, they joined the enemy because they saw that instruction from Assyria remained far from them and that no governors went to their aid. Eridu and Kullab, *which were remaining* (*loyal*) *as best they could*, have (now) stood with enemy. Now all the Gurasimmu have become hostile. There are no cities which stand on the side of Assyria except Ur, Kissik, and Šāt-iddin ... The Puqūdu and Sealand hate us and plan to do harm to your temples; they have ruined us by murder and plundering.[155]

The loss of the Gurasimmu was particularly disastrous because they went on to aid the enemy and because their defection served to further isolate Ur from its hinterland and Uruk.[156] Finally an appeal by Sîn-tabni-uṣur to Uruk and the Assyrian governor Aplaya produced results. Kudurru of Uruk, Aplaya, and the governor of Zamū went to the aid of Ur.[157] This expedition was presumably successful although it is unlikely that all pressure was removed for good.

It is possible that relief to the southern towns came at some point in 650. This is suggested by *ABL* 942, which was written by the people of Šāt-iddin before aid had come and records that they had kept guard for the king for two (or possibly more) years,[158] by *ABL* 290, in which Ashurbanipal states that Sîn-tabni-uṣur had endured the enemy and famine for two years,[159] and by *ABL* 523, apparently written after the worst pressure on Ur had been relieved, in which Ashurbanipal writes to Sîn-tabni-uṣur to commend him for having done his duty for a third year.[160] If one assumes that rebel pressure on Ur had begun in 652, at the start of the revolt, this might suggest that Ur had been relieved in 650.[161] This date seems all the more likely because early in that year the Assyrians appear to have been gaining the upper hand in the

155 *ABL* 1241+*CT* 54 112:4'-rev. 5 (cf. Dietrich, *Aramäer*, pp. 200-201 nos. 155-56). The translation "Eridu and Kullab, *which were remaining* (*loyal*) *as best they could*" is tentative and the passage could be interpreted in other ways, including "As soon as they were able, the remainder of Eridu and Kullab."

156 *ABL* 1236 appears to describe an attempt to win the Gurasimmu over to the rebellion, but due to damage to the text and difficulties of interpretation, details are unclear. See Dietrich, *Aramäer*, pp. 117-18 and 204-205 no. 162 for one interpretation. Note also *ABL* 1089+47-7-2,120 (date uncertain) in which the author, Iddin-Marduk, begs for troops and states that the Gurasimmu and Puqūdu support the king (see Dietrich, *Aramäer*, pp. 204-205 no. 163). (Note that *ABL* 1089+47-7-2,120:17-19 and rev. 2-10 are similar to *CT* 54 182 rev. 4-6 and 9-15; the authors of the latter letter appear to be members of the Gurasimmu.)

157 *ABL* 754(+)*CT* 54 250:4-13.

158 *ABL* 942:5-6.

159 *ABL* 290 rev. 7-10. Durand, however, suggests that *ABL* 290 was written shortly before the revolt (*RA* 75 [1981]: 184-85).

160 *ABL* 523 rev. 3-5; read ^{m}30-DÙ!-⸢PAB!⸣ in line 1 (collation courtesy S. Parpola).

161 Since, however, we do not know exactly when Sîn-tabni-uṣur was appointed governor of Ur, this suggested date for the relief of the city must be taken as most tentative.

north (with the commencement of the siege of Babylon in the fourth month of 650) and around Uruk (see above) and because Ashurbanipal appointed Bēl-ibni to the Sealand in the second month of 650 (see below). The situation was presumably stable enough in the third month of that year that Sîn-tabni-uṣur felt able leave Ur and go to the town of Ninā, though it is also possible that his journey there was part of some military manoeuvre.[162] The situation was certainly not back to normal. Fighting continued in the Sealand and supplies of food remained limited due to the effects of military actions. Texts dated on the twenty-third day of Simanu (III) in 650 and the twenty-ninth day of Nisannu (I) in 649 at Ninā and Ur respectively reflect the scarcity of food in those cities since in each individuals sold something in order to acquire money to buy food to eat.[163]

At some point Sîn-tabni-uṣur appears to have been forced by Ur's pitiable condition to offer some kind of submission to Šamaš-šuma-ukīn, but there is no proof that Ur itself was ever occupied by the rebels. Possibly Sîn-tabni-uṣur had only begun to negotiate with the rebels for the surrender of the city when help arrived. The people of Ur had written to Ashurbanipal that conditions were so bad that due to starvation they had had to resort to cannibalism. They claimed that Sîn-tabni-uṣur had submitted to the rebels only out of desperation and that he was indeed loyal to the king.[164] Ashurbanipal forgave him and expressed faith in him, stating that he did not believe the slanders made against Sîn-tabni-uṣur by Sîn-šarra-uṣur and Ummanigaš.[165]

---

162 BM 113929 (*B-K* J.11). Note the presence of an individual who was a *qurrubūtu*-attendant at the head of the witness list following the mention of Sîn-tabni-uṣur (line 35). The exact function of the *qurbūtu*/*qurrubūtu* is unknown. He may have been a bodyguard or, as suggested by Tadmor (*Mesopotamien und seine Nachbarn*, p. 451), a special courier.

163 BM 113929 and BM 113928 (*B-K* J.11 and J.13).

164 *ABL* 1274 (heavily damaged; see Dietrich, *Aramäer*, pp. 202-203 no. 160 for a restoration of lines 11-17). *CAD* 2 (B), p. 301 takes the statement about eating their children as a question ("Should we eat ...?"). Since there is no other evidence to suggest that Ur was held by the rebels, this submission by Sîn-tabni-uṣur is difficult to explain. Durand (*RA* 75 [1981]: 184-85) dates the letter to before the revolt, thus eliminating the problem. However, the references to famine in the city (lines 9-11) and "want [and exhau]stion in the service [of the king], our lord" (*ekûti* [*u bub*]*ūti ina maṣṣarti* [*ša šarri*] *bēlini*, lines 13-15) would point to a date during the revolt. In connection with the possible defection of Sîn-tabni-uṣur, note that Ashurbanipal had had extispicies performed to determine if Sîn-tabni-uṣur would be loyal to him or if he would support Šamaš-šuma-ukīn (Starr, *SAA* 4, nos. 300-301; see above).

165 *ABL* 290. Presumably Sîn-šarra-uṣur was trying to stir up trouble for his brother and hoping to regain control of Ur. If we accept a date during the revolt for this letter, Ummanigaš can not be identified with the king Ḫumban-nikaš II (Babylonian Ummanigaš) since it is unlikely that the king of Elam would have been corresponding with Ashurbanipal about Sîn-tabni-uṣur while at the same time aiding Šamaš-šuma-ukīn against Assyria. Ḫumban-nikaš II appears to have been killed early in the revolt (see below) and Sîn-tabni-uṣur did not become governor of Ur until after the revolt had begun (see above).

Ur may have had some help from Bēl-ibni.[166] Certainly his subjugation of the Gurasimmu, which is described in *ABL* 790+*CT* 54 425 (see below) and which possibly commenced in the second month of 650 with his appointment over the Sealand, helped to relieve the pressure on the city. Ur, in turn, appears to have aided Bēl-ibni in his subjugation of the Sealand.[167]

IV. The Arameans

As mentioned, edition A of Ashurbanipal's annals states that the Arameans joined the rebel cause. Just as during the entire period 689-627, the Puqūdu and the Gambūlu are the only Aramean tribes about whom much is known during the rebellion. While both tribes played a major role on the rebel side, the Gambūlu appear to have acted only in association with Elam and some of the Puqūdu must have been loyal to Ashurbanipal, or at least neutral in the dispute, since at one point it was feared that some Puqudians would revolt if they heard that the king of Elam had come to fight Assyria.[168]

The Puqūdu were a mainstay of the rebel movement in the south, active against the pro-Assyrian towns there and often co-operating with the people of the Sealand; however, they may not have been undivided in their loyalty to Šamaš-šuma-ukīn. As mentioned earlier, Ashurbanipal appears to have sought to determine the truth of reports that that tribe and the Sealand would support Assyria if he appointed Sîn-šarra-uṣur of Ur over them.[169] If these reports had come from individuals among the Puqūdu, they could reflect some measure of support for Ashurbanipal among that tribe, but it is also possible that these reports were a trick, an attempt to have Ashurbanipal give a major appointment to an individual whose loyalty to Assyria was in question and one whom the Puqūdu knew was truly a rebel at heart.

Reference is frequently made to this tribe in the letters of the period; however, only rarely is the context sufficiently preserved to make it clear exactly why they are mentioned. As stated earlier, Nabû-ušēzib and his brother Saḫdu sent forces into the vicinity of Uruk to discover why Assyrian troops were gathering there. They managed to take a number of prisoners

---

Ashurbanipal stated in *ABL* 523 that he did not believe Sîn-šarra-uṣur's statements against Sîn-ṭabni-uṣur.

166 *ABL* 754(+)*CT* 54 250:21-24; see Dietrich, *Aramäer*, pp. 202-203 no. 158.

167 *ABL* 1129 rev. 13'-16'; see Brinkman, *Or*. NS 34 (1965): 255. Although Bēl-ibni is not mentioned in *ABL* 920, the author, Sîn-[ṭabni-uṣur?], claims to have taken prisoners from the Sealand (lines 7-8). The exact date of *ABL* 920 is uncertain.

168 Starr, *SAA* 4, no. 289 rev. 1-5; on the date of the report, see pp. 149-50. *ABL* 267 rev. 3-6 (see Dietrich, *Aramäer*, pp. 182-83 no. 114) states that Puqudians had been expecting an Elamite attack, which could indicate that they opposed Elam and thus the rebellion or that they were waiting for the attack to carry out some action of their own in support of the rebellion.

169 Starr, *SAA* 4, no. 302. On this report, see p. 164 n. 153.

before their forces were defeated.[170] Nabû-ušēzib may have been active against Ur[171] and in league with the rebels among the Bīt-Amukāni (see below). Ashurbanipal was eager to capture Nabû-ušēzib and association with him was cause for suspicion. He may even have had to flee from his own tribesmen, after Assyrian forces won the upper hand over them, in order to avoid being delivered up to Ashurbanipal.[172]

As described above, Ur and its neighbouring towns were the main objectives of the rebel forces in the south. In alliance with Nabû-bēl-šumāti and the Sealand, the Puqūdu plundered those loyal to Assyria, wreaking havoc in the south. Out of desperation, the towns of Kullab and Eridu and the Gurasimmu tribe deserted to the rebel side, and Ur's governor may have been forced to submit briefly. The actions of the Puqūdu were so effective that they appear to have been able to take two or three thousand captives from Ur and the town of Bīt-Il-aḫtir.[173] As was suggested above, relief may have come to Ur early in 650, ending, at least temporarily, the desperate conditions there.

Another leader of the Puqūdu was Natan. At some point during the revolt, presumably after Bēl-ibni's commission to rewin the Sealand early in 650, he may have stolen sheep and oxen from Uruk.[174] Probably while Indabibi was king of Elam (*c.* 649), Natan and some Puqudians went to make an alliance with Nabû-bēl-šumāti in the town of Targibātu.[175] If the Puqudian Natan is to be identified with the Natan mentioned in *ABL* 1437, he was eventually captured in company with another rebel.[176] However, when Natan was making his alliance with Nabû-bēl-šumāti, Bēl-ibni felt that Ashurbanipal could command (or at least threaten) Natan not to deal with Nabû-bēl-šumāti and Elam, suggesting thereby that Natan would obey the Assyrian king.[177]

During his campaign to win the Sealand from Nabû-bēl-šumāti, Bēl-ibni appears to have claimed victory over the Puqūdu on several occasions and to

---

170 *ABL* 1028:1'-16'.

171 *ABL* 754(+)*CT* 54 250:28. The passage is so damaged as to preclude any conclusions. One cannot be certain that the Nabû-ušēzib mentioned in line 28 is the Puqudian by that name, although reference is made to the Puqūdu in lines 24 and 26.

172 *ABL* 896.

173 *ABL* 1028 rev. 4-8 (see above).

174 *ABL* 1129 rev. 10'-13'; see Dietrich, *Aramäer*, pp. 188-89 no. 127 for possible restorations.

175 *ABL* 282:17-rev. 14. Indabibi's presence on the throne of Elam at the time this letter was written is suggested by the statement that one Šumaya, a relative of the former king, Tammarītu, had fled from Elam and was then with Bēl-ibni (lines 6-16). Šumaya may have been one of those who fled from Elam with Tammarītu when the latter was deposed (Piepkorn, *Asb.*, pp. 78-81 vii 54-70), although it is conceivable that he fled at another time, for example at the time Ḫumban-ḫaltaš III seized the throne of Elam.

176 *ABL* 1437:9'-10'.

177 *ABL* 282 rev. 15-23. Natan is mentioned with the sheikhs of the Puqūdu in *ABL* 622+1279 rev. 3-6, but the exact interpretation of the incident described is unclear.

have taken a number of captives.[178] At one point he considered buying barley from the Puqūdu to order to feed the Sealand because that area was without food; this was probably after the rebellion had been essentially crushed.[179] The author of *ABL* 275 states that in an attack the Puqūdu had destroyed Bīt-Amukāni and settled in the area of that Chaldean tribe. He said that servants of the king were being attacked and killed and advised the king that the crimes of the Puqūdu should not go unpunished.[180] This fighting between the Aramean Puqūdu and the Chaldean Bīt-Amukāni likely dates to the time either during the revolt or shortly thereafter since the letter also mentions a military officer (*rab kiṣri*) by the name of Nabû-šarra-uṣur, who is known to have been active in the first few years after the revolt.[181] If it does date from the time of the revolt it would indicate that at least some of the Bīt-Amukāni tribe had not been supporting that rebellion. The Puqūdu were thus a major force in the rebel alliance in the south, although they were not solidly behind Šamaš-šuma-ukīn; indeed, some members of this tribe actively aided Ashurbanipal. It is uncertain exactly when they were finally subdued or submitted.

The Gambūlu tribe (attested at this time mainly by the actions of the people of Ḫilmu/Ḫilimmu),[182] situated on the Elamite-Babylonian border, were occasionally involved on the rebel side. Parû, the chieftain of Ḫilmu (LÚ.EN.URU KUR *ḫi-il-mu*), presumably with military levies, was among those sent by Ḫumban-nikaš II to aid Šamaš-šuma-ukīn early in the revolt; he was defeated and killed by the Assyrian forces.[183] At one point Nabû-bēl-šumāti appears to have hired members of the Ḫilmu and other tribes, who were suffering from famine, to raid the Sealand. Bēl-ibni responded by sending a retaliatory strike-force which inflicted a defeat upon the Ḫilmu and Pillatu tribes and took many captives.[184] Thus Elam seems to have allowed

---

178 *ABL* 790+*CT* 54 425:10-12; see Dietrich, *Aramäer*, pp. 188-89 no. 128 for possible restorations.

179 *ABL* 792 rev. 8'-11'.

180 Kudurru, the author of *ABL* 275, may not be the Urukian by that name since the introductory section of the letter refers to the gods Bēl and Nabû while Kudurru of Uruk's letters refer to Ištar of Uruk and Nanaya. It has sometimes been thought that there was a Kudurru who was governor of the Bīt-Amukāni (e.g., Dietrich, *Aramäer*, pp. 30-31); however, while an individual by this name did write to the Assyrian king about that tribe, exactly what position (if any) he held is unclear.

181 He also appears in *ABL* 462 rev. 27'; the letter should date around the time of Ashurbanipal's campaigns against Ḫumban-ḫaltaš (see lines 14-17).

182 Sargon refers to the land of Ḫilmu as one of six districts of Gambūlu (Lie, *Sar.*, pp. 48-49:1).

183 Piepkorn, *Asb.*, pp. 76-77 vii 3-35. Also sent by Ḫumban-nikaš was Zazaz, chieftain of the Pillatu, a tribe which frequently appears with the Ḫilmu (see Brinkman, *PKB*, p. 396).

184 *ABL* 1000; date uncertain. The tribes used by Nabû-bēl-šumāti were the Ḫilmu, Pillatu, Nuguḫu (LÚ ⸢*nu*⸣-*gu-ḫu*, collated), Yašiʾ-il (LÚ *i-ši*-DINGIR), and Lakabru.

the rebels to acquire military aid from the Gambūlu and other border tribes and to use their area as a base from which to harry the Assyrian forces and the latter's Babylonian allies.[185]

There is no clear evidence that any other Babylonian tribe known to have been Aramean played a role in the revolt. However, the Gurasimmu tribe, which is never specifically called Aramean but which may have been,[186] was involved. This tribe was under the jurisdiction of Ur in the time of Sîn-balāssu-iqbi and apparently also at the start of the Šamaš-šuma-ukīn Revolt (see above). In general, they appear to have been loyal to Ashurbanipal during the opening stages of the rebellion, but harassment by the Puqūdu and Sealanders and the absence of any aid from Assyria caused them to join the rebels. Having deserted, they proceeded to aid the rebels in their actions against Ur and an individual by the name of Balāssu appears to have been their leader.[187] Sîn-šarra-uṣur of Ur may also have become involved with them. Probably one of Bēl-ibni's first steps in dealing with Nabû-bēl-šumāti was the subjugation of the Gurasimmu. Bēl-ibni claims that during the previous six months he had subdued them for over one hundred and twenty kilometres, from the town of Kapru to the watercourse É.MEŠ-GAL (reading uncertain), and to have been aided in doing so by the Assyrian governor of Zamū, Nūrea, and a force of 200 soldiers and 50 horses.[188] Some of the Gurasimmu fled with Nabû-bēl-šumāti to the Elamite border region and aided him in his raids against Bēl-ibni.[189]

V. The Chaldeans

According to edition A of Ashurbanipal's annals, Šamaš-šuma-ukīn incited the people of Chaldea to revolt against Assyria,[190] but some Chaldeans are known to have remained loyal to Ashurbanipal and Assyria.[191] Bīt-Yakīn probably played a major role on the rebel side, led by Nabû-bēl-šumāti, a member of the ruling family of that tribe. The Bīt-Yakīn, however, are never mentioned explicitly by name, but only via the larger term Sealand. The

---

185 The Šamaš-šuma-ukīn Chronicle (Grayson, *Chronicles*, no. 15:12) may record some activity involving the town of Ša-pī-Bēl, the old Gambulian capital, in 651. Millard has attempted to interpret the incident to indicate that Nabû-bēl-šumāti had taken prisoners of some Assyrians who had been sent by Ashurbanipal to him in Ša-pī-Bēl (*Iraq* 26 [1964]: 26-27), but severe damage to the text makes any conclusions uncertain.

186 See chapter 4.

187 *ABL* 1236:14'-15'.

188 *ABL* 790+*CT* 54 425:4-10.

189 *ABL* 1000; see below.

190 Streck, *Asb.*, pp. 30-31 iii 96-100 and note Thompson, *AAA* 20 (1933): 86, 95, and pl. 94:111.

191 Starr, *SAA* 4, no. 280 rev. 9-14.

people of the town of Kissik, which was situated in Bīt-Yakīn territory,[192] claimed that the Chaldeans hated them because of their loyalty to Assyria;[193] most likely the Chaldeans referred to were the Bīt-Yakīn. Since the Bīt-Yakīn seem to have been closely connected to the Sealand, they will be discussed more fully under that heading (section VI).

The Bīt-Dakkūri tribe is mentioned clearly only once during the revolt, in a damaged epigraph for one of Ashurbanipal's reliefs. The epigraph appears to state that a member of the tribe, whose name is not preserved, had been flayed and had had his hands burned. Presumably he was being punished for fighting on the rebel side.[194] Late in 649, on the first day of Addaru (XII), the town of Iltuk, a fortified settlement located in Bīt-Dakkūri territory, may have been under Assyrian control. On that day, a document recording the sale of an orchard and dated by Ashurbanipal's regnal years may have been composed at that site.[195] Thus, there is not enough information to know the exact position or actions of this tribe during the revolt.

During the reign of Ashurbanipal, the only clear references to the Bīt-Amukāni tribe come from the time around the revolt. It is equally impossible to plot the course of this tribe during the period, but some of its members are known to have supported the Babylonian king. An Aramaic letter written on a potsherd and found at the city of Assur reports on one incident involving this tribe.[196] Regrettably, the text is badly damaged and difficult to understand; as a result, it is difficult to use the letter for detailed historical reconstructions with any degree of confidence. It appears to have been written by an individual by the name of Bēl-ēṭir (possibly acting from Uruk) to his brother Pir'i-Amurrî and to state that he and one Arbaya had captured four individuals at Hafīrū in the desert and that these had had in their possession a letter from Šamaš-šuma-ukīn. It is possible that the letter had

192 Luckenbill, *Senn.*, p. 53:48-49.

193 *ABL* 210 rev. 5-6.

194 Weidner, *AfO* 8 (1932-33): 194-95 no. 60. Weidner's restoration of the text suggests that the individual's hands were singled out for mutilation because they had been used to hold a bow, i.e., to shoot Assyrian soldiers. It is unlikely that the *mukīl appāti* Nabû-ušallimšunu mentioned in another epigraph is to be identified with the Nabû-ušallim who was appointed ruler of the Bīt-Dakkūri by Esarhaddon in 678 (*ibid.*, pp. 196-97 no. 62 and n. 88). Another individual punished for supporting Šamaš-šuma-ukīn was Nabû-zēra-ukīn son of Nabû-šuma(?)-[...] (*ibid.*, pp. 194-95 no. 59); his tribal or city affiliation is unknown, although Bauer (*Asb.*, p. 98) restores the passage to indicate that he was a Chaldean ([... LÚ *kal-d*]*a-a-a*, K 4453++ b 6). Since these three individuals were mentioned by name in the epigraphs, they must have been important members of the rebel movement.

195 Pohl, *AnOr* 9 4 v 48-vi 46 (part of a composite text; *B-K* J.15); the reading of the name of the site at which the text was composed as Iltuk is not completely certain. An official (*qīpu*) by the name of Zērūtu was witness to the sales transaction (vi 34-35). Luckenbill, *Senn.*, pp. 52-53:38-39.

196 Assur Ostracon. For recent editions of this text, see Donner and Röllig, *KAI*, no. 233 and Gibson, *TSSI* 2, no. 20.

been addressed to the Bīt-Amukāni, whose name appears at this point and who are mentioned several times in the text. The letter and the prisoners were sent to the Assyrian king, who gave the prisoners to Bēl-ēṭir as slaves. Bēl-ēṭir had left the slaves in Assyria but now wrote to ask that they be sent on to him. Bēl-ēṭir and Arbaya are presumably to be identified with two army captains by those names whom Ashurbanipal had sent to the aid of Uruk.[197] Some editors of the text believe that the author advised the king to carry out a military action against the Bīt-Amukāni.[198]

The town of Šamēlē was one of the rebel strongholds in Bīt-Amukāni territory. At one point, probably before the second month of 650, a number of persons in Šamēlē appear to have surrendered to an official in Uruk; these included Bēl-ušallim and Nabû-gāmil.[199] Possibly they abandoned the rebel cause because by that time the Assyrians had turned the rebel tide in the area.[200]

The Bīt-Amukāni leader Ea-zēra-qīša[201] was held hostage in Assyria during all or part of the rebellion as security for his tribe's loyalty. Because he had been accused of complicity in the rebellion and of being an associate of the Puqudian rebel Nabû-ušēzib, he wrote the letter *ABL* 896 to his mother, Ḫumbušti,[202] asking her to assure Ashurbanipal of Bīt-Amukāni's loyalty and to deliver Nabû-ušēzib and his family to the Assyrians if it were true, as it had been reported, that Nabû-ušēzib had fled from the Puqūdu to Bīt-Amukāni.

> They are slandering me in the presence of the king, saying: "He and Nabû-(u)šēzib are friends of the king of Babylon. They have conspired (literally "known these matters") with the king of Babylon from the beginning." The king questioned me. I *persisted*, saying: "I will undergo an ordeal! I will lift up the iron axe! I swear that I do not know anything and have not been informed of anything!" Now, because I have heard it said that Nabû-(u)šēzib has extracted his women and family from the Puqūdu and settled them in Bīt-Amukāni, and now, (since) the king of Babylon has been defeated, I have also heard it said that he (Nabû-ušēzib) has fled to the Bīt-Amukāni, I have made the

197 *ABL* 273, 543, 1108, and 1244.

198 Donner and Röllig, *KAI* 2, p. 288.

199 *CT* 54 507:16-18; see p. 161.

200 *CT* 54 92:4'-9' may indicate that Šamaš-šuma-ukīn had appointed Šulaya, son of Ibnaya (ᵐ*ib-na-*⌈*a?*⌉ [(...)]), to be *šatammu* of Šamēlē (see Dietrich, *Aramäer*, pp. 174-75 no. 97 for restorations); however, the text is badly broken and it is unclear exactly when to date the incident.

201 The reading of the final element of this individual's name as a form of the imperative (*qīša*) instead of the preterit (*iqīša*) is suggested by the writing *-qi-šá* in *ABL* 896:1; elsewhere it is generally written -BA-*šá* (e.g., *ABL* 517:7, *CT* 35 pl. 17:8, and BM 118970:31 [*B-K* I.22]).

202 Her name is written ᶠ*ḫu-um-bu-uš-ti* in this letter (line 2), while in *ABL* 517:13 it appears as ᶠ*ḫum-bu-us-te*.

following agreement with the king: "... May the king understand from (this) how loyal I am to the king. If it is acceptable to the king, I will write to Bīt-Amukāni (and) if Nabû-(u)šēzib is there, I will make the hands of his king reach him and his people. If he is not there, I will place (his) people who are in Bīt-Amukāni into the hands of the king. From this may the king understand that I am loyal to the king, that all Bīt-Amukāni knows nothing about it, and that they are true (literally "complete") servants of the king!" Now, if you (Ḫumbušti) say "Let my son live," the steward (Nabû-ušēzib), his people, and the message (confirming) the loyalty of Bīt-A[mukāni] should reach the king quickly or else I am lost ...[203]

ABL 896 may well have been written by Ea-zēra-qīša under pressure from his Assyrian captors. Certainly he would have expected them to examine it. The accusation that Ea-zēra-qīša had been conspiring with Šamaš-šuma-ukīn and Nabû-ušēzib "from the beginning" suggests that he may not have been taken to Assyria until after the rebellion had begun, but rather been forced to go there part way through the revolt.[204] Even if it was true as Ea-zēra-qīša claimed that he had not been involved in the rebellion, it seems likely that some of his sons had. An epigraph for an Assyrian relief refers to "the sons of Ea-zēra-qīša of Bīt-Amukāni." It was not the normal practice of the scribes of these epigraphs, or of Assyrian royal inscriptions in general, to refer by name to subordinates or supporters of the Assyrian king, and enemies of the king were usually not mentioned unless they had submitted, or been defeated. Thus, it seems likely that these sons of Ea-zēra-qīša had been punished for involvement in anti-Assyrian activities.[205]

---

203 The translation assumes the following readings: *ḫur-sa-an lal!-lik* AN.BAR *ka-la!-pu la!-an-tuḫ* (obv. 10-11; cf. *ABL* 390 rev.16-18); M[Í!].ME!-*šú* (obv. 14); *lìb-bi!* (obv. 15); *ki-i* GAZ!-*tú* (obv. 18); *di!-kàt-u-ni* (obv. 19); *la-áš-pur a!-na!* (rev. 2); *lu!-šak-šid-su* (rev. 5); *šá i-na!* (rev. 6); [*mar gab*]-⌜*bu*⌝-*u-ni* (rev. 10); *ma!-a* ⌜DUMU!⌝-*a-a* (rev. 13); and *lib-luṭ!* LÚ.KUŠ.E.SIR! (rev. 14, see Parpola, *OLZ* 74 [1979]: 26 for latter part). New readings were kindly provided by S. Parpola.

204 The defeat of Šamaš-šuma-ukīn which is mentioned in the letter could refer to the final fall of Babylon, the commencement of the siege of Babylon, or some major battle in which the Assyrians proved victorious, and is thus of limited value for dating the text. Ea-zēra-qīša is called *mār Amukānu* in BM 118970:31 (duplicate BM 118976, *B-K* I.22-23), dated at Šapiya on 5-VII-673; he is the first person mentioned in the witness list, a position often reserved for governors and/or *šatammu*-officials in other texts of the period.

In *JCS* 5 (1951): 74, Waterman published a Neo-Babylonian letter from one Ea-zēra-(i)qīša to Nabû-šarra-uṣur and identified the author with the author of *ABL* 896 and the recipient as an Assyrian officer in the time of Ashurbanipal. The contents of the letter, however, do not support these identifications and it seems preferable to assign the letter, which deals with logs and wells, among other matters, to some minor official in the Neo-Babylonian period. Nabû-šarra-uṣur is well-attested as an official at Uruk in the time of Nabonidus (see Frame, *ZA* 81 [in press]).

205 Weidner, *AfO* 8 (1932-33): 196-97 no. 63. The epigraph simply reads "The sons of Ea-zēra-qīša of Bīt-Amukāni" (i.e., without any context). That the epigraph should be

As mentioned earlier, having abandoned the rebellion, Bēl-ušallim reported to Ashurbanipal on matters among the Bīt-Amukāni, including actions of Ḫumbušti. Bēl-ušallim was complimented for what he had done with regard to the son of Ea-zēra-qīša and the elders of the tribe in a letter composed on the nineteenth day of Ayyaru (II) in 650. He also sent information to Ashurbanipal about Ḫumbušti and the Assyrian king wished to have him report in person on the matter.[206] Clearly, Ashurbanipal was concerned about the actions of this important tribe, and in connection with this it may be noted that *ABL* 1117 states that Aḫu-ṭāb, a Ḫitayan, had been sent by the Assyrian king to take a message to Bīt-Amukāni (or to the city of the Bīt-Amukāni), at some point after the capture of Cutha by the rebels (VI_2-651) and before the siege of Babylon (IV-650).[207] What Bēl-ušallim had done with the son of Ea-zēra-qīša and the elders of the Bīt-Amukāni is unknown. Had he punished them or given them new duties? While some of Ea-zēra-qīša's sons appear to have been punished for their support of the rebellion (see above), this son may not have been one of these. He may even have been made leader of the tribe in his father's absence since at one point during the revolt Ashurbanipal considered appointing someone over the tribe's men or troops (LÚ.ÉRIN.MEŠ).[208] However, all this is mere speculation. Although Ea-zēra-qīša may have been in league with the Puqudians and the latter's leader Nabû-ušēzib, it is also clear that the Puqūdu attacked the Bīt-Amukāni at some point, either during the revolt or soon thereafter.[209] If the attack dates to the time of the rebellion, the Puqūdu may have been fighting those elements among the Bīt-Amukāni who had abandoned the rebellion.

An economic text has been preserved which is dated at the town of Ša-ṣur-Adad under Ashurbanipal on the twenty-seventh day of Araḫsamna (VIII) in 649.[210] If this place is to be identified with Ša-iṣṣūr-Adad, a fortified town considered to belong to the Bīt-Amukāni by Sennacherib's scribes,[211] then a part of that tribe's territory was under Assyrian control at that date.

At the very end of the year 648, the Assyrians carried off a number of literary texts written on writing boards from Bīt-Ibâ, which may be located in

connected with the time of the Šamaš-šuma-ukīn Revolt is suggested by the fact that epigraphs on the same tablet describe the plundering of Babylon by Ashurbanipal and the sending of troops by Tammarītu, the king of Elam, to fight Ashurbanipal's troops (*ibid.*, nos. 61 and 64).

206 *ABL* 517. For a translation of this letter, see p. 162 n. 137. It is not known when the letter was composed in relation to that of Ea-zēra-qīša to his mother.

207 *ABL* 1117, note especially lines 6-12 and rev. 11'-15'.

208 Starr, *SAA* 4, no. 290 rev. 6-9.

209 *ABL* 275 and see discussion above.

210 BM 118982 (*B-K* J.14). The text records the sale of an orchard located in the *ugāru* of Uruk.

211 Luckenbill, *Senn.*, p. 53:42 and 47. See Zadok, *RGTC* 8, p. 12 sub Ālu-ša-Iṣṣur-Adad.

the territory of the Bīt-Amukāni, not far from Uruk.[212] Quite possibly Bīt-Ibâ was being looted as punishment for supporting the rebellion. Certainly one of its leaders, Bēl-ēṭir, is known to have opposed Assyria at one point during the reign of Ashurbanipal and to have been the subject of two vituperative denunciations.[213]

In sum, there is very little clear evidence about the sympathies and actions of the Bīt-Amukāni and Bīt-Dakkūri tribes during the rebellion. Not all Chaldeans joined the rebel alliance, although it seems likely that for the most part they sympathized with the rebel movement. A number of reliefs from the North Palace at Nineveh depict individuals who have sometimes been identified as Chaldeans fighting, surrendering, or being led away as prisoners (see for example figs. 7-8). It is generally unclear with which particular events during the reign of Ashurbanipal these should be associated, but some undoubtedly represent events during the rebellion of 652-648.[214]

VI. The Sealand

The Sealand, the traditional base and refuge of Babylonian rebels, played an important role in the Šamaš-šuma-ukīn Revolt. The rebels in the Sealand were led by Nabû-bēl-šumāti, a member of the ruling family of the Bīt-Yakīn tribe and probably the governor of the Sealand, who joined the rebellion by the first month 651 at the latest, if indeed he had not been instrumental in bringing it about.[215] On the fourth day of that month, an extispicy was performed for Ashurbanipal to determine the truth of a rumour that Nabû-bēl-šumāti, who is said to have arrogantly broken his sworn word to Ashurbanipal, had assembled archers in Elam and to learn if he would lead them into battle against the forces loyal to Ashurbanipal.[216] Nabû-bēl-šumāti may have feigned loyalty to Ashurbanipal at the beginning of the revolt.[217] Editions B and C of Ashurbanipal's annals state that the Assyrian king had sent some Assyrians to aid Nabû-bēl-šumāti and that by trickery the latter had seized and imprisoned these individuals who had trusted him and gone about

212 See Parpola, *JNES* 42 (1983): 11 and 20-21 no. 3. For the location of Bīt-Ibâ, see Zadok, *RGTC* 8, p. 91.

213 See p. 118.

214 See Barnett, *North Palace*, pls. 28?, 29-30, 34, 60-61, 66, and 68. Although Barnett describes these individuals as Chaldeans, no epigraphs identify them as such. Can we be certain that some were not Arameans or Akkadians? A thorough study of the depictions of Babylonians—including Akkadians, Chaldeans, and Arameans—on Assyrian wall reliefs is needed.

215 With regard to Nabû-bēl-šumāti, see also pp. 127-29. The career of Nabû-bēl-šumāti has been studied by Malbran-Labat in *JA* 263 (1975): 7-37.

216 Starr, *SAA* 4, no. 280; the omens were unfavourable. The final element of the name is erroneously written -*šīmāti* (NAM.MEŠ) in rev. 1.

217 See also pp. 128-29.

with him like friends, protecting his land.[218] It is uncertain if these Assyrians had been sent before or after the revolt began, although the former seems more likely. The continued detention of these Assyrians proved a cause of dispute between Ashurbanipal and Elam, where they had presumably been taken (see below). The importance of Nabû-bēl-šumāti in the rebel coalition is indicated by the fact that Ashurbanipal ranked him with Šamaš-šuma-ukīn and the king of a land whose name is not preserved (likely Elam) as the most prominent rebel leaders,[219] and by the fact that inscriptions often vilified him when mentioning his name (e.g., "Nabû-bēl-šumāti, the prostitute of Menanu," "the one rejected by the god Bēl and cursed by the gods, Nabû-bēl-šumāti," and "Nabû-bēl-šumāti, whose skin the god Nabû will sell").[220] The mere fact that he is mentioned frequently in royal inscriptions and letters proves that he played an important role in events.[221] Following the precedent set by earlier members of his family (Merodach-Baladan II and Nabû-ušallim), Nabû-bēl-šumāti associated himself with Elam, hiring troops in its border region and using Elamite territory as a base of operations.[222]

The relationship between Nabû-bēl-šumāti and Šamaš-šuma-ukīn is unclear. *ABL* 1326 shows them in contact with one another ("the messenger of Nabû-bēl-šumāti who we[nt] into the presence of Šamaš-šuma-ukīn"), but a pre-revolt date for this text cannot be excluded.[223] A chronicle entry for the year 651[224] may record that Nabû-bēl-šumāti took someone or something to Šamaš-šuma-ukīn, but the poor state of preservation of the text makes any conclusions uncertain. Probably Nabû-bēl-šumāti acted independently of Šamaš-šuma-ukīn, particularly after Babylon was besieged and communication became difficult or impossible. Šamaš-šuma-ukīn and Nabû-

---

218 Piepkorn, *Asb.*, pp. 80-81 vii 81-86; Bauer, *Asb.*, p. 17 and pl. 12 ix 59-62. The incident may also be mentioned in a chronicle entry for 651, but the passage is too damaged to be certain (Grayson, *Chronicles*, no. 15:11-16; see Millard, *Iraq* 26 [1964]: 26-27). The first entry in the chronicle for the year 651 mentions the intercalary sixth month (line 7); thus, it is likely that the incident of concern here took place in or after that month. Since Nabû-bēl-šumāti is known to have joined the rebellion by the first month of that year (Starr, *SAA* 4, no. 280, see above), it would seem unlikely that he had waited several months to arrest these Assyrians.

219 Starr, *SAA* 4, no. 290 rev. 6-12. The text asks if an individual would ally himself with Šamaš-šuma-ukīn, Nabû-bēl-šumāti, or the king of the *la*[*nd* of ...] if Ashurbanipal put him in charge of the troops/men (LÚ.ÉRIN.MEŠ) of Bīt-Amukāni. The only kings known to have actively aided the rebellion were those of Elam and two Arab tribal groups.

220 *ABL* 289:7-8, 460:14', and 1000:11'-12'. Menanu is possibly an abbreviation of the Elamite name Ḫumban-nimena and could refer to the Elamite king who reigned 692-689 or to some other Elamite by the same name (cf. *ABL* 1380:1? and p. 184 below). Note also the description of the suicide of Nabû-bēl-šumāti in Streck, *Asb.*, pp. 60-63 vii 16-50.

221 Note that Elam's refusal to return Nabû-bēl-šumāti to Assyria for punishment is described as one of the reasons for Ashurbanipal's invasions of that land.

222 E.g., *ABL* 1000.

223 *ABL* 1326 rev. 4-6.

224 See below.

bēl-šumāti were active in different regions, the former in the north and the latter in the south. One may wonder if Nabû-bēl-šumāti, a descendant of kings of Babylonia, supported the rebellion not so much out of any real loyalty to Šamaš-šuma-ukīn (an Assyrian after all) as out of the desire for Babylonian independence. Perhaps conflict would have eventually arisen between the two parties if the revolt had proved successful. Nabû-bēl-šumāti maintained his own contacts with outside forces, in particular Elam. Property belonging to him was later found to be in Dilmun. Possibly he had sent some of his possessions there in order to keep them safe from the Assyrians and to be available if he should ever need to flee down the Gulf. Or possibly he had commercial ties with that land. At the same time, he may have been attempting to win the support of Ḫundaru, the ruler of Dilmun. That Dilmun may have aided the rebels is indicated by the fact that a supporter of Assyria in the Sealand later asked Ashurbanipal if he wanted to pardon Ḫundaru.[225]

We do not know if Nabû-bēl-šumāti had any particular base of operations within the Sealand, although after fleeing to the Elamite border region he may have used the town of Targibātu as one; he is said to have received a deputation from the Puqūdu there on one occasion.[226] As it was throughout Babylonian history, the Sealand with its swamps and marshlands was an ideal place from which to launch operations against a town-bound enemy and to serve as a place of refuge from pursuers.

The extent of Nabû-bēl-šumāti's support in the Sealand is unknown although the core of his forces likely came from his own Bīt-Yakīn tribe. The towns of Eridu, Kullab, and Kissik, which Sennacherib's inscriptions assigned to the Bīt-Yakīn, supported the Assyrians, but they were probably not inhabited by Chaldeans.[227] Since Ashurbanipal wrote reassuringly to some Sealanders in Ayyaru (II) of 650 and sent Bēl-ibni to lead them,[228] he must have had some support there.[229] Later in the revolt it is known that a

---

225 *ABL* 791. A letter from Ashurbanipal to Ḫundaru dated to the eponymy of Nabû-nādin-[aḫḫē] (647 or 646) mentions Nabû-bēl-šumāti and says that Ashurbanipal had given the kingship of Dilmun to Ḫundaru (Thompson, *AAA* 20 [1933]: 103-105 and pl. 100. See also Kessler in Potts, *Dilmun*, pp. 150-51. Thus, if Ḫundaru had indeed supported the rebellion, it seems that Ashurbanipal pardoned him.

226 *ABL* 282:17-rev. 14. *ABL* 521 rev. 21-24 appears to connect Nabû-bēl-šumāti with the town Ḫudimiri, indicating that he may have moved his possessions in Elam to that town (see Zadok, *RGTC* 8, p. 164 on the reading of the place name and Dietrich, *Aramäer*, pp. 206-207 no. 166). Although Nabû-bēl-šumāti's name is not preserved in the text, the epithets used to describe the individual were those used elsewhere for Nabû-bēl-šumāti (see *CAD* 15 [S], p. 245b). A damaged chronicle entry may also connect Nabû-bēl-šumāti with Ša-pī-Bēl (see Grayson, *Chronicles* no. 15:12-13, commentary).

227 Luckenbill, *Senn.*, p. 53:48-49. See *ABL* 210 rev. 5-6 where the people of Kissik clearly distinguish themselves from the Chaldeans.

228 *ABL* 289.

229 Note also the view conveyed to Ashurbanipal by some individuals (presumably from the Puqūdu and Sealand, but possibly from Ur) that if the Assyrian king appointed Ningal-

number of Gurasimmu, as well as individuals from Ur and Kissik, were active with Nabû-bēl-šumāti[230] and that some Puqūdu were in (friendly) contact with him.[231] As head of the powerful Bīt-Yakīn tribe, Nabû-bēl-šumāti would have had at his disposal the wealth of the tribe to provision his men and to hire troops elsewhere.[232] Furthermore, the various kings of Elam may have provided him with additional forces. According to Ashurbanipal, the kings of Elam—Ḫumban-nikaš II, Tammarītu, Indabibi, and Ḫumban-ḫaltaš III—all aided Nabû-bēl-šumāti.[233] While only Ḫumban-nikaš II is specifically stated to have sent military aid to the rebels (and then to Šamaš-šuma-ukīn, not Nabû-bēl-šumāti), the others at least allowed Nabû-bēl-šumāti to gather troops in Elamite territory, and to use their region as a base of operations and, eventually, as a refuge. The exact course of events in the Sealand during the revolt and the actions of the various combatants are not clear. In all likelihood the struggle for control of the Sealand, particularly after Bēl-ibni arrived, was a see-saw series of actions, with now one side and now the other momentarily the stronger. Some incidents described in letters may even have taken place after Babylon fell to the Assyrians.

Probably Nabû-bēl-šumāti's first endeavour was to try to gain control of the pro-Assyrian towns of the south. With Puqudian help, he managed to cut off Assyrian aid to these towns and to the Gurasimmu tribe and to place them in a precarious position.[234] As described earlier, he was eventually successful in making Eridu, Kullab, and the Gurasimmu join the revolt and the governor of Ur, Sîn-tabni-uṣur, may have been forced to submit briefly. The Šamaš-šuma-ukīn Chronicle may record some action by Nabû-bēl-šumāti in the second half of 651, possibly stating that he had defeated an Assyrian army and taken someone or something to Šamaš-šuma-ukīn; however, the broken context makes any readings extremely uncertain.[235]

One coup carried out by Nabû-bēl-šumāti or his followers was the capture of Marduk-šarra-uṣur, an official sent by Ashurbanipal to aid in putting down

---

iddin's son Sîn-šarra-uṣur over them, the Puqūdu and Sealand would support Assyria (Starr, *SAA* 4, no. 302). This could indicate that the Sealand was not whole-hearted in its support for Šamaš-šuma-ukīn, but note the earlier comments on the date of the text mentioning this matter and on the possibility that the individuals saying this may have been lying (see pp. 164 and 167).

230 *ABL* 1000:11'-19'.

231 *ABL* 282:17-rev. 14. For the date of the letter, see p. 168.

232 Note Starr, *SAA* 4, no. 280 rev. 1-8; there is no proof that he was hiring, as opposed to simply assembling, troops in Elam in this text.

233 Streck, *Asb.*, pp. 60-61 vii 16-24.

234 Note in particular *ABL* 1236:7'-9', *ultu* [*bīt?*] *Nabû-bēl-šumāti ana gurasim ūridi šēpani! kî taparsu*, "Because our access has been cut off ever since Nabû-bēl-šumāti went down to the Gurasimmu," and *ABL* 1241+*CT* 54 112.

235 Grayson, *Chronicles*, no. 15:13-18; the name Nabû-bēl-šumāti is mostly restored. This passage may be connected with the statement in edition B that Nabû-bēl-šumāti had seized some Assyrians whom Ashurbanipal had sent to help him (but see above).

the rebellion.[236] Marduk-šarra-uṣur appears to have been detained or imprisoned in Elam, since he was there when Tammarītu fled Elam after being deposed by Indabibi; Tammarītu brought Marduk-šarra-uṣur back to Assyria with him. Again, the exact details of this incident are unclear. Perhaps we are dealing with more than one individual by the name of Marduk-šarra-uṣur since edition B of Ashurbanipal's annals seems to state that Tammarītu brought him to Assyria by force, implying that he did not wish to go to Assyria.[237]

The Assyrians may have begun to gain the upper hand in the Sealand in 650. By the second month of that year a number of Sealanders apparently had surrendered, giving themselves up to an official in Uruk.[238] On the fifth day of Ayyaru (II) in 650 Ashurbanipal wrote to the Sealanders to tell them that he did not associate them with the crimes of Nabû-bēl-šumāti and that he had appointed to be their leader one Bēl-ibni, who is described as a servant/slave (*ardu*) of Ashurbanipal and a member of his court (*manzaz pāniya*).[239] According to *ABL* 1106, Bēl-ibni was the son of Nabû-kudurrī-uṣur to whom Ashurbanipal had given the Sealand, presumably in the place of the rebel Nabû-bēl-šumāti.[240] Elsewhere Bēl-ibni is called a general

---

236 Marduk-šarra-uṣur is perhaps to be identified with the son of Gabê by that name who had been one of those helping Uruk (see *ABL* 1106:11'-15').

237 *ABL* 963:2'-10' (see Dietrich, *Aramäer*, pp. 206-207 no. 165 for possible restorations) and Piepkorn, *Asb.*, pp. 78-81 vii 58-70. Edition B states that in order to glorify the gods Aššur and Ištar (the gods who had deposed Tammarītu at Ashurbanipal's request), Tammarītu and his followers, "together with Marduk-šarra-uṣur, an official of mine, whom they had carried off by force" (*itti Marduk-šarra-uṣur šūt rēšiya ša ibšimūšu ina danāni*), crawled naked before Ashurbanipal and grasped his royal feet. Instead of indicating that Marduk-šarra-uṣur had been brought to Ashurbanipal unwillingly, could his having been carried off by force refer to his original capture by the rebels or to Tammarītu having had to use force to gain control of him from the new king of Elam? Dietrich thinks that *ABL* 960:4'-12' indicates that Marduk-šarra-uṣur had gone to Elam of his own free will, in order to obtain food (see Dietrich, *Aramäer*, pp. 172-73 no. 86), but the letter is so damaged as to preclude any certainty about the matter. In *Iraq* 26 (1964): 28, Millard suggests that Marduk-šarra-uṣur's capture may be mentioned in the Šamaš-šuma-ukīn Chronicle and date the incident to 651, but the passage is broken and the name of Marduk-šarra-uṣur is not preserved. Note also Hämeen-Anttila, *SAAB* 1 (1987): 13-16.

238 *CT* 54 507:5-9 (partially restored). See above, p. 161 n. 134, for the date of this incident.

239 *ABL* 289; and see *ABL* 291:14. Bēl-ibni may have been active in the Sealand before this date. With regard to Bēl-ibni, see Schawe in *RLA* 1, pp. 477-79.

240 *ABL* 1106 rev. 13'-14'. It is not inconceivable that like Nabû-bēl-šumāti, Bēl-ibni was a descendant of Merodach-Baladan II and thus a member of Bīt-Yakīn's ruling family (as suggested in Olmstead, *Assyria*, p. 453), but there is no direct evidence of this. However, the reason Bēl-ibni expressed great pleasure at being given a statue of Merodach-Baladan by Ashurbanipal (*ABL* 521:9-11) may be because Merodach-Baladan was one of his ancestors. It is unclear if the statue was in the likeness of Merodach-Baladan or merely one which had previously belonged to him.

(*turtānu*) and a royal official (*ša rēši ša* [*šarri*]).[241] The fragmentary letter *CT* 54 545 may refer to a Bēl-ibni with the normal Babylonian title for governor, *šākin ṭēmi* (⌜LÚ⌝.GAR.K[U?]); thus he may have been sent to take over the governorship of the Sealand and to lead the loyal forces in that region.[242]

Bēl-ibni recognized that, because of the marshes, fighting in the Sealand required special tactics and equipment. Thus he requested that the king send him lumber and twenty Sidonians to build ten boats.[243] With the boats, he would be able to pursue the rebels into the depths of the marshes and, if necessary, into Elam itself. It was probably at about the time of this appointment in Ayyaru (II) of 650 that Bēl-ibni and Nūrea, the Assyrian governor of Zamū, went to the aid of Ur and subjugated a large part of the Gurasimmu.[244] He also claims to have defeated the Puqūdu and the Sealand three of four times.[245] In the course of taking up his position in the Sealand Bēl-ibni may have received oaths of allegiance from some people of the Sealand, beginning in Kissik, as recorded in *ABL* 521; however, it may be that this was done later, when the revolt in the Sealand had been essentially crushed and Nabû-bēl-šumāti had fled to Elam.[246] At one point during Bēl-ibni's pacification of the Sealand, Tammarītu of Elam, having been defeated and deposed by the usurper Indabibi, fled to Ashurbanipal via the Sealand. He, his family, and his retinue came into the hands of Bēl-ibni, who sent them on to Assyria, where they were given asylum.[247] Not all of Bēl-ibni's actions met with Ashurbanipal's approval. On one occasion the king wanted

---

241 *ABL* 795:4-6 (allusion not entirely certain) and 267 rev. 11-12. On the *ša rēši* official, see p. 234 n. 126.

242 *CT* 54 545:6'. Because of the lack of context, it is possible that the title does not in fact refer to Bēl-ibni or that a different Bēl-ibni is meant. The reference to Nabû-bēl-šumāti (line 10') supports the identification of this Bēl-ibni with the official of that name who was sent by Ashurbanipal to the Sealand. The usual title for governors of the Sealand was, however, *šaknu* (see Appendix B sub 12).

243 *ABL* 795 rev. 7'-12'.

244 *ABL* 790+*CT* 54 425:4-10. Note *ABL* 1129 rev. 13'-16'; the passage can be understood in several ways, including "not even Bēl-ibni and a thousand bowmen (stationed) in Ur could restrain Nabû-bēl-šumāti" (see Brinkman, *Or.* NS 34 [1965]: 255) and "Nabû-bēl-šumāti must not be allowed to restrain Bēl-ibni and the one thousand bowmen (with him) at Ur" (see Dietrich, *Aramäer*, pp. 188-89 no. 127).

245 *ABL* 790+*CT* 54 425:10-12 (partially restored); see Dietrich, *Aramäer*, pp. 188-89 no. 128.

246 Parpola and Watanabe (*SAA* 2, p. XXXII) suggest that the oath of loyalty *SAA* 2, no. 9 (*ABL* 1105) may have been imposed upon Sealanders who had initially taken part in the rebellion but later changed sides and that *ABL* 521 refers to the imposition of this oath of loyalty. It is uncertain, however, that the Sealanders were the ones taking the oath represented by *SAA* 2, no. 9 (see above, p. 141).

247 E.g., Weidner, *AfO* 8 (1932-33): 198-99 nos. 68-70; *ABL* 284; and cf. *ABL* 282:6-16. For the date of this incident, see below.

to know how one as devoted to the king as Bēl-ibni had done what he had done.[248]

The struggle between the two parties for control of the Sealand caused a shortage of food there; the fighting undoubtedly hindered the cultivation and collection of food supplies. Hunger forced a number of prominent rebel supporters of Nabû-bēl-šumāti to surrender to Bēl-ibni.[249] When Nabû-bēl-šumāti became unable to maintain himself in the Sealand as a result of Bēl-ibni's actions, he fled to Elam. *ABL* 282 suggests that he was there in Targibātu when Indabibi's revolt occurred (by 649 at the latest).[250] Nabû-bēl-šumāti took some captives with him to Elam, including a number of Assyrians (whose detention in Elam became a bone of contention between Ashurbanipal and Indabibi),[251] people from Kissik,[252] and a brother of Bēl-ibni.[253] Those from Kissik managed to escape, only to be arrested by Bēl-ibni when they entered the Sealand, presumably because Bēl-ibni regarded with suspicion any persons coming from Elam.[254] Four years after his brother had been captured, Bēl-ibni managed to free him by sending a force of troops to his aid.[255]

Bēl-ibni had his own contacts with Elam, undoubtedly trying both to discover Nabû-bēl-šumāti's movements and plans and to persuade Elam to give the rebel up to Assyria.[256] From the Elamite border region, Nabû-bēl-šumāti continued to harass Bēl-ibni. One such action is reported in *ABL* 1000. Nabû-bēl-šumāti hired[257] members of various tribes (Ḫilmu, Pillatu,

248 *ABL* 291.

249 *ABL* 963 rev. 3'-10'; see Dietrich, *Aramäer*, pp. 192-93 no. 137.

250 See above, p. 168.

251 E.g., Streck, *Asb.*, pp. 142-43 viii 47-61 and see below, pp. 185-86.

252 *ABL* 736:7-9.

253 *ABL* 460 rev. 3-8. Although the name of the author of the letter is not preserved, the contents and language suggest that it was Bēl-ibni. For example, only letters of Bēl-ibni and Ashurbanipal refer to Ummanšibar and the epithets used to describe Nabû-bēl-šumāti are used elsewhere only by Bēl-ibni.

254 *ABL* 736:7-13.

255 *ABL* 460 rev. 8-12. The reference to the author having been held captive for four years (rev. 3-8) points to his rescue having taken place in 649 at the earliest (if we assume he had not been taken captive before the Šamaš-šuma-ukīn Revolt began in 652). It could, however, have taken place after the end of the rebellion since Nabû-bēl-šumāti remained alive and possibly active until some time after Ashurbanipal's second campaign against Ḫumban-ḫaltaš III.

256 *ABL* 1170, a letter from Ashurbanipal to the Elamite Ummanši[bar] dated on 25-IV-648, appears to refer to a message from Ummanšibar to Bēl-ibni (lines 8-9). An Ummanšibar also appears in *ABL* 281:11-12 (via his herald), 460:3, 792:5, and possibly *CT* 54 282:11' (partially restored).

257 The meaning of *ú-tag-gi-ra* (*ABL* 1000:16') is not absolutely certain. Neither *CAD* nor *AHw* includes it in its *agāru* article; according to these two dictionaries, a D-stem of *agāru* is attested only in the Old Assyrian period. Since no verbal root tgr is cited in *AHw*, since none of the *nagāru*/*nugguru* verbs appear to make sense in this passage, and since a

Nuguḫu, Yaši'-il, and Lakabru) who were suffering from famine. They, together with his own troops, including 250 Gurasimmu and persons from Ur and Kissik, made a raid into the Sealand by boat and plundered the tribes there. In retaliation, Bēl-ibni sent out four hundred archers, who crossed the Gulf by boat and entered Elam. They defeated the Ḫilmu and Pillatu, and took many captives.[258] Nabû-bēl-šumāti remained in refuge in Elam for at least two years after the end of the Šamaš-šuma-ukīn Revolt, sheltered by Ḫumban-ḫaltaš III or other Elamite nobles.[259]

VII. Elam

Elam and its kings proved to be the most important non-Babylonian supporters of the rebellion. This is to be expected in view of long-standing Elamite enmity toward Assyria and in view of the fact that Elam was Babylonia's only other important neighbouring state. Despite the fact that there were several kings of Elam in rapid succession during the course of the rebellion, each having taken the throne from his predecessor by force of arms, they were unanimous in their support of the rebellion in Babylonia, although one (Indabibi) considered making peace with Assyria at one point. While Elam continued to support anti-Assyrian movements in Babylonia, it also continued to provide that support for a fee.[260] Ashurbanipal states that both Ḫumban-nikaš and Tammarītu received a present (*ṭa'tu*) from Šamaš-šuma-ukīn for their support,[261] and it is known that Nabû-bēl-šumāti acquired the help of tribes on the Elamite border in return for food and slaves.[262] Unfortunately for Elam, the revolt failed and Elam had to pay a heavy price for its support of the rebels—two campaigns by Ashurbanipal.

Although Ashurbanipal had given Ḫumban-nikaš II asylum from Teumman and installed him as king of Elam, Ḫumban-nikaš disregarded his agreement with the Assyrian king and accepted a gift from Šamaš-šuma-ukīn's messengers. He then sent military forces made up of Elamites and

---

meaning "hire" would fit the context, a D-stem of *agāru* is tentatively accepted here. For a second possible example of a D-stem form of *agāru* in the Neo-Assyrian period, in *ABL* 201:10, see Postgate, *Taxation*, p. 263.

258 The date of *ABL* 1000 is uncertain; the letter could conceivably come from after the fall of Babylon.

259 See chapter 9.

260 See Brinkman, *JCS* 25 (1973): 91-93 and *JNES* 24 (1965): 161-66.

261 Piepkorn, *Asb.*, pp. 76-79 vii 3-8 and 43-47, and Streck, *Asb.*, pp. 32-33 iii 136-137. Veenhof (*Aspects*, pp. 219-302) has discussed the meaning of the term *dātu* (*ṭa'tu*/*ṭātu*), primarily in the Old Assyrian period. In historical texts of the later period, he has demonstrated that this word indicates "an amount of money paid or a gift donated in order to buy off a superior enemy, to maintain good relations with a powerful neighbour, or to win the support of a possible ally" (*ibid.*, p. 223).

262 *ABL* 1000:11'-16'.

border tribes to the aid of the Babylonian king against the Assyrian troops "who were going about the land of Karduniaš (and) subduing the land of Chaldea." These reinforcements were led by Undasu (a son of the former king Teumman), Attametu (the chief archer), Nēšu (the leader of Elam's armies), and two Arameans (Zazaz, the chieftain of Pillatu, and Parû, the chieftain of Ḫilmu). The Elamites and their allies were defeated by the Assyrians, who advanced from their base at Mangisi, apparently located on the Tigris near the confluence of the Diyala River. The heads of all of the enemy leaders were cut off and sent to Ashurbanipal.[263] Ashurbanipal wrote to Ḫumban-nikaš about the latter's treacherous action but the Elamite king refused to reply and restrained the Assyrian king's messenger.

The position of Ḫumban-nikaš became precarious after the defeat of his forces. Edition B of Ashurbanipal's annals implies that it was fairly soon after this battle that Tammarītu—possibly a second individual by this name, and not the brother of Ḫumban-nikaš II whom Ashurbanipal had put on the throne of Ḫîdalu—succeeded Ḫumban-nikaš as king of Elam.[264] Tammarītu revolted against Ḫumban-nikaš and killed both him and his family. It is not known if those supporting the deposition of Ḫumban-nikaš were doing so simply because they preferred Tammarītu to Ḫumban-nikaš, because they

---

263 Piepkorn, *Asb.*, pp. 76-79 vii 3-39; Aynard, *Asb.*, pp. 42-43 iii 6-9; Streck, *Asb.*, pp. 32-33 iii 136-138. Although Ashurbanipal's inscriptions state that Nēšu went to the aid Šamaš-šuma-ukīn, his name is not among those mentioned as having been defeated by the Assyrian forces. K 4500, a fragmentary Assyrian inscription draft, refers to Undasu (obv.? 4' and 15'), Attametu (5'), and Zazaz (15', partially restored), as well as Šamaš-šuma-ukīn (6' and 12', partially restored). See also Appendix D on this battle. Although all the kings of Elam during the time of the revolt are said to have supported the rebels, this is the only occasion on which Elamite troops are clearly known to have taken part in a battle on Babylonian soil.

264 Some scholars (e.g., Hinz, *Elam*, p. 185, and Cameron, *HEI*, pp. 192 and 231) have argued that this Tammarītu was not the brother of Ḫumban-nikaš II. This belief is based primarily upon the reference to a statue of "Tammarītu, the second (*arkû*), who did obeissance to me [Ashurbanipal] at the command of the gods Aššur and Ištar," which editions A and F state had been carried off to Assyria from Elam after Ashurbanipal's second campaign against Ḫumban-ḫaltaš III (Streck, *Asb.*, pp. 54-55 vi 55-57; Aynard, *Asb.*, pp. 54-55 v 38-39). A fragmentary text, K 3062, bears a similar statement: "[Statue of Tammarītu], the second, [who] fled [from] Elam [at the command] of the gods Aššur [and] Ištar, [grasp]ed [my feet], (and) did obeissance to me" (Streck, *Asb.*, pp. 214-15:1-4). The Tammarītu who revolted against Ḫumban-nikaš later fled to Assyria and submitted to Ashurbanipal "to glorify" the gods Aššur and Ištar (see p. 179 n. 237). Further support for the belief in a second Tammarītu at this time comes from references to the successor of Ḫumban-nikaš on the throne of Elam as "Tammarītu, the son/heir of Ḫumban-nikaš, the brother of his father" and as "[Tammarīt]u, who is not the brother of Ḫumban-nikaš" (Streck, *Asb.*, pp. 180-83:34-35 and Bauer, *Asb.*, pp. 51-52 obv. 14-rev. 1), although the latter passage is damaged and could also be translated as "[Tammarīt]u, the unbrotherly brother of Ḫumban-nikaš" (compare *ABL* 301:4). This Tammarītu is sometimes referred to as Tammarītu II. On this matter, see in particular the references cited in Carter and Stolper, *Elam*, p. 96 n. 404.

wished to appease Assyria, or because they wanted to put a stronger leader on the throne, one who would carry on the fight against Ashurbanipal. A letter from about this time sent by Ashurbanipal to an Elamite by the name of Menanu would suggest that at least some Elamites supported Ashurbanipal, or at least were unwilling to anger him. Ashurbanipal states that Menanu had sent the following message to him: "I have killed Simbur, to whom you showed favour ... but who sinned against (his) sworn agreement with you. ... We will fight with Ḫumban-nikaš, to whom you showed great favour but who sinned against (his) sworn agreement with you, sided with your enemy, and crossed your border."[265] Whether or not Tammarītu had been aided by those who wished to appease Ashurbanipal, once on the throne of Elam he too accepted a present from Šamaš-šuma-ukīn and made an alliance with him. Tammarītu is said to have sent military aid to Šamaš-šuma-ukīn, rushing his armed forces into battle (*ana mitḫūṣi ummānāteya urriḫa kakkēšu*), although no actual battle is ever mentioned.[266] On 5-II-650, Ashurbanipal described Nabû-bēl-šumāti as "the prostitute of Menanu."[267] If this refers to the same Menanu as the earlier letter, he must have supported Tammarītu in the deposition of Ḫumban-nikaš and then gone on to help Tammarītu against Assyria, presumably by giving aid to Nabû-bēl-šumāti.

As mentioned earlier, Ashurbanipal had an extispicy performed in 651 to determine if the Elamite army would be mobilized and fight with Assyrian forces between the eighth day of Abu (V) and the eighth day of Ulūlu (VI). The omens were unfavourable (i.e., the Elamite forces would not be mobilized).[268] Since we do not know the exact date Tammarītu replaced Ḫumban-nikaš on the throne of Elam, it is not possible to tell which of the two would have been king of Elam at the time. Possibly Ashurbanipal had requested this information immediately after the deposition of Ḫumban-nikaš in an attempt to discover if the new king would also support the rebellion.

At some point in or before 649, a rebellion took place against Tammarītu and he was defeated in open battle. Indabibi, who had instigated the rebellion, seized the throne. Tammarītu, his family, relatives, and eighty-five Elamite nobles who supported him fled to Ashurbanipal for refuge. In their flight they passed through the Sealand and Bēl-ibni sent them on to Ashurbanipal.

---

265 *ABL* 1380:5-13; in line 10 read ⌜*a-na*⌝ not KÙ.BABBAR (collated). The tablet is broken and large parts of it are difficult to interpret. Simbur is probably to be identified with the Elamite herald by that name who is mentioned in an Assyrian epigraph as having submitted to Ashurbanipal (Weidner, *AfO* 8 [1932-33]: 178-79 no. 2).

266 Aynard, *Asb.*, pp. 42-43 iii 10-16; Piepkorn, *Asb.*, pp. 78-79 vii 40-51; Streck, *Asb.*, pp. 32-35 iv 1-8; Weidner, *AfO* 8 (1932-33): 191-203 (various epigraphs). Edition B implies that Ḫumban-nikaš was deposed by the gods because of his action in sending aid to Šamaš-šuma-ukīn.

267 *ABL* 289:7-8.

268 Starr, *SAA* 4, no. 281.

They came before the Assyrian king, crawling naked on their bellies and bringing with them Nabû-bēl-šumāti's prisoner Marduk-šarra-uṣur. They undoubtedly hoped to placate Ashurbanipal's anger with them by returning Marduk-šarra-uṣur and to win support in recovering the throne of Elam. Ashurbanipal forgave Tammarītu's treachery and insolent words which the Elamite had earlier said about Assyria and gave him a place in his palace.[269] The fact that Tammarītu fled to Ashurbanipal and not to Šamaš-šuma-ukīn would indicate that he felt that either the Babylonian revolt was doomed to failure or that Indabibi would certainly ally with the rebels in Babylonia, making hope of refuge with them unlikely. The exact date of Indabibi's revolt is not known though he is attested on the throne of Elam at some point in 649, when Ashurbanipal wrote to him (*ABL* 1151). Tammarītu, his predecessor, is known to have been on the throne of Elam at some point after the ninth month of 651 since an extispicy report raises the possibility that he might attack Nippur and he is likely to have done so only after that city fell to the Assyrians.[270] Since Bēl-ibni was in the Sealand to receive Tammarītu when he fled from Indabibi, the revolt of Indabibi is likely to have taken place only after Bēl-ibni was put in charge of that area.

Indabibi considered establishing peace with Assyria by returning the Assyrians whom Nabû-bēl-šumāti had taken captive to Elam. According to edition of B of Ashurbanipal's annals, Indabibi released the captives from prison, sent a messenger to Ashurbanipal to establish friendly relations with Assyria, and promised "not to trespass (beyond) the boundary of his land" (i.e., not to send troops to aid the rebels).[271] It was probably at this time in 649 that Ashurbanipal sent *ABL* 1151 to Indabibi, calling him "brother" and wishing him well. Only the introductory section and the date are preserved and we are thus deprived of the real contents of the letter. Possibly because Indabibi became angry at the Assyrian king for giving refuge to Tammarītu, this friendly state of affairs ended and the Elamite king refused to return the Assyrian captives. There is no evidence that Indabibi sent military aid to the Babylonian rebels, although he did give refuge to Nabû-bēl-šumāti. Ashurbanipal sent an angry message to Indabibi complaining that he had not returned Nabû-bēl-šumāti and the captive Assyrians and threatening that he would ravage Elam and put someone else on the throne of that land. This message never reached Indabibi. Hearing of the approach of Ashurbanipal's

---

269 Aynard, *Asb.*, pp. 42-45 iii 17-32; Piepkorn, *Asb.*, pp. 78-81 vii 52-76; Streck, *Asb.*, pp. 34-37 iv 9-41; Weidner, *AfO* 8 (1932-33): 191-203 (various epigraphs); *ABL* 284; and possibly *CT* 54 487 (see Dietrich, *Aramäer*, p. 121 and 194-95 no. 140). See also p. 179 n. 237.

270 Starr, *SAA* 4, no. 289.

271 Piepkorn, *Asb.*, pp. 80-81 vii 77-92.

messenger, Ḫumban-ḫaltaš III revolted, killed Indabibi, and took the throne of Elam.[272]

Exactly when Indabibi was deposed is unknown; it is not even clear if this took place before or after the fall of Babylon. Only C of Ashurbanipal's annals clearly describes both the rebellion of Ḫumban-ḫaltaš against Indabibi and the end of the Šamaš-šuma-ukīn Revolt and it mentions the deposition of Indabibi after describing the fall of Babylon.[273] Edition A which also describes the fall of Babylon and knew of the accession of Ḫumban-ḫaltaš to the throne of Elam does not mention that individual's actual seizure of the throne from Indabibi. Since Assyrian annals often did not follow strict chronological order (at times geographical location and other considerations played a part), it must remain uncertain whether Indabibi was deposed before or after Babylon fell to the Assyrians. There is no clear evidence to indicate that Ḫumban-ḫaltaš III was on the throne of Elam while the Šamaš-šuma-ukīn Revolt was in progress.[274] Is it possible that the fall of Babylon played a part in the deposition Indabibi? With the rebellion in Babylonia finally put down, Ashurbanipal could now turn his attention to Elam and some Elamites may have hoped to appease him by deposing a ruler who had aided the rebellion and by replacing him with an individual who might be more acceptable to Assyria.

Conclusion

The rebellion of 652-648 was the first widespread uprising in Babylonia against Assyrian domination since the revolt of 694-689. It too won support from non-Babylonians who were interested in seeing Assyria's power diminished. Though it was led by a brother of the Assyrian king, the revolt

---

272 Streck, *Asb.*, pp. 142-45 viii 47-74. It is possible that this text is in error in implying that the rebellion against Indabibi was brought about because of Indabibi's refusal to release these Assyrians since it is not clear that his rebellion took place during the time of the Šamaš-šuma-ukīn Revolt in Babylonia.

273 For edition C, see Bauer, *Asb.*, pp. 17-18 and pl. 12 (heavily restored); the description of the Šamaš-šuma-ukīn Revolt ends on ix 53 and that of the revolt of Ḫumban-ḫaltaš III against Indabibi begins on ix 89 (cf. Streck, *Asb.*, pp. 144-45 viii 68-74). A brief reference to Indabibi's accession appears in edition K after the description of the fall of Babylon; see Cogan and Tadmor, *Or.* NS 50 (1981): 232-33 BM 134436 a 38'-39' (restored from ND 814 b 16'-17'). Cogan and Tadmor state that the defeat of Indabibi appears in more detail before the surrender of Babylon is mentioned (*ibid.*, p. 238), but the passage in question (Piepkorn, *Asb.*, pp. 102-103 iv) is badly damaged and could instead describe the revolt of Indabibi against Tammarītu.

274 *ABL* 462, which refers to Ḫumban-ḫaltaš III as king of Elam (lines 16-17), may suggest that messengers of Šamaš-šuma-ukīn were in Elam at that time (rev. 6'-10'). (In view of the spelling ^{d}GIŠ.NU$_{11}$-[...] in rev. 7' it is likely that Šamaš-šuma-ukīn's name is to be read here.) But the messengers may have gone to Elam in the time of Indabibi and simply remained there for their own safety when Babylon fell.

was supported by Chaldeans, Arameans, Sealanders, and Akkadians—by both settled and nomadic groups. These groups, however, were not totally united in rebellion. In particular, a number of towns in southern Babylonia remained loyal to Assyria despite intense pressure exerted upon them by the rebels. While Babylon did not fall until the middle of 648 at the earliest (and by the end of that year at the latest), it seems likely that the rebellion had begun to wind down in the northern part of the country around the time Babylon was besieged in the middle of 650, and it is possible that the same holds true for the southern part of the land. This is supported, albeit passively, by the fact that neither the Šamaš-šuma-ukīn Chronicle nor the Akītu Chronicle mentions any military incidents occurring after the siege of Babylon began; thus, the compilers of these chronicles may have considered that no actions worthy of mention had taken place.[275] This revolt marked the last known attempt by Babylonians to regain their independence from Assyria before the final successful attempt led by Nabopolassar, which resulted in the formation of the Neo-Babylonian empire. The four-year-long Šamaš-šuma-ukīn Revolt put a great strain on Assyria and its resources and undoubtedly marked the beginning of its decline, even though Assyrian troops went on to other victories in the Near East, including the defeat of Elam on two separate occasions.[276]

---

275 They may, however, have had no information on events taking places outside Babylon after the city was besieged, or none that was of interest to a possibly "Babylon-centric" point of view.

276 Ashurbanipal's military campaigns after the revolt were directed mainly against Šamaš-šuma-ukīn's non-Babylonian supporters (the nomadic tribes of the western desert region and the Elamites). These were major hard-fought campaigns in their own right, taking place outside Babylonia, and one should not consider them mere mopping up exercises.

TABLE 2

The Šamaš-šuma-ukīn Revolt: A Chronological Outline

652	II through X	The *rab bīti* ("steward") carried out some activity (*biḫirti ibteḫir*) in the land of Akkad. (Grayson, *Chronicles*, no. 16:9-10)
	23-II	Ashurbanipal appealed to the people of Babylon not to join Šamaš-šuma-ukīn in rebellion and promised that he would not hold against them the fact that they had initially sided with his brother. (*ABL* 301)
	17-IV	An extispicy was performed to determine if Šamaš-šuma-ukīn would be captured if Assyrian forces entered Babylon. Report unfavourable. (Starr, *SAA* 4, no. 279)
	19-X	Hostilities began. (Grayson, *Chronicles*, no. 16:11)
	8-XI	Šamaš-šuma-ukīn withdrew before the enemy into Babylon. (Grayson, *Chronicles*, no. 15:6 and cf. no. 16:12)
	12-XII	A battle took place between the armies of Babylonia and Assyria. (Sachs, *Astronomical Diaries* 1, no. -651 iv 10')
	27-XII	A Babylonian army was defeated at Ḫirītu, in the province of Sippar. (Grayson, *Chronicles*, no. 16:13-15 and Sachs, *Astronomical Diaries* 1, no. -651 iv 18'-19')
651	-	There were [*insu*]*rrections* in Assyria and Akkad. The New Year's festival was not celebrated. (Grayson, *Chronicles*, no. 16:17-19)
	4-I	An extispicy was performed to determine if Nabû-bēl-šumāti had assembled archers in Elam and was coming to oppose the pro-Assyrian forces. Report unfavourable. (Starr, *SAA* 4, no. 280)
	[?]-V?	An extispicy was performed to determine if the Elamite army would assemble, march, and fight with the troops of Ashurbanipal between 8-V and 8-VI. Report unfavourable. (Starr,

		SAA 4, no. 281)[1]
	9-VI$_2$	Babylonian forces captured Cutha. (Grayson, *Chronicles*, no. 15:7-10)
	15-VII	An extispicy was performed to determine if the report that Šamaš-šuma-ukīn was fleeing to Elam was true. Report unfavourable. (Starr, *SAA* 4, no. 282)
	16-VIII	An extispicy was performed to determine if Šamaš-šuma-ukīn would be captured by Assyrian troops if they advanced against him. Report favourable. (Starr, *SAA* 4, no. 283)
	between 3(+)-IX and 18-XI	Nippur was captured by, or went over to, the Assyrians.[2]
	11-XI	An extispicy was performed to determine if Šamaš-šuma-ukīn would go out from Babylon and flee. (Starr, *SAA* 4, no. 285)
	13-[?]	An extispicy was performed to determine if an individual would join Ashurbanipal's enemies. Report unfavourable(?). (Starr, *SAA* 4, no. 293)
	[?]-[?]	An extispicy was performed to determine if Assyrian troops should go to Bāb-Sāme and do battle with the forces of Šamaš-šuma-ukīn. Report favourable. (Starr, *SAA* 4, no. 287)
650	-	The New Year's festival was not celebrated. (Grayson, *Chronicles*, no. 16:20-21)
	5-II	In a letter to the people of the Sealand, Ashurbanipal stated that he had appointed Bēl-ibni over that area. (*ABL* 289)
	11-IV	Babylon was besieged by the Assyrians. (Grayson, *Chronicles*, no. 15:19)
	13-VIII	Composition of the first of several "siege documents" at Babylon referring to hardship and severe famine in the land. (Budge, *PSBA* 10 [1887-88]: 146 and pls. 4-6 [*B-K* K.119])

---

[1] For the date of the extispicy (possibly in the twelfth month), see p. 145 n. 56.

[2] On 3(+)-IX-651 a text was dated at Nippur by the regnal years of Šamaš-šuma-ukīn (IM 57923; *B-K* K.116), but on 18-XI-651 a transaction was dated by Ashurbanipal's regnal years (IM 57901 and duplicate IM 57902; *B-K* J.8-9).

649	-	The New Year's festival was not celebrated. (Grayson, *Chronicles*, no. 16:22)
	-	Ashurbanipal wrote a friendly letter to Indabibi, the king of Elam. (*ABL* 1151)
648	-	The New Year's festival was not celebrated. (Grayson, *Chronicles*, no. 16:23)
	28-V	Last economic document from Borsippa dated by the regnal years of Šamaš-šuma-ukīn. (BM 134973 [*B-K* K.142])
	30-V	Last economic document from Babylon dated by the regnal years of Šamaš-šuma-ukīn. (BM 40577 [*B-K* K.143])

CHAPTER 9

ASHURBANIPAL, KING OF ASSYRIA, AND KANDALĀNU, KING OF BABYLONIA (647-627)

Babylonian desire for independence was obviously deeply rooted for the people to have attempted to challenge the might of Assyria and to have withstood warfare, siege, and starvation for several years. They were now exhausted, cowed into submission by Assyrian actions; and the information we have suggests that they were kept more closely under Assyrian control. The Babylonian people were ready for a period of peace so that they could repair the damage caused by the war and recover their strength. There is no record of any anti-Assyrian action in Babylonia from the fall of Babylon in 648 to the death of Kandalānu in 627,[1] but then there are few texts which deal with political and military matters in Babylonia, or Assyria, during these years. Much of what information there is involves Elam and the Arabs in the three to five years immediately following the revolt. Although little is known about the political situation, it would be incorrect to describe this time as a period of decline in Babylonia since numerous legal and administrative texts attest to considerable activity in the economic sphere.

Although edition A of Ashurbanipal's annals records that having put down the rebellion the Assyrian king appointed new governors and officials (LÚ.GAR.KUR.MEŠ LÚ.TIL.GÍD.DA.MEŠ) over the people of Babylonia, no mention is made of their new king. However, at some point after the revolt, Ashurbanipal installed Kandalānu as ruler of Babylonia.[2] Kandalānu[3]

---

[1] There may have been some unrest in the last few years of this period but this has not been established clearly as yet (see below).

[2] Kandalānu is cited as the successor of Šamaš-šuma-ukīn in Babylonian Kinglist A iv 22', the Synchronistic Kinglist iv 15, and the Ptolemaic Canon (see Grayson in *RLA* 6, pp. 93, 120, and 101 respectively) and may have followed him the synchronistic kinglist fragment *KAV* 182 iv 6 (name restored, as is that of his predecessor; see *ibid.*, p. 125). He is cited in Uruk Kinglist line 3' (name of his predecessor uncertain; see *ibid.*, p. 97) and in a Babylonian chronicle (first ruler mentioned after Šamaš-šuma-ukīn; Grayson, *Chronicles*, no. 16:24)

[3] In kinglists and chronicles the name is spelled as follows: *kan-dal* (Babylonian Kinglist A iv 22'), *k[an-da]*-⌜*la*⌝-*an* (Uruk Kinglist 3'; while the traces of the first sign might suggest *k[a-* instead of *k[an-*, this is not certain and the spacing would suggest the writing proposed [following *UVB* 18, p. 53 and against van Dijk, *Rēš-Heiligtum*, p. 27]), *kan-dàl-a-nu* (Synchronistic Kinglist iv 15 and 20), *kan-da-la-nu* (Grayson, *Chronicles*, no. 16:24) and

is first mentioned as king in an economic document dated at Babylon on sixth day of Ṭebētu (X) in 647 (year 1 of Kandalānu).[4] In date formulae he was usually called "king" or "king of Babylon."[5] As with Šamaš-šuma-ukīn, no date formula ever refers to his accession year and this could suggest that he ascended the throne at the New Year's festival in 647. The fact, however, that documents were dated by Ashurbanipal's regnal years in 647 at Uruk and Borsippa up until the twelfth day of Du'ūzu (IV) and the eighteenth day of Kislīmu (IX) respectively could indicate that he was appointed only after that time.[6] Kandalānu's reign was to last for twenty-one years and to end with his death in 627.[7]

Kandalānu appears to have been acknowledged king over as wide an area as Šamaš-šuma-ukīn, with the important exception of Nippur. While texts were dated by Kandalānu's regnal years at Babylon, Borsippa, Dilbat, Ḫursagkalama, Sippar, and Uruk, all of the texts from Nippur during these twenty-one years were dated by Ashurbanipal, who was given the title "king

---

Κινηλαδάνου (Ptolemaic Canon). In the astronomical text *LBAT* 1417 iv 1 and in the nineteen-year cycle text BM 33809:6, the name is spelled *kan-dal-an*-[(x)] and ⌜*kan-dal-an*⌝ respectively; in the Neo-Assyrian letter *CT* 53 966:10 it appears as *kan-dàl-a-nu* (if the passage is understood correctly; see below). In date formulae of the period, the royal name is spelled *kan-da-la-nu* about ninety per cent of the time. Other spellings are as follows: *kan-da-la-an-nu* (Hunger, *Bagh. Mitt.* 5 [1970]: 278 no. 6:40 [*B-K* L.107]); *kan-dal-la-nu* (Ellis, *JCS* 36 [1984]: 51 no. 16:14 [*B-K* L.88]); *kan-da-la-nu-u* (Jakob-Rost, *FB* 10 [1968]: 51 no. 9:18 [*B-K* L.192]) *kan-da-la-a-nu* (Ellis, *JCS* 36 [1984]: 43 no. 7:17 and Jakob-Rost, *FB* 10 [1968]: 44 no. 3:9 [*B-K* L.17 and 95]); *kan-dal-a-nu* (BM 50298 rev. 7' [*B-K* L.126]); *kan-da-la-an* (*LIH* 1 70:24); *kan-dal-an* (PTS 2479:22' [*B-K* L.14]); *kan-da-la-na* (Pinches, *Berens Coll.*, no. 103:19 [*B-K* L.123]); *kan-dal-na* (BM 41174 rev. 6' [*B-K* L.34]); *kan-da-la-ni* (Oppert, *RA* 1 [1886]: 4 line 15; Dalley, *Edinburgh*, no. 61:7; PRS 9:20; and BM 29531:17 [*B-K* L.16, 43, 50a, and 58]); and *kan-dal-a-ni* (Ellis, *JCS* 36 [1984]: 39 no. 4:30 and Jastrow in *Oriental Studies*, pl. facing p. 136 line 28 [*B-K* L.4 and 10]). The personal determinative appears in about twenty-five per cent of the cases. The name is preceded by the divine determinative on three occasions—*AnOr* 9 4 v 45; B.78:17; and Pinches, *Berens Coll.*, no. 103:19 (*B-K* L.23, L.109 and L.123 respectively).

4 *VAS* 5 3 (*B-K* L.1).

5 He bore the title LUGAL URU.DÙG in Weidner, *AfO* 16 (1952-53): pl. 5 no. 6:6 (*B-K* L.76) and note *OECT* 10 1 rev. 8' ([LU]GAL URU.DÙG.KI; royal name not preserved; *B-K* Ln.1). For the writing of URU.DÙG for Babylon, see Brinkman, *PKB*, p. 116 n. 653.

6 BM 29171; W 18874; YBC 7166; *OECT* 10 9; and Jakob-Rost, *FB* 10 (1968): 57-58 no. 13 (*B-K* J.18-22). Though note below that a transaction was dated according to Ashurbanipal's reign at Dilbat in the first month of 646.

7 Uruk Kinglist 3' (van Dijk, *Rēš-Heiligtum*, no. 88). Berossos states that the successor to Šamaš-šuma-ukīn as ruler of Babylonia reigned for twenty-one years (Schnabel, *Berossos*, p. 269:29 and p. 270:7 and 35-36). The Ptolemaic Canon gives Kandalānu a reign of twenty-two years, but see below. The date formulae of economic texts show that Kandalānu died sometime between 8-III-627 (year 21 Kandalānu) and 1(+)-VIII-627 (year 21 "after Kandalānu"); see below.

of (all) lands," "king of Assyria," or "king of the world."[8] Nippur had been taken by the Assyrians in 651 and used as a military base by them during the remainder of the Šamaš-šuma-ukīn Revolt. Presumably Ashurbanipal continued to keep Nippur directly under his control because it had been the most consistently troublesome of all the Babylonian cities since the time of Sennacherib and because it could serve as a centrally located military base in the event of further rebellion in Babylonia. Assyrian forces may simply have remained in Nippur after Babylon fell in 648. Assyria maintained control of Nippur for some time after 627 in spite of the efforts of Nabopolassar, suggesting that the city was under military occupation at that time.[9] It appears that not all the other cities in Babylonia were placed under Kandalānu's jurisdiction, or chose to recognize his position, at the same time. Although he was acknowledged as king at Babylon on the sixth day of Ṭebētu (X) in 647, a document was dated by Ashurbanipal at Dilbat on the twenty-ninth of Nisannu (I) in the following year.[10] Possibly the administration of Dilbat was not handed back to civilian (Babylonian) control by the military (Assyrian) authorities until after that date. There is no information about Ur during this period, so it is not possible to know whether that city was under the authority of Kandalānu or of Ashurbanipal. Indeed, no text dated at Ur after 649 and before the reign of Nebuchadnezzar II has been preserved.[11] While documents dated to the reign of Nabopolassar have been found at Ur, none were specifically dated there and some state that they were drawn up elsewhere (e.g., Babylon and Borsippa).[12] Thus, they may have been taken to Ur after the reign of Nabopolassar. The reason for this lack of texts is unknown. Had Ur been so severely hurt by rebel actions during the revolt that it now lapsed into a period of obscurity and neglect? Had trouble continued with the surrounding tribal groups and weakened its position? Or with the lessening of its importance as a bastion against these groups had it stagnated into a provincial backwater?

It has frequently been suggested that Kandalānu and Ashurbanipal were one and the same person because statements attributed to Berossos record that Šamaš-šuma-ukīn was succeeded by his brother (variant: Sardanapallos [=Ashurbanipal]), because Kandalānu and Ashurbanipal appear to have died

---

8 See Appendix A, tables 2 and 4. Approximately one half of the Babylonian economic texts dated by Ashurbanipal's regnal years gave him the title "king of the lands," one quarter the title "king of Assyria," and one fifth the title "king of the world."

9 Texts were dated at Nippur under Aššur-etil-ilāni, Sîn-šumu-līšir, and Sîn-šarra-iškun (see *B-K* sub M, N, and O; there are no texts from Nippur dated by Nabopolassar until his nineteenth year (*ROMCT* 2 7; see Kennedy, *JCS* 38 [1986]: 210 no. T.19.55).

10 *OECT* 10 399 (*B-K* J.24).

11 BM 113928 (*B-K* J.13) was dated at Ur on 29-I-year 20 of Ashurbanipal; for texts dated at Ur during the reign of Nebuchadnezzar II, see *UET* 4, p. 3.

12 See *UET* 4, pp. 3 and 6 and Brinkman, *Or.* NS 34 (1965): 256-57.

in the same year (627), and because Kandalānu has been attested only in kinglists and date formulae, and not in letters or historical texts. While there is no conclusive evidence on the matter, it seems more likely that they were separate individuals.[13] The tradition that has preserved the statements of Berossos is very involved and cannot be accepted without question. It is not impossible that Kandalānu was forgotten, overshadowed by the Assyrian king, because he had little or no authority over Babylonia and had carried out no actions worthy of record. Although Kandalānu is not attested in historical texts, there are in fact comparatively few royal records from Assyria that deal with events after the fall of Susa. Šamaš-šuma-ukīn left few royal inscriptions and he clearly had more authority than Kandalānu.

A few fragmentary Assyrian inscriptions and one dedicatory text from Nippur include among Ashurbanipal's many titles and epithets "king of Sumer and Akkad" and/or "viceroy of Babylon," and at least one of the Assyrian texts clearly dates to the period after Kandalānu would have ascended the throne of Babylonia. This would suggest that Ashurbanipal claimed the rulership of Babylonia and could be used to support the identification of Ashurbanipal with Kandalānu. However, some of the texts which give him these titles may date to periods when there was no king of Babylonia recognized by Assyria (e.g., during the revolt and before the appointment of Kandalānu) and others may be the products of sloppy or overzealous scribes. The major Assyrian texts from this period do not give Ashurbanipal these titles.

There is no evidence that alternate "throne names" were ever used by Assyrian kings during their lifetimes and in any case it would have been strange for Ashurbanipal to chose to rule Babylonia under a name that presumably means "shaped like a *kandalu*-utensil" and that could reflect some physical deformity. Also, if Ashurbanipal were Kandalānu, one might expect some confusion or alternation of the royal names in date formulae from Babylonia, but none is found. After the twenty-ninth day of Nisannu (I) of 646 the only economic texts from Babylonia dated by Ashurbanipal are from Nippur, and there are no texts at all dated by Kandalānu from that city. It is, of course, possible that Kandalānu and Ashurbanipal died in the same year. Kandalānu may have been deposed (and killed) during unrest at the death of the Assyrian king (see below). Finally, a fragment of a recently published Neo-Assyrian letter may mention Kandalānu in connection with the Assyrian

---

[13] At least this is the view of the author and many current scholars (e.g., Brinkman in *RLA* 5, p. 368). In a recent study of the matter, however, S. Zawadzki has argued strongly for an identification of Kandalānu with Ashurbanipal (*Fall of Assyria*, pp. 57-62). In view of his support for this contrary view, it has seemed best to re-examine the matter in detail. This re-examination is presented in Appendix F; what follows here is a summary of the major matters discussed there.

royal family. *CT* 53 966 refers to Kandalānu and Šērū'a-ēṭerat in successive lines: [...] x ^{f}*še-ru-u-a*-KAR-*at*(?!) and [...] ^{m}*kan-dàl-a-nu* (lines 9-10). Since Šērū'a-ēṭerat was the name of a sister of Ashurbanipal and since references to [Bīt]-Ibâ(?) (line 6) and the king of Elam (rev. 2) point to a southern focus for the letter, it seems likely that this letter refers to the individual who was, or was to become, king of Babylonia.[14] The mention of Kandalānu in a letter together with Šērū'a-ēṭerat might suggest that he was connected with the Assyrian royal family, but since the letter is badly damaged and appears to deal with political, not family matters, any conclusions must be considered extremely tentative.

Little is known about Kandalānu, undoubtedly because he was a mere figurehead with no real power or authority. Ashurbanipal would not have wanted to risk another revolt in Babylonia by giving actual control to anyone else. Not wishing to follow the example of his grandfather Sennacherib and abolish the position of king of Babylonia, and thereby add to the grievances of the Babylonians, Ashurbanipal probably decided to appoint a puppet ruler in the southern kingdom. Various proposals have been made for the identification of Kandalānu in addition to Ashurbanipal. Following Berossos, he might have been another son of Esarhaddon.[15] Possibly he was a son of Ashurbanipal[16] or a Babylonian whose loyalty Ashurbanipal felt was unquestioned. He may even have been someone who was deformed[17] or simple-minded, and thus unlikely to be able to win the support of his people in any action against Assyria; however, the appointment of such an individual might well have been regarded as a grave insult by Babylonians and caused further trouble. It has also been suggested that Kandalānu was actually a statue that represented Ashurbanipal at the Akītu festival.[18] However, if this were true, why was Kandalānu not acknowledged at Nippur also? In the absence of any conclusive evidence, Kandalānu remains an enigma, but, although the identification of Ashurbanipal with Kandalānu cannot be totally ruled out, on the basis of the evidence currently available it is more likely that they were two separate individuals.

---

14 The writing of the name Kandalānu in the letter would be unique (see pp. 191-92 n. 3 above) but then this would be the only reference to Kandalānu in a letter, and in an Assyrian letter at that.

15 Thus, for example, Ahmed, *Asb.*, p. 108.

16 In her unpublished dissertation, "A Survery of Neo-Babylonian History" (University of Michigan, 1963), pp. 8-9, E.N. von Voigtlander suggested that Kandalānu may be identified with Aššur-etil-ilāni and that the texts dated by him as Aššur-etil-ilāni at Nippur are contemporary with the later texts dated by him as Kandalānu elsewhere (i.e., Ashurbanipal died before 627 and Aššur-etil-ilāni then ruled Nippur by his Assyrian name since Nippur was kept under direct Assyrian rule). See, however, J. Oates, *CAH* 3/2 (in press).

17 See p. 304.

18 Reade, *JCS* 23 (1970-71): 1.

After Ashurbanipal reconquered Babylonia, he appointed new governors and officials who he hoped would be loyal and submissive to him and imposed the payment of new taxes, tribute, and offerings for Assyrian gods.[19] No major Babylonian officials are known to have held office both during the Šamaš-šuma-ukīn Revolt and into the reign of Kandalānu except Bēl-ibni and Kudurru, and their respective offices during the revolt are unclear. As was suggested, Kandalānu's authority over Babylonia was undoubtedly severely limited, if not non-existent. Officials in Uruk and the Sealand continued to report to Ashurbanipal on both domestic and military matters and to take orders from him.[20] One of the officials appointed by Ashurbanipal after the conquest of Babylon was likely Šamaš-danninanni, who is variously called governor—*šaknu* or *šakin māti*—of Akkad and (provincial) governor—(*ša*) *pīḫati*—of Babylon. The former title could suggest that he had some authority over northern Babylonia in general and his importance is further indicated by the fact that he is mentioned as eponym in Assyrian texts composed shortly after the revolt (*c*. 643).[21] All other "Babylonian" officials who were considered to be eponyms in Assyrian texts governed areas annexed to Assyria (Dēr, Laḫīru, and perhaps Dūr-Šarrukku).[22] Although the presence of Kandalānu on the throne of Babylon (and the dating of texts there by his regnal years) indicates that Babylonia was not annexed to Assyria at this time, Šamaš-danninanni's eponymate may well reflect closer Assyrian control over Babylonia than had been the case earlier in the reign of Ashurbanipal.

Ashurbanipal continued to carry out building projects in Babylonia and did so without reference to Kandalānu. Some of this work may have been the repair of damage done during the revolt, especially in the conquest of the rebel cities. Editions C and K of Ashurbanipal's annals, both compiled soon after the end of the revolt, have lengthy introductory sections that describe the Assyrian king's good works, in particular his restoration of temples in Assyria and Babylonia. Just as he felt it necessary to justify his actions in Babylonia by claiming that Enlil and Marduk, the chief gods of Babylonia, had allowed him to defeat Šamaš-šuma-ukīn,[23] this work might have been his

---

19 Streck, *Asb*., pp. 40-41 iv 104-109.

20 E.g., *ABL* 274 and 281. The author of *ABL* 274, Kudurru, uses the traditional Urukian introductory formula and does not refer to warfare or Nabû-ušabši; thus, it is likely that his letter was composed after the revolt when Kudurru was governor of Uruk. The references in *ABL* 281 to Assyrian troops having gone against Elam and to Ḫumban-ḫaltaš wanting to deliver up Nabû-bēl-šumāti to Assyria indicate that this letter was composed after a campaign against Ḫumban-ḫaltaš III, thus likely after the revolt.

21 See chapter 3 and Appendix B sub 1 and 2a. Zawadzki (*Fall of Assyria*, pp. 61-62) argues that Šamaš-danninanni controlled all of Babylonia, but see pp. 301-302.

22 See pp. 222-24.

23 Thompson, *AAA* 20 (1933): 86, 95, and pl. 94:111-112.

way of apologizing for the damage (and sacrilege) suffered by Babylon and the Esagila temple at the capture of the city.[24] Ashurbanipal's inscriptions dating after the revolt refer to work done by him at Babylon (Esagila, its ziggurat, and possibly the temple of Gula), Borsippa (Ezida), Cutha (Emeslam, the temple of the god Nergal), and Dēr (Edimgalkalamma, the temple of the god Ištarān);[25] however, it is not possible to know whether these projects were undertaken before or after the revolt.

A great deal of construction was carried out at Nippur in the seventh century and Ashurbanipal was responsible for at least some of it. He has left inscriptions in which he claims to have renovated the temple of the god Enlil (Ekur) and to have restored its ziggurat. These texts do not mention Šamaš-šuma-ukīn and while the brick inscriptions may simply not have had room to do so, this can not be said for the one cylinder inscription. The fact that this cylinder inscription, which describes the restoration of the ziggurat, gives Ashurbanipal the title "king of Sumer and Akkad" might also suggest that it came from a time when Ashurbanipal (or the scribes at Nippur) did not acknowledge the authority of any other person over Babylonia, or at least over the city of Nippur. This could suggest the time of the rebellion of 652-648 but it would seem unlikely that the ziggurat would have been restored then. Thus, this inscription and Ashurbanipal's work on the ziggurat probably date to the time of Kandalānu, who was a mere puppet ruler and one with no authority over Nippur.[26] Archaeological evidence would suggest that his work in the Ekur resulted in changes in circulation and in the functioning of that temple.[27] A brick with an inscription recording Ashurbanipal's work on Ekur has also been found in a pavement associated with the socle of the Inanna temple at Nippur and this would suggest that he also authorized some

---

24 Tadmor in *HHI*, p. 49.

25 Nassouhi, *AfK* 2 (1924-25): 97-106; Streck, *Asb.*, pp. 146-51 x 17-46 and 186-87 rev. 24-25; Thompson, *AAA* 20 (1933): 82-84, 92-93, and pl. 92:42-59 and 69-70 (Ištarān is called [A]N.GAL [likely Anu-rabû]); Thompson, *PEA*, pp. 29-30, 32-33, and pls. 14-16 i 21-ii 6 and iii 15-37. See Bergamini, *Mesopotamia* 12 [1977]: 149 for work on the ziggurat at Babylon done at some point during the reign of Ashurbanipal. For inscriptions referring to work by Ashurbanipal at Akkad (temple of the goddess Ištar), Babylon (ziggurat), Dūr-Kurigalzu (structure possibly associated with the god Enlil), and Tell Haddad (temple of the god Nergal) which might also date to this period, see pp. 112-13.

26 Bricks: Streck, *Asb.*, pp. 352-53 no. 3b (Ekur; the inscription is modelled upon one by Adad-šuma-uṣur which may have come to light during the work ordered by Ashurbanipal [see *ibid.*, p. LXIV]); *PBS* 15 74 (é-zi-DAR-x); Gerardi, *ARRIM* 4 (1986): 37 (possibly a well, pú!?-galam!?, located inside Eḫursaggalamma; new reading courtesy P. Gerardi). Cylinder: Gerardi, *Sjöberg Festschrift*, pp. 207-15 (possibly referring to the temple on top of the ziggurat and not to the ziggurat itself); with regard to the date of the text, see also pp. 304-305.

27 For archaeological evidence of work on the Ekur during the Assyrian period (including the presence of bricks with inscriptions of Ashurbanipal in the floor of level II), see McCown and Haines, *Nippur* 1, pp. 18 and 27.

repairs on this structure even though there is no textual evidence for this.[28] A new city wall was built about this time and its excavators have suggested that Ashurbanipal is the most likely candidate to have ordered its construction.[29] All this work may well date to the period after the Šamaš-šuma-ukīn Revolt when Nippur was under direct Assyrian control.

While Ashurbanipal was restoring temples throughout Babylonia, the statues of the gods in them were being repaired and given new and rich adornments.[30] At the same time, the Assyrian king's agents were collecting and copying inscriptions for the archives in Nineveh. While some of these texts were forfeited as spoils of war, others may have been taken or copied by explicit command.[31] It is possible that *CT* 22 1, a letter from an Assyrian king, is to be assigned to this time; it records an order for the collection of various literary works in private and temple libraries in Borsippa and for their delivery to Assyria. The king had written to the governor and temple administrator (*šatammu*) about the matter and no one was to be permitted to withhold tablets.[32] Evidence of scholarly work in Babylonia at this time is meagre, though a building inscription dealing with the Ezida in Borsippa from the time of Marduk-šāpik-zēri, a ruler of the Second Dynasty of Isin, was recopied in Kandalānu's fifteenth year.[33] Astronomical observations, however, continued to be made and recorded. One document from the reign of Kandalānu records observations of planetary movements in terms of the king's reign, the lunar month and state of the moon, and also the part of the sky in which the planet (saturn) was visible. This tablet has been described as having "the earliest observations in any civilization giving you all the data one needs to date astronomical observations."[34]

Only a few documents bear witness to economic activity in Babylonia in the first five years after the revolt (647-643); on average about four texts a year come from this time.[35] Undoubtedly the country was still suffering from the ravages of war. Beginning in 642, business and commerce appear to

---

28 See R.L. Zettler, "The Ur III Inanna Temple at Nippur" (unpublished doctoral dissertation, University of Chicago, 1984), pp. 83-84 n. 1.

29 Gibson, Zettler, and Armstrong, *Sumer* 39 (1983): 177 and 189.

30 E.g., *VAS* 6 1 (*B-K* L.56; gold ornaments for Aya). Streck, *Asb.*, pp. 276-87 refers to a dedication of a gold incense altar for Marduk in Esagila .

31 See Parpola, *JNES* 42 (1983): 1-29, particularly pp. 10-12, and above, p. 156 n. 107. Note also *CT* 54 57 and 106 (see Moren, *RA* 74 [1980]: 190-91).

32 Lieberman points out that we only have two students' copies of the letter and argues that it is unlikely that Ashurbanipal was the king mentioned in it (*Moran Festschrift*, pp. 310 and 312); however, the points he raises to support this belief are not particularly strong and the matter must remain open.

33 King, *LIH* 70.

34 See Walker, *BSMS* 5 (1983): 20-21.

35 This and the following statements are based upon a study of the patterns discernable in the tables presented in Appendix A and assumes (perhaps erroneously) that a representative sample of texts has been preserved from the various sites.

have increased; for the years 642-627 there is an average of eleven texts per year. By far the majority of those that can be assigned to a given locality came from the north (Babylon, Borsippa, Dilbat, and Sippar), a pattern found also during the reign of Šamaš-šuma-ukīn. Documents from Nippur are more common than in the reign of Šamaš-šuma-ukīn,[36] which may reflect an increase in the importance of the city as the Assyrian base of operations. Conditions in the south appear to have been less prosperous. No documents are known from Ur during this period and Uruk provides only about six per cent of the total number of documents known for the period 647-627, as compared with about thirteen per cent for the years 669-648.[37]

The economic documents of the period most commonly record sales of land (houses, field, orchards, vacant lots), loans, and inventories of livestock. Accounts of the current disposition of sheep and goats make up about seven per cent of the total number of texts and are of a type which is hitherto unattested, but which continued in use into the reign of Cambyses II (529-522).[38] Presumably they reflect some change in the administration of livestock which now required these records. As in the reign of Šamaš-šuma-ukīn, temple prebends were sold; transactions are attested which involve prebends in temples at Babylon (the office of butcher in Esagila), Uruk (office of baker before the goddess Ištar of Uruk), and Dilbat (the office of

---

36 Almost three times as many texts from Nippur are dated to the years 647-627 than to 668-653, though the former period is only a third longer that the latter.

37 Matters may have declined at Uruk at some point after the revolt. While the city provides almost thirty per cent of the documents from 648-642, only about five per cent of the texts for 641-627 come from Uruk. As Brinkman notes (*Prelude*, p. 108), accident of discovery may be particularly significant here.

38 E.g., Wellcome Collection 1971.08; Ellis, *JCS* 36 (1984): 47 nos. 10 and 11; PTS 2791; Ellis, *JCS* 36 (1984): 48-49 nos. 12, 13 and 14; PTS 3011; PTS 2377; and Ellis, *JCS* 36 (1984): 56 no. 20 (*B-K* L.26, L.30-33a, L.37, L.53, L.54, and L.133 respectively). In each the format is basically the same: a list of various types of sheep and goats with the respective numbers of animals, the total number of animals (ranging from 125 to 795), the current disposition of the animals ("under the control of PN"), and the date. The place from which the documents come is never stated, nor is the name of the scribe. The texts tend to come in clusters (for example, five between 22-III and 24-III of Kandalānu's ninth year), suggesting that they were found together. An examination of this type of text from the various reigns during which it is attested reveals other such clusters of texts; however, it also indicates that the texts come from every month of the year (though the third month is particularly common) and from almost every day of the month. The shearing of sheep generally took place in the spring, in February-May (see Waetzoldt, *Textilindustrie*, pp. 10-11 and Postgate, *JSS* 20 [1975]: 4) though today May-June is the normal time in southern Iraq. Possibly the preponderance of documents from the third month reflects some regular accounting of the sheep and goats after their shearing. Quite likely these texts represent accounts of a large temple or estate whose herds were under the supervision of various herdsmen. See San Nicolò, *Or.* NS 20 (1951): 133-39, especially p. 134 n. 1; and Frame, *JAOS* 104 (1984): 751-52.

"temple-enterer" in Eimbi-Anum, the sanctuary of the god Uraš).[39] Several documents deal with iron and iron implements, one of which refers to an ironsmith and one talent of iron from Cilicia;[40] documents involving oil and sesame are also particularly common.[41] In comparison to the case with the documents from the reign of Šamaš-šuma-ukīn, a much larger percentage do not indicate the place at which they were composed. The reason for this is that a higher percentage of the economic texts from the reign of Kandalānu are records of accounts (e.g., the livestock accounts mentioned above and documents recording the issue or receipt of various commodities). These tend to be less formal than legal documents recording major business transactions (sales of property and loans) which may have been needed later in court.

Nippur remained under direct Assyrian control, dated its documents by the regnal years of the king of Assyria, and may well have housed an Assyrian garrison. The presence of glazed pottery similar to Assyrian palace wares would suggest an Assyrian presence or at least strong Assyrian influence in the city. Although the exact date of the pottery is uncertain, a date during the period of Assyrian domination would seem likely.[42] As already mentioned, it is probable that at least some of the extensive work carried out in the city in the name of Ashurbanipal is to be dated to the time after the rebellion of 652-648 rather than to the time before it. The main body of the family archive of Ninurta-uballiṭ son of Bēl-usāt begins at Nippur during this period and stretches into the reigns of Aššur-etil-ilāni and Sîn-šarra-iškun. Ninurta-uballiṭ himself appears in at least fifteen legal transactions, from 651 until the third year of Sîn-šarra-iškun. In most texts, he is depicted as creditor (loan agreements) or purchaser (sales of children and land).[43]

---

[39] Weidner, *AfO* 16 (1952-53): 45 and duplicate Ellis, *JCS* 36 (1984): 41-42 no. 6; Hunger, *Bagh. Mitt.* 5 (1970): 278 no. 6; *OECT* 10 398 and duplicate Ellis, *JCS* 36 (1984): 54-55 no. 19 (from Babylon but dealing with a temple in Dilbat); note also BM 40542 in which a number of days of the office of butcher appear to be given as security for a loan (*B-K* L.11-12, L.107, L.116-117, and L.185 respectively).

[40] NCBT 1093 (*B-K* L.144). See Brinkman in Curtis, *Bronzeworking Centres*, p. 155 n. 49 for information on this text and *ibid.*, pp. 135-68 for textual evidence of the use of bronze and iron in the first half of the first millennium. Other texts mentioning iron include BM 54030, BM 62730, *CT* 55 222, and IM 64669 (*B-K* L.99, L.141, L.150, and L.173 respectively).

[41] E.g., BM 49326; Dalley, *Edinburgh*, no. 61; Weidner, *AfO* 16 (1952-53): pl. 3 no. 4; BM 49201; Weidner, *AfO* 16 (1952-53): pl. 5 no. 6; BM 49167; and BM 49279 (*B-K* L.2, L.43-44, L.71, L.76, L.82, and L.86 respectively).

[42] See pp. 23-24.

[43] The archive comprises 2 NT 280-307 and was found in TA/52, 30 cm above level III/1 floor. See Oppenheim, *Iraq* 17 (1955): 69-89 for an initial study of this archive. Some texts from the archive date before 651, to the reigns of Sargon II, Bēl-ibni, and Sennacherib. While Ninurta-uballiṭ's father appears in the one document from the reign of Bēl-ibni (2 NT

Uruk is the only Babylonian city for which there is substantial information during the reign of Kandalānu, yet most of it deals with the first few years after the revolt.[44] During this period the city was undoubtedly attempting to recover from the damage caused during the revolt.[45] It seems reasonable that the Kudurru who was governor of Uruk in 647 and 646 is the same Kudurru active at Uruk during the rebellion while Nabû-ušabši was governor; however, this cannot be proven.[46] There are a few letters between Kudurru and Ashurbanipal which may date from the first few years after the Šamaš-šuma-ukīn Revolt,[47] but unfortunately they provide little historical information. Kudurru reported to the Assyrian king on domestic matters, Elam, and Bēl-ibni's actions. In addition he appears to have become involved in a legal dispute with Šamaš-danninanni, the governor of the province of Akkad, over some Puqudians who had been dedicated to the goddesses Ištar of Uruk and Nanaya by the Assyrian kings Sargon and Sennacherib. A problem had arisen over their status already in the time of Esarhaddon but that king had confirmed that they belonged to the goddesses. The outcome of the matter is unknown.[48] Kudurru had either left office or was dead by the twenty-fourth day of Simanu (III) of 642, when Nabû-zēru-līšir is attested as governor of Uruk.[49] No *šatammu* (chief administrator) of the Eanna temple at Uruk is attested during the reign of Kandalānu after 642, when Bēl-uballiṭ is known to have held office. Šamaš-ilaya, who held the title "*qīpu* of Uruk and Eanna," is given prominence in the witness lists during the years 642 to 637 and appears in office only a few months after the last *šatammu* is attested.[50] The temple administration at Uruk had presumably been restructured with the *qīpu* now holding the dominant position.

---

284 [IM 57904]; *B-K* E.3), the reason for the presence of some other texts in the archive is not clear.

44 Note the drop in the number of economic texts from Uruk after 642 (see p. 199 n. 37).

45 Note the reference to houses being in ruins in *ABL* 880+*CT* 54 43 rev. 2-3.

46 See chapter 8. There is no evidence of any other governor of Uruk between Nabû-ušabši (last attested on 20-I-649) and Kudurru (first attested as governor on 20-I-647).

47 *ABL* 274, 277, and 518. The third letter is dated to 24-II-eponymy of Nabû-šar-aḫḫēšu; the first two should probably be assigned to the period after the Šamaš-šuma-ukīn Revolt since Kudurru used in them an introductory formula usually employed by governors of Uruk (see Frame in *Cuneiform Archives*, pp. 262-65), since Kudurru is only attested as governor after the revolt, and since neither letter gives the impression that warfare (the Šamaš-šuma-ukīn Revolt) was in progress in Babylonia.

48 *BIN* 2 132. Lines 12-13 read ⌜^{md}UTU-*di-na-an-ni* LÚ⌝.[GAR].⌜KUR URU.KI⌝ *it-ti* ⌜^{m}NÍG.DU LÚ.GAR.KU UNUG.KI *di-i-ni*⌝ *ig-r*[*e-e-ma* ...], "Šamaš-danninanni, the [gov]ernor of Akkad, brou[ght] a lawsuit against Kudurru, the governor of Uruk [and ...]" (collation courtesy J.A. Brinkman).

49 PTS 2479 (*B-K* L.14).

50 See Appendix B sub 15. The *šatammu* Bēl-uballiṭ may be identified with the author of *ABL* 880+*CT* 54 43 and *ABL* 1129.

A statue of the goddess Nanaya of Uruk had been taken to Elam in the distant past, likely carried off from Uruk in the course of an Elamite raid. According to Ashurbanipal, Ḫumban-ḫaltaš III of Elam had refused to return the statue to Babylonia. During the course of his second campaign against Ḫumban-ḫaltaš (*c*. 646), Ashurbanipal recovered the statue from Susa and sent it back to the Eanna in Uruk.[51] As punishment for Elam's abduction of the statue, Ashurbanipal may have ordered that statues of several Elamite gods be sent to Uruk to sit in captivity before the goddess Nanaya. A chronicle states that in his accession year "Nabopolassar sent back to Susa the gods of Susa whom Assyria had carried off and settled in Uruk"[52] and the mostly likely Assyrian king to have sent Elamite statues from Susa to Uruk is Ashurbanipal.

There appears to have been some action by Ashurbanipal and Kandalānu (or their officials) affecting the ownership or tenancy of certain large plots of land in the area of Uruk;[53] however, it is not clear if the land was being redistributed or if usual arrangements were being confirmed or simply recorded. On the one hand, it has been suggested that the texts indicate that the Assyrian king took a number of date palm orchards which belonged to the goddesses Ištar of Uruk and Nanaya and which were managed by officials or prebendaries of Eanna and gave them to individuals to work for the benefit of the god Ninurta. Those benefiting were supporters of Ashurbanipal and by implication those being deprived of land were individuals who had not supported Ashurbanipal during the revolt of 652-648.[54] On the other hand, it has been argued that since the god Ninurta was also worshipped in Eanna, the texts merely record and confirm the donation of land to Eanna, land meant specifically for Ninurta.[55]

Towards the end of the period is first attested the career of Nabû-ušallim son of Bēl-iddin, an individual whose archive was found in a house in the southwest of the Eanna precinct (Nd XVI 5) at Uruk. Although his activities began in 631 (and continued into the reign of Nabopolassar), one of the texts from the archive comes from the reign of Aššur-nādin-šumi, four from the reign of Šamaš-šuma-ukīn, and one from the reign of Ashurbanipal (time of the Šamaš-šuma-ukīn Revolt). The reason for the presence of some of these earlier texts with the texts of Nabû-ušallim is uncertain; however, all of them

---

51 Streck, *Asb.*, pp. 58-59 vi 107-124 and 175-76 no. 2 rev. 6-8; Aynard, *Asb.*, pp. 58-59 v 72-vi 11; Thompson, *AAA* 20 (1933): 85, 94, and pl. 93:102-104; Thompson, *PEA*, p. 35 and pl. 17 v 9-32. Note Cogan's discussion of this incident in *Imperialism*, pp. 13-15.

52 Grayson, *Chronicles*, no. 2:15-17.

53 *AnOr* 9 2 (reign of Ashurbanipal, *B-K* Jn.6); *AnOr* 9 3 and *BIN* 1 159 (years 2 and 8 of Kandalānu, *B-K* L.5 and L.29).

54 Cocquerillat, *WO* 7 (1973-74): 107. See also Cocquerillat, *Palmeraies*, pp. 23-25.

55 Zawadzki, *FO* 18 (1977): 187-97.

were composed at Uruk and involve prebends (purchases of prebends or loans with prebends as security) and during his own career Nabû-ušallim was interested in acquiring prebends at Uruk. Only two of the fifteen texts mentioning Nabû-ušallim date to the reign of Kandalānu. In one, Nabû-ušallim purchased a field in the district of the great gate inside Uruk and in the other he purchased fifteen days of a prebend in the office of baker before the goddess Ištar of Uruk.[56]

In between sections dealing with campaigns by Ashurbanipal against Ḫumban-ḫaltaš III of Elam (see below), one Assyrian royal inscription records that the Assyrian king carried off from Elam to Assyria "[the people] of Uruk, Nippur, Larak, [Bīt]-Dakkūri, and Bīt-Amukāni [who] had cut back [*on the gif*]*ts* (due) to Assyria ([*ša ina tāma*]*rti māt aššur iḫarraṣū*) (and) [*had fled*] to Elam." This may refer to Babylonians who had acted either during or immediately after the Šamaš-šuma-ukīn Revolt. The former seems more likely since it is improbable that Babylonians would have risked another rebellion so soon after the last. The inscription goes on to say that having investigated the matter Ashurbanipal killed the captives.[57] The situation described in Ezra 4:9-10 may be connected to this incident. In this preamble to a letter to Artaxerxes, reference is made to people of Uruk, Babylon, and Susa whom one Asnappar (variant: Osnappar) had deported and settled in Samaria and the rest of the province "Beyond-the-River."[58] If people from all these cities had been deported by one king, Ashurbanipal is the most likely, for he had conquered both Babylonia and Elam and had cause to punish both lands. The mention of Susa would suggest a date after his conquest of that city which took place *c.* 646 (see below and Appendix E). Since Uruk as a whole had remained loyal to Ashurbanipal during the rebellion, presumably it would have been individual supporters of Šamaš-šuma-ukīn from that city who were deported.

Most of the detailed evidence available for this period deals with Elam and Bēl-ibni of the Sealand in the first two or three years after the rebellion. One of the few other incidents that might date to this time is the attack by the Aramean Puqūdu tribe upon the Chaldean tribe of Bīt-Amukāni reported in *ABL* 275. This attack was discussed in the previous chapter since it could also date to the time of the revolt. Conflict between Assyria and Elam was

---

56 For the archive of Nabû-ušallim, see van Dijk, *UVB* 18, pp. 41-43; Hunger, *Bagh. Mitt.* 5 (1970): 193-304 (nos. 2 and 6 date to the reign of Kandalānu); and Zawadzki, *FO* 20 (1979): 175-84. Note Brinkman, *Or.* NS 41 (1972): 245 for the date of the one document from the reign of Aššur-nādin-šumi (*B-K* F.1).

57 Knudsen, *Iraq* 29 (1967): 57-60. On the matter of the payment of tribute to Assyria, see pp. 238-39.

58 Earlier, when Samaria was captured by the Assyrians and the Israelites were deported, people from Babylonia were settled in the towns of Samaria according to 2 Kings 17:24. Note also Ezra 4:2 which refers to people settled in Palestine by Esarhaddon.

inevitable in view of Elam's support of the Babylonian rebels and its refusal to deliver up the arch-rebel Nabû-bēl-šumāti, who had taken refuge in Elam. Ashurbanipal undoubtedly also wished to capture and punish supporters of Nabû-bēl-šumāti and Šamaš-šuma-ukīn who had been given refuge in Elam and to free Assyrian and Babylonian prisoners taken there.[59] The campaigns of Ashurbanipal against Ḫumban-ḫaltaš III and Bēl-ibni's involvement in them can not be treated in any detail in this study, since they deserve a monograph of their own. However, since the Sealand was used as a base of operations against Elam and since a Babylonian, Nabû-bēl-šumāti, was a major cause of these wars, a few words will be said about them.

Two campaigns were conducted by Ashurbanipal against Elam and its ruler Ḫumban-ḫaltaš III during the years 648-645 in retaliation for their aid to Šamaš-šuma-ukīn and Nabû-bēl-šumāti.[60] The first campaign likely took place in 647, commencing in the third month. Several tribal groups and towns along the Elamite-Babylonian border immediately submitted to Ashurbanipal. These included some Gambulians and the town of Laḫīru. If the town of Laḫīru refers to the capital of the province by that name which was located to the northeast of Babylonia and whose governor had aided in crushing the rebellion of 652-648, then the town must have fallen to the Elamites or revolted towards the end of the Šamaš-šuma-ukīn Revolt, or immediately thereafter. It is possible, however, that it is to be identified with a separate town, perhaps located to the southeast of Dēr, which belonged to the Aramean tribe of Laḫīru who dwelt along the Babylonian-Elamite border.[61] It is also possible that the term town (URU) was used loosely and referred simply to the tribe by that name. After the Assyrian army captured the Elamite border fortress of Bīt-Imbî, punished its defenders, and entered Elam proper, Ḫumban-ḫaltaš abandoned the city of Madaktu and fled to the mountains. Tammarītu (II), who had sought refuge in Assyria when overthrown by Indabibi, was installed as ruler in Susa by Ashurbanipal, but soon removed when he objected to the plundering being carried out by Assyrian troops. Ashurbanipal claims to have captured, looted, and destroyed twenty-nine Elamite cities before returning to Assyria.[62]

The second campaign, probably dating to the second half of 647 or more likely to 646, was even more extensive and destructive than the first. As in the previous campaign, the Assyrian troops first headed for the border city of Bīt-Imbî. When it and its nearby regions were taken, Ḫumban-ḫaltaš again

59 With regard to prisoners, see *ABL* 460 and perhaps 1430.

60 For the date of these campaigns, see Appendix E.

61 See Zadok, *WO* 16 (1985): 71, but note the contrary opinion of Brinkman in *PKB*, p. 178 n. 1093. With regard to Laḫīru, note also the episode described in *ABL* 280; see pp. 205-206.

62 Streck, *Asb.*, pp. 40-47 iv 110-v 62; Aynard, *Asb.*, pp. 44-49 iii 33-iv 16; Cogan and Tadmor, *Or.* NS 50 (1981): 233-34 col. b 29-37; and note *CT* 54 567.

fled from Madaktu. The Assyrians captured, looted, and destroyed numerous cities, towns, and regions as they advanced further and further into Elamite territory; in particular, fourteen royal cities, including Susa and Madaktu, fell to the invaders. Susa, the most important city of the country, was thoroughly looted and ruthlessly destroyed. Among the great plunder taken by the Assyrians were items given to Elamite monarchs by Šamaš-šuma-ukīn and previous Babylonian kings to win Elamite aid. The statues of numerous Elamite gods were carried off to Assyria and their temples razed; the tombs of the Elamite kings were desecrated and their bones exposed to the sun; fields were sown with salt and cress in order to destroy their productivity. The statue of the goddess Nanaya which had been taken to Elam from Uruk in the distant past was recovered and sent back to Uruk.[63] By the time Ashurbanipal left Elam, taking with him a large part of its wealth and vast numbers of people and animals, Elam lay devastated.[64]

Bēl-ibni, a loyal servant of Assyria in the Sealand during and after the revolt, was ideally suited to report on conditions in Elam and to lead efforts against that country. The dates of the incidents described in his letters are often unclear since Nabû-bēl-šumāti may have continued to stir up trouble in the south even after Babylon fell. Bēl-ibni was involved in at least one of Ashurbanipal's two campaigns against Ḫumban-ḫaltaš III.[65] He reported to the king that Elam lived in fear because of Assyrian actions, that it was in a state of turmoil due to internal unrest, and that famine had swept that land.[66] He wrote about garrisoning various border positions, making raids against the border tribes and into Elam, killing the enemy, and taking large numbers of prisoners, and much booty.[67] On one occasion he sent five hundred soldiers to man the town of Zabdānu and to raid Elam. These troops marched against the Elamite city of Irgidu, slew two hundred of the enemy, including several of their leaders, and took one hundred and fifty prisoners. Because of this military action, the sheikhs of the town of Laḫīru and the Nugū' people submitted to Bēl-ibni's nephew Mušēzib-Marduk, took an oath of loyalty to

---

[63] One text indicates that a primary reason for the campaign was to recover the statue of Nanaya which Ḫumban-ḫaltaš had refused to return (Streck, *Asb.*, pp. 174-75 no. 2 rev. 6-8 and see Cogan, *Imperialism*, p. 14).

[64] Streck, *Asb.*, pp. 46-64 v 63-vii 81; Aynard, *Asb.*, pp. 48-61 iv 17-vi 21; Thompson, *PEA*, pp. 34-35 and pls. 16-17 iv 36-v 32; and Thompson, *AAA* 20 (1933): 85, 94, and pl. 93:102-104.

[65] *ABL* 462:14-16. Although the name of the author is not preserved, the introduction used (blessing by the gods Aššur, Šamaš, and Marduk) and the contents (e.g., references to a request for the extradition of Nabû-bēl-šumāti and the sea) point to Bēl-ibni as being the author. See also *ABL* 794.

[66] *ABL* 280 rev. 15-23, 281:5-23, and 521 rev. 15-20 (date uncertain).

[67] E.g., *ABL* 280, 462 (name of author restored), 520, 792, and 794.

Assyria, and aided in actions against Elam.[68] On another occasion, Bēl-ibni sent troops against the regions of Aqbānu and 'Alē, where they killed a number of the enemy, carried off one hundred and thirty captives, and destroyed those regions with fire. The enemy laid an ambush for them, but they avoided it and in an ensuing battle again won the upper hand. About the same time, Bēl-ibni took six hundred archers and fifty horsemen to Bāb-Marrati ("Gate-of-the-Sea"). From there forces went on by raft into hostile territory, to the town of Maḫmītu, and carried off 1500 cattle belonging to the king of Elam and the sheikh of the tribe of Pillatu.[69] Large numbers of the enemy are known to have fallen into the hands of Bēl-ibni; two letters refer to one thousand prisoners having been taken by him.[70] He appears to have had a sizeable number of troops under his command and he continued to request further support from the king, although these requests were not always answered.[71] It is difficult, however, to fit all of Bēl-ibni's reports neatly into the actions of the campaigns as described in the annals of the Assyrian king, and some may refer to actions during the rebellion of 652-648 against rebels in the border region.

As was mentioned, the question of Nabû-bēl-šumāti's sanctuary in Elam was a major cause of the Assyrian offensive in Elam,[72] although the main reason for these campaigns was undoubtedly Ashurbanipal's desire to punish Elam for its aid to Šamaš-šuma-ukīn, to crush the threat of that country once and for all, and to set up a king of Assyria's choosing. Several of Bēl-ibni's letters report on the continuing attempts to seize Nabû-bēl-šumāti or to have him handed over to Assyria and it is clear that Bēl-ibni was actively involved in the matter.[73] According to one of Bēl-ibni's letters, Ḫumban-ḫaltaš III claimed that he had wanted to surrender Nabû-bēl-šumāti earlier in order to prevent the Assyrian king from sending troops against Elam but that Nabû-bēl-šumāti had had Elamite supporters who had protected him. Bēl-ibni recommended that Ashurbanipal send him a sealed letter addressed to

---

68 *ABL* 280; for a translation, see Oppenheim, *Letters*, no. 120. Irgidu is said to have lain "two double hours this side of Susa." Since the Laḫīru submitted during Ashurbanipal's first campaign against Ḫumban-ḫaltaš III (see above), this letter may well date to that time. Ashurbanipal wrote to Bēl-ibni about Mušēzib-Marduk in *ABL* 399. It is possible that the Nugū' are to be identified with the Nuguḫu tribe who had aided Nabû-bēl-šumāti against Bēl-ibni (see pp. 181-82 and Zadok, *RGTC* 8, p. 243).

69 *ABL* 520. The locations of most of the places mentioned are unknown; according to Zadok (*RGTC* 8, p. 59), Bāb-Marrati "was considered to be, in a way, the southernmost place in Babylonia."

70 *ABL* 792 rev. 5'-6' and 794 rev. 15'.

71 *ABL* 462 rev. 17'-26'.

72 Edition A of the annals actually describes Ashurbanipal's demand for the extradition of Nabû-bēl-šumāti after the conclusion of the second campaign (Streck, *Asb.*, pp. 60-61 vii 16-27).

73 *ABL* 281, 460 (name of author not preserved), 792, and 1286 (name of author not preserved).

Ḫumban-ḫaltaš which requested the arrest of Nabû-bēl-šumāti and said that he would sent it secretly to the Elamite king. He warned that if the king wrote directly to Ḫumban-ḫaltaš, Nabû-bēl-šumāti would learn of it and bribe Elamite nobles to protect him. Fortunately, Umḫuluma', who had been Nabû-bēl-šumāti's patron, was now dead and Nabû-bēl-šumāti's position more precarious. The rebel was currently under detention at the Elamite court for having diverted to his own use rations belonging to certain *šarnuppu*-individuals.[74]

Ashurbanipal continued to demand the surrender of Nabû-bēl-šumāti and in Šabaṭu (XI) of the eponymy of Nabû-nādin-aḫḫē (647 or 646) he wrote to the elders of Elam to warn them of what would happen to them if they did not surrender the rebel.[75] At some point after the second of the Assyrian campaigns which devastated Elam, Nabû-bēl-šumāti heard that the Assyrian king had again written to Ḫumban-ḫaltaš III about his extradition. He became afraid, and he and his groom slew each other with their swords.[76] The inability of Ḫumban-ḫaltaš to have Nabû-bēl-šumāti extradited earlier shows that Elam was not united behind its king. Ashurbanipal's campaigns had no doubt helped to destabilize Elam and weaken the king's authority. Ashurbanipal's annals indicate that when Ḫumban-ḫaltaš fled to the mountains during Ashurbanipal's first campaign an individual by the name of Umbaḫabua briefly took his place on the throne and they also refer to one Pa'e, who is said to have exercised the rulership in place of Ḫumban-ḫaltaš III.[77] In addition, letters refer to other upheavals in Elam.[78] All these are signs that Elam was internally divided. Ḫumban-ḫaltaš had the corpse of Nabû-bēl-šumāti preserved in salt and sent it and the head of Nabû-bēl-šumāti's groom to the Assyrian king.[79] In *ABL* 879, a letter to the Assyrian king written either to accompany the body or after it had been sent, and dated on the twenty-sixth day of Du'ūzu (IV) of the eponymy of Nabû-šar-aḫḫēšu (646 or 645), the Elamite king attempted to pacify Ashurbanipal by putting the blame for Nabû-bēl-šumāti's presence in Elam and the subsequent battles between the two countries on the Martenaya (perhaps a tribal group living along the border) and promised to punish them. Ashurbanipal did not allow the body of Nabû-bēl-šumāti to be buried, but rather made it "more dead than

[74] *ABL* 281. On this letter, see also Stolper, *ZA* 68 (1978): 261-69. He argues that *šarnuppu* designates "intended recipients of rations apportioned."

[75] BM 132980. With regard to this letter, see p. 123 n. 114.

[76] Streck, *Asb.*, pp. 60-61 vii 28-37; Thompson, *AAA* 20 (1933): 85-86, 94-95, and pl. 94:107-109.

[77] Streck, *Asb.*, pp. 44-45 v 11-17 and pp. 62-63 vii 51-52. It is possible that the passages merely indicate a misunderstanding by the Assyrians of the complicated structure of the Elamite monarchy (see p. 29 n. 16).

[78] *ABL* 280 and 281.

[79] Streck, *Asb.*, pp. 60-63 vii 38-44.

before" by cutting off its head and hanging it around the neck of Nabû-qātē-ṣabat, an official of Šamaš-šuma-ukīn who had gone with Nabû-bēl-šumāti to incite Elam against Assyria.[80] Ḫumban-ḫaltaš did not survive much longer on the throne of Elam. According to edition A of Ashurbanipal's annals, the land rose against him and he fled to the mountains; Ashurbanipal sought him out and brought him back to Assyria.[81] Little is known about Babylonian-Elamite relations during the remainder of Ashurbanipal's reign (645-627). Elam was undoubtedly recovering from the Assyrian invasions and attempting to cope with hostile elements from the Iranian plateau. In destroying Elam as a military power, Ashurbanipal ironically eliminated a buffer between Assyria and other groups in Iran, namely the Medes and the Persians, and contributed to the eventual fall of Assyria.

A few years after the revolt, *c.* 645, Ashurbanipal conducted military actions in the west against the cities of Ušû (near Tyre) and Akko and against Arabs who had supported Šamaš-šuma-ukīn or who had made use of the troubles during the revolt for their own ends, in particular Abiyate' (king of Qedar) and his brother Ayamu, Uaite' (king of Sumu'ilu), and Natnu (king of the Nabayateans). According to Ashurbanipal's scribes the campaigns were successful. The Arabs were defeated, plundered, and many were carried off into captivity. Ušû and Akko were also punished; at Akko, the corpses of rebels were impaled on stakes surrounding the city, to serve as a reminder of what could happen to those who did not faithfully obey Assyria.[82] Uaite' and three captured Elamite rulers (Tammarītu, Pa'e, and Ḫumban-ḫaltaš III) were forced to take part in Ashurbanipal's victory celebration in Nineveh and to pull Ashurbanipal's carriage in a procession.[83]

The last major edition of Ashurbanipal's annals was composed about 643 (edition A). Assyrian royal inscriptions composed after that time record little new military activity, although the poorly preserved edition H (compiled in 639) and Ištar Temple text do mention abortive attacks on Assyria by Dugdammê.[84] By the time edition A was written Šamaš-šuma-ukīn's erstwhile allies (the Arabs and Elam) had been subdued. Undoubtedly

---

80 Streck, *Asb.*, pp. 62-63 vii 45-50 and Thompson, *AAA* 20 (1933): 86, 95, and pl. 94:109-110.

81 Streck, *Asb.*, pp. 82-83 x 6-16. Note also Barnett, *North Palace*, p. 46 and pl. 34 (BM 124793; relief and epigraph likely describing the capture of Ḫumban-ḫaltaš).

82 These campaigns are recorded in greatest detail in edition A of Ashurbanipal's annals (Streck, *Asb.*, pp.64-83 vii 82-x 5) and on a slab inscription from the temple of Ištar at Nineveh (Thompson, *AAA* 20 [1933]: 86-87, 95-96, and pls. 94-95:113 and 123-129). See Eph'al, *Ancient Arabs*, pp. 157-65 for the details of these campaigns; he suggests that the campaign against Natnu may be of later date.

83 Streck, *Asb.*, pp. 82-85 x 17-39, 272-73:6-10, and 274-75:6-10; Thompson, *AAA* 20 (1933): 86-87, 95, and pl. 94:118-121.

84 With regard to the identity and actions of Dugdammê, see A.Th.L. Kuhrt in *RLA* 7, pp. 186-89 sub Lygdamis.

Ashurbanipal's demonstration of Assyria's might had made the various parts of the empire and its neighbours realize that it would be foolhardy to risk Assyrian anger by supporting or carrying out anti-Assyrian actions. The impact of Ashurbanipal's military victories was felt throughout the Near East. Edition A of Ashurbanipal's annals states that fear of Ashurbanipal's mighty deeds prompted Sardur (Ištar-dūrī), the king of Urartu, to send valuable presents to him[85] and edition H records that after the Assyrian conquest of Elam Kuraš, ruler of Parsumaš (presumably Cyrus I), and Pišlumê, ruler of Ḫudimeri, sent gifts to Ashurbanipal in order to secure his favour and to establish friendly relations.[86] A number of other rulers, including Ḫundaru, king of Dilmun, and at least one of his neighbours, also submitted, although exactly when is uncertain.[87]

Politically, practically nothing is known about Babylonia from about 643 until 627. Both Ashurbanipal and Kandalānu appear to have died in 627. Kandalānu is last heard of on the eighth day of Simanu (III); in the month of Araḫsamna (VIII) of that year a document was dated at Babylon "after (the death of) Kandalānu."[88] His death may have taken place before the sixth month. It is not mentioned in a Babylonian chronicle which may well describe events in that year; the chronicle's first preserved entry is for that month and seems to refer to fighting in Babylon before that point (see below). It may be that Kandalānu did not die a natural death, but rather was deposed and killed in unrest at the time of Ashurbanipal's death. Ashurbanipal is last attested on the twentieth day of Simanu (III) in 631,[89] but a later inscription of the mother of Nabonidus states that Ashurbanipal reigned forty-two years;[90] this would indicate that Ashurbanipal died in 627. Although this text presents some chronological problems with regard to the length of the life of the mother of Nabonidus, there is no proof that the error affects the statement about Ashurbanipal's reign.[91] Ashurbanipal had the "House-of-Succession" in Nineveh restored shortly after the end of the Šamaš-šuma-ukīn Revolt,[92]

---

85 Streck, *Asb*. pp. 84-85 x 40-50. See also Thompson, *AAA* 20 (1933): 87, 95, and pl. 94:121-123.

86 Weidner, AfO 7 (1931-32): 3-5 ii' 7'-25'; according to this text, Kuraš sent his eldest son to Nineveh "to do obeisance" (*ana epēš ardūtu*). See also Thompson, *AAA* 20 (1933): 86, 95, and pl. 94:115-118.

87 Thompson, *AAA* 20 (1933): 87-88, 96, and pl. 95:129-138 (some may have submitted before the rebellion of 652-648); *ABL* 458; Heimpel, *ZA* 77 (1987): 90. For the possibility that Ḫundaru had aided the rebels in Babylonia and been in contact with Nabû-bēl-šumāti, see p. 135.

88 BM 50270 and BM 36514 (Wiseman, *Chronicles*, pls. 20-21); *B-K* L.159-160.

89 N 4016 (*B-K* J.38).

90 Gadd, *AnSt* 8 (1958): 46-47 i 30.

91 See above, p. 27.

92 Editions A and F of Ashurbanipal's annals describe the rebuilding of this structure (Streck, *Asb*., pp. 84-91 x 51-108 and Aynard, *Asb*., pp. 60-63 vi 22-61).

but there is no evidence that he made any specific plans for the succession[93] and this may have been one of the reasons for the period of uncertainty in Assyria and Babylonia following his death and that of Kandalānu. According to one synchronistic kinglist fragment, Ashurbanipal was succeeded as ruler of Assyria by Aššur-etil-ilāni, but the lengths of the reigns are not preserved and thus we cannot determine exactly when Aššur-etil-ilāni became king or when he died. By not stating that Aššur-etil-ilāni was "king of Assyria and Babylon" (titles given to Sennacherib and Esarhaddon but not Ashurbanipal), the text implies that someone else was on the throne of Babylonia.[94]

A period of political uncertainty in Babylonia is clearly attested by the fact that texts at Babylon were dated posthumously to the reign of Kandalānu in the eighth month of 627 and on the second day of the eighth month of 626.[95] The Uruk Kinglist assigns the year following Kandalānu and preceding the first regnal year of Nabopolassar to two kings (jointly)—Sîn-šumu-līšir and Sîn-šarra-iškun[96]—while the Ptolemaic Canon gives Kandalānu a reign of twenty-two years, thus presumably assigning this year of confusion to him.[97] The Akītu Chronicle refers to a time "after Kandalānu, in the accession year of Nabopolassar" when there were insurrections in Assyria and Babylonia and the New Year's festival did not take place.[98] The New Year's festival that did not take place must have been the one at the beginning of 626 since there is no obvious reason for that festival not to have been celebrated at the beginning of 627, when Kandalānu was still on the throne. Thus, this chronicle avoided assigning the period following the death of Kandalānu and preceding the accession of Nabopolassar to any particular person.

A second Babylonian chronicle mentions trouble in the land around this time. It states that Nabopolassar ascended the throne in the eighth month of the first year in which there was no king in the land (626). It also records several military actions between Assyrian and Babylonian troops preceding that event and some of these may have taken place in 627. In brief, the chronicle mentions the following: fighting in the city of Babylon; individuals connected with Sîn-šarra-iškun fleeing to Assyria; a military action at Šaznaku in the month of Ulūlu (VI) in which Assyrian forces entered the town and set fire to the temple; the removal of the gods of Kish to Babylon in the month of Tašrītu (VII); an Assyrian army forcing Nabopolassar to retreat from Nippur

---

93 See also Parpola, *LAS* 2, p. 4 n. 4.

94 *KAV* 182 iv 7'.

95 BM 36514 and 40039 (Wiseman, *Chronicles*, pls. 20-21 and 18-19 respectively; *B-K* L.160 and L.163).

96 Van Dijk, *Rēš-Heiligtum*, no. 88:4'-5'. The reign of Sîn-šumu-līšir and the beginning of the reign of Sîn-šarra-iškun would then have taken place during the period between the two "after Kandalānu" texts.

97 See Grayson in *RLA* 6, p. 101.

98 Grayson, *Chronicles*, no. 16:24-27

to Uruk, where the Assyrians and their supporters from Nippur were in turn driven back by Nabopolassar's forces; the departure of an Assyrian army for Babylonia in the month of Ayyaru (II); and the defeat of an Assyrian army by forces coming out from Babylon on the twelfth day of Tašrītu (VII). The chronicle then states: "The first year in which there was no king in the land: On the twenty-sixth day of Araḫsamna (VIII), Nabopolassar ascended the throne in Babylon."[99] If the whole section refers to 626, the order of months is listed out of sequence because the chronicle refers to events in the sixth, seventh, second, and seventh months before the accession of Nabopolassar in the eighth month. However, if we assume that it refers to events in two years, namely 627 and 626, with the change being with the mention of the Assyrian army's departure for Babylonia in Ayyaru (II), contrary to normal practice no line ruling would separate the entries for the two years and the first entry for 626 would not begin with a statement about the year (which is mentioned only with the accession of Nabopolassar). As one scholar has suggested, it is also possible the entry describing Nabopolassar's accession to the throne was the only entry for 626, with the earlier statements referring to 628 and 627 (i.e., assigning the events before the month of Ayyaru to 628 and the remainder to 627); however, the same difficulties arise.[100] The absence of any mention of the death or deposition of Kandalānu would suggest that that event had taken place before any of the entries preserved in the chronicle, with either all the statements dating to 626 or some to 627 and the remainder to 626. The actions described in the chronicle are more closely connected with the following period than the period under consideration and thus will not be discussed in detail here.

Thus, upon the deaths of Ashurbanipal and Kandalānu, a number of persons became locked in a struggle for the thrones of Babylonia and Assyria. The eventual victor in Babylonia was Nabopolassar, who may have been a native of the Sealand, or an official originally in charge of that area. Eusebius records that Nabopolassar had been sent to Babylon as general by an Assyrian king to fight against a force invading from the sea.[101] Although the later Greek authors are not always reliable and there is no contemporary evidence to support this, it would not be surprising if Nabopolassar had held some official or tribal position before he began his rebellion. That he had some connection with the Sealand is suggested by a reference to him as king of the Sealand at the end of a ritual text from the Seleucid period and possibly by an historical-literary document in which Nabopolassar says that Marduk

---

99 Grayson, *Chronicles*, no. 2:1-15.

100 See Brinkman, *Prelude*, p. 109 n. 546 and note also Zawadzki, *Fall of Assyria*, pp. 48-54 on the problem of determining the precise dates of the events recorded in the chronicle.

101 Schnabel, *Berossos*, p. 271, lines 1-4.

had looked favourably upon him "from the midst of the lower sea."[102] After an initial struggle with Assyrian forces he ascended the throne in Babylon on the twenty-sixth day of Araḫsamna (VIII) in 626, although he had already been given the title "king of Babylon" in an economic text dated just over two months earlier.[103] Nabopolassar founded the Neo-Babylonian dynasty that was to last for eighty-seven years. The other contenders for power were Aššur-etil-ilāni (son of Ashurbanipal and his immediate successor as king of Assyria),[104] Sîn-šarra-iškun (another son of Ashurbanipal and the one who sat on the throne of Assyria when Nineveh fell in 612), and Sîn-šumu-līšir. As mentioned, Sîn-šumu-līšir and Sîn-šarra-iškun are acknowledged in the Seleucid Uruk Kinglist as rulers of Babylonia in the year preceding the accession of Nabopolassar.[105] Because Ashurbanipal is not attested as king in any contemporary text after 631 scholars have sometimes postulated that he died about that time and was succeeded by Aššur-etil-ilāni or that Aššur-etil-ilāni was co-ruler with Ashurbanipal during the last few years of his reign.[106] Since Aššur-etil-ilāni states that Sîn-šumu-līšir had put him on the throne of Assyria in succession to Ashurbanipal,[107] and since the Uruk Kinglist indicates that Sîn-šumu-līšir was Kandalānu's immediate successor over Babylonia, it seems reasonable to assume that some time would have elapsed between Sîn-šumu-līšir's aiding Aššur-etil-ilāni and his gaining control over part of Babylonia—enough time for Sîn-šumu-līšir to enter into rebellion and

---

102 Thureau-Dangin, *Rit.Acc.*, p. 65:47; Gerardi, *AfO* 33 (1986): 35 lines 10-11. The latter text does not mention Nabopolassar by name but Gerardi has reasonably argued that the text must have been composed in his time. Is it possible that Nabopolassar was related to the Bēl-ibni whom Ashurbanipal put in charge of the Sealand during the Šamaš-šuma-ukīn Revolt? Names were frequently re-used in a family (e.g., an individual often bore the same name as his grandfather) and Bēl-ibni's father and Nabopolassar's son were both named Nabû-kudurrī-uṣur. Since this name form was fairly common, this suggestion must remain mere speculation. With regard to the supposed "Chaldean" background of Nabopolassar and the Neo-Babylonian kings, see Brinkman's cautionary remarks in *Prelude*, p. 110 n. 551.

103 Grayson, *Chronicles*, no. 2:14-15; Wiseman, *Chronicles*, pp. 93-94 and pl. 21; Kennedy, *JCS* 38 [1986]: 178 no. T.0.1. A later economic text refers to 10-IV of his accession year (see Brinkman, *Prelude*, p. 111 n. 551).

104 E.g., *KAV* 182 iv 7' and Streck, *Asb.*, pp. 380-81. In Babylonia, texts dated by his regnal years are only found at Nippur and come from his accession year through to his fourth year (20-VII-accession year to 1-VIII-year 4; see *B-K* M.1-12).

105 Date formulae of economic texts from Babylonia show that Sîn-šumu-līšir had only an accession year, attested between 12-III and 15-V (see *B-K* N.1-7). Sîn-šarra-iškun apparently succeeded Aššur-etil-ilāni as king of Assyria and died in 612; his earliest Babylonian year date comes from 8-VII of his accession year (Falkner, *AfO* 16 [1952-53]: pl. 16 no. 3; *B-K* O.1).

106 In particular, it has been suggested that Ashurbanipal abdicated in favour of Aššur-etil-ilāni about 631 and retired to Harran. See van Dijk, *UVB* 18, p. 57; von Soden, *ZA* 58 (1967): 248-49 and 254; Reade, *JCS* 23 (1970-71): 1. An accession date of 627 for Aššur-etil-ilāni does present some problems (e.g., in the possession of Nippur).

107 Postgate, *Royal Grants*, nos. 13 and 14.

win Nippur, since some texts dated by his accession year there call him "king of Assyria."[108] Several attempts have been made to come to terms with the various, apparently conflicting, pieces of information about the order of events and rulers at this time; however, none has won general acceptance and all seem to fail to account for all the data.[109] To the best of my knowledge, of these four contenders for control of Babylonia only Nabopolassar ever used the title "king of Babylon" or "king of the land of Sumer and Akkad," or was called "king of Babylon" in the date formulae of Babylonian economic texts. In these economic texts, Aššur-etil-ilāni, Sîn-šumu-līšir, and Sîn-šarra-iškun were called either "king of Assyria," "king of (all) lands," "king of the world," or simply "king." The Babylonian scribes obviously wished to avoid stating that any of these three was a true king of Babylonia.

The years following the deaths of Ashurbanipal and Kandalānu were a difficult time for Babylonia and Assyria. As already mentioned, the Akītu Chronicle records that in 626 "there were insurrections in Assyria and Akkad. There was war; fighting continued." The gods Nabû and Marduk could not leave their temples (or their cities) to take part in the New Year's festival.[110] It is not the purpose of this study to consider the problem of the successors to Kandalānu and Ashurbanipal since this would involve us with the whole question of the fall of Assyria; thus this matter will not be considered further. One must reckon with the possibility, however, that Ashurbanipal died or relinquished office before 627, that Aššur-etil-ilāni was ruler of Assyria, and effectively Babylonia, before that time, and that the fight for control of Babylonia had begun before Kandalānu's death.

---

108 E.g., *BE* 8 141 (*B-K* N.4).

109 The most recent discussions about the succession to the thrones of Assyria and Babylonia at this time are the following: Borger, *WZKM* 55 (1959): 62-76 and *JCS* 19 (1965): 59-78; Oates, *Iraq* 27 (1965): 135-59 and *CAH* 3/2 (in press); Reade, *JCS* 23 (1970-71): 1-9; van Dijk, *UVB* 18, pp. 53-57; von Soden, *WZKM* 53 (1956-57): 316-21 and *ZA* 58 (1967): 241-55; and Zawadzki, *Fall of Assyria*, pp. 23-63.

110 Grayson, *Chronicles*, no. 16:24-27.

CHAPTER 10

THE BABYLONIAN STATE

I. The Monarchy

At the head of the Babylonian state was the king, an absolute monarch with political, military, and judicial power. Between the fall of Babylon to Sennacherib in 689 and the accession of Esarhaddon to the thrones of Assyria and Babylonia in 681, however, there was no "king of Babylon." Sennacherib ruled the southern kingdom as "king of Assyria"[1] and Babylonia was apparently considered to have been incorporated directly into the Assyrian provincial system. Esarhaddon, Sennacherib's successor, claimed the title "king of Babylon" and attempted to rule the south as a true king of Babylonia. To that end he carried out various building projects in Babylonia and showed favour to that land, and in particular to the residents of its old, important cult centres. However, he was essentially an absentee ruler; it is not clear how often or for how long he visited Babylonia.[2] In addition, as long as the statue of the god Marduk remained absent, the important New Year's festival could not take place in Babylon, the revered capital of the land.[3] During the reign of Ashurbanipal as king of Assyria, the separate kingship of Babylonia was re-established as Šamaš-šuma-ukīn and Kandalānu occupied the throne of Babylon in succession. With the return of Marduk to Babylon in the second month of 668, the New Year's festival resumed. However, neither of these two kings of Babylonia held full authority and power over his realm. In particular, Kandalānu appears to have been a mere puppet ruler.

Thus, it is impossible to present a comprehensive picture of the Babylonian monarchy during the years 689-627 since there were only three kings of Babylonia and since one of these was primarily a king of Assyria and the other two were dependent upon the king of Assyria for their positions.[4] In theory, the rulership of Babylonia was hereditary and one

---

[1] At least the few Babylonian economic texts dated by Sennacherib from this period give him the title "king of Assyria" (see Appendix C) and he did not claim this title in his inscriptions from Assyria.

[2] See pp. 89-90.

[3] Or at least, not take place in its full and proper form.

[4] From what little is known about the Babylonian monarchy during these years, however, it appears that the general picture presented by Brinkman for the years 1158-722 in *PKB*,

could argue that it did pass in a hereditary line from Sennacherib to Esarhaddon, and thence to Šamaš-šuma-ukīn.[5] As was mentioned, however, Sennacherib never claimed to be "king of Babylon." Primarily because of Assyrian actions, no Babylonian ruler had been succeeded on the throne by his son since 734, when Nabonassar had been followed by his son Nabû-nādin-zēri. The rulership of the land was nevertheless comparatively stable during the years 689-627, at least in contrast to preceding decades when the reigns of the kings were of much shorter duration.[6] Šamaš-šuma-ukīn and Kandalānu each ruled for about twenty years and Esarhaddon for twelve.

The king of Babylonia ruled a realm made up of various groups that had varying life-styles and interests and that rarely acted in concert. As has been mentioned (chapter 4), no single term existed for Babylonia as a whole in common usage; rulers generally assumed the title "king of Babylon" or "viceroy of Babylon," that is, ruler of the most important city and the traditional seat of government for Babylonia. To ensure the safety and prosperity of his country, and to proclaim his own power and generosity, the king of Babylonia carried out various public and religious building projects. The extent and nature of the crown lands and royal revenue during this period are unknown, but we may note that Šamaš-šuma-ukīn confirmed land ownership in the area of Bīt-Ḫa'raḫu,[7] granted a prebend in the Ebabbar temple at Sippar,[8] gave monetary inducements to Elamite kings to gain their support,[9] and carried out building projects in various cities.[10] There is, however, little evidence that Šamaš-šuma-ukīn had any real military power or authority, except after he rebelled against Assyria in 652, and no evidence that Kandalānu ever held such power. While Ashurbanipal claims to have provided his brother with troops,[11] Šamaš-šuma-ukīn had to wait for Ashurbanipal to send an army from Assyria to deal with Urtak's invasion. After Šamaš-šuma-ukīn began his rebellion, he raised military forces from within his realm and on at least one occasion went out to battle along with his

---

pp. 289-96, holds true for this period also. See also Brinkman in *Palais*, pp. 409-15, where the period of concern here is included within the larger period 1150-625.

5 Kandalānu's background is unknown; some have argued that he may have been a member of the royal family (see above).

6 Brinkman (*Prelude*, p. 16) points out that between 733 and 689 fourteen different individuals had been accepted as ruler of Babylonia, an average of just 3.2 years per ruler.

7 *BBSt* 10 (*B-K* K.169). Bīt-Ḫa'raḫu appears to have been located in the area inhabited by the Bīt-Dakkūri since the ruler of that tribe gave testimony about the ownership of the land in question; see Zadok, *RGTC* 8, p. 90.

8 Steinmetzer, *Deimel Festschrift*, pp. 302-306 (*B-K* K.163).

9 E.g., Piepkorn, *Asb.*, pp. 76-77 vii 3-11 and pp. 78-79 vii 43-51. See p. 182 n. 261 on the meaning of *ṭa'tu*.

10 See p. 108.

11 Streck, *Asb.*, pp. 28-29 iii 74-75.

troops.[12] Ashurbanipal was keenly interested in events and conditions in the important southern kingdom and Babylonian officials looked to him for final authority. He involved himself in internal Babylonian affairs, issuing orders to officials and acting freely in the realm. In particular, he kept a close eye on Babylonia's relations with Elam and maintained a military protectorship over Babylonia. As a result, neither Šamaš-šuma-ukīn nor Kandalānu was an independent ruler; rather they were vassals of Assyria. Any ruler of Babylonia about this time would have had difficulty keeping tight control over his realm and his people due to their heterogeneous nature. In particular, he would have had to deal with the numerous tribal groups who maintained a semi-independent existence within the land and the old cult centres which were used to receiving special privileges with regard to such matters as taxation, corvée duty, and the administration of justice.

The administration of justice was a fundamental duty of the Babylonian ruler and was often expressed in his royal epithets (e.g., *šar mīšari*, "king of justice/just king"), in contrast to Assyria where such epithets do not really appear until the time of the Sargonid kings.[13] This duty also found expression in the statement by Ashurbanipal that he had appointed his brother to rule Babylonia in order to provide the Babylonians with justice ("in order that the strong should not oppress the weak").[14] *BBSt* 10 records how Šamaš-šuma-ukīn was personally involved in settling at least one legal matter. An individual appealed directly to Šamaš-šuma-ukīn to issue a royal decree confirming his ownership of some land which had previously been seized by officials and later returned by Esarhaddon. The king questioned the leader of the Bīt-Dakkūri about the matter and then issued the desired decree stating that the land belonged to the individual in question and that no one, whether ruler or official, should ever appropriate that land for official or private use. A document was drawn up stating this and sealed with the royal seal guaranteeing that the land would not be given to someone else at some future date or be reclaimed. It was important that the document receive that seal; Esarhaddon had not given the owner a document sealed with the royal seal and as a result he could not currently bequeath the land to his heirs. The presence of the royal seal was thus important to help ensure that the proper ownership of the property was not questioned in the future. When Šamaš-

---

12 *ABL* 326 rev. 1'-2' reads "... after Šamaš-šuma-ukīn went out [to] Kār-Nergal against the camp of the king, my lord." Although troops are not mentioned explicitly, he would not have gone against the Assyrian camp alone. There is no evidence that the king of Babylonia fought in person or that battle took place, although a rebel is said to have killed a supporter of Ashurbanipal (lines 3'-5'). The important point is that he was willing to put his personal safety in jeopardy by leaving the fortified towns. For the possibility that he may have been wounded in battle, see p. 148.

13 See Seux, *Épithètes*, pp. 316-17 and Postgate in *Palais*, p. 417.

14 E.g., Streck, *Asb.*, pp. 240-41 no. 5:11-12.

Šuma-ukīn had granted a prebend in the temple of the god Šamaš at Sippar, the document had also received the royal seal.[15] Otherwise there is no direct evidence of the king's personal intervention in legal matters at this time, although individuals were often sent to Ashurbanipal to be questioned, and perhaps tried, about various (usually political) matters.

While the execution of justice was basically the responsiblility of local officials and local assemblies (see below), it appears that the citizens of the old, important cult centres, who had been granted special privileges by the crown, had the right to have their cases tried by the king. J.N. Postgate has argued that the phrase appearing in several letters "to speak 'the word of the king'" implied an appeal directly to the king of Assyria, bypassing local officials, and that this procedure was intended to protect individuals from oppression by the local administration.[16] Babylonian letters from the reigns of Esarhaddon and Ashurbanipal refer to persons appealing thus to the Assyrian king on at least three occasions. The chief administrator (*šatammu*) of Esagila, Šuma-iddin, sent four individuals to Esarhaddon "because they had spoken 'the word of the king.'" When a prisoner escaped and "spoke 'the word of the king' in the assembly of the people," local officials had no option but to send him to the king to be questioned. Nabû-balāssu-iqbi, however, once complained to Ashurbanipal that when he had spoken "the word of the king," his appeal had been ignored and he had been deprived of his property.[17] Officials, in their turn, often complained to the king about unjust treatment they had received at the hands of other officials, obviously hoping that the king would intervene on their behalf. The king also empowered officials to sort out legal problems. The author of *ABL* 716 reports how Ashurbanipal had sent the *sukkallu* and the *sartennu* (vizier and chief judge) to provide justice in the land.[18]

II. The Provincial Administration

The provincial administrative system of Babylonia during the years 689-627 has too much in common with that found before and after this time to justify a separate study of the administration of these particular years; furthermore, the insufficiency of reliable data would make any such

---

15 Steinmetzer, *Deimel Festschrift*, p. 305 rev. 7-8 (*B-K* K.163). On the royal seal, see Brinkman, *RA* 61 (1967): 72-73; Kienast, *Reiner Festschrift*, pp. 167-74; and Brinkman and Dalley, *ZA* 78 (1988): 92.

16 Postgate in *Palais*, pp. 417-26. Note also Postgate, *RA* 74 (1980): 180-82 and Garelli in *Finet Festschrift*, pp. 45-46.

17 Landsberger, *Brief*, pp. 8-13 lines 26-31; *ABL* 344 rev. 1-10 and 716:9-13.

18 *dīnu kitti* [*u*] *mīšaru ina mātiya dīnā*, rev. 12-13. Note that it was the Assyrian king who did this, showing again Ashurbanipal's involvement in Babylonian affairs.

systematic discussion difficult.[19] While the letters of the Kuyunjik collection contain a great deal of data about the actions of various officials within Babylonia, much of it is unilluminating or ambiguous. In particular, it is usually impossible to ascertain the exact official position of an individual who wrote a letter, or was mentioned in one. Even if a particular individual is known to have held a specific post at one point in time, it cannot simply be assumed that he held that post when he wrote, or was mentioned in, a particular letter. Although it seems reasonable that only high officials and important individuals would write directly to the king, there may well have been exceptions. In any case, officials at more than one level in the administrative structure could write to the king from the same province at the same time.[20] There is evidence to suggest that a particular type of introductory blessing may well have been used exclusively by the governors of Uruk;[21] however, this cannot be proven conclusively as yet, and no similar formula has been shown for any other city (or province).

For earlier periods, kudurrus have provided a wealth of data for the study of the provinical administration. Unfortunately, only two imperfectly preserved kudurrus are attested for this period and the many economic texts available provide only a limited amount of information on the actions and duties of officials. However, it was common practice for a governor, or a *šatammu* official (administrative head of a temple), or both, to be present at the conclusion of certain business transactions, and to be mentioned as such in the documents recording these transactions. This practice makes it possible to determine the names of a number of the people who held important positions in Babylonia at this time. A list of these officials is presented in Appendix B.

During this period of Assyrian domination and control, the native Babylonian provincial administration may have been influenced and changed by Assyrian practices.[22] In general, however, the Assyrians tended to leave the internal administrative structure of a vassal state intact.[23] The fact that officials could report to, and rely upon, the Assyrian king while there was a king of Babylonia presents some problems. It is difficult to be certain what authority the king of Babylonia actually held over these officials. While all

---

19 A thorough study of Babylonian administration in the first millennium is much needed.

20 Nabû-ušabši and Itti-Marduk-balāṭu (presumably the governor and *šatammu* of Uruk respectively) wrote to the king about what may be the same matter (*ABL* 268 and 831; see p. 127 n. 138).

21 See Brinkman, *Or.* NS 46 (1977): 312 and Frame in *Cuneiform Archives*, pp. 261-65.

22 The practice of dating by eponyms was used at Babylon on at least three occasions (see Appendix C) and Šamaš-šuma-ukīn's choice of court officials may have been influenced by Assyrian practices (see below).

23 For a survey of Assyrian administrative practices, see Pečírková, *ArOr* 55 (1987): 162-75.

authority and pretense of authority rested in Assyria during the later years of Sennacherib (689-681) and the reign of Esarhaddon (681-669), the lack of a strong central government at Babylon may have encouraged the various provincial governors to become more "independent," particularly in the south. It was probably during the years 689-681, when there was not even the pretense of a separate Babylonian kingship, that texts at Ur were dated by the years of office of its governor and that the ruler of the Bīt-Dakkūri seized land belonging to citizens of Babylon and Borsippa.[24]

Most of our information revolves around the important cities of the land. With their long and rich histories, they had a leading role in the cultural, intellectual, and economic life of the country. Here were the seats of the provincial governors, with their administrative staffs; here were the temples where the major religious needs and duties of the community were looked after; and here were found the various scholars and scribal schools. The wealth of the country was concentrated in the hands of the royal family, the temples, and a few prominent families, who were found in these cities.[25] Some of them, primarily Babylon, Borsippa, Nippur, and Sippar, had even received special status from the crown, which relieved the citizens of at least some duties and taxes and gave them privileges with regard to legal matters.[26]

Administrative Districts

The arrangement of administrative districts within Babylonia follows the pattern discerned by Brinkman for the years 1158-722.[27] Babylonia was divided into a number of administrative units, each called a *pīḫatu* (logogram: NAM).[28] These units, which we call provinces, were independent of each other and were directly under the jurisdiction of the king. In general, the provinces appear to have been quite limited in size, formed by one major (or minor) settlement and its immediately surrounding territory and to have been named after that settlement (e.g., Uruk). Only the governor of Ur, who also controlled Eridu, is known to have governed a second important settlement.[29]

---

24 See Appendix C and Borger, *Esarh.*, p. 52 §27 episode 12.

25 Tribal leaders could also control great wealth, being able to mobilize the resources of their tribes.

26 See above, chapter 4.

27 Brinkman, *PKB*, pp. 296-97.

28 On the writing of the term *pīḫatu*, see Brinkman, *PKB*, p. 296 n. 1940 and *AHw*, p. 862 sub voce *pīḫātu(m)* I.

29 *UET* 1 168:5-6, 170: 6-7, and 8 102:8-9. The fact that Eridu is rarely mentioned in texts from this time could indicate that it was no longer an important or sizeable town, located as it was in an isolated spot on the desert fringe. It should be noted, however, that the southern mound of Eridu covered 22 hectares in the Neo-Babylonian through Seleucid periods; at the same time Ur was 40 hectares in size. See H.T. Wright in Adams, *Heartland of Cities*, pp. 334, 338 no. 10, and 342-43 no. 108.

The one significant exception to this arrangement is the province of the Sealand. Located around the swamp-marsh region in southernmost Babylonia, it covered a wide area and is not known to have contained any major centre at this time.[30] The following provinces are attested by being expressly called provinces (nos. 1-3 and 7-10) or by having a *bēl piḫati* or (*ša*) *piḫati* "(provincial) governor" (nos. 1 and 4-6):[31]

1. Babylon[32]
2. Bīt-Raḫ'e[33]
3. Bīt-Uškuru[34]
4. Dēr[35]
5. Dūr-Šarrukku[36]
6. Laḫīru[37]
7. Marad[38]

---

30 A number of the cities and towns attributed by Sennacherib to the Bīt-Yakīn tribe, who appear to have lived in the Sealand (see chapter 4), either do not figure prominently in this period or do not actually appear to have been controlled by that tribe. It is not impossible, however, that others were under the authority of the governor of the Sealand.

31 Dēr, Laḫīru, and possibly Dūr-Šarrukku had actually been annexed to Assyria at this time (see below). Note also the reference to a *bēl piḫati* of the city of Šamaš-nāṣir in *ABL* 32:11-12 (*LAS*, no. 29) which may have lain in the Diyala region (see *LAS* 2, p. 33), possibly in the area annexed to Assyria.

32 E.g., *VAS* 5 4:2 (*B-K* L.122). See Appendix B sub 2a and note the *šākin ṭēmi* sub 2b.

33 *AnOr* 9 4 v 3 and 13, *pi-ḫat* É-ʳ*ra-aḫ-'-e* (*B-K* L.23), possibly located in the Bīt-Dakkūri area (San Nicolò, *BR 8/7*, p. 39 and Zadok, *RGTC* 8, p. 101).

34 BM 54193:6, *pi-ḫat* É ᵐ*uš-ku-ru* (*B-K* K.148). Since this text was composed at Babylon, Bīt-Uškuru may have been located near that city.

35 *ABL* 140:7 and rev. 6, possibly dating to the reign of Esarhaddon or Ashurbanipal (Waterman, *RCAE* 3, p. 62). See also pp. 222-24 and Appendix B sub 5a.

36 *ABL* 339:7 (*LAS*, no. 293). See also Appendix B sub 7a The town (and province) was also called Sippar-Aruru (2 *R* 50:64a and see Landsberger, *Brief*, pp. 55-56 n. 106). The exact location of Dūr-Šarrukku is unclear but various pieces of evidence suggest that it was situated on or near the Diyala, likely near Opis or Sippar. See Unger in *RLA* 2, p. 249; *LAS* 2, p. 299; Nashef, *RGTC* 5, p. 99; Zadok, *RGTC* 8, p. 124; and Black, *NAPR* 1 (1987): 19. For a location near Opis (Upī), note that a kudurru which was found at Tulūl al-Mugēli' (Mujailī'āt) and recently published by al-Adami (*Sumer* 38 [1982]: 121-33) also connects the Babylonian city with Opis; the kudurru was dated at Upī (ii 18) and deals with land located in the *ugāru* of Dūr-Šarrukku (i 2). Al-Adami suggests that Dūr-Šarrukku (Dur-sharrukin) is a later name for the city of Akkad (*ibid.*, pp. 121-22), but this seems unlikely since both names appear in texts of the period (e.g., in letters of Mār-Ištar). Dūr-Šarrukku has been identified with Tell ed-Dēr (see de Meyer *apud* Groneberg, *RGTC* 3, p. 209), but that site seems to be Sippar-Anunītu (see Charpin, *RA* 82 [1988]: 13-32).

37 E.g *ABL* 1244:9'. See also Appendix B sub 9a. Laḫīru is attested as a city, a land, and a people. The city may have been located in the region where the Diyala River cuts through the Jebel Ḫamrīn (see Brinkman, *PKB*, p. 178 n. 1093); Kessler tentatively suggests Eski Kifrī (*TAVO* map B IV 10). See also Zadok, *RGTC* 8, p. 208.

38 FLP 1314:2 (*B-K* L.39). Note also the references to a governor (*šākin ṭēmi*) of Marad in *ABL* 238:9 (see Appendix B sub 10a) and 853:13 (GN mostly restored). For the possible identification of modern Wannat as-Sa'dūn with Marad, see Zadok, *RGTC* 8, p. 220.

8. (URU) Qutayanu[39]
9. Sippar[40]
10. Uruk[41]

In addition, the following places are known to have had a governor (*šākin ṭēmi*, *šandabakku*, *šaknu*, *šakin māti*, or *šakkanakku*):[42]

11. (KUR) Akkad[43]
12. Borsippa[44]
13. Cutha[45]
14. Dilbat[46]
15. Ḫaṭallu?[47]
16. (KUR) Kaldu[48]
17. Nippur[49]
18. Sealand[50]
19. Ur[51]

---

[39] Budge, *PSBA* 10 (1887-88): pl. 4:2 (facing p. 148; *B-K* K.119). Since the text was dated at Babylon, this province may have been situated in the general area of that city. Zadok (*RGTC* 8, p. 256 sub Qutajin) thinks the town may have been part of Bīt-Dakkūri.

[40] Sachs, *Astronomical Diaries*, no. -651 iv 18' (see Appendix D).

[41] *TCL* 12 8:2 and MMA 86.11.217:2 (*B-K* K.149 and L.103). See also Appendix B sub 15a for several governors (bearing the title *šākin ṭēmi*) of this province.

[42] For the uses of these terms, see below.

[43] See Appendix B sub 1a. Presumably this refers to the region around Babylon since Šamaš-danninanni was called both *šaknu* (or *šakin māti*) of Akkad and (*ša*) *pīḫati* of Babylon.

[44] See Appendix B sub 3a (title *šākin ṭēmi*).

[45] See Appendix B sub 4a (title *šākin ṭēmi*).

[46] See Appendix B sub 6a (title *šākin ṭēmi*).

[47] Oppert, *RA* 1 (1886): 3:3 (*B-K* L.16); GN written URU *ḫa?-ṭal-la* (collated). Since the text was composed at Sippar, this locality may have been located near that city (see Zadok, *RGTC* 8, p. 425). Or should this place be identified with Ḫaṭallūa, a locality which Zadok describes as a suburb of Bīt-Zabīni in the region of Nippur (*ibid.*, p. 157)? The Aramean tribe LÚ *ḫaṭallu* (*ibid.*, p. 157) could also be connected to this site, but this remains unproven. It is possible that *šaknu* does not refer to a governor here but rather to a lower official since it could be used to describe both governors and other (lower) officials.

[48] *BBSt* 10 rev. 4-5 (and cf. rev. 13, partially restored; *B-K* K.169). The term *šaknu* (LÚ *šá-kan*) of Kaldu (Chaldea) may refer here to a lower official, and not to a governor. The inscription refers to a *šaknu* and a *šāpiru* of Kaldu illegally seizing land, to the return of the land to its legitimate owner by Esarhaddon, and to the ruler of the Bīt-Dakkūri giving testimony about the matter. It is possible that the seizure of the land should be connected with the actions of Šamaš-ibni and that the two unnamed officials were actually members of his tribe, the Bīt-Dakkūri, or even that the *šaknu* was Šamaš-ibni himself. The land in question, and thus the "province" of Kaldu (if one did exist), may have been located in the northern half of Babylonia where the Bīt-Dakkūri were concentrated. There may be a connection between the land of Kaldu in this text and the province of the city Kaldu mentioned in *OECT* 10 400:2 (*B-K* N.3, time of Sîn-šumu-līšir).

[49] See Appendix B sub 11a (title *šandabakku*).

[50] See Appendix B sub 12a (title *šaknu*).

[51] See Appendix B sub 14a (titles *šaknu* and *šakkanakku*).

Undoubtedly there were other provinces about which we have no information. Kish-Ḫursagkalama, for instance, was likely the centre of a province; texts were dated at Kish and Ḫursagkalama during these years (see Appendix A) and Ḫursagkalama is known to have had a *qīpu* official.[52] Although Larsa is practically unattested at this time,[53] it may also have been the centre of a province, and Bīt-Dakkūri is referred to as a province in the time of Nabopolassar.[54] Bīt-Ada, Bīt-Piri'-Amurrû, Bīt-Sîn-māgir, Bīt-Sîn-šeme, Dūr-Kurigalzu, Ḫalman, Ḫudadu, Isin, and Namar are attested as provinces at some point between 1158 and 722; however, although some of these places are still mentioned in texts, none of them is attested as a province at this time.[55] In view of the almost total obscurity of some of the places listed above, we may wonder if all provinces had the same status. For example, did the governor of Bīt-Raḫ'e have the same powers over his province as did the governor of Uruk?[56]

Two or three of the provinces listed above now formed parts of Assyria and thus on strict grounds should perhaps not be mentioned here. Dēr and Laḫīru had been incorporated directly into Assyria, annexed in the second half of the eighth century;[57] and Dūr-Šarrukku also may have been annexed by Assyria. They have, however, been included in the list because of their close ties to Babylonia, particularly those of Dēr and Dūr-Šarrukku, the furthest from Assyria proper. Their incorporation within Assyria is indicated by the appearance of governors of these cities in the canon of Assyrian eponym officials during the period of concern here—Der: 670; Dūr-Šarrukku: 672 and 664 (as well as in the post-canonical period); and Laḫīru: 673.[58] The only governor of what is clearly a Babylonian province to appear as an eponym in Assyrian texts was Šamaš-danninanni (the governor of Babylon/Akkad) but he appears *c*. 643, in the post-canonical period.[59] The

---

52 *ABL* 1214 rev. 6-8 (*LAS*, no. 291); the passage refers to *qīpu*-officials of the temples of Sippar, Cutha, Ḫursagkalama, and Dilbat.

53 Esarhaddon returned the statue of its god Šamaš (Borger, *Esarh.*, p. 84 §53 rev. 43-44) and the city is mentioned in *ABL* 1293+*CT* 54 61 rev. 2-6 (see Dietrich, *Aramäer*, pp. 176-77 no. 100). Dietrich suggests a date during the time of the revolt of 652-648 for the latter source (*ibid.*, p. 88).

54 *AnOr* 9 4 i 2.

55 Some of these areas would likely have been annexed to Assyria (e.g., Ḫalman and Namar). See Brinkman, *JESHO* 6 (1963): 234 for provinces attested under the Second Dynasty of Isin and *PKB*, p. 297 (esp. n. 1941) for the period 1158-722.

56 Brinkman points out that just as there were different types of *šaknu* (see below) there may also have been different levels of *bēl pīḫati* (private communication).

57 See Brinkman in *Studies Oppenheim*, p. 13 n. 42 and *PKB*, p. 178 n. 1093.

58 See Appendix B sub 5a, 7a, and 9a; Falkner, *AfO* 17 (1954-56): 119 n. 58; Dalley and Postgate, *TFS*, p. 63; and Kwasman, *NALD*, no. 132:26'-27'.

59 The fact that economic texts from Babylon were dated by the reign of Kandalānu indicates that Babylon had not been annexed to Assyria.

eponyms for the years 672 and 664 are usually understood to have been the governors of the Assyrian city of Khorsabad (Dūr-Šarrukīn), but the names of the Assyrian and the Babylonian cities can be written the same way[60] and the Babylonian city is well attested in the texts of this period. Thus, even though it is clear that Khorsabad was not totally abandoned after the death of Sargon II, is it possible that the city (and province) mentioned in the eponym dates was actually the Babylonian city of Dūr-Šarrukku and not the Assyrian one of Khorsabad?[61] If the Babylonian city is meant, this would mean that three of the four Assyrian eponym officials between 673 and 670 came from provinces along the northeastern border of Babylonia, and this may be no accident.[62] No texts dated by the reigns of Babylonian kings are known from Dēr, Dūr-Šarrukku, or Laḫīru during the years 689-627; however, Dēr has not been excavated and the exact locations of the other two cities have not yet been determined. Dēr, the most important city, gave the Assyrians a strategically located base for dealing with Elam, lying across the best route between Elam and the Mesopotamian plain; the other two would have been useful for maintaining control of the route to Dēr. The Assyrians were clearly interested in maintaining authority over this region which was located at the juncture of Assyria, Babylonia, and Elam.

H. Lewy has suggested that Laḫīru served as the administrative centre of Babylonia during the reign of Esarhaddon, first administered by Zakūtu, the king's mother, and later by Šamaš-šuma-ukīn, the crown prince of Babylon.[63] The two certainly had some connections with Laḫīru and their servants are sometimes attested there, but, as described earlier, there is really no evidence that Zakūtu ever had any authority over Babylonia or that Šamaš-šuma-ukīn lived in Laḫīru for any period of time. *ABL* 1214 (*LAS*, no. 291), a letter of Mār-Ištar possibly dating to 669,[64] states that a personal attendant (*qurbūtu*), presumably of the king, had come with a deputy (*šanî*, LÚ.2-*i*) from Laḫīru, dismissed various temple officials in Sippar, Cutha, Ḫursagkalama, and Dilbat, and appointed new ones. This could suggest that Laḫīru had some authority over at least northern Babylonia at that time,[65] but one should note that the two individuals acted only after announcing a royal

---

60 See Parpola, *Toponyms*, pp. 112-14 and Zadok, *RGTC* 8, p. 124. The reading Dūr-Šarrukku is used for the Babylonian city in this study in order to distinguish it from the Assyrian one.

61 The identification of the eponym of 672 as the governor of the Babylonian city is also suggested by Parpola (*LAS* 2, p. 300 sub no. 293 line 7'; read 672 for 673) and Watanabe (*Vereidigung*, p. 209, commentary to line 665). Three economic texts dated by eponyms from the post-canonical period were found at Khorsabad (see Brinkman, *Prelude*, p. 54 n. 254) and these thus attest to continued habitation at the site.

62 The eponym in the remaining year (671) was the chief judge (*sartennu*).

63 *JNES* 11 (1952): 272-77.

64 For the date, see Parpola in *LAS* 2, pp. 291-94.

65 As recently argued by Parpola in *LAS* 2, p. 264.

order, that the official from Laḫīru is mentioned after the *qurbūtu*-attendant, and that the latter was probably a royal official sent from Assyria with the order. *ABL* 746 (*LAS*, no. 275)[66] states that the deputy of the chief steward of Laḫīru had been ordered to send offerings to the goddess (Ištar) of the city of Akkad. This cannot be used as proof that the city of Akkad was under the jurisdiction of Laḫīru; it may simply indicate that the king was having the neighbouring provinces provide offerings for the goddess of the newly restored city. The idea that Laḫīru had a special place in the administration of Babylonia during the reign of Esarhaddon remains to be proven.

During the revolt of 652-648, the governor of Laḫīru acted in co-ordination with the governors of the Assyrian provinces of Arrapḫa and Zamū in order to aid Uruk.[67] However, Laḫīru submitted to Ashurbanipal during his first campaign against Ḫumban-ḫaltaš III, suggesting that the city had declared its independence of Assyria, presumably in connection with the Šamaš-šuma-ukīn Revolt.[68] Dūr-Šarrukku and Laḫīru are mentioned together on several occasions and people from Laḫīru appear in various Assyrian economic documents.[69] Because of their location on the northeastern frontier of Babylonia, however, Dēr, Dūr-Šarrukku, and Laḫīru are mentioned frequently in connection with Babylonia. For example, Mār-Ištar's letters report on these cities as well as on other Babylonian ones,[70] Laḫīru was obliged to provide offerings for the Lady-of-Akkad,[71] and Esarhaddon includes Dēr and Dūr-Šarrukku (as Sippar-Aruru) in a list of Babylonian cities to whose gods he had shown favour.[72]

Except for the Sealand, Ur, and Uruk, all the provinces are definitely or most likely in central or northern Babylonia. This supports the evidence from

---

66 Dated by Parpola to late 670 (*LAS* 2, pp. 262-63).

67 *ABL* 543, 1108, and 1244.

68 Streck, *Asb*., pp. 42-43 iv 116-123 and note *ABL* 280:19-rev. 4. It is perhaps more likely, however, that Laḫīru does not refer here to the city or province by that name, but rather to the tribe or to a separate town which was connected with that tribe and located near Dēr (see p. 204).

69 See for example *ABL* 558, *CT* 54 557, and various references cited in Parpola, *Toponyms*, pp. 222-23. Note that the situation at Dūr-Šarrukku is contrasted with that at Nineveh, Arbela, and (presumably) Assur in *ABL* 339 (*LAS*, no. 293), though these particular cities may be mentioned simply because the king would have been more fully aware of the circumstances there. The mention of the gods Šimalū'a and Ḫumḫum in connection with Dūr-Šarrukku (lines 7-11) indicates that the Babylonian city, not Khorsabad, is meant. With regard to the two deities, see Parpola, *LAS* 2, p. 300.

70 *ABL* 339, 476, 746, 1014, and 1214 (*LAS*, nos. 293, 277, 275, 292, and 291 respectively).

71 *ABL* 746 (*LAS*, no. 275).

72 Borger, *Esarh.*, p. 74 §47:16-25 and p. 84 §53 rev. 40-44. Note also the mention of both Dēr and Dūr-Šarrukku in Grayson, *Chronicles*, no. 1 iii 44-46; Esarhaddon was presumably returning to these two cities statues of gods which had been previously carried off to Assyria.

the period 1158-722 that the bulk of the Babylonian population was concentrated in the central and northern parts of the country.[73] Possibly Ur and Uruk were maintained in part as bastions of settled life in the south, intended to keep an eye on, and facilitate control over, the tribal groups who occupied the surrounding area of swamp-marsh.

Governors

Various titles are used by the Babylonian and Assyrian sources to refer to the head of a Babylonian province and it is sometimes difficult to determine whether any real difference in function or authority is indicated by the different terms. The normal title used by governors of Babylonian provinces at this time was *šākin ṭēmi*, (LÚ).GAR.KU, freely translated "one who gives orders."[74] *Šaknu*, the term generally used for "governor" in Babylonia until around the middle of the ninth century,[75] could be used both here and, more commonly, in Assyria. In neither place, however, did it refer exclusively to governors.[76] As in earlier periods, and presumably as a reflection of the traditional religious importance of the city, the governor of Nippur bore the special title *šandabakku*, (LÚ).GÚ.EN.NA.[77] There is no evidence, however, that he had any more authority or power than his fellow governors and we may note that in a letter to the people of Nippur the Assyrian king refers to "the *šandabakku* who is your *šaknu*."[78] At Ur, where one family held the post of governor for an extended period of time, various titles were used. Ningal-iddin chose to be called *šaknu* of Ur.[79] Of the three sons who

---

73 Brinkman, *PKB*, p. 297.

74 For the earlier use of the term, see Brinkman, *PKB*, pp. 307-309.

75 Brinkman, *PKB*, p. 297.

76 See Postgate, *AnSt* 30 (1980): 69-72 and *CAD* 17/1 (Š), pp. 180-92.

77 Despite Brinkman's doubts on the correct reading of the logogram in *Prelude*, p. 17 n. 68, the reading *šandabakku* is certain. See the two lists of officials from Nippur published by S. Cole which give *šá-an-da-bak-ku* as the pronunciation for LÚ.GÚ.EN.NA (*JAC* 1 [1986]: 129-31 and 140 12 N 129:4 and 12 N 148:4). In addition, Borger has pointed out to me that Nabû-šuma-ēreš who is called LÚ.GÚ.EN.NA in Streck, *Asb.*, p. 28 iii 63 is given the title *šandabakku* (written syllabically) in Bauer, *Asb.*, p. 93 K. 4530:15 and p. 101 80-7-19,102 rev. 14 (both passages heavily restored; title written [...]-*an-da-bak-ku* and [...]-*da-bak-ku* respectively).

78 The full passage reads *ḫi-iṭ-ṭu* ⌜*ša* LÚ⌝ *šá-an-da-bak-ki ša* LÚ *šak-ni-ku-nu šu-u ù šá-ni-ia-ʾ-nu ša* LÚ *šá* IGI É.GAL *ša la ú-še?!-rib-ak-ku-nu-ši i-na pa-ni-ia*, "It is the fault (firstly) of the *šandabakku* who is your *šaknu* and secondly of the palace overseer who did not allow you to enter into my presence" (*ABL* 287 rev. 1-7). *CAD* 17/1 (Š), pp. 188 and 373 take the section down to *šū* to mean "it is the fault of the *šandabakku* and your *šaknu*," but this would require an *u* ("and") to be understood after *šandabakki* and would take *šū* to be the subject of *ḫiṭṭu* rather than of *šaknikunu*. If *šū* referred to *ḫiṭṭu* it should be at the end of the whole passage.

79 It is sometimes difficult to determine if the title *šaknu* or *šakin māti* is meant in Akkadian texts, i.e., if the writing (LÚ) GAR.KUR should be read syllabically (LÚ) *šá-kìn*

in turn succeeded him in office, Sîn-balāssu-iqbi and Sîn-šarra-uṣur, preferred the more grandiose term *šakkanakku*, (LÚ).GÌR.NÍTA,[80] while Sîn-tabni-uṣur, like his father, preferred *šaknu*.[81] Possibly the use of these titles at Ur reflects greater authority or independence of the governors of this city. Because of Ur's somewhat isolated position in an area dominated by tribal groups, its governors may have needed, or found it easy to acquire extra authority and power to maintain their position and that of Assyria. Ningal-iddin of Ur is the only governor known to have dated texts by the years of his own tenure in office. Sîn-balāssu-iqbi could lay claim to govern Eridu and the Gurasimmu tribe as well as Ur,[82] and apparently snubbed his legitimate king (Šamaš-šuma-ukīn) in his building inscriptions.[83] The use of *šaknu* by Ningal-iddin and Sîn-tabni-uṣur, however, may reflect nothing more than a conservative desire to retain the traditional title for governor at this old religious centre. The governor of the Sealand also used this title.[84]

The title *bēl pīḫati*, (LÚ).EN.NAM ("lord of a province"), could also be used to refer to the head of a province.[85] This title is attested in Babylonia already in the Old Babylonia period, but only for low level officials; it was not used for governors until the eighth century.[86] The title was often reserved for Assyrian officials or for use in "Assyrian" contexts, such as for Babylonian officials in eponym dates. There does not seem to be any definable difference in function and authority between the *bēl pīḫati* and the *šākin ṭēmi*, and it may well be that the two terms could actually refer to the same office, just as appears to be the case with *šaknu* and (*bēl*) *pīḫati* in Assyria.[87] There is no evidence of a locality having both a *šākin ṭēmi* and a *bēl pīḫati* at the same time; and only Babylon is known to have had both during the years 689-627. Šamaš-danninanni was called both (*ša*) *pīḫati* of

---

or be taken as a logogram to stand for *šakin māti* or *šaknu*. This is particularly true when the title is followed by a toponym which is normally preceded by KUR (e.g., the Sealand and Akkad). See in particular Borger, *AfO* 23 (1970): 9-10; Postgate, *AnSt* 30 (1980): 69-70; Parpola, *LAS* 2, p. 300; and *CAD* 17/1 (Š), p. 191.

80 A title often borne by kings (see Seux, *Épithètes*, pp. 276-80).

81 See Appendix A sub 14a.

82 *UET* 8 102:6-9.

83 At least Sîn-balāssu-iqbi dedicated some of his building projects for the life of Ashurbanipal while never mentioning Šamaš-šuma-ukīn.

84 See Appendix B sub 12a. Note also *CT* 54 545:6' (see above, p. 180).

85 See for example Appendix B sub 2a. The Babylonian form *bēl pīḫati*, not the Assyrian form *bēl pāḫiti/pāḫati/paḫāti* (see Brinkman, *PKB*, p. 296 n. 1940 and Postgate, *AnSt* 30 (1980): 69 on these forms), is used in this study. For a possible reading *bēl pāḫat/pāḫaš*, see Cole, *JAC* 1 (1986): 129-36, 12 N 129:5, 12 N 148:5, and 12 N 163:1.

86 See Brinkman, *PKB*, pp. 303-304.

87 Postgate (*AnSt* 30 [1980]: 70) can see no difference in Assyria between the post of *šaknu* of a province and that of (*bēl*) *pāḫiti*. The same individual could be called both *šaknu* and *bēl pāḫiti* in Assyrian texts (e.g., Grayson, *AfO* 20 [1963]: 96:126 and Postgate, *Iraq* 32 [1970]: 148 no. 14 rev. 5'-6').

Babylon and the *šaknu* (or *šakin māti*) of Akkad in post-canonical eponym dates.[88] While the use of different localities could indicate that he held two distinct offices and that he held authority over more that just the city of Babylon and its immediately surrounding region, he may simply have been given the wider title by Assyrian scribes because he was governor of the most important city in the region of Akkad. Quite likely the two titles refer to the same position, the governorship of the province of Babylon.

The governor was the highest official in his province. He was appointed and dismissed by the king and was responsible only to him.[89] Governors, as well as other officials, were tied to the king by oaths of loyalty (*adê*-agreements).[90] In particular, they promised not to support any rebellion against the king, to report any talk of rebellion to the king, and to arrest any individuals attempting to foment rebellion. These oaths did not have to be taken in the presence of the king but rather could be administered by other officials who were acting upon instruction from the king. Because he had been absent when oaths were taken at Babylon, Kabtiya went to the palace overseer and took the oath at Nippur and Uruk. These oaths were not restricted to officials; Kabtiya mentioned that it might be requested that not only he but also his soldiers, and their sons and wives, should take oaths of loyalty.[91] On some, if not all, occasions, individuals swore their allegiance in the presence of the gods (i.e., statues of gods) and they may have performed some ritual or symbolic act.[92] To break an oath of allegiance was a sin against the gods as well as man.[93] The governor and other officials were bound by their oaths to keep the king informed about conditions and events both in their own province and elsewhere. They could say: "It is written [in] the *adê*-agreement: 'Write (and tell) me (the Assyrian king) whatever you see and hear!'"[94] The governor reported to the king on his own actions and those of other officials, individuals, and tribal groups, conditions in neighbouring

---

88 See Appendix B sub 1a and 2a-b. One legal text (Pinches, *AfO* 13 [1939-41]: pls. 3-4; *B-K* S.7) is dated at Babylon in the eponymy of a *šākin ṭēmi* of Babylon and a *bēl pīḫati* of an unspecified locality appears as a witness, but it is not clear that the latter was the *bēl pīḫati* of Babylon. There was a *šākin ṭēmi* of Babylon in 654 and a *bēl pīḫati* of Babylon sometime likely *c.* 656-653 (see Appendix B sub 2), but it is possible that their tenures in office did not overlap.

89 While Šamaš-šuma-ukīn was crown prince of Babylonia he held some authority over Babylonia and persons there reported to him (Parpola, *Iraq* 34 [1972]: 21-34 and pl. 19).

90 On the term *adê*, see p. 11 n. 27.

91 *ABL* 202; for a translation, see Oppenheim, *Letters*, no. 91.

92 E.g., *ABL* 202 rev. 4-7; Borger, *Esarh.*, p. 43 §27 episode 2:50-51. See Watanabe, *Vereidigung*, p. 26.

93 E.g., Streck, *Asb.*, pp. 12-13 i 132-133.

94 *ABL* 831 rev. 1'-5' and compare for example 472:1-5. One letter (Parpola, *Iraq* 34 [1972]: 21-34 and pl. 19:9-12) states that Esarhaddon had made an *adê*-agreement with certain Babylonians which required them to report whatever they heard to Šamaš-šuma-ukīn. See also Malbran-Labat, *Armée*, pp. 31-57.

countries (especially Elam), building programmes, and even what seem to us to be trivial matters. The king earnestly desired these reports in order to be prepared for possible trouble and officials were complimented for keeping the king informed. Ashurbanipal wrote to Bēl-ibni and praised him, saying: "With regard to what you wrote to me concerning the Puqūdu who live along the canal, just as a man who loves the house of his masters informs his masters whatever he sees and hears, in the same way it is good that you wrote and informed me (about this)."[95] Messages from the king had to be acted upon without delay if one wished to avoid angering him. Kudurru was forced to return to Uruk while already on the way to visit the king when it was reported to him that a messenger had arrived in Uruk with a letter from the king,[96] and it was a matter of concern if royal messengers and their messages were delayed in reaching their destinations.[97] The fact that Babylonian officials continued to report to the king of Assyria after Šamaš-šuma-ukīn became king, whether in accordance with Esarhaddon's plans or not, was undoubtedly one of the causes of the Šamaš-šuma-ukīn Revolt. While the governor was the highest official in his province, he could not do as he pleased because he knew that other officials and individuals were watching him and reporting on his activities to the king.[98]

Where the ancestry can be traced, the holders of the two highest offices in a city or province—governor and *šatammu*—often prove to have been related to previous holders of those offices. Thus certain families in a city or province, presumably the leading families, constituted a "ruling class" which tended to provide the chief officials. This is most clearly demonstrable at Borsippa, where the families Arkât-ilī-damqā, Iliya, and Nūr-Papsukkal appear to have controlled these offices.[99] At Ur, the governorship was in effect a hereditary postion during this time in that Ningal-iddin was succeeded as governor by three of his sons, and no other persons are known to have held that post during these years. The family of Saggilaya supplied a *bēl pīḫati* of Babylon during the reign of Kandalānu and a *šākin ṭēmi* during the reign of Šamaš-šuma-ukīn.[100] In one case, a *šatammu*-official may have become governor of Babylon[101] and at least one other governor appears to

95 *ABL* 288; for a translation, see Oppenheim, *Letters*, no. 117. The use of the plural term "masters" (EN.MEŠ) is unexpected.

96 *ABL* 274; for a translation, see Oppenheim, *Letters*, no. 93. In returning to Uruk, Kudurru acted upon the advice of the chief baker.

97 See *ABL* 238 rev. 8'-12'.

98 E.g., Landsberger, *Brief*, pp. 8-13 lines 58-59.

99 See Appendix B sub 3 and Frame, *JCS* 36 (1984): 67-80.

100 See Appendix B sub 2a-b.

101 Bēl-lē'i-(kalama) son of (E)saggilaya (see Appendix B sub 2b-c).

have held high office before he became governor.[102] There is no evidence that governors were moved from one city to another during this time. A governor could hold office for a considerable period. Nabû-ušabši governed Uruk for at least thirteen years (and a maximum of eighteen years).[103] Terms of office could also be short, particularly if the individual proved unacceptable to the Assyrian king. One letter from Nippur from the time of Esarhaddon states: "The king, your father, allowed ten-year (terms of office) for governors, but now three governors *have been ousted* (⌈*it-te?!-bu?!-ú?*⌉) in a (single) year."[104]

During the decade preceding Šamaš-šuma-ukīn's declaration of independence there appears to have been an unusual development in the governorship at Borsippa. Nabû-bēl-šumāti (not to be confused with the Sealander of that name) and Nabû-šuma-uṣur, both called "son/descendant (*mār*) of Iliya," are attested as governors of Borsippa, the former in 662 (or later), 661, 656, 654, and 653 or 652, and the latter in 660, 658, and 656.[105] In 656 Nabû-bēl-šumāti was called governor in a text dated on the thirteenth day of Kislīmu (IX) and Nabû-šuma-uṣur in one dated less than a month later, on the seventh day of Ṭebētu (X). Possibly they were brothers (or relations of some other degree) who were sharing or alternating in the governorship of that city, but either arrangement would have been unprecedented.[106]

The governor was the usual channel of communication between his province and the king. He passed on reports to the king and received orders from him. The king sometimes wrote to him and the people of his province jointly.[107] Perhaps these letters had to be read in public or at least to the elders of the city. On occasion the governor would claim to be writing to the king jointly with the people or officials of his province, presumably to indicate that the matter in question was important and of common concern.[108] The king was concerned about the welfare of his loyal officials and Kudurru of Uruk reports that Ashurbanipal had sent a doctor to cure him of an illness.[109] Governors appears to have desired and felt obliged to visit the king periodically, although they sometimes sent individuals to represent them and their provinces. On one occasion, the governor of Nippur felt compelled to

---

102 Kudurru, who was governor of Uruk after the Šamaš-šuma-ukīn Revolt, is probably to be identified with the Kudurru acting at Uruk during the revolt.

103 See Appendix B sub 15a.

104 *CT* 54 22 rev. 9-11; see Dietrich, *Aramäer*, pp. 158-59 no. 55 and *CAD* 17/1 (Š), p. 373.

105 See Appendix B sub 3.

106 See Frame, *JCS* 36 (1984): 70-71.

107 E.g., *ABL* 292 (to Enlil-bāni and the people of Nippur; see p. 276 n. 50) and 518 (to Kudurru and the people of Uruk).

108 E.g., *CT* 54 15 (*ABL* 240+) (from Enlil-bāni, the people of Nippur, the *nešakku*-dignitaries, and the *ērib bīti*-personnel).

109 *ABL* 274 (Oppenheim, *Letters*, no. 93).

send his brother and ten citizens (*mār banî*) to see the king when he was ill and could not go in person; on other occasions, fifteen elders of Nippur and the *šatammu*, *qīpu*, and scribe of the temple of Uruk visited the king.[110] Personal contacts with the king and his advisors were important for an individual who wished to obtain an official position, to maintain it, and, eventually, to secure favours and positions for his friends and relatives. The king was unlikely to bestow offices on, or show favour to, someone he had not already met or someone who had not been vouched for by an individual he trusted. Thus officials tended to come from the same families since they automatically had access to the court. Officials in the provinces wished to make sure that they had friends at court who would ensure that their letters reached the king, mention their names when it could prove advantageous, and defend them when necessary from the complaints of other individuals. Even if an individual went to Nineveh, he could not be sure of seeing the king. Palace officials might not inform the king of his presence or recommend that he was worthy of being given an audience,[111] although governors are unlikely to have had this problem. Officials portrayed their own actions in the best possible light. They flattered, supplicated, and begged the king and his advisors in the hope of obtaining favours;[112] in order to show their zealousness for the Assyrian cause and to gain an advantage over rivals, they sometimes criticized the actions of other officials.

The governor would have had some force under his control to maintain the internal order of his city and province. This force was likely quite small, but he did have sufficient men and authority to arrest (runaway) captives (*ḫabtūte*) and fugitives (*munnabittu*). He also appears to have borne the responsibility to raise a larger body of armed men from his region if required to do so by the king. He could be ordered to prepare troops in his district and send them out to battle.[113] The governor could levy assessments to keep the city's military resources at full strength and appears to have been responsible for the collection of at least some taxes, in particular the *ṣibtu*-tax on oxen and sheep on behalf of temples (i.e., to provide them with offerings).[114]

---

110 *ABL* 327 (Oppenheim, *Letters*, no. 121), 287, and 476 (*LAS*, no. 277). Parpola (*LAS* 2, p. 265) suggests that the Assyrian king received visiting officials in early Nisannu (I) or Tašrītu (VII), at the time of the New Year's festival. With regard to the term *mār banî*, see p. 231.

111 See *ABL* 287.

112 Note for example the comment of Šuma-iddin, likely the *šatammu* of Esagila, that he had no friend or relative at court and that he had to rely solely on the king (Landsberger, *Brief*, pp. 8-13 lines 50-54).

113 *ABL* 839:16-20 and 269.

114 *ABL* 340 rev. 4-9 (*LAS*, no. 276); see below p. 242 n. 162. *ABL* 464 rev. 1-3; see Postgate, *Taxation*, pp. 167, 171, and 215 n. 1, where Postgate suggests the various Babylonian provinces and neighbouring districts may have been required to provide offerings for Esagila on a regular basis.

The governor's presence was desirable at the conclusion of certain legal transactions in his province, in particular matters involving the transfer of ownership of real estate and temple prebends. Of the economic texts that mention a governor as witness, about 80 per cent involve land (e.g., sales and exchanges) and about 15 per cent are sales of temple prebends. The governor could preside in court cases and send persons to the water ordeal,[115] although court cases are said to have taken place more often before an assembly of citizens, with or without the governor.[116] Such assemblies might include citizens from other cities, possibly because the parties involved in the dispute being judged came from different cities. For example, *UET* 4 200 refers to a dispute settled in the presence of Sîn-balāssu-iqbi (presumably at that time governor of Ur) and men from Babylon, Borsippa, and Ur.[117] Exactly who was eligible to form part of the assembly is uncertain, though probably only full citizens. In *UET* 4 201, the assembly is said to be comprised of the *mār banî* (LÚ.DUMU.MEŠ ⌜DÙ⌝.MEŠ). The term *mār banî* is usually translated "free person," "citizen," or "nobleman," and taken to refer to persons with full citizen rights, but its exact meaning remains uncertain.[118] These assemblies could give judgement in legal disputes, impose monetary payments, and decide on the ownership of land and prebends. They could also send litigants to undergo an ordeal in order to help determine the matter. Decisions, however, could be appealed to the king and citizens

115 BM 33905 (governor and the people of Cutha); Budge, *ZA* 3 (1888): 228-29 no. 5 (governor of Babylon); BM 118983 (assembly of the people of Babylon and the governor); and compare *TCL* 12 4 (Bēl-īpuš [governor?] and the people of Dilbat) (*B-K* K.51, K.84, K.101, and I.25 respectively).

116 Assemblies, or groups of citizens acting to decide legal matters, are attested at Babylon (Strassmaier, *8e Congrès*, no. 4, BM 77907, BM 118983 [*B-K* I.6, K.1, and K.101 respectively]), Cutha (BM 33905 [*B-K* K.51]), Dilbat (*TCL* 12 4 [*B-K* I.25]), and Ur (*UET* 4 200 and 201 [*B-K* Kn. 2 and K.166 respectively]). Note also the assembly of Babylonians at Ḫîdalu (Leichty, *AnSt* 33 [1983]: 153-55 and pl. 34; *B-K* R.1) and see San Nicolò, *BR 8/7*, pp. 146-47, commentary to line 5. With regard to city assemblies in Babylonia, see in particular Dandamaev in Šulmu. *Papers on the Ancient Near East Presented at International Conference of Socialist Countries (Prague, Sept. 30-Oct. 3, 1986)*, ed. P. Vavroušek and V. Souček (Prague, 1988), pp. 63-71.

117 The date of the text is not preserved, but it probably comes from the period Sîn-balāssu-iqbi held office in Ur (*B-K* Kn.2). BM 47480+47783 (*B-K* K.9, composed at Dilbat) refers to an assembly comprised of the *rab alāni* and people from Babylon and Borsippa and BM 29029 (*B-K* K.107, composed at Dilbat) mentions an assembly of people from Babylon and Dilbat.

118 See for example *CAD* 10/1 (M), pp. 256-57; Dandamaev, *Klio* 63 (1981): 45-49 and *Slavery*, p. 44. The final part of the term is sometimes transcribed *banî* and sometimes *bānî*; there is at present no scholarly consensus on the matter. M. Roth has recently published an important document from the reign of Cyrus II which indicates that the status of *mār banî* did not have to be acquired at birth, but could be conferred upon a former slave, and that the *mār banî* was answerable to temple authorities (see *Sjöberg Festschrift*, pp. 481-89 and especially her discussion *ibid.*, pp. 486-87).

with privileged status could demand that their cases be heard by the king himself (see above).

Other Officials

It is generally not possible to determine the relative ranking of many of the subordinate officials within the provincial structure of Babylonia during the years 689-627 or to understand their exact duties and responsibilities. Sometimes it is unclear whether an official held responsibilites at the local, provincial, or national level. For earlier periods (especially for the Isin II period), kudurrus provide valuable data for examining the hierarchy and responsibilities of officials.[119] Only two kudurrus are attested for this period, both from the pre-revolt reign of Šamaš-šuma-ukīn, and only a limited picture of the hierarchy of officials can be obtained from the witness lists (unfortunately damaged) of these two texts.[120]

	VA 3614			**BM 87220**
1.	^{md}IŠKUR-*da-a-ni* LÚ.SUKKAL	*	1.	[^{m}]⸢^{d}⸣IŠKUR-*da-an* LÚ.SUKKAL
2.	^{md}AG-EN-PAP ⸢LÚ⸣.GAR *ma-*⸢*a?*⸣-[*ti* ...]	*	2.	^{md}PA-EN-*ú-ṣur* ⸢LÚ.GAR.KUR⸣ [...][121]
3.	^{m}AN.GAL-*mu-šal-lim* LÚ.GAL.SAG		3.	[...] [...]
4.	^{m}ŠEŠ-*li*-[*i*]*a* LÚ *šá* ⸢IGI!? É⸣.[...]	*	4.	[^{m}ŠE]Š-⸢DINGIR⸣-*ia* LÚ *šá* IGI É.GAL
5.	^{md}AG-*kil-la-an-ni* LÚ *mu-kil ap-pa-a-ti*	*	5.	^{md}AG-*kil-an-ni* LÚ *m*[*u-* ...]
6.	^{m}*nu-ra-nu* LÚ *q*[*í-*(*i*)*-pi?* ...]		6.	[...] [...]
7.	^{md}AG-MU-GAR-*un* LÚ.DUB.SAR É.GAL		7.	[^{m}*r*]*i-ḫa-nu* LÚ *qí-i-pi šá é-sag-gíl*
8.	^{m}⸢*tak?-lak*⸣-*ana*-^{d}⸢AG?⸣ LÚ *qí*-[*p*]*a? šá* [...][122]		8.	[...] [...]

[119] For the following Neo-Babylonian period, evidence is available for the ranking of officials at Uruk; see Kümmel, *Familie*, pp. 137-38.

[120] Steinmetzer, *Deimel Festschrift*, p. 306 rev. 17-26 (VA 3614; *B-K* K.163) and King, *BBSt* 10 rev. 42-50 (BM 87220, collated; *B-K* K.169).

[121] With regard to province he governed, see p. 234 n. 128.

[122] Landsberger, (*Brief*, p. 59 n. 110) suggests that Taklāk-ana-Nabû was the *qīpu* of Ezida.

			9. [^{m}]⸢^{d}⸣PA-GI DUMU ⸢^{m}*da-ku*⸣-*ru*
			10. [...] [...]
9.	^{md}AMAR.UTU-NUMUN-DÙ A ^{md}30-*šad-ú-ni* ⸢LÚ⸣.TU.É ^{d}AMAR.UTU x [...]	*	11. [^{m}]⸢^{d}⸣AMAR.UTU-NUMUN-⸢*ib*⸣-*ni* A ^{md}⸢30⸣-*šá-du-nu* LÚ.TU.⸢É⸣ [...]
			12. [...] [...]
10.	^{m}*a-qar*-^{d}EN-*lu-mur* A ^{m}ÌR-⸢^{d}*é*⸣-*a* L[Ú ...][123]		13. [^{m}]⸢^{d}⸣AG-EN-MU.MEŠ A ^{m}DINGIR-*iá* LÚ.⸢GAR.KU⸣ *bar-sip*.⸢KI⸣
			14. ^{m}[...] [...]
11.	^{md}EN-DA-DÙ.A.BI A ^{m}*é-*[*s*]*a*[*g-gí*]*l-a-a* L[Ú ...]	*	15. ⸢^{m}⸣^{d}EN-⸢DA⸣-DÙ.A.BI A ^{m}*é-sag-gíl-a-a* LÚ.ŠÀ.TAM ⸢*é*⸣-[...][124]
			16. [...] [...]
12.	^{md}AG-ÙRU-*ir* DUMU ^{md}ILLAT-I [...]		17. ⸢^{md}⸣U.GUR-SAG.⸢KAL⸣ A ^{md}30-SÍSKUR-*iš*-⸢*me*⸣ LÚ.⸢GAR⸣ [...][125]
13.	^{md}AG-*na-din*-ŠEŠ A ^{m}GAL-*a-šá*-^{d}MAŠ [...]		18. [...] [...]
14.	^{md}EN-SUM.NA DUMU ^{m}*ši-gu-u*-⸢*a*⸣ [...]	*	19. ⸢^{md}EN-SUM⸣.NA A ^{m}*ši-gu-ú-a* LÚ.⸢ŠIM×A?⸣ [...]

(* indicates that the individual is mentioned in both texts)

Although both lists are damaged and one originally contained several more entries than the other, it is obvious that a similar ordering was used in each.

---

123 His place of office was probably at Babylon, where several members of the family of Arad-Ea had previously held the postion of governor (see Lambert, *JCS* 11 [1957]: 2-3 and 9-10, and add *VAS* 1 37 v 2-3). One member of this family may have held office at Borsippa (see Frame, *JCS* 36 [1984]: 75).

124 Possibly *šatammu* of Esagila; see Appendix B sub 2c.

125 It seems probable the title was *šākin ṭēmi* of Cutha. Nergal-ašarid belonged to the same family (Sîn-karābī-išme) as Išum-bāni, who was governor of Cutha during the reign of Merodach-Baladan II (*VAS* 1 37 v 12-13). He may be identical with Ašaridu, the governor of Cutha in 656 (see Appendix B sub 4a).

Court officials dominate the first part of each list: the *sukkallu* (a high official, sometimes translated "vizier") Adad-dān(i); the *rab* (*ša*) *rēši* (an important official of some type) AN.GAL-mušallim;[126] the *ša pān ekalli* (palace overseer) Aḫi-iliya; the *mukīl appāti* (chariot driver, literally "the one who holds the reins") Nabû-killanni; and the *ṭupšar ekalli* (palace scribe) Nabû-šuma-iškun.[127] The governor of a province (Nabû-bēla-uṣur), however, is the second witness in each case.[128] The presence of court officials is not surprising since at the time these texts were composed there was a separate king in Babylon with his own court and since kudurrus were royal grants or decrees. These five court positions were important in Assyria at this time and their prominence in the two kudurrus may therefore reflect some Assyrian influence on the structure of the court at Babylon.[129] This would not be unexpected since at the time these texts were composed the king of Babylonia was an Assyrian prince, Šamaš-šuma-ukīn. The fact that Nabû-killanni, the *mukīl appāti*, appears among a number of Assyrian officials in the administrative document *ADD* 860 (i 18) suggests, but does not prove, that he was of Assyrian origin. Ashurbanipal claims to have given soldiers, horses, and chariots to Šamaš-šuma-ukīn[130] and Nabû-killanni may have been

---

[126] While the term *ša rēši* is often thought to have stood for "eunuch" in Assyria, there is as yet no proof that it did so in Babylonia and the exact relationship between the *ša rēši* and the *rab ša rēši* is not necessarily certain. See for example Brinkman, *PKB*, pp. 309-11, Oppenheim, *JANES* 5 (1973): 325-34, and Brinkman and Dalley, *ZA* 78 (1988): 85-86. With regard to the reading of the first element of the personal name, see p. 282 n. 92.

[127] Due to damage to BM 87220, it is not certain if all five of these officials were mentioned in that text.

[128] It is not clear which province Nabû-bēla-uṣur governed because neither entry is fully preserved. One of the two kudurrus (Steinmetzer, *Deimel Festschrift*, pp. 302-306) was dated at Sippar and dealt with the grant of a prebend there; thus one might expect the governor of that city to have been present. Alternatively, Nabû-bēla-uṣur may have been governor of Babylon, the most important province, as suggested by Johns in *PSBA* 25 (1903): 86-87. Or should he be identified with the like-named governor of Dūr-Šarrukku who was eponym in 672 (see Appendix B sub 7a)? Since the title *šakin māti* seems to have been used more by governors of Assyrian provinces than Babylonian ones (see *CAD* 17/1 [Š], p. 160), since Dūr-Šarrukku may have been annexed to Assyria at this time, and since Dūr-Šarrukku was located not far from Sippar, this identification would seem obvious. One of the kudurrus (*BBSt* 10), however, was composed sometime between 662 and 659 (in either year 6, 7, 8, or 9 of Šamaš-šuma-ukīn). The Nabû-bēla-uṣur who was governor of Dūr-Šarrukku is known to have left office before that time and to have been replaced by Šarru-lū-dāri, who was eponym in 664 (see Appendix B sub 7a). Thus, if he was the individual mentioned in that kudurru, he must returned to office at some point after 664.

[129] Note the mention of four of these five officials in the same order in the Assyrian letter *ABL* 568 rev. 12', 16', 17', and 20'. On these officials, see in particular: Klauber, *Beamtentum*; Kinnier Wilson, *Wine Lists*, pp. 36-37, 46-48, 52-53, and 62-64; Garelli in *RLA* 4, pp. 448-51; Dalley and Postgate, *TFS*, pp. 37-38; and the references in n. 126. Compare this order of officials with that mentioned in kudurrus from the post-Kassite period (see Brinkman, *PKB*, pp. 301-303).

[130] Streck, *Asb.*, pp. 28-29 iii 74-75.

sent by the Assyrian king to serve as commander of the chariotry. Whether the individuals holding the other four positions were Babylonians or Assyrians is unknown; their names give no certain clues. Similar influence may be detected at the court of Aššur-nādin-šumi, the son of Sennacherib who reigned at Babylon from 699 to 694. In addition to the *ša pān ekalli*, the *mukīl appāti*, and the *ṭupšar ekalli*, the witness list of a kudurru fragment from that time (Ashmolean 1933.1101) includes the *tašlīšu* (the third man on a chariot), the *rab kiṣri* (the commander of an army unit), and the *ša muḫḫi bītāni* (the person in charge of the inner quarters), all officials well attested in Assyria. While not mentioned in the two kudurrus from the time of Šamaš-šuma-ukīn, the *rab kiṣri* does appear in Babylonia during the period of concern here, although often as an official sent from Assyria.[131] The beginning of the witness list of Ashmolean 1933.1101 is broken and may originally have included other "Assyrian" officials. Babylonian officials mentioned in that kudurru include the *qīpu* of Esagila (also appearing in at least one of the two lists from the time of Šamaš-šuma-ukīn), *šatammu* officials of Ezida and possibly Esagila, and at least one governor (*bēl pīḫ*[*ati*]).[132]

The *sukkallu* headed each of the two witness lists from the time of Šamaš-šuma-ukīn. There is no clear evidence of an individual holding this position in Babylonia during the years 689-627 except while there was a separate king of Babylonia (i.e., during the time Ashurbanipal reigned in Assyria).[133] In addition to the court functionaries the lists included provincial governors (Nabû-bēla-uṣur, Nabû-bēl-šumāti of Borsippa, and probably Nergal-ašarid), individuals clearly or possibly associated with local temples—including a *šatammu* (Bēl-lē'i-kalama of the family of Esaggilaya), two or three *qīpu*-officials (Rīḫānu, Taklāk?-ana-Nabû?, and possibly Nūrānu), and an *ērib bīti* of the god Marduk (Marduk-zēra-ibni of the family of Sîn-šadûni)—the ruler of a Chaldean tribe (Nabû-ušallim of Bīt-Dakkūri), and several individuals whose titles (if any) are not preserved (Aqar-Bēl-lūmur of the family of Arad-

---

131 See, for example, *ABL* 273 rev. 1-8 and 275 rev. 4-6. In a legal document from Babylon, the *rab kiṣri* Mannu-kî-Arba'il is mentioned as the first of several important witnesses (Pinches, *AfO* 13 [1939-41]: pl. 3:28 [*B-K* S.7]; individual's name partially restored). He also appears in texts from Assyria (one of which is dated to 680) and in view of his name, he is likely to have been an Assyrian (see Tallqvist, *APN*, p. 125).

132 See Brinkman and Dalley, *ZA* 78 (1988): 76-98, especially 85-93; as Brinkman and Dalley note, the office of *ṭupšar ekalli* had already appeared at the court of Merodach-Baladan II (*VAS* 1 37 v 15) and the positions of *ša pān ekalli*, and *ša muḫḫi bītāni* eventually came to be used under the native Babylonian monarchy as well.

133 This is undoubtedly due to the fact that we have not yet found the official archives at Babylon for this time. *ABL* 716 which may date after the Šamaš-šuma-ukīn Revolt (see lines 10 and rev. 6-8) states that the king had installed a *sukkallu* and a *sartennu* in the land (Babylonia) to make just decisions there (rev. 11-13). Possibly Ashurbanipal was appointing officials to run Babylonia in the name of Kandalānu.

Ea, Nabû-nāṣir of the family of Baliḫ-na'id,[134] and Nabû-nādin-aḫi of the family of Rabâ-ša-Ninurta). One witness (Bēl-iddin of the family of Šigū'a) appears to have been a brewer; he may have been in charge of providing beer to the palace or some important temple complex. The fact that the head of the Bīt-Dakkūri tribe, was mentioned before the governor of Borsippa points out his important place within the provincial structure of Babylonia.[135]

As was mentioned, a thorough study of Babylonian officialdom would involve using material from outside the period of concern here and would require a book of its own. A few words, however, must be said about the *šatammu*, logogram (LÚ).ŠÀ.TAM.[136] After the governor, the *šatammu* was the next most important official in a city, or at least the official mentioned the next most often in the texts. He was the chief official in charge of the administration of the major temple of a city. It may be wrong to consider him *de jure* part of the provincial administration since he was basically a local temple official; however, because of his eminence within the city, he was probably a person whom the king used in maintaining control of the city. The major temples in the land—such as Esagila in Babylon, Ebabbar in Sippar, Ezida in Borsippa, and Eanna in Uruk—had great influence in their communities. Besides caring for the (formal) religious life of the people, the temples controlled great wealth, which was derived from their large estates and economic enterprises, as well as from gifts and donations from the crown and populace. Thus the *šatammu* was a force to be reckoned with in the affairs of a city. The *šatammu* was normally a member of a prominent family in the city and the post of *šatammu* could be a stepping stone to that of governor. Holders of this office tended to be related to previous holders of the position; in particular, during all this period of time, only members of the family Nūr-Papsukkal are known to have held the position of *šatammu* of Ezida.[137] Like the governor, the *šatammu* often attended the formalization of certain business transactions; of the texts that have a *šatammu* as witness, about 70 per cent involve land (sales and exchanges) and about 10 per cent deal with temple prebends. He was responsible to the king, reporting directly to him on political as well as cultic matters, and could go to visit him.[138]

---

[134] This witness may have been *šatammu* at Sippar (see p. 277 n. 56).

[135] The fact that he gives testimony in the proceeding described on the kudurru may play a part in this placement.

[136] The title has been translated in various ways, including "bishop" (Landsberger, *Brief*, p. 58) and "dean" (McEwan, *Priest and Temple*, p. 25). I prefer to leave the title untranslated.

[137] See Appendix B sub 3b and Frame, *JCS* 36 (1984): 67-80. In addition to the individuals mentioned in the latter article, note also Zākir of the family of Nūr-Papsukkal who held the office of *šatammu* of Ez[ida] at one point during the reign of Aššur-nādin-šumi (see Brinkman and Dalley, *ZA* 78 [1988]: 81, 83-84, and 89-90 iii 15').

[138] E.g., *ABL* 476 (*LAS*, no. 277) and 831; for the authorship of the latter letter, see p. 127 n. 138.

While he was the chief administrator of a city's temple, his exact role in the functioning of the temple is uncertain. There is no clear evidence that he had authority over all of a city's temples or that he took part in temple rituals.[139]

Tribal Groups

Tribal groups appear to have lain outside the normal provincial structure for the most part, although the Gurasimmu were under the jurisdiction of the governor of Ur at one point and there may have been a province called Chaldea (KUR *kaldu*), which would have included undoubtedly some Chaldeans.[140] Assyrian kings are known to have appointed (or confirmed) and deposed tribal rulers at this time. The tribal chieftains probably had the same kinds responsibilities for their tribes as governors had for their provinces. This is to be expected; it would have been difficult and impractical to impose a system based upon the requirements of city populations on tribal structures with their own traditional leaders, or to have the tribes with their often nomadic lifestyle supervised by a city-bound bureaucracy. Officials in cities, however, did keep an eye on the tribal groups in the neighbouring area and reported on their activities to the king. It was best for the Assyrian king to recognize the tribal leader with his traditional authority and support from his own tribe as the person responsible for that tribe, and simply to replace him with another member of that tribe's leading family if he proved troublesome. One may wonder if Babylonian law (criminal and civil) extended to the tribal groups, particularly the nomadic elements. Likely they would have followed tribal law, although there is some evidence that Babylonian law may have been used among the more settled (and Babylonized) tribesmen in cases of land ownership.[141] The internal administrative structure of the various tribes is unknown. In effect, the tribal groups seems to have formed semi-independent units within the state as a whole.

These tribal leaders could be powerful individuals, supported by their followers and making use of their tribes' economic resources. Šamaš-ibni

---

139 This is not the place to present a thorough study of the role of this official in temple matters or of the temple hierarchy. Landsberger commenced such a study (*Brief*, pp. 58-63), but much work remains to be done. In addition, see the important article by M. Gallery on the *šatammu*, primarily in the Old Babylonian period, in *AfO* 27 (1980): 1-36. For the hierarchy at Uruk during the sixth century, see Kümmel, *Familie*, pp. 137-48, especially 138. Note in particular the order *šatammu*, *qīpu*, and temple scribe of Uruk in *ABL* 476:28-29 (*LAS*, no. 277); without the presence of these, Mār-Ištar could not check the gold in the temple treasury of Uruk which was available for restoring divine statues.

140 See p. 221 n. 48 where it is suggested that *šaknu* of KUR *kaldu* may actually refer to the leader of the Bīt-Dakkūri or a lower official of that tribe.

141 E.g., *BBSt* 10 (*B-K* K.169).

was called the king of Bīt-Dakkūri by Esarhaddon and Na'id-Marduk of Bīt-Yakīn held the lordship (*bēlūtu*) of the Sealand.[142] In an economic text from Šapiya, the ruler of the Bīt-Amukāni tribe was accorded the pre-eminent position in the witness list usually reserved for governors and *šatammu*-officials,[143] and in a kudurru the ruler of the Bīt-Dakkūri was one of eleven important witnesses listed.[144] Nabû-ušallim was made ruler of the Bīt-Dakkūri by Esarhaddon and reported to Assyria about events in his area. He was powerful enough to refuse to hand over persons without a royal order[145] and could give testimony to Šamaš-šuma-ukīn on the question of land ownership.[146] The administration of those Aramean tribes with more than one sheikh (e.g., the Puqūdu) is unknown, although the Gambūlu appear to have been united under one leader during part of this period (Bēl-iqīša and later his son Dunanu). The division of power within the Puqūdu may have been one of the reasons for their disruptive role in Babylonian life.

Tribute and Taxes

There is little information about the payment of tribute or taxes by Babylonia to Assyria or to its own king (when that king was distinct from the king of Assyria) during this time. Earlier, Tiglath-pileser III had imposed tribute on the Chaldean sheikhs and Sargon II had required tribute from various Babylonian groups, including Arameans (the Puqūdu in particular), the "whole land of Chaldea" (the Bīt-Amukāni and Bīt-Dakkūri in particular), and the city of Dūr-Kurigalzu; finally Sennacherib received tribute and/or gifts from an official of Ḫararātu, a place likely located east of the Tigris.[147] On one occasion, Sargon had also required defeated Arameans to send animals annually to the gods Marduk and Nabû; presumably these animals were to be used as offerings in the temples of these deities at Babylon and Borsippa.[148] Only two Babylonian tribal groups are known to have sent tribute (*biltu* and *mandattu*) or "gifts" (*tāmartu*) to Assyria in the time of Esarhaddon. Na'id-Marduk, the head of the Sealand and ruler of Bīt-Yakīn, sent yearly gifts to

---

142 Borger, *Esarh.*, p. 52 §27 episode 12 A iii 63 and p. 47 §2 episode 4 A ii 61-62.

143 As the first witness, preceded by the phrase *ina ušuzzi ša* ("in the presence of"). BM 118970:31 and duplicate BM 118976 (*B-K* I.22-23). Šapiya (Sapiya) lay within the area controlled by the Bīt-Amukāni (Luckenbill, *Senn.*, p. 53:42-47) and appears to have been its "capital" during the time of (Nabû)-mukīn-zēri (see Brinkman in *Studies Oppenheim*, p. 11 and n. 28).

144 *BBSt* 10 rev. 45 (*B-K* K.169); he is cited simply as Nabû-ušallim *mār* Dakkūru.

145 *ABL* 336:8-13.

146 *BBSt* 10 (*B-K* K.169).

147 Rost, *Tigl. III*, pp. 44-45:14-15; Lie, *Sar.*, pp. 2-5:6-10, 48-49:4-330, and 56-57:376-377 (partially restored); and Luckenbill, *Senn.*, pp. 25-26 i 54-57 and 54:57.

148 Lie, *Sar.*, pp. 50-51:331-332.

Esarhaddon and Bēl-iqīša of the Gambūlu sent tribute.[149] There is no evidence that the city populations sent tribute to Assyria at this time; instead, they often received favours and gifts from Esarhaddon and from Ashurbanipal, at least in the first half of the latter's reign (see chapter 4). It has sometimes been suggested that it was the payment of tribute that caused Šamaš-šuma-ukīn to rebel, but there is in fact no clear evidence that he ever did send tribute to Ashurbanipal.[150] After Ashurbanipal put down the rebellion of 652-648, he did, however, require those Babylonians who had rebelled to send him tribute yearly and to provide Aššur, Bēlet, and the other gods of Assyria with various types of offerings (*sattukkī ginê rēšēti*).[151] As mentioned in chapter 9, shortly after the revolt some individuals from Uruk, Nippur, Larak and the Chaldean tribes of Bīt-Dakkūri and Bīt-Amukāni appear to have been punished for not sending "gifts" (*tāmartu*) to Assyria, but exactly when they had done so is uncertain. Since they were not accused of having aided Šamaš-šuma-ukīn, or of having fought against Assyria, it may be that they were being punished for not paying the tribute imposed upon them after the revolt of 652-648, but one would not expect them to have done this so soon after the crushing of the earlier rebellion. If because of the special privileges granted to them by Esarhaddon and Ashurbanipal, the citizens of some Babylonian cities did not pay tribute to Assyria, one can, however, assume that they still paid taxes for the administration and defence of their cities and temples. Due to the absence of documentary evidence from Babylon, we are unable to determine if the various Babylonian cities and tribes sent taxes to Šamaš-šuma-ukīn and Kandalānu to help them maintain their courts in Babylon, though this would seem likely. They may also have been required to send offerings to Babylon to help maintain the cult of Marduk, the national deity.[152]

Assyrian Involvement

Assyrian involvement in the internal administration of Babylonia was extensive, even though the basic structure was not changed and there was at

149 Borger, *Esarh.*, p. 47 §27 episode 4 A ii 63-64 (*tāmartu*) and pp. 52-53 §27 episode 13 A iii 75-78 (*biltu* and *mandattu*).

150 See p. 131 n. 1 for sometimes proposed references to tribute in *ABL* 301 and Amherst papyrus 63. Grayson's translation of *ABL* 1105:28'-31' (=Parpola and Watanabe, *SAA* 2, no. 9) indicates that Ashurbanipal had some Babylonians swear to help the Assyrian king in collecting any tribute which was due from Šamaš-šuma-ukīn, or more accurately from individual(s) under his authority ("[*If* ...] of Šamaš-šuma-ukīn, or of another land will not deliver [*his tribute* to Ashurbanipal, king of Assyria] ..."; *JCS* 39 [1987]: 144 and see 140); the crucial word "tribute" is, however, restored.

151 Streck, *Asb.*, pp. 40-41 iv 106-109.

152 See p. 230 n. 114.

times a king of Babylonia who was not also the king of Assyria. The Assyrian king appointed or confirmed the most important Babylonian officials and these were expected to make full reports to, and to carry out the orders of, the Assyrian king. Assyrians could also be sent south to carry out duties there and to report to the king on the activities of Babylonian officials. There was an Assyrian[153] official (*šaknu*) stationed at Nippur during the reign of Ashurbanipal to forward sealed orders and messengers of the king[154] and Esarhaddon sent a trusted official by the name of Mār-Ištar to Babylonia to supervise and report on the restoration of temples and the reorganization of cultic services. A large number of his letters have been preserved and they provide a wealth of data on his activities. Mār-Ištar appears to have operated over a wide area; his letters refer to Akkad, Babylon, Borsippa, Cutha, Dēr, Dilbat, Dūr-Šarrukku, Ḫursagkalama, Laḫīru, Nippur, Sippar, and Uruk. He seems to have borne royal orders to officials in the south, seen that they were carried out, and reported on this to the king. There is an emphasis in the letters upon temple-cultic matters (such as sacrifices, divine statues and their repair, the substitute-king ritual, and the repair of temples), but these were not his only concerns. He wrote to the king about the actions (both legal and illegal) of local officials, repair work on bridges, and relations with Elam. The Assyrian kings undoubtedly realized that local officials might have their own reasons to disguise the true nature of conditions and events and send unreliable reports to the king. Thus the kings sent trusted individuals such as Mār-Ištar to check up on matters, to carry out special tasks, and perhaps to co-ordinate operations between various jurisdictions. These special agents acted openly and were officially recognized—they were the eyes and the ears of the king.[155]

As a further means of controlling Babylonia, it seems that the Assyrian kings sometimes had Babylonians held as hostages in Assyria, presumably as guaranty for their families' or tribes' loyalty. Some were there in the guise of welcome "guests" while others were youths being educated in Assyria, with the intention (on the part of the Assyrians) that they would become favourably disposed towards Assyria and remain so when they later took up positions of authority back home. Bēl-ibni, who had been appointed ruler of Babylonia

---

153 Or at least the individual's name included the divine name Aššur.

154 *ABL* 238 rev. 8'-10'. In Assyria, *šaknu* can refer to both governors and other officials (probably military officials of fairly high rank); see Postgate, *AnSt* 30 (1980): 67-76. It seems likely that Aššur-bēla-taqqin was a military official posted in Nippur by the Assyrian king to keep an eye on matters in that frequently rebellious town and to facilitate communication between Babylonia and Assyria. The Assyrians relied upon an efficient system of messengers to keep them up to date about what occurred in the south.

155 See Parpola, *LAS*, nos. 275-297 and 2, p. XVI; see also chapter 6.

by the Assyrians in 703, was described as the son of a *rab banî* who had been brought up in Sennacherib's palace "like a young dog."[156]

III. The Military

Preferring Babylonia to be militarily weak and dependent upon Assyria for its defence, the Assyrian rulers saw to it that no Babylonian standing army existed, or at least no large body of forces on permanent duty. They did not wish to see the creation of a potentially hostile military force in Babylonia and this would have been facilitated by the fact that Babylonia did not have a tradition as a militaristic state.[157] In edition A of his annals, Ashurbanipal claimed to have given military forces—literally "soldiers, horses, (and) chariots"—to his brother, Šamaš-šuma-ukīn.[158] This was a defence of Ashurbanipal's goodness and magnanimity towards his brother, in contrast to Šamaš-šuma-ukīn's perfidy at the time of the revolt, and should be weighed accordingly. It is uncertain if these "troops" were comprised of Assyrians or Babylonians, how many were involved, or to whom they were loyal. Perhaps they simply comprised Šamaš-šuma-ukīn's palace guard or were his personal bodyguards, since he was after all an Assyrian in Babylonia.

Since relatively unsophisticated weaponry and techniques were universally employed[159] and since Babylonia was not then attempting to conquer or hold other areas, it needed no large standing army. Each city would have had some armed forces to maintain at least minimum security and these would have been supplemented by levies formed from the citizenry in times of trouble. The tribal groups could also supply a large number of men for combat if they were so ordered and so inclined. Šamaš-šuma-ukīn did not rely solely on outside, non-Babylonian forces to fight his war with Assyria; he was able to raise sufficient troops to capture Nippur and Cutha and to keep the Assyrians busy for more than four years. The tribal groups may have provided a large part of his (mobile) army, with the inhabitants of the cities

---

156 Luckenbill, *Senn.*, pp. 54:54 and 57:13. The exact meaning of the term *rab banî* and its exact relation to the term *mār banî* is uncertain. In recent studies, Zadok has taken it to mean "noble" or something similar (*RA* 77 [1983]: 189-90) and Brinkman and Dalley as a family name, similar to such family names as "Fuller" (LÚ *ašlāku*) and "Weaver" (LÚ *išparu*) (*ZA* 78 [1988]: 90-91). On the question of Babylonian hostages in Assyria, see Parpola, *Iraq* 34 (1972): 33-34 and the case of Ea-zēra-qīša (*ABL* 896). Note also the presence of Babylonian economic texts drawn up at the city of Assur (*B-K* I.4 and I.7). Despite Parpola, *Iraq* 34 (1972): 33, there is really no proof that the Kudurru mentioned as doing scholarly work in Nineveh was the Kudurru who was a son of the Chaldean Šamaš-ibni; Kudurru was a common name at this time.

157 During the post-Kassite period (1158-722), Babylonia appears to have had only a small army (Brinkman, *PKB*, p. 312).

158 Streck, *Asb.*, pp. 28-29 iii 74-75.

159 Thus a large body of "professional" troops was not required.

being more disposed to maintain the security of their cities, but this is mere supposition. Earlier, Merodach-Baladan II had been able to raise a sizeable force against Assyria[160] and later Nabopolassar was able to do the same. The force supporting Šamaš-šuma-ukīn in 652-648 probably cannot be described as a unified army. In all probability, it would have been comprised of both urban citizenry and tribal groups, with the latter probably led by their tribal leaders. It is not clear how much contact there was between the various groups, particularly between Šamaš-šuma-ukīn in the north and Nabû-bēl-šumāti in the south, and after the Assyrians began to gain ground by 650.

A provincial governor could prepare and send out *ḫiyālu*-troops from his own area if ordered to do so by the (Assyrian) king[161] and Babylonian cities were responsible for maintaining a certain number of chariots, presumably for military use.[162] Possibly provinces were required to raise and equip a set number of troops if the king requested them. For major disturbances, troops were sent from Assyria. There is no clear evidence that there were normally Assyrian garrisons in Babylonian cities, except during the rebellion of 652-648, although Nippur was likely garrisoned after the revolt.[163] Ša-pī-Bēl, a Gambulian centre bordering Elam, was not garrisoned by Esarhaddon when its ruler submitted to him; Esarhaddon simply considered the native troops there to be a garrison against Elam.[164] However, garrisons were sometimes installed in forts located outside urban centres, particularly in border regions. Auxiliaries made up of Aramean tribesmen may occasionally have been stationed in Babylonian cities, but it is uncertain if they were there on permanent duty or how large their numbers were. At one point, men of the Utu', Yādaqu, and Reḫīqu tribes were stationed in Borsippa to keep watch.[165] The Assyrian kings maintained an efficient network for gathering intelligence in Babylonia in order to ensure that they received immediate word of potentially dangerous situations and outbreaks of trouble in that land and in order to be able to react quickly if military aid from Assyria proved necessary.

---

160 See for example, Lie, *Sar.*, pp. 44-45:274-277.

161 *ABL* 269. Postgate (*BiOr* 41 [1984]: 422) points out that *ḫiyālu*-troops appear only in Babylonian letters and did not constitute part of the regular Assyrian army. Exactly what their particular function was is unclear.

162 *ABL* 340 (*LAS*, no. 276) appears to indicate that the governors of Babylon, Borsippa, and Cutha made the citizens of their cities bring up the numbers of their chariotry to its former strength: *re-eš* GIŠ.GIGIR.MEŠ-*ku-nu iṣ-ṣa*, "make up your chariots (to their former strength)" (rev. 5-6). Parpola (*LAS* 2, p. 264) suggests that this was done to make up for losses occurring in the Egyptian campaign of 671 or in preparation for that campaign.

163 See chapter 9.

164 Borger, *Esarh.*, p. 53 §27 episode 13 A iii 80-83. Esarhaddon may simply have been accepting as a fact the presence of Bēl-iqīša's troops in that city.

165 *ABL* 349. They served with Nabû-šar-aḫḫēšu who was to guard the house of an individual by the name of Nabû-lē'i. The date of the letter is uncertain; Röllig (*RLA* 5, p. 232) suggests a date *c.* 675, but presents no evidence for this.

Babylon was about 450 kilometres from Nineveh. A messenger could cover this distance in about six days[166] and an army marching 25 kilometres a day could cover it in about 18 days.[167] When Urtak invaded Babylonia early in the reign of Šamaš-šuma-ukīn, the Babylonian king had to wait for Ashurbanipal to send troops from Assyria to drive out the Elamites.[168]

In 677, 652, and probably 679, chronicles record the following: *rab bīti ina māt Akkadî biḫirtu* (var. *biḫirti*) *ibteḫir*, "The steward did/made *biḫirtu* in the land of Akkad"; for 652, it is stated that the official did this from the second month until the tenth month.[169] Since these events are mentioned in the chronicles, they must have been considered important. The phrase *biḫirtu beḫēru* occurs only here, and the verb *beḫēru* occurs only once otherwise, in a Neo-Babylonian letter in connection with the choosing of cattle.[170] Thus the exact meaning of the phrase cannot be derived from the context alone. Many scholars translate the phrase as "to levy/conscript troops,"[171] taking the root bḫr to be a loan from Aramaic. Although the meaning "choose" or "examine" is well attested for the Aramaic verb בְּחַר and the Hebrew בָּחַר, in neither language does the verb have a clear military connotation. In Hebrew, the related noun can occasionally have a military connection, referring to a "chosen/selected man," "young man," or "warrior";[172] however, ideally one would wish for a clearer connection for the Neo-Babylonian usage than this. The title *rab bīti*, "steward," could denote an individual ranging from an overseer of a private household to an important government official. The references in the chronicles must, however, refer to a high official. Postgate argues that in Assyria a *rab bīti* "despite his title, usually acted as military deputy to a provincial governor" and this would support a military connotation for the phrase *biḫirtu beḫēru*.[173] The fact that the action in

---

166 See Parpola, *LAS* 2, p. 31.

167 Twenty-five to thirty kilometres a day was a reasonable march for an army; see Hallo, *JCS* 18 (1964): 63 and Eph'al in *HHI*, p. 99. Note also Wall-Romana, *JNES* 49 (1990): 216 on boat trips from Mosul to Baghdad lasting three to six days.

168 Piepkorn, *Asb*., pp. 58-59 iv 33-52.

169 Grayson, *Chronicles*, no. 1 iii 48 (restored) and iv 4, no. 14:6 (mostly restored) and 12, and no. 16:9-10.

170 *BIN* 1 68:24.

171 See Grayson, *Chronicles*, p. 83, commentary to no. 1 iv 4; *CAD* 2 (B), pp. 186 and 223; and *AHw*, pp. 117-18 and 125 (following Landsberger and Bauer, *ZA* 37 [1927]: 74).

172 See Jastrow, *Dictionary*, p. 155; *BDB*, pp. 103-104 and Ludwig Koehler und Walter Baumgartner, *Hebräisches und aramäisches Lexikon zum alten Textament*, 3rd edition (Leiden, 1967), volume 1, pp. 114-15. The best examples are 1 Chron. 19:10, 2 Chron. 25:5, and Judg. 20:15-16. Note also Z. Weisman's study of bāḥūr in the Old Testament which argues that the connotations of "young man" and "selected warrior" "originated from a primary common background that had to do with trial and testing" (*Vetus Testamentum* 31 [1981]: 441-50).

173 Postgate, *Iraq* 35 (1973): 31 n. 19 and see also Dalley and Postgate, *TFS*, p. 193 sub i 8'-9' and iii 22'.

question was carried out in 652, commencing in the same month in which the rebellion is first attested and ending in the same month in which actual warfare first broke out, might well suggest a military connotation, and the levying of troops at that time would certainly have been appropriate.[174] Although it seems likely that the *rab bīti* was choosing/collecting something/some persons, and although the meaning "to levy troops" seems reasonable for the phrase *biḫirtu beḫēru*, the exact connotation of this phrase cannot be considered certain.[175]

How large a force could be raised in Babylonia during the years 689-627 is unknown but we do have some figures for individual actions. During the Šamaš-šuma-ukīn Revolt, Uruk raised 500 or 600 archers to go to the aid of Ur; on another occasion, 1000 bowmen are mentioned as being stationed in Ur. In addition, 250 Gurasimmu were involved with Nabû-bēl-šumāti after he abandoned the Sealand to Bēl-ibni.[176] Archers, *ḫiyālu*-troops, and chariotry are attested as part of the Babylonian military during this period,[177] although their numbers are unknown. During the revolt of 652-648, Šamaš-šuma-ukīn is known to have gone out himself with troops to oppose the Assyrians,[178] but, for the most part, the urban populations tended to rely upon their city walls. The tribal groups and Elam often appear to have provided the bulk of active combatants. In summary, very little is known about the Babylonian military establishment at this time, probably because no formal unified military establishment existed. On occasion, Arameans, Chaldeans, and urban citizenry from Babylonia supported Assyria militarily (possibly even forming part of the Assyrian armed forces themselves), though some of these may have been no longer resident in Babylonia (e.g., deportees or their descendants).[179]

---

174 Brinkman (*Prelude*, p. 77 n. 375) suggests it may not be simply an accident that in all three cases political upheavals occurred in Babylonia within two years of the *rab bīti* acting.

175 See also Brinkman, *Prelude*, p. 77 n. 375. The chronicles may simply refer to a palace official who assembled a few individuals for some duty, but one might not have expected them to bother mentioning such an occurrence or for it to have taken place (and have lasted eight months) in 652.

176 *ABL* 754:10-13, 1129 rev. 13'-16', and 1000:16'-17'. Figures may have been rounded off or exaggerated. Earlier Merodach-Baladan II had sent 600 cavalry and 4000 garrison troops to aid Dūr-Atḫara against the army of Sargon II (Lie, *Sar.*, pp. 44-45:274-277).

177 E.g., *ABL* 754:10, 269:7-10, and 340 rev. 5-6; Streck, *Asb.*, pp. 28-29 iii 74-75.

178 See above, p. 148.

179 See Parker, *Iraq* 23 (1961): 38 ND 2619; Dalley and Postgate, *TFS*, pp. 35-39; Zadok, *WO* 16 (1985): 65; *ABL* 564:5-8; and Starr, *SAA* 4, no. 280. On the Assyrian army, see in particular Manitius, *ZA* 24 (1910): 97-149 and 185-224; Reade, *Iraq* 34 (1972): 87-112; Malbran-Labat, *Armée* (though note Postgate, *BiOr* 41 [1985]: 420-26); Postgate in *Power and Propaganda*, pp. 207-13; and Dalley and Postgate, *TFS*, pp. 27-47. See Eph'al in *HHI*, pp. 88-106, for a useful discussion of warfare and military control in the ancient Near East.

CHAPTER 11

BABYLONIA, ASSYRIA, AND ELAM

Throughout its history, Babylonia had much to do with Assyria to the north and Elam to the east. This is not surprising since these were the only two unified states bordering Babylonia. To the south of Babylonia was the Persian Gulf, with its route to Dilmun and beyond, and to the west was the Syro-Arabian desert, with its nomadic tribal groups. Because the three countries adjoined one another geographically, were connected by trade routes, and had similar religious, literary, and political traditions and interests, they maintained close relations. Not all contacts between the lands were hostile. Trade was carried out across border-lines. Individuals and tribal groups travelled from one land to another and at times took up residence in the new country. Inevitably a large part of the information on Babylonia during the years 689-627 deals with its relations with Assyria and Elam—especially Assyria since that land controlled Babylonia at this time. This chapter will attempt to provide some idea of the nature of these relations.[1]

During most of the years from 689 to 627 Babylonia was not an independent sovereign state; it had no formal foreign policy or diplomatic relations with other states. Only during the Šamaš-šuma-ukīn Revolt was there a truly independent ruler of Babylonia, but then the country was not united under him and Assyrian troops moved throughout his land. At other times during the reign of Ashurbanipal in Assyria, although Šamaš-šuma-ukīn and Kandalānu ruled nominally in Babylonia, the Assyrian king seems to have been the final authority and Babylonian foreign policy was, in effect, Assyrian foreign policy. Since Babylonia did not act as a sovereign state during almost all of this period, it will be useful to examine the actions of individual persons and groups within Babylonia, keeping in mind that such actions were not necessarily representative of the entire country. Our sources in themselves may provide a one-sided view of affairs, being written mostly by or for Assyrians; there are no real first-hand accounts that give the sentiments of individual Babylonians.

---

[1] The documentation for most of the statements presented in this chapter has been provided earlier in this study, primarily in chapters 5-10. Commercial relations will not be considered here, though not because of their irrelevance or lack of importance.

I. Babylonian "Foreign Policy"

During the years 689-627 Babylonian resistance to Assyrian domination was never far from the surface. There were frequent efforts on the part of various elements, particularly the tribal groups, to throw off the Assyrian yoke and establish their independence. They did not shy away from armed resistance, and there were a number of revolts in Babylonia during this time. Whenever Assyrian control seemed weak, or Assyria was pre-occupied with other matters rebellion might break out (for example during the unrest in Assyria at the death of Sennacherib). The Šamaš-šuma-ukīn Revolt showed that many Babylonians were willing to follow a foreigner, even an Assyrian, into rebellion if there was a good chance of success. There also is the possibility that at times rebellion may have been fuelled by nothing more than greed for wealth and power on the part of the "rebel leaders." Though Babylonia was a rich country, it appears to have had no well-organized army, so that outside support was desirable in order to provide both military aid and a place of refuge if necessary. Many Babylonian rebels sought Elamite support and Šamaš-šuma-ukīn, at least, was willing to pay for such support, as had earlier kings of Babylonia.[2]

Various forces and motives came into play in different localities that effected the impetus behind, and support for, rebellion. These would have included fear of Assyrian reprisal, proximity to Assyrian troops, preparedness for rebellion (e.g., presence or absence of city walls and military equipment), ability to flee from Assyrian troops, internal divisions and antipathies, and self-interest (e.g., some officials were dependent on Assyria for their positions while others had relatives being held hostage in Assyria). Nomadic and semi-nomadic tribal groups who could readily pick up their possessions and flee, were well versed in the arts of fighting and survival, and had relatively few tangible possessions to lose, might be more willing to risk rebellion than settled, urban populations who could be more easily trapped in their cities and towns, stripped of their possessions, and forced to watch their houses and crops destroyed.[3] Sennacherib's destruction of Babylon was likely a much more vivid memory for urban populations (especially the inhabitants of Babylon) than for non-urban groups, and would remind them of the possible consequences of rebellion. The tribal chieftains traditionally had great respect and authority which might have made it easier for them to unite their people in one purpose than for city governors who

---

2 See Brinkman, *JNES* 24 (1965): 161-66.

3 This does not mean to imply that tribal groups had no permanent settlements which could be attacked or that they were poor.

were dependent upon the Assyrian king for their positions.[4] Thus, it is not surprising that the major revolts were led or supported mainly by tribal groups, and in particular by the leaders of the Chaldean Bīt-Yakīn tribe who had provided kings for Babylonia in the past and could use the swamp-marsh area of the Sealand as a convenient base of operations and place of retreat.[5]

Unity of action even among the tribal groups, however, was extremely rare. The fragmented nature of the Babylonian state did not encourage united action or a common policy.[6] Internal divisions and various interests and concerns made uniting the people in a common purpose difficult if not impossible; Šamaš-šuma-ukīn came closest to doing so during the period in question. Of course, he had the advantage of having been the acknowledged ruler of Babylonia for sixteen years beforehand, sufficient time for him to build up a base of support and power.[7] The absence of a universally acknowledged native ruling family was a major factor in preventing the formation of a common response to Assyria. The throne of Babylonia had not remained in the possession of any one family for any length of time since the ninth century, when the family of Nabû-šuma-ukīn ruled Babylonia for four generations. This was mainly as a result of foreign interference and internal revolts, revolts which often involved tribal groups.

It has occasionally been suggested that there was a pro-Assyrian party in Babylonia during the time of the late Neo-Assyrian kings (Tiglath-pileser III to Ashurbanipal) and that this party was found in the cities of northern Babylonia, particularly among the temple personnel of Babylon and Borsippa.[8] This argument depends on (a) the belief that there were persons of Assyrian descent among the temple personnel of Borsippa, (b) statements of the Assyrian kings Tiglath-pileser III and Sargon II that after they had defeated tribal groups in Babylonia they were welcomed by individuals in northern Babylonian cities, and (c) the knowledge that Babylonian cities did not always support anti-Assyrian movements and sometimes aided Assyria

---

4 While tribal rulers may have been confirmed in their positions by the Assyrian king (e.g., Borger, *Esarh.*, p. 47 §27 episode 4 A ii 62), in general they seem to have come from the native ruling families of the tribes.

5 Although Nippur, or at least some of its governors, frequently gave trouble to Esarhaddon and Ashurbanipal, and a number of cities in northern Babylonia strongly supported Šamaš-šuma-ukīn during the revolt of 652-648, the city populations otherwise appear to have remained submissive to Assyria.

6 For example, the Aramean Puqūdu fought with the Chaldean Bīt-Amukāni (*ABL* 275).

7 The fact that he was an Assyrian may have been one of the reasons why not all Babylonians rallied to his cause against the king of Assyria.

8 E.g., Ahmed, *Asb.*, pp. 48-50, and Brinkman in *Studies Oppenheim*, p. 20 n. 103 and p. 39 (subsequently retracted in *PKB*, p. 225 n. 1420).

against Babylonian rebels.[9] However, the idea that some temple personnel were of Assyrian descent was based upon the mistaken interpretation of the term A ᵐAŠ-ŠUR to mean "descendant of the Assyrian" rather than "descendant of Ēda-ēṭir"[10] and the statements of the Assyrian kings that they had been welcomed by Babylonians can not be accepted uncritically. Our knowledge of the welcome given to the victorious Assyrian kings Tiglath-pileser III and Sargon II by persons from Babylon, Borsippa, and possibly Cutha comes from those kings' own inscriptions[11] and naturally they would have wished to present themselves as the saviours of Babylonia from evil and impious tribal leaders and as the legitimate and acknowledged rulers of that country.[12] If indeed they were welcomed by inhabitants of these cities, one may wonder if these persons were not merely trying to pacify the Assyrian kings and prevent hostile actions being directed against them and their cities.

One does not find much actual evidence of pro-Assyrian support in Babylonia. Although Assyrian kings showed favour to the inhabitants of Babylonia's cities and on occasion presented themselves as defenders and champions of the cities (particularly against the tribal groups), during the period from Tiglath-pileser's defeat of Nabû-mukīn-zēri (729) until the death of Ashurbanipal, only once did any cities actively support Assyria against Babylonian rebels. This, of course, was the Šamaš-šuma-ukīn Revolt, in which various cities and towns in southern Babylonia (Uruk, Ur, Eridu, Kissik, Šāt-iddin, and Kullab), as well as Cutha,[13] aided Ashurbanipal against his own brother (i.e., another Assyrian). Before 689, cities had often given military support to rebel movements led by tribal rulers (e.g., Nabû-mukīn-zēri, Merodach-Baladan II, and Mušēzib-Marduk).[14] During the years 689-627, several cities of northern Babylonia supported the revolt of Šamaš-šuma-ukīn, and Nippur was frequently involved in anti-Assyrian actions. Even though active urban support for rebels is otherwise unattested during these years, it does not necessarily reflect a pro-Assyrian attitude in those cities. Recognizing Babylonia's internal disunity and military weakness, Assyria's overwhelming military might, their own vulnerable position, and the fact that the interests of the tribal groups which usually led the rebel

---

9 Cutha and the cities of southern Babylonia remained loyal to Assyria during the Šamaš-šuma-ukīn Revolt. Babylonians are attested fighting on the side of the Assyrians on several occasions.

10 See Stamm, *Namengebung*, p. 170.

11 Rost, *Tigl. III*, pp. 2-3:6-7 and Lie, *Sar.*, pp. 54-57:371-375.

12 Lie, *Sar.*, pp. 42-43:267-273.

13 It is possible that Cutha supported Assyria at the beginning of the Šamaš-šuma-ukīn Revolt only because of the presence of Assyrian troops in or near that city (see p. 146).

14 In particular, Babylon underwent a long siege by Assyrian troops for supporting Mušēzib-Marduk. Babylonian cities did not, however, always support rebellions; for example, Dilbat and Nippur may have supported Assyria against Nabû-mukīn-zēri (see Brinkman, *PKB*, p. 237).

movements were not always the same as theirs, the urban population may have remained neutral simply out of a desire for self-preservation and stability. The cities may not have regarded the tribal leaders as legitimate candidates for the throne of Babylonia. While the descendants of Merodach-Baladan II could point to him and Erība-Marduk as ancestors who had been kings of Babylonia, and attempt to claim the kingship on the basis of inheritance, other Babylonians who were not related to them had been accepted as legitimate rulers of Babylonia in the meantime. The neutral position on the part of the city populations may have been one of the reasons rebel leaders occasionally carried out hostile actions against them.[15]

If there was a pro-Assyrian party in Babylonia, it is more likely to be found in the cities and towns of the south rather than in northern Babylonia. These centres were located in an area that was inhabited primarily by tribal groups and that might have been less prosperous because of the poorer agricultural condition of the land (part was swamp-marsh and part perhaps highly salinated).[16] Yet during this period the city of Ur experienced a time of prosperity, as attested by the building programme of Sîn-balāssu-iqbi. Some of the cities and towns of the south undoubtedly derived economic benefits from their location on trade routes to and from the Persian Gulf;[17] and Uruk, Ur, and probably Eridu likely gained because of their long-standing religious importance. Still it is quite possible that Assyrian kings were at least partially responsible for the prosperity of some of these cities and towns. Somewhat isolated from the important centres of northern Babylonia, the southern centres may have been intended to form bastions of pro-Assyrian sentiment, or stability, in this tribal area. These cities would have been natural antagonists of the tribal groups in the area, and favourable Assyrian actions may simply have reinforced their opposition to rebellion and the tribes who supported it. Sargon II had settled persons from Kummuḫu in the area of Bīt-Yakīn.[18] Could these immigrants have also supported Assyria because they felt insecure in their new homes? Thus, some of these cities and towns may have been in part artificially supported in order to help facilitate control over the tribes concentrated in the area.[19] Members of high-ranking families in

---

15 This could be why Merodach-Baladan II took captives from Sippar, Nippur, Babylon, and Borsippa to Dūr-Yakīn (Lie, *Sar.*, pp. 64-65:7-9).

16 Note that according to Wright's surface survey of the area of Ur the population reached its maximum height in the late Larsa-Old Babylonian period and declined markedly thereafter (despite a slight increase in Neo-Babylonian-Persian times) and Ur itself shrank in size between 1800 and 400, after which the area was practically abandoned (see Wright in Adams, *Heartland of Cities*, pp. 295-345, especially p. 336).

17 For Ur's contacts with the west, see Brinkman, *Or.* NS 34 (1965): 258.

18 Lie, *Sar.*, pp. 64-65:13-16.

19 Note also the case of Kissik in which the inhabitants of the town clearly distinguished themselves from the surrounding Chaldeans and stated that they were hated by them (*ABL* 210).

Babylonian cities who were dependent upon Assyria for their official positions and who were especially favoured by them probably helped maintain Assyrian control in the southern kingdom. In this connection, we may think of Nabû-ušabši at Uruk and the family of Ningal-iddin at Ur who kept their cities loyal to Ashurbanipal during the Šamaš-šuma-ukīn Revolt. Possibly they may be considered to have held "pro-Assyrian" views, but how large such a "party" may have been is unknown. In general, those who did not actively support rebel movements against Assyria might be classified more accurately as political pragmatists or realists rather than as pro-Assyrians or collaborators. Indeed, a common, negative view of Assyrian rule may have been one of the few factors unifying the heterogeneous population of Babylonia.

II. Assyria and Babylonia

The purpose of Assyria's policy toward Babylonia at this time seems clear. It was to keep Babylonia within Assyria's sphere of influence and under Assyria's control. Assyria was essentially successful in this since Babylonia was ruled by the Assyrian king, directly or indirectly, during all but a few years of this period. For many reasons the possession of Babylonia was desirable to the Assyrian empire. The most important may be summarized as follows:

1. Babylonia was a rich country, located on several important trade routes,[20] and thus a source of wealth for its Assyrian overlords.
2. For Assyria's security, it would be unwise to have an independent and potentially hostile neighbour.[21]
3. It was the practice for Assyrian kings to try to expand the area under their, and the god Aššur's, control.
4. If Babylonia were allowed to gain its freedom, other vassals would view it as a sign of Assyrian weakness and be encouraged to revolt.
5. Any Assyrian king who gave up Babylonia might find his position threatened in Assyria itself by those who thought such an action a sign of weakness.

In addition, historically, culturally, and religiously, Assyria and Babylonia were closely linked. Assyrians seem to have respected Babylonian

---

20 The most practical route from the coast of the Mediterranean to the Persian Gulf ran down the Euphrates, one end passing through Babylonia. Major trade routes ran from Babylonia to Elam (via Dēr) and the Iranian plateau (via Kermanshah).

21 This is particularly important because there was no natural barrier between the two countries, because Babylonia was historically a major force in the Near East, and because Babylonia was frequently in alliance with Elam, a perennial foe of Assyria.

culture and scholarship and often adopted Babylonian manners and customs.[22] Certainly some Assyrian monarchs appear to have taken personal pleasure in being honoured by the citizens of Babylonian cities and in worshipping in their ancient and highly revered temples (e.g., Esagila in Babylon and Ezida in Borsippa) and they were proud of the benefits they had bestowed upon Babylonian gods and temples. Tiglath-pileser III and Sargon II recorded how they had been welcomed by the officials and people of Babylonian cities and been honoured to partake of leftover offerings which had been dedicated to Babylonian gods.[23] Thus, some Assyrians felt that it would be proper for the two countries to be connected politically, whether directly (under the same king) or indirectly (under separate kings but with the king of Babylonia dependent upon the king of Assyria for his position). By equating their tutelary god Aššur with the Babylonian god Anšar, one of Marduk's forbears, they could defend their control of Babylonia on religious grounds. As Anšar, Aššur was of an older generation than Marduk in the divine order; thus, Marduk was subordinate to Aššur and Marduk's realm should be subordinate to Aššur's vicar on earth, the Assyrian king.[24]

In recognition of Babylonia's importance within the Assyrian empire, Assyrian kings made particular efforts to win the support of its people and it was given special status and privileges. It is true that toward the end of his reign Sennacherib broke with this policy and dealt roughly with Babylonia, but at that time he was acting under severe provocation caused in part by the loss of his son Aššur-nādin-šumi. When Esarhaddon reversed his father's policy toward Babylonia, he endeavoured to blunt any Babylonian criticism of Sennacherib's actions by stressing that Marduk had abandoned Babylon because of the sins of its own people and any Assyrian objection to the restoration of the city by avoiding criticism of Sennacherib and by stating that the gods had indicated their support for the rebuilding by means of omens. Assyria normally ruled subject states either by incorporating them directly into Assyria as provinces or by leaving them as vassal states under their own rulers. For the most part, Babylonia was incorporated into the empire as a unified state, with its own provinces and administrative structure intact,[25] and with its own king (though that king was at times also king of Assyria). Some

---

22 For example, Assyrian royal inscriptions were generally written in a Babylonian literary dialect and Babylonian gods were worshipped in Assyria.

23 See p. 248 n. 11.

24 However, evidence that this claim was made widely in Babylonia is meagre. The claim that the god Marduk had been begotten by the god Aššur is found in a few of Ashurbanipal's texts from Babylonia (Streck, *Asb.*, pp. 232-33:7-9, 242-43:23-26, and 244-45:36-41). On this matter, see chapter 5.

25 Sargon II had divided the land into two parts, one under the governor of Babylon and the other under the governor of Gambūlu (Lie, *Sar.*, pp. 66-67:1); however, there is no evidence that that division remained in effect after his reign.

areas of Babylonia east of the Tigris (Dēr, Laḫīru, and possibly Dūr-Šarrukku) were, however, annexed to Assyria because of their strategic location—they faced Elam and were relatively easily accessible from Assyria. During the reign of Sennacherib after 689, when there was no separate kingship, Babylonia was apparently incorporated directly into the Assyrian empire under the king of Assyria. The importance of Babylonia to the Assyrian rulers is also reflected in the fact that the rulership of Babylonia was the only specific foreign title that the Neo-Assyrian kings generally included in their royal titulary.[26]

For over one hundred years (*c.* 730 to 615) the Neo-Assyrian kings attempted to control Babylonia and tried several different methods to govern the country. None of these methods proved effective for long, undoubtedly due in part to the heterogeneous nature of the Babylonian state and population. During the period in question, they tried abolition of the kingship of Babylonia and direct rule by the king of Assyria (Sennacherib), and assumption of the throne of Babylonia by the king of Assyria (Esarhaddon), by the brother of the king of Assyria (Šamaš-šuma-ukīn), and by a third party (Kandalānu);[27] and previously, Sennacherib had tried entrusting the rulership of Babylonia to his heir, Aššur-nādin-šumi. The continuing question of how to govern Babylonia was Assyria's "Babylonian problem."[28] Assyrian kings were reluctant to delegate authority within Babylonia, and, even when there were kings of Babylonia during the reign of Ashurbanipal, the Assyrian king continued to interfere there.

For Assyria to maintain control over its southern neighbour, Babylonia had to be kept militarily weak and dependent upon Assyria. It should not have any substantial standing military force of its own lest that prompt it to revolt, and Babylonian contacts with foreign countries should be carefully monitored, lest they result in the making of alliances against Assyria. Babylonia should have no central government of its own with any real power and authority in order to prevent united action by the Babylonian people against Assyria.

---

[26] See Seux, *Épithètes*, pp. 278 and 301-303. As titles reflecting the rulership of Babylonia, I include "viceroy of Babylon," "king of Babylon," "king of Karduniaš," and "king of Sumer and Akkad." Esarhaddon also took the titles "king of Egypt" (e.g., Borger, *Esarh.*, p. 36 §24:5), "king of Subartu, Amurrû, Gutium, and vast Ḫatti" (e.g., *ibid.*, p. 80 §53:27-28), "king of the kings of Egypt, Patros, and Kush" (e.g., *ibid.*, p. 72 §44:4-5), and "king of the kings of Dilmun, Magan, and Meluḫḫa" (e.g., *ibid.*, p. 80 §53:28-29).

[27] As noted above (p. 195), it is possible that Kandalānu was a brother of Ashurbanipal or a member of the Assyrian royal family.

[28] With regard to Assyria's "Babylonian problem," see in particular Brinkman, *JCS* 25 (1973): 89-95 and Machinist, *WBJ* 1984-85, pp. 353-64.

Neo-Assyrian kings frequently resettled rebellious and defeated groups far from their original homes as a means of punishment and pacification.[29] Before this period began, Babylonia (especially the southern part of the country) had been the area most effected by Assyrian deportations, both with regard to the number of individuals removed and to the frequency of deportations. No contemporary evidence exists of mass deportations from Babylonia during the years 689-627, though Ashurbanipal may have deported some people from Babylonia to Syria-Palestine, quite likely after the rebellion of 652-648. On the contrary, Esarhaddon claims to have returned to Babylon its people who had been enslaved and dispersed after the destruction of the city by Sennacherib.[30] No mass atrocities are recorded as having been committed against Babylonians, although bodies of important rebels could be subject to degradation[31] and, after the capture of Babylon in 648, a number of rebels were killed by cruel methods (see chapter 8).

As discussed in chapter 10, oaths of allegiance were regularly imposed on local officials; they were required to swear loyalty to the Assyrian king and to report to him whatever they saw or heard. Failure to observe the oaths could result in swift punishment. It is possible that attempts were made to educate individual Babylonians in pro-Assyrian views so that they might one day hold official positions, but this is not absolutely proven as yet. At times individual Babylonians were held in Assyria, presumably as hostages for their families' or tribes' loyalty; however, there is no evidence how widespread this practice was. For the most part, Assyria seems to have relied upon the quick response of its troops stationed in nearby Assyria to deal with any unrest in Babylonia that the local authorities could not handle.[32] There is no clear evidence of Assyrian garrisons in Babylonia itself.[33] Thus they fostered and

---

29 On the Assyrian practice of deportation, see Oded, *Deportations*, and note Postgate, *BiOr* 38 (1981): 636-38. Deportations were also used to populate other areas (e.g., vulnerable border areas) and to provide labourers for imperial building projects.

30 Ezra 4:9-10 and Borger, *Esarh.*, p. 25 §11 episode 37. Note also the unnamed Assyrian king (Sennacherib or Ashurbanipal?) mentioned in 2 Kings 17:24 who settled people from Babylon and Cutha in Samaria and the reference to people having been settled in Syria-Palestine by Esarhaddon in Ezra 4:2, though where they came from is not stated.

31 For example, the head of Nabû-bēl-šumāti was hung around the neck of Nabû-qātē-ṣabat (Streck, *Asb.*, pp. 60-63 vii 39-50). Rich rewards could be promised for the capture of prominent rebels (*ABL* 292).

32 Note however Ashurbanipal's delay in sending troops to aid Babylon against Urtak's invasion (see above, p. 120). The necessity of having to wait for troops to arrive from Assyria to deal with disturbances may not have found favour with Babylonians. Military forces from the nearby provinces of Arrapḫa and Zamū, led by their governors, were active in Babylonia during the Šamaš-šuma-ukīn Revolt (e.g., *ABL* 754). Parpola (*ARINH*, p. 132) points out that the seats of office of these two governors were situated along watercourses by which they could quickly reach Babylonia.

33 See chapter 10; though as suggested there, Nippur may well have been garrisoned after the Šamaš-šuma-ukīn Revolt.

maintained an efficient intelligence-gathering network (both official and unofficial) to report in detail on conditions in Babylonia.[34] Although the Assyrian kings attempted to keep the Babylonian populace quiet by various means, on occasion military campaigns were necessary. While these were usually directed against disruptive tribal groups, they could also be against rebellious urban citizenry. On occasion, the Assyrians had recourse to siege warfare to reduce Babylonian cities. A siege necessitated tying up a large body of troops for a considerable period of time, as for instance for the two-year siege of Babylon during the Šamaš-šuma-ukīn Revolt, and was ordered only when other means had failed.[35]

It may have been a policy of the Assyrian kings to facilitate control of Babylonia by attempting to divide that country internally, or at least to take advantage of already existing divisions, and in doing so to champion the cause of the urban populations as opposed to that of the tribal groups. Prior to the period 689-627, Tiglath-pileser III and Sargon II had described themselves in their inscriptions as persons who had saved Babylonia from tribal groups, and emissaries of Tiglath-pileser III may have attempted to incite Babylonian city dwellers against Chaldeans by appealing to the citizens of Babylon to abandon Nabû-mukīn-zēri because he was a Chaldean.[36] The cities were undoubtedly chosen for special consideration since the urban populations were naturally less prone to rebellion than the tribal groups and formed the core (and majority?) of the Babylonian state and since the city dwellers were the bearers of the classical Babylonian culture which at least some Assyrians admired and imitated. It would also be easier to confer favours upon a settled population than on unsettled, or partially settled, tribes with their own native hierarchical structures. Special privileges, including the exemption from at least some taxes and duties, were granted to the inhabitants of certain towns; temples and fortification works of cities were built or restored; divine statues were refurbished and honoured with sacrifical offerings. While some tribal groups are known to have paid tribute to Esarhaddon, there is no clear evidence of the city populations doing so until after Ashurbanipal's victory over Šamaš-šuma-ukīn in 648. Unconsciously the Assyrians may have championed the urban populations simply because they were more submissive than the tribal groups, but some notion of cause and effect cannot be excluded from consideration. It must be stressed again,

---

[34] See Brinkman in *Power and Propaganda*, p. 235.

[35] See Eph'al, *HHI*, pp. 93-94.

[36] Saggs, *Iraq* 17 (1955): 23-26 and pl. 4 no. 1:14-16; the exact interpretation of the relevant section of this letter is uncertain. In addition, in his royal inscriptions, Esarhaddon pointed out that it was Nabû-zēr-kitti-līšir, a member of the Bīt-Yakīn tribe and governor of the Sealand, who had opposed Ur in 680, and the Chaldean Bīt-Dakkūri who had seized control of land belonging to the citizens of Babylon and Borsippa (Borger, *Esarh.*, pp. 46-48 and 52 §27 episodes 4 and 12).

however, that we are dependent upon Assyrian or Assyrian-oriented sources for most of our information; and this may render our view of conditions and events unreliable or distorted. Policy alone may not have prompted the Assyrian monarchs to treat these cities well; as mentioned earlier, many may have admired Babylonian culture, as exemplified in these ancient cities.

III. Elam and Babylonia

The general purpose of Elam's policy toward Babylonia was clearly to remove it from Assyrian control and to eliminate it as a possible threat to Elam's own security. Elamite kings undoubtedly wished to gain an ally against powerful Assyria and to turn Babylonia into a buffer state between itself and Assyria, or at least to keep Assyria occupied in Babylonia and out of Elam. With its close ties to Babylonia,[37] Elam wanted to draw that country into its own sphere of influence and, in particular, to gain control over the border region (in particular the Sealand and the area of the Gambūlu). The border between Elam and Babylonia had always been fluid and penetrable as tribes moved to exploit the natural resources of the region, as marshes expanded and receded, as towns and groupings changed their formal and informal allegiance, and as military ventures proved successful or unsuccessful.[38] To these ends Elam on occasion invaded Babylonia, provided military aid and other support for rebel movements, and gave refuge to rebel fugitives, as it had done in the past. Not all of their interventions in Babylonia were caused by anti-Assyrian feeling alone; one must not ignore the possibility that some were motivated simply by greed. Certainly Elamite kings often accepted a monetary inducement for their support of Babylonian rebels.

Nevertheless, Elamite kings were not unswerving in their policy of aiding anti-Assyrian movements in Babylonia. During the seventh century, there was a rapid turn-over in rulers of Elam, the result of illnesses, foreign invasions, and internal revolts. This, and the Elamite system of having several rulers at the same time, prevented Elam from maintaining any one policy with regard to Assyria and Babylonia for a long time.[39] In addition, Elamite rulers undoubtedly realized that at times it would have been sheer

---

[37] Note for example the presence of Babylonians resident in Ḫādalu (=Ḫīdalu) and forming an assembly there (Leichty, *AnSt* 33 [1983]: 153-55 and pl. 34). Leichty suggests that these Babylonians had gone to the city when Ashurbanipal put Tammarītu on the throne there.

[38] With regard to the border between Babylonia and Elam between 750 and 625, see Brinkman in *Steve Festschrift*, pp. 199-207.

[39] The control which Elamite kings had over their own subjects and territory fluctuated. Babylonian rebels who had taken refuge in Elam and their Elamite supporters could even flout the Elamite king (see *ABL* 281).

folly to risk incurring Assyrian wrath—when Assyria was strong, united, and unoccupied elsewhere and, possibly, when there was internal dissension or division in Elam itself. Elamites were even willing to turn to Assyrian kings for aid against their own countrymen. Ḫumban-nikaš II and Tammarītu both sought aid from Ashurbanipal in their efforts to gain control of Elam. Elamite supporters of deposed rulers or pretenders to the throne are likely to have aided the Assyrians in restoring them.[40] In order to win favour with Assyria, Elamites had killed the Babylonian rebel leader Nabû-zēr-kitti-līšir when he sought refuge in Elam in the time of Ḫumban-ḫaltaš II. In addition, Urtak maintained peaceful relations with Assyria in the time of Esarhaddon and at the beginning of Ashurbanipal's reign and Indabibi contemplated establishing friendly relations in 649. Still, both Urtak and Indabibi eventually supported Babylonian rebels, and the action of Ḫumban-ḫaltaš II may have been prompted by the knowledge that Assyrian troops were advancing south. Around the time of the Šamaš-šuma-ukīn Revolt, several persons ruled Elam in rapid succession, each having taken the throne after the violent deposition of his predecessor; but each new monarch aided the rebels in Babylonia.

Depending upon their personal loyalties, Babylonians could see in Elam an enemy or a helper. Elamite kings could send troops into Babylonia, at times aiding Babylonians against Assyria and at times simply for their own aggrandizement and profit; they could also give refuge to Babylonian rebels or deny it to them. Babylonians seeking outside help against Assyria, or their fellow Babylonians, naturally turned to Elam because that country was its only other neighbour that was also a well-organized state, because it was a perennial foe of Assyria, and because it had been known to provide aid in the recent past (to Merodach-Baladan II and Mušēzib-Marduk). Elamite contacts were particularly close with the tribal groups located along the border, especially the Gambūlu tribe (who at times appear to have been subject to Elam) and the rulers of the Chaldean Bīt-Yakīn (who usually supported or led the anti-Assyrian movements at this time). However, as a result of Assyrian military operations directed against it, and its own internal problems, by the end of the period in question Elam appears to have been effectively destroyed as a political force in the Near East. Elam was no longer able to stand as a barrier between the Mesopotamian lowland and the tribes of the Iranian plateau.

---

[40] Reade points out that individuals in Elamite clothing are depicted as fighting alongside Assyrians on reliefs of Sennacherib and Ashurbanipal (*Iraq* 34 [1972]: 107) and military personnel are known to have accompanied Ḫumban-nikaš II when he fled to Assyria from Teumman (e.g., Piepkorn, *Asb.*, pp. 60-61 iv 74-86).

CHAPTER 12

CONCLUSION

At the end of 689 Babylonia had reached a low point in its political existence. The country was totally controlled by Assyria, and was incorporated directly into the Assyrian empire. There was no longer a "king of Babylon" (even one who was also ruler of Assyria), and Babylon, the venerable capital of the land, lay devastated and abandoned. Finally, the statue of Marduk, the head of the Babylonian pantheon and tutelary god of Babylon, had been destroyed or carried off to Assyria, a fact that was to make the celebration of the important New Year's festival impossible for twenty years. During the years 689-627, Babylonia remained weak, disunited, and subject to Assyria. Although revolts did occur sporadically throughout these years, only once was Assyria's domination seriously challenged, during the Šamaš-šuma-ukīn Revolt of 652-648; even then, Assyria never lost control of all the country and eventually crushed the rebels. Nevertheless, a few short years after this period ended, Babylonia was to rise to its greatest height under the Neo-Babylonian dynasty, to destroy its former overlord, Assyria, and to win from that country hegemony over western Asia.

Our knowledge of Babylonia and its political history during these important years is uneven, even though this is one of the better documented periods in Babylonian history. Only two portions of this period are fairly well known—the reign of Esarhaddon (in particular the second half of his reign) and the years around the Šamaš-šuma-ukīn Revolt. While various types of sources provide information for this study, most of the textual sources are Assyrian or Assyrian-oriented in character; thus, a pro-Assyrian bias is inevitably reflected in our data.

Babylonia's internal disunity was its major weakness, making it difficult for the country to unite behind one leader. A number of different population groups made up the Babylonian state and these had varying backgrounds and lifestyles, interests and purposes. Because of Assyrian and Elamite interference and internal rebellions, not one Babylonian family had held the kingship of Babylonia for any length of time in the recent past. Thus there was no one individual or family who could make a claim to the throne which would find ready acceptance by the people as a whole and who could unite the country against the Assyrians. Only once did a large segment of the population unite against Assyria, and then it was behind a brother of the

Assyrian king. It is characteristic of this period that it was the tribal groups, especially the Chaldean tribes, who were the most active in opposing Assyria. In particular it was the ruling family of the Chaldean Bīt-Yakīn tribe, the descendants of the infamous rebel Merodach-Baladan II, who led the opposition. With their base in the marshes of the Sealand, their close relations with Elam, and their reasonable claim to the throne of Babylonia,[1] rulers of the Bīt-Yakīn were the natural leaders of the resistance. Also characteristic of this period was a close connection between Elam and Babylonian rebels, a continuation of the arrangement attested earlier in the first millennium.

Assyrian kings made a special effort to reconcile Babylonians to Assyrian rule, by experimenting with various methods of governing the southern kingdom, and by showing favour to its cities, people, and gods. Although a large number of rebels were executed after the revolts of 694-689 and 652-648, no mass atrocities committed by Assyrian troops against Babylonians are recorded for the years 689-627 and no large-scale deportations are known to have occurred. Yet, despite Babylonia's internal divisions, its lack of a militaristic tradition, and its vulnerable position in relation to its powerful northern neighbour, Babylonia remained restless and refused to be absorbed by Assyria. Although the two countries possessed similar cultures, and their histories had been connected for many centuries, Babylonia had a long history as a separate, independent state—albeit under numerous short-lived dynasties of various origins. Indeed, it was only after about 730 that Assyrian kings had seriously tried to make Babylonia part of their empire.[2] Thus, nationalistic sentiment on the part of the Babylonians was undoubtedly a major cause of their resistance to Assyrian overlordship. Despite various attempts to find a solution to the thorny problem of how to govern Babylonia, the Assyrian kings could not find an answer which met Babylonian approval and was effective for any length of time. The knowledge that Assyrian kings put Assyria's interests before those of Babylonia, and that Assyrian-appointed kings in Babylonia did not have real independence of action, would have been galling to the Babylonians. Some jarring of sensitivities may have resulted simply from daily contact between conquered and conqueror. Possibly the Babylonians even regarded their northern neighbours as their cultural inferiors since the Assyrians esteemed, and frequently imitated, Babylonian customs while the Babylonians did not tend to adopt Assyrian

---

[1] Although both Erība-Marduk and Merodach-Baladan II of the Bīt-Yakīn tribe had been kings of Babylonia, their reigns had not been successive and other individuals had been acknowledged as rulers of the country in the meantime. This meant that that family's claim to the throne could be disputed.

[2] Tiglath-pileser III assumed the kingship of Babylonia in 729 after defeating Nabû-mukīn-zēri (Grayson, *Chronicles*, no. 1 i 19-23).

ways or manners. The harsh actions of Assyrian kings in the past (such as the large-scale deportations of tribal groups, the destruction of Babylon, and the removal of Babylonian gods to Assyria) probably continued to rankle in Babylonian hearts in spite of Esarhaddon's actions to redress Babylonia's grievances. Assyria's troubles elsewhere (for example in Egypt) may have provided the occasion for those opposed to Assyrian rule to revolt. Likely some of the anti-Assyrian feeling was fed or fomented by individuals who hoped to use Babylonian antipathy toward Assyria as a springboard to increase their own power and wealth. Elamite kings undoubtedly encouraged anti-Assyrian feeling in Babylonia in order to weaken Assyria's hold over that country and thereby to make their own positions more secure. These are only a few suggestions that might help explain Babylonia's continual opposition to Assyrian domination during the years 689-627; none can be proven, though all may have been present.[3]

The last twenty years of the period are poorly known. The conditions that were developing in Babylonia and the Near East in general during these years led to the rise of Nabopolassar, who became king of Babylonia in 626, and to the beginning of Assyria's decline. A major cause of Assyria's rapid collapse between 627 and 609 was probably the fact that Esarhaddon and Ashurbanipal had over-extended the strength of Assyria with their conquests of Egypt and Elam. Neither country was held by the Assyrians for long; it was really only while the Assyrian army was present on their soil that they formed part of the Assyrian empire. Assyria proper was just not large enough to maintain this empire,[4] and the lengthy revolt of Šamaš-šuma-ukīn probably strained its men and resources to the limit. For four long years Assyria was kept occupied in Babylonia, and losses in men and equipment may well have been high in view of the intensity of the fighting. In the three or four years immediately following the fall of Babylon in 648, Assyria was forced to expend further time and energy dealing with Šamaš-šuma-ukīn's erstwhile allies, Elam and the Arabs, and with others who had made use of Assyria's preoccupation with the rebellion in Babylonia to declare their own independence (the cities of Akko and Ušû). The Assyrians are not known to have conducted any major campaigns during the remainder of the reign of Ashurbanipal. While this may be simply because we have not found the Assyrian king's annals for the later part of his reign, it also may be because no important campaigns took place during that time. Ashurbanipal's demonstration of Assyria's power may have cowed its vassals into

---

3 In addition, there is the possibility that Babylonians were conscripted into the Assyrian army, or compelled to serve in Assyria's wars, on two or three occasions (see chapter 10 on the use and meaning of the phrase *biḫirtu beḫēru*); this practice would surely not have found favour in Babylonia.

4 Assyria had to draw upon non-Assyrians for military support.

submission and made its neighbours wary of provoking Assyria's anger. At the same time, however, Assyria may well have been worn out from dealing with Šamaš-šuma-ukīn and his allies, and needed time to recover militarily and politically and to reaffirm and strengthen its position over the lands it held. Of course, in the years following 627, the internal struggle over the Assyrian throne between Aššur-etil-ilāni, Sîn-šumu-līšir, and Sîn-šarra-iškun, and the emergence of a new and powerful foe in Iran, the Medes, were the final events which doomed the Assyrian empire. Olmstead describes Esarhaddon's restoration of Babylon and his later division of the empire between Ashurbanipal and Šamaš-šuma-ukīn as colossal blunders leading to the collapse of the empire. He concludes that the Assyrians "had not, save in Sennacherib alone, rulers who had the moral courage to force Babylon to come within the system [the Assyrian imperial organization]. Babylon remained an open sore and from this infection of the body politic came destruction ..."[5] We can basically agree with this view. It was in large part Assyria's inability to find an effective and long-lasting method of controlling Babylonia and its resurrection of Babylon, a long-time foe and rival, which led to Assyria's downfall. However, we are speaking with the benefit of hindsight. A Babylonia lacking its ancient capital and incorporated politically within the empire might still have found sufficient courage and support to continue its opposition to Assyria. Indeed, Assyrian oppression may have strengthened Babylonia's will to oppose its northern neighbour. Esarhaddon's actions were noble and innovative measures which under certain circumstances might have succeeded in making Assyrian dominion palatable to the Babylonians.

Although Babylonian culture exerted great influence on Assyria, almost no Assyrian influence on Babylonia can be detected at this time in spite of the fact that Babylonia had been under Assyrian rule, off and on, since the reign of Tiglath-pileser III. Babylonia was affected greatly by Assyria, but influenced little. There is even little direct evidence of trade between Assyria and Babylonia during the years 689-627 although goods must have moved from one country to the other, at least in the form of booty, gifts, and taxes.

Babylonia remained in political eclipse throughout the period 689-627, but Babylonian life and culture flourished, continuing an improvement in conditions already detectable in the last part of the previous century. Temples were built or restored; religious and scholarly works were composed or copied; and the Sumerian language continued to be used for some royal inscriptions. Astronomical sightings were made and recorded; indeed, the oldest astronomical diary known was written during this period. The

[5] *American Political Science Review* 12 (1918): 76-77. He also suggests that if Ashurbanipal had destroyed Babylon after he took the city in 648 the fall of the Assyrian empire might have been indefinitely postponed.

increasing number of documents attesting to business transactions likely mirrors improving economic conditions in the land. Although numerous texts indicate the continuing importance of the cuneiform script and the Akkadian language, it is probable that Aramaic was continuing to make inroads as the everyday language of the people.[6] The population of parts of Babylonia may have increased in size,[7] and at Babylon and Ur evidence of increased prosperity may be detected in the archaeological remains.[8]

Although 689-627 may be characterized as a period of political weakness and disunity in Babylonia, a time when the land was dominated by its northern neighbour Assyria, it was also a period of internal vigour and a turning point in Babylonia's existence. During this low point in Babylonia's history, momentum was building up which was to result in the founding of the Neo-Babylonian kingdom by Nabopolassar. This was undoubtedly sparked in part by an increasingly common and negative response to Assyria, a response which helped unite the heterogeneous population of Babylonia. Many factors, nationalistic feeling undoubtedly not the least, engendered a growing resistance to Assyrian rule; and, just as it was tribal groups who had led Babylonia to its most important periods in the past (the Amorites in the Old Babylonian period and the Kassites in the Middle Babylonian), so it was the Chaldean tribes who were the main champions of Babylonian independence during these years.

---

6 With regard to the use and influence of the Aramaic language in Babylonia, see p. 48.

7 See chapter 2.

8 In the Merkes quarter at Babylon, the level identified by the excavator as representing the rebuilding by Esarhaddon and his successors had more substantial remains than had the "pre-destruction" level (see chapter 5). It must be pointed out, however, that the dating of the various levels cannot be considered proven because clear chronological linkage is lacking. During the time of Sîn-balassu-iqbi as governor of Ur, an ambitious building programme was carried out at that city. This was the first major building activity attested at Ur since the Kassite period.

APPENDIX A

Babylonian Economic Texts: A Tabular Summary

The following four tables (nos. 3-6) summarize the information about Babylonian economic documents dated by the regnal years of Esarhaddon, Ashurbanipal, Šamaš-šuma-ukīn, and Kandalānu which is presented by J.A. Brinkman and D.A. Kennedy in their study "Documentary Evidence for the Economic Base of Early Neo-Babylonian Society: A Survey of Dated Babylonian Economic Texts, 721-626 B.C.," *JCS* 35 (1983): 1-90, with supplement in *JCS* 38 (1986): 99-106.[1] Full bibliographies for each document are given in that study. Because there are only three documents dated by the regnal years of Sennacherib from the period of concern, no table was prepared for these; they are discussed in Appendix C.

1 Abbreviated as *B-K* in this study.

APPENDIX B

Babylonian Officials

In order to view the numerous letters of the period against their historical background and to arrive at an understanding of the complex interrelationships at work, it is necessary to determine who held the various important positions within the provincial administration of Babylonia and when they did so. The list presented below is an attempt to help provide such a framework and is composed primarily of officials mentioned in the witness lists of economic texts. These are our most reliable sources of information; in addition to giving the official's name, title, and occasionally family or paternal name, they are usually dated, thus indicating that the individual held office on that particular date. A number of officials who are specifically given official titles in other documents (for example, chronicles, royal inscriptions, and letters) have also been included if we can determine with a reasonable degree of certainty when that person held office. In including individuals in this list and indicating their dates, I have preferred to take a conservative viewpoint. Thus, for example, such important individuals as Nabû-bēl-šumāti and Bēl-ibni are not included because there is no clear statement as to what office(s) they held, even though we may assume that these two held some post over the Sealand (see above).[1] Unless a date is clearly given (as in economic texts and chronicles) or obtainable with only minimal argument (as in the case of Ningal-iddin holding the governorship of Ur in Esarhaddon's first regnal year),[2] an indication such as "time of RN," "early in the reign of RN," or occasionally "*c.* 656-653?" is given.[3] For the purposes of this list, I have not assumed that an individual held any office at the time he corresponded with the king, even though on (apparently) official business, and even if the individual is known to have held a particular office at some other point in time, unless he is specifically given a title in the letter. In addition, the date a royal inscription was composed or copied is not automatically assumed as the

---

[1] Leaders of the tribal groups have also not been included nor for the most part have individuals given titles in letters of the period whose place of office and dates are unknown or uncertain.

[2] No one inscription states that Ningal-iddin held this office on that date; however, one of Esarhaddon's inscriptions states that Ningal-iddin was governor of Ur when that city was besieged by Nabû-zēr-kitti-līšir and a chronicle says that (Nabû)-zēr-kitti-līšir camped against Ur in Esarhaddon's first regnal year.

[3] I have sometimes proposed a more exact dating in the text, generally in chapters 5-9.

date for an official mentioned in that text. Royal inscriptions tend to describe events covering several years and it cannot be taken for granted that the individual was still in office when the events relating to him were finally recorded.[4]

[4] In the notes connected with the entries below, references to individuals (usually without their titles) in other texts are sometimes given; such references are to be considered illustrative and not necessarily exhaustive.

1. AKKAD

a) Šamaš-danninanni[5]	*šaknu/šakin māti*	eponymy of Šamaš-danninanni (*c*. 643-642?)

2. BABYLON[6]

a) Aqara[7]	*bēl pīḫati*	eponymy of Aqara (*c*. 656-653?)
Marduk-[(...)] [*mār*?] Saggilaya[8]	*bēl pīḫati*	year 15 Kan. (633)
Šamaš-danninanni[9]	*(ša) pīḫati*	eponymy of Šamaš-danninanni (*c*. 643-642?)
b) Ubāru[10]	*šākin ṭēmi*	eponymy of Ubāru (early in reign of Esar.?)
Bēl-lē'i-(kalama) *mār* Saggilaya[11]	*šākin ṭēmi*	year 14 Ššu (654)
Nabû-nādin-aḫi *mār* Egibi[12]	*šākin ṭēmi*	time of Kan.
[PN? *mār*? Ši?]gū'a[13]	*šākin ṭēmi*	time of Kan.
c) Šuma-iddin[14]	*šatammu* of Esagila	eponymy of Ubāru (early in reign of Esar.?)

---

[5] See Falkner, *AfO* 17 (1954-56): 106, 116 and 118, and note also *BIN* 2 132:10 and 12 (collation J.A. Brinkman). His title is written LÚ.GAR.KUR KUR URI.KI (5 *R* pl. 10 x 122); with regard to this title (*šaknu/šakin māti*), see pp. 225-26 n. 79. He also bore the title (*ša*) *pīḫati* (LÚ.NAM) of Babylon. For the date of his eponymy, see chapter 3. His tenure as governor of Akkad overlapped that of Kudurru as governor of Uruk; see *BIN* 2 132:12-13 and p. 201.

[6] It was once thought that the eponym in 655 was the governor of Babylon (e.g., Ungnad in *RLA* 2, pp. 428 and 441), but see Weidner, *AfO* 13 (1939-41): 206-207.

[7] Frame, *RA* 76 (1982): 160 line 44 and 8-B-10 (*B-K* S.1-2). See Appendix C.

[8] Weidner, *AfO* 16 (1952-53): pl. 5 no. 7:14 (*B-K* L.87).

[9] See above, n. 5.

[10] Pinches, *AfO* 13 (1939-41): pl. 4 rev. 26 (*B-K* S.7; name written ᵐ*ú-bar*). See Appendix C for other references to this individual and the date of his career.

[11] Budge, *ZA* 3 (1888): 228 no. 5:4-5 and *TCL* 12 11:9-10 (*B-K* K.84 and K.86). Possibly this person is to be identified with Bēl-lē'i-kalama *mār* Esaggilaya who bore the title *šatammu* in year 6(+) of Šamaš-šuma-ukīn; see below.

[12] *VAS* 5 5:28-29 (*B-K* L.176).

[13] BM 50749:5' (*B-K* L.184); [...]-*gu-ú-a* LÚ.GAR.KU TIN.TIR.[KI].

[14] Pinches, *AfO* 13 (1939-41): pl. 4 rev. 1 (*B-K* S.7). He is likely to be identified with the author of TKSM 21/676 (Landsberger, *Brief*, pp. 5-13 and 63-64). See also *CT* 54 439:6'?

? Bēl-lēʾi-kalama *mār* Esaggilaya[15]	*šatammu* of E[sagila?]	year 6(+) Ššu (662[-])
[...] x-*ia*[16]	*šatammu*	time of Kan.
d) Rībānu[17]	*qīpu* of Esagila	year 6(+) Ššu (662[-])
Marduk-rāʾim-šarri[18]	*qīpu* of Esagila	year 15 Kan. (633)
e) Bēl-ēṭir[19]	*dayyānu* of Babylon	acc. year Ššu (668)

3. BORSIPPA[20]

a) Šamaš-zēra-iqīša *mār* Arkât-ayīti-damqā[21]	*šākin ṭēmi*	year 5 Esar. (676)
Nabû-bēl-šumāti *mār* Iliya[22]	*šākin ṭēmi*	years 6(+), 7, 12, 14, and 15/16 Ššu (662[-], 661, 656, 654, and 653/652)

---

15 Steinmetzer, *Deimel Festschrift*, p. 306 rev. 23 (title not preserved; dated at Sippar) and *BBSt* 10 rev. 48 (*B-K* K.163 and K.169); see above, p. 233. The latter text was composed sometime between the sixth (662) and the ninth (659) years of Šamaš-šuma-ukīn (collated); the published copies have year nine. This official is possibly to be identified with the governor of Babylon in 654. The restoration E[sagila] was proposed by Landsberger in *Brief*, p. 59. *CAD* 17/1 (Š), p. 163 restores E[zida]; however, Nabû-nādin-šumi is attested as *šatammu* of Ezida from at least 676 to 653 and the two kudurrus must date from that period.

16 *VAS* 5 5:30 (*B-K* L.176). The temple in which he served is not mentioned; however, he is also given the title *ērib bīti* of Marduk and is mentioned in the witness list after the governor of Babylon. San Nicolò and Ungnad (*NRVU*, p. 53 no. 33) suggest that the name be read Kabtiya ([Ka]bti-ja).

17 *BBSt* 10 rev. 44 (*B-K* K.169); see above, p. 232. Landsberger (*Brief*, p. 59) seems to suggest that Nūrānu, who bears the title LÚ *q*[*í*-(*i*)-*pi*? ...] in Steinmetzer, *Deimel Festschrift*, p. 306 rev. 19 (*B-K* K.163; dated at Sippar), was also *qīpu* of Esagila.

18 Weidner, *AfO* 16 (1952-53): pl. 5 no. 7:10-11 (*B-K* L.87).

19 Grayson, *Chronicles*, no. 1 iv 38 and no. 14:39 (name not given in the latter source). The term "judge of Babylon" could refer to a title or to an occupation together with the location at which it was practised. In the second of the two chronicle references, the individual's personal name is not given. If this omission was not a scribal error, it would suggest that the scribe took the term to refer to a particular office.

20 See in particular Frame, *JCS* 36 (1984): 67-80. A possible *qīpu* of Ezida in the time of Šamaš-šuma-ukīn may have been Taklāk?-ana-Nabû?; see below sub 16.

21 BM 26523:12-13 and Speleers, *Recueil*, no. 278 rev. 6-7 (*B-K* I.10 and I.28). See also Legrain, *RA* 10 (1913): 68 no. 46:20 (first witness, but without title; *B-K* K.14, Borsippa year 4 [664] of Šamaš-šuma-ukīn). On the family name (likely an error for Arkât-ilī-damqā), see Frame, *JCS* 36 (1984): 68-69.

22 *BBSt* 10 rev. 47 (see above, p. 233); *TCL* 12 9:24-25; L 4724 rev. 4 (partially restored; information courtesy F. Joannès); YBC 11426:20; NBC 8397:23-24; CBS 7756 rev. 1-2; VAT 13392:24; and *TuM* 2-3 17:25-26 (*B-K* K.169, K. 23, K.50a, K.55, K.56, K.83, K.151, and K.173). Cf. *ABL* 834; see Frame, *JCS* 36 (1984): 70 n. 16.

Nabû-šuma-uṣur *mār* Iliya[23]	*šākin ṭēmi*	years 8, 10, and 12 Ššu (660, 658, and 656)
Marduk-nāṣir *mār* Nūr-Papsukkal[24]	*šākin ṭēmi*	year 7 Kan. (641)
Nabû-zēru-līšir *mār* Arkât-ilī-damqā[25]	*šākin ṭēmi*	year 13 Kan. (635)
b) Nādinu[26]	*šatammu* of Ezida	eponymy of Ubāru (early in reign of Esar.?)
Nabû-nādin-šumi *mār* Nūr-Papsukkal[27]	*šatammu* of Ezida	year 5 Esar. (676); years 7, 10, 12, 14, and 15/16 Sšu (661, 658, 656, 654, and 653/652)
Nabû-apla-iddin *mār* Nūr-Papsukkal[28]	*šatammu* of Ezida	year 7 Kan. (641)
Zēr-Bābili *mār* Nūr-Papsukkal[29]	*šatammu* of Ezida	year 13 Kan. (635)

4. CUTHA

a) Ašaridu[30]	*šākin ṭēmi*	year 12 Ššu (656)

---

[23] *TuM* 2-3 11:19, 12:21-22, and 23:18' (title not preserved, but fully preserved in duplicate MAH 16232), and *OECT* 12 pl. 22 A 131:23 (*B-K* K.29, K.34, K.60-61, and K.67). The individual's name could also be read Nabû-nādin-aḫi since in every case the name is written ^{md}AG-MU-ŠEŠ.

[24] *TCL* 12 6:27-28 (*B-K* L.21); he is also given the title of *ērib būti* of Nabû.

[25] *TuM* 2-3 14:23-24 (*B-K* L.68).

[26] Pinches, *AfO* 13 (1939-41): pl. 4 rev. 2 (*B-K* S.7).

[27] BM 26523:14-15 and Speleers, *Recueil*, no. 278 rev. 8 (*B-K* I.10 and I.28). *TCL* 12 9:26; *TuM* 2-3 12:23-24; L 4724 rev. 2-3 (partially restored; information courtesy F. Joannès); YBC 11426:21-22; NBC 8397:21-22; *TuM* 2-3 23:19' (title not preserved, but fully preserved in duplicate MAH 16232); *OECT* 12 pl. 22 A 131:24-25; CBS 7756 rev. 3-4; VAT 13392:22-23; and *TuM* 2-3 17:27-28 (partially restored) (*B-K* K.23, K.34, K.50a, K.55, K.56, K.60-61, K.67, K.83, K.151, and K.173). He also bore the title *ērib būti* of Nabû (e.g. *TuM* 2-3 12).

[28] *TCL* 12 6:29-30 (*B-K* L.21); he is also given the title *ērib būti* of Nabû.

[29] *TuM* 2-3 14:25-26 (*B-K* L.68).

[30] BM 33905:5-6 (*B-K* K.51). Note also *ABL* 254, *CT* 54 510:8-9, and perhaps *CT* 54 37:6-7 and 463:7-8. Quite possibly he is to be identified with Nergal-ašarid *mār* Sîn-karābī-išme who is mentioned in *BBSt* 10 rev. 49 (*B-K* K.169) as LÚ.GAR.[...]; that text dates to year 6(+) of Šamaš-šuma-ukīn (662 or later). See also p. 233.

5. DĒR[31]

a) Šulmu-bēli-lašme[32]	*šaknu/šakin māti*	eponymy of Šulmu-bēli-lašme (670)
b) Šuma-iddin[33]	*šatammu* of Dēr	time of Asb.?

6. DILBAT[34]

a) Šulaya[35]	*šākin ṭēmi*	time of Ššu
? Šullumu[36]	*šākin ṭēmi*	year 13?[(+)] Kan. (635?[(-)])
b) Bēl-ēṭir[37]	*šatammu*	year 13 Ššu (655)

[31] Dēr was actually annexed to Assyria at this time; see p. 222. *ABL* 140, which Waterman suggests may be dated to the reign of Esarhaddon or Ashurbanipal (*RCAE* 3, p. 62), also refers to a *bēl piḫati* of Dēr (line 7).

[32] See Ungnad in *RLA* 2, pp. 428-29 and 456 and references in Tallqvist, *APN*, p. 224. The first element of the name should perhaps be read šulum or šulam rather than šulmu. The title is written GAR.KUR *de-ri* in the eponym list *KAV* 20 v 10; in other sources the title appears as (LÚ).GAR.KUR (URU) *de-(e)-ri*/BÀD.AN.KI.

[33] *ABL* 412:14-15. Could he be the *šatammu* of Dēr mentioned in *ABL* 476 rev. 13-14 (*LAS*, no. 277), which is dated to 671 by Parpola (*LAS* 2, pp. 265-66)?

[34] Bēl-īpuš may have been an official (governor?) of Dilbat in the eighth year of Esarhaddon (673); on 21-XI of that year a law case was carried out in the presence of him and the people of Dilbat (*ina pa-ni* ᵐᵈEN-DÙ-*uš u* LÚ *dil-bat*.KI-*iá*; *TCL* 12 4 [*B-K* I.25]).

[35] *ABL* 326:8-9; he was appointed governor of Dilbat by Šamaš-šuma-ukīn. According to the letter, which was written during the revolt of 652-648, Šulaya was the grandson of Bēl-iddin, an enemy of Assyria.

[36] BM 47482:6 (*B-K* L.170); the exact interpretation of the passage is uncertain.

[37] BM 29084:1 and BM 29086:9 (*B-K* K.68 and K.71). No temple name follows the title in the former text and it is not sufficently preserved in the latter for identification (⌜*é*⌝-x-[x]). The texts are from Dilbat and the title is quite likely generic.

7. DŪR-ŠARRUKKU[38]

a) Nabû-bēla-uṣur[39]	*šaknu*, (*šakin māti*)	eponymy of Nabû-bēla-uṣur (672)
Šarru-lū-dāri[40]	*šaknu*/*šakin māti*	eponymy of Šarru-lū-dāri (664)

8. KISH

a) Nādinu[41]	*šatammu* of Kish	eponymy of Ubāru (early in reign of Esar.?)

---

38 This assumes that the individuals (all eponym officials) were governors of the Babylonian city Dūr-Šarrukku/Šarrukīn, and not of the Assyrian city Dūr-Šarrukīn (Khorsabad)—a most uncertain assumption since the Assyrian city still existed (see p. 223). The Babylonian city would then have been annexed to Assyria at this time. It has sometimes been stated that either the eponym in 693 or the one in 688 was governor of this city, but the one text suggesting this (*ADD* 400) is now thought to refer to a govenor in the post-canonical period (see below). An individual whose name is not preserved, but who was governor of this city, is cited as eponym in *ADD* 425 rev. 23-24 (Kwasman, *NALD*, no. 37:45'-46'): *lim-mu* [...] LÚ.GAR.KUR URU.BÀD-^{m}MAN-⸢*uk*⸣-[*ku*/*kin*]; the individual in question may be Nabû-bēla-uṣur, Šarru-lū-dāri, or some other individual. With regard to post-canonical eponyms, note Kanūnaya, *bēl pīḫati* of URU.BÀD-<MAN>-GI.NA (possibly just after our period ends; see Dalley and Postgate, *TFS*, pp. 5, 55, and 62-63), and Iddina-[aḫḫē?] (^{m}⸢SUM.NA⸣-[PAP.MEŠ?]) *ša* URU.BÀD-^{m}MAN-GI[N] (*ADD* 400 rev. 10-11; see Kwasman, *NALD*, no. 132 for reading and date [part of an archive dated by Falkner to just after our period ends]). Note also Falkner's suggestion that the post-canonical eponym Upāq-ana-Arba'il, assigned by her to 631, was governor of this city (*AfO* 17 [1954-56]: 119). Unnamed *bēl pīḫatis* of Dūr-Šarrukku/Khorsabad are mentioned in *ADD* 27:4 (dated to 667; Kwasman, *NALD*, no. 213) and 372 rev. 4 (name not preserved), and *ABL* 339:7 (*LAS*, no. 293; identified with Nabû-bēla-uṣur by Parpola in *LAS* 2, p. 300; reign of Esarhaddon) and 558 rev. 5.

39 See Ungnad in *RLA* 2, pp. 428-29 and 451; Parpola and Watanabe, *SAA* 2, no. 6:665; and references in Tallqvist, *APN*, p. 147. The title is written GAR BÀD-^{m}MAN-[...] in the eponym list *KAV* 20 v 6; in other sources the title appears as LÚ.GAR.KUR (URU) BÀD-MAN/LUGAL-GIN/*uk-ka*/*uk-ku*. For the possibility that he returned to office after 664, see p. 234 n. 128.

40 See Ungnad in *RLA* 2, pp. 428-29 and 455 and references in Tallqvist, *APN*, p. 219. The title is written GAR.KUR BÀD-^{m}MAN-[...] in the eponym list *KAV* 20 v 20. In other sources it appears as [LÚ.GA]R.KUR URU BÀD-^{m}MAN-GI[N] (*ADD* 377 rev. 10'; see Parpola, *Assur* 2/5 [1979]: 57 for collations) and LÚ.GAR.KUR URU BÀD-[...] (*ADD* 398 rev. 14).

41 Pinches, *AfO* 13 (1939-41): pl. 4 rev. 3 (*B-K* S.7).

9. LAḪĪRU[42]

a) Atar-ilī[43]	*šaknu*, *bēl pīḫati*, (*šakin māti*)	eponymy of Atar-ilī (673)
Nergal-ilaya[44]	*bēl pīḫati*	eponymy of Šulmu-bēli-lašme (670)

10. MARAD

a) Šuma-iddin[45]	*šākin ṭēmi*	time of Asb.

11. NIPPUR

a) DN-aḫḫē-šullim[46]	*šandabakku*[47]	year 3 Esar. (678)
Šuma-iddin[48]	*šandabakku*	year 6 Esar. (675)
Nabû-šuma-ēreš[49]	*šandabakku*	early in reign ofŠšu
Enlil-bāni[50]	*šandabakku*	year 7 Ššu (661)

---

42 Laḫīru had actually been annexed to Assyria at this time. Unnamed governors (*bēl pīḫati*) of Laḫīru are mentioned in several other texts, including *ABL* 543 rev. 5' (and parallels 1108 and 1244; time of Šamaš-šuma-ukīn Revolt) and 558 rev. 4.

43 The name can also be written Atri-ilī, Itri-ilī, and Itri. He is described as GAR *la-ḫi-r*[*i*] in the eponym list *KAV* 20 v 4 and elsewhere as LÚ.EN.NAM (*šá*)/LÚ.GAR.KUR KUR/URU *la-ḫi-ra*/*ri*/*ru*. He, or a similarly named individual, was called *ša rēši* of the crown prince of Babylon in 670 (*ADD* 625:13-14). See Ungnad in *RLA* 2, pp. 428-29 and 445; Borger, *Esarh.*, p. 64 §27; *LAS* 2, p. 271 and n. 489; Cogan, *AfO* 31 (1984): 72; Kwasman, *NALD*, pp. 63-64; and the references in Tallqvist, *APN*, p. 47.

44 *ADD* 625:1-2 (LÚ.EN.NAM *ša* KUR *la-ḫi-ri*; Kwasman, *NALD*, no. 46).

45 *ABL* 238:9; likely from before the revolt of 652-648. Enlil-bāni (of Nippur) refers to "Šuma-iddin whom the king, my lord, sent to be governor of Marad" (*ana šākin ṭēmūti ša Marad*).

46 Grayson, *Chronicles*, nos. 1 iv 1-2 and 14:10-11.

47 For the reading *šandabakku* for LÚ.GÚ.EN.NA, see p. 225 n. 77. The *šandabakku* was described as the *šaknu* of Nippur in *ABL* 287 rev. 2-3. It is assumed here that every *šandabakku* was an official at Nippur.

48 Grayson, *Chronicles*, nos. 1 iv 14-15 and 14:19. He was apparently also governor in 676; see *CT* 54 22 rev. 1 (collated by Brinkman in *Or.* NS 46 [1977]: 318 sub. 24), dated to the year after the capture of Sidon (obv. 13-15), i.e., 676.

49 He was one of those inciting Urtak to invade Babylonia, likely in 664 (see p. 119 and Piepkorn, *Asb.*, pp. 56-61 iv 18-63).

50 BM 78903 rev. 12'-13' (*B-K* Kn.9); final element of the name written *-ba-na*. Note also the following letters written by him: *ABL* 238, 239, 292 (restore names of addressees to read ^{md}EN.[LÍL-*ba-ni*] *ù* LÚ.EN.[LÍL.KI.MEŠ GAL].MEŠ ù TUR.MEŠ [ÌR.MEŠ-*ia*]), 617+699 (restore names of addressees to read ^{md}EN.LÍL-*b*[*a?-ni*] ⌜^{m}⌝AN.ŠÁR-EN-GAR-*in ù* LÚ.⌜EN⌝.[LÍL.KI.MEŠ]; possibly an error for Aššur-bēla-taqqin [cf. *ABL* 238]), 1465 and *CT* 54 15 (*ABL* 240+); note also *ABL* 797:16-18 and possibly *ABL* 1124 rev. 8.

12. SEALAND[51]

a) (Nabû)-zēr-kitti-līšir *mār* Marduk-apla-iddina[52]	*šaknu*	year 1 Esar. (680)
Na'id-Marduk *mār* Marduk-apla-iddina[53]	(*šaknu*)	time of Esar.
? Nabû-ēṭir[54]	*šaknu*	time of Esar.?

13. SIPPAR[55]

a) Nabû-nāṣir[56]	*šatammu* of Sippar	eponymy of Ubāru (early in reign of Esar.?)
Šulaya *mār* Baliḫ-na'id[57]	*šatammu* of Ebabbar	year 6 Kan. (642)
[...]-x[58]	*šatammu* of Ebabbar	year 9 Kan. (639)

---

51 In addition to the individuals listed below, it seems likely that Nabû-bēl-šumāti *mār* Marduk-apla-iddina (Merodach-Baladan II) became governor of the Sealand at some point before the Šamaš-šuma-ukīn Revolt (see above, pp. 127-28). He was expelled from the Sealand during the revolt by Bēl-ibni, who too is likely to have held some office over that province (see above, pp. 179-80). Note also Bēl-ibni's father, Nabû-kudurrī-uṣur, to whom Ashurbanipal "gave the Sealand" (*ABL* 1106 rev. 13'-14').

52 Grayson, *Chronicles*, no. 1 iii 39-42 (name abbreviated and paternal name not given) and Borger, *Esarh.*, p. 33 §21:21 and pp. 46-48 §27 episode 4; his title is written (LÚ).GAR KUR *tam-tim*. See also *ABL* 589, 965, 1248, and *CT* 54 22. (Marduk-apla-iddina is Merodach-Baladan II.)

53 Esarhaddon appointed Na'id-Marduk as the successor of Nabû-zēr-kitti-līšir over the Sealand (likely in 680; Borger, *Esarh.*, p. 47 §27 episode 4 ii 58-64; see also ibid., p. 121 §109 sub 680/79 Aa). For the possibility that he remained in office until at least 673, see p. 89 n. 126. He was author of *ABL* 917; see also *ABL* 223 (*LAS*, no. 30), 576, 839, and 1114. (Marduk-apla-iddina is Merodach-Baladan II.)

54 *ABL* 540 rev. 6-7 (title written LÚ.GAR KUR *tam-tim*). See above, p. 86.

55 For the officials of Sippar during the Neo-Babylonian period, see San Nicolò, *Prosopographie*, pp. 33-39 and Frame, *JAOS* 104 (1984): 750. For a possible governor of this city in the time of Šamaš-šuma-ukīn, see p. 234 n. 128.

56 Pinches, *AfO* 13 (1939-41): pl. 4 rev. 4 (*B-K* S.7). Dietrich (*WO* 4 [1967-68]: 237-38) argues that this individual is also mentioned in *CT* 54 170:7 ([md]AG-ÙRU-*ir* LÚ.ŠÀ.T[AM? ...]). Although this is possible, the letter could be referring to the *šatammu* at Uruk by this name. Should the official at Sippar be identified with the Nabû-nāṣir *mār* Baliḫ-na'id mentioned in the witness list of the kudurru from Sippar dated to the time of Šamaš-šuma-ukīn (Steinmetzer, *Deimel Festschrift*, p. 306 rev. 24; see above p. 233)? Note that the next individual known to have been *šatammu* at Sippar, Šulaya, was also *mār* Baliḫ-na'id.

57 Oppert, *RA* 1 (1886): 4:7-8 (*B-K* L.16); family name written [md]ILLAT-I.

58 BM 50186:2 (*B-K* L.41); the traces of the name are as follows:  (collation courtesy of G.J.P. McEwan).

Šamaš-mudammiq[59]	*šatammu* of Ebabbar	year 20 Kan. (628)
b) Šamaš-rā'im-šarri[60]	*qīpu*	years 6 and 9 Kan. (642 and 639)
Bēl-īpuš[61]	*qīpu* of Ebabbar	years 20 and 21 Kan. (628 and 627)

14. UR

a) Ningal-iddin[62]	*šaknu*	year 1 Esar. (680) and years 8 and 12 of Ningal-iddin (as governor or Ur)
Sîn-balāssu-iqbi *mār* Ningal-iddin[63]	*šakkanakku*	years 10 and 11 Ššu (658 and 657)
Sîn-šarra-uṣur *mār* Ningal-iddin[64]	*šakkanakku*	time of Ššu

59 PRS no. 10 rev. 1-2 (information courtesy of M. Gallery Kovacs) and BM 75779:6-7 (*B-K* L.145a and L.151); the exact reading of the second part of the name (written -SIG$_5$-*iq*) is not certain.

60 Oppert, *RA* 1 (1886): 4:9 (collated) and BM 50186:1 (*B-K* L.16 and L.41). The temple with which he was associated is not given in the first text and is not preserved in the second; however, in the first text, he is mentioned in the witness list after the *šatammu* of Ebabbar, and in the second, the *šatammu* of Ebabbar appears in the next line.

61 PRS no. 10 rev. 2-3 (information courtesy of M. Gallery Kovacs), BM 75779:8, and MMA 86.11.187:9 (*B-K* L.145a, L.151, and L.156; temple name not given in last text).

62 Grayson, *Chronicles*, no. 1 iii 39-40 (name and title not given) and Borger, *Esarh.*, pp. 46-47 §27 episode 4 sub A (esp. ii 43-45); *UET* 4 27:17-18, 90 rev. 10' (without title), and 9:32 (*B-K* S.5, S.6, and Sn.3). For the possibility that he remained in office until at least 673, see p. 100. His title is written LÚ.GAR.KUR ŠEŠ.UNUG.KI. Sîn-balāssu-iqbi refers to his father as having been *šakkanakku* of Ur, the same title he himself used (*UET* 1 169:5-8 and 183:5-10). See also *ABL* 223 rev. 3 (*LAS*, no. 30), *CT* 54 527 rev. 5 (name written [m]⌈d⌉*nin-kal-la*-SUM.NA), and Appendix C sub 2.

63 BM 113927:32 and *UET* 4 32:17 (*B-K* K.40 and K.45); see also *UET* 1 169:5-6, 171:5-6, 172:33-34, 173:3-4, 174:3-4, 175:3-4, 176:3-4; 177:3-4; 178:3-4, 179:3-4, 180:3–4, 181:3-4, 182:3-4, and 183:5-7. He bears the title *šakkanakku* of Ur and Eridu in *UET* 1 168:4-6 and 170:5-7 and the title *šakkanakku* of Ur, Eridu, and the Gurasimmu in *UET* 8 102:6-9. The paternal name is learned from *ABL* 445:5-6, *UET* 1 169:5-8 and 183:5-10, and *UET* 8 102:6-7. See also *ABL* 426, 839, and 1106.

64 *TCL* 12 13:1 and duplicate Scheil, *RT* 36 (1914): 189:1 (*B-K* Kn.11; for a new copy of the latter exemplar, see Durrand, *DCEPHE* 1, HE 144). The paternal name comes from *CT* 53 175:2. See also *ABL* 290, 947, 1121, and 1207. Durand (*RA* 75 [1981]: 181-85) has reasonably argued that Sîn-šarra-uṣur is likely to have held office between the tenures of Sîn-balāssu-iqbi and Sîn-tabni-uṣur, being appointed some point before the outbreak of the revolt of 652-648.

Sîn-tabni-uṣur *mār* Ningal-iddin[65]	*šaknu*	years 19 and 20 Asb. (650 and 649)

15. URUK[66]

a) Ina-tēšî-eṭir[67]	*šākin ṭēmi*	year 3 Esar. (678)
Aḫḫēšaya[68]	*šākin ṭēmi*	years 6, 7, and 8 Esar. (675, 674, and 673); accession year Asb. (669); years 1 and 2 Ššu (667 and 666)

---

65 BM 113929:34, BM 113928:30, and *UET* 4 23:24. (*B-K* J.11, J.13, and J.39); the title is written LÚ.GAR.KUR ŠEŠ.UNUG.KI. Note also U 30656 rev. 6' (*B-K* Jn.9); only the last part of the name is preserved ([...]-ŠEŠ), but the use of the title *šaknu* (LÚ.GAR.KUR ŠEŠ.UNUG.KI) suggests that the name is more likely to be restored [Sîn-tabni]-uṣur than [Sîn-šarra]-uṣur because the latter individual was given the title *šakkanakku* on the only occasion he clearly appears as governor (see above). The paternal name comes from Starr, *SAA* 4, nos. 300:5'-6' and 301 rev. 8-9. See also *ABL* 290, 523 (^{m}30-DÙ!-⌜PAB!⌝ in line 1; collation courtesy S. Parpola), 754, 1207, etc.

66 For the officials of Uruk during the Neo-Babylonian period, see San Nicolò, *Prosopographie*, pp. 12-32 and Kümmel, *Familie*, pp. 137-46. In addition to the individuals listed below, one should note Marduk-nāṣir, *šatammu* of Eanna, and Nabû-rēmanni, *qīpu* of Eanna, who are mentioned in *BIN* 1 114:10-11, *TCL* 13 211:8-9, and PTS 2981:9-10 (see *B-K* In.7; information on the third text courtesy of E. Leichty). None of the texts refers to the year of the king under which it was composed; however, individuals mentioned in the documents can be found in other documents dated between 718 and 666 (see Kümmel, *Familie*, p. 141 n. 246 and *B-K* In.7). San Nicolò (*Prosopographie*, p. 26 n. 38a) dates these two officials to the reign of Ashurbanipal, without however giving any reason for this proposal. Note also Nabû-nāṣir whom Šamaš-šuma-ukīn may have appointed governor of Uruk, although there is no evidence he ever actually held office (*CT* 54 496:3'-5', partially restored; and see chapter 8). The name of the province controlled by the Sîn-šarra-uṣur who appears as (post-canonical) eponym in *ADD* 1252:24-25 is indistinct and probably to be read Nineveh (NINA.KI) not Uruk (UNUG.KI) (collation by C.B.F. Walker, with Johns copy and against Postgate, *FNALD*, p. 117 and Kwasman, *NALD*, p. 28). Falkner (*AfO* 17 [1954-56]: 116 and 118) tentatively dates this eponymy to 639 but presents no strong reason for this. Even if Uruk is to be read here, the eponymy may well date after 627 when control of Uruk appears to have fluctuated between the Assyrians and Babylonians.

67 BM 118964:26 (*B-K* I.5). He may also appear in Ellis, *JCS* 36 (1984): 63 no. 26:5' (mostly restored; *B-K* In.2).

68 BM 118965:23; BM 118979:27 (mostly restored); A 3674:26; BM 118972:24; and W 21339 rev. 1 (*B-K* I.11, I.19 , I.20, I.24, and In.6). BM 118975:27 (with duplicates BM 118969:28 and MAH 15976:26) (*B-K* J.2-4). BM 118981:24 and Weidner, *AfO* 16 (1952-53): 44:35 (*B-K* K.5 and K.8). He was possibly the son of Nanaya-uṣalli; see Kümmel, *Familie*, p. 139 and n. 222. See also *ABL* 965 and 1062.

	Nabû-ušabši[69]	*šākin ṭēmi*	years 7, 9, 10, and 12 Ššu (661, 659, 658, and 656); years 18 and 20 Asb. (651 and 649)
	Kudurru[70]	*šākin ṭēmi*	year 22 Asb. (647); year 2 Kan.? (646)
	Nabû-zēru-līšir[71]	*šākin ṭēmi*	year 6 Kan. (642)
	Na'id-Marduk[72]	*šākin ṭēmi*	year 17 Kan. (631)
b)	Nabû-nāṣir[73]	*šatammu* of Eanna	years 3 and 6 Esar. (678 and 675)
	Balāṭu[74]	*šatammu* of Eanna	years 7 and 8 Esar. (674 and 673); possibly year 2 Ššu? (666)
	Nabû-iqīša[75]	*šatammu* of Eanna	years 9, 10, and 12 Ššu (659, 658, and 656)

---

69 BM 118984:23; BM 118967:25; *TCL* 12 10:27 (and duplicate AO 10347 rev. 5 [Durand, *TBER*, pl. 33, labelled obverse]); *UET* 4 15:26 (and duplicate BM 118966:25); BM 118985:25 (and duplicate BM 118988:25); *TCL* 12 8:31; Hunger, *Bagh. Mitt.* 5 (1970): 276 no. 4:21; and Durand, *DCEPHE* 1, HE 469 rev. 2 (*B-K* K.22, K.33, K.36-37, K.38-39, K.64-65, K. 149, K.165, and Kn.6). Hunger, *Bagh. Mitt.* 5 (1970): 277 no. 5:21-22; and Smith, *MAT*, pl. 28:26 (*B-K* J.6, and J.12). He also appears in many letters. Note especially *ABL* 517 dated to 19-II-650. See Frame in *Cuneiform Archives*, pp. 260-72.

70 *AnOr* 9 13:27 (royal name left blank but king's title was *šar mātāti*) and possibly Ellis, *JCS* 36 (1984): 39 no. 4 rev. 21 (*B-K* Jn.8 and L.4). See also *BIN* 2 132:8 and 12 (collation courtesy J.A. Brinkman); since this text refers to Šamaš-danninanni as governor of Akkad (see above), the two individuals' tenures in office must have overlapped. Kudurru appears in several letters of the period (see in part Frame in *Cuneiform Archives*, p. 262). Note especially *ABL* 518, dated to 24-II of the eponymy of Nabû-šar-aḫḫēšu and sent by the king to Kudurru and the Urukians. He may be the son of Nabû-nāṣir mentioned in *ABL* 880+*CT* 54 43:15-16.

71 PTS 2479:14' (*B-K* L.14).

72 Hunger, *Bagh. Mitt.* 5 (1970): 278 no. 6:31 and 274 no. 2:29 (*B-K* L.107 and L.108). He is probably to be identified with the son of ᵐUD.20.1.LÁ.KÁM-PAB mentioned in *ABL* 1387 rev. 1 (and cf. 815:1) and *BIN* 1 159:18 (*B-K* L.29); see Kümmel, *Familie*, p. 139 and n. 227.

73 BM 118964:27 and BM 118965:24 (*B-K* I.5 and I.11). See also p. 277 n. 56.

74 BM 118979:28 (title mostly restored); A 3674:27; BM 118972:25; and W 21339 rev. 2 (*B-K* I.19, I.20, I.24, and In.6 respectively); possibly Weidner, *AfO* 16 (1952-53): 44:35-36 (only traces of the last sign of the name are preserved; C.B.F. Walker informs me that the restoration would fit the spacing and that the remains of the last sign are "entirely consistent with its being ⸢*ṭu*⸣" [private communication]; *B-K* K.8). He is likely to be indentified with the *šatammu* Itti-Marduk-balāṭu who is mentioned in *ABL* 476 (*LAS*, no. 277) and the Itti-Marduk-balāṭu who wrote *ABL* 831. Parpola dates *ABL* 476 to the year 671 (*LAS* 2, pp. 265-66). Note also *CT* 54 60 rev. 3'?

75 BM 118967:26; *TCL* 12 10:28 (and duplicate AO 10347 rev. 6 [Durand, *TBER*, pl. 33, labelled obverse]); *UET* 4 15:27 (and duplicate BM 118966:26); BM 118985:26 (and

	Nabû-šuma-iddin[76]	*šatammu* of Eanna	year 18 Asb. (651)
	Bēl-uballiṭ[77]	*šatammu* of Eanna	year 6 Kan. (642)
c)	Aššur-bēla-uṣur[78]	*qīpu* of Eanna	at some point while Nabû-ušabši governor of Uruk
	Šamaš-ilaya[79]	*qīpu* of Urukand Eanna	years 6, 9, and 11 Kan. (642, 639, and 637)
d)	Nabû-ušallim *mār* Sîn-leqi-unninnī[80]	*ṭupšarru* of Eanna	year 2 Kan. (646)
	Širikti-Marduk *māršu ša* Ibni-Ištar[81]	*ṭupšarru* of Eanna	year 4 Kan. (644)
	Širikti-Marduk *māršu ša* Nabû-ušallim *mār* Ḫunzû[82]	*ṭupšarru* of Eanna	year 6 Kan. (642)

16. MISCELLANEOUS

Nādin-aḫi[83]	*bēl pīḫati*	eponymy of Ubāru(early in reign of Esar.?)
[Mannu]-kî-Arba'il[84]	*rab kiṣri*	eponymy of Ubāru (early in reign of Esar.?)
Nergal-nāṣir[85]	*gugallu*	eponymy of Ubāru(early in reign of Esar.?)

duplicate BM 118988:26); and Hunger, *Bagh. Mitt.* 5 (1970): 276 no. 4:22 (*B-K* K.33, K.36-37, K.38-39, K.64-65, and K.165 respectively).

76 Hunger, *Bagh. Mitt.* 5 (1970): 277 no. 5:22 (*B-K* J.6).

77 PTS 2479:15' (*B-K* L.14). See also *ABL* 880+*CT* 54 43 and *ABL* 1129?

78 Durand, *DCEPHE* 1, HE 469 rev. 3 (*B-K* Kn.6).

79 Ellis, *JCS* 36 (1984): 43 no. 7:6-7 and 45 no. 8:33; A 3658:33; and Ellis, *JCS* 36 (1984): 50 no. 15:9-10 (*B-K* L.17, L.18, L.38, and L.52 respectively).

80 *AnOr* 9 3:62-64 (*B-K* L.5). He was also *kalû*-priest of Ištar and *šangû*-priest of Nusku. His father's name was probably Balāṭu; see Weidner, *AfO* 16 (1952-53): 44:47-48 (*B-K* K.8). A temple scribe of Uruk (LÚ.DUB.SAR É DINGIR *ša* UNUG.KI) appears associated with the *šatammu* and the *qīpu* in the time of Esarhaddon (*ABL* 476:28-29 [*LAS*, no. 277]); Parpola dates the letter of the year 671 (*LAS* 2, pp. 265-66).

81 Ellis, *JCS* 36 (1984): 40 no. 5:20-21 (*B-K* L.8). Could he or the like-named son of Nabû-ušallim (see below) be identified with the Širiktu mentioned in *ABL* 815:2?

82 Ellis, *JCS* 36 (1984): 45 no. 8:34-35 (*B-K* L.18).

83 Pinches, *AfO* 13 (1939-41): pl. 4:5 (*B-K* S.7); text dated at Babylon.

84 Pinches, *AfO* 13 (1939-41): pl. 3:28 and see p. 53 (*B-K* S.7); text dated at Babylon. Since he appears to have been an Assyrian, possibly sent to perform some commission in Babylonia, he should perhaps not appear in this list. A number of other individuals bearing the title of *rab kiṣri* appear in Babylonia during this time; some at least appear to have been Assyrians. See p. 235.

85 Pinches, *AfO* 13 (1939-41): pl. 4:6 (*B-K* S.7); text dated at Babylon.

Bēl-ēṭir[86]	šākin ṭēmi	late in reign of Esar.
Zēra-iddin[87]	rab ālāni	year 2 Ššu (666)
Adad-dān(i)[88]	sukkallu	year 6(+) Ššu (662[-])
Nabû-bēla-uṣur[89]	šakin māti, (šaknu)	year 6(+) Ššu (662[-])
Aḫi-iliya[90]	ša pān ekalli	year 6(+) Ššu (662[-])
Nabû-killanni[91]	mukīl appāti	year 6(+) Ššu (662[-])
AN.GAL-mušallim[92]	rab (ša) rēši	time of Ššu
Nabû-šuma-iškun[93]	ṭupšar ekalli	time of Ššu
Taklāk?-ana-Nabû?[94]	LÚ qí-[p]a? šá [...]	time of Ššu
Ṣalam-šarri-iqbi[95]	šaknu ša šarri	time of Ššu
[ᵐ(x)]-TI-DINGIR[96]	šaknu ša šarri!?	time of Ššu
Šu[maya?][97]	šatammu of Ningal	time of Ššu revolt or shortly thereafter
Bābilaya[98]	ša rēši ṭupšarru ša šar bābili	time of Asb.

---

[86] ABL 276 rev. 10. For the date of the letter (in or after 671), see Landsberger, *Brief*, pp. 34-36 and Parpola, *LAS* 2, p. 64 and n. 120. Note also *CT* 54 63:6'?
[87] BM 47480+47783:9'-10' (*B-K* K.9); dated at Dilbat and reportedly found at that site.
[88] Steinmetzer, *Deimel Festschrift*, p. 306 rev. 17 (dated at Sippar) and *BBSt* 10 rev. 42 (*B-K* K.163 and K.169); see p. 232.
[89] *BBSt* 10 rev. 42 (*B-K* K.169). Steinmetzer, *Deimel Festschrift*, p. 306 rev. 17 (*B-K* K.163; year not preserved); text from Sippar. With regard to the writing of his title, see p. 232. With regard to the province he governed, see p. 234 n. 128.
[90] Steinmetzer, *Deimel Festschrift*, p. 306 rev. 18 (dated at Sippar) and *BBSt* 10 rev. 43 (*B-K* K.163 and K.169); see p. 232. See also *ABL* 270:5 (letter written by Nabû-ušabši of Uruk).
[91] Steinmetzer, *Deimel Festschrift*, p. 306 rev. 19 (dated at Sippar) and *BBSt* 10 rev. 43 (*B-K* K.163 and K.169); see p. 232. See also *ADD* 860 i 18.
[92] Steinmetzer, *Deimel Festschrift*, p. 306 rev. 18 (*B-K* K.163); dated at Sippar; see p. 232. On the reading of AN.GAL, see Borger, *Zeichenliste*, p. 61 (Angal or Anu-rabû) and Zadok, *West Semites*, p. 20 (possibly Ḫumban).
[93] Steinmetzer, *Deimel Festschrift*, p. 306 rev. 20 (*B-K* K.163); dated at Sippar; see p. 232.
[94] Steinmetzer, *Deimel Festschrift*, p. 306 rev. 20 (*B-K* K.163); dated at Sippar. The reading of the name is uncertain. Landsberger (*Brief*, p. 59 n. 110) assigns him to the Ezida temple, but the approximately corresponding entry in the second kudurru from the time of Šamaš-šuma-ukīn (*BBSt* 10 rev. 44) mentions the qīpu of Esagila (see above, p. 232).
[95] *UET* 4 201:12 (*B-K* K.166); text found at Ur. The title is written ⌈LÚ⌉ šak-nu šá LUGAL.
[96] *UET* 4 201:13 (*B-K* K.166); text found at Ur. The reading of the personal name is not certain. The title is written LÚ šak-⌈nu⌉ šá LUGAL!(copy: LÚ).
[97] *ABL* 1000:18-19; the individual is described as being from Kissik. The tentative restoration of the name comes from *ABL* 963 rev. 4' (following Dietrich, *Aramäer*, p. 195 no. 142).
[98] BM 29391:22 (*B-K* Jn.5). The document likely dates to early in the reign of Ashurbanipal in view of the presence of three witnesses—Marduk-šuma-uṣur (GAL

Zērūtu *mār* Bēl-iraššī[99]	*qīpu*	year 20 Asb. (649)
Bēl-x-x[100]	*šaknu/šakin māti*	year 4 Kan. (644)
Ša-Nabû-šū[101]	*rab ālāni ša šakni/šakin māti*	year 20 Kan. (628)
Šarrukkaya[102]	*rab ālāni ša kiṣir eššu*	year 20 Kan. (628)
Bēl-šarra-uṣur[103]	*ša rēš šarri bēl piqittu ša kāri*	year 20 Kan. (628)
Aḫu-dūrī[104]	*rab kiṣri*	year 21 Kan. (627)[105]

LÚ.ḪAL, chief diviner), Nāṣiru (LÚ.ḪAL, diviner), and Aqara (LÚ.ḪAL, diviner) (lines 19-21)—who held office in Assyria at the end of the reign of Esarhaddon and at the beginning of the reign of Ashurbanipal (see *LAS*, no. 115, with commentary). A number of other officials appear as witnesses in the document who may have served in Babylonia (e.g., Šamaš-balāṭu, the palace overseer—*šá* ⌈*pa*⌉-*an* É.G[AL], line 16), but they more likely served in Assyria as did some other witnesses (e.g., the mayor of Nineveh—[...]-⌈*ia*⌉ LÚ *ḫa-za-an šá* URU *ni-ná*-⌈*a*⌉, line 14).

99 *AnOr* 9 4 vi 34-35 (*B-K* J.15); exact reading of family name (⌈m⌉1dEN-TUK-*ši*) uncertain. Kümmel suggests that he was *qīpu* of Eanna in Uruk (*Familie*, p. 140); however, the text was dated at Iltuk, which may be identified with the town located in Bīt-Dakkūri (Luckenbill, *Senn.*, pp. 52-53:38-39).

100 Ellis, *JCS* 36 (1983): 40 no. 5:6 (*B-K* L.8); dated at Uruk. The text is damaged and it is not absolutely certain that the title (LÚ.GAR.KUR) refers to the individual even though it immediately follows his name.

101 Weidner, *AfO* 16 (1952-53): pl. 6 no. 8:9-10 (*B-K* L.143); text dated at Ṣibti-ša-šakni/šakin-māti. The title is written LÚ.GAL URU.MEŠ *šá* LÚ.GAR.KUR. An individual with the same title is attested during the reign of Sîn-šarra-iškun (BM 50762:3-4, *B-K* O.46).

102 Weidner, *AfO* 16 (1952-53): pl. 6 no. 8:11-12 (*B-K* L.143); text dated at Ṣibti-ša-šakni/šakin-māti. The title is written LÚ.GAL URU.MEŠ *šá ki-ṣir eš-šú*.

103 BM 97376:3-4 (*B-K* L.146a); text dated at Sippar.

104 MMA 86.11.187:10 (*B-K* L.156); text dated at Sippar.

105 In addition to the above, officials also dating to this period may be the *šākin ṭēmi* Marduk mentioned in *ABL* 1204:4' and the *šatammu* Bēl-iqīša mentioned in *ABL* 914:4 and rev.19. *CT* 54 92:4'-7' appears to refer to one Šulaya son of Ibnaya (m*ib-na*-⌈*a?*⌉ [(...)]) whom Šamaš-šuma-ukīn had appointed *šatammu* (for restorations, see Dietrich, *Aramäer*, pp. 174-75 no. 97).

APPENDIX C

Some Notes on Dating Methods in Babylonian Economic Texts

Changing and at times ambiguous political circumstances during the period 689-627, and in the year thereafter, resulted in several variations of recording year dates in private economic documents from Babylonia. Atypical formulae are attested for the "kingless" years (688-681) and the year following the death of Kandalānu. The Assyrian practice of dating by eponyms was also employed, sometimes using Assyrian eponyms and sometimes new Babylonian eponyms. Since Babylonia was in effect under Assyrian control during all of this period, this is not surprising, though the use of eponym dating at Babylon while a king of Babylonia sat on the throne is unexpected, even if he was the brother of the king of Assyria.[1]

(1) Babylonian economic texts dated by the regnal years of Sennacherib exhibit two different systems of reckoning the year of the king's reign. IM 57905 and UM 29-13-568 (*B-K* C.1-2) are dated at Nippur by "Sennacherib, king of Assyria" on the ninth day of Nisannu (I) of his third year and on an unknown day in Kislīmu (IX) of his fourth year respectively. The former document records a payment and the latter the sale of land. Since Sennacherib ruled Babylonia directly for only two years before he made Bēl-ibni king of Babylonia in 703, they cannot be dated to that period and should come from the period after the destruction of Babylon, with year one likely being considered 688—the first of the eight "kingless" years recorded by the Ptolemaic Canon and one of the Babylonian chronicles.[2] In contrast, *VAS* 5 1 (*B-K* C.3), which may describe the sale of a slave, was dated at Ḫursagkalama on the twenty-fourth day of Simanu (III) in the twenty-fourth year of "Sennacherib, king of Assyria"; the document would come from 681, with 704 being counted as Sennacherib's first regnal year.[3] Thus, in the

---

1 This assumes that the eponymy of Aqara is to be dated to the reign of Šamaš-šuma-ukīn (see below).

2 Grayson, *Chronicles*, no. 1 iii 28.

3 There was also some confusion in Assyria in reckoning the first regnal year of Sennacherib, as J. Lewy pointed out in *Deimel Festschrift*, pp. 225-31. (See also Brinkman in *Studies Oppenheim*, p. 22.) Lewy notes that 705, 704, and 703 were variously reckoned as Sennacherib's first regnal year. In the case of this Babylonian text (*VAS* 5 1), the year 703 can be ruled out since it would put year 24 in 680, the first year of

absence of a king of Babylonia there was some confusion over the reference points for starting to enumerate the regnal years of the Assyrian overlord.

(2) Two documents dated by the years of office of a governor are known—*UET* 4 27 and 90 (*B-K* S.5-6); the former records the sale of a slave, while the latter deals with a loan of silver. Both texts were found at Ur and *UET* 4 27 specifically states that it was composed at that site; the place at which *UET* 4 90 was composed is not preserved. They were drawn up on the eleventh day of Addaru (XII) in the eighth year and on the twenty-eighth (or later) day of Tašrītu (VII) in the twelfth year of Ningal-iddin respectively; in the former text, Ningal-iddin is given the title governor (*šākin ṭēmi*) of Ur. Exactly when these two texts are to be dated in absolute terms is not clear. The only secure date within Ningal-iddin's term as governor of Ur is 680, when he was attacked by Nabû-zēr-kitti-līšir of the Sealand. The dates of both his and his successor's appointment to the office are unknown. *ABL* 445 may suggest that his son Sîn-balāssu-iqbi had already succeeded him as governor in the reign of Esarhaddon, but this is uncertain.[4] It is probable that Ningal-iddin held the governorship under both Sennacherib and Esarhaddon,[5] especially in view of the absence of texts dated by either king at Ur, and thus these texts could come from either reign. It seems more likely, however, that texts would have been dated by a governor's years of office during a "kingless" period rather than during the reign of an acknowledged king of Babylonia. Whereas Sennacherib never claimed the title "king of Babylon" and was not recognized as such during his lifetime, Esarhaddon was acknowledged to be a legitimate ruler of Babylonia. If the two texts dated by Ningal-iddin come from the "kingless" period in Babylonia, rather than the reign of Esarhaddon, as would seem more likely, Ningal-iddin must have been appointed governor of Ur either before or shortly after the beginning of the rebellion of 694-689.[6]

(3) Three documents from this period are of particular significance because they show the adoption and adaptation of the Assyrian practice of eponym dating by Babylonian scribes. In each case, the text comes from

---

Esarhaddon's reign. Since scholarly opinion accepts 704 as Sennacherib's first regnal year, and since none of the texts reckoning 705 as year one are Babylonian, it is best to assume that the author of the *VAS* 5 1 used 704 as year one, and that this text is to be dated to 681.

4 On *ABL* 445, see p. 99.

5 Since there is no definite proof that anyone but Ningal-iddin held the governorship of Ur until 658, when Sîn-balāssu-iqbi was expressly called governor of Ur, one cannot rule out the possibility that Ningal-iddin governed Ur down into the reign of Šamaš-šuma-ukīn. But, as discussed in chapter 6, this is unlikely. Inscriptions of Esarhaddon composed in 673 still mention him as governor of Ur (see p. 100).

6 On the date of these texts, see also p. 61.

Babylon and is dated by the eponymy (*limmu*) of an official who does not appear in the Assyrian canon and who held office in Babylon.

The first text, formerly no. 224 in the collection of Lord Amherst,[7] records the redemption of an individual and is dated at Babylon on the fourth day of Abu (V) in the eponymy of ^{m}*ú-bar*, the *šākin ṭēmi* of Babylon. The person named as eponym is also known from *ABL* 327, 418, and 702.[8] In each case, Ubār(u) is associated with Babylon, and twice expressly called *šākin ṭēmi* of that city.[9] Internal evidence from two of the letters indicates that they were written during the reign of Esarhaddon.[10] In addition, the first witness in the economic text in question here, [Mannu]-kî-Arba'il, the *rab kiṣri*, also appears in texts from Assyria datable to the reign of Esarhaddon, including one from the end of the second month of 680.[11] Since it is unlikely that there would have been a governor of Babylon until after Esarhaddon had resettled that city, this text likely dates to the reign of Esarhaddon, possibly soon after Babylon was restored. Ubāru may have been appointed eponym in order to help commemorate that restoration. However, since no other individual is attested as governor of Babylon until 654, it is not impossible that Ubāru held office into the early part of the reign of Šamaš-šuma-ukīn and that his eponymy comes from that time.[12]

Two documents are dated at Babylon by the eponymy of ^{m}*a-qar-a*, the governor (*bēl pīḫati*) of Babylon, on the fifth day of Abu (V) and the eighteenth day of Šabaṭu (XI) respectively (BM 118973 and 80-B-10; *B-K* S.1-2).[13] The former text records the sale of an orchard; information on the latter text is not available. Individuals with the name of Aqara (possibly to be read Aqarâ, Aqaraya, or Aqar-aplu) appear in many letters, economic texts, reports, and other documents; however, there is no clear evidence to associate any of them with the eponym of this name.[14] Prosopographic evidence from the former text might suggest that it dates from *c.* 656-653, the period during

---

7 Pinches, *AfO* 13 (1939-41): 51-52 and pls. 3-4 (*B-K* S.7) and see Landsberger, *Brief*, pp. 29-30.

8 He may also be the Ubāru mentioned in *CT* 54 439:6' (see Dietrich, *WO* 4 [1968]: 214-15).

9 *ABL* 327 rev. 11 and 418:2-3.

10 *ABL* 418 (reference to the king having repopulated Babylon in rev. 4-9) and 702 (references to the resettlement of Babylon and to Ṣillaya in lines 9-10 and rev. 7; see Landsberger, *Brief*, pp. 32-33 for a translation based upon restorations).

11 See the references in Tallqvist, *APN*, p. 125, especially *ADD* 360 (Kwasman, *NALD*, no. 152).

12 See Frame, *RA* 76 (1982): 157 and 159, and *JCS* 36 (1984): 79-80 n. 77.

13 See Frame, *RA* 76 (1982): 157-66 for the former text. The city over which he was governor is not given in the latter text.

14 The most likely other reference to the governor by this name might be as the recipient of *ABL* 912 (date uncertain); the individual in that text had the power to appoint officials (see rev. 4-6).

which the main participant in the transaction described in the document was active in Babylon, but the evidence is not overwhelming.[15]

This adoption of an Assyrian dating practice at Babylon, however modified for Babylonian usage, is surprising and presumably could only have taken place while Assyria exercised control over that country. The exact reason why it was done remains uncertain.

(4) A few documents may have been dated in Babylonia according to Assyrian eponym officials. Two tablets, both numbered IM 63773 (*B-K* S.3-4), are dated in the eponymy of Nabû-šarra-uṣur, the palace(?) scribe; they were found at Dūr-Kurigalzu and appear to have been composed at Opis. Nabû-šarra-uṣur was a post-canonical eponym official who may have held office *c.* 626.[16] Since Dūr-Kurigalzu and Opis are on Babylonia's northern border, close to Assyria, it is not surprising that Assyrian dating practices were at times employed there.[17]

B.79 (*B-K* Sn.1) is an Assyrian-style economic text written in the Neo-Assyrian script and dated on the twenty-second day of Šabaṭu (XI) in the eponymy of Aššur-gimilla-tīr, the *chief* ... (GAL x [...]), *c.* 641.[18] Since this text comes from the Babylon collection in Istanbul, it may have been found at that city. It would seem more likely, however, that the tablet was either wrongly assigned to this collection or brought to Babylon from Assyria in ancient (or modern) times.

(5) On occasion, documents were dated according to the years of a previous, deceased ruler. This type of dating had been used at Targibātu in 693: "first year after (*arki*) Nergal-ušēzib, king of Babylon" (*UET* 4 204; *B-K* G.1).[19] Similarly, two documents were given *arki* dates during the

---

15 See Frame, *RA* 76 (1982): 163-65. Mušēzib-Marduk was active in business matters at Babylon from 656 to 653, but he also appears in texts from Uruk as early as 678. Thus this eponymy could conceivably date close in time to that of Ubāru. Another possibility might be the accession year of Šamaš-šuma-ukīn (668), for which no documents are attested.

16 The eponym's name and/or title is not fully preserved in either text. He was first identified by Brinkman with the like-named individual who was eponym in 682 (*JCS* 25 [1973]: 95 n. 33), but this view was retracted in *Power and Propaganda*, p. 244 n. 66. For an approximate date of 626 for the post-canonical eponymy, see Falkner, *AfO* 17 (1954-56): 114 and 119. Note the study by Fales of the various individuals bearing the name Nabû-šarra-uṣur in the Neo-Assyrian archives (*SAAB* 2 [1988]: 105-24).

17 In view of the uncertainty over the exact location of the Assyrian border at this time, it is possible that these two cities, particularly the latter, were then under direct Assyrian control. On the location of Opis, see Frame, *AOF* 13 (1986): 209 and Black, *NAPR* 1 (1987): 18-19.

18 For the date of the eponymy, see Falkner, *AfO* 17 (1954-56): 109-10 and 118.

19 Note also the unpublished text BM 17310 (*B-K* Bn.1) which refers to the nineteenth year of Sargon even though that king reigned only seventeen years.

"kingless" years, while Sennacherib was officially in control of Babylonia. BM 46916 and L 1672 (*B-K* Fn.2 and Fn.5) were composed at Borsippa on the twenty-fourth day of an unknown month in the twelfth year and on the twenty-second day of intercalary Ulūlu (VI_2) in the thirteenth year "after Aššur-nādin-šumi, the king" respectively (688 and 687).[20] Thus, these tablets were dated according to the years of the last Babylonia ruler to be considered legitimate by both the Assyrians and Babylonians.

Two tablets with similar date formulae are BM 36514 and 40039 (Wiseman, *Chron.*, p. 89 and pls. 20-21 and 18-19 respectively; *B-K* L.160 and L.163). Both documents were composed at Babylon and deal with the payment of debts or the settlement of accounts. The former text was dated on the first (or a later) day of Araḫsamna (VIII) in the twenty-first year "after Kandalānu"[21] and the latter one on the second day of Araḫsamna (VIII) in the twenty-second year "after Kandalānu, king of Babylon," i.e., in 627 and 626 respectively. The use of this type of date formula reflects uncertainty in Babylon as to who should be acknowledged ruler in the period of strife following the deaths of Kandalānu and Ashurbanipal.

---

20 BM 46916 describes a loan of ten shekels of silver and L 1672 a transaction involving a house (exact interpretation uncertain). Information on L 1672 was kindly supplied by F. Joannès.

21 Kandalānu's title is not preserved in the document.

APPENDIX D

The Battle of Ḫirītu and Ashurbanipal Edition B

The Akītu Chronicle states that in the sixteenth year of Šamaš-šuma-ukīn Babylonian rebel forces were defeated by an Assyrian army at Ḫirītu on the twenty-seventh day of Addaru (XII):

> ŠE 27 ÉRIN-*ni* KUR *aš-šur u* ÉRIN KUR URI.KI
> *ṣal-tu₄ ina ḫi-rit* DÙ.MEŠ-*ma* ÉRIN KUR URI.KI
> *ina* MÈ EDIN BAL.ME-*ma* BAD₅.BAD₅-*šú-nu ma-a-diš* GAR-*in*

> On the twenty-seventh (day) of Addaru the army of Assyria and the army of Akkad did battle at Ḫirīt. The army of Akkad retreated from the battlefield and a major defeat was inflicted upon them.[1]

BM 32312, an astronomical diary for the year 652 (the year -651 according to astronomical citation), contains the following historical comment after an entry for the twenty-seventh day of the twelfth month and before one for the twenty-eighth day:

> [x x x x] *ḫi-ri-tu₄* NAM UD.KIB.NUN.KI ÉRIN KUR URI.KI *u* KUR *aš-šur*
> [*ṣal-tú* KI *a-ḫa*]-*meš* DÙ.MEŠ-*ma* ÉRIN KUR URI.KI BAL.ME *ma-ʾ-diš* GAZ

> The armies of Akkad and Assyria did [battle with each] other [... at] Ḫirītu, (in the) province of Sippar. The army of Akkad retreated (and) was soundly defeated.[2]

Obviously the two sources refer to the same battle—a battle in which Babylonian forces were decisively defeated by Assyrian troops and forced to

---

1 *BHT*, pl. 4:13-15 (Grayson, *Chronicles*, no. 16).

2 Sachs, *Astronomical Diaries* 1, no. -651 iv 18'-19'. A.J. Sachs kindly provided me with a transliteration of the two historical passages in this text in 1979 and allowed me to use it in my doctoral dissertation (University of Chicago, 1981).

retreat[3]—and thereby confirm that the sixteenth year of Šamaš-šuma-ukīn is to be identified with the year 652. The exact location of Ḫirītu, however, is unclear. Up until now it has been assumed that the Ḫirītu mentioned in the Akītu Chronicle was located in southeastern Babylonia,[4] but BM 32312 states that it was in the province of Sippar. This would place it in northern Babylonia, closer to the Assyrian border,[5] unless one wished to assume either an error in the text or a second, and otherwise unattested, province of Sippar in the south—both obviously undesirable assumptions. It is not improbable for a major battle to have taken place early in the revolt in the area around the border between the two countries, since as a rule the Assyrians kept no major forces stationed in Babylonia. Ḫirītu means "ditch," "canal," or "moat"[6] and it is thus not surprising that several places have this name, making it difficult to connect the Ḫirītu of our texts with any other place of a similar name.[7] We may note, however, that a Ḫirītu is attested in the Ur III period in the province of Urum (possibly located just north of Sippar).[8] Millard has suggested that the Ḫirītu of the chronicle is to be connected to Ḫarutu (URU *ḫa-ru-tu*), a border fortress between Babylonia and Assyria situated east of the Tigris in the time of Tukultī-Ninurta II and Ashurnasirpal II, and possibly to Ḫararātu (URU *ḫa-ra-ra-tu₄*), a town destroyed by Sennacherib in 702.[9] There may be a Ḫirītu River (ÍD *ḫi-ri-te*) located in the East Tigris region[10] and a Ḫirutu ([KUR] *ḫi-ru-tu*) is attested as one of the provinces of Gambūlu. The latter could be connected with our Ḫirītu,[11] but only a short, unstressed /a/ in an open syllable undergoes vowel harmony in Assyrian. The Gambūlu, however, are usually found in southern Babylonia along the Elamite border,

---

3 For minor differences in the two accounts (e.g., Assyria is mentioned first in the former account and Akkad in the latter) which might suggest that neither account was directly derived from the other, see Brinkman, *Moran Festschrift*, pp. 95-96.

4 E.g., Grayson, *Chronicles*, p. 257 and Zadok, *RGTC* 8, p. 162.

5 The exact location of the Assyro-Babylonian border during the years 689-627 is uncertain, although it must have lain north of Sippar. At this time, Dēr, Laḫīru, and possibly Dūr-Šarrukku appear to have been annexed to Assyria (see pp. 222-24). Since Babylonia was under Assyrian control or supervision during this time, there may have been no clearly defined border.

6 *CAD* 6 (Ḫ), p. 198.

7 Note in particular Röllig in *RLA* 4, p. 418.

8 See Edzard and Farber, *RGTC* 2, p. 76 and Steinkeller, *JCS* 32 (1980): 33. For the location of the province of Urum, see Frayne, *AOS* (in press).

9 Millard, *Iraq* 26 (1964): 25 n. 52. Thompson, *Archaeologia* 79 (1929): 117 and pl. 41 no. 1:7-8; *AKA*, p. 163:15-17; and Grayson, *Chronicles*, no. 1 ii 24-25.

10 Lie, *Sar.*, p. 46:289. Three towns (in the district) of ÍD *ḫi-ri-te* were captured by Sargon during his campaign against Dūr-Atḫara, which Unger suggests may be located on the Tigris near Kut el-Amara (*RLA* 2, p. 242). In addition, an URU *ḫi-ri-te* appears in a letter of Šamaš-ēmuranni (*ABL* 312:7), in broken context, and an URU ⌜*ḫi*⌝-*ri-t*[*i*] in a list of towns (including Arbela) making deliveries of grain (Parker, *Iraq* 23 [1961]: 54 and pl. 28 ND 2791:2').

11 Lie, *Sar.*, p., 48:1.

not in the vicinity of Sippar. Although an exact location for the Ḫirītu of the chronicle and astronomical diary cannot be ascertained, there is no reason not to locate it in northern Babylonia, in the province of Sippar.[12]

Edition B of Ashurbanipal's annals states that during the Šamaš-šuma-ukīn Revolt Assyrian forces stationed in Mangisi within Sumandir (URU [var. KUR] *man-gi-si ša qé-reb* URU *su-man-dir*) defeated some troops that had been sent by Ḫumban-nikaš II, king of Elam, to aid Šamaš-šuma-ukīn.[13] No other reference to Mangisi is attested in this period. A place by the name of Sumandar located in the region of Uruk is well-attested in Neo-Babylonian texts;[14] however, a location in the southwest would present some problems. It would be strange to find Elamite troops fighting with troops stationed near Uruk. Although the Elamites could have entered Babylonia via the Sealand, it is much more likely that their army would have come via Dēr, the normal invasion route. In this case, either the Elamite or Assyrian troops would have had to cross all of Babylonia in order to meet the opposing force. A location for the battle in the northeast would seem more likely and, in fact, it is possible to locate Mangisi and Sumandir there. A town by the name of Mankisum was located on the Tigris in the area of the Diyala in the Old Babylonian period.[15] Neo-Babylonian texts also appear to refer to a Sumandar river, and perhaps a town by the name of Sumundar, located near Babylon and Sippar;[16] and a Simudar was apparently located in the Diyala region in the Ur III period.[17]

Millard has suggested that the Akītu Chronicle and edition B describe one and the same battle.[18] In both accounts, rebel forces in the north were

---

[12] Could this Ḫirītu be identified with the town by that name besieged by Elamite troops in the Old Babylonian period? When they were unable to take the town, the Elamites appear to have returned to Eshnunna; this could suggest that the town besieged by them had been within striking distance of Eshnunna (see *AEM* 1/2 327:6'-7', 328:21-22, 376: 5-10, and 384:23'). These references were kindly brought to my attention by D.R. Frayne.

[13] Piepkorn, *Asb.*, pp. 76-77 vii 3-35. Edition C (Bauer, *Asb.*, pl. 11 and p. 17 viii 3-20) does not appear to add any information of value about this incident that is not contained in edition B.

[14] See Zadok, *RGTC* 8, p. 275. McEwan connects the Sumandir of edition B with this place (*RA* 74 [1980]: 171).

[15] See Goetze, *JCS* 7 (1953): 56; Groneberg, *RGTC* 3, pp. 158-59. Beitzel has located the town near the ford at modern Tarmiya (*Iraq* 46 [1984]: 37 n. 50). The association of Mangisi with this location was first proposed by Millard in *Iraq* 26 (1964): 24. The place or places called Mangiṣṣi/Mankiṣṣi in Middle Babylonian texts and located in the area of Nippur and the province of Bīt-Sîn-māgir are to be distinguished from the town in the northeast. See Edzard in *RLA* 7, pp. 339-40 and Nashef, *RGTC* 5, p. 183; the province of Bīt-Sîn-māgir apparently lay near the Sealand (*ibid.*, pp. 68-69), though note that a Bīt-Sîn-māgir is located near Dūr-Kurigalzu on the *TAVO* map B III 7 which is associated with Nashef's volume.

[16] See Zadok, *RGTC* 8, pp. 275 and 382-83, and Nashef, *RGTC* 5, p. 316.

[17] Edzard and Farber, *RGTC* 2, pp. 166-67.

[18] *Iraq* 26 (1964): 24-25.

defeated early in the revolt by an Assyrian army[19] and it would not be surprising if the one specific battle of the revolt considered worthy of mention in Ashurbanipal's annals[20] was also the one battle mentioned in the Akītu Chronicle. If identified with the earlier site on the Tigris in the region of the Diyala, Mangisi would have lain quite close to Sippar, in whose province the battle at Ḫirītu took place. The identification of the battle mentioned in edition B with the one in the Akītu Chronicle and the astronomical diary does, however, present at least one problem. The Babylonian chronicle and diary state that it was Babylonians (troops of Akkad) who fought with the Assyrians, while edition B, an Assyrian document, only refers to Elamite forces on the opposing side. One could argue that the difference is due to the different orientations of the texts (i.e., Babylonian versus Assyrian). Similar conflicting reports about who took part in fighting (as well as who won) are preserved about the battle at Dēr in 720, where scholars give greater credence to a statement found in a chronicle—regrettably not in the same chronicle as the one in question here—than to those found in Assyrian (and Babylonian) royal inscriptions.[21] However, in view of the detail involved in edition B (e.g., the names of the various Elamite officials taking part in the battle and their fates), it seems certain that a battle between Elamite and Assyrian forces actually took place. Possibly the Babylonian sources subsumed the Elamite troops under the term "army of Akkad" since the Elamites had come to aid Babylonia, induced by a "gift" from Šamaš-šuma-ukīn to Ḫumban-nikaš (i.e., in Babylonian employ). Nevertheless, since several military engagements undoubtedly took place in northern Babylonia during the early years of the revolt—the chronicle states that "there was war; fighting continued" (MUNUS.KÚR GAR-*at ṣal-tu₄ sad-rat*) immediately following its entry about the battle at Ḫirītu[22]—and in view of the differences in the two accounts over who fought in the battle, it is likely that two battles, not one, are described in the sources.

19 Edition B does not give a precise date for the battle; however, since the Elamite army was sent by Ḫumban-nikaš II, it must have taken place before his death partway through the revolt.

20 Excluding the battles with the Arabs (see above).

21 See Grayson in *Studies Landsberger*, pp. 340-42.

22 Grayson, *Chronicles*, no. 16:16.

APPENDIX E

The Dating of Ashurbanipal's Campaigns against Ḫumban-ḫaltaš III

The problem of the exact dates of Ashurbanipal's two campaigns in Elam against Ḫumban-ḫaltaš III has been discussed for a number of years but as yet no consensus has been reached. The information available offers several possibilities, none of which is in any way conclusive. In attempting to determine the dates of the two campaigns, the following points must be kept in mind:

1) The previous king of Elam, Indabibi, is known to have been on the throne for at least part of 649.[1]

2) Neither edition B nor edition D of Ashurbanipal's annals mentions Indabibi having been replaced by Ḫumban-ḫaltaš III or a campaign to Elam which could be identified with one against Ḫumban-ḫaltaš III. Various copies of these editions were composed in 649 and 648.[2]

3) Ḫumban-ḫaltaš III is first mentioned as ruler of Elam in editions K and C of Ashurbanipal's annals, which mention the first campaign against the Elamite king. No date is preserved for edition K, but edition C was composed in the eponymy of Nabû-nādin-aḫḫē (647 or 646).[3]

4) Both campaigns are described in edition F of Ashurbanipal's annals, the earliest copy of which was composed on the twenty-fourth day of Ayyaru (II) of the eponymy of Nabû-šar-aḫḫēšu (646 or 645).[4]

5) Both campaigns are described before the death of Nabû-bēl-šumāti in edition A and that death appears to have taken place no earlier than the month

---

1 *ABL* 1151 (letter from Ashurbanipal to Indabibi, "king of Elam," composed in 649).

2 Piepkorn, *Asb.*, pp. 90-91 and Millard, *Iraq* 30 (1968): 102-103. One copy was composed in the fifth month of 648 (K 2732++). For a tentative assignment of all copies composed in 648 to edition D, see Cogan, *JCS* 32 (1980): 148-49.

3 For the dates of the eponymy of Nabû-nādin-aḫḫē and edition C, see chapter 3. Cogan and Tadmor argue that edition K was composed before edition C and suggest 647 and 646 for editions K and C respectively (*Or.* NS 50 [1981]: 238-39). With regard to Indabibi's loss of the throne, see pp. 185-86.

4 See Aynard, *Asb.*, p. 12 and n. 3. For the date of the eponymy of Nabû-šar-aḫḫēšu, see chapter 3. Both campaigns are also described in editions T and A; edition T, the earlier edition of the two, was copied on 24-VI of the eponymy of Nabû-šar-aḫḫēšu (Thompson, *PEA*, p. 36 and pl. 18 vi 51-53) and edition A somewhat later (eponymy of Šamaš-danninanni).

of Šabaṭu (XI) of the eponymy of Nabû-nādin-aḫḫē and no later than 26-IV of the eponymy of Nabû-šar-aḫḫēšu.[5]

6) The first campaign began in the month of Simanu (III).[6]

7) The second campaign lasted at least one month and twenty-five days.[7]

8) Editions A, F, and T record that Ashurbanipal escorted back to Uruk the statue of Nanaya which he had recovered from Elam in the course of the second campaign and that he set it up in the temple Eḫilianna. Edition A adds that the statue entered Uruk on the first day of the month of Kislīmu (IX).[8]

Although Ḫumban-ḫaltaš III must have replaced Indabibi as ruler of Elam sometime between 649 and the eponymy of Nabû-nādin-aḫḫē (647 or 646), the exact date cannot be determined at present. While he may have become king before the end of the Šamaš-šuma-ukīn Revolt, there is no evidence to prove this.[9] In addition, it seems likely that the two campaigns took place before the eponymy of Nabû-šar-aḫḫēšu. This suggests the following possible dates for Ashurbanipal's two campaigns against Ḫumban-ḫaltaš III:

	First Campaign	Second Campaign
1.	III-648	648 (after III)
2.	III-648	647
3.	III-648	646
4.	III-647	647 (after III)
5.	III-647	646
6.	III-646	646 (after III)

The first three proposals require one or both campaigns to have taken place before Babylon fell to the Assyrians (sometime after 30-V-648) and Ḫumban-ḫaltaš III to have replaced Indabibi by the beginning of 648 at the latest;[10] the first, fourth, and sixth require the two campaigns to have been in the same year; and the third, fifth, and sixth require the eponymy of Nabû-šar-aḫḫēšu

---

5 Nabû-bēl-šumāti was still alive on the former date, when Ashurbanipal wrote to the elders of Elam demanding the surrender of the rebel (BM 132980; see above, p. 207). *ABL* 879, a letter from Ḫumban-ḫaltaš III to Ashurbanipal, was composed on the latter date and mentions the arrest and return of the rebel (presumably his body); that the body had already been sent to Ashurbanipal at the time the letter was written is inferred from the use of the perfect *ussēbilka* in line 8.

6 Aynard, *Asb.*, pp. 44-45 iii 33-36 and Streck, *Asb.*, pp. 40-43 iv 110-13.

7 Aynard, *Asb.*, pp. 56-57 v 55 and Streck, *Asb.*, pp. 56-57 vi 77-78. Note, however, that edition A also states that Ashurbanipal overthrew Elam in one month (literally "in a month of days"); Streck, *Asb.* pp. 56-57 vi 99-100.

8 Aynard, *Asb.*, pp. 58-59 v 72-vi 11; Streck, *Asb.*, pp. 58-59 vi 107-24; and Thompson, *PEA*, p. 35 and pl. 17 v 9-32.

9 See also p. 186.

10 Proposal 2 has recently been suggested by Grayson in *ZA* 70 (1980): 231.

to be dated to 645 rather than 646. If Ashurbanipal campaigned in Elam before Babylon fell, he must have felt very confident about the situation in Babylonia, believing that the fall of the city was imminent and would not require his own presence or that of all his army. In this case, it may have been word of his victory over the Elamites, the usual supporters of the Babylonian rebels, which caused the people of Babylon to despair and submit. A campaign against Ḫumban-ḫaltaš in Simanu of 648, however, also means that at least one copy of edition D of Ashurbanipal's annals mentioning Indabibi as king of Elam would have been made even after a campaign had been carried out against Indabibi's successor as king of Elam.[11] The possibility of two campaigns in the same year cannot be ruled out; however, the descriptions in Ashurbanipal's annals do not give the immediate impression that they were conducted in the same year.[12] If the statue of Nanaya went directly from Susa to Uruk, then the second campaign must have been over by the ninth month and the two campaigns must have been completed within seven months (III-IX), with the second having begun no more than four months after the first. Thus, if we assume that it is unlikely that any campaign took place before Babylon fell and that two long and arduous campaigns were conducted in the same year, we are left with the fifth proposal (first campaign in the third month of 647 and second campaign in 646), a scheme which, as noted above, requires the eponymy of Nabû-šar-aḫḫēšu to date to 645.[13] Since this latter dating is contested, and all the other proposals present some problem or other, we must await further information to help clarify matters.

---

11 See p. 293 n. 2.

12 The description of the campaigns in K 2631+2653+2855:12-rev. 23 (Streck, *Asb.*, pp. 178-87) is confused and appears to refer to three campaigns against Ḫumban-ḫaltaš (in rev. 9 we should probably read ^{m}*um-man-*[*al-da-si*] rather than Streck's ^{m}*um-man-*[*i-gaš*]); however, this source also seems to refer to campaigns in two consecutive years (*ibid.*, pp. 184-85 rev. 8-9). In her unpublished dissertation "Assurbanipal's Elamite Campaigns: A Literary and Political Study" (University of Pennsylvania, 1987), P.D. Gerardi argues that a study of the literary structure of the Assyrian campaign accounts suggests that both campaigns took place in the same year, in 647.

13 This proposed dating is the one used in the most recent study of Elamite history (Carter and Stolper, *Elam*, pp. 51-52).

APPENDIX F

The Identification of Ashurbanipal as Kandalānu

The present study has taken the view that while currently available data do not exclude the possibility of identifying Ashurbanipal with Kandalānu (i.e., the Assyrian king ruling Babylonia after the death of Šamaš-šuma-ukīn under the "throne name" of Kandalānu), the two were more probably distinct individuals.[1] In a recent work dealing with the fall of Assyria, Stefan Zawadzki has studied the question anew and strongly asserted the opinion that the two should be identified: "the identification of Ashurbanipal as Kandalanu, the subject of many heated discussions, should be no longer questioned."[2] In view of the importance of the matter to our understanding of the history of the period it seems necessary to re-examine the question here. The arguments presented by Zawadzki will be used as starting points for this review.

(1) Zawadzki points out that according to Berossos Šamaš-šuma-ukīn was succeeded by Sardanapallos (=Ashurbanipal) and he compares this to the statements in Babylonian Kinglist A and the Ptolemaic Canon that Šamaš-šuma-ukīn was succeeded by Kandalānu.[3]

The strongest, and in fact only direct piece of evidence for the identification of the two individuals has always been the statement attributed to Berossos that Šamaš-šuma-ukīn was succeeded as king of Babylonia by Ashurbanipal. The tradition that preserves Berossos' statements, however, is late in date and very involved.[4] It cannot be accepted without question since other statements attributed to Berossos can be proven to be incorrect historically. In addition, while it is recorded in one place that Berossos stated that Šamaš-šuma-ukīn was succeeded by Ashurbanipal, two other places omitted the name of Ashurbanipal and simply stated that Šamaš-šuma-ukīn

---

1 See pp. 193-95. This view has been expounded most recently by Brinkman in *RLA* 5, p. 368 and *Prelude*, pp. 105-106. Note also A.T. Clay's useful summary of the evidence and scholarly opinion (up until about 1908) in *BE* 8/1, pp. 6-11.

2 *Fall of Assyria*, pp. 24 and 57-62.

3 *Fall of Assyria*, pp. 24 and 57. Schnabel, *Berossos*, p. 270 lines 35-36; Grayson in *RLA* 6, p. 93 iv 21-22 and p. 101. The name of the king who preceded Kandalānu in the Uruk kinglist is not preserved (*ibid.*, p. 97 line 2).

4 See Brinkman, *PKB*, pp. 34-35 and Burstein, *SANE* 1/5 (1978): 6 and 10-11.

was succeeded by his brother.[5] Perhaps Kandalānu was a third son of Esarhaddon and later tradition erroneously supplied the name of Šamaš-šuma-ukīn's more famous brother. Or perhaps both statements are incorrect and Kandalānu was totally forgotten since he was a mere figurehead, with Ashurbanipal holding all real power over Babylonia.

(2) According to Zawadzki, Ashurbanipal and Kandalānu died in the same year (627) and if Ashurbanipal were indeed Kandalānu each of the three sources mentioned above would give him a total reign of 42 years (by adding the lengths of reigns accorded to Šamaš-šuma-ukīn and Kandalānu). This would accord with the length of Ashurbanipal's reign stated in the Harran inscription of Nabonidus' mother.[6]

The total length of Šamaš-šuma-ukīn's reign and that of Kandalānu is 42 years in both Berossos and the Ptolemaic Canon and this does match the figure given for Ashurbanipal in the only source recording the length of that king's reign. It should actually be one less than the length of the reign of Ashurbanipal since Šamaš-šuma-ukīn ascended the throne in the year following Ashurbanipal's accession; however, the Ptolemaic Canon and Berossos each made a "mistake" of one year in one or the other of the kings' lengths of reign. Berossos presumably assumed Šamaš-šuma-ukīn ascended the throne at the same time as Ashurbanipal and thus allotted him a reign of twenty-one instead of twenty years. The Ptolemaic Canon gave Kandalānu a reign of twenty-two years, instead of twenty-one, presumably allotting to him the "kingless" year following the end of his reign and preceding the accession of Nabopolassar to the throne of Babylonia. The lengths of reign for Šamaš-šuma-ukīn and Kandalānu in the third source, Babylonian Kinglist A, are not preserved. Allowing for these "corrections" (which are also accepted by Zawadzki) and assuming that Kandalānu's and Ashurbanipal's reigns ended in the same year, the total number of regnal years assigned for Šamaš-šuma-ukīn and Kandalānu by the Ptolemaic Canon and Berossos would naturally equal those commonly assigned to Ashurbanipal. We know that there was civil strife immediately following the death of Ashurbanipal, and quite likely preceding it, and it would not be surprising if a puppet ruler's reign over Babylonia had ended during that time.

(3) Economic texts were dated at Nippur by Ashurbanipal's regnal years (using 668 as his first regnal year), while after the first month of 646 texts elsewhere from Babylonia used only Kandalānu's years (with 647 as his first regnal year). Brinkman has argued that it is difficult to understand why the

---

5 See Schnabel, *Berossos*, p. 269 line 29 and p. 270 line 7.

6 *Fall of Assyria*, pp. 24 and 57. Gadd, *AnSt* 8 (1958): 46-47 and pl. 5 i 30.

two different systems of dating were used if the two individuals were one. Zawadzki contends that the reason for the two systems is that "Nippur was not under Babylonian control but directly under Assyrian administration" and was considered to be "almost [an] integral part of Assyria."[7]

Certainly Ashurbanipal appears to have kept Nippur under his own control after the end of the revolt of 652-648, but this is also noted by Brinkman.[8] The problem is that even if Nippur was directly under Assyrian administration, why would Ashurbanipal wish to emphasize the fact (and cause Babylonian resentment) by requiring that his "Assyrian" rather than his "Babylonian" name be used? There is no reason the "Babylonian" name could not have been used by the local scribes at Nippur when dating everyday business documents even if there was an Assyrian garrison in the city or if that city was considered to be more closely connected to Assyria than were other Babylonian cities. The absolute consistency in the use of the royal names, and the titles associated with them, is important. After the first month of 646 no economic text from Babylonia was dated by Ashurbanipal's regnal years at any site except Nippur and none from Nippur were dated by Kandalānu's regnal years. Ashurbanipal was "king of the lands," "king of the world," or "king of Assyria" in date formula, while Kandalānu was "king of Babylon." In view of the large number of texts, scribes, and places involved, one might expect to have found at least one case where the scribe used a wrong name or title if Ashurbanipal and Kandalānu were indeed the same person.

(4) No texts dated by the accession year of Kandalānu are known; the first document mentioning him comes from Babylon and is dated late in his first year (6-X-647). However, texts were dated by Ashurbanipal's years at Nippur in 648, at Borsippa, Nippur, and Uruk in 647, and at Dilbat in 646. Zawadzki argues that this can not be explained if 648 was Kandalānu's accession year and feels that the only explanation can be that Ashurbanipal decided to use the name of Kandalānu in Babylonian business documents in 647. Since the king had already had his accession year in the past (669) and only his name had changed, there was no reason to have another one.[9]

---

7 *Fall of Assyria*, pp. 58-59. *B-K* J and L; Brinkman, *Prelude*, p. 106. Zawadzki (*Fall of Assyria*, pp. 58-59) also argues that Nippur remained under Assyrian control and was not handed over to Šamaš-šuma-ukīn before the middle of 664 since a document was dated at that city according to Ashurbanipal's regnal years in the fifth month of 664 and since the first document dated by the Babylonian king's regnal years at Nippur comes from 660 (NBC 6142 and *TuM* 2-3 10; *B-K* J.5 and K.26). A different explanation for the former dating is presented in chapter 7.

8 *Prelude*, pp. 106-107.

9 *Fall of Assyria*, pp. 59-60. IM 57906, IM 57912, BM 29171, W. 18874, YBC 7166, Ashmolean 1924.1260 (*OECT* 10 9), VAT 17904 (Jakob-Rost, *FB* 10 [1968]: 57-58 no.

The absence of accession year texts for Kandalānu may be explained in one of two ways. First, we may simply have not yet found these documents. We have after all only two texts for 648 which are not dated by the regnal years of Šamaš-šuma-ukīn; both come from Nippur and would have used Ashurbanipal's regnal years in any case. Since we do not know exactly when Babylon fell in 648, Kandalānu may not have been appointed king until near the end of that year, making his accession year very brief. The Šamaš-šuma-ukīn Revolt had only just been crushed and matters were still unsettled, thus we should not expect many texts from this period. Second, Kandalānu may have been nominated and installed as king of Babylonia at the Near Year's festival at the beginning of 647. Thus he may have had no accession year, although it must be admitted that this would have been unprecedented. It is a problem that a few texts were dated by Ashurbanipal in 647 at Borsippa (three texts) and Uruk (two texts) and in the first month of 646 at Dilbat (one text), i.e., to the period after Kandalānu ascended the throne of Babylonia.[10] This can, however, be explained if we assumed that Assyrian troops which had come to put down the rebellion had not yet left those cities and their administration had not yet been returned to Babylonians. Thus these cities may simply have not yet been handed over to Kandalānu's jurisdiction. On the other hand, if Ashurbanipal was Kandalānu, why was not Kandalānu's name used in the text from Dilbat in 646, since that name had already been used at Babylon? Or would this be an example of the inconsistency desired above, but supporting the identification of Ashurbanipal with Kandalānu?

(5) According to Zawadzki, the fact that the Synchronistic Kinglist from Assyria gives the name of Ashurbanipal twice, once opposite Šamaš-šuma-ukīn and once opposite Kandalānu, cannot provide an argument either for or against the identification. Whether he was Kandalānu or not the list would have looked the same since in Babylonia the ruler's name was Kandalānu.[11]

While the evidence of the Synchronistic Kinglist is not strong, I would argue that the lack of any indication that one person was meant by the different names is *prima facie* evidence that two separate individuals were

13), IM 58813 (McCown, Haines, and Biggs, *Nippur* 2, pp. 75 and 87 no. 28), Ashmolean 1924.484 (*OECT* 10 399), and VAT 2963 (*VAS* 5 3); *B-K* J.16-24 and L.1 respectively. Zawadzki also refers to texts which he says probably come from Sippar and date to Ashurbanipal's twenty-second year (647). The texts in question (BM 49326 and 62469; *B-K* L.2-3) date to Kandalānu's first year (as correctly shown on Zawadzki's chart, *Fall of Assyria*, p. 58). While the two texts are part of the Sippar collection of the British Museum, that collection includes texts from other sites than just Sippar; thus it is not certain that they came from that city or were composed there.

10 The presence of texts dated by Ashurbanipal at Nippur is not a problem since Nippur was kept under Assyrian control throughout this part of his reign.

11 *Fall of Assyria*, p. 60.

meant. Ashurbanipal and Kandalānu appear twice in the text opposite one another (once in the body of the text and once in the summary statement about the length of the period considered in the document) and never with an indication that the two were one.[12] The Assyrian compilers of this text had already called Sennacherib king of both Assyria and Bablyonia for the period after the destruction of Babylon in 689, even though he never appears to have claimed the kingship of Babylonia during that time. One may wonder if they would have "disguised" the fact that Ashurbanipal had ruled Babylonia by using two separate names for him without any indication that the two referred to the same person.

(6) Kandalānu's name appears only in chronological texts and date formulae. Official documents recording the construction or restoration of temples in Babylonia at that time ascribed these acts to Ashurbanipal. Zawadzki states that it was the duty and privilege of the sovereign to carry out such actions and that "it is easy ... to imagine that even though Ashurbanipal wanted business documents to be dated by the name of Kandalanu, he still chose that his activities as a benefactor be associated with his supremacy over the whole Empire, not only Babylonia."[13]

We may have no official inscriptions of Kandalānu's because he was a mere figurehead; after the experience with Šamaš-šuma-ukīn, Ashurbanipal would not have wanted the new king to have any real power. Kandalānu was to be merely a symbol, an indication that Babylonia still existed as a separate kingdom with its own ruler. Or possibly we may simply have not yet found Kandalānu's building inscriptions. We should note that Šamaš-šuma-ukīn left few official texts and, in fact, there are few official inscriptions of Ashurbanipal from Babylonia clearly dating from after about 643. Since Ashurbanipal left inscriptions describing his building projects in Babylonia during the reign of Šamaš-šuma-ukīn (who surely held more authority than Kandalānu), it is not surprising that he left some from the time of Kandalānu as well. A copy of edition H of Ashurbanipal's annals comes from Babylon and is dated to the sixth day of Ayyaru (II) of his thirtieth year (639) as "king of Assyria";[14] however, it is not surprising that an inscription of the Assyrian king would be dated by his regnal years and not those of his vassal.

Kandalānu now appears to be attested in a letter, *CT* 53 966, but it is uncertain if this would sustain the identification or not. The fact that the letter also mentions Šērū'a-ēṭerat could connect Kandalānu with the Assyrian royal family, and thus possibly with her brother Ashurbanipal. However, it has

---

12 Grayson in *RLA* 6, p. 120 iv 15 and 17-20.

13 *Fall of Assyria*, p. 61.

14 Nassouhi, *AfK* 2 (1924-25): 101 and 104-105 viii 14-16; title partially restored.

always been possible that Kandalānu was another member of the royal family and the text is too damaged to determine the exact context in which he appears.[15]

(7) In Zawadzki 's opinion, the identification is sustained by the fact that there are no date formulae which would be similar those used in 538: "the first year of Cyrus, king of lands, and of Cambyses, king of Babylon."[16]

This type of date formula, however, was unusual and appears approximately one hundred years after the time of Kandalānu. Babylonia had just been conquered by the Persians and this formula may reflect Persian tradition or have been invented by Babylonian scribes to describe a particular political/administrative structure new to them. No such date formulae have been found mentioning Sennacherib and Bēl-ibni or Aššur-nādin-šumi, or Ashurbanipal and Šamaš-šuma-ukīn; yet in each case the Assyrian king was overlord of the Babylonian ruler, just as would be the case with Ashurbanipal and Kandalānu.

(8) Zawadzki believes that Šamaš-danninanni, a Babylonian official who bore the titles *šakin māti* of Akkad and *(ša) pīḫati* of Babylon in eponym dates from this time, administered all of Babylonia and compares his position to that of Gubaru who was appointed governor of all of Babylonia by Cyrus after the Persian conquest in 539. He then argues that if Kandalānu was distinct from Ashurbanipal, Šamaš-danninanni would have "duplicated Kandalanu's powers of jurisdiction."[17]

The fact that Šamaš-danninanni was an eponym official clearly indicates that he held an important post, but there is no evidence that he was more than governor of Babylon and its surrounding territory. Gubaru held office over one hundred years after the time of Šamaš-danninanni and under different political circumstances; there is no reason to assume that Šamaš-danninanni held a similar position to that of Gubaru. Borsippa and Uruk are known to have had their own governors during the reign of Kandalānu (see Appendix B) and there is no evidence that they were subject to Šamaš-danninanni. Zawadzki argues that the term Akkad in Šamaš-danninanni's title was being used in an archaic fashion to refer to all of Babylonia and finds support for this in the fact that Šamaš-danninanni appears with the title governor of Akkad in *BIN* 2 132. In that text, Šamaš-danninanni took part in a proceeding involving a dispute over some Puqudians who had earlier been presented to the goddesses Ištar of Uruk and Nanaya. The fact that Šamaš-

---

15 That the letter deals with political, not family matters is suggested by the references to the king of Elam and [Bīt]-Ibâ. On the letter, see pp. 194-95.

16 *Fall of Assyria*, p. 61.

17 *Fall of Assyria*, pp. 61-62. Falkner, *AfO* 17 (1954-56): 106.

danninanni appears in this text is not evidence that he administered all of Babylonia. The text is damaged, but does not appear to indicate that he settled the dispute as the superior official. Instead, it appears to indicate that Šamaš-danninanni and Kudurru were on opposing sides.[18] Nor can the fact that Šamaš-danninanni was a eponym official be used to indicate that he held authority over all Babylonia since provincial governors (albeit not Babylonian ones) regularly appeared as eponym officials. While the term Akkad can refer to Babylonia as a whole, it does not have to mean more than northern Babylonia, the region in which Babylon was the main centre, and Šamaš-danninanni's other title, (*ša*) *pīḫati*, "provincial governor" of Babylon, would support this interpretation. The assignment of the administration of all of Babylonia to one official (i.e., not a vassal ruler) would have been unprecedented; as a rule the Assyrians left the provincial structure of Babylonia alone and the subjugation of one governor to another governor would have been most unusual. Thus, there is no reason to assume that Šamaš-danninanni had authority over exactly the same area as Kandalānu.

(9) Finally, Zawadzki points out that while edition A of Ashurbanipal's annals states that after the Assyrian king put down Šamaš-šuma-ukīn's revolt he appointed new governors and officials for Babylonia, this edition makes no mention of the appointment of Kandalānu to be king of Babylonia.[19]

The fact that Ashurbanipal's annals do not mention the appointment of a new king of Babylonia is surprising, particularly since edition A was composed a few years after Kandalānu's first appearance in date formulae. Perhaps the reason was that Assyrian scribes felt that after describing the long revolt of Šamaš-šuma-ukīn the mention of a new king of Babylonia would have made the reader wonder if the latter would also cause problems for Assyria by leading Babylonians into rebellion. Or perhaps the scribes were subtly attempting to denigrate Kandalānu by considering him among the governors and officials appointed by Ashurbanipal. All this is mere supposition, but one may also point out that the annals also do not state that Ashurbanipal assumed the rulership of Babylonia, or sat on the throne of Babylon, or took the hand of Bēl in the New Year's ritual.

Two further matters are germane to the question of the identification of Ashurbanipal with Kandalānu: Did Assyrian kings ever use two names[20] and

---

[18] For a collation of the relevant lines, see p. 201 n. 48. Zawadzki states that Kudurru arbitrated the matter and if so, this would not indicate that he was subordinate to Šamaš-danninanni. Damage to the text, however, makes it unclear who actually settled the matter.

[19] *Fall of Assyria*, p. 62. Streck, *Asb.*, pp. 40-41 iv 104-105.

[20] On this matter, see only Zawadzki's brief statement in *Fall of Assyria*, p. 24.

did Ashurbanipal ever claim the rulership of Babylonia under the name Ashurbanipal?

(10) It is clear that at least a few Assyrian rulers did take a new name when they were appointed heir to the throne or when they assumed power. Although individuals other than the monarch did occasionally bear the name Sargon,[21] it is unlikely that Sargon II of Assyria was originally given a name meaning "The-King-Is-Legitimate" (or something similar);[22] and Esarhaddon was given the name Aššur-etil-ilāni-mukīn-apli ("Aššur-Lord-Of-The-Gods-The-One-Who-Preserves-The-Heir") at some point before he became king. Sargon, however, did not continue to use his old name; in fact we have no idea what it was. Esarhaddon's new name was used in only two official inscriptions and he soon reverted to his original name.[23] In addition, it is sometimes thought that the name Ashurbanipal may have been given to that individual when he was appointed heir and that his old name had been Sîn-nādin-apli since at one point Esarhaddon had considered appointing Sîn-nādin-apli his heir.[24] While Tiglath-pileser III is called Pūlu (or a similar name) in some non-contemporary sources—for example, Babylonian Kinglist A, the Old Testament, Berossos, Josephus, and the Ptolemaic Canon—he was never given this name in Assyrian and Babylonian texts of the period. Shalmaneser V appears as Ulūlayu (or with a similar name) in Babylonian Kinglist A, the Ptolemaic Canon, the Assur Ostracon, and a few Nimrud letters. The Nimrud letters were of contemporary date, but they were not formal, official documents. Undoubtedly Shalmaneser was using a family nickname in these letters, which were written by him to his father.[25] There is

---

21 Several Babylonians bore this name in the first millennium (see Tallqvist, *NBN*, p. 201), but it is unclear if it was used by private individuals in Assyria. An individual by the name of Sargon does appear in an extispicy report for Ashurbanipal (Starr, *SAA* 4, no. 305 rev. 6'), but he may have been a Babylonian.

22 Sargon II does not appear to have been directly in line for the throne, but rather to have been a usurper or a member of a junior branch of the royal house (see Brinkman, *Studies Oppenheim*, p. 12). With regard to the meaning of the name Sargon, see B. Lewis, *The Sargon Legend* (American Schools of Oriental Research, Dissertation Series 4) (Cambridge, Massachusetts, 1980), p. 30.

23 Borger, *Esarh.*, p. 9 §7:1 (two exemplars) and p. 68 §30:1 (mostly restored). In addition, he appears with both names in *ABL* 1452 (the newer one abbreviated to Aššur-etillu-mukīn-apli), where it is stated that Esarhaddon had been renamed, and in *ABL* 308 (newer name abbreviated to Aššur-etil-ilāni-mukinni), a private family letter. Only Borger, *Esarh.*, p. 9 §7 does not date to the time of Sennacherib. Could the agate bead with an inscription of Aššur-etil-ilāni-mukīn-apli which was found in a post-Assyrian grave at Assur (Haller, *Gräber*, p. 71) have originally belonged to Esarhaddon?

24 See Starr, *SAA* 4, no. 149 and Parpola, *LAS* 2, p. 106 (with references).

25 The name Ulūlayu presumably indicates the month in which Shalmaneser was born; the meaning of the name Pūlu is unknown, although it may have been an abbreviation for the last part of Tiglath-pileser's name.

no evidence that Tiglath-pileser III and Shalmaneser V were ever referred to as Pūlu and Ulūlayu in contemporary official documents.[26] Scholars have sometimes attempted to argue that the later Assyrian kings Aššur-etil-ilāni and Sîn-šarra-iškun were one and the same person;[27] however, this view has never gained wide acceptance and it is clear that one was not the "Assyrian" throne name and the other the "Babylonian" throne name of one individual.[28]

In sum, there is no proof that Assyrian kings ever used alternate throne names, let alone separate "Assyrian" and "Babylonian" throne names. However, even if Ashurbanipal had wanted a separate throne name for use in Babylonia, why would he have chosen the name Kandalānu? The name appears to mean "shaped like a *kandalu*-utensil" and may have indicated some physical deformity (a clubfoot?).[29] If he was physically deformed he would surely not have wished to emphasize the fact by choosing to use a name indicating this, even if it was a family nickname. When new official names for Sargon II and Esarhaddon had been adopted or considered, the new names reflected ideas of royal legitimacy and divine sponsorship. Perhaps Ashurbanipal chose someone with a physical deformity and/or a pejorative name to be the new ruler of Babylonia as an insult to the Babylonians or because he wanted the new ruler of Babylonia to be someone who would find it difficult to inspire the Babylonians and lead them into rebellion.

(11) If Ashurbanipal was Kandalānu, and thus king of Babylonia, we might expect to find some indication in the titles and epithets accorded him in royal inscriptions that Ashurbanipal claimed to be ruler of Babylonia (i.e., specific titles claiming the rulership of Babylonia as opposed to such general titles as "king of the world" and "king of the four quarters"). Certainly, his son Sîn-šarra-iškun referred to his father as "king of Sumer and Akkad," but that was after the fact.[30] No inscription, whether royal or economic in nature, refers to Ashurbanipal as "king of Babylon," but an inscription from Nippur describing the restoration of the Egiginû, the ziggurat of that city, does refer to Ashurbanipal as "king of Sumer and Akkad"[31] and several fragmentary Assyrian inscriptions (apparently all from Nineveh) accord him this title

---

[26] This matter is discussed in greater depth by Brinkman in *PKB*, pp. 61-62, 240-41 n. 1544, and 243-44 nn. 1560 and 1564, and by von Soden in *ZA* 58 (1967): 243-44.

[27] E.g., Borger, *WZKM* 55 (1959): 68.

[28] See, for example, von Soden, *ZA* 58 (1967): 244. Both names were used extensively in Babylonian sources. Zawadzki discusses this identification in connection with other scholars' reconstructions of the history of the period but does not give his opinion on the matter (e.g., *Fall of Assyria*, p. 31).

[29] See *CAD* 8 (K), p. 148; *AHw*, p. 436; and Stamm, *Namengebung*, p. 266 n. 5.

[30] See Donbaz and Grayson, *Clay Cones*, p. 56:1-2 and Schroeder, *KAH* 2 134:2-3.

[31] L-29-632+633+636 and duplicate UM 55-21-384 line 10 (Gerardi, *Sjöberg Festschrift*, pp. 207-15).

and/or the title "viceroy of Babylon."[32] The dates of most of these texts are merely a matter of conjecture and could come from any time in the king's reign, but at least one Assyrian piece clearly dates to the period after the appointment of Kandalānu to be king of Babylonia.[33] In the inscription from Nippur, Ashurbanipal was also called "viceroy for the gods Aššur (AN.ŠÁR), Enlil, and Ninurta." The fact that Aššur, even under the "guise" of Anšar, was given precedence over Enlil in an inscription dedicated to Enlil from Enlil's own city would indicate a date when Nippur was under Assyrian control, likely during or after the rebellion of 652-648; and building projects are more likely to have taken place after the rebellion than during it.

These texts could suggest that at some point(s) Ashurbanipal claimed the rulership of Babylonia, or at least that his scribes claimed it for him, and this could support the idea that Ashurbanipal was king of Babylonia and thus Kandalānu. However, the title "king of Sumer and Akkad" was a traditional one associated with the holder of the city of Nippur and scribes there may have felt it politic to accord this title to the Assyrian king since he had not turned that city over to Kandalānu (assuming the text does date after the ascension of Kandalānu). More importantly, in the major inscriptions from the time after the rebellion (e.g., editions A, F, and apparently C), Ashurbanipal was not called "viceroy of Babylon" or "king of Sumer and Akkad."[34] Edition T, which dates from the eponymy of Nabû-šar-aḫḫēšu (646 or 645), describes Ashurbanipal as having conducted various building projects in Babylonia (and Assyria) and yet gives him no title indicating that

---

[32] Tablet fragments: K 3079+K 3080 i 4-5 (both titles partly restored; Bauer, *Asb.*, p. 19 and pl. 34); K 2813+K 8394+79-7-8,134:22 (latter title, possibly referring to Esarhaddon; *ibid.*, p. 38 and pl. 29); 80-7-19,141:9 (former title, partially restored; ascription to Ashurbanipal uncertain; *ibid.*, p. 48 and pl. 56); DT 133:3' (latter title, partly restored; *ibid.*, p. 54 and pl. 52); possibly 81-7-27,70:4' (latter title, restoration uncertain; *ibid.*, p. 49 and pl. 58). Prism fragments: BM 123410:14 (both titles, former mostly restored; Millard, *Iraq* 30 [1968]:107 and pl. 24); and BM 134455 col. B 12'-13' (both[?] titles, mostly restored and most likely referring to Esarhaddon; Thompson, *Iraq* 7 [1940]: 103 and fig. 13 no. 23). Note also the "cylinder" mentioned in Smith, *Assyrian Discoveries*, p. 377 and Streck, *Asb.*, p. 409 (possibly one or more of the pieces published by Bauer; both titles). Cf. Seux, *Épithètes*, p. 278.

[33] BM 123410; according to Millard the piece is part of edition H, but this remains to be proven. If the text found by G. Smith is related to edition C (see previous note) that piece would also date to this period (see Streck, *Asb.*, pp. 408-409). Note also K 3079+3080 which Bauer also connects to edition C; this text may deal with the temple of Nergal at Cutha (see ii 23-26 and iv 2), whose restoration is described in 3 *R* pl. 38 no. 1, a text composed after the revolt and the destruction of Susa. On the other hand, K 2813++ is a dedicatory inscription to Nusku of Harran and Ashurbanipal is known to have carried out work there at the start of his reign (Streck, *Asb.*, pp. 158-75, note rev. 51).

[34] Note also the inscriptions dedicated to Nergal of Cutha and Marduk of Babylon (Streck, *Asb.*, pp. 176-89 and 276-87) which date to this period which do not accord him titles reflecting the rulership of Babylonia.

he held the rulership of Babylonia. Would the Assyrian scribes have refrained from according him such titles just because he was not using his "Babylonian" name in the text? Sennacherib's texts omitted such titles but that Assyrian king had renounced them because he was furious with Babylonia after the death of his son Aššur-nādin-šumi. There is no evidence that Ashurbanipal felt the same way, particularly not if one assumes that he bore them under another name. Perhaps the texts which accorded him the titles "king of Sumer and Akkad" and "viceroy of Babylon" were written by careless or over-zealous scribes who gave greater weight to the fact that Ashurbanipal was the real ruler of Babylonia than to the fact that someone else (a non-entity with no actual authority) sat on the throne of Babylon. On the one hand, the fact that Ashurbanipal is accorded the titles "king of Sumer and Akkad" and "viceroy of Babylon" in a few texts (mainly miscellaneous dedicatory inscriptions from Assyria) and that at least one of these texts clearly dates to the period when Kandalānu was on the throne of Babylonia, could provide some support for the identification of Ashurbanipal with Kandalānu. On the other hand, the omission of such titles in the major inscriptions of the period argues against it.

In conclusion, Zawadzki has raised a number of new points on the question of the identification of Ashurbanipal as Kandalānu, but has not proven his case. Although an identification of the two solves some problems, it raises new ones. The data currently available suggest, but do not prove, that Ashurbanipal and Kandalānu were more likely two individuals than one.[35]

[35] The question of who Kandalānu may have been is discussed in chapter 9.

BIBLIOGRAPHY

al-Adami, K. "A New Kudurru of Marduk-nadin-ahhe: IM. 90585." *Sumer* 38 (1982): 121-33.

Adams, R.McC. *Heartland of Cities: Surveys of Ancient Settlement and Land Use on the Central Floodplain of the Euphrates.* Chicago, 1981.

———. *Land Behind Baghdad: A History of Settlement on the Diyala Plains.* Chicago, 1965.

———. "Settlement and Irrigation Patterns in Ancient Akkad." In *The City and Area of Kish*, by McG. Gibson, pp. 182-208. Coconut Grove, Florida, 1972.

——— and Nissen, H.J. *The Uruk Countryside: The Natural Setting of Urban Societies.* Chicago, 1972.

Ahmed, S.S. "Ashurbanipal and Shamash-shum-ukin during Esarhaddon's Reign." *Abr-Nahrain* 6 (1965-66): 53-62.

———. "Causes of Shamash-shum-ukin's Uprising, 652-651 B.C." *Zeitschrift für alttestamentliche Wissenschaft* 79 (1967): 1-13.

———. *Southern Mesopotamia in the Time of Ashurbanipal.* The Hague and Paris, 1968.

Aro, J. "Remarks on the Practice of Extispicy in the Time of Esarhaddon and Assurbanipal." In *La divination en Mésopotamie ancienne et dans les régions voisines*, pp. 109-17. Paris, 1966.

Aynard, J.-M. *Le Prisme du Louvre AO 19.939.* Bibliothèque de l'École des Hautes Études 309. Paris, 1957.

Barnett, R.D. *Sculptures from the North Palace of Ashurbanipal at Nineveh (668-627 B.C.).* London, 1976.

Bauer, T. *Das Inschriftenwerk Assurbanipals.* 2 volumes. Assyriologische Bibliothek, Neue Folge 1-2. Leipzig, 1933.

Becking, B. "The Two Neo-Assyrian Documents from Gezer in Their Historical Context." *JEOL* 27 (1981-82): 76-89.

Beitzel, B.J. "Išme-Dagan's Military Actions in the Jezirah: A Geographical Study." *Iraq* 46 (1984): 29-42.

Bergamini, G. "Levels of Babylon Reconsidered." *Mesopotamia* 12 (1977): 111-52, figures 71-81, and plates 1-3.

Black, J.A. "Ḥabl aṣ-Ṣaḫr 1983-1985: Nebuchadnezzar II's Cross-Country Wall North of Sippar. Part 4: Babylonian Textual Evidence." *NAPR* 1 (1987): 15-21.

Borger, R. "Der Aufstieg des neubabylonischen Reiches." *JCS* 19 (1965): 59-78.

———. *Die Inschriften Asarhaddons, Königs von Assyrien.* AfO Bei. 9. Graz, 1956.

———. "König Sanheribs Eheglück." *ARRIM* 6 (1988): 5-11.

———. "Mesopotamien in den Jahren 629-621 v. Chr." *WZKM* 55 (1959): 62-76.

———. "Vier Grenzsteinurkunden Merodachbaladans I. von Babylonien." *AfO* 23 (1970): 1-26.

———. "Zur Datierung des assyrischen Königs Sinšumulīšir." *Or.* NS 38 (1969): 237-39.

———. "Zur Königsliste aus Uruk." *AfO* 25 (1974-77): 165-66.

———. Review of B. Landsberger, *Brief eines Bischofs von Esagila an König Asarhaddon. BiOr* 29 (1972): 33-37.

Börker-Klähn, J. *Altvorderasiatische Bildstelen und vergleichbare Felsreliefs.* 2 volumes. Baghdader Forschungen 4. Mainz am Rhein, 1982.

Bottéro, J. "Le substitut royal et son sort en Mésopotamie ancienne." *Akkadica* 9 (1978): 2-24.

Braun-Holzinger, E.A. "Bronze Objects from Babylonia." In *Bronzeworking Centres of Western Asia c. 1000-539 B.C.*, edited by J. Curtis, pp. 119-34 and figures 90-96. London and New York, 1988.

———. *Figürliche Bronzen aus Mesopotamien.* Munich, 1984.

Brinkman, J.A. "Babylonia under the Assyrian Empire, 745-627 B.C." In *Power and Propaganda: A Symposium on Ancient Empires*, edited by M.T. Larsen, pp. 223-50. Mesopotamia 7. Copenhagen, 1979.

———. "The Babylonian Chronicle Revisited." In *Lingering Over Words: Studies in Ancient Near Eastern Literature in Honor of William L. Moran*, edited by T. Abusch, J. Huehnergard, and P. Steinkeller, pp. 73-104. Harvard Semitic Studies 37. Atlanta, 1990.

———. "The Early Neo-Babylonian Monarchy." In *Le palais et la royauté (archéologie et civilisation)*, edited by P. Garelli, pp. 409-15. Paris, 1974.

———. "The Elamite-Babylonian Frontier in the Neo-Elamite Period, 750-625 B.C." In *Fragmenta Historiae Elamicae: Mélanges offerts à M.J. Steve*, edited by L. De Meyer, H. Gasche, et F. Vallat, pp. 199-207. Paris, 1986.

———. "Elamite Military Aide to Merodach-Baladan." *JNES* 24 (1965): 161-66.

———. "Foreign Relations of Babylonia from 1600 to 625 B.C.: The Documentary Evidence." *American Journal of Archaeology* 76 (1972): 271-81.

———. "From Destruction to Resurrection: The Antecedents of Babylonia's Birth as a World Power in the Seventh Century B.C." *Sumer* 41 (1985): 110-12.

———. "Kandalānu." *RLA* 5, pp. 368-69.

———. *Materials and Studies for Kassite History.* Volume 1: *A Catalogue of Cuneiform Sources Pertaining to Specific Monarchs of the Kassite Dynasty.* Chicago, 1976.

———. "Merodach-Baladan II." In *Studies Presented to A. Leo Oppenheim*, edited by R.D. Biggs and J.A. Brinkman, pp. 6-53. Chicago, 1964.

———. "Mesopotamian Chronology of the Historical Period." In *Ancient Mesopotamia: Portrait of a Dead Civilization*, by A.L. Oppenheim, revised edition completed by Erica Reiner, pp. 335-48. Chicago and London, 1977.

———. "Notes on Arameans and Chaldeans in Southern Mesopotamia in the Early Seventh Century B.C." *Or.* NS 46 (1977): 304-25.

———. *A Political History of Post-Kassite Babylonia, 1158-722 B.C.* AnOr 43. Rome, 1968.

———. *Prelude to Empire: Babylonian Society and Politics, 747-626 B.C.* Occasional Publications of the Babylonian Fund 7. Philadelphia, 1984.

———. "Provincial Administration in Babylonia under the Second Dynasty of Isin." *JESHO* 6 (1963): 233-42.

———. "Remarks on Two Kudurrus from the Second Dynasty of Isin." *RA* 61 (1967): 70-74.

———. "Sennacherib's Babylonian Problem: An Interpretation." *JCS* 25 (1973): 89-95.

———. "Settlement Surveys and Documentary Evidence: Regional Variation and Secular Trend in Mesopotamian Demography." *JNES* 43 (1984): 169-80.

———. "Textual Evidence for Bronze in Babylonia in the Early Iron Age, 1000-539 BC." In *Bronzeworking Centres of Western Asia c. 1000-539 B.C.*, edited by J. Curtis, pp. 135-68. London and New York, 1988.

———. "Through a Glass Darkly: Esarhaddon's Retrospects on the Downfall of Babylon." *JAOS* 103 (1983): 35-42.

———. "Ur: 'The Kassite Period and the Period of the Assyrian Kings.'" *Or.* NS 38 (1969): 310-48.

———. "Ur: 721-605 B.C." *Or.* NS 34 (1965): 241-58.

——— and Dalley, S. "A Royal Kudurru from the Reign of Aššur-nādin-šumi." *ZA* 78 (1988): 76-98 and 2 plates following p. 80.

——— and Kennedy, D.A. "Documentary Evidence for the Economic Base of Early Neo-Babylonian Society: A Survey of Dated Babylonian Economic Texts, 721-626 B.C." *JCS* 35 (1983): 1-90.

——— and Kennedy, D.A. "Supplement to the Survey of Dated Neo-Babylonian Economic Texts, 721-626 B.C. (*JCS* 35 [1983] 1-90)." *JCS* 38 (1986): 99-106.

Budge, E.A.W. "On Some Recently Acquired Babylonian Tablets." Copies by J.N. Strassmaier. *ZA* 3 (1888): 211-30.

———. "Sale of a Garden." *PSBA* 10 (1887-88): 146 and plates 4-6 following p. 148.

——— and King, L.W. *Annals of the Kings of Assyria: The Cuneiform Texts with Translations, Transliterations, etc., from the Original Documents in the British Museum.* Volume 1. London, 1902.

Burstein, S.M. *The* Babyloniaca *of Berossus.* SANE 1/5. Malibu, 1978.

Cameron, G.G. *History of Early Iran.* Chicago, 1936.

Carter, E., and Stolper, M.W. *Elam: Surveys of Political History and Archaeology.* Berkeley, Los Angeles, and London, 1984.

Charpin, D., et al. *Archives épistolaires de Mari I/2.* Archives Royales de Mari 26. Paris, 1988.

Civil, M. "Note sur les inscriptions d'Asarhaddon à Nippur." *RA* 68 (1974): 94.

Clay, A.T. *Babylonian Business Transactions of the First Millennium B.C.* BRM 1. New York, 1912.

———. *Legal and Commercial Transactions Dated in the Assyrian, Neo-Babylonian and Persian Periods Chiefly from Nippur.* BE 8/1. Philadelphia, 1908.

Cocquerillat, D. *Palmeraies et cultures de l'Eanna d'Uruk (559-520).* Ausgrabungen der Deutschen Forschungsgemeinschaft in Uruk-Warka 8. Berlin, 1968.

———. "Recherches sur le verger du temple campagnard de l'Akītu ($KIRI_6$ ḫallat)." *WO* 7 (1973-74): 96-134.

Cogan, M. "Ashurbanipal Prism F: Notes on Scribal Techniques and Editorial Procedures." *JCS* 29 (1977): 97-107.

———. *Imperialism and Religion: Assyria, Judah and Israel in the Eighth and Seventh Centuries B.C.E.* Missoula, Montana, 1974.

———. "New Additions to the Corpus of Esarhaddon Historical Inscriptions." *AfO* 31 (1984): 72-75.

———. "Omens and Ideology in the Babylon Inscription of Esarhaddon." In *History, Historiography and Interpretation: Studies in Biblical and Cuneiform Literatures*, edited by H. Tadmor and M. Weinfield, pp. 76-87. Jerusalem and Leiden, 1983.

———. "A Plaidoyer on Behalf of the Royal Scribes." In *Ah, Assyria ... Studies in Assyrian History and Ancient Near Eastern Historiography Presented to Hayim Tadmor*, edited by M. Cogan and I. Eph'al, pp. 121-28. Scripta Hierosolymitana 33. Jerusalem, 1991.

——— and Tadmor, H. "Ashurbanipal's Conquest of Babylon: The First Official Report—Prism K." *Or.* NS 50 (1981): 229-40.

——— and Tadmor, H. "Gyges and Ashurbanipal: A Study in Literary Transmission." *Or.* NS 46 (1977): 65-85.

Cole, S.W. "Four Early Neo-Babylonian Lists of Officials and Professions from Nippur." *JAC* 1 (1986): 127-43.

Combe, É. *Histoire du culte de Sin en Babylonie et en Assyrie.* Paris, 1908.

Contenau, G. *Contrats néo-babyloniens.* Volume 1: *De Téglath-phalasar III à Nabonide.* TCL 12. Paris, 1927.

Crawford, V.E. "Nippur, the Holy City." *Archaeology* 12 (1959): 74-83.

Curtis, J. "Assyria as a Bronzeworking Centre in the Late Assyrian Period." In *Bronzeworking Centres of Western Asia c. 1000-539 B.C.*, edited by J. Curtis, pp. 83-96 and figures 74-89. London and New York, 1988.

Dalley, S. *A Catalogue of the Akkadian Cuneiform Tablets in the Collections of the Royal Scottish Museum, Edinburgh, with Copies of the Texts.* Edinburgh, 1979.

——— and Postgate, J.N. *The Tablets from Fort Shalmaneser.* Cuneiform Texts from Nimrud 3. London, 1984.

Dandamaev, M.A. "The Neo-Babylonian Citizens." *Klio* 63 (1981): 45-49.

———. "The Neo-Babylonian Popular Assembly." In Šulmu. *Papers on the Ancient Near East Presented at International Conference of Socialist Countries (Prague, Sept. 30-Oct. 3, 1986)*, edited by P. Vavroušek and V. Souček, pp. 63-71. Prague, 1988.

———. *Slavery in Babylonia from Nabopolassar to Alexander the Great (626-331 BC).* Revised edition. Translated by V.A. Powell and edited by M.A. Powell and D.B. Weisberg. DeKalb, Illinois, 1984.

———. "Social Stratification in Babylonia (7th-4th Centuries B.C.)." *Acta Antiqua* 22 (1974): 433-44.

Delaunay, J.A. *Nouvelle édition de A.B. Moldenke, Cuneiform Texts in the Metropolitan Museum of Art (New York).* Paris, 1977.

Deller, K. "Die Briefe des Adad-šumu-uṣur." In lišān mitḫurti: *Festschrift Wolfram Freiherr von Soden zum 19.VI.1968 gewidmet von Schülern und Mitarbeitern*, edited by W. Röllig, with the assistance of M. Dietrich, pp. 45-64. AOAT 1. Kevelaer and Neukirchen-Vluyn, 1969.

———. "Drei wiederentdeckte neuassyrische Rechtsurkunden aus Aššur." *Bagh. Mitt.* 15 (1984): 225-51 and pls. 24-25.

De Meyer, L. *Tell ed-Dēr.* Volume 3: *Soundings at Abū Ḥabbah (Sippar).* Louvain, 1980.

Dietrich, M. *Die Aramäer Südbabyloniens in der Sargonidenzeit (700-648).* AOAT 7. Kevelaer and Neukirchen-Vluyn, 1970.

———. "Gurasimmu." *RLA* 3, pp. 702-703.

———. *Neo-Babylonian Letters from the Kuyunjik Collection.* CT 54. London, 1979.

———. "Neue Quellen zur Geschichte Babyloniens, I." *WO* 4 (1967-68): 61-103.

———. "Neue Quellen zur Geschichte Babyloniens, II." *WO* 4 (1967-68): 183-251 and 5 (1969-70): 51-56.

———. "Neue Quellen zur Geschichte Babyloniens, III." *WO* 5 (1969-70): 176-90.

———. "Neue Quellen zur Geschichte Babyloniens, IV." *WO* 6 (1970-71): 157-62.

van Dijk, J. "Die Inschriftenfunde." In *XVIII. vorläufiger Bericht über die von dem Deutschen Archäologischen Institut und der Deutschen Orient-Gesellschaft aus Mitteln der Deutschen Forschungsgemeinschaft unternommenen Ausgrabungen in*

Uruk-Warka Winter 1959/60, by H. Lenzen et al, pp. 39-62 and plates 20 and 27-28. ADOG 7. Berlin, 1962.
——— and W.R. Mayer. *Texte aus dem Rēš-Heiligtum in Uruk-Warka.* Baghdader Mitteilungen Beiheft 2. Berlin, 1980.
Donbaz, V., and Grayson, A.K. *Royal Inscriptions on Clay Cones from Ashur now in Istanbul.* Royal Inscriptions of Mesopotamia, Supplements 1. Toronto, Buffalo, and London, 1984.
Donner, H., and Röllig, W. *Kanaanäische und aramäische Inschriften.* Revised edition. 3 volumes. Wiesbaden, 1969-73.
Dossin, G. "L'inscription de fondation de Iaḫdun-Lim, roi de Mari." *Syria* 32 (1955): 1-28 and plates 1-2.
Dougherty, R.P. *Archives from Erech, Neo-Babylonian and Persian Periods.* GCCI 2. New Haven, 1933.
———. *The Sealand of Ancient Arabia.* Yale Oriental Series, Researches 19. New Haven, 1932.
van Driel, G. Review of S.S. Ahmed, *Southern Mesopotamia in the Time of Ashurbanipal. BiOr* 26 (1969): 367-68.
Driver, G.R. "The Sale of a Priesthood." *JRAS* Centenary Supplement 1924, pp. 41-48 and plates 4-5 following p. 48.
Dubberstein, W.H. "Assyrian-Babylonian Chronology (669-612 B.C.)." *JNES* 3 (1944): 38-42.
———. "Comparative Prices in Later Babylonia (625-400 B.C.)." *AJSL* 56 (1939): 20-43.
Durand, J.-M. *Documents cunéiformes de la IVe Section de l'École pratique des Hautes Études.* Volume 1: *Catalogue et copies cunéiformes.* Hautes Études Orientales 18. Geneva and Paris, 1982.
———. "Note à propos de la date d'*ABL* 290." *RA* 75 (1981): 181-85.
———. *Textes babyloniens d'époque récente.* Recherche sur les grandes civilisations, Cahier 6. Paris, 1981.
Edzard, D.O. "Kaldu." *RLA* 5, pp. 291-97.
———. "Kullab." *RLA* 6, p. 305.
———. "Mankisum." *RLA* 7, pp. 339-40.
——— and Farber, G. *Die Orts- und Gewässernamen der Zeit der 3. Dynastie von Ur.* RGTC 2. Wiesbaden, 1974.
Ellis, M. deJ. "Neo-Babylonian Texts in the Yale Babylonian Collection." *JCS* 36 (1984): 1-63.
Eph'al, I. *The Ancient Arabs: Nomads on the Borders of the Fertile Crescent, 9th-5th Centuries B.C.* Jerusalem and Leiden, 1982.
———. "'Arabs' in Babylonia in the 8th Century B.C." *JAOS* 94 (1974): 108-15.
———. "On Warfare and Military Control in the Ancient Near Eastern Empires: A Research Outline." In *History, Historiography and Interpretation: Studies in Biblical and Cuneiform Literatures*, edited by H. Tadmor and M. Weinfeld, pp. 88-106. Jerusalem and Leiden, 1983.
———. "The Western Minorities in Babylonia in the 6th-5th Centuries B.C.: Maintenance and Cohesion." *Or.* NS 47 (1978): 74-90.
Fales, F.M. "Prosopography of the Neo-Assyrian Empire, 2: The Many Faces of Nabû-šarru-uṣur." *SAAB* 2 (1988): 105-24.
Falkenstein, A. *Literarische Keilschrifttexte aus Uruk.* Berlin, 1931.
Falkner, M. "Die Eponymen der spätassyrischen Zeit." *AfO* 17 (1954-56): 100-20.

———. "Neue Inschriften aus der Zeit Sin-šarru-iškuns." *AfO* 16 (1952-53): 305-10.

Fecht, G. "Zu den Namen ägyptischer Fürsten und Städte in den Annalen des Assurbanipal und der Chronik des Asarhaddon." *MDAIK* 16 (1958): 112-19.

Figulla, H.H. *Business Documents of the New-Babylonian Period.* UET 4. London, 1949.

Finkel, I.L. "A Neo-Assyrian Exchange Tablet." *SAAB* 3 (1989): 65-68.

Fisher, C.S. *Excavations at Nippur.* Philadelphia, 1905.

Fisher, W.B. *The Middle East: A Physical, Social and Regional Geography.* Seventh edition. London, 1978.

Forrer, E. "Aramu." *RLA* 1, pp. 131-39.

Frame, G. "Another Babylonian Eponym." *RA* 76 (1982): 157-66.

———. "Babylonia 689-627 B.C.: A Political History." Ph.D. dissertation, University of Chicago, 1981.

———. "The Correspondence of Nabû-ušabši, Governor of Uruk." In *Cuneiform Archives and Libraries: Papers Read at the 30ᵉ Rencontre Assyriologique Internationale, Leiden, 4-8 July 1983*, edited by K.R. Veenhof, pp. 260-72. Leiden, 1986.

———. "The 'First Families' of Borsippa during the Early Neo-Babylonian Period." *JCS* 36 (1984): 67-80.

———. "A Kudurru Fragment from the Reign of Adad-apla-iddina." *AOF* 13 (1986): 206-11.

———. "Neo-Babylonian and Achaemenid Economic Texts from the Sippar Collection of the British Museum." *JAOS* 104 (1984): 745-52.

Frymer-Kensky, T. "The Tribulations of Marduk: The So-Called 'Marduk Ordeal Text.'" *JAOS* 103 (1983): 131-41.

Gadd, C.J. "The Harran Inscriptions of Nabonidus." *AnSt* 8 (1958): 35-92 and plates 1-16.

———. "Inscribed Prisms of Sargon II from Nimrud." *Iraq* 16 (1954): 173-201 and pls. 44-51.

——— and Kramer, S.N. *Literary and Religious Texts, Second Part.* UET 6/2. London, 1966.

——— et al. *Royal Inscriptions.* 2 parts. UET 1. London, 1928.

Gallery, M. "The Office of the šatammu in the Old Babylonian Period." *AfO* 27 (1980): 1-36.

Galter, H.D. "Die Zerstörung Babylons durch Sanherib." *StOr* 55 (1984): 161-73.

Garelli, P. "L'appel au roi sous l'empire assyrien." In *Reflets des deux fleuves. Volume de mélanges offerts à André Finet*, edited by M. Lebeau and P. Talon, pp. 45-46. Akkadica Supplementum 6. Leuven, 1989.

———. "Hofstaat. B. Assyrisch." *RLA* 4, pp. 446-52.

———. "Les sujets du roi d'Assyrie." In *La voix de l'opposition en Mésopotamie*, edited by A. Finet, pp. 189-213. Brussels, n.d.

Gerardi, P. "Assurbanipal and the Building of the Egigunû." In *dumu-e$_2$-dub-ba-a: Studies in Honor of Åke W. Sjöberg*, edited by H. Behrens, D. Loding, and M.T. Roth, pp. 207-15. Occasional Publications of the Samuel Noah Kramer Fund 11. Philadelphia, 1989.

———. "Assurbanipal's Elamite Campaigns: A Literary and Political Study." Ph.D. dissertation, University of Pennsylvania, 1987.

———. "Declaring War in Mesopotamia." *AfO* 33 (1986): 30-38.

———. "Epigraphs and Assyrian Palace Reliefs: The Development of the Epigraphic Text." *JCS* 40 (1988): 1-35.

———. "A New Assurbanipal Brick Inscription from Nippur." *ARRIM* 4 (1986): 37.

Gibson, J.C.L. *Aramaic Inscriptions, including Inscriptions in the Dialect of Zenjirli.* Textbook of Syrian Semitic Inscriptions 2. Oxford, 1975.

Gibson, McG. *The City and Area of Kish.* Coconut Grove, Florida, 1972.

———. "Current Oriental Institute Excavations in Iraq." *BSMS* 3 (1982): 16-32.

———. "Nippur." In *The Oriental Institute 1987-88 Annual Report*, edited by J.H. Johnson, pp. 18-29. Chicago, 1989.

———. "Nippur. Back to Tablet Hill: Sixteenth Season at Nippur, 1985." In *The Oriental Institute 1984-85 Annual Report*, edited by J.H. Johnson, pp. 20-30. Chicago, 1985.

———. "Nippur under Assyrian Domination: 15th Season of Excavation, 1981-1982." In *The Oriental Institute 1981-82 Annual Report*, edited by R.McC. Adams, pp. 40-48. Chicago, 1982.

———. "16th Season at Nippur." *Sumer* 43 (1984): 252-54.

———, Zettler, R.L., and Armstrong, J.A. "The Southern Corner of Nippur: Summary of Excavations during the 14th and 15th Seasons." *Sumer* 39 (1983): 170-90.

——— et al. *Excavations at Nippur, Eleventh Season.* OIC 22. Chicago and London, 1975.

——— et al. *Excavations at Nippur, Twelfth Season.* OIC 23. Chicago, 1978.

Godbey, A.H. "The Esarhaddon Succession." *AJSL* 22 (1905-1906): 63-80.

Goetze, A. "Additions to Parker and Dubberstein's Chronology." *JNES* 3 (1944): 43-46.

———. "Esarhaddon's Inscription from the Inanna Temple in Nippur." *JCS* 17 (1963): 119-31.

———. "An Old Babylonian Itinerary." *JCS* 7 (1953): 51-72.

Gonçalves, F.J. *L'expédition de Sennachérib en Palestine dans la littérature hébraïque ancienne.* Louvain-la-Neuve, 1986.

Grayson, A.K. "Akkadian Treaties of the Seventh Century B.C." *JCS* 39 (1987): 127-60.

———. *Assyrian and Babylonian Chronicles.* Texts from Cuneiform Sources 5. Locust Valley, New York, 1975.

———. "Assyrian and Babylonian Kinglists: Collations and Comments." In lišān mitḫurti: *Festschrift Wolfram Freiherr von Soden zum 19.VI.1968 gewidmet von Schülern und Mitarbeitern*, edited by W. Röllig, with the assistance of M. Dietrich, pp. 105-18. AOAT 1. Kevelaer and Neukirchen-Vluyn, 1969.

———. *Assyrian Royal Inscriptions.* 2 volumes. Wiesbaden, 1972 and 1976.

———. "The Chronology of the Reign of Ashurbanipal." *ZA* 70 (1980): 227-45.

———. "Königslisten und Chroniken, Akkadisch." *RLA* 6, pp. 86-135.

———. "Problematical Battles in Mesopotamian History." In *Studies in Honor of Benno Landsberger on His Seventy-fifth Birthday, April 21, 1965*, edited by H.G. Güterbock and T. Jacobsen, pp. 337-42. Assyriological Studies 16. Chicago, 1965.

———. "The Walters Art Gallery Sennacherib Inscription." *AfO* 20 (1963): 83-96.

——— and Redford, D.B. *Papyrus and Tablet.* Englewood Cliffs, New Jersey, 1973.

Greenfield, J. "Babylonian-Aramaic Relationship." In *Mesopotamien und seine Nachbarn: Politische und kulturelle Wechselbeziehungen im Alten Vorderasien vom 4. bis 1. Jahrtausend v. Chr.*, edited by H.-J. Nissen and J. Renger, pp. 471-82. Berliner Beiträge zum Vorderen Orient 1. Berlin, 1982.

Groneberg, B. *Die Orts- und Gewässernamen der altbabylonischen Zeit.* RGTC 3. Wiesbaden, 1980.

Gurney, O.R. "Three Contract Tablets from Babylon." In *Societies and Languages of the Ancient Near East: Studies in Honour of I.M. Diakonoff*, edited by M.A. Dandamayev et al., pp. 120-28. Warminster, 1982.

Haller, A. *Die Gräber und Grüfte von Assur*. WVDOG 65. Berlin, 1954.

Hämeen-Anttila, J. "A New Text Relating to Ashurbanipal's Elamite Wars." *SAAB* 1 (1987): 13-16.

Hannoun, N. "Tell al-Seeb and Tell Haddad." *BSMS* 2 (1982): 5-6.

Hansen, D.P., and Dales, G.F. "The Temple of Inanna, Queen of Heaven, at Nippur." *Archaeology* 15 (1962): 75-84.

Hansman, J.F. "The Mesopotamian Delta in the First Millennium B.C." *Geographical Journal* 144 (1978): 49-61.

Harper, R.F. *Assyrian and Babylonian Letters Belonging to the K(ouyunjik) Collection(s) of the British Museum*. 14 volumes. Chicago, 1892-1914.

Heidel, A. "A New Hexagonal Prism of Esarhaddon (676 B.C.)." *Sumer* 12 (1956): 9-37 and plates1-12 following.

Heimpel, W. "Das Untere Meer." *ZA* 77 (1987): 22-91.

Heltzer, M. *The Suteans*. Naples, 1981.

Hilprecht, H.V. *Explorations in Bible Lands during the 19th Century*. Philadelphia, 1903.

Hinz, W. *The Lost World of Elam: Re-creation of a Vanished Civilization*. Translated by J. Barnes. London, 1972.

Hulin, P. "The Inscriptions on the Carved Throne-Base of Shalmaneser III." *Iraq* 25 (1963): 48-69 and plate 10.

Hunger, H. "Das Archiv des Nabû-ušallim." *Bagh. Mitt.* 5 (1970): 193-304.

———. "Kalendar." *RLA* 5, pp. 297-303.

Ishida, T. "The Succession Narrative and Esarhaddon's Apology: A Comparison." In *Ah, Assyria ... Studies in Assyrian History and Ancient Near Eastern Historiography Presented to Hayim Tadmor*, edited by M. Cogan and I. Eph'al, pp. 166-73. Scripta Hierosolymitana 33. Jerusalem, 1991.

Jacobsen, T. "Abstruse Sumerian. In *Ah, Assyria ... Studies in Assyrian History and Ancient Near Eastern Historiography Presented to Hayim Tadmor*, edited by M. Cogan and I. Eph'al, pp. 279-91. Scripta Hierosolymitana 33. Jerusalem, 1991.

———. *Salinity and Irrigation Agriculture in Antiquity. Diyala Basin Archaeological Projects: Report on Essential Results, 1957-58*. Bibliotheca Mesopotamica 14. Malibu, California 1982.

Jacoby, F. *Die Fragmente der griechischen Historiker*. Volume III/C/1: *Aegypten-Geten Nr. 608a-708*. Leiden, 1958.

Jakob-Rost, L. "Ein neubabylonisches Tontafelarchiv aus dem 7. Jahrhundert v.u.Z." *FB* 10 (1968): 39-62.

———. "Urkunden des 7. Jahrhunderts v.u.Z. aus Babylon." *FB* 12 (1970): 49-60.

Jastrow, M. "A Legal Document of Babylonia Dealing with the Revocation of an Illegal Sale." In *Oriental Studies: A Selection of the Papers Read before the Oriental Club of Philadelphia 1888-1894*, pp. 116-36 and plate opposite p. 136. Boston, 1894.

Joannès, F. *Archives de Borsippa: La famille Ea-ilûta-bâni. Étude d'un lot d'archives familiales en Babylonie du VIII*[e] *au V*[e] *siècle av. J.-C.* Hautes Études Orientales 25. Geneva, 1989.

———. *Les tablettes néo-babyloniennes de la Bodleian Library conservées à l'Ashmolean Museum*. OECT 12. Oxford, 1990.

———. *Textes économiques de la Babylonie récente (Étude des texts de TBER - Cahier n*[o] *6)*. Recherche sur les civilisations, Cahier 5. Paris, 1982.

Johns, C.H.W. *Assyrian Deeds and Documents Recording the Transfer of Property, Including the So-Called Private Contracts, Legal Decisions and Proclamations Preserved in the Kouyunjik Collections of the British Museum, Chiefly of the 7th Century B.C.* 4 volumes. Cambridge, 1898-1923.

———. "The Chronology of Ašurbânipal's Reign, B.C. 668-626. II." *PSBA* 25 (1903): 82-89.

Johnston, C. "Šamaš-šum-ukîn, The Eldest Son of Esarhaddon." *JAOS* 25 (1904): 79-83.

Jordan, J. *Uruk-Warka nach den Ausgrabungen durch die Deutsche Orient-Gesellschaft.* WVDOG 51. Leipzig, 1928.

al-Jumaily, A.I. "Investigations and Restoration at the Ziggurat of Aqarquf (10th-13 seasons)." *Sumer* 27 (1971): 63-98 and plates 1-16 (Arabic section).

Keiser, C.E. *Letters and Contracts from Erech Written in the Neo-Babylonian Period.* BIN 1. New Haven, London, and Oxford, 1917.

Kennedy, D.A. "Documentary Evidence for the Economic Base of Early Neo-Babylonian Society. Part II: A Survey of Babylonian Texts, 626-605 B.C." *JCS* 38 (1986): 172-244.

Kessler, K. *Untersuchungen zur historischen Topographie Nordmesopotamiens nach keilschriftlichen Quellen des 1. Jahrtausends v. Chr.* TAVO Beiheft B/26. Wiesbaden, 1980.

———. "Zu den keilschriftlichen Quellen des 2./1. Jahrtausends v. Chr. über Dilmun." In *Dilmun: New Studies in the Archaeology and Early History of Bahrain*, edited by D.T. Potts, pp. 147-60. Berliner Beiträge zum Vorderen Orient 2. Berlin 1983.

Kienast, B. "NA4 KIŠIB LUGAL *ša šiprēti.*" In *Language, Literature, and History: Philological and Historical Studies Presented to Erica Reiner*, edited by F. Rochberg-Halton, pp. 167-74. American Oriental Series 67. New Haven, 1987.

King, L.W. *Babylonian Boundary-Stones and Memorial Tablets in the British Museum.* 2 volumes. London, 1912.

———. *Cuneiform Texts from Babylonian Tablets, &c., in the British Museum.* Volume 34. London, 1914.

———. *The Letters and Inscriptions of Hammurabi, King of Babylon, about B.C. 2200, to Which Are Added a Series of Letters of Other Kings of the First Dynasty of Babylon.* 3 volumes. London, 1898-1900.

Kinnier Wilson, J.V. "An Introduction to Babylonian Psychiatry." In *Studies in Honor of Benno Landsberger on His Seventy-fifth Birthday, April 21, 1965*, edited by H.G. Güterbock and T. Jacobsen, pp. 289-98. Assyriological Studies 16. Chicago, 1965.

———. *The Nimrud Wine Lists: A Study of Men and Administration at the Assyrian Capital in the Eighth Century, B.C.* Cuneiform Texts from Nimrud 1. London, 1972.

Kitchen, K.A. *The Third Intermediate Period in Egypt (1100-650 B.C.).* 2nd edition with supplement. Warminster, 1986.

Klauber, E.G. *Assyrisches Beamtentum nach Briefen aus der Sargonidenzeit.* LSS 5/3. Leipzig, 1910.

———. *Politisch-religiöse Texte aus der Sargonidenzeit.* Leipzig, 1913.

Knudsen, E.E. "Fragments of Historical Texts from Nimrud, II." *Iraq* 29 (1967): 49-69 and plastes 14-29.

Knudtzon, J.A. *Assyrische Gebete an den Sonnengott für Staat und königliches Haus aus der Zeit Asarhaddons und Asurbanipals.* 2 volumes. Leipzig, 1893.

Koldewey, R. *Das Ischtar-Tor in Babylon.* WVDOG 32. Leipzig, 1918.

———. *Die Pflastersteine von Aiburschabu in Babylon.* WVDOG 2. Leipzig, 1901.

———. *Die Tempel von Babylon und Borsippa.* WVDOG 15. Leipzig, 1911.

———. *Das wieder erstehende Babylon. Die bisherigen Ergebnisse der deutschen Ausgrabungen.* 4th edition. Leipzig, 1925.

———. *Die Königsburgen von Babylon.* Volume 1: *Die Südburg.* Edited by F. Wetzel. WVDOG 54. Leipzig, 1931.

———. *Die Königsburgen von Babylon.* Volume 2: *Die Hauptburg und der Sommerpalast Nebukadnezars im Hügel Babil.* Edited by F. Wetzel. WVDOG 55. Leipzig, 1932.

König, F.W. *Die elamischen Königsinschriften.* AfO Bei. 16. Graz, 1965.

———. *Die* Persika *des Ktesias von Knidos.* AfO Bei. 18. Graz, 1972.

Krückmann, O. *Neubabylonische Rechts- und Verwaltungstexte.* TuM 2-3. Leipzig, 1933.

Kümmel, H.M. *Familie, Beruf und Amt im spätbabylonischen Uruk: prosopographische Untersuchungen zu Berufsgruppen des 6. Jahrhunderts v. Chr. in Uruk.* ADOG 20. Berlin, 1979.

Kuhrt, A.Th.L. "Lygdamis." *RLA* 7, pp. 186-89.

Kwasman, T. *Neo-Assyrian Legal Documents in the Kouyunjik Collection of the British Museum.* Studia Phol: Series Maior 14. Rome, 1988.

Labat, R. "Asarhaddon et la ville de Zaqqap." *RA* 53 (1959): 113-18.

———. *Traité akkadien de diagnostics et pronostics médicaux.* 2 volumes. Paris, 1951.

Laessøe, J. *Studies on the Assyrian Ritual and Series* bît rimki. Copenhagen, 1955.

Lambert, W.G. *Babylonian Wisdom Literature.* Reprint edition with corrections. Oxford, 1967.

———. "Esarhaddon's Attempt to return Marduk to Babylon." In *Ad bene et fideliter seminandum: Festgabe für Karlheinz Deller zum 21. Februar 1987*, edited by G. Mauer and U. Magen, pp. 157-74. AOAT 220. Kevelaer and Neukirchen-Vluyn, 1988.

———. "An Eye-Stone of Esarhaddon's Queen and Other Similar Gems." *RA* 63 (1969): 65-71.

———. "The God Aššur." *Iraq* 45 (1983): 82-86.

———. "An Incantation of the Maqlû Type." *AfO* 18 (1957-58): 288-99 and plates 11-16.

———. "Two Texts from the Early Part of the Reign of Ashurbanipal." *AfO* 18 (1957-58): 382-87.

——— and Millard, A.R. *Catalogue of the Cuneiform Tablets in the Kouyunjik Collection of the British Museum. 2nd Supplement.* London, 1968.

Landsberger, B. *Brief des Bischofs von Esagila an König Asarhaddon.* Mededelingen der Koninklijke Nederlandse Akademie van Wetenschappen, Afd. Letterkunde, N.R. 28/6. Amsterdam, 1965.

———. "Einige unerkannt gebliebene oder verkannte Nomina des Akkadischen." *WO* 3 (1964-66): 48-79.

——— and Bauer, T. "Zu neuveröffentlichten Geschichtsquellen aus der Zeit von Asarhaddon bis Nabonid." *ZA* 37 (1927): 61-98 and 215-22.

Lanfranchi, G.B. "Scholars and Scholarly Tradition in Neo-Assyrian Times: A Case Study." *SAAB* 3 (1989): 99-114.

Langdon, S. *Excavations at Kish.* Volume 1. Paris, 1924.

———. "Kandalānu and Ašurbanipal." *JRAS* 1928, pp. 321-25.

———. *Die neubabylonischen Königsinschriften.* Vorderasiatische Bibliothek 4. Leipzig, 1912.

———. "The Religious Interpretation of Babylonian Seals and a New Prayer of Shamash-shum-ukin (BM. 78219)." *RA* 16 (1919): 49-68.

Larsen, C.E. "The Mesopotamian Delta Region: A Reconsideration of Lees and Falcon." *JAOS* 95 (1975): 43-57.

——— and Evans, G. "The Holocene Geological History of the Tigris-Euphrates-Karun Delta." In *The Environmental History of the Near and Middle East Since the Last Ice Age*, edited by W.C. Brice, pp. 227-44. London, New York, and San Francisco, 1978.

Larsen, M. "Unusual Eponymy-Datings from Mari and Assyria." *RA* 68 (1974): 15-24.

Leemans, W.F. "*Kidinnu*: un symbole de droit divin babylonien." In *Symbolae ad jus et historiam antiquitatis pertinentes Julio Christiano van Oven dedicatae*, edited by M. David et al., pp. 36-61. Leiden, 1946.

Leeper, A.W.A. *Cuneiform Texts from Babylonian Tablets, &c., in the British Museum.* Volume 35. London, 1918.

Lees, G.M., and Falcon, N.L. "The Geographical History of the Mesopotamian Plains." *Geographical Journal* 118 (1952): 24-39 and 2 folding sheets.

Legrain, L. "Collection Louis Cugnin: textes cunéiformes, catalogue, transcription et traduction." *RA* 10 (1913): 41-68.

Lehmann, C.F. "Der babylonische Königsname Saosduchin." *ZK* 2 (1885): 360-64.

———. "Die Mondfinsternis vom 15. Šabaṭu unter Šamaššumukîn." *ZA* 11 (1896): 110-16.

———. *Šamaššumukîn, König von Babylonien 668-648 v. Chr., inschriftliches Material über den Beginn seiner Regierung.* 2 volumes. Assyriologische Bibliothek 8. Leipzig, 1892.

Leichty, E. "Bel-epuš and Tammaritu." *AnSt* 33 (1983): 153-55.

———. "Esarhaddon's 'Letter to the Gods.'" In *Ah, Assyria ... Studies in Assyrian History and Ancient Near Eastern Historiography Presented to Hayim Tadmor*, edited by M. Cogan and I. Eph'al, pp. 52-57. Scripta Hierosolymitana 33. Jerusalem, 1991.

Lenzen, H.J. et al. *XVIII. vorläufiger Bericht über die von dem Deutschen Archäologischen Institut und der Deutschen Orient-Gesellschaft aus Mitteln der Deutschen Forschungsgemeinschaft unternommenen Ausgrabungen in Uruk-Warka Winter 1959/60.* ADOG 7. Berlin, 1962.

———. *XIX. vorläufiger Bericht über die von dem Deutschen Archäologischen Institut und der Deutschen Orient-Gesellschaft aus Mitteln der Deutschen Forschungsgemeinschaft unternommenen Ausgrabungen in Uruk-Warka Winter 1960/61.* ADOG 8. Berlin, 1963.

Levine, L. "Sennacherib's Southern Front: 704-689 B.C." *JCS* 34 (1982): 28-58.

Lewis, B. *The Sargon Legend: A Study of the Akkadian Text and the Tale of the Hero Who Was Exposed at Birth.* American Schools of Oriental Research, Dissertation Series 4. Cambridge, Massachusetts, 1980.

Lewy, H. "Nitokris-Naqî'a." *JNES* 11 (1952): 264-86.

Lewy, J. "The Chronology of Sennacherib's Accession." In *Miscellanea orientalia dedicata Antonio Deimel annos LXX complenti*, pp. 225-31. AnOr 12. Rome, 1935.

Lie, A.G. *The Inscriptions of Sargon II, King of Assyria.* Part 1: *The Annals.* Paris, 1929.

Lieberman, S.J. "Canonical and Official Cuneiform Texts: Towards an Understanding of Assurbanipal's Personal Tablet Collection." In *Lingering Over Words: Studies in Ancient Near Eastern Literature in Honor of William L. Moran*, edited by T.

Abusch, J. Huehnergard, and P. Steinkeller, pp. 305-36. Harvard Semitic Studies 37. Atlanta, 1990.

Livingstone, A. *Court Poetry and Literary Miscellanea.* SAA 3. Helsinki, 1989.

———. *Mystical and Mythological Explanatory Works of Assyrian and Babylonian Scholars.* Oxford, 1986.

Luckenbill, D.D. *Ancient Records of Assyria and Babylonia.* 2 volumes. Chicago, 1926-27.

———. *The Annals of Sennacherib.* OIP 2. Chicago, 1924.

Lutz, H.F. "Neo-Babylonian Administrative Documents from Erech." *UCP* 9/1 (1927).

———. *Selected Sumerian and Babylonian Texts.* PBS 1/2. Philadelphia, 1919.

———. "The Warka Cylinder of Ashurbanipal." *UCP* 9/8 (1931).

MacFadyen, W.A., and Vita-Finzi, C. "Mesopotamia: The Tigris-Euphrates Delta and Its Holocene Hammar Fauna." With an appendix by J.E. Robinson. *Geological Magazine* 115 (1978): 287-300.

MacGinnis, J.D.A. "Ctesias and the Fall of Nineveh." *Sumer* 45 (1987-88): 40-43.

Machinist, P. "The Assyrians and Their Babylonian Problem: Some Reflections." *WBJ* 1984-85, pp. 353-64.

Malbran-Labat, F. *L'armée et l'organisation militaire de l'Assyrie d'après les lettres des Sargonides trouvées à Ninive.* Geneva and Paris, 1982.

———. "La Babylonie du sud, du XIIe au VIIe siècle avant notre ère d'après deux ouvrages récents." *JA* 260 (1972): 15-38.

———. "Nabû-bēl-šumâte, prince du Pays-de-la-Mer." *JA* 263 (1975): 7-37.

Mantius, W. "Das stehende Heer der Assyrerkönige und seine Organisation." *ZA* 24 (1910): 97-149 and 185-224.

Matsushima, E. "Les Rituels du Mariage Divin dans les Documents Accadiens." *ASJ* 10 (1988): 95-128.

Mattila, R. "The Political Status of Elam after 653 B.C. According to *ABL* 839." *SAAB* 1 (1987): 27-30.

McCown, D.E., and Haines, R.C. *Nippur.* Part 1: *Temple of Enlil, Scribal Quarter and Soundings.* Assisted by D.P. Hansen. OIP 78. Chicago, 1967.

McCown, D.E., Haines, R.C., and Biggs, R.D. *Nippur.* Part 2: *The North Temple and Sounding E.* Assisted by E.F. Carter. OIP 97. Chicago, 1978.

McEwan, G.J.P. "Agade after the Gutian Destruction: The Afterlife of a Mesopotamian City." In *Vorträge gehalten auf der 28. Rencontre Assyriologique Internationale in Wien 6.-10. Juli 1981*, edited by H. Hunger and H. Hirsch, pp. 8-15. AfO Bei. 19. Horn, 1982.

———. *The Late Babylonian Tablets in the Royal Ontario Museum.* ROMCT 2. Toronto, 1982.

———. *Late Babylonian Texts in the Ashmolean Museum.* OECT 10. Oxford, 1984.

———. *Priest and Temple in Hellenistic Babylonia.* Freiburger altorientalische Studien 4. Wiesbaden, 1981.

Meissner, B. "Šamaš-ibni von Bît-Dâkûri." *OLZ* 21 (1918): 220-23.

Messerschmidt, L. *Keilschrifttexte aus Assur historischen Inhalts.* Part 1. WVDOG 16. Leipzig, 1911.

Michalowski, P. "Presence at the Creation." In *Lingering Over Words: Studies in Ancient Near Eastern Literature in Honor of William L. Moran*, edited by T. Abusch, J. Huehnergard, and P. Steinkeller, pp. 381-96. Harvard Semitic Studies 37. Atlanta, 1990.

Michel, E. "Die Assur-Texte Salmanassars III. (858-824) 11. Fortsetzung." *WO* 4 (1967-68): 29-37.

Millard, A.R. "Another Babylonian Chronicle Text." *Iraq* 26 (1964): 14-35.

———. "Ashurbanipal's Ultimatum to Elam." In *Abstracts of the XXXVIe Rencontre Assyriologique Internationale, 10-14 July 1989*, [p. 17]. Ghent, [1989].

———. "Fragments of Historical Texts from Nineveh: Ashurbanipal." *Iraq* 30 (1968): 98-111 and plates 19-27.

———. "Some Esarhaddon Fragments Relating to the Restoration of Babylon." *AfO* 24 (1973): 117-19.

Miller, J.M., and Hayes, J.H. *A History of Ancient Israel and Judah.* Philadelphia, 1986.

de Miroschedji, P. "La localisation de Madaktu et l'organisation politique de l'Elam à l'époque néo-élamite." In *Fragmenta Historiae Elamicae: Mélanges offerts à M.J. Steve*, edited by L. De Meyer, H. Gasche, et F. Vallat, pp. 209-25. Paris, 1986.

Moldenke, A.B. *Cuneiform Texts in the Metropolitan Museum of Art.* 2 volumes. New York, 1893.

Moore, E.W. *Neo-Babylonian Business and Administrative Documents with Transliteration, Translation and Notes.* Ann Arbor, 1935.

Moorey, P.R.S. *Kish Excavations 1923-1933, with a Microfiche Catalogue of the Objects in Oxford Excavated by the Oxford-Field Museum, Chicago Expedition to Kish in Iraq, 1923-1933.* Oxford, 1978.

Moran, W.L. "Assurbanipal's Message to the Babylonians (*ABL* 301), with an Excursus on Figurative *biltu*." In *Ah, Assyria ... Studies in Assyrian History and Ancient Near Eastern Historiography Presented to Hayim Tadmor*, edited by M. Cogan and I. Eph'al, pp. 320-31. Scripta Hierosolymitana 33. Jerusalem, 1991.

Moren, S.M. "Note brève." *RA* 74 (1980): 190-91.

Moritz, B. "Die Nationalität der Arumu-Stämme in Südost-Babylonien." In *Oriental Studies Published in Commemoration of the Fortieth Anniversary (1883-1923) of Paul Haupt as Director of the Oriental Seminary of the Johns Hopkins University, Baltimore, Md.*, edited by C. Adler and A. Ember, pp. 184-211. Baltimore and Leipzig, 1926.

Mullo-Weir, C.J. "The Return of Marduk to Babylon with Shamashumukin." *JRAS* 1929, pp. 553-55.

Myhrman, D.W. *Babylonian Hymns and Prayers. PBS* 1/1. Philaelphia, 1911.

Nashef, K. *Die Orts- und Gewässernamen der mittelbabylonischen und mittelassyrischen Zeit.* RGTC 5. Wiesbaden, 1982.

Nassouhi, E. "Prisme d'Assurbânipal daté de sa trentième année, provenant du temple de Gula à Babylone." *AfK* 2 (1924-25): 97-106.

Nies, J.B., and Keiser, C.E. *Historical, Religious and Economic Texts and Antiquities.* BIN 2. New Haven, 1920.

North, R. "Status of the Warka Excavation." *Or.* NS 26 (1957): 185-256.

Nougayrol, J. "Nouveau fragment de prisme d'Asarhaddon relatant la restauration de Babylone." *AfO* 18 (1957-58): 314-18 and plates 21-22.

———. "Parallèles, duplicata, etc." *RA* 36 (1939): 29-40.

Oates, D. "Dilmun and the Late Assyrian Empire." In *Bahrain through the Ages: The Archaeology*, edited by H. Ali Al Khalifa and M. Rice, pp. 428-34. London, New York, Sydney, and Henley 1986.

Oates, J. "Assyrian Chronology, 631-612 B.C." *Iraq* 27 (1965): 135-59.

Oded, B. *Mass Deportations and Deportees in the Neo-Assyrian Empire.* Wiesbaden, 1979.

Oelsner, J. "Erwägungen zum Gesellschaftsaufbau Babyloniens von der neubabylonischen bis zur achämenidischen Zeit (7.-4. Jh. v.u.Z.)." *AOF* 4 (1976): 131-49.

Olmstead, A.T.E. "Assyrian Government of Dependencies." *American Political Science Review* 12 (1918): 63-77.

———. *Assyrian Historiography: A Source Study*. Columbia, 1916.

———. "The Fall and Rise of Babylon." *AJSL* 38 (1921-22): 73-96.

———. *History of Assyria*. Chicago and London, 1923.

Oppenheim, A.L. *Letters from Mesopotamia: Official, Business, and Private Letters on Clay Tablets from Two Millennia*. Chicago, 1967.

———. "Neo-Assyrian and Neo-Babylonian Empires." In *Propaganda and Communication in World History*. Volume 1: *The Symbolic Instrument in Early Times*, edited by H.D. Lasswell, D. Lerner, and H. Speier, pp. 111-44. Honolulu, 1979.

———. "A Note on *ša rēši*." *JANES* 5 (1973): 325-34.

———. "'Siege Documents' from Nippur." *Iraq* 17 (1955): 69-89.

Oppert, J. "Le nom de Saosduchin." *ZA* 6 (1891): 328-29.

———. "La vraie personnalité et les dates du roi Chiniladan." *RA* 1 (1886): 1-11.

Owen, D., and Watanabe, K. "Eine neubabylonische Gartenkaufurkunde mit Flüchen aus dem Akzessionsjahr Asarhaddons." *OrAnt* 22 (1983): 37-48.

Parker, B. "Administrative Tablets from the North-West Palace, Nimrud." *Iraq* 23 (1961): 15-67 and plates 9-30.

Parker, R.A., and Dubberstein, W.H. *Babylonian Chronology 626 B.C.-A.D. 75*. Brown University Studies 19. Providence, Rhode Island, 1956.

Parpola, S. "Assyrian Library Records." *JNES* 42 (1983): 1-29.

———. "Assyrian Royal Inscriptions and Neo-Assyrian Letters." In *Assyrian Royal Inscriptions: New Horizons in Literary, Ideological and Historical Analysis*, edited by F.M. Fales, pp. 117-42. Rome, 1981.

———. "Collations to Neo-Assyrian Legal Texts from Nineveh." *Assur* 2/5 (1979): 1-89.

———. "A Letter from Šamaš-šumu-ukīn to Esarhaddon." *Iraq* 34 (1972): 21-34.

———. *Letters from Assyrian Scholars to the Kings Esarhaddon and Assurbanipal*. 2 volumes. AOAT 5/1-2. Kevelaer and Neukirchen-Vluyn, 1970 and 1983.

———. "The Murderer of Sennacherib." In *Death in Mesopotamia: Papers Read at the XXVIe Rencontre Assyriologique Internationale*, edited by B. Alster, pp. 171-82. Mesopotamia 8. Copenhagen, 1980.

———. *Neo-Assyrian Letters from the Kuyunjik Collection*. CT 53. London, 1979.

———. *Neo-Assyrian Toponyms*. AOAT 6. Programming and computer printing by K. Koskenniemi. Kevelaer and Neukirchen-Vluyn, 1970.

———. "Neo-Assyrian Treaties from the Royal Archives of Nineveh." *JCS* 39 (1987): 161-89.

———. "The Royal Archives of Nineveh." In *Cuneiform Archives and Libraries: Papers Read at the 30^e Rencontre Assyriologique Internationale, Leiden, 4-8 July 1983*, edited by K.R. Veenhof, pp. 223-36. Leiden, 1986.

———. Review of J.N. Postgate, *Taxation and Conscription in the Assyrian Empire*. *ZA* 65 (1975): 293-96.

——— and Watanabe, K. *Neo-Assyrian Treaties and Loyalty Oaths*. SAA 2. Helsinki, 1988.

Parr, P.J. "Settlement Patterns and Urban Planning in the Ancient Levant: The Nature of the Evidence." In *Man, Settlement and Urbanism*, edited by P.J. Ucko, R. Tringham, and G.W. Dimbleby, pp. 805-10. London, 1972.

Parrot, A., and Nougayrol, J. "Asarhaddon et Naq'ia sur un bronze du Louvre (AO 20.185)." *Syria* 33 (1956): 147-60 and plate 6.

Pečírková, J. "The Administrative Organization of the Neo-Assyrian Empire." *ArOr* 45 (1977): 211-28.

Pedersén, O. Review of S. Dalley and J.N. Postgate, *The Tablets from Fort Shalmaneser*. *AfO* 35 (1988): 169-73.

Peiser, F.E. *Texte juristischen und geschäftlichen Inhalts*. Keilinschriftliche Bibliothek 4. Berlin, 1896.

Peters, J.P. *Nippur or Explorations and Adventures on the Euphrates, The Narrative of the University of Pennsylvania Expedition to Babylonia in the Years 1888-1890*. 2 volumes. New York and London, 1897.

Petschow, H. *Neubabylonisches Pfandrecht*. Abhandlungen der Sächsischen Akademie der Wissenschaften zu Leipzig, Philologisch-historische Klasse 48/1. Berlin, 1956.

Pfeiffer, R.H. *State Letters of Assyria*. American Oriental Series 6. New Haven, 1935.

Piepkorn, A.C. *Historical Prism Inscriptions of Ashurbanipal*. Volume 1: *Editions E, B_{1-5}, D, and K*. Assyriological Studies 5. Chicago, 1933.

Pinches, T.G. "Babylonian Contract-Tablets with Historical References." *RP* NS 4 (1890): 96-108.

———. *The Babylonian Tablets of the Berens Collection*. Asiatic Society Monographs 16. London, 1915.

———. "Ein babylonischer Eponym." *AfO* 13 (1939-41): 51-54 and plates 3-4.

———. *Cuneiform Texts from Babylonian Tablets, &c., in the British Museum*. Volume 4. London, 1898.

———. *Miscellaneous Texts*. CT 44. London, 1963.

———. "Notes upon Some of the Recent Discoveries in the Realm of Assyriology, with Special Reference to the Private Life of the Babylonians." *JTVI* 26 (1893): 123-71.

Pinckert, J. *Hymnen und Gebete an Nebo*. LSS 3/4. Leipzig, 1920.

Pohl, A. *Neubabylonische Rechtsurkunden aus den Berliner Staatlichen Museen*. 2 volumes. AnOr 8 and 9. Rome, 1933-34.

Porada, E. "Suggestions for the Classification of Neo-Babylonian Cylinder Seals." *Or.* NS 16 (1947): 145-65.

Porter, B.N. "Symbols of Power: Figurative Aspects of Esarhaddon's Babylonian Policy (681-669 B.C.)." Ph.D. disertation, University of Pennsylvania, 1987.

Postgate, J.N. "Assyrian Texts and Fragments." *Iraq* 35 (1973): 13-36

———. "The Economic Structure of the Assyrian Empire." In *Power and Propaganda: A Symposium on Ancient Empires*, edited by M.T. Larsen, pp. 193-221. Mesopotamia 7. Copenhagen, 1979.

———. *Fifty Neo-Assyrian Legal Documents*. Warminster, 1976.

———. "Itu'." *RLA* 5, pp. 221-22.

———. "More 'Assyrian Deeds and Documents.'" *Iraq* 32 (1970): 129-64 and pls. 18-31.

———. *Neo-Assyrian Royal Grants and Decrees*. Studia Pohl: Series Maior 1. Rome, 1969.

———. "The Place of the *šaknu* in Assyrian Government." *AnSt* 30 (1980): 67-76.

———. "'Princeps Iudex' in Assyria." *RA* 74 (1980): 180-82.

———. "Royal Exercise of Justice under the Assyrian Empire." In *Le palais et la royauté*, edited by P. Garelli, pp. 417-26. Paris, 1974.

———. "Some Old Babylonian Shepherds and their Flocks." With a contribution by S. Payne. *JSS* 20 (1975): 1-21.

———. *Taxation and Conscription in the Assyrian Empire.* Studia Pohl: Series Maior 3. Rome 1974.

———. Review of F. Malbran-Labat, *L'armée et l'organisation militaire de l'Assyrie d'après les lettres Sargonides trouvées à Ninive.* *BiOr* 41 (1984): 420-26.

———. Review of B. Oded, *Mass Deportations and Deportees in the Neo-Assyrian Empire.* *BiOr* 38 (1981): 636-38.

Powell, M.A. "Identification and Interpretation of Long Term Price Fluctuations in Babylonia: More on the History of Money in Mesopotamia." *AOF* 17 (1990): 76-99.

Prince, J.D. "A New Šamaš-šum-ukîn Series." *AJSL* 31 (1914-15): 256-70.

Pritchard, J. B., ed. *Ancient Near Eastern Texts Relating to the Old Testament.* 3rd edition with supplement. Princeton, 1969.

Rashid, F. "A Royal Text from Tell Haddad." *Sumer* 37 (1981): 72-80 (Arabic section).

Reade, J.E. "The Accession of Sinsharishkun." *JCS* 23 (1970-71): 1-9.

———. "Narrative Composition in Assyrian Sculpture." *Bagh. Mitt.* 10 (1979): 52-110 and plates 14-25.

———. "The Neo-Assyrian Court and Army: Evidence from the Sculptures." *Iraq* 34 (1972): 87-112 and plates 33-40.

———. "Neo-Assyrian Monuments in Their Historical Context." In *Assyrian Royal Inscriptions: New Horizons in Literary, Ideological and Historical Analysis,* edited by F.M. Fales, pp. 143-67 and plates 1-10. Rome, 1981.

———. "Rassam's Excavations at Borsippa and Kutha, 1879-82." *Iraq* 48 (1986): 105-116 and plates 13-19.

——— and Walker, C.B.F. "Some Neo-Assyrian Royal Inscriptions." *AfO* 28 (1981-82): 113-22.

Reiner, E.; with an appendix by M. Civil. "The Babylonian Fürstenspiegel in Practice." In *Societies and Languages of the Ancient Near East: Studies in Honour of I.M. Diakonoff,* edited by M.A. Dandamayev et al., pp. 320-26. Warminster, 1982.

Reuther, O. *Die Innenstadt von Babylon (Merkes).* WVDOG 47. Leipzig, 1926.

Revillout, V. "Un nouveau nom royal Perse." *PSBA* 9 (1886-87): 233-40.

Reviv, H. "*Kidinnu*: Observations on Privileges of Mesopotamian Cities." *JESHO* 31 (1988): 286-98.

Röllig, W. "Ḫirītum." *RLA* 4, p. 418.

———. "Jadaqqu." *RLA* 5, p. 232.

———. "Kisiga, Kissik." *RLA* 5, pp. 620-22.

Rost, P. *Die Keilschrifttexte Tiglat-Pilesers III. nach den Papierabklatschen und Originalen des Britischen Museums.* 2 volumes. Leipzig, 1893.

Roth, M.T. "A Case of Contested Status." In *dumu-e$_2$-dub-ba-a: Studies in Honor of Åke W. Sjöberg,* edited by H. Behrens, D. Loding, and M.T. Roth, pp. 481-89. Occasional Publications of the Samuel Noah Kramer Fund 11. Philadelphia, 1989.

———. Review of S. Parpola, *Letters from Assyrian Scholars to the Kings Esarhaddon and Assurbanipal,* volume 2. *ZA* 75 (1985): 307-10.

Roux, G. "Recently Discovered Ancient Sites in the Hammar Lake District (Southern Iraq)." *Sumer* 16 (1960): 20-31.

Sachs, A.J. *Astronomical Diaries and Related Texts from Babylonia.* Volume 1: *Diaries from 652 B.C. to 262 B.C.* Completed and edited by H. Hunger. Vienna, 1988.

———. "Babylonian Observational Astronomy." In *The Place of Astronomy in the Ancient World*, edited by F.R. Hodson, pp. 43-50. London, 1974.

———. *Late Babylonian Astronomical and Related Texts Copied by T.G. Pinches and J.N. Strassmaier*. With the cooperation of J. Schaumberger. Providence, 1955.

Safar, F. "Soundings at Tell Al-Laham." *Sumer* 5 (1949): 154-72.

Saggs, H.W.F. *The Might That Was Assyria*. London, 1984.

———. "The Nimrud Letters, 1952, Part I." *Iraq* 17 (1955): 21-56.

———. "The Nimrud Letters, 1952, Part III." *Iraq* 18 (1956): 40-56 and plates 9-12.

San Nicolò, M. *Babylonische Rechtsurkunden des ausgehenden 8. und des 7. Jahrhunderts v. Chr.* Abhandlungen der Bayerischen Akademie der Wissenschaften, Philosophisch-historische Klasse, Neue Folge 34. Munich, 1951.

———. *Beiträge zu einer Prosopographie neubabylonischer Beamten der Zivil- und Tempelverwaltung*. Sitzungsberichte der Bayerischen Akademie der Wissenschaften, Philosophisch-historische Abteilung, Jahrgang 1941, 2/2. Munich, 1941.

———. "Materialien zur Viehwirtschaft in den neubabylonischen Tempeln. III." *Or.* NS 20 (1951): 129-50.

——— and Ungnad, A. *Neubabylonische Rechts- und Verwaltungsurkunden übersetzt und erläutert.* Volume I: *Rechts- und Wirtschaftsurkunden der Berliner Museen aus vorhellenistischer Zeit*. Leipzig, 1935.

Scheil, V. "Catalogue de la collection Eugène Tisserant." *RA* 18 (1921): 1-33.

———. "Notes d'épigraphie de d'archéologie assyriennes." *RT* 16 (1894): 90-92; and 17 (1895): 27-41.

———. "Notules." *RA* 15 (1918): 75-86.

———. "Nouvelles notes d'épigraphie et d'archéologie assyriennes." *RT* 36 (1914): 179-92.

———. *Une saison de fouilles à Sippar*. Cairo, 1902.

Schmidt, J., et al. *XXVI. und XXVII. vorläufiger Bericht über die von dem Deutschen Archäologischen Institut und der Deutschen Orient-Gesellschaft aus Mitteln der Deutschen Forschungsgemeinschaft unternommenen Ausgrabungen in Uruk-Warka 1968 und 1969*. ADOG 16. Berlin, 1972.

Schmidtke, F. Asarhaddons Statthalterschaft in Babylonien und seine Thronbesteigung in Assyrien 681 v. Chr. AOTU 1/2. Leiden, 1916.

Schnabel, P. *Berossos und die babylonisch-hellenistische Literatur*. Leipzig, 1923.

Schollmeyer, A. *Sumerisch-babylonische Hymnen und Gebete an Šamaš*. Paderborn, 1912.

Schrader, E. "Kineladan und Asurbanipal." *ZK* 1 (1884): 222-32.

Schroeder, O. *Keilschrifttexte aus Assur historischen Inhalts*. Part 2. WVDOG 37. Leipzig, 1922.

———. *Keilschrifttexte aus Assur verschiedenen Inhalts*. WVDOG 35. Leipzig, 1920.

Seidl, U. "Die babylonischen Kudurru-Reliefs." *Bagh. Mitt.* 4 (1968): 7-220 and plates 1-32.

Seux, M.-J. *Épithètes royales akkadiennes et sumériennes*. Paris, 1967.

———. "Königtum. B. II. und I. Jahrtausend." *RLA* 6, pp. 140-73.

Smith, G. *Assyrian Discoveries; an Account of Explorations and Discoveries on the Site of Nineveh, during 1873 and 1874*. 3rd edition. London, 1875.

———. *History of Sennacherib Translated from the Cuneiform Inscriptions*. Edited by A.H. Sayce. London and Edinburgh, 1878.

Smith, S. *Babylonian Historical Texts Relating to the Capture and Downfall of Babylon*. London, 1924.

———. *The First Campaign of Sennacherib, King of Assyria, B.C. 705-681*. London, 1921.

Smith, S.A. *Miscellaneous Assyrian Texts of the British Museum, with Textual Notes*. Leipzig, 1887.

von Soden, W. "Aramäische Wörter in neuassyrischen und neu- und spätbabylonischen Texten. Ein Vorbericht." *Or.* NS 35 (1966): 1-20; 37 (1968): 261-71; and 46 (1977): 183-97.

———. "Aššuretellilāni, Sînšarriškun, Sînšum(u)līšer und die Ereignisse im Assyrerreich nach 635 v. Chr." *ZA* 58 (1967): 241-55.

———. "Gibt es ein Zeugnis dafür, dass die Babylonier an die Wiederauferstehung Marduks geglaubt haben?" *ZA* 51 (1955): 130-66.

———. "Gibt es Hinweise auf die Ermordung Sanheribs im Ninurta-Tempel (wohl) in Kalaḫ in Texten aus Assyrien?" *NABU* 1990, pp. 16-17 no. 22.

———. "Der neubabylonische Funktionär *simmagir* und die Feuertod des Šamaš-šum-ukīn." *ZA* 62 (1972): 84-90.

———. "Ein neues Bruchstücke des assyrischen Kommentars zum Marduk-Ordal." *ZA* 52 (1957): 224-34.

———. "Sanherib vor Jerusalem 701 v. Chr." In *Antike und Universalgeschichte. Festschrift Hans Erich Stier*, pp. 43-51. Münster, 1972.

Sollberger, E. "The Cuneiform Collection in Geneva." *JCS* 5 (1951): 18-20.

———. *Royal Inscriptions, Part II*. UET 8. London, 1965.

Spalinger, A. "Assurbanipal and Egypt: A Source Study." *JAOS* 94 (1974): 316-28.

———. "Esarhaddon and Egypt: An Analysis of the First Invasion of Egypt." *Or.* NS 43 (1974): 295-326.

van der Spek, R.J. "The Struggle of King Sargon II of Assyria against the Chaldaean Merodach-Baladan (710-707 B.C.)." *JEOL* 25 (1977-78): 56-66.

Speleers, L. *Recueil des inscriptions de l'Asie antérieure des Musées Royaux du Cinquantenaire à Bruxelles*. Brussels, 1925.

Starr, I. "Historical Omens Concerning Ashurbanipal's War Against Elam." *AfO* 32 (1985): 60-67.

———. *Queries to the Sungod: Divination and Politics in Sargonid Assyria*. SAA 4. Helsinki, 1990.

Stamm, J.J. *Die akkadische Namengebung*. Mitteilungen der Vorderasiatisch-Ägyptischen Gesellschaft 44. Leipzig, 1939.

Steiner, R.C., and Nims, C.F. "Ashurbanipal and Shamash-Shum-Ukin: A Tale of Two Brothers from the Aramaic Text in Demotic Script. Part 1." *RB* 92 (1985): 60-81 and plates 1-4.

Steinkeller, P. "On the Reading and Location of the Toponyms ÚR×Ú.KI and A.ḪA.KI." *JCS* 32 (1980): 23-33.

Steinmetzer, F.X. "Die Bestallungsurkunde des Königs Šamaš-šum-ukîn von Babylon." In *Miscellanea orientalia dedicata Antonio Deimel annos LXX complenti*, pp. 302-306. AnOr 12. Rome, 1935.

———. "Die Bestallungsurkunde Königs Šamaš-šum-ukîn von Babylon." *ArOr* 7 (1935) 314-18.

Stephens, F.J. "A Tablet from the Reign of Šamaš-šum-ukin." *JCS* 1 (1947): 273-74.

Stigers, H.G. "A Neo-Babylonian Quit-Claim Deed." *Jewish Quarterly Review* 63 (1972-73): 171-74.

Stol, M. "A Cadastral Innovation by Hammurabi." In zikir šumim: *Assyriological Studies Presented to F.R. Kraus on the Occasion of his Seventieth Birthday*, edited by G. van Driel et al, pp. 351-58. Leiden, 1982.

———. "Old Babylonian Fields." *BSA* 4 (1988): 173-88.

Stolper, M.W. "The Neo-Babylonian Text from the Persepolis Fortification." *JNES* 43 (1984): 299-310.

———. "*šarnuppu.*" *ZA* 68 (1978): 261-69.

Strassmaier, J.N. "Einige kleinere babylonische Keilschrifttexte aus dem Britischen Museum." In *Actes du Huitième Congrès International des Orientalistes, tenu en 1889 à Stockholm et à Christiania*, 2/IB, pp. 279-283 and Beilage Leiden, 1893.

———. *Inschriften von Nabonidus, König von Babylon (555-538 v. Chr.).* Leipzig, 1889.

———. *Inschriften von Nabuchodonosor, König von Babylon (604-561 v. Chr.).* Leipzig, 1889.

Streck, M. *Die alte Landschaft Babylonien nach den arabischen Geographen.* 2 volumes. Leiden, 1900-1901.

———. *Assurbanipal und die letzten assyrischen Könige bis zum Untergange Niniveh's.* 3 volumes. Vorderasiatische Bibliothek 7. Leipzig, 1916.

———. "Die nomadischen Völkerschaften Babyloniens und des angrenzenden Elams." *MVAG* 11 (1906): 203-46.

Tadmor, H. "The Aramaization of Assyria: Aspects of Western Impact." In *Mesopotamien und seine Nachbarn: Politische und kulturelle Wechselbeziehungen im Alten Vorderasien vom 4. bis 1. Jahrtausend v. Chr.*, edited by H.-J. Nissen and J. Renger, pp. 449-70. Berliner Beiträge zum Vorderen Orient 1. Berlin, 1982.

———. "Autobiographical Apology in the Royal Assyrian Literature." In *History, Historiography and Interpretation: Studies in Biblical and Cuneiform Literatures*, edited by H. Tadmor and M. Weinfeld, pp. 36-57. Jerusalem and Leiden, 1983.

———. "The Last Three Decades of Assyria" [in Russian]. In *Proceedings of the 25th International Congress of Orientalists*, volume 1, pp. 240-41. Moscow, 1962.

———. "Monarchy and the Elite in Assyria and Babylonia: The Question of Royal Accountability." In *The Origins and Diversity of Axial Age Civilizations*, edited by S.N. Eisenstadt, pp. 203-24. Albany, 1986.

———. "The 'Sin of Sargon'" [in Hebrew, with a summary in English]. *Eretz Israel* 5 (1958): 150-63 and 93*.

———. "Treaty and Oath in the Ancient Near East: A Historian's Approach." In *Humanizing America's Iconic Book: Society of Biblical Literature Centennial Addresses 1980*, edited by G.M. Tucker and D.A. Knight, pp. 127-52. Chico, California, 1982.

———, Landsberger, B., and Parpola, S. "The Sin of Sargon and Sennacherib's Last Will." *SAAB* 3 (1989): 3-51.

Tallqvist, K.L. *Assyrian Personal Names.* Acta Societatis Scientiarum Fennicae 43/1. Helsinki, 1914.

———. *Neubabylonisches Namenbuch zu den Geschäftsurkunden aus der Zeit des Šamaššumukîn bis Xerxes.* Acta Societatis Scientiarum Fennicae 32/2. Helsinki, 1902.

Thompson, R.C. *The Prisms of Esarhaddon and Ashurbanipal found at Nineveh, 1927-8.* London, 1931.

———. *The Reports of the Magicians and Astrologers of Nineveh and Babylon in the British Museum.* 2 volumes. Leondon, 1900.

———. "A Selection from the Cuneiform Historical Texts from Nineveh (1927-32)." *Iraq* 7 (1940): 85-131.

——— and Hutchinson, R.W. "The Excavations on the Temple of Nabû at Nineveh." *Archaeologia* 79 (1929): 103-48 and plates 41-65.

——— and Mallowan, M.E.L. "The British Museum Excavations at Nineveh, 1931-32." *AAA* 20 (1933): 71-186 and pls. 35-106.

Thureau-Dangin, F. *Rituels accadiens*. Paris, 1921.

Unger, E. *Babylon, die heilige Stadt nach der Beschreibung der Babylonier*. Introduction by R. Borger. 2nd edition. Berlin, 1970.

———. "Bît-Bunak(k)u/i." *RLA* 2, p. 38.

———. "Dûr-Atḫara." *RLA* 2, p. 242.

———. *Sargon II. von Assyrien der Sohn Tiglatpilesers III*. Istanbul Asarıatika Müzeleri Nesriyatı 9. Istanbul, 1933.

———. "Topographie der Stadt Dilbat." *ArOr* 3 (1931): 21-48 and pl. 1.

Ungnad, A. "Eponymen." *RLA* 2, pp. 412-57.

———. "Figurenzauber für den kranken König Šamaš-šumu-ukîn." *Or.* NS 12 (1943): 293-310.

———. *Vorderasiatische Schriftdenkmäler der Königlichen Museen zu Berlin*. Volumes 4, 5, and 6. Leipzig, 1907-1908.

Veenhof, K.R. *Aspects of Old Assyrian Trade and its Terminology*. Studia et Documenta ad Iura Orientis Antiqui Pertinentia 10. Leiden, 1972.

Vita-Finzi, C. "Recent Alluvial History in the Catchment of the Arabo-Persian Gulf." In *The Environmental History of the Near and Middle East since the Last Ice Age*, edited by W.C. Brice, pp. 255-61. London, 1978.

Vleeming, S.P., and Wesselius, J.W. *Studies in Papyrus Amherst 63. Essays on the Aramaic Texts in Aramaic/Demotic Papyrus Amherst 63*. Volume 1. Amsterdam, 1985.

von Voigtlander, E.N. "A Survey of Neo-Babylonian History." Ph.D. dissertation, University of Michigan, 1963.

Wachsmuth, C. *Einleitung in das Studium der alten Geschichte*. Leipzig, 1895.

Waetzoldt, H. *Untersuchungen zur neusumerischen Textilindustrie*. Rome, 1972.

———. "Zu den Strandverschiebungen am Persischen Golf und den Bezeichnungen der Ḥōrs." In *Strandverschiebungen in ihrer Bedeutung für Geowissenschaften und Archäologie*, edited by J. Schäfer and W. Simon, pp. 159-83 and figs. 1-3. Ruperto Carola Sonderheft 1981. Heidelberg, 1981.

Walker, C.B.F. "Babylonian Chronicle 25: A Chronicle of the Kassite and Isin II Dynasties." In zikir šumim: *Assyriological Studies Presented to F.R. Kraus on the Occasion of his Seventieth Birthday*, edited by G. van Driel et al, pp. 398-417. Leiden, 1982.

———. *Cuneiform Brick Inscriptions in the British Museum; the Ashmolean Museum, Oxford; the City of Birmingham Museums and Art Gallery; the City of Bristol Museum and Art Gallery*. London, 1981.

———. "Episodes in the History of Babylonian Astronomy." *BSMS* 5 (1983): 10-26.

Wall-Romana, C. "An Areal Location of Agade." *JNES* 49 (1990): 205-45.

Watanabe, K. *Die* adê-*Vereidigung anlässlich der Thronfolgeregelung Asarhaddons*. Baghdader Mitteilungen Beiheft 3. Berlin, 1987.

Watelin, L.C., and Langdon, S. *Excavations at Kish*. Volumes 3 and 4. Paris, 1930 and 1934.

Waterman, L. *Royal Correspondence of the Assyrian Empire*. 4 volumes. Ann Arbor, 1930-36.

———. "Texts and Fragments. 12." *JCS* 5 (1951): 74.

Weidner, E.F. "Die älteste Nachricht über das persische Königshaus: Kyros I. ein Zeitgenosse Aššurbânaplis." *AfO* 7 (1931-32): 1-7.

———. "Assurbânipal in Assur." *AfO* 13 (1939-41): 204-18 and plates 11-16.

———. "Assyrische Beschreibungen der Kriegs-Reliefs Aššurbânaplis." *AfO* 8 (1932-33): 175-203.

———. "Die Feldzüge und Bauten Tiglatpilesers I." *AfO* 18 (1957-58): 342-60.

———. "Die grosse Königsliste aus Assur." *AfO* 3 (1926): 66-77.

———. "Hochverrat gegen Asarhaddon." *AfO* 17 (1954-56): 5-9.

———. "Keilschrifttexte nach Kopien von T.G. Pinches. Aus dem Nachlass veröffentlicht und bearbeitet. 1. Babylonisches Privaturkunden aus dem 7. Jahrhundert v. Chr." *AfO* 16 (1952-53): 35-46.

Weippert, M.H.E. "Die Kämpfe des assyrischen Königs Assurbanipal gegen die Araber." *WO* 7 (1973-74): 39-85.

———. "Nieuwassyrische Profetieën." In *Schrijvend Verleden: Documenten uit het Oude Nabije Oosten Vertaald en Toegelicht*, edited by K.R. Veenhof, pp. 284-89. Leiden, 1983.

Weisman, Z. "The Nature and Background of bāḥūr in the Old Testament." *Vetus Testamentum* 31 (1981): 441-50.

Wetzel, F. *Die Stadtmauern von Babylon*. WVDOG 48. Leipzig, 1930.

——— and Weissbach, F. *Das Hauptheiligtum des Marduk in Babylon, Esagila und Etemenanki*. WVDOG 59. Leipzig, 1938.

Winckler, H. *Altorientalische Forschungen*. 3 volumes. Leipzig, 1893-1905.

———. *Die Keilschrifttexte Sargons nach den Papierabklatschen und Originalen*. 2 volumes. Leipzig, 1889.

Wiseman, D.J. *Chronicles of Chaldaean Kings (626-556 B.C.) in the British Museum*. London, 1956.

———. "Two Historical Inscriptions from Nimrud." *Iraq* 13 (1951): 21-26 and plates 11-12.

———. "The Vassal-Treaties of Esarhaddon." *Iraq* 20 (1958): 1-99 and pls. I-XII and 1-53.

Woolley, L. *The Kassite Period and the Period of the Assyrian Kings*. UE 8. London, 1965.

———. *The Neo-Babylonian and Persian Periods*. UE 9. London, 1962.

———. *Ur 'of the Chaldees'*. Revised and updated by P.R.S. Moorey. London, 1982.

Wright, H. "The Southern Margins of Sumer: Archaeological Survey of the Area of Eridu and Ur." In *Heartland of Cities: Surveys of Ancient Settlement and Land Use on the Central Floodplain of the Euphrates*, by R.McC. Adams, pp. 295-345. Chicago, 1981.

Young, T.C. "The Iranian Migration into the Zagros." *Iran* 5 (1967): 11-34.

Zadok, R. "Arabians in Mesopotamia during the Late-Assyrian, Chaldean, Achaemenian and Hellenistic Periods Chiefly according to the Cuneiform Sources." *ZDMG* 131 (1981): 42-84.

———. "Assyrians in Chaldean and Achaemenian Babylonia." *Assur* 4/3 (1984).

———. "Elements of Aramean Pre-History." In *Ah, Assyria ... Studies in Assyrian History and Ancient Near Eastern Historiography Presented to Hayim Tadmor*, edited by M. Cogan and I. Eph'al, pp. 104-17. Scripta Hierosolymitana 33. Jerusalem, 1991.

———. *Geographical Names According to New- and Late-Babylonian Texts*. RGTC 8. Wiesbaden, 1985.

———. "N/LB *rab-bānê* < Aram. *rabbānē* 'nobles' or sim." *RA* 77 (1983): 189-90.

———. "On Some Egyptians in First-Millennium Mesopotamia." *Göttinger Miszellen* 26 (1977): 63-68.

———. "On Some Foreign Population Groups in First-Millennium Babylonia." *Tel Aviv* 6 (1979): 164-81.

———. *On West Semites in Babylonia during the Chaldean and Achaemenian Periods: An Onomastic Study*. Jerusalem, 1977.

———. "The Topography of the Nippur Region during the 1st Millennium B.C. within the General Framework of the Mesopotamian Toponymy." *WO* 12 (1981): 39-69.

———. "Zur Geographie Babyloniens während des sargonidischen, chaldäischen, achämenidischen und hellenistischen Zeitalters." *WO* 16 (1985): 19-79.

Zawadzki, S. "The Economic Crisis in Uruk during the Last Years of Assyrian Rule in the Light of the So-Called Nabu-ušallim Archives." *FO* 20 (1979): 175-84.

———. *The Fall of Assyria and Median-Babylonian Relations in Light of the Nabopolassar Chronicle*. Translated by U. Wolko and P. Lavelle. Poznan, 1988.

———. "Some Remarks Concerning the Property of the Eanna Temple in Uruk (7th c. B.C.)." *FO* 18 (1977): 187-97.

Zettler, R.L. "The Ur III Inanna Temple at Nippur." 2 volumes. Ph.D. dissertation, University of Chicago, 1984.

GENERAL INDEX

SELECTED TEXT REFERENCES

ABL 210:11-16, 164
ABL 287 rev. 1-7, 225
ABL 288:6-rev. 4, 228
ABL 292:1-3, 276; 14-17, 121
ABL 301:3-rev. 16, 138-39
ABL 326 rev. 1'-2', 216
ABL 327:13-20, 86
ABL 403:8-12, 80
ABL 418:10-rev. 13, 73
ABL 517, 162
ABL 617+699:2-3, 276; rev. 5, 154
ABL 754(+)*CT* 54 250:4-9, 160-61
ABL 804 rev. 8-16, 144
ABL 831 rev. 1'-5', 227
ABL 896:4-rev. 18, 172-73
ABL 972 rev. 8-9, 154
ABL 1002 rev. 3-9, 163
ABL 1236:7'-9', 178
ABL 1241+*CT* 54 112:4'-rev. 5, 164-65
ABL 1380:5-12, 184
ABL 1385:7-rev. 17, 111

BBSt 10 rev. 42-50, 232-33

BIN 2 132:12-13, 201

CT 35 pl. 38 rev. 14-17, 155
CT 54 22 rev. 9-11, 229

Grayson, *Chronicles*, no. 15:11, 148
Grayson, *Chronicles*, no.16:13-15, 289; 16, 292

Al-Jumaily, *Sumer* 27 (1971): pl. 14 fig. 30:1-3 (Arabic section), 113

Knudsen, *Iraq* 29 (1967): 53 and pl. 20 i' 5-7, 148
Knudsen, *Iraq* 29 (1967): 59-60 ii 23-26, 203

Lehmann, *Ššmk*, no. 1 i 6 and ii 6, 96

Luckenbill, *Senn.*, p. 149 no. 5:1-4, 57

Sachs, *Astronomical Diaries*, no. -651 iv 18'-19', 289

Steinmetzer, *Deimel Festschrift*, p. 306 rev. 17-26, 232-33

Illustrations

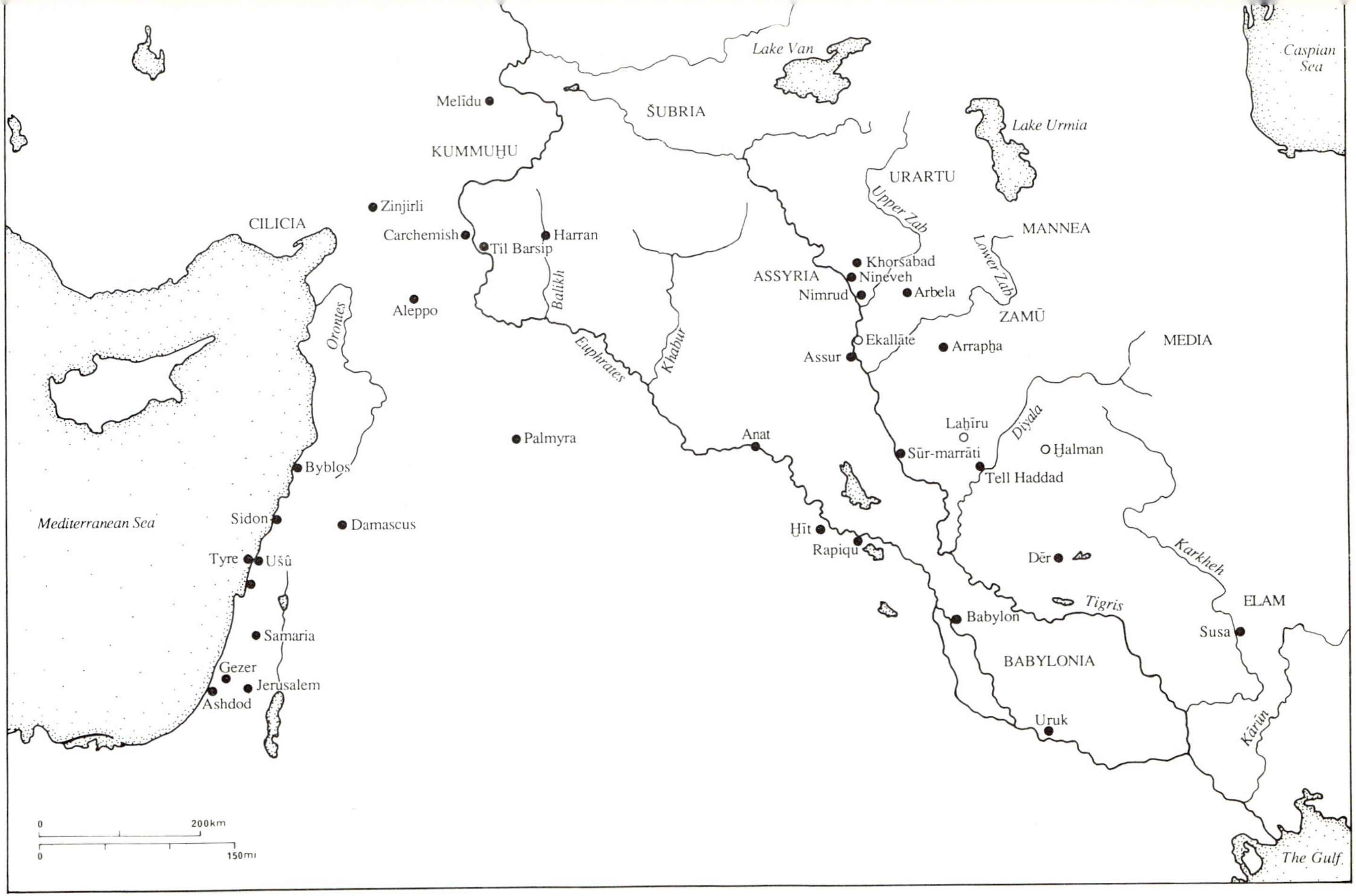

Map 1 – The Ancient Near East

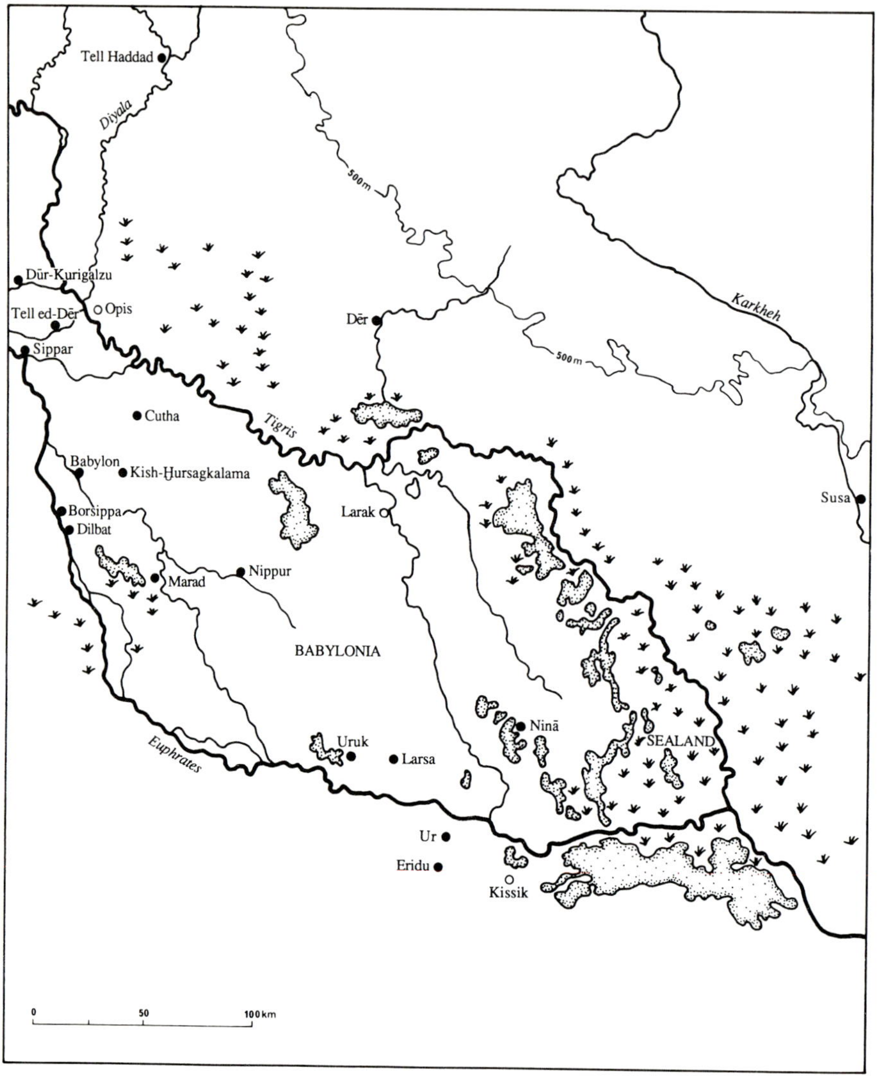

Map 2 – Babylonia

Figure 1 – Stela of Esarhaddon from Zinjirli (VA 2708)

Figure 2 – Stela of Ashurbanipal from Borsippa (BM 90865)

Figure 3 – Stela of Šamaš-šuma-ukīn from Borsippa (BM 90866)

Figure 4 – Wall relief from the Palace of Sennacherib (BM 124801)

Figure 5 – Wall relief from the North Palace of Ashurbanipal (BM 124945-6)

Figure 6 – Wall relief from the North Palace of Ashurbanipal (BM 124945-6)

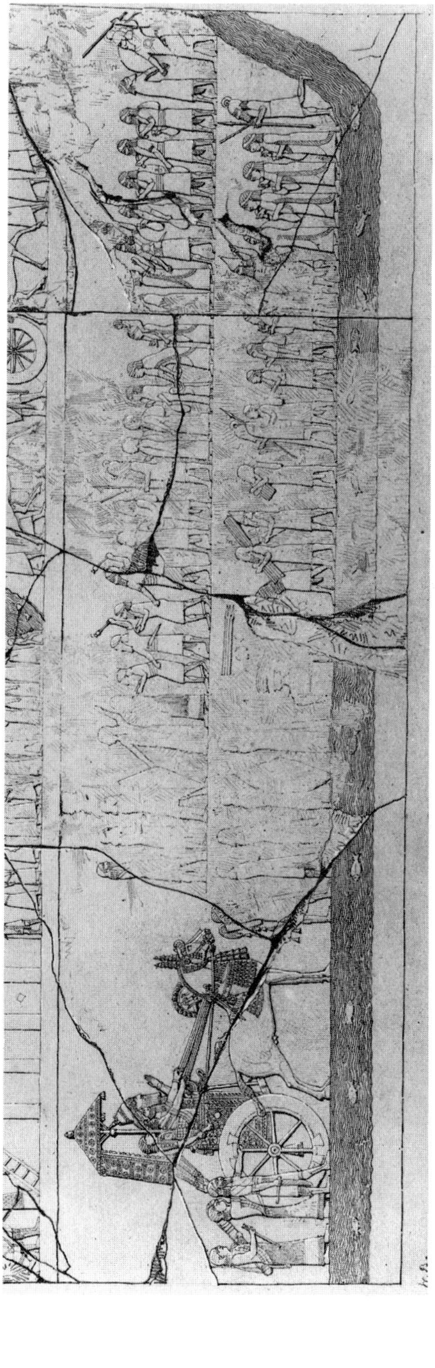

Figure 7 – Wall relief from the North Palace of Ashurbanipal (BM drawing Or.DR V,24)

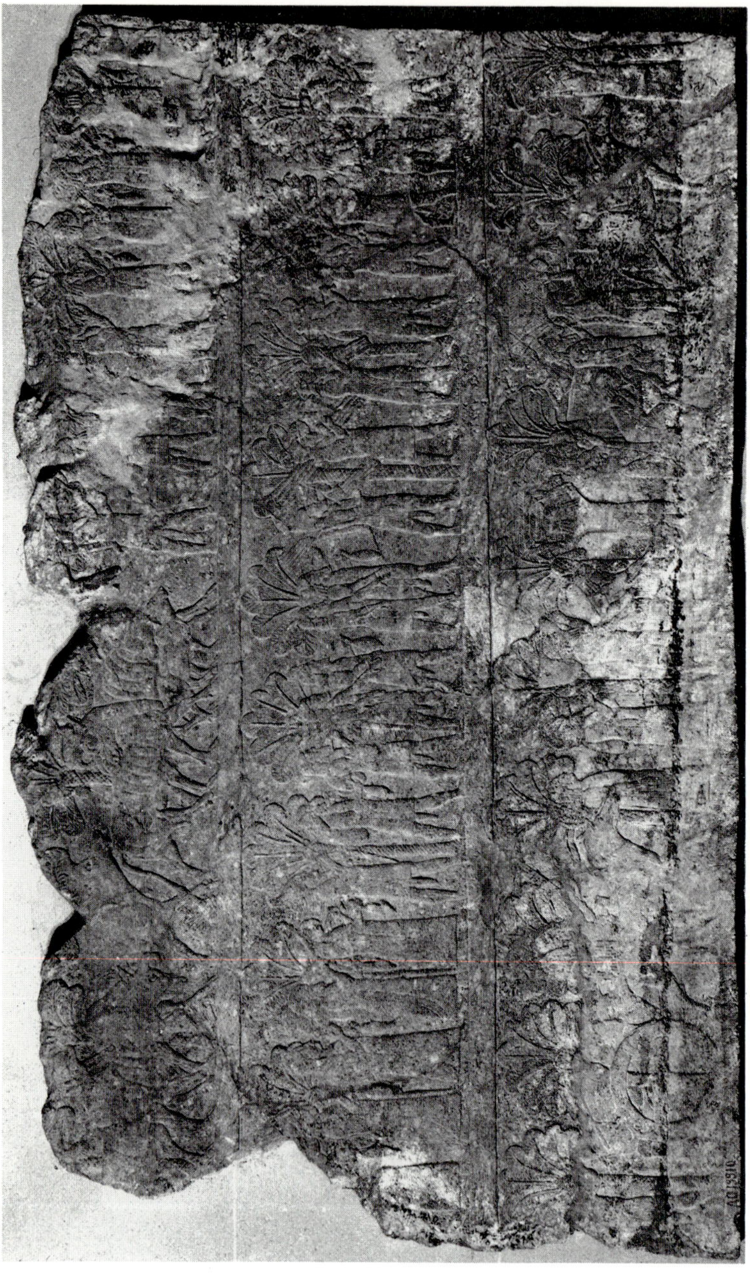

Figure 8 – Wall relief from the North Palace of Ashurbanipal (AO 19910)